HISTORY OF THE GREAT WAR
GALLIPOLI

HISTORY OF THE GREAT WAR

BASED ON OFFICIAL DOCUMENTS
BY DIRECTION OF THE HISTORICAL SECTION
COMMITTEE OF IMPERIAL DEFENCE

MILITARY OPERATIONS
GALLIPOLI

COMPILED BY
BR.-GENERAL C. F. ASPINALL-OGLANDER
C.B., C.M.G., D.S.O., *p.s.c.*

MAPS AND SKETCHES COMPILED BY
MAJOR A. F. BECKE
R.A. (RETIRED), HON. M.A. (OXON.)

VOL. I
INCEPTION OF THE CAMPAIGN
TO MAY 1915

The Naval & Military Press Ltd

Published by

The Naval & Military Press Ltd
Unit 5 Riverside, Brambleside
Bellbrook Industrial Estate
Uckfield, East Sussex
TN22 1QQ England

Tel: +44 (0)1825 749494

www.naval-military-press.com
www.nmarchive.com

In reprinting in facsimile from the original, any imperfections are inevitably reproduced and the quality may fall short of modern type and cartographic standards.

From the painting by Charles Dixon, R.I.
Reproduced by permission of the officers 2nd Bn, Hampshire Regiment

PREFACE

THE records of the Great War contain no story more full of moving interest for the general reader, or of vital lessons for the soldier, the sailor, and the statesman, than the story of Britain's efforts to force the Dardanelles. The campaign was enacted upon the most historic of all stages for a noble feat of arms; it offered to a successful solution far-reaching and perhaps decisive advantages; and its lack of success was due in great part to the neglect of age-old principles of war. It witnessed on the part of all the belligerents engaged—whether British, Australian, New Zealand, French, or Turk—a heroism and self-sacrifice that reached the topmost pinnacle of human endeavour; it furnished the only instance in the war of combined naval and military operations on a large scale, and the only example in history of the storming of open beaches defended by wire and machine guns.

In the original scheme for the official war histories it was decided that the operations in Gallipoli and the Dardanelles should be dealt with in two distinct compartments, the naval historian telling the story of the fleet's efforts, and the military historian that of the campaign on land. The naval story has already been told in Volumes II. and III. of the Naval History of the War. But just as the late Sir Julian Corbett found it impossible to describe the doings of the fleet without dealing at some length with the operations on land, so in describing the events on shore, the present writer has had to retrace to some extent the steps of his colleague, and to include an outline of the naval side of the story. Particularly has this been necessary in relating the events of the landings, where the two senior services were working in close and intimate co-operation.

The military history of the campaign will be completed in two volumes. The present volume deals with the course of events from Turkey's entry into the war up to the middle of May 1915. The second volume will describe the subsequent operations on the peninsula up to and including the final evacuation.

From the outset of the Great War it was fully realized by the War Office and the Admiralty, as by the responsible ministers of the Crown, that the capture of the Dardanelles would involve a military rather than a naval operation; and the idea of such an enterprise, discussed for the first time by the War Council in November 1914, was temporarily laid on one side for lack of sufficient troops. Later in the year, in the belief that a condition of stalemate had been reached in France, the British Government began to consider the advisability of finding some new theatre for the employment of their growing military strength, where Britain's sea-power might be turned to greater account, and where the enemy could be struck at his weakest rather than his strongest point of concentration. This policy was strongly deprecated in France. There the Western Front was still regarded as the only theatre where final victory could be won, and both the French High Command and the British General Headquarters in France were sternly opposed to any weakening of the main British effort by the pursuit of a subsidiary enterprise.

Whether or not this view was correct is a problem that will doubtless exercise the military student for many years to come. Certainly the state of Britain's military resources in January 1915 did not admit of any new and immediate commitments in addition to a spring offensive in France. But strong support is not lacking for the view that a wiser policy at this time would have been to regard the importance of the Western front as latent, to cancel the spring offensive in France, and to order a temporary defensive attitude in that theatre while striking a strong and sudden blow in the Near East with the object of destroying Turkey, succouring Russia, and rallying the Balkan states to the side of the Entente.

To the student of the Gallipoli campaign, the opinion of eminent German naval and military authorities on this point cannot fail to be of interest, and it is noteworthy that as early as 12th March 1915 Admiral von Tirpitz was writing: "The " question of the Dardanelles excites the Balkans. It is a " dangerous situation: the capsizing of one little State may " affect fatally the whole course of the war." Again on 21st March he wrote: "The forcing of the Dardanelles would be " a severe blow to us. . . . We have no trumps left." And in General Ludendorff's War Memories, that eminent soldier explained: "If the enemy fleets, by occupying the Straits, had " commanded the Black Sea, Russia could have been supplied " with the war material of which she stood in need. The " fighting in the East would then have assumed a much more " serious character. The Entente would have had access to the " rich corn supplies of Southern Russia and Rumania, and would " have persuaded that kingdom to yield to their wishes even " sooner than it actually did. . . . These details clearly show " the importance of the Straits, and therefore of Turkey, for " the Eastern Front and for our whole position."

Unfortunately, when the critical decision had to be made at the beginning of 1915, the British Government was without the assistance of an authoritative General Staff at the War Office, to advise them with a broad and independent review of the whole military situation. As a result, with barely enough munitions for one theatre, offensive operations were sanctioned in two at the same time, and neither attained success. Early in January 1915, at the earnest request of the Russians, it was decided to carry out a naval demonstration at the Dardanelles, with a view to relieving Turkish pressure in the Caucasus, and the pages of this volume will show the fateful chain of cause and consequence which led to the enlargement of this simple operation first into an unaided attempt by the fleet to force the Dardanelles, next, but only when all chance of surprise had disappeared, into a combined naval and military operation for the reduction of the Narrows forts, and finally into a great military campaign for the capture of the peninsula.

It may be doubted whether any army has operated under more demoralizing conditions than those which faced Sir Ian Hamilton's forces at the Dardanelles. Though for a brief period in early spring the Gallipoli peninsula and the waters that wash its shores offer a picture of unsurpassed beauty, the restricted areas occupied by the Allied troops throughout the campaign were in general a barren wilderness. Local supplies of food and fuel were wholly lacking, and the problem of drinking-water, though eventually solved at Helles and Suvla, was at Anzac throughout the campaign a source of daily anxiety.

The climate in May was ideal for campaigning, but later it varied from tropical heat in July and August to such intense cold in the autumn that in one instance 16,000 cases of frost-bite and exposure had to be evacuated in two days. For three summer months there was an indescribable and revolting plague of flies, as a result of which endemic and epidemic disease was rampant. The dangers and discomforts inseparable from trench life had often to be borne by units and individuals for weeks on end without a break. Unlike the Turks, who had unlimited space for resting troops in the well-watered valleys behind their lines, the invading forces had no adequate rest camps on the peninsula. There was scarcely a corner of the ground in Allied occupation that was immune from hostile shelling, and every officer and man, from highest to lowest, went day and night in constant and almost equal danger of their lives.

The unsuccessful termination of the Gallipoli operations induced a widespread feeling not only that the campaign had been an unrelieved failure, but that the problem of the Dardanelles was so essentially difficult that no attempt to solve it could ever have succeeded. But a close study of the events of the campaign, and of the subsequent episodes of the war, goes far to prove that both these views were wrong. Whether or not the capture of the peninsula, and the arrival of the fleet off Constantinople, would have secured the prizes hoped for, is a question that none can answer. But there is at least abundant proof to-day that in 1915 the problem of the Dardanelles was by no means incapable of solution. Three times at least during the course of the operations, first at the naval attack on 18th March, secondly when the Expeditionary Force landed on 25th April, and again at the time of the August offensive at Anzac and the landing at Suvla Bay, the issue hung in the balance, and there can be little doubt that a combined naval and military attack, carefully planned in every detail before the troops embarked, and carried out in April with all the essential advantages of surprise, could scarcely have failed to succeed. "Mr. Churchill's bold idea", says the German official account of the campaign, "was decidedly not a fine-spun " fantasy of the brain, and this is borne out by the state of " things at the beginning of March 1915."

In war it is only the sum of failures and successes that is of importance, and in weighing the results of the Gallipoli operations, with all their high hopes, their bitter disappointments, and their records of matchless heroism, it is right to remember that at the expense of a casualty list which was less than double that incurred on the first day of the Battles of the Somme, 1916, the Mediterranean Expeditionary Force in Gallipoli destroyed the flower of the Turkish Army, safeguarded the Suez Canal, and laid the foundation of Turkey's final defeat.

I have been greatly assisted in the compilation of this volume by the staff of the Historical Section, and especially by Captain W. Miles, who has collected, arranged, and scrutinized the vast number of official records of the campaign. I have also received valuable assistance from the loan of private diaries and letters dealing with the operations, and from the criticisms of a large number of officers who took part in the fighting. The late Admiral Sir John de Robeck read the book in manuscript and sent me a number of valuable notes on questions of fact regarding the co-operation of the fleet. I tender sincere thanks to Mr. W. B. Wood, M.A., for his helpful comments when reading the chapters in draft form ; to Brigadier-General A. T. Beckwith for the loan of the photographs reproduced to face pages 79, 189, and 276; and to the officers of the 2/Hampshire Regiment for permission to reproduce their picture of the landing from the *River Clyde*. The maps and sketches have been drawn for reproduction by Mr. H. Burge.

Every attempt has been made to ensure the accuracy of the history, but it is hoped that if any errors are noticed they may be communicated to the Secretary, Historical Section, Committee of Imperial Defence, 2 Whitehall Gardens, S.W.1.

C. F. A.-O.

1st October 1928.

CONTENTS

PART I

BEFORE THE LANDINGS

CHAPTER		PAGE
I.	TURKEY BEFORE THE WAR	1
	The Turkish Army in 1914	17
	Turkish Lines of Communication	20
	The Turkish Navy	21
	MILITARY SITUATION IN THE BALKAN STATES—AUGUST 1914	21
II.	THE DARDANELLES PROBLEM 1807–1914	25
	The Defences of the Dardanelles	31
III.	THE INITIATION OF THE DARDANELLES CAMPAIGN	39
IV.	THE INITIATION OF THE CAMPAIGN (*continued*)	63
V.	THE INITIATION OF THE CAMPAIGN (*concluded*)	93
VI.	PRELIMINARY PREPARATIONS AT ALEXANDRIA	108
VII.	FINAL PREPARATIONS AT MUDROS	130
VIII.	FINAL PREPARATIONS BY THE TURKS	153

PART II

THE BATTLES OF THE BEACHES

IX.	THE LANDING AT ANZAC:	
	The News at Turkish Headquarters	162
	The Demonstration off Bulair	163
	The Anzac Plan	165
	The Landing of the Covering Force	173
X.	THE LANDING AT ANZAC (*concluded*):	
	The Main Body	181

GALLIPOLI

CHAPTER		PAGE
XI. THE LANDING AT Y BEACH		201
XII. THE LANDINGS AT HELLES:		
The Plan		216
The Covering Force		222
The Landing at X Beach		224
The Landing at W Beach		226
The Landing at V Beach		230
The Landing at S Beach		236
XIII. THE LANDINGS AT HELLES (*concluded*):		
The Main Body		238
Review of the Operation		251
XIV. THE FRENCH DIVERSION AT KUM KALE		257

PART III

THE STRUGGLE FOR ACHI BABA

XV. THE DAY AFTER THE LANDING:		
Events at Anzac		266
Helles and Sedd el Bahr		273
XVI. OPERATIONS 27TH–30TH APRIL:		
The Advance at Helles, 27th April		281
Preparations for the First Battle of Krithia		284
The First Battle of Krithia, 28th April		288
Operations at Anzac		295
XVII. REINFORCEMENTS		300
XVIII. OPERATIONS 1ST–5TH MAY:		
British Submarines in the Marmara		308
The Attack on Baby 700, 2nd May		309
Raids at Suvla and Gaba Tepe		312
The Situation at Helles, 1st May		315
The Turkish Night Attacks, 1st–3rd May		317
Preparations for an Allied Advance		320
XIX. THE SECOND BATTLE OF KRITHIA, 6TH–8TH MAY		333
XX. THE END OF THE FIRST PHASE		348

SKETCHES

(*Bound in Volume*)

[*N.B.*—The spelling of the place-names in the Sketches and Maps agrees with the rulings, where such have been given, of the Royal Geographical Society's Permanent Committee on Geographical Names.]

1. The Theatre of Operations			*End-paper*
2. Germany's Eastern Ambition, 1914		*Facing page*	3
3. Constantinople and the Bosporus		,, ,,	19
4. The Objectives for 25th April		,, ,,	133
5. Turkish Dispositions before the Landings		,, ,,	157
5A. Dispositions of the Turkish 9th Division, Dawn, 25th April		,, ,,	159
6. The Three Anzac Ridges	} *Between pages*	{ 168	
7. Anzac		{ 169	
8. Y Beach		*Facing page*	207
8A. The Helles Beaches on 25th April		,, ,,	223
9. V Beach 9 A.M., 25th April		,, ,,	231
10. Kum Kale and Yeni Shehr		,, ,,	259
11. The Landings. Situation at Dusk, 25th April		,, ,,	261
12. Gully Ravine (from British Map)	} *Between pages*	{ 282	
13. Gully Ravine (from Turkish Map)		{ 283	
14. First Battle of Krithia		*Facing page*	285
15. Anzac. Approximate British Front Line, end of April		,, ,,	297
16. Attack on Baby 700, 2nd May		,, ,,	309
17. Turkish Night Attack, 1st/2nd May		,, ,,	317
18. Objectives for the Second Battle of Krithia		,, ,,	327
19. The Second Battle of Krithia, 6th–8th May		,, ,,	347

APPENDICES
(*At end*)

1. Lord Kitchener's Instructions to Sir Ian Hamilton.
2. Order of Battle, Mediterranean Expeditionary Force.
3. Sir I. Hamilton's Order for Landing, 25th April.
4. Instructions for Helles Covering Force.
5. Instructions to G.O.C. A. & N.Z.A.C.
6. Instructions for Kum Kale Landing.
7. Epitome of Orders issued by Vice-Admiral de Robeck.
8. Composition of Naval Squadrons
9. Epitome of Orders issued by Rear-Admiral Wemyss.
10. General Orders to Masters of Transports.
11. Medical Arrangements for the Landings.
12. Epitome of Orders issued by Rear-Admiral Thursby.
13. Suggested Action in event of Failure.
14. Gen. Birdwood's Order for Anzac Landing.
15. Gen. Birdwood's Instructions to 1st Australian Division.
16. 1st Australian Division Order for Landing.
17. 29th Division Order for Landing.
18. 29th Division Instructions for Covering Force.
19. 86th Brigade Operation Order No. 1.
20. Instructions to G.O.C. C.E.O.
21. Extracts from Signal Log, H.M.S. *Euryalus*.
22. 29th Division Order, First Battle of Krithia.
23. 87th Brigade Order, First Battle of Krithia.
24. G.H.Q. Order, Second Battle of Krithia.
25. 29th Division Order, Second Battle of Krithia.
26. 29th Division Order, Second Battle of Krithia (2nd Day).
27. G.H.Q. Order, Second Battle of Krithia (3rd Day).
28. 29th Division Order, Second Battle of Krithia (Final Phase).
29. Notes on Signal Arrangements.

ILLUSTRATIONS

The Landing from the *River Clyde*	*Frontispiece*
	Facing page
Sedd el Bahr and Morto Bay from the Air	79
Embarking Mules at Alexandria	126
Achi Baba from the High Ground above V Beach	137
The Seaward Face of First Ridge	167
Full Face View of the Sphinx	167
Anzac Cove	174
The Sphinx from the North	178
Walker's Ridge and Russell's Top	189
Gully Ravine	204
Diagram of the Helles Landings	217
W Beach	226
Sketch of V Beach, 9 A.M. 25th April	231
V Beach from the *River Clyde*, 8 A.M. 25th April	234
Turkish Wire Entanglement at Cape Helles	242
The Old Fort, Sedd el Bahr, and the Asiatic Shore	257
The Postern Gate, Sedd el Bahr	276
V Beach in May 1915	321
Naval Officers coming from Observation Station	356

PART I
BEFORE THE LANDINGS

CHAPTER I

Turkey Before the War

(Map 1 ; Sketches 1, 2, 3)

"Who is to have Constantinople? That is always the crux of Map "the problem."[1]

So wrote Napoleon to his ambassador in St. Petersburg in May 1808. The French fleet had been destroyed at Trafalgar two and a half years earlier, and the Emperor was nervous of Russian activity in the Mediterranean. "If Russia should hold "the Dardanelles," he explained in the same letter, "she would "be at the gates of Toulon, of Naples, and Corfu."

With the Turkish empire crumbling to decay, this question of the future guardianship of the Dardanelles was destined to exercise the statesmen of Europe for the next hundred years. Little by little it became the cardinal policy of the western capitals that neither Russia nor any other great Power could be tolerated as Turkey's successor. Regard for the safety of India and the whole position in the East kept Britain a firm adherent to this policy and induced her to take up arms in Turkey's support in the Crimean war. By the Treaty of Paris, which ended that war, the principle[2] was reaffirmed that foreign war vessels were prohibited from entering the Straits whilst Turkey was at peace.

Twenty-two years later a similar fear of Russian expansion persuaded the whole Concert of Europe, at Britain's instigation, to revise the Treaty of San Stefano, signed by the Russians and the Turks at the end of the Russo-Turkish war. As a result of the Congress of Berlin the provision made by that treaty for

---

[1] " Le fond de la grande question est toujours là: Qui aura Con-" stantinople? " " Lettres inédites de Napoléon Ier." Léon Lecestre. Tome i. No. 286.

[2] This principle had previously been affirmed by the Congress of London in 1841. The Sultan, in accordance with his ancient rights, notified his intention of prohibiting the entry of foreign war vessels into the Straits whilst Turkey was at peace; and the signatory Powers (England, France, Russia, Austria, and Prussia) agreed to respect those rights.

a "Big Bulgaria" under Russian influence was annulled by the great Powers, who feared that such a state might well become Russia's jumping-off place for a new attack on Constantinople.[1] The Congress also confirmed the principle that the Bosporus and the Dardanelles should be closed to foreign warships so long as Turkey remained at peace.

Up to 1914 this principle had never been abrogated, though the fear of a Russian fleet in the Mediterranean had practically disappeared. Individual war vessels could visit Constantinople by permission of the Sultan in times of peace; but in the event of a European war it was still incumbent upon Turkey, so long as she remained neutral, to prohibit foreign warships from passing through the Straits, and to intern any foreign man-of-war which remained in the Straits for more than twenty-four hours. But the treaty made no stipulation regarding merchant vessels; and so long as Turkey remained at peace trading ships of all nations had the right to use the Straits without let or hindrance from the Sublime Porte. It is important to bear this point in mind when considering the strategic situation at Constantinople at the outbreak of the Great War.

Thus it will be seen that up to 1914 Turkey owed her continued possession of Constantinople to the multiple and diverse interests of the Western Powers rather than to the justice of her cause or the strength of her own right arm. The history of Turkey had been darkened by so many and such appalling atrocities that little could be said in her defence. At best she was an awkward ally for nations who professed and called themselves Christian. But by the accident of her geographical position she helped to maintain the balance of European power; and no practicable alternative could be found for the custody of the Dardanelles.

Britain's not altogether disinterested generosity to the Turk at the time of the Crimean war was warmly appreciated at Constantinople, and for another forty years British prestige and influence were supreme at the Ottoman capital. This happy result was due not so much to British effort as to the fact that the Turk, though slow to form his convictions, is equally slow to relinquish them. British policy in Egypt, in Persia, in Macedonia, and in Crete was in many respects opposed to Turkish interests. Heedless of the advantages to their country in maintaining the *status quo* at Constantinople, the British public, burning with indignation at the long tale of Turkish

---

[1] Germany, at that time anxious for Russia's goodwill (see next page), was in favour of supporting the Tzar, but was outvoted by the other Powers. Sir Sidney Lee, " King Edward VII." i. p. 436.

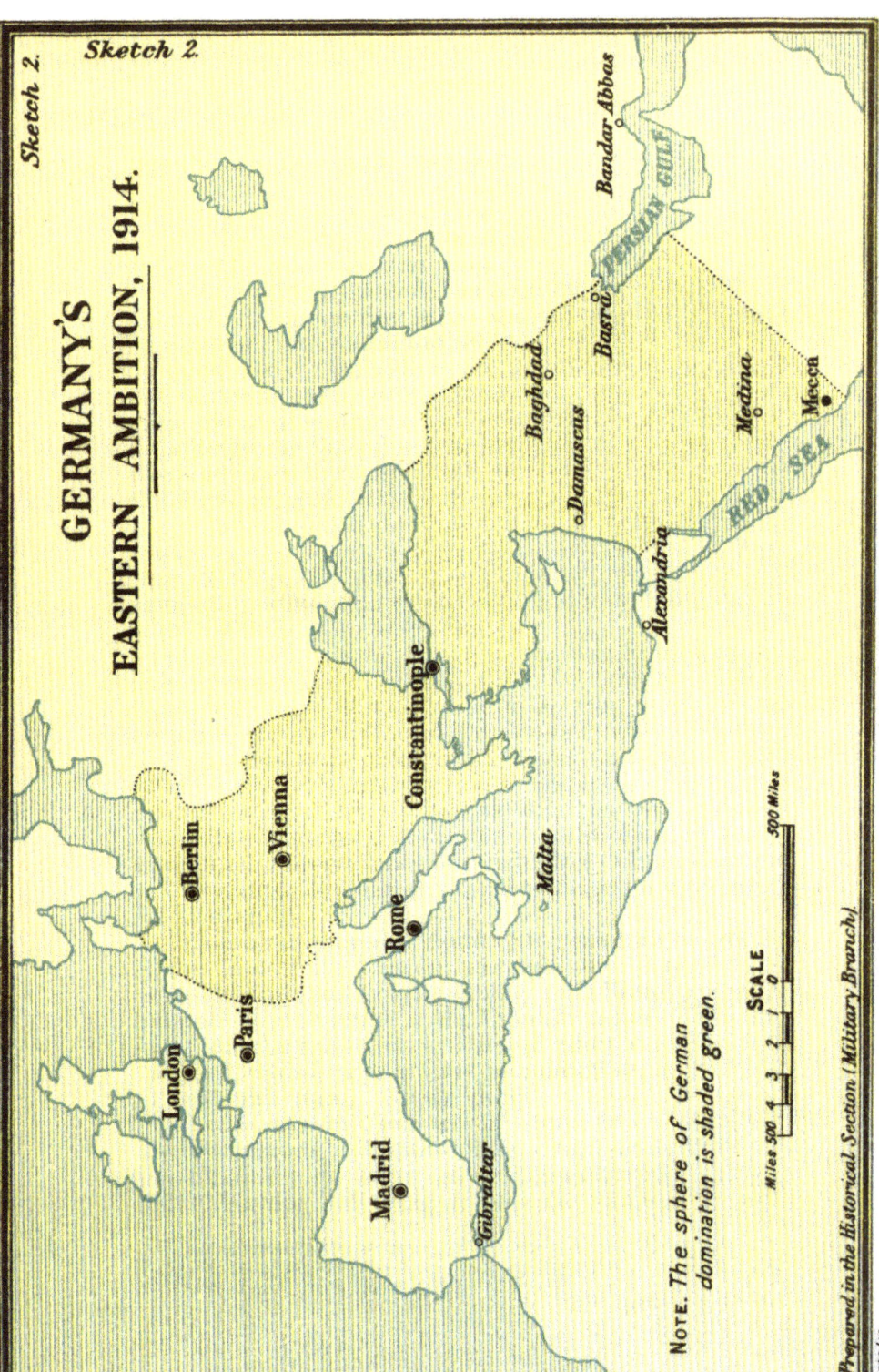

atrocities, had lost all patience with the Porte. The British press, and the public utterances of British statesmen, had left Turkey under no illusions regarding their abhorrence of her misdeeds. Nevertheless, for many years the Turks continued to regard Britain as their hereditary friend, as surely as Russia was their hereditary foe. Unable to stand alone, it was to Britain that they confidently looked for help from Russian aggression. But by the closing years of the nineteenth century this confidence had begun to wane, and though the effect was contrary to British interests, it was undoubtedly produced by outraged public opinion in England, and no British statesmanship could have conjured it away.

But if moral influences drew Britain away from Turkey, it was material interest which finally induced the Turks to widen the gulf. The conclusion of the Anglo-Russian agreement in 1907 gave definite point to Ottoman distrust in British policy, and confirmed the conviction that Turkey must look elsewhere for protection from Tzarist ambitions. This was the situation which Germany had long awaited, and Turkish suspicions of Britain were soon to be fostered by Berlin with every means open to a resourceful diplomacy.

Previous to 1875 the German Government took little personal interest in Turkish affairs. In that year, indeed, anxious to bring further pressure to bear on France, Germany approached the Court of St. Petersburg with an offer to withdraw her opposition to a Russian occupation of Constantinople if the Tzar would give her a free hand in the west. But on the summary rejection of this offer, Germany was forced to look east instead of west for expansion, and the resulting dream of an empire stretching from the North Sea to the shores of the Persian Gulf turned her thoughts for the first time in the direction of Constantinople.

Quietly, unobtrusively, and with infinite patience, she set herself from that moment to usurp Britain's predominant position at the Turkish capital. Whilst the rest of Europe resounded with indignation at Turkish atrocities, in Germany alone was no voice of criticism to be heard. In Germany alone, after England and France had refused, could a new Turkish loan be raised. It was Germany who sent a military mission to reorganize the army, and it was Germany who encouraged Turkish officers to complete their military education at Berlin. As soon as the Anglo-Russian Entente raised definite suspicions of British honesty of purpose, redoubled efforts were made by the German Embassy in Constantinople. No stone was left unturned to depreciate the value of British friendship. No opportunity was lost for pointing out that Germany was Turkey's only true friend, and that the future welfare of one country depended upon that of the other.

The German Foreign Office took the precaution of selecting none but their best men to represent them at Constantinople, and seldom has an ambassador been able to secure, by the exercise of his own personality, such important results for his country as did Baron Marschall von Bieberstein at the Turkish capital in the early years of the twentieth century. Appointed to Constantinople in 1897 he remained there for fifteen years. His ability and his knowledge of Turkish affairs were both profound, but it was not by these alone that his great success was won. He scored by his personality, by the impression he gave of brute strength, resolution, and ruthlessness. His giant stature, heavy build, and scarred face were all turned to account. To Turkish officers and officials, to the Turkish man in the street, he personified their idea of Germany's position in the world. During the last five years of his tenure of office he could do almost what he liked with the Turk.

Probably the one Englishman who could have countered Bieberstein's influence was Lord Kitchener, and this point seems to have been recognised by Kitchener himself. Writing from Simla to a friend in 1908 he said:

> I have always as you know been very much interested in the Eastern question.... Please let me know all you can on the subject. In old days I used to know Constantinople well, and speaking Turkish gave me rather a pull in seeing what was going on behind the scenes. It seems to me that we have now a great opportunity of retrieving our position in the Moslem world. The Turkish army is composed of some of the very best fighting material, and we have only to look at the Baghdad railway and the conduct of Russia in Persia to see how important it is for us to support Turkey and be the one to help her to reorganize her forces. I do not see how much could be done except as Ambassador. That post would, however, place whoever occupies it in a position to do a great deal, and unless we have a really good man there Russia or Germany will assuredly pull the chestnuts out of the fire. I still hold the rank and Sultan's commission of a Lieut.-General in the Turkish army, and should rather like to re-visit old haunts and see old friends, but it is not easy to see how this could be done.[1]

It certainly was not easy. Lord Kitchener was at that time Commander-in-Chief in India, and it can be no matter for

---

[1] Sir George Arthur, "Life of Lord Kitchener," ii. p. 281.

surprise if the idea of appointing him ambassador at Constantinople was never officially considered.

Baron von Wangenheim, who succeeded Bieberstein at Constantinople, was a man of similar pattern, and his dominating personality, cloaked by a somewhat suaver manner, exerted a similar influence. It was to him that Berlin looked in 1914 to induce Turkey to side with Germany in the event of a European war. Thus might the Dardanelles be closed, Russia cut off from France, a large portion of the Russian army sent to fight in the Caucasus, and, if Britain joined France, the British Empire distracted by threats against the Suez Canal.

Though even up to July 1914 a majority in the Turkish Cabinet was well disposed to England, its two most prominent members, Talaat Bey and Enver Pasha, had for long been anxious to accept German assistance to reconstruct their country. At first Talaat Bey does not seem to have been actively hostile to Britain. But it was his firm opinion that Germany was the only Great Power whose interests nowhere clashed with those of his own country. Enver Pasha, on the other hand, ever since a tour of duty as military attaché in Berlin in 1909, had been under the spell of German influence, and by 1913 was violently in favour of a German entente. This man, soon to become the German Ambassador's principal tool for bringing Turkey into the war, was at that time thirty-one years of age. Imbued with great force of character and unbounded conceit, he was to succeed in making himself Minister of War in January 1914, and after the outbreak of hostilities to be for all practical purposes the only Turk who counted.

With the help of these two men Germany was able at the end of 1913 to make a great stride towards the goal of her ambition. Previous to the Balkan war of 1912 the Turkish army had been reorganized by General von der Goltz,[1] but since his departure there had been no permanent German mission in Constantinople. A few German officers were employed as directors of the arsenal and the munition factory, but they had no outside power or influence. In many quarters, moreover, Germany was still being blamed for Turkey's defeat in the war. Little, however, had been done by the Turks to pull their army together after its defeat, and the whole service was suffering from official neglect. This was the situation when in December 1913, through the exertions of Baron von Wangenheim, an important German military mission of seventy officers, under General Liman von Sanders, was sent to Constantinople with

[1] He first arrived in Constantinople in 1883 as Director of Military Education.

greatly extended powers. The effect of this move was remarkable. Within three months of the mission's arrival German influence in the Turkish army was supreme.

About the same time a clever step was taken by Berlin to impress the Turk with a sense of Germany's growing power on the sea. British naval prestige was still pre-eminent at Constantinople, and the Turkish fleet was under the tuition of a British naval mission. In an endeavour to minimize that prestige, the German Admiralty sent out the *Goeben*, one of their newest battle cruisers, and the largest war vessel that had hitherto entered the Dardanelles, to pay an extended visit to the Turkish capital. The presence of this ship did more than undermine British naval prestige at Constantinople. She acted as an emblem of Germany. Anchored off the German Embassy, a palatial building which overlooks the entrance to the Golden Horn, many receptions were given in her, and at night she was a blaze of light from stem to stern. The little steamers which ply up and down the Bosporus would pass as close to her as possible, and the interested comments of their passengers were eloquent of the impression this mighty war vessel was building up in favour of Germany. No peace-time move of a single ship was ever fraught with more momentous consequence. A few months later, the presence of this one vessel in the Mediterranean was to secure Turkey as Germany's ally.

Thus, whilst the spring of 1914 ripened into summer, Turkey, with ever-growing momentum, was hurried along the path from which there was soon to be no escape. When the Serajevo assassinations threw over Europe the shadow of the approaching storm, the situation at Constantinople was ripe for a final and intensive effort by Germany to secure not only the goodwill of the Turkish Cabinet but the certainty of their active support. Extravagant promises were made by Baron von Wangenheim. The perpetual menace from Russia could be averted by a timely alliance. Caucasia, North-West Persia, and the Trans-Caspian provinces could be the reward of Germany's active ally at the end of a successful war.[1] India and other Moslem countries groaning under Christian oppression could be kindled into a flame of infinite possibilities for the Khalifate of Constantinople. Turkey would emerge from the war the one great Power of the East, even as Germany would be the one great Power of the West.

Even at this late hour, perhaps, the situation was not yet

---

[1] It is certain that Germany held out this promise of the realization of one of the dreams of the Pan-Turkish movement, and almost certain that a secret agreement on the subject was signed.

hopeless for the Entente. Traditional respect for British power was still a potent though fast diminishing factor. Enver Pasha, urging his colleagues forward, was meeting with strong opposition. The natural prudence of Talaat was inclining him towards neutrality until the general situation became more clear. The majority of the Turkish Cabinet, in addition to the Sultan and the heir apparent, were actively opposed to war.

A friendly gesture by Britain and France at that time, coupled with a guarantee of Turkish independence and integrity, might perhaps have recalled Turkey to her old attitude and ensured a benevolent neutrality in the Dardanelles.

But fate had decided otherwise. England, still unconscious that she herself was about to be plunged into war, and without any wish or intention that Turkey should become involved, was unaware of the fateful decision which the Turkish Cabinet was being called upon to make, and unmindful of the terrific consequences entailed. Through all the critical days of July and early August, the British Ambassador at Constantinople was absent on leave. By the time he returned on the 18th August the die was already cast.

As the war clouds gathered at the latter end of July the predominating anxiety of the Turks was to obtain a trustworthy guarantee of their own territorial integrity, and to secure the greatest possible advantages for their country from the rapidly approaching storm. Imbued, as the strongest members of the Turkish Cabinet were at this time, with a belief in German invincibility, unaware that Britain would enter the war, and convinced that the British Government would no longer stand in the way of Tzarist ambitions with regard to the Dardanelles, one course only appeared to be open to Turkey. From Germany alone, it seemed, could certain help be secured in the coming emergency. Thus it happened that Wangenheim's aims were attained. Late in the evening of the 27th July,[1] according to German documents, the Grand Vizier, prompted no doubt by the forceful persuasion of Enver, sent for the German Ambassador and formally "asked" for a secret defensive and offensive alliance between Germany and Turkey against Russia. In less than twenty-four hours Berlin had officially "accepted" this proposal.[2] Three

[1] The day before Austria-Hungary declared war on Serbia.
[2] Karl Kautsky, "Die deutschen Dokumente zum Kriegsausbruch," 1914, ii. The following translated extracts from telegrams show the sequence of events:
German Ambassador to Berlin. Constantinople 1.45 A.M. 28th July.
" The Grand Vizier has just sent for me and begged me to submit to
" the Emperor the Sultan's request for a secret defensive and offensive

days later, on the 31st July,[1] forcefully anticipating the consent of his Cabinet, Enver Pasha issued the order for immediate mobilization. On the 2nd August the treaty with Germany was signed. The following day the first mines were laid in the Dardanelles. Germany had won a bloodless victory. From that moment Constantinople became to all intents and purposes a German town.

Famous though the Dardanelles had been throughout the ages for their immense strategic importance, and greatly though the question of their ownership had exercised the mind of Europe for the last hundred years, it was left for the events of 1914–1918 to underline the full significance of Napoleon's dictum of 1808. Even Germany, who had worked so diligently to obtain control of the Straits, would not appear in August 1914 to have realized the full value of her achievement. She saw, no doubt, that in the course of the brief war which was all she then anticipated, it would be of great value to sever the only direct line of communication between France and Russia, and to detain a large Russian force in the Caucasus by a mere threat of Turkish invasion. She saw, too, that should Britain throw in her lot with France, it would be advantageous to distract her attention by a Turkish attack on the Suez Canal, and by the violent insurrections which could surely be fostered in India through Mahommedan sympathy with the Turk. But Germany's Turkish plans were connected not so much with the war as with what might happen afterwards. Once Russia and France had been defeated, and the Balkans reduced to a state

---

" alliance between Germany and Turkey against Russia. The *casus*
" *foederis* would arise if Russia attacked Turkey or Germany or Austria,
" or if Germany or the Triple Alliance attacked Russia. Against other
" countries than Russia Turkey does not ask for protection. . . . The
" Grand Vizier wishes the treaty kept secret even from the Turkish Ministers
" and from my colleagues. . . ."
    Bethmann Hollweg to German Ambassador. Berlin 9.30 P.M. 28th July.
" His Majesty accepts the Grand Vizier's proposals. The treaty should
" be concluded on the following basis. . . ."
    The actual treaty, signed on 2nd August, was practically similar to Bethmann Hollweg's proposals, except that Bethmann Hollweg suggested that it should last only " till the end of the war ". The Turks, according to Kautsky, objected to this short period as not giving them sufficient safeguards against Russian vengeance after the war. It was finally agreed that the treaty should last for the duration of Liman von Sanders's tour of duty in Turkey, *i.e.* till 31st December 1918. Few people anticipated at this time that the war would last longer than a few months.
    The signature of the treaty was kept secret from the majority of the Turkish Cabinet for several weeks. The text given by Kautsky is the only version ever seen in this country, but an additional document is believed to have been signed. See f.n. 1, page 6.
    [1] The date of Russia's general mobilization.

TURKEY BEFORE THE WAR

of vassalage, the dream of a Teutonic Empire stretching to the Persian Gulf could at last become a reality. This was the real focus of German vision, a focus which obscured the more immediate significance of the Straits. In company with the rest of the world, Germany had yet to realize that the closing of the Dardanelles could stop the life-blood of Russia's millions and seal their country's doom. At a later date the cabinets of the Entente, no less than that of Germany, were to learn this lesson. They were to learn, too, that the Dardanelles was the enemy's heel of Achilles; that a success at this point might rally the wavering Balkans to the banner of the Entente; that the forcing of the Straits might prove the beginning of the end.[1] But by the time this knowledge had been assimilated the opportunity for successful action had gone.

Wangenheim had negotiated his treaty; but Britain's sudden entry into the war was nearly to prevent its ratification.[2] Drawn up before the storm of 1914 had burst, and signed before it was realized that Britain would throw in her lot with France, Turkey's new alliance had exposed her to a peril which neither Enver nor Talaat had dreamed of. Till this moment their chief source of anxiety had been the Russian Black Sea fleet. This anxiety had been removed by Wangenheim undertaking that the *Goeben*, then in the Adriatic, together with the light cruiser *Breslau*, should at once return to Constantinople.[3] The German Admiral Souchon could then take command of the Turco-German fleet, which would be more than a match for the Russians, and the Turkish concentration in the Caucasus would be safe from interference.[4] But scarcely was the ink

[1] " Should the Dardanelles fall," wrote Admiral von Tirpitz on 8th August 1915, the day after the British troops had landed at Suvla, " the " world war has been decided against us." " Erinnerungen," p. 491.

[2] The treaty, according to Kautsky, had to be ratified one month after signature.

[3] The *Goeben* had just undergone a refit at Pola. The *Breslau*, the only other German warship in the Mediterranean at the outbreak of war, was at Durazzo.

[4] The following translated telegram from Admiral von Tirpitz to Baron von Wangenheim, despatched on 3rd August, explains the situation:
" *Goeben* and *Breslau* have been ordered to Constantinople forthwith. " The appointment of Admiral Souchon to command the Turkish fleet " rests with you. Please reply by telegram whether we can assist the " Turkish fleet with German personnel."
The German Foreign Minister (Herr von Jägow) telegraphed to Wangenheim the same day:
" As we must anticipate that England will attack us please make necessary " preparations in order that the British naval mission with the Turkish " fleet cannot act to our disadvantage and that Mahommedan loyalty in the " English colonies, especially India, will be upset. A revolution in the " Caucasus would be welcome," Kautsky, iv.

on the new treaty dry when, as the result of the invasion of Belgium, Britain sent her ultimatum to Berlin, and the nature of Turkey's danger at once stood clearly revealed.

Turkey's situation, especially *vis-à-vis* Russia, was certainly precarious. The chances of the *Goeben* eluding the British Mediterranean fleet seemed problematical. The Turkish arrangements for mobilization were far from complete, and the process of raising the army to a war footing would be slow and difficult. There was a grave shortage of war material, particularly of artillery, machine guns, and all classes of ammunition. Germany had engaged to supply these deficiencies; but the attitude of Bulgaria was uncertain, and if she should join the Entente the only communication between the German frontier and Constantinople would be severed. Even if Bulgaria remained neutral the amount of munitions that could arrive would be far below requirements, and owing to the dearth of factories at home it was vital for Turkey to be able to count on a constant supply from abroad. The Caucasian frontier would now be exposed to Russian attack, as also the Bosporus. Most important of all, in the opinion of everyone in Constantinople, the Dardanelles at that moment was at the mercy of the British fleet.

The Turkish ministers concerned with the treaty at once took counsel of their fears, and for the next few days at least there was undoubtedly a desire to withdraw from this new and dangerous commitment. As a preliminary measure the German Ambassador was informed that, treaty or no treaty, the most that Turkey could now do was to maintain a benevolent neutrality until her army was mobilized.[1] Wangenheim was quick to see the logic of this argument, and to realize that the temporary neutrality of Turkey was actually in Germany's favour. If the war should last only a few weeks, as was then expected, Turkey the friendly neutral would be as useful as Turkey the active ally, and her claims for consideration at the peace conference could be ignored. But well though he knew the Turks, the German Ambassador can have had little idea

---

[1] ". . . not only would it be of no benefit to Germany for us to take an active part in the war before our mobilisation was complete, but it would simply mean suicide on our part. If the English, French, and Russians, who knew perfectly well that we had not a single man at the Dardanelles, in Constantinople, or on the Russian frontier, made a sudden attack on the Dardanelles and the Bosphorus, simultaneously advanced on Erzerum, and after occupying Constantinople and Erzerum approached the interior of Anatolia through Sivas, our army would be unable to complete its mobilisation during the war, and the downfall of the Ottoman Empire would be decreed at the very outset." Djemal (Jemal) Pasha, "Memories of a Turkish Statesman," p. 116.

at that moment of the full depth of their duplicity. On the day after Britain's declaration of war Enver Pasha approached the Russian military attaché, General Leontev, with definite proposals for a Russo-Turkish alliance.[1]

Whether or not the terms offered by the Turkish War Minister could have been agreed to by France and Britain, even if they had proved acceptable to Russia, is a matter of vain speculation. The opportunity, even if genuine, was only a fleeting one. A few days later, with the safe arrival of the *Goeben*, Enver's mood had changed. The proposal, moreover, was never reported by Russia to England or France. The Triple Entente was not yet working as a team.

With Enver in doubtful mood it is not surprising that the waverers in the Turkish Cabinet were shaken to their foundations by Britain's entry into the war. It seems possible that these men might have resisted every persuasion to throw off the cloak of neutrality had it not been for two events which enormously strengthened Baron von Wangenheim's hand at this time.

The first of these events was the sudden appropriation by Britain of two Turkish battleships at that time building in British yards. The question of these ships lay very near to every Turkish heart. Ever since the seizure of the islands of Lemnos, Imbros, and Mitylene by the Greeks in 1912 Turkey had longed for a new war with Greece in order to get them back. With this object the battleships had been ordered, and so great was the popularity of the cause that, the national exchequer being empty, the money for their purchase had been largely raised by public subscription. The "man-in-the-street", therefore, no less than the government, was taking keen interest and pride in the approaching completion of these vessels, and it was an open secret that their usefulness was to be put to a practical test at the earliest opportunity. One of these ships was ready for delivery at the end of July 1914, and its Turkish crew had actually reached the Tyne when the critical situation in Europe decided the British Government on the 3rd August to inform Turkey that they proposed to take over the contract.

---

[1] See "The Partition of Asiatic Turkey," 1924, an official Russian publication of war documents. The Russian Ambassador (M. de Giers) and General Leontev appear to have been convinced of Enver's sincerity, and begged in vain for the immediate acceptance of his terms, which were briefly as follows:

(1) Turkey withdraws from the Caucasus and places an army at Russia's disposal in Thrace.

(2) All German officers dismissed from Turkish service.

(3) Western Thrace and the Ægean islands to be returned to Turkey after the war.

(4) A defensive Russo-Turkish alliance for 5-10 years.

The full wisdom of this step was not to be realized at the time, for not until long afterwards was it known that a treaty with Germany had been signed at Constantinople the previous day. But even on general grounds the decision was justified. Britain's very existence depended upon her retaining command of the sea, and her margin in dreadnoughts was only seven. To forgo this welcome and timely addition to their number was unthinkable. Still more unthinkable was it to let them pass into the hands of even a potential enemy. Nevertheless, though no other action was possible, the retention of these vessels was to prove of inestimable assistance to Wangenheim in developing the situation which eventually forced Turkey into war. Even without external pressure the Turk would have deeply resented what he looked upon as highway robbery. But external pressure was at once exerted with overwhelming force, and violent articles on Britain's perfidy at once began to fill the Turkish press.[1]

The second event, intimately connected, as it was made to appear, with the foregoing incident, was the arrival of the *Goeben* and the *Breslau* in the Dardanelles on the 10th August.

The arrival of these two vessels in Turkish waters was a momentous incident. When, at midnight on the 3rd August, they received Admiral von Tirpitz's telegram,[2] they were proceeding west to interfere with the transport of French troops from Africa. On receiving his new instructions Admiral Souchon at once headed back for Messina; but there, in consequence of Turkey's subsequent refusal to abandon her neutrality, further

---

[1] "Wangenheim's agents now filled columns of purchased space in the newspapers with bitter attacks on England for taking over these vessels. The whole Turkish press rapidly passed under the control of Germany. Wangenheim purchased the *Ikdam*, one of the largest Turkish newspapers, which immediately began to sing the praises of Germany and to abuse the Entente. The *Osmanischer Lloyd*, published in French and German, became an organ of the German Embassy. Although the Turkish Constitution guaranteed a free press, a censorship was established in the interests of the Central Powers. All Turkish editors were ordered to write in Germany's favour and they obeyed instructions. . . . A certain Baron Oppenheim travelled all over Turkey manufacturing public opinion against England and France. . . . Huge maps were pasted on walls, showing all the territory lost by Turkey in a century. Russia was portrayed as the nation chiefly responsible for these ' robberies ', and attention was drawn to the fact that England had now become Russia's ally. . . . Germany was pictured as Turkey's friend; the Kaiser suddenly became " ' Hadji Wilhelm ', the great protector of Islam, and stories were even printed that he had become a convert to Mahommedanism. The Turkish populace was informed that the Moslems of India and of Egypt were about to revolt and throw off their English ' tyrants ' . . . and the motive power of this infamous campaign was German money." Morgenthau, " Secrets of the Bosphorus," pp. 65-6.

[2] See f.n. 4, page 9.

orders were received on the 5th August, cancelling the move to Constantinople, and ordering him, in view of Britain's declaration of war, to seek temporary shelter at Pola. Later in the day, Austria having protested that she was not yet ready to risk being drawn into war with Britain, these orders, too, were cancelled, and Souchon was directed to choose his own line of escape. There were two alternatives: the Dardanelles or the Atlantic. Though his admission into the Straits was by no means certain, Admiral Souchon decided on the Dardanelles, and well was his choice rewarded. Leaving Messina on the afternoon of the 6th he successfully shook off the only fraction of the British fleet which caught sight of him, and after two anxious days in the Ægean, waiting for Wangenheim to persuade the unwilling Turkish Cabinet to break their neutrality, he was finally admitted by Enver's orders on the evening of the 10th.[1] Not only had he escaped from what seemed like certain destruction: he had brought his ships to the one place in the world where they could be of greatest use. Their presence at Constantinople was to have consequences which for many weeks few people in England dreamed of. They were to force Turkey into the war and Russia out of it, and were to be responsible for half the troubles of the Entente.

The safe arrival of these vessels—one more proof of German naval prowess—persuaded Enver and the bolder spirits of the war party to stand by the new treaty. But the majority of the Cabinet were still against them, and even to those who were most inclined for war it seemed advisable to keep up the pretence of neutrality till the defences of the Dardanelles had been improved. In common, therefore, with the rest of the Turkish Cabinet the war party continued to insist on Turkey's peaceful intentions, and every possible device was utilized for throwing dust in the eyes of the Entente. The British demand that, in accordance with existing treaty obligations, the *Goeben* and *Breslau* should at once either be interned or forced to leave the Straits was met with the transparent but unanswerable fiction that these vessels had been bought by Turkey; and, further, that the sole reason for their purchase was the recent detention of the two ships building in England. A formal undertaking was given that the German crews should at once be sent back to Berlin, but though this promise was vehemently reiterated by every responsible statesman for the next six weeks, it was never kept. On the 15th August the British

---

[1] According to a German eye-witness Enver issued these orders on his own responsibility without consulting the Cabinet. Kannengiesser, "Gallipoli," pp. 20-1.

naval mission under Vice-Admiral A. H. Limpus was suddenly removed from its executive command, and instructed, if it cared to remain, to continue work at the Ministry of Marine. A few days later Admiral Souchon was appointed Commander-in-Chief of the Turkish navy, and from that moment the Ottoman fleet, as well as the army, passed under German domination.

From this time onward, the evidence of Turkey's approaching entry into the war began daily to increase. Men, guns, and ammunition, smuggled through the neutral Balkan states, began to trickle into the capital by train from Germany; British and French ships were detained at Constantinople and their wireless destroyed; more mines were laid in the Dardanelles;[1] and the seaward defences of the Straits began to be improved under German direction. Throughout this period the British Embassy at Constantinople did not fail to keep Whitehall informed of the increasing menace of the situation; but swayed by the protestations of Turkish ministers, who to the end insisted on Turkey's peaceful intentions,[2] it continued at the same time to hold out hope that war might be averted.

The British Government were straining every nerve to maintain peace with Turkey, or at least to put off the evil day for as long as possible. Not only had Britain nothing to gain by an extension of the war area to the Near East, but her every interest appeared to be opposed to it. Turkey's first aggressive action would undoubtedly be an attack on the Suez Canal. Not a man could be spared from France for its defence; some weeks must

---

[1] Three lines of mines had been placed in position by 24th August. Between 16th August and the end of the month the British Embassy in Constantinople sent repeated reports of minelaying in the Straits and of the mounting of Hotchkiss guns to cover the minefields. On 26th August the German Ambassador was quoted as saying that the Germans had taken steps to make the Dardanelles impregnable. On 28th August German military reservists were reported as already allotted as part of the garrison at the forts. By the middle of September the Embassy had traced the arrival in Constantinople of a battery of field guns, several heavy howitzer batteries and thousands of rifles, as well as 3,000 rounds of ammunition for the *Goeben*. German reservists were said to have received instructions to enrol for service with the Turkish army, and on 20th September it was estimated that there were between 4,000 and 5,000 German soldiers and sailors in the Turkish capital. A special train with 500 German marines and sailors for Constantinople passed through Bucharest on 27th August.

[2] Jemal Pasha, Minister of Marine and member of the war party, took pride in the measure of success attained by his duplicity. Writing of an interview with Sir Louis Mallet, the British Ambassador, in which he assured him that Turkey would remain neutral, and that if the Germans tried to force her hand by committing an act of war in the Black Sea he would open the Dardanelles to the British fleet, he remarked: " It is certainly " astounding that this very perspicacious English diplomat believed my " words." " Memories of a Turkish Statesman," p. 126.

elapse before Indian troops could reach Egypt, and several months before the Dominion troops could cross the seas. Every week's delay before Turkey should take her probably inevitable plunge was therefore held to be of great military advantage, even though it similarly enabled the Turks to complete their arrangements. Further, it was considered essential to the position of Great Britain in Asia, with her millions of Moslem subjects, that if and when Turkey joined the Central Powers, it should be clear that it was the deliberate act of the Ottoman Government, with whom Britain had wished to remain at peace. In pursuance of this policy the British Government continued to overlook Turkey's constant and outrageous breaches of neutrality, and on the 22nd August 1914 went so far as to guarantee, with France and Russia, that if she would immediately dismiss the German officers and crews and re-open the Dardanelles to merchant shipping, the terms of peace at the end of the war should in no way prejudice Turkish independence and integrity.

In one particular alone would England permit herself to make a firm stand. She refused to admit the legality of the sale of the *Goeben* and *Breslau* so long as German crews remained on board, and categorically declared that if they attempted to leave the Dardanelles they would be treated as German vessels and sunk. Similarly, so long as German crews remained at Constantinople she would allow no Turkish war vessel to leave the Dardanelles. To give effect to this declaration, a British squadron was ordered to watch the entrance of the Straits.

By the beginning of September the position of the British naval mission at Constantinople had become so undignified that, on the advice of the Ambassador, it was withdrawn. The Admiralty now determined to utilize the local knowledge of Admiral Limpus, the chief of the mission, by appointing him to command the British Dardanelles squadron, and orders to that effect were actually issued. But with a chivalry which surely outstripped common sense this order was subsequently cancelled on the grounds that it would be unfair and unduly provocative to employ at the Dardanelles a man who had just acquired an intimate inside knowledge of the Turkish fleet.[1] While it is impossible not to take pride in such an example of fair play, even when confronted by every form of duplicity and deception, the effect of the generous gesture was to forgo the advantage of having at this vital point the admiral who, better than any other, knew the Turks and the Dardanelles.

[1] Churchill, " The World Crisis, 1911-1914," p. 491.

Great Britain's patience and magnanimity were all in vain. Turkey had now lost her independence, and the date of her entry into the war would depend solely upon German dictation. On the 27th September, in retaliation for the British squadron's refusal to allow a Turkish torpedo boat to enter the Ægean, the Turkish commandant of the Dardanelles, Jevad Bey, was persuaded by Vice-Admiral Merten, his German artillery adviser, to close the Straits. This was quickly done by filling the gap in the outer minefield with four mines.[1] This act, despite the protestations of the peace party in the Cabinet, was officially approved. Two days later the gaps in the other two existing lines of mines were filled and a fourth line added to the minefield. From that date, in contravention of all treaty rights, no vessel of any kind was allowed to enter the Straits.

So long as the war in France continued to move according to plan, Germany remained well content with the existing situation at Constantinople. No further pressure was exercised from Berlin during that period. In the absence of such pressure the peace-party believed that they were gaining the upper hand; and this impression was reflected in the more hopeful telegrams which began to reach England from Constantinople at the beginning of September. By the beginning of October, however, the German defeat on the Marne, and the successes of Russia in Galicia, had extinguished the hope of a speedy decision on which the whole German plan of campaign was originally framed.[2] The Austrians were begging for a reinforcement of 30 divisions from the Western front to restore the situation in Galicia, a demand which, owing to the serious situation in France and Belgium, could not be entertained. In the view of the German High Command the whole issue of the war was trembling in the balance, and an immediate diversion in the Near East was imperative. Unless Turkey could at once be dragged into the war, a further Russian success might finally deter her from joining the Central Powers.

It was in these circumstances that Wangenheim was given his final instructions by the Kaiser. Turkey's procrastination must be ended forthwith. If the consent of a united Cabinet could be obtained, so much the better. If not, the country

---

[1] The Germans had endeavoured to persuade the Turkish Government to close the minefield on 8th September, but Enver refused, owing to a fear that this would lead to an ultimatum from the Entente. The closing on 27th September was a great relief to the German mission at the Dardanelles, who reported subsequently that in the event of a sudden attack this work could not have been carried out in time, owing to the supineness of the Turks.

[2] Falkenhayn, "General Headquarters and its Critical Decisions," p. 28.

TURKEY BEFORE THE WAR

must be irrevocably committed to war by some sudden and flagrant act of the army or the fleet.

The acquiescence of the peace party still proving unobtainable, Turkey's German masters adopted the alternative course. Already, on the responsibility of Enver, several hostile raids, each forming a definite breach of neutrality, had been carried out on the Egyptian frontier. But it was clear that Britain's patience was well-nigh inexhaustible. Nothing short of a definite threat on the Canal would force her into war, and for this the Turkish army was not yet ready. But the fleet was capable of a not too dangerous task, and it was rightly considered that a rupture with the Entente could best be provoked by an attack on the Russian Black Sea ports.

On this sinister mission, probably without the consent of anyone but Enver, Admiral Souchon led the Turkish fleet quietly into the Black Sea on the evening of the 27th October. Before dawn on the 29th a wanton attack was made upon Odessa and other neighbouring towns; the *Goeben* sank the Russian minelayer *Prut* and bombarded Sevastopol; and a Russian gunboat was sunk at anchor without warning.

The inevitable had happened at last. Turkey had been forced across the Rubicon. On the 30th October the Russian Ambassador demanded his passports. After a final and ineffective demand for the immediate dismissal of the German military and naval missions, his British and French colleagues followed suit.

Now at last, without offending the susceptibilities of their Moslem subjects, Britain and France might have endeavoured to reopen by force of arms the vital communications with Russia which, in contravention of all treaty rights, had been closed for more than a month. The task would already have been more difficult than in September; it might already have been impossible of accomplishment. But engrossed as they were with the problems on their immediate fronts, the war councils of the Entente had not yet realized the fateful importance of the Dardanelles. The advice of those who had already recognized the immense value of a success in that theatre was for several weeks more to fall on deaf ears.

THE TURKISH ARMY IN 1914

When General Liman von Sanders arrived at the head of the new German military mission in December 1913 he was placed in command of the *I. Corps*, with headquarters in Constantinople. The appointment of a foreigner to the executive command of the troops in the Turkish capital was strongly resented by Russia and France. Diplomatic pressure was brought to bear upon the Sublime Porte to cancel the appointment, and shortly afterwards Liman von Sanders was given the rank of a Turkish marshal and appointed Inspector-General of the army.

It needed but a few weeks' experience of his surroundings to show the new Inspector-General that from top to bottom the Turkish army was thoroughly unready for war. As a result of their recent defeats in the Balkans, the morale of the troops was at a low ebb, and the dangerous effect of this condition was being increased by official neglect. No pay had been issued for months. Except in the capital the men were ill-fed. Their uniforms were in rags. The infantry were physically unfit to execute any manœuvre, and in many cases could not march for lack of boots. Staff and regimental officers alike were for the most part ignorant of their duties. Hospitals were in a deplorable state, and the disorder in the administrative services was chaotic.

German criticism was at first unwelcome. A Turkish divisional commander, who had the imprudence to tell the Inspector-General the truth, was, by Enver's orders, immediately dismissed. For some time, indeed, the German mission had considerable difficulty in overcoming the proverbial obstruction with which every request for reform had hitherto been met.[1] Able soldier though he was, diplomatic tact formed no part of the equipment of the new marshal. Intolerant of inefficiency, he was too impatient for reform to accept the official excuses for procrastination, and it was probably for this reason that considerable friction soon developed between himself and Enver, a friction which was never wholly eliminated.

Despite this serious disadvantage the work of the German mission was so far successful that during the spring and summer of 1914 the efficiency of the army rapidly improved. The recent defeats of Kirk Kilisse and Lule Burgas were useful object lessons in the necessity for reform, while the national hope for a new war with Greece provided a yet stronger inducement to the War Ministry to listen to German advice. On the 31st July, therefore, when mobilization was ordered, the army had gone far to recover from its plight of the previous December, and thenceforward it enjoyed the advantage of three undisturbed months in which to place itself on a war footing. Furthermore, though Liman von Sanders found fault with the training of the

[1] Liman, " Fünf Jahre Türkei," pp. 19-23.

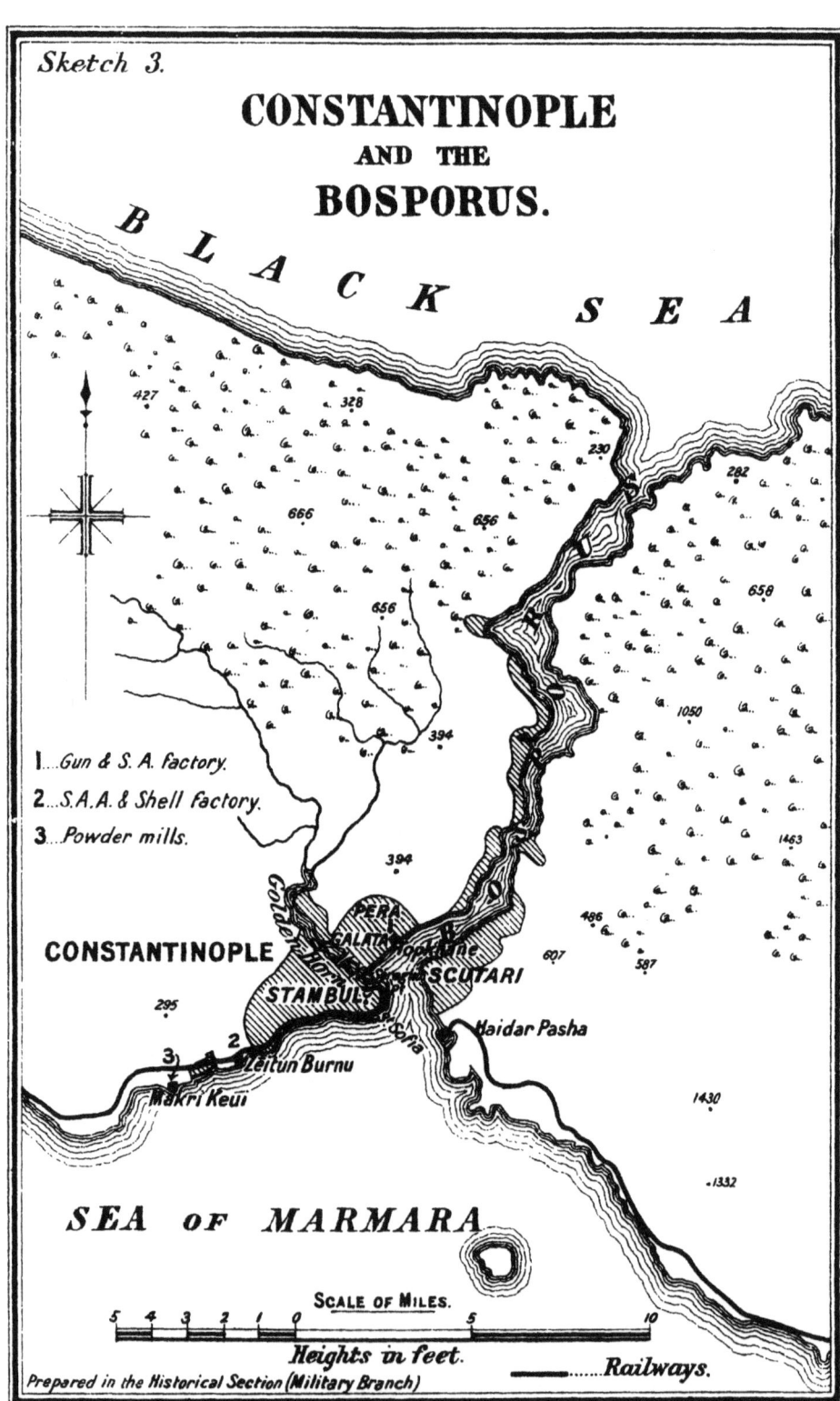

THE TURKISH ARMY

officers, the majority of them, unlike their Allies, had had the advantage of recent experience of warfare under modern conditions. It may be assumed therefore that, in spite of serious deficiencies in equipment and material, the Turkish army in November 1914 was at least as ready for war as in any recent period in its history. It must also be remembered that two months more were to elapse before any serious fighting occurred, and that by the time the army was called upon to meet the Allied landing in Gallipoli it had been on a war footing for nearly nine months.

So far as can be ascertained, about 800,000 men were called up during the 1914 mobilization, and early in 1915 the peacetime establishment of 36 divisions had probably been increased to 45. In the course of the war some 70 divisions were raised, but this number was never in being at the same time, as new formations were often broken up in order to keep first-line divisions up to strength.

The nominal composition of a Turkish army corps was one cavalry brigade (1,400-2,000 sabres, 12 machine guns and 8 horse artillery guns) and three—in some cases two—infantry divisions with a varying number of artillery and ancillary units.

An infantry division comprised, as a general rule, three regiments, each consisting of three battalions and one machine-gun company of 4 Maxim or Hotchkiss guns.

There were four companies to an infantry battalion, and the war establishment of a company was 266 all ranks; but at the outbreak of war the rifle strength of a division was probably never more than 9,000. The men were armed with 1903 pattern Mauser rifles, but on mobilization there was a deficiency of these weapons and a large number were imported during the autumn of 1914.

The divisional field artillery—organized in battalions, each of three 4-gun batteries—was supposed to consist of from twenty-four to thirty-six field or mountain guns.

A khaki uniform had been adopted for the whole army.

The air service in November 1914 was still in an inefficient state, nor was there much improvement during the following year, though a number of aeroplanes arrived from Germany.

Supply and transport arrangements, though fairly well organized near Constantinople, were indifferent in other parts of the empire, where they depended chiefly on local improvisation.

There was a gun and rifle factory in Constantinople, and a

small arm ammunition and shell factory at Zeitun Burnu.[1] Turkey would have to depend largely upon Germany for her requirements. There were no shell factories in Asia Minor.

Map 1. By the end of 1914 the distribution of the Turkish army was as follows: in Turkey in Europe there were concentrated under Marshal Liman von Sanders, who commanded the *First Army*, 10 Regular divisions,[2] (including one in the Gallipoli peninsula), 3 provisional divisions, and 3 cavalry brigades. On the Asiatic side from Scutari to Smyrna was the *Second Army* of 4 Regular divisions (including one on the Asiatic shore of the Straits), and one or two provisional divisions. In the Caucasus was the *Third Army* of 11 Regular divisions, of which one came from Constantinople, and one from the Baghdad area, with 2 cavalry brigades and a large number of Kurdish levies.

Between Aleppo and the Egyptian frontier were 7 Regular divisions and one provisional division. This force, together with 10,000-12,000 Arab irregulars, formed the *Fourth Army*, which included the Egyptian expeditionary force for the attack upon the Suez Canal. Jemal Pasha, formerly minister of Marine, who reached Damascus in November, was in command of this group.

Two Regular divisions were in the Yemen, two in Mesopotamia, and two in the Hejaz and Asir districts.

Over and above these formations there were numerous fortress troops, chiefly artillery and engineers, and a number of battalions of gendarmerie. The latter were all old soldiers, and bore a high reputation for steadfastness in defence.

TURKISH LINES OF COMMUNICATION

The paucity of railway communications in the Turkish Empire, and the shortage of locomotives, rolling stock, and fuel, were a severe military handicap, and rendered the transfer of troops from one theatre to another a matter of great difficulty. In peace time the main line of communication between Constantinople and the Asia Minor coast, and the coasts of Syria and Armenia, was by sea. This line was now closed, and no through railway communication was in existence. The main line of communication with the Gallipoli peninsula was also by sea, the only alternative being by rail to Uzun Keupri on the Adrianople line, and thence by road *via* Keshan and the

---

[1] On the Marmara coast just outside the capital.
[2] The word division is somewhat misleading, as many of the divisions were much below strength both in infantry and guns.

THE TURKISH NAVY

isthmus of Bulair. The distance from Uzun Keupri to the Narrows by road was 100 miles.

Strategically the most important railway was the Baghdad line, which was eventually to link Scutari (on the Asiatic side of the Bosporus, opposite Constantinople) with Mesopotamia, Syria, and Arabia. But the value of this line was discounted by two large gaps where tunnels were incomplete, one through the Taurus mountains, the other through the Amanus range. Troops and stores coming from the west, on reaching the Taurus mountains, had to be detrained and despatched by a well-graded road to Tarsus, 30 miles distant. Here railway transport across the plain of Adana again became available as far as the Amanus range, when once more the only route was a difficult road over mountains four thousand feet high. A temporary narrow-gauge line was completed through the Amanus tunnel by the end of 1915, but the Taurus tunnel remained unpierced until 1918.

East of the Amanus range the railway ran to Aleppo, and thence to the Euphrates, whilst another line (the Hejaz railway) connected Aleppo and Medina, with branches to the Syrian ports.

THE TURKISH NAVY

Apart from the *Goeben* and *Breslau*, the Turkish navy consisted of three old battleships, two protected cruisers, two torpedo cruisers, eight destroyers, ten torpedo boats, and seven minelayers. When Admiral Souchon took over command he regarded only the two German vessels as fit for active operations, and relegated all other ships to the reserve. Exercises were arranged for these latter vessels, and as individual ships became more efficient they were gradually added to the active squadron, which at the end of October consisted of the *Goeben, Breslau,* one Turkish battleship (*Messudieh*), one protected cruiser, two torpedo cruisers, and eight destroyers.

MILITARY SITUATION IN THE BALKAN STATES, AUGUST 1914

It remains to notice briefly the military situation in the neighbouring Balkan states at the beginning of August 1914. Since Germany first cast envious glances in the direction of the Persian Gulf, British diplomacy had worked for a confederation of these states to bar the German path. But the age-long hatreds and jealousies of the Balkans had frustrated the growth of mutual confidence, and every effort in this direction had so far met with failure.

After the Balkan war of 1912, in which Bulgaria, Serbia, Montenegro, and Greece, formed into a Balkan League by King Ferdinand, had for once joined forces against the Turk, the victors came to blows over the division of the spoils. Before the war, Serbia had promised large portions of the districts of Uskub and Monastir to Bulgaria. But in view of the unexpected capture of Adrianople by the Bulgars, Serbia contended that, having won so great a prize in the east, Bulgaria should be content to let both the western districts of Macedonia pass to her. At the invitation of Britain a conference was held in London to decide the issue, and a treaty was concluded in May 1913, by which Bulgaria was given a large increase of territory, including Adrianople, but was excluded from all the parts of Macedonia to which she laid claim. Scarcely had the treaty been signed before Bulgaria turned upon her old Allies and invaded Macedonia. Here her advance was countered by an alliance between Serbia and Greece. During the fighting which ensued, Rumania jumped on the back of her old Bulgarian enemy, and Turkey, seizing her opportunity, reoccupied Adrianople. The result of this second war was disastrous to Bulgarian ambition. Though by the resulting treaty of Bucharest her territory was considerably greater than before 1912, she had lost the valuable prize of Adrianople without any compensating gain in Macedonia, and was in addition obliged to cede to Rumania more than 3,000 square miles of corn-growing lands hitherto in her undisputed possession.

The year 1914 dawned therefore upon a restless situation in the Balkans. Though peace had been restored, the heat engendered by the recent war had not abated. In Bulgaria, where deep grudges were being nursed against Serbia, Rumania, and Turkey alike, the smouldering embers of discontent were ready to leap into flame with the first breath of opportunity. The Bulgarian king, though his personal sympathies were entirely German, was expected, in the event of a European conflagration, to offer his sword to that side which seemed most likely to win; and in August 1914 it was rightly anticipated that he would remain neutral until the probable issue of the struggle became more clear. He longed to take Macedonia from the Serbs, and Adrianople from the Turks. But to achieve both aims was impossible. Serbia, through force of circumstances rather than from choice, was in the Entente group; Turkey was probably joining the Central Powers. Hostility with one would necessitate friendship with the other. For the moment, therefore, though inclined to believe that the Central Powers would win, King Ferdinand was anxious to postpone his fateful choice of friends.

The war strength of the Bulgarian army was about 300,000, and despite its recent reverses it had fought with such distinction against the Turks in 1912 that its reputation still stood very high.

Serbia, whose war strength stood at 250,000, had already been committed to the side of the Entente in August 1914 by the Austrian ultimatum, and her position, should Bulgaria join Germany, was precarious.

The Greek army had a mobilization strength of 250,000, of whom at the moment only 180,000 could be equipped. Greece was still under an obligation to assist Serbia if attacked by "a third power"; but as the first article of the military convention distinctly laid down that such help would only be given "in circumstances foreseen by the Greco-Serb treaty", *i.e.* in the event of an attack by Bulgaria, the Greek Government had not unnaturally informed their Ally that they would be forced to remain neutral until Bulgaria showed her hand. With regard to Greece's attitude towards the Great Powers, though King Constantine was the Kaiser's brother-in-law he fully realized that to join the Central Powers would be to place his capital, his coasts, and his islands at the mercy of the British fleet. The country as a whole was in sympathy with the Entente, feeling that its interests as a maritime nation, and its hopes of future expansion, were dependent upon the victory of Britain and France. This sympathy was likely to become even more pronounced if Turkey, the hereditary enemy of Greece, should definitely join the Central Powers. Nevertheless, in Greece as in Bulgaria, there was a general feeling that the Central Powers would win, and self-interest was tending to keep that sympathy within strictly passive bounds. On the whole, therefore, the country was in favour of neutrality, at any rate until the probable result of the struggle could be seen more clearly. But this caution was not shared by the Greek Premier. Within a fortnight of Britain's declaration of war, M. Venizelos, with the King's unwilling concurrence, placed his country's naval and military resources at the unreserved disposal of the Entente.

Finally, on the borders of the Balkan states was Rumania, with an army of 350,000 men and huge resources in grain and oil—a valuable ally for either side in the coming struggle. Strategically, Rumania's position was of great importance, especially from the point of view of an Anglo-French campaign against Turkey, for so long as the Serbian boundary remained intact the only route between Germany and Constantinople passed through Rumanian territory. The King was a German; but his son had French sympathies and was married to an English princess, and the Government and people were strongly pro-Entente. But Rumania too was waiting to guess the probable direction of the wind. She had many aspirations and many fears. To a certain extent she might gain great advantages from the victory of either side. She coveted Transylvania from Austria - Hungary, and Bessarabia, beyond her eastern frontier, from Russia. But she was in uneasy possession of the valuable province of Dobruja, snatched from Bulgaria in 1912, and the attitude of Bulgaria was shrouded in mystery. For the moment, therefore, prudence dictated a non-committal attitude. The Government decided on a rôle of strict neutrality, and in the first days of August they invited representatives of Bulgaria, Turkey, and Greece to a conference at Bucharest with a view to the establishment of a solid neutral *bloc* in the Balkans. It is of interest that at this conference Talaat Bey, the Turkish representative, admitted that Turkey was "no longer free" to accede to Rumania's request.

In point of fact the Rumanians were even more friendly to the Entente than was for some time recognized in London, for certain arrangements likely to be of advantage to the Entente were concluded with Russia in September 1914, although not communicated to the British Foreign Office by St. Petersburg till the following April. But in Bucharest it was held to be dangerous to help the Russians, or even Serbia, while the attitude of Bulgaria, thirsting for her lost Dobruja, remained in any doubt.

CHAPTER II

THE DARDANELLES PROBLEM, 1807–1914

(Maps 1, 2; Sketch 1)

To force the passage of the Dardanelles, and to retain command of its narrow waterway, had been for a hundred years regarded as one of the most difficult yet most interesting operations of war. The problems to be solved were such as fire the imagination. They were presented upon the most historic of all stages for a noble feat of arms. They offered to a successful solution the most far-reaching and decisive advantages. Interest in them was excited rather than diminished by the notorious risks involved.

The first comparatively modern attempt to force the Straits was made by the British Admiral Duckworth in 1807, with ships alone. The motive on this occasion was to some extent the same as in 1915. England was asked to assist Russia against Turkey, and to assist her at once. The order came from home, and it was in vain that Sir John Moore, then second-in-command of the Sicily garrison, protested against a scheme which included no troops to secure the passage, although troops for that purpose were available.[1] The British Navy has never

1807.

---

[1] Almost at the same moment 7,000 British troops were sent on a fruitless expedition to Alexandria. Sir John Moore's comments on this episode (see " The Diary of Sir J. Moore," ii. p. 151) would have repaid study in 1915. " My opinion ", he wrote on 5th February 1807, " is that " the expedition to Alexandria is ill-judged. . . . It would have been well " to have sent 7,000 or 8,000 men with the fleet to Constantinople, which " would have secured their passage through the Dardanelles and enabled " the admiral to destroy the Turkish fleet and arsenal, which, from the " want of such force, he may not be able to effect." Again on 15th April 1807 he wrote: " If the Alexandria expedition had been deferred, and " 7,000 troops had accompanied Sir John Duckworth's squadron, Con-" stantinople and the Turkish fleet might have been destroyed."

Duckworth's despatch without troops is also criticised by Lieut.-General Sir H. Bunbury in his " Narratives of some Passages in the Great " War with France 1799–1810," p. 283. Discussing the Alexandria expedition, Bunbury wrote: " Another mode appeared to be this: That " 20 sail of the line instead of 7, and with 10,000 troops on board, should " have been despatched direct to Constantinople. . . . But instead of

been in the habit of quarrelling with an order on the ground of its impracticability. Duckworth, with seven ships of the line, ran the batteries, destroyed a Turkish squadron, and was making for Constantinople when he was caught by a head wind while still eight miles from the city, which in the last resort he had been ordered to destroy. The Turkish authorities refused to listen to an admiral who could do nothing to hurt them. His overtures and threats were alike unheeded. After waiting another week for a wind, he at last retired; and his fleet suffered the loss of 150 men in repassing the batteries of the Dardanelles. No ships were lost, and the casualty list was the least serious consequence of this unfortunate enterprise. A heavy blow was dealt to British prestige, and Russia, a few months later, signed the peace of Tilsit with Napoleon.

The lesson, for that time, was learned. The British naval expedition despatched later in the year to demand the surrender of the Danish fleet at Copenhagen was accompanied by a landing force of 27,000 men, and the combined operation was brilliantly successful.

The Duckworth episode also led to a strengthening of the belief, already current in the Services, that ships alone cannot be expected to command decisions on shore without the assistance of troops. The belief hardened into a maxim, which remained virtually unchallenged throughout the century.

But to a Power whose principal strength lay on the sea, and who, in a Near-Eastern crisis, would be more likely to have ships than an army available, this maxim could never be very popular. In successive Governments, therefore, despite the fact that numerous official reports confirmed the current opinion of the Services, the hope that ships alone might be able to open and keep open the Dardanelles was never wholly extinguished.

1877. An instance of this occurred in 1877, when, at the time of the Russo-Turkish war, there was a possibility of Britain entering the struggle on the side of the Turks. In view of this possibility the British Mediterranean Fleet was assembled at Besika Bay, with orders to be ready to proceed to Constantinople. But the thought of entering the Marmara without first ensuring that the Russians could not occupy the Gallipoli peninsula, drew many expostulations from the naval commander-in-chief, Admiral Sir Geoffrey Phipps Hornby, who urged that a British garrison should first be landed to assist the Turks to hold the Bulair

---

" acting vigorously in either one or the other direction our Cabinet came
" to the miserable determination of sending 5 or 6 men-of-war, without
" soldiers, to the Dardanelles, and 5,000 soldiers, without a fleet, to
" Alexandria."

lines. Writing on the 10th August 1877 to Lord Derby, the British Foreign Secretary, he agreed that the fleet could force the Dardanelles with little trouble. But he pointed out that it would be impossible to keep the passage open for transports and colliers if the European shore of the Narrows was held by hostile troops. In such a case mobile guns would be used to defend the waterway, and it "would be most difficult for "men-of-war to silence them". On the 13th February 1878, after the signature of the armistice between the Turks and the Russians, the British fleet was ordered to proceed to the Marmara,[1] and it remained in the vicinity of Constantinople till peace was finally signed. But though a Turkish garrison was in occupation of the Bulair isthmus, Admiral Hornby was still nervous for the safety of his communications. On the 19th February he wrote to the First Lord of the Admiralty: "There " seems to be an idea that this fleet can keep the Dardanelles " and Bosphorus open. Nothing can be more visionary. " Not all the fleets in the world can keep them open for un- " armoured ships."[2]

The re-arming and reorganization of the coast defence batteries in 1885 and the following years were held by professional opinion to have increased the difficulties of the Dardanelles problem. From that date, not only was the idea of a naval raid generally considered impracticable, but even a combined naval and military operation began to be regarded in the Services as a doubtful enterprise.

Here the question was allowed to rest till, in 1904, a sudden emergency led to a fresh examination of the problem by Admiral Sir John Fisher, newly appointed First Sea Lord. It was a subject on which that officer was well qualified to speak. He had commanded a battleship under Admiral Hornby in 1878, and during the last three years, while in command of the Mediterranean Fleet, he had made a close study of the Dardanelles problem on the spot. Now, in his new capacity, he was again to ponder over the famous riddle, and his conclusion was not a hopeful one. He satisfied himself that even with military co-operation the enterprise would be "mightily " hazardous".

1904.

Two years later a dispute arose between Turkey and Britain over the Turco-Egyptian boundary. Turkey eventually admitted

[1] The fleet passed through the Dardanelles, with the tacit consent of the Turks, on the morning of 13th February. A north-east gale was blowing, with heavy snow, and the weather was very thick. The fleet consisted of *Alexandra, Agincourt, Achilles, Swiftsure, Téméraire, Sultan, Salamis, Hotspur,* and *Ruby.*
[2] Mrs. Fred Egerton, " Admiral Sir Phipps Hornby, G.C.B.," p. 253.

1906. the justice of the British claim, but the British Government, uncertain as to the best way of bringing pressure to bear on the Porte, should such a step ever become necessary, assembled a joint naval and military conference to consider the matter for the future guidance of British diplomacy.

In their memorandum on this conference, dated the 19th December 1906, the General Staff concurred in the opinion of the Naval Intelligence Department that an attempt to force the Dardanelles with ships alone was unlikely to attain any useful purpose. It might be possible for a squadron of "His Majesty's "least valuable ships" to rush the Straits and reach Constantinople. But if the Turkish Government kept their heads, and retired into the interior, leaving Constantinople an undefended city, little would have been gained. The squadron must in the end return to the Ægean, and, as in the case of Admiral Duckworth, would probably again suffer heavily in the Straits. Such an operation, therefore, was "much to be "deprecated".

The General Staff memorandum next examined the possibility of a sudden *coup de main* by a force of 5,000 troops, secretly embarked at night at Malta and thrown ashore on the Gallipoli peninsula as a complete surprise. It was considered that a surprise of this nature might be effected, the forts taken in rear, and a passage opened for the fleet. On the other hand, it would be so difficult for the military force subsequently to extricate itself, or to hold on till reinforced, that this scheme was as much to be deprecated as the first.

Finally the General Staff examined the question of a combined naval and military operation on a large scale. They agreed that such an operation, having for its object the capture of the Gallipoli peninsula and the destruction of the forts, would, if successful, lead to immediate and decisive results. But two grave factors were held to prejudice the chances of success. First, following a period of profound peace, it would be impossible to prevent the Turks from knowing about the mobilization and despatch of the expeditionary force and its obvious objective. By the time the troops arrived, every possible landing-place would be defended, and at least 100,000 men would be waiting to oppose their disembarkation. Secondly, it was considered that a landing could not be effected in the face of modern weapons unless the covering squadron could guarantee with its guns that the troops would reach the shore unmolested, and would find after disembarkation a large enough area free from hostile fire to enable them to form up for battle on suitable ground. The General Staff were not persuaded that this absolute guarantee could be given, and their strategical study ended with the following words:

> However brilliant as a combination of war, and however fruitful in its consequences such an operation would be if crowned with success, the General Staff, in view of the risks involved, are not prepared to recommend its being attempted.

The Naval Intelligence Department, on the other hand, whilst concurring in the great risks involved, were of opinion that the General Staff underrated the value of naval artillery support. They held that such an attack could succeed, but that the Government would have to be prepared to use a considerable force and to face heavy casualties.

In 1908 the operation was again considered in the War Office. It was then suggested that, if secrecy could be maintained by despatching troops ostensibly for the protection of Egypt, and deflecting their course after Malta had been passed, and if the fleet and the expeditionary force could arrive at the peninsula unexpectedly and together, the forcing of the Dardanelles would be a feasible operation. The scheme included an attack on the forts by naval gunfire, simultaneously with a landing of 20,000 men south of Gaba Tepe to assault the western slopes of the Kilid Bahr plateau, at that time said to be undefended.

1908.

Three years later, in 1911, the question was again reviewed by the General Staff. This time the opinion of 1906 was confirmed, that owing to the impossibility of effecting a surprise, an attempt to disembark an army on the Gallipoli peninsula would be too hazardous to be recommended.

1911.

From this time to the outbreak of the Great War no further study of the Dardanelles problem was made, even though from 1910 onwards the opinion of the General Staff [1] was hardening into a certainty that Turkey would join the Central Powers in the event of a European conflagration.

This lack of further official interest in the question was not wholly due to a belief that the last word on the subject had already been written, for various new conditions, non-existent before 1911, had recently been accumulating, some of which undoubtedly tended to reduce the hazards of the enterprise. The great advance in range and power of naval guns; the increasing practicability of artillery observation by aircraft; the rapidity with which, in the new dreadnought era, ships

---

[1] Letter from the Director of Military Operations, War Office, to the Chief of the General Staff, India, dated 13th December 1910.

became obsolescent and surplus to main fleet requirements—all these were factors which might facilitate the solution of this century-old problem and enable vessels of unexpected power to be classed among "His Majesty's least valuable ships". Certain bombarding experiments, too, had recently attained an unexpected degree of accuracy; and in many quarters it was beginning to be felt that a duel between ships and forts need no longer be so one-sided a contest as in the past. Above all, there was the important point that previous studies of the problem had taken into consideration a war between Turkey and England alone, following a period of profound peace, when the mobilization, departure, and probable destination of an expeditionary force could scarcely escape notice, and when the whole of Turkey's armed forces would be available to support the defence. An attempt to force the Dardanelles which formed merely a single episode in a world war, which could be undertaken by two or more allies, which would find Turkey's attention deflected by campaigns in other parts of her empire, and which could be set on foot with complete secrecy, thus enjoying the advantages of surprise, would be free from many of the objections foreseen by the memorandum of 1906.

But despite these hitherto unexamined possibilities, the idea of an attack upon the Straits formed no part of Britain's pre-war plans to meet the emergency of a world-wide struggle in which Turkey might be found in the opposite camp. Should Britain be drawn into such a war it was held that the only place for the employment of her expeditionary force would be in line with the French armies. The defeat of Germany would mean the collapse of the Central Powers. This end could be attained most quickly on the Western front. Every available man must therefore be concentrated in France for this purpose; and whether Turkey should be a belligerent or not, no British troops could be spared for a major enterprise in another theatre of war. It was confidently believed, not only by Britain, but by France and Germany as well, that a great European war could not last for six months. The German Great General Staff held that one great battle in France would decide the issue, and that it would take place in the sixth week after mobilization. It appeared certain, therefore, that no opportunity would arise for a large expansion of the British army during the course of hostilities, and that the only action open to Britain against a hostile Turkey would be the passive defence of Egypt and the safeguarding of British interests in the Persian Gulf. This view still represented accepted military opinion at the outbreak of the Great War, and it was this view

THE DARDANELLES DEFENCES, 1914 31

which strengthened the Government's desire in August 1914 to maintain peace with Constantinople.

How this opinion began to be changed, and this policy reversed, first by an offer of troops from an unexpected quarter for an attack upon the Dardanelles, and afterwards by the apparent deadlock in the Western theatre and by the mighty growth of Britain's military strength, will be related in the next chapter.

THE DEFENCES OF THE DARDANELLES

Up to the end of October 1914 the main facts concerning the seaward defences of the Dardanelles were well known to the Entente, and though, after Turkey's entry into the war, information regarding later improvements became increasingly difficult to obtain, the British Government succeeded up to the end of 1914 in gaining a fair knowledge of what was going on inside the "fortress".[1] In one important particular, however, it will be seen that British information was at fault. At the beginning of the war the strength of the Turkish defences, and their readiness to resist attack, were undoubtedly rated too high, whereas, at the beginning of 1915, the great improvements carried out at German instigation were insufficiently realized.

The total length of the passage of the Dardanelles from its mouth at Cape Helles to the Sea of Marmara is about forty-one statute miles. For the whole of this distance the narrow waterway is dominated by the frowning heights of the Gallipoli peninsula, and by lesser eminences on the Asiatic shore. At the beginning of the war only the mouth of the Straits, and the four miles' course from the northern point of Kephez Bay to the Narrows at Chanak, had been prepared for defence.

Four thousand yards wide at their mouth, the Straits rapidly broaden out after the entrance has been passed, till at five miles from that point they attain their maximum breadth of four and a half miles in Eren Keui Bay. Thenceforward they gradually contract till at Kephez Point, eleven miles from the entrance, the width is only about 1¾ miles. Beyond Kephez they expand once more with the sweep of Sari Sighlar Bay, but at the Narrows, between Chanak and Kilid Bahr, fourteen miles from the entrance, the width is less than 1,600 yards from shore to shore. From this point, turning left-handed, the channel opens out again and bears due north for four miles to Nagara

[1] The Turks used the word "fortress" to describe the sea-defences on both sides of the Straits, from Chanak to the mouth.

1914. Point, where the course once more bears north-east for the remaining twenty-three miles to Gallipoli and the Sea of Marmara.

It would be difficult to imagine a stretch of land and water more lavishly endowed with natural advantages for defence than this narrow, winding, land-locked channel, with its rapid current continually setting for the Ægean. Given a modern and well-sited armament, an abundance of ammunition, a carefully planned system of infantry positions to protect the sea-defences from the land side, and a stout-hearted garrison, it needed only capable direction and a sound scheme of defence to render the Dardanelles impregnable. But at the beginning of August 1914 not one of these necessary conditions had been fulfilled.

Aug. At the outbreak of the war in August 1914 the first line of defence of the Straits, known as the "Outer Defences", consisted of two permanent forts near the toe of the Gallipoli peninsula, and two on the Asiatic shore. These four forts contained a total of 19 guns, of which only four were really serviceable. The range of these four guns was 16,000 yards, while the remainder had a range of only 6,000-8,000 yards. In addition there was a small earthwork at Cape Tekke (Tekke Burnu), on the European shore, armed with four field howitzers.

From the toe of the peninsula for the first ten miles, the Straits were entirely undefended in August 1914, but in the neighbourhood of Kephez Point were four works, with a fifth on the opposite European shore. The principal object of these works, known as the "Intermediate Defences" was to protect the minefield, which on the 3rd August consisted of one line of mines laid between Kephez Point and the European shore. At no period were any mines laid at the mouth of the Straits. The principal fort of the Intermediate Defences was Fort Dardanos, armed with two modern 6-inch naval guns, while the remaining four works contained a miscellaneous collection of ten small shielded quick-firing guns.

The "Inner Defences", situated at the Narrows, formed the third and last line of resistance of the Straits. Here were collected all the heaviest guns available, as well as a number of light howitzers, field guns, and other mobile artillery. On the European shore were five forts, and on the Asiatic shore six, with a total armament of 72 heavy and medium guns. The majority of these were comparatively out of date, and the only ones capable of long-range fire were five 14-inch guns and three 9·4-inch, with ranges of 17,000 and 15,000 yards respectively. The remainder of the armament of the Inner Defences could in no case shoot beyond 10,000 yards, and mostly consisted of old-pattern short guns with a far shorter range.

To summarize, out of a total of over 100 guns of heavy and medium calibre mounted in the defences of the Straits at the beginning of the war, only fourteen were modern long-range weapons. The others were old-pattern guns on old-pattern carriages, mounted in works of antiquated design. The gun detachments were badly trained; ammunition was scarce, especially for the heavier pieces, and its replenishment would be a matter of great difficulty. For the illumination of the whole area there existed on mobilization only two searchlights, one at the entrance to the Straits, the other at the Narrows. Amongst other weaknesses in the defensive arrangements, the forts were of a very conspicuous character; guns of many different types and calibres were grouped in the same battery; gun-shields, and cover for personnel, were lacking; the method of range-finding, and of fire observation and control, was very poor, and was dependent on a poorly developed aerial telephone system.

The unreadiness of the defence in August 1914 is frankly admitted in the Turkish official account of the Dardanelles campaign. "On mobilization," it is stated, "the fortification and " armament of the Dardanelles were very inadequate. Not only " were the majority of the guns of old pattern, with a slow rate " of fire and short range, but their ammunition supply was also " limited."

Faced with this dangerous situation—for the arrival of an Allied squadron off the mouth of the Straits left no doubt as to the menace with which the capital was threatened—the Germans at Constantinople at once began to press for energetic measures to increase the defences of the Dardanelles. The first step was the appointment of the German General Weber, of the military mission, as delegate of Turkish G.H.Q. to advise and assist the fortress commander. This step was followed towards the end of the month by the despatch from Germany of Vice-Admiral von Usedom with a number of special service officers, and a detachment of over 500 men to stiffen the garrisons of the Dardanelles and Bosporus forts.[1] On his arrival at the beginning of September, Usedom was **Sept.** made Inspector-General of Coast Defences and Mines, with headquarters at Constantinople; an officer of his mission, Admiral Merten, was despatched to Chanak to take over the duties hitherto assigned to General Weber; and a large detach-

[1] The Bosporus defences were in as unsatisfactory a condition as those of the Dardanelles.

ment of German marines accompanied him to man the more modern guns.

From this date the defences of the Straits began steadily to improve. Whereas at the beginning of September the Germans had to report that neither the guns nor their detachments were ready to meet an attack, they were able to inform headquarters at the middle of the month that at least the guns at the Narrows had been put in order and were ready for action. A month later the more important batteries had been manned almost entirely with German personnel, with the double purpose of acting as instructional batteries and of ensuring that in an emergency some at least of the forts would do their work properly.

Oct. Meanwhile plans were drawn up for the construction of additional works in the intermediate zone, and for increasing the efficiency of the defence by the addition of mobile howitzers and quick-firing guns from the older ships of the fleet. Several heavy howitzers were also brought to the Dardanelles during October. But owing to the poor efficiency of the Turkish gunners, the out-of-date armaments, and the great shortage of ammunition,[1] Admiral von Usedom soon decided that he must trust mainly to the minefield for the protection of the Straits. Three lines of mines had been laid at the time of his arrival, but it is characteristic of the Turks that further work on this service had been stopped, as they believed they had no more mines. After a thorough search 145 more mines were found and put into working order, with the result that five lines had been laid by

Nov. the beginning of November. Protection against sweepers had by the same date been improved by the addition of a number of small quick-firing guns, and the number of searchlights had been increased from two to six.[2]

At the date of Turkey's entry into the war, therefore, a good deal had been done to increase the efficiency of the defences of the Dardanelles against naval attack. The whole position, however, was still far from secure, and the Intermediate Defences, on which the Germans principally relied, were still weak and ill-organized as regards guns, mines, and searchlights.

On the 3rd November, two days after the British Ambassador left Constantinople, the Allied fleet carried out a short bombardment of the outer forts. Up to this time the German efforts to effect a more rapid improvement in the defences of the

---

[1] Admiral von Usedom reported in October that there was only enough big-gun ammunition to meet one energetic attack.
[2] Two more lines of mines were laid in November and two in January. By the end of February there were ten lines of mines and twelve searchlights.

Straits had met with considerable obstruction from the Turks. The effect of the bombardment was temporarily to sweep this obstruction aside. "The bombardment of 3rd November "warned me," said Jevad Pasha, commander of the fortress, after the war, "and I realized that I must spend the rest of my "time in developing and strengthening the defences by every "means."

The unfortunate effect of the bombardment was aggravated by its astonishing success. Though the firing lasted only twenty minutes, it succeeded, owing to two lucky shots, in causing more damage than any subsequent attack. The forts at Sedd el Bahr were destroyed, and the explosion of the magazine dismounted all the guns.[1] The severity of this damage impressed both Turks and Germans with the fact that however much the Outer Defences were reinforced with available armament, a hostile fleet could obliterate them at leisure while itself keeping out of range. The forts were repaired, but no attempt was made to add to their strength, and it was determined to concentrate future efforts on protecting the Inner Defences from sharing a similar fate, and more especially on protecting the minefield.

To prevent the inner forts from being demolished at leisure from a point within the Straits before their short-range guns could open fire, large numbers of howitzers and other mobile pieces were gradually placed on each side of the Straits to cover the unprotected area between Dardanos Fort and the entrance. The rugged nature of the country was well suited for concealing these pieces, which, it was hoped, would prevent a hostile fleet from anchoring and compel it to keep on the move. With their aim thus disturbed, it was thought that ships would be unable to destroy the inner forts at long range, and even if a large proportion of them succeeded in passing the minefields, the short-range guns at the Narrows would then be able to develop their maximum power.

Still further to protect the inner forts from long-range fire, work was started on a number of batteries to be armed with small guns firing black powder, which would serve as dummies to attract the fire of an attacking fleet.

For more than five weeks after the bombardment of the 3rd November, the Allied fleet in the Ægean remained inactive. The nervousness created by that episode was in consequence beginning to evaporate when the defenders of the Straits were again aroused by a warning blow, this time from a totally unexpected quarter. On the 13th December a British submarine,

Dec.

---

[1] Some of these guns were again in action in February 1915.

commanded by Lieut. N. D. Holbrook, R.N., performed the hitherto unprecedented feat of diving under the five rows of Turkish mines and sinking an old warship at anchor in Sari Sighlar Bay. This very gallant exploit, for which Lieut. Holbrook was awarded the Victoria Cross, undoubtedly furnished the Turks with a second reminder of the danger with which their capital was threatened, and gave them a new incentive to work on their defences with all possible speed. Nevertheless only a small proportion of the additional batteries were ready for action by the end of the year, and it was March before the various new measures decided upon began to approach completion.

By the end of December 1914 Admiral von Usedom was able to report a considerable improvement in Turkish gunnery, but he still considered that a strong fleet could break through to the Marmara with a loss of four or five ships. During January and the first half of February several more batteries were completed, three torpedo tubes were mounted in the Narrows, and heavy armament began to arrive from the Adrianople defences. But up to the 18th March the majority of Turks and Germans alike continued to believe in the power of the Entente to force the Straits with ships alone. Despite the measures taken by Liman von Sanders to protect the capital from the possible results of a hostile fleet arriving at the Golden Horn, the opening of the naval bombardment on the 19th February created something like consternation in Constantinople.[1]

The Turkish official account is silent on the subject of early preparations to meet a land attack carried out in co-operation with the navy, but little would seem to have been done in this respect until six months after mobilization began. From the outbreak of the war to the end of February 1915 no attempt was made to increase the mobile forces at the Dardanelles

---

[1] Liman von Sanders gives the opinion that an Allied fleet arriving alone at Constantinople would have been in an almost untenable position. So long as the Turks held the Dardanelles, no supplies could reach the fleet by sea, and he believes that the measures he took would have made it impossible to land parties to collect local supplies. He felt at the time that a decisive result could only be gained if the Allies landed " a respectable " number " of troops at the same time as the fleet forced the passage, or if a Russian force succeeded in landing simultaneously at the mouth of the Bosporus. But to make the stay of the fleet off Constantinople as difficult as possible, Liman mounted a number of guns to bring cross fire to bear between San Stefano and Seraglio Point; also on the Asiatic shore and on the adjacent islands. Flying detachments were posted to guard the coast, with reserves in rear. Similar measures were taken to protect the Bosporus against a Russian landing. Mobile detachments watched the coast, and the *VI. Corps*, specially trained in night exercises for the purpose, was held in reserve. " Fünf Jahre Türkei," pp. 65-6.

beyond two divisions, of which only one was quartered on the peninsula. Throughout the autumn and winter months little addition was made to the trenches which had been constructed the previous year to meet the possibility of a landing by the Greeks. These trenches had been dug principally on the western slopes of the Kilid Bahr plateau, a position which, dominating the Inner Defences on both sides of the Straits, was in effect the key of the Dardanelles.[1] A certain amount of work was done in the winter of 1914 for the local protection of batteries, and trenches of a sort were undoubtedly dug by the numerous detachments into which the solitary division on the peninsula was divided to watch various landing places along the coast.[2] But nothing in the shape of a defensive position, to meet the emergency of a landing in force, was attempted, and the massive hills of Achi Baba[3] and Sari Bair,[4] second in importance only to the Kilid Bahr plateau in the influence which their capture would exert upon the fate of the Dardanelles, for several months continued virgin soil.

A further weakness — and one never eradicated during the course of the campaign — lay in the divided system of command. Engaged in the defence of the area were no less than three commanders, each independent of the other two. First there was Colonel Jevad Bey, the commander of the "Dardanelles Fortress", which comprised the coast defences with their artillery and engineers, the mine-laying personnel, and a small infantry garrison detached from the two divisions in the neighbourhood to defend the works and batteries from land attack. This small garrison consisted of three companies of infantry on the southern half of the Gallipoli peninsula, below the line Gaba Tepe—Maidos, and a similar number on the Asiatic shore. Secondly, there was General Essad Bey, who was responsible for guarding the central and northern portions of the peninsula with one division of his corps, and probably had a call on the other division on the Asiatic side of the Straits. Thirdly, there was the admiral commanding the fleet, who retained under his immediate command all vessels allotted to co-operate in the defence.

[1] The Greek plan of campaign is believed to have included a landing south of Gaba Tepe, at the foot of this plateau.
[2] The whole division was split up in this way, and until the end of February there was no general reserve on the peninsula.
[3] The Turkish name for this hill is Alchi Tepe. It was wrongly called Achi Baba on the first British map issued to the troops, and remained known by this name to the British forces throughout the campaign.
[4] Sari Bair was the name given on the English map to the whole range of hills culminating in Hill 971. The Turks used this name only for some yellow precipices facing the sea north of Ari Burnu.

Feb. 1915. As soon as the naval bombardment began in February 1915, measures were taken to increase the Turkish military strength in the Dardanelles area, but reinforcements moved slowly. "Up to 25th February", says the Turkish official account, "it "would have been possible to effect a landing successfully at "any point on the peninsula, and the capture of the Straits by "land troops would have been comparatively easy."

Guided by the various studies of the Dardanelles problem outlined in this chapter, by a post-war knowledge of the actual state of the defences in the winter of 1914–15, and by the defenders' opinion of their strength, it will be obvious to the reader that, though sustained attack on the Straits by ships alone might have resulted in a portion of the Allied fleet reaching the Sea of Marmara and appearing off Constantinople, the value of their arrival would have depended partly on the political effect which such a success might have had upon the Turkish Government and the neutral Balkan states, and partly on whether the Turks could have supplied their troops in Asia Minor with ammunition in spite of the presence of a hostile fleet in the Marmara.[1] It will further be obvious that from a military point of view the greatest chance of success lay in a combined operation taking the form of a surprise landing by a large army, supported by ships' guns, and the capture of the Narrows defences with the object of opening the Straits for the fleet.

In the course of the following chapters it will be shown that this point was from the first fully realized both at the War Office and at the Admiralty. The chain of events will be described which led, first to a purely naval attack on the Straits; secondly to a naval attack supported by a small number of troops; thirdly, but only when all hope of surprise had vanished, to a military operation, still in insufficient strength, "to assist the fleet to force the Dardanelles", and finally to a great military campaign for the capture of what was at last a veritable fortress.

[1] See page 20.

CHAPTER III

THE INITIATION OF THE DARDANELLES CAMPAIGN

(Map 1; Sketch 1)

THREE days before the opening of the Battle of Mons, when **Aug.** every soldier's eyes were fixed on the Western front, and **1914.** every sailor's on the horizon of the North Sea, two telegrams were received at the Foreign Office, which, read in conjunction with a third on the 27th August, thus early in the war attracted the attention of ministers to the Dardanelles.

The first of these messages was from the British chargé d'affaires at Athens. It announced that M. Venizelos, the Greek Prime Minister, with the full approval of King and Cabinet, had formally placed all the naval and military resources of Greece at the disposal of the Entente.

The second telegram was from Sir Louis Mallet, British Ambassador at Constantinople. It suggested the consideration of how far the forcing of the Dardanelles would be an effective and necessary step towards winning the war.

The third telegram, also from Sir Louis Mallet, suggested that, although an Allied squadron could probably force the Straits unaided—the mines would be their only difficulty—they would be unable to command the situation without the assistance of troops. Success would depend on rapidity of action, but if the operation were decided upon, there must be a minimum risk of failure. A failure, or even a partial success, might prove disastrous.

At that moment the Entente still cherished the hope of preserving peace with the Turks. England, France, and Russia were united in their anxiety to keep Turkey neutral, and to avoid another war in the Balkans. In addition, they were endeavouring to form Rumania and the Balkan states into a solid neutral *bloc*. To accept Greece as an ally would obviously frustrate that scheme, and, owing to her bitter quarrel with the Porte, might be expected to force Turkey into the opposite camp, even though no attack upon Turkish territory were attempted. Again, if Bulgaria also should join the Central Powers, the safety of Greece would be jeopardized without the Entente being able to spare a man to help her.

For all these reasons Greece's offer of help was for the moment unacceptable. But on the 29th August the surprising news reached London from Sir Francis Elliot [1] that, owing to the numerous proofs of German ascendancy at Constantinople, the Russian minister at Athens had asked the Greek King point-blank whether, in certain eventualities, he would supply an expeditionary force to assist in an attack on the Dardanelles. The King had given a positive though reluctant consent, but had subsequently stipulated that the neutrality of Bulgaria must first be guaranteed. This request by the Russian minister is noteworthy, for a few months later [2] it was the Russian Government that opposed the suggestion of employing Greek troops in an attack on Constantinople.

The considerations which were inducing the British Government to overlook Turkey's flagrant breaches of neutrality have already been related,[3] and it will be remembered that only the previous week Britain, with France and Russia, had offered on certain conditions to guarantee Turkish integrity and independence at the end of the war. But from a military point of view, if means permitted, there was much to be said in favour of anticipating the obviously hostile intentions of the Turkish war-party, and of forcing Turkey either to dismiss her German masters and remain neutral, or to take up arms before her mobilization was complete. If war was inevitable, the military advantages of precipitating hostilities at a time of British rather than of German choosing were self-evident. It might need only a definite threat against the Dardanelles to secure the downfall of Enver and the triumph of the peace-party. Alternatively, even if the passage of the fleet were opposed, the Gallipoli peninsula could possibly be captured with little trouble while its defences were still unprepared. A successful combined operation might well result in the immediate capitulation of Turkey and the removal of all anxiety regarding Egypt and the Suez Canal. The matter was in any case of sufficient importance to call for immediate consideration in view of the Greek offer of military help. On the 31st August the problem was discussed by Mr. Churchill, the First Lord of the Admiralty, and Lord Kitchener, the Secretary of State for War.

The next day, in the absence of Lord Kitchener in Paris,

---

[1] British minister at Athens.
[2] See Chapter IV.   See page 14.

INITIATION OF DARDANELLES CAMPAIGN 41

Mr. Churchill asked the Chief of the Imperial General Staff to appoint two officers to examine and work out, with two officers from the Admiralty, a "plan for the seizure of the Gallipoli " peninsula, by means of a Greek army of adequate strength, " with a view to admitting a British fleet to the sea of " Marmara". The matter was said to be urgent as "Turkey " may make war on us at any moment".

Sept. 1914.

Two points in this letter demand attention. In the first place, nothing but a military operation was contemplated. The Greek army, after capturing the peninsula, would " admit " the British fleet to the Marmara". Secondly, there was no idea of precipitating hostilities. The operation was only to be examined in view of the imminent risk of Turkey declaring war.

On the 3rd September, as a result of the First Lord's letter, Major-General C. E. Callwell, Director of Military Operations,[1] formulated the opinion of the General Staff. He stated that an attack on the Gallipoli peninsula would be an extremely difficult operation. During the war of 1911-12 the protection of the land faces of the various works dominating the Straits had been taken in hand, and it was believed that they were now secure against anything in the nature of a surprise attack. The normal garrison of the peninsula was 27,000 men, but it had probably been strengthened considerably.[2] Recent reports stated that there was an army corps on the Asiatic side of the Straits, which could quickly be brought across to the European shore in case of attack. He did not consider it justifiable to undertake the operation with less than 60,000 men and strong siege ordnance.

It will be seen, therefore, that in September 1914 the operation was considered feasible by the General Staff, though extremely difficult, and General Callwell, who had assisted in drawing up the 1906 memorandum, evidently agreed that its concluding sentence [3] was no longer applicable.

On the 4th September Sir Edward Grey informed the British minister at Athens that the British Government were still anxious that Turkey should remain neutral, but that if she were to join the Central Powers, Britain would welcome and

---

[1] General Callwell, one of the retired officers recalled to the War Office on mobilization to replace officers who had proceeded to France, had lately relieved Major-General (later Field-Marshal Sir) H. H. Wilson as Director of Military Operations.

[2] In point of fact, there was only one division, between 5,000 and 6,000 rifles, on the peninsula at this time, and apart from bringing the division up to war strength, 9,000 rifles, this number was not increased till 25th February 1915. [3] See page 29.

support Greece as an ally. The Admiralty would therefore instruct Rear-Admiral Mark Kerr[1] to discuss with the Greek naval and military authorities the best measures to be taken in the event of war. But it was to be made clear to Greece that so long as Turkey kept the peace she must on no account be provoked.

Admiral Kerr was instructed in the above sense. He was told that the Admiralty's idea would be to reinforce the Greek fleet to such a strength as to give it superiority over the enemy, and to place Admiral Kerr in command of the Allied fleets. The Admiralty believed that the best method of subduing Turkey would be to strike at Constantinople, and that with this object, in the event of war, a Greek army should seize the peninsula, open the Straits, and admit the fleet.[2]

After an interview with King Constantine, and consultations with the War Ministry, Admiral Kerr replied on the 8th September that the Greek staff were of opinion, and he agreed, that provided Bulgaria could be prevented from attacking Greece, the Greek army could capture the peninsula. But Athens would not rely on a Bulgarian promise of neutrality. Unless the Bulgarian army simultaneously attacked Turkey, the Greeks would not move. Subject to that proviso, the Greek plan was ready, and could be put into operation at once. The Greek fleet should be reinforced by two or three British battle cruisers, some cruisers and destroyers, and a flotilla of minesweepers.

The Greek plan for forcing the Dardanelles, drawn up to meet the case of a single-handed war between Greece and Turkey, left nothing to chance.[3] It was based on the assumption that no fleet could enter the Marmara till the minefields were swept; that the mines could not be swept till the forts protecting them had been captured; and that the forts could not be captured without extensive landing operations on both sides of the Straits. After the fall of the forts, other distant points would have to be taken and held to prevent the arrival of troops to recapture the Straits. In broad outline the plan was as follows:

> 60,000 men to land south of Gaba Tepe, to take the European forts in rear.
> Two battalions to land on the Asiatic shore and capture Kum Kale fort at the entrance to the Straits.

[1] Chief of the British naval mission to Greece.
[2] Here, as in Mr. Churchill's letter of 1st September, reliance was placed on military operations to enable the fleet to enter the Marmara.
[3] These details are from information given to Rear-Admiral Kerr in September 1914. No copy of the Greek plan was ever seen in England.

INITIATION OF DARDANELLES CAMPAIGN 43

These operations were to be followed by the landing of

30,000 men near Bulair, to seize and hold the isthmus.
20,000 men to land at Alexandretta, to cut the railway line from the south.
20,000 men to land in the Gulf of Adramyti, to neutralize the Smyrna army corps.[1]

As for the Greek stipulation that Bulgaria should simultaneously attack Turkey, the task of bringing King Ferdinand to the side of the Entente would doubtless have proved as difficult in September 1914 as it did later. But the situation did not then arise. Turkey for the moment continued to refrain from any overt act of hostility. The Entente, in accordance with their settled policy, continued to be patient. The Germans continued to fortify the Dardanelles.

But even had the Entente decided to declare immediate war on Turkey, it is highly unlikely that Greece would have drawn her sword. Before Admiral Kerr's telegram reached London, King Constantine had changed his mind. Owing to a belief that Bulgaria was already pledged to Germany, he now declared that he would not attack Turkey unless Turkey attacked him first.[2]

For some time the question of operations against the Dardanelles was not again discussed in London. Not only was there a lack of troops for the enterprise: even the British navy could ill afford to increase its strength in the Mediterranean until the last of the German commerce-destroyers had been swept from the sea. But towards the end of October, in view of the unmistakable imminence of a Turkish rupture, the First Lord of the Admiralty, who had early recognized the immense importance of the Straits, again discussed the matter with the Director of Military Operations. General Callwell reiterated his opinion that the capture of the Straits must be mainly a soldier's task, and that it would be extremely difficult. He repeated his fears that the Turks would mass a strong force to oppose a landing, and that the attacking troops would at once find themselves confronted by elaborate entrenchments. Oct. 1914.

A few days later Admiral Souchon bombarded the Black Sea ports, and Turkey was at last forced into the war.

On the 3rd November the British blockading squadron carried out the short bombardment of the outer forts already alluded to.[3] This operation formed no part of any settled plan Nov. 1914.

---

[1] In view of existing circumstances, and Turkey's probable commitments elsewhere, it is possible that the Alexandretta and Adramyti portions of the scheme would not have been included in the Greek plan of attack in 1914.
[2] Greek White Book (Supplement) No. 6, p. 10.   [3] See page 34.

for an attack on the Straits. Its sole object was to test existing information regarding the armament of the forts.

Three weeks later, at the initial meeting of the newly constituted War Council, the question of attacking the Dardanelles was for the first time considered in session by the ministers responsible for the higher direction of the war. Measures were being considered for the protection of Egypt and the Suez Canal, and Mr. Churchill pointed out that the ideal way of achieving this object would be to capture the Gallipoli peninsula. This would give Britain control of the Dardanelles, and enable her to dictate terms at Constantinople. He added that it would be a very difficult operation and would require a large military force. After a brief discussion the operation was considered unfeasible owing to lack of troops. Mr. Churchill then suggested a feint at Gallipoli while pressing home an attack on some other part of the Turkish coast, such as Haifa. Lord Kitchener concurred in the probable necessity of cutting the Turkish communications, but he considered that the moment had not yet arrived. Egypt was in no immediate danger, and in any case no troops were at present available even for this minor project. The First Lord finally suggested that transports should gradually be collected at some British port in the Mediterranean for use if and when required, but this proposal, too, was rejected, on account of the already great shortage of merchant shipping.

Dec. 1914. For several weeks no further allusion was made to the Dardanelles. But towards the end of December, in view of the absence of any outstanding success to the credit of the Entente, the Government began to question the wisdom of continuing to send every available soldier to France; and in several quarters efforts began to be made to discover an alternative and easier theatre in which to strike an effective blow at the enemy.

On the Western front the First Battles of Ypres had been fought and won, and the German effort to secure the Channel ports seemed definitely and finally to have failed. But the opposing fronts now extended in an unbroken line from the Alps to the North Sea. With the advent of winter a condition of stalemate appeared to have been reached, and the belief was gaining ground in ministerial circles that no attack in the West could hope for a success in any way commensurate with the enormous losses entailed.

In the Eastern theatre the situation was disquieting. The Russian successes in Galicia had not been maintained, and the alarming news had reached England that this was due to a

INITIATION OF DARDANELLES CAMPAIGN 45

grave shortage of arms and ammunition. Meanwhile Germany, realizing that though unable to make headway in the West she could at least maintain her positions with a greatly reduced garrison, was sending heavy reinforcements to the East.

In Serbia the situation was no less menacing. Though the Serbs had recaptured Belgrade on the 14th December, there was every sign of a renewed Austro-German attack in the near future. And if Serbia should be crushed, Bulgaria would almost certainly join the Central Powers and open the road for increased German assistance to the Turks in their impending advance on the Suez Canal. Help for Serbia could come only from Greece or Rumania. But both these countries, though friendly to the Entente, were determined to maintain their neutrality unless Bulgaria agreed to attack Turkey with all her forces. And every effort of British diplomacy to secure the co-operation of Bulgaria had hitherto ended in failure. Moreover, it was becoming clear that the cause of diplomatic failure was the absence of military success. Without military success, diplomacy in war is bankrupt. Yet up to the present the Entente could point to no outstanding victory, and there was for the moment no sign of a turn in the tide.

To gain a clear picture of the military problem at this time, it is necessary to glance at the state of Britain's growing armies at the end of December 1914. In France were 300,000 men, including three British and two Indian cavalry divisions, nine British [1] and two Indian infantry divisions, and a number of Territorial battalions. In England were the 28th and 29th Divisions,[2] mainly composed of Regular units brought home from India and the Colonies and now being organized and equipped, and the 1st Canadian Division. These three divisions would soon be ready to take the field; two of them, the 28th and the Canadians, had already been promised to France. Behind them stood eleven first-line [3] and thirteen second-line Territorial divisions, all the divisions of the New Army, the Royal Naval Division, and about fourteen Yeomanry brigades. Apart from the first-line Territorials, the majority of whom were employed in home defence duties, none of these divisions were expected to be ready for service for several months, and the second-line Territorials had not as yet been asked to undertake foreign service obligations.

[1] The six divisions of the original Expeditionary Force (1st-6th) and the 7th, 8th, and 27th Divisions, all composed of Regular units.
[2] All the units of the 29th Division had not yet reached England.
[3] The efficiency of some of these first-line T.F. divisions had been affected by 23 T.F. battalions being sent independently to reinforce the B.E.F. in France, and 8 to relieve Regular battalions in overseas garrisons.

In Egypt, in addition to a garrison of one Territorial[1] and two Indian divisions, the 1st Australian Division, one brigade of New Zealand infantry, and three mounted brigades had assembled by the middle of December. But the training of these troops would not be completed before the end of February.

From the foregoing it will be seen that, apart from the 28th Division and the Canadians, already ear-marked for France, the only troops available for foreign service in the immediate future were the 29th Division and perhaps two of the first-line Territorial divisions at that time allotted to home defence. But the number of troops required for home defence was still a controversial point. An attempt to invade England was in certain quarters still held to be probable, and Lord Kitchener was strongly opposed to any immediate reduction of the home garrison. On the other hand, a large number of divisions would be ready to take the field in the early summer, and it was hoped that, provided the ammunition problem could be solved, Britain in 1915 would be able to play an important, and perhaps a decisive, part in the military struggle.

The question where all these growing forces could be employed to the best advantage demanded an immediate answer. Though nothing big could be attempted for some months, it was essential that the military policy for the ensuing year should be decided as soon as possible.

The difficulties of the Government in deciding this vital problem were gravely increased by the fact that the General Staff, so far as the weight of their authority was concerned, had temporarily ceased to exist. The first responsibility of the General Staff is "to advise His Majesty's Government upon "all questions of military policy affecting the security of the "Empire".[2] Yet throughout this critical period their advice was never asked by the Secretary of State for War, and ministers were not afforded the assistance of a detailed examination by the General Staff of the various courses within the capabilities of the troops likely to be available in 1915.

This regrettable eclipse of the General Staff had its origin in an early misconception regarding the duration of the war. Believing that a great European war could not last six months, that there would be no time for creating new formations, and that Britain's maximum military commitment, if she were involved in the struggle, could not greatly exceed the six divisions of her Expeditionary Force, the Army Council had formed the opinion that once the war started, there would be

---

[1] The 42nd (East Lancs.) Division.
[2] "F.S. Regs., 1924," ii. (4).

INITIATION OF DARDANELLES CAMPAIGN 47

little more work of outstanding military importance in Whitehall, and that the cream of the War Office staff should be appointed on mobilization to accompany the army to France. Thus it happened that in the early days of August 1914 the General Staff branch at the War Office was denuded of all its most experienced officers. Vacancies were quickly filled; but rightly or wrongly Lord Kitchener was unwilling either to take into his confidence or ask the opinion of a body of officers who for the most part had still to win their spurs. Throughout the winter of 1914, so far from being required to submit plans for the ensuing year, the General Staff were kept in almost complete ignorance of the various courses under discussion by the Government.

The effect of this eclipse of the General Staff was nowhere more felt than in the case of the Dardanelles campaign. As will be shown in the course of this history the decision to launch a purely naval attack against the Straits, and the subsequent decision to send out troops to assist the fleet in case of need, were both arrived at without the General Staff being called upon to review the military aspect of the problem. The troops to render this assistance were embarked without any preliminary scheme for their disembarkation and subsequent action. And when, at the last moment, the army was suddenly called upon to make plans for a landing in face of a now thoroughly awakened enemy, the absence of initial Staff preparation had already resulted in the violation of most of the principles the observance of which is essential to the success of an amphibious campaign.

In the fog and uncertainty of war distracting influences are always present to cloud the judgment and shake the resolution of those on whom the chief responsibility lies. Towards the end of December, while the majority of ministers were inclining to a belief that the British and French fronts in the West were impregnable, a sudden gust of nervousness hurried some of their number to an entirely contrary view. So persistent were the rumours that Germany was sending heavy reinforcements to the West, and was even planning an invasion of the English coast, that Sir John French was hastily summoned to England to discuss the situation. On the 28th December, after a conference with General Joffre, the British Commander-in-Chief was able to assure the Government that the French had no fears regarding their ability to deal with any possible break that might occur in the Franco-British line, and that they now believed such a contingency to be more than ever remote. This assurance temporarily allayed any nervousness about the security of the Western front, and the movement in favour of an alternative theatre for Britain's main effort continued to gain strength.

It is important to realize the various influences which at this time were inducing the Government to seek for an alternative and easier theatre in which to strike a decisive blow. Uppermost in the mind of the Government was the urgent importance of achieving a signal military success at an early date, both for diplomatic reasons and to hearten the spirits of the nation. The deadlock in the West was tending more and more to shake the confidence of ministers in the possibility of an appreciable advance in that quarter. Side by side with this feeling, Britain's traditional dislike of continental warfare was beginning to assert itself. There was an uneasy suspicion that the teachings of history were being neglected, and that the country was making insufficient use of its amphibious power. History declared, it was said, that the army of a sea-power wholly committed to continental fighting loses half its strength. If every available man and gun were hurled into the apparently bottomless pit of Flanders, would not the strength which arises from a well-adjusted combination of land and sea forces be thrown away? The French Government were insistent that the only correct strategy for Britain was to send every trained soldier to the Western front. Sir John French fully shared this view, and persistently impressed it on Lord Kitchener. But British ministers, though actuated by the utmost loyalty to France, were unwilling to allow their military policy to be dictated by the necessarily more limited outlook of their Allies. While fully conscious of the importance of massing where decisive blows were to be struck, they were no longer unanimous that France should be regarded as the decisive theatre. Even those who felt that the final decision must be sought on the Western front, were anxious that Britain, by use of her amphibious power, should try to strike an early and resounding blow elsewhere, with such troops as might fairly be considered surplus to the immediate requirements of the British Army in France.

Lord Kitchener, whose personality dominated the War Council at this time, never wavered in his opinion that France must be regarded as the main theatre for British arms. He was, however, fully alive to the importance of an early success, and with this object was in favour of a small diversion as soon as troops could be spared. The operation which he most favoured was a landing at Alexandretta, where he hoped that a small force astride the railway could secure results out of all

INITIATION OF DARDANELLES CAMPAIGN 49

proportion to the number of troops engaged. But throughout this period he insisted that, until the situation became more clear, nothing must be done to endanger either the British line in France or the security of England from invasion, and that for some time to come no troops would be available for any other theatre.

In addition to the suggested diversion in the Mediterranean, two other schemes were under consideration in England during the month of December 1914. First there was a project evolved by Sir John French and the First Lord of the Admiralty for turning the German right flank in Flanders with the help of the fleet, and capturing the enemy's rapidly growing submarine bases at Zeebrugge and Ostend. Mr. Churchill, sanguine of the value of naval artillery against shore targets, had promised Sir John French the assistance of "100 or 200 " guns from the sea, in absolutely devastating support". Secondly, there was a project, emanating from Lord Fisher, for naval and military operations on the Baltic coast. This scheme, the details of which were still known only to Lord Fisher, could not be ready for many months, but permission had been accorded for the building of a number of special vessels required for the operation.[1]

Consideration of both these ideas, however, gave way to the study of two remarkable papers circulated to members of the War Council at the beginning of the New Year.

Jan. 1915.

The first was a paper prepared by the Secretary of the Council, Lieut.-Colonel Maurice Hankey, by direction of the Prime Minister. After calling attention to the dead-lock on the Western front, Colonel Hankey suggested that some new method, or failing that, some new outlet, must be found for utilizing the large forces which would be available for service in a few months' time. Weight of numbers alone could not achieve a victory on the Western front. We must either develop some new device for capturing trenches protected by wire and machine guns, or else we must go elsewhere. He suggested that Germany could be struck most easily through her Allies, and particularly through Turkey. In a few months Britain would be able to supply three army corps for an attack on Turkey, and if Greece and Bulgaria could be induced to co-operate, it should be possible to capture Constantinople. The advantages accruing from such an operation would be

---

[1] " This scheme had often been mentioned before the war and as often " opposed by the General Staff. From a military standpoint it was not a " practicable proposition." Field-Marshal Sir W. Robertson, " Soldiers " and Statesmen," i. p. 83.

numerous. In addition to gaining the adherence of the Balkan states and destroying Turkey's armed resistance, communication with the Black Sea would be re-opened. This would at once bring down the price of wheat and release 350,000 tons of merchant shipping now locked up in Russian and Danube ports.

The second paper was written by Mr. Lloyd George. In it he pointed out that Britain would soon have half a million men ready for service. He urged that they should not be thrown away on fruitless enterprises on the Western front. Half a million reinforcements there could make no appreciable difference. The time had come for realizing that the Western front was impregnable. The garrison of the Allied line should be provided by the French, and, with the exception of a large British reserve to be kept near the coast for use in case of emergency, the whole British army should be taken bag and baggage from France and despatched to some new theatre. He suggested that the Government should at once prepare for two independent operations to be undertaken in the Mediterranean in the spring. The main operation should be an attack on Austria, based on Salonika, or some port on the Dalmatian coast. For this operation, in addition to 600,000 British troops, the Foreign Office should try to secure the help of the Rumanians, Serbs, and Greeks. The subsidiary operation should consist of a landing on the Syrian coast, with the object of severing Turkey's line of communication with Egypt.

Mr. Lloyd George pointed out that unless some steps of this nature were taken it would be impossible to end the existing stalemate. Preparations would, however, take months. The first essential would be to decide where to land the army and what should be its eventual line of attack. The necessary transport should then be collected, and the forces concentrated in the Mediterranean, ostensibly for the defence of Egypt. "Expeditions", he prophetically declared, " which are decided " upon and organized with insufficient care and preparation " generally end disastrously", and he urged that as similar considerations would apply to any other operation contemplated, the matter should be pressed to a decision at once, so that all the necessary plans could be put in hand.

The result of this memorandum was the despatch on the 2nd January 1915 of the following letter from Lord Kitchener to Sir John French:

There does not appear to be much sign of the contemplated push through on the part of the French Army.
Probably they find themselves up against the same problem all

INITIATION OF DARDANELLES CAMPAIGN 51

along the line as you do in your part, viz.: trenches that render attack only a waste of men for a few yards gained of quite worthless ground. The feeling here is gaining ground that, although it is essential to defend the line we hold, troops over and above what is necessary for that service could be better employed elsewhere. . . . The question of *where* anything effective can be accomplished opens a large field and requires a good deal of study. What are the views of your staff?[1] Russia is hard-pressed in the Caucasus and can only just hold her own in Poland. Fresh forces are necessary to change the deadlock. Italy and Rumania seem the most likely providers; therefore some action that would help to bring these out seems attractive, though full of difficulties.

In his reply Sir John French denied that it was impossible to break the German lines, provided he were given sufficient guns and high-explosive shell. In any case the safety of the Channel ports was vital to England; and if the Germans should defeat Russia and bring the bulk of their forces to the West, all the troops at Britain's disposal would be no more than required to save the situation.[2] If the Government desired an alternative theatre he considered an expedition to Serbia *via* Salonika the least objectionable, though the difficulties of land communication would be immense. An attack on Turkey would be barren of results, and would merely play Germany's game by deflecting much-needed troops from the decisive spot. The best plan of all would be to use the British army to oust the Germans from Zeebrugge and Ostend in co-operation with the fleet.

Before this reply arrived, on the very date, in fact, of Lord Kitchener's letter, namely, 2nd January, a telegram of momentous consequence reached London from the British Ambassador at Petrograd, a telegram which was destined to lead the Government, by slow and almost insensible degrees, to the Gallipoli campaign, with all its high hopes, its immortal heroisms, and its final and heart-breaking failure.

This telegram stated that early in the week beginning Sunday, 27th December the situation in the Caucasus had caused grave anxiety owing to a serious enveloping movement

---

[1] This request for the opinion of Sir John French's staff is of interest in view of the remarks on page 47. But for the policy of denuding the War Office on the outbreak of war, these officers, whose opinion Lord Kitchener desired, would have been available in London to make an unbiassed and detached study of the situation. In their present position, in touch with the enemy, and fully occupied with the problems on their immediate front, they would have been almost more than human had they been able to take a detached view.

[2] Compare Sir J. French's statement after seeing Joffre on 28th December, page 47.

by the Turks.[1] The Grand Duke Nicholas had refused the request of the Russian local commander for reinforcements, on the ground that every available man was needed on the Austro-German front. The Grand Duke, however, had asked the chief of the British military mission if Lord Kitchener could arrange for some demonstration either naval or military against the Turks elsewhere, and if he could spread reports which might cause the Turks to withdraw troops from the Caucasus and thus ease the situation.

The tragedy of this telegram, so direful in its results, lies in the fact that even while the means of making a demonstration were being discussed in London, the necessity for making it had already disappeared. By the 3rd January the Turkish enveloping movement had failed, and the remnants of the forces engaged in it had surrendered at Sarikamish.[2] But this information was not known in England; and the British Government felt bound to strain every nerve to help an ally whose danger in the Caucasus had arisen from his endeavour to relieve the pressure against France.

Having no troops available at the moment, Lord Kitchener discussed with Mr. Churchill the possibility of a purely naval demonstration against the Turks. No definite plan was decided upon, but in view of the necessity of helping a hard-pressed ally, Lord Kitchener sent the following telegram to Petrograd on the evening of the 2nd January:

Please assure the Grand Duke that steps will be taken to make a demonstration against the Turks. It is feared however that any

---

[1] The conduct of the Caucasus campaign by the Turks, had it been fully understood in England, would have afforded significant proof of the improvements effected in the Turkish army by the German military mission, and of the opposition to be expected by any force attempting the invasion of the Gallipoli peninsula. Turkish troops in the Caucasus were being moved and maintained in exceedingly difficult country with comparative facility. The Russians were reporting them to be well armed and equipped, cleverly commanded, and abundantly supplied with stores. But these facts were very improperly understood in England at the time.

[2] Though Sarikamish was a great and opportune Russian victory, it is now known that the battle was one of the most fiercely contested actions ever fought between Russian and Turkish troops, and that at one stage the Turks came near to a sweeping success. Their failure was mainly due to an attempt at an almost impossible turning movement by Enver Pasha. This operation was carried out in deep snow, at an altitude of 10,000 feet. There were violent blizzards; the temperature was 30° below zero; and the later stages of the turning movement were made without artillery and supply convoys. For three days before Sarikamish was reached the men had been without food. Eventually the survivors surrendered *en masse*, but eye-witnesses have declared that Turkish soldiers never exhibited greater endurance and bravery.

INITIATION OF DARDANELLES CAMPAIGN 53

action we can devise and carry out will be unlikely to affect seriously the numbers of enemy in the Caucasus or cause their withdrawal.

This telegram had the concurrence of the Foreign Minister, who afterwards told the Dardanelles Commission that it would have had a bad effect to refuse the assistance for which the Russians had asked.

At the same time Lord Kitchener wrote to Mr. Churchill:

I do not see that we can do anything that will very seriously help the Russians in the Caucasus. . . . We have no troops to land anywhere. A demonstration[1] at Smyrna would do no good and probably cause the massacre of Christians. Alexandretta has already been tried[2] and would have no great effect a second time. The coast of Syria would have no effect. The only place that a demonstration might have some effect in stopping reinforcements going east would be the Dardanelles. Particularly if, as the Grand Duke says, reports could be spread at the same time that Constantinople was threatened.

We shall not be ready for anything big for some months.

Thus, for a reason which had already ceased to exist, Britain stood pledged to make a demonstration against the Turks. The place for the demonstration had yet to be decided on, though Lord Kitchener was of opinion that it should be at the Dardanelles. It is obvious from his letter to the First Lord

[1] Lord Kitchener obviously referred only to a naval demonstration, for " we have no troops to land anywhere ".
[2] The British light cruiser *Doris* landed a party north of Alexandretta on 18th December which tore up the railway line without opposition. An hour later a train coming from the northward was derailed. The next day an ultimatum was sent ashore demanding the surrender of all engines and military stores, under penalty of bombardment, and pending a reply another party, landed north of Payas (10 miles north of Alexandretta), drove in a patrol, blew up a railway bridge, wrecked the railway station, and cut the telegraph wires. The ultimatum was then accepted, and the Turks agreed to blow up the two locomotives in the town provided the British would lend them some explosives. A torpedo-lieutenant went ashore with some gun-cotton, but in the words of the official naval account (Corbett, " Naval Operations," ii. p. 76) " a new difficulty then arose. " Turkish dignity could not submit to our men having anything to do with " the destruction. . . . Hours were spent over the difficulty, but eventually " it was overcome by formally rating the torpedo-lieutenant as a Turkish " naval officer for the rest of the day. . . . The comedy was ended by a " party of Turkish cavalry rounding up the locomotives and bringing them " to the place of execution, when they were duly blown up."

This ludicrous episode was largely responsible for the faulty opinion then formed as to the degree of resistance which might be expected from the Turks in the Dardanelles. Mr. Churchill told the Dardanelles Commission that the incident gave him the idea that we were not dealing with a thoroughly efficient military power, and that it was quite possible that we might get into parley with them.

that he had not yet thought of a serious attack on the Straits. The last thing he would have wanted to do in that case would be to stop the Turks from denuding the Dardanelles, or to spread a report that Constantinople was threatened.

On the 3rd January Lord Fisher, who knew of the events of the previous day, and had seen the Russian telegram, wrote a letter to the First Lord which had an important bearing on the decision now to be reached. He strongly supported an attack on Turkey, but only if it could be carried out immediately. He suggested that all the Indians in France and 75,000 seasoned British troops should immediately be replaced by Territorials and embarked at Marseilles, ostensibly for the protection of Egypt. They should then be disembarked as quickly as possible at Besika Bay, preceded by a demonstration at Haifa and a landing in force at Alexandretta. Simultaneously the Greeks should be landed on the Gallipoli peninsula, the Bulgarians should be induced to march on Adrianople, and the Rumanians to join the Russians and Serbs in an attack on Austria. Finally, Admiral Sturdee should at the same time "force the Dardanelles" with ships of the *Majestic* and *Canopus* class. The letter ended: "But as the great Napoleon said, 'Celerity—'without it Failure'." [1]

This grandiose proposal, in many respects a mixture of the recent suggestions of Colonel Hankey and Mr. Lloyd George, was undoubtedly a counsel of perfection. Put into force in its entirety, had this been possible, the plan might have brought not only victory but peace. But at least three of the premises on which the plan was based were false. It had proved impossible to gain Bulgarian co-operation without an initial military success, or without making promises of territorial expansion at the expense of other Balkan states which it was not in Britain's power to fulfil. It was equally impossible at the moment to persuade Greece to march while Bulgaria's attitude remained uncertain. And to extract 75,000 seasoned British troops from France, without creating an open breach with the French Government, would have been even more difficult than to force the Dardanelles.

It is a fair assumption that when assigning to Admiral Sturdee the task of forcing the Straits Lord Fisher had no intention that this part of his scheme should be read without its context. To force the Straits while 100,000 British and

---

[1] Lord Fisher followed this letter up next day with an official minute stating that the naval advantages of the possession of Constantinople were so overwhelming that a plan for operations against Turkey, as outlined by Col. Hankey, was "vital, imperative, and very pressing".

INITIATION OF DARDANELLES CAMPAIGN 55

Indian troops were landing in Besika Bay, the Bulgarians marching on Adrianople, and a Greek army attacking the Gallipoli peninsula, was a very different proposition to an unaided attack by the fleet.

Nevertheless, this was the first time in the present war that the forcing of the Straits by fleet action had even been mentioned by a responsible sailor, and the words attracted the earnest attention of the minister to whom it was addressed. Hitherto the matter had been looked upon as a military problem and a difficult one at that, and discussion had ranged on the possibility of capturing the shores of the Straits with a view to admitting the fleet. But here was the First Sea Lord, with an intimate knowledge of the Dardanelles, plainly suggesting that the Straits might be forced by vessels of the *Majestic* and *Canopus* class, both of which came under the category of " His Majesty's " least valuable ships ". To be content with a demonstration off the mouth of the Dardanelles, if the same ships could force their way unaided into the Marmara, was unthinkable. An achievement of this nature might well be expected to break the vicious circle which was at once preventing the adherence of Bulgaria for lack of a military success, and a military success for lack of Bulgarian help. Hitherto Mr. Churchill had been convinced that the capture of the Straits was an affair for soldiers. But as no troops were available, the question raised by Lord Fisher's plan was at least worthy of further investigation. Later in the day, with the full concurrence of Lord Fisher, he telegraphed to the admiral at the Dardanelles, with a view to eliciting the views of the man on the spot: [1]

January 3rd, 1915. Do you consider the forcing of the Straits by ships alone a practicable operation?

It is assumed older battleships fitted with mine-bumpers would be used, preceded by colliers as mine-bumpers and sweepers. Importance of result would justify severe loss. Let me know your views.

Two days later Admiral Carden's answer arrived:

January 5th. I do not consider Dardanelles can be rushed. They might be forced by extended operations with large number of ships.

The following day Admiral Carden was asked to elaborate his views. But the Government were not as yet greatly interested

[1] Admiral Carden, on whom this weight of responsibility was suddenly cast, until his appointment to command the Dardanelles squadron in September, had been Admiral Superintendent of Malta dockyard since 1912.

in the promised demonstration against Turkey, and at the War Council meetings of the 7th and 8th January the project was not discussed.

The Council meeting of the 7th January was concerned principally with Sir John French's project for an advance towards Zeebrugge in co-operation with the fleet. After a long discussion, which elicited the fact that not enough ammunition was yet available for a big attack, it was decided to veto this scheme, its possible advantages not being commensurate with the losses certain to be incurred.

At the meeting of the 8th January discussion ranged over the possible alternative theatres for the New Armies. It was considered that a sea-base in the Adriatic would be unsuitable, owing to the danger of submarines, and that Salonika could only be used if Greece became an ally. Furthermore, the single line of rail from Salonika could not support a large army. Lord Kitchener suggested that the Dardanelles would be the most suitable objective, as an attack there could be made in co-operation with the fleet. He thought that 150,000 troops would suffice for the operation, but would reserve judgment till a clearer study had been made. Meanwhile a landing at Alexandretta would be a useful minor operation. But he repeated that at present no troops were available even for this project. He believed that a new German attack on the Western front was imminent, and not a man should be detached to a subsidiary theatre till this attack was over.

As a result of this meeting, the Government decided that the main theatre for British arms should be alongside the French army so long as France required armed support. But if the result of the next German attack should prove that no serious advance in the West was possible, British troops should be sent to some other theatre, where operations might lead to more decisive results. With this object in view alternative courses were at once to be studied by a sub-committee of the Council, so that, when the new forces were fit for action, plans would be ready to meet any eventuality that might be deemed expedient, either from a diplomatic point of view, or to enable British troops to co-operate with other nations throwing in their lot with the Entente.

The effect of these decisions was the return of Sir John French to England to urge again the advantages of his Zeebrugge scheme. At a subsequent meeting on the 13th January, the whole subject was reopened. Sir John French admitted that neither he nor General Joffre believed that a complete success in the West was probable; nevertheless the decision of the 7th January

INITIATION OF DARDANELLES CAMPAIGN 57

was reversed. It was now agreed to press on with the arrangements for an attack along the coast, though final permission for the enterprise was reserved for future consideration.

The question of Admiral Carden's telegrams was then brought before the Council, but, before recounting the decision arrived at, mention must now be made of the events of the two previous days.

On the 11th January Admiral Carden had replied to the Admiralty's telegram of the 6th with a detailed plan for forcing the Dardanelles by ships alone. The scheme was divided into four distinct stages:

1. Reduction of the forts at the entrance.
2. Destruction of the inside defences as far as Kephez.
3. Reduction of the forts at the Narrows.
4. Clearing the minefield, reduction of defences above the Narrows, and final advance into the Marmara.

The duration of the operations would depend on the weather. Gales were now frequent, but the Marmara could probably be reached in a month.

Everyone at the Admiralty would have preferred a combined operation, and it was generally agreed that troops would be required at least to follow up and complete a naval success.[1] But Lord Kitchener had said that no troops were yet available. In these circumstances it was felt by the Admiralty War Staff that, if immediate action was a political necessity, there would be little harm in making the naval attempt, particularly as, now that von Spee had been accounted for, the ships wanted for the attack could be supplied without detriment to the requirements of other theatres. Even a failure could not assume the magnitude of a disaster. If unsuccessful the operations could be regarded as a mere demonstration and broken off at any minute.

[1] In a memorandum dated 5th January, Admiral Sir Henry Jackson wrote: "Though the fleet might dominate the city (Constantinople) and "inflict enormous damage, their position would not be an enviable one "unless there was a large military force to occupy the town. . . . The "capture of Constantinople would be worth a considerable loss, but the "bombardment alone would not greatly affect the distant military operations, "and even if it surrendered, it could not be held without troops, and would "probably result in indiscriminate massacres."

Sir H. Jackson's connection with the campaign at this time was intermittent and with no responsibility. He held no official appointment at the Admiralty, but was chairman of a sub-committee of the Committee of Imperial Defence to control naval and military operations against the German colonies and overseas wireless stations. He merely wrote appreciations on points connected with the attack on the Dardanelles when asked to do so.

This was the situation when, on the 13th January, Mr. Churchill first introduced and explained Admiral Carden's plan for forcing the Dardanelles.

It is essential to recall the atmosphere in which this momentous question was now discussed by the Government. Diplomacy was calling for an immediate military success. Except in France, where there was insufficient ammunition to deal with the enemy's strong positions, and where no important advance seemed possible, not a man was available to strike a new blow. Russia was languishing for material of all kinds. Serbia was in immediate danger of extinction. Greece and Rumania, though believed to be ready to join the Entente and assist the Serbs, were held back by fear of Bulgaria. Bulgaria, impressed by German successes, was inclining more and more to the Central Powers. Here was the suggestion of a captivating enterprise, which apparently required no troops, which apparently was approved by the Admiralty experts,[1] and which called only for vessels surplus to naval requirements elsewhere. The arrival of the *Goeben* had been mainly responsible for plunging Turkey into war. The forcing of the Dardanelles, and the sinking of the German ships, might lead to a revolution in Constantinople and an appeal for a separate peace. Bulgaria, Greece, and Rumania, perhaps even Italy, might be attracted to the banners of the Entente. The Central Powers would in that case be enclosed by an iron ring. The way would be open for an advance up the Danube. Russia could receive her much-needed war material, and the depreciation of her exchange would be arrested by the export of Russian wheat.

By a misunderstanding which, even if it stood alone, would demonstrate that the General Staff had temporarily ceased to exist, the recent achievements of heavy howitzers against the forts of Liége and Namur were generally believed by ministers to presage the success of modern naval gunfire— especially of the new 15-inch guns—against the antiquated works at the Dardanelles. Above all was it felt that no great harm would be done, even if the operation failed. If satisfactory progress were not made, the bombardment could be broken off and the fleet could steam away. This was the

---

[1] The First Report of the Dardanelles Commission suggests that Mr. Churchill had obtained his advisers' consent to a less extent than he imagined. It, however, points out that Lord Fisher approved a minute written by the First Lord on 12th January, in which, after stating that the forcing of the Dardanelles as proposed by Admiral Carden would be a victory of first importance, Mr. Churchill gave a provisional list of vessels available for the task. The new battleship *Queen Elizabeth*, with our first 15-inch naval guns, was added to Mr. Churchill's list on Lord Fisher's own recommendation.

INITIATION OF DARDANELLES CAMPAIGN 59

consideration which weighed most strongly with the Government, and though the operation was not on this occasion finally approved, it was decided that the Admiralty should at once complete the necessary arrangements. Taken in its literal sense, the official wording of the decision contemplated a strange task for a fleet. The Admiralty were ordered "to " prepare for a naval expedition in February, to bombard and " take the Gallipoli peninsula, with Constantinople as its " objective".[1]

Directly the meeting was over, Mr. Churchill addressed a minute to the Naval Chief of Staff, through Lord Fisher, informing him that the Government regarded the Dardanelles enterprise as "of the highest urgency and importance", and outlining the various preparatory measures to be undertaken forthwith. An officer of the Naval War Staff was to analyse Admiral Carden's proposals, in order to show exactly what guns the ships would have to face, "but", the minute added, "this " officer is to assume that the principle is settled, and all that " is necessary is to estimate the force required".

On the 15th January Admiral Carden was informed that the Government had approved his scheme in principle, and that the Admiralty agreed with his plan of piecemeal reduction of the forts. The operations would be entrusted to him; he was to continue to perfect his arrangements; and the sooner the attack could begin the better. The *Queen Elizabeth* would be added to the number of vessels for which he had asked.

A few days later, with the full concurrence of the Prime Minister, Lord Kitchener, and Sir Edward Grey, as well as that of the First Sea Lord and the Naval Chief of Staff, Mr. Churchill informed the French Government of Admiral Carden's scheme, and added that it was hoped to begin the attack on the 15th February. The French Government promised a squadron to co-operate; and it was agreed that the Allied fleets should be under Admiral Carden's command.

On the 19th January Mr. Churchill informed the Grand Duke Nicholas that, in addition to the minor demonstration promised by Lord Kitchener, the Government had determined to attempt to force the Dardanelles. He hoped that the Russians would

[1] Dealing with the wording of this decision, the Dardanelles Commission calls attention to the atmosphere of vagueness and want of precision which seems to have characterized the proceedings of the War Council. The majority of ministers present believed that the attack had already been approved, unless some unforeseen event should render it unnecessary. Some, including the Prime Minister, who read out the decision, imagined that they had merely sanctioned the making of provisional plans. A few, among them Lord Fisher and Admiral Wilson, left the meeting before the decision was read out, and were unaware that anything definite had been settled.

assist the operation by simultaneously attacking the Bosporus with ships and troops, though this operation had better be deferred until the outer forts had fallen, so that, if failure in this first enterprise should result, it would not have the appearance of a serious reverse. Mr. Churchill added, however, that it was the British Government's intention to press the matter to a conclusion.

The following day Mr. Churchill informed Lord Kitchener that, in order to guard against the appearance of a serious rebuff, he did not wish to concentrate the full naval force at the Dardanelles until the outer forts had fallen. He suggested that a landing at Alexandretta should be practically simultaneous with the attack on the Dardanelles, so that, in the event of a check, the bombardment of the forts would look like a mere demonstration to cover the seizure of Alexandretta. The Admiralty wanted to begin the attack on the Dardanelles about the 15th February. Could troops be ready to land at Alexandretta about that date?

Lord Kitchener replied that no troops could be spared at present, even for Alexandretta. The training of the Australians was not yet completed, and the whole garrison of Egypt might be required to defeat the impending attack on the Suez Canal.

Meanwhile Lord Fisher, whose original wish had been only for an immediate and combined operation, was becoming more and more opposed to the whole scheme.[1] This attitude, so far as could be elicited by the Dardanelles Commission, was due, not so much to a belief that the attack would fail, as to a realization that the length and magnitude of the operations would prohibit the great combined undertaking in the Baltic on which for years he had set his heart.[2]

Such was the situation when the War Council next assembled on the 28th January.

The decision reached at this meeting was so important that it will be of interest to quote an extract from the Dardanelles Commission's account of the proceedings. After detailing the various steps taken by the Admiralty since the last meeting, with regard to Admiral Carden's scheme and the arrangements made with the French, Mr. Churchill asked if the War Council

[1] Lord Fisher was equally or even more opposed to the Zeebrugge scheme, preparations for which had been authorized on 13th January. He explained to the Commission that it was the loss of valuable ships' crews that he dreaded. The ships were obsolescent, but " you cannot go round " the corner to find a naval officer or seaman like you can a person to let " off a rifle in a trench ".

[2] " The Baltic was the real focus of all my purposes at the Admiralty. " Mr. Churchill dropped it for the Dardanelles. That was the real point " of separation." Lord Fisher before the Dardanelles Commission.

INITIATION OF DARDANELLES CAMPAIGN 61

attached importance to the operation, which undoubtedly involved some risks. Lord Fisher, who with Mr. Churchill had just had an interview with the Prime Minister, in the course of which he had urged the greater value of his Baltic project, said that "he understood this question would not be " raised to-day". The Prime Minister replied that in view of the steps which had already been taken the question could not well be left in abeyance. Lord Kitchener said that in his opinion the naval attack was vitally important. If successful its effect would be equivalent to that of a successful campaign fought with the New Armies.

Mr. Balfour remarked that it was difficult to imagine a more helpful operation. Sir Edward Grey thought that it would finally settle the attitude of Bulgaria and the whole of the Balkans. Mr. Churchill said that the naval Commander-in-Chief believed that it could be done, and that it would take three weeks to a month. The necessary ships were on their way to the Dardanelles.

When Lord Fisher realized that a final decision was about to be taken, he rose from the table, meaning to tender his resignation. Lord Kitchener at once drew him to the window and strongly urged him not to resign, pointing out that he was the only dissentient. The First Sea Lord was persuaded to return to his seat, and the Council then agreed that the Admiralty should be definitely charged to carry out the operation.

It was arranged to hold a second meeting of the War Council later in the day, to hear the final Admiralty view. Between the two meetings Mr. Churchill sent for Lord Fisher, and succeeded in persuading him to undertake the operation.[1] Accordingly, at the evening session, the First Lord was able to announce that the Admiralty definitely agreed to carry out the task.

The matter had now passed into the domain of action. An attack was to be made as soon as possible, by the fleet alone, with Constantinople as its ultimate objective.

The decision thus arrived at on the 28th January marks the first great landmark in the history of the Dardanelles campaign. In an effort to satisfy the urgent needs of diplomacy, Britain's fleet was to attempt, without the aid of a single soldier, an enterprise which in the earlier days of the war both the

---

[1] " To forbid, before it had been tried, an experiment on which rested " so many sanguine hopes, would have been an impracticable step. The " experiment had to be made, and I did accept in that connection, responsi- " bility, though reluctant responsibility." Lord Fisher before the Dardanelles Commission.

Admiralty and the War Office had regarded as a military task.[1] The operation would, moreover, be many times more difficult than in the early days of the war. The Germans had already had six months in which to improve the defences of the Straits, and the minefields were continually growing.

The enterprise was perhaps still capable of accomplishment, if the Government were ready to face the inevitable loss of ships. This was the opinion of the German Admiral von Usedom, who knew better than anyone the strength and the weakness of the fortress and the capacity of its defenders. But there must be no indecision, no faltering, and no delay. Nothing but iron will and grim determination, both at home and on the spot, could snatch the hazardous victory.

[1] Speaking in the House of Commons on 15th November 1915, Mr. Asquith said: " It is the duty of any Government . . . to rely very largely " upon the advice of its naval and military counsellors. But in the long " run a Government which is worthy of the name, must bring all these " things into some kind of proportion one to the other, and sometimes it " is not only expedient but necessary to run risks and to encounter dangers " which pure naval and military policy would warn you against."

CHAPTER IV

THE INITIATION OF THE DARDANELLES CAMPAIGN (*continued*)

(Maps 1, 2, 4; Sketch 10)

GRIM determination to succeed was, however, avowedly absent from the Government's initial resolve to force the Dardanelles. If the door were to prove too strongly barred, the fleet was to be called away, and the onlooking world persuaded that no attempt had been made to break it open. A great merit of the scheme, in the eyes of those influenced by current French doctrine, was the belief that it would lead to no diversion of troops from the Western front. It was this factor that helped to win for the plan its espousal by the French Government.
 Jan. 1915.

The enterprise was in fact a compromise between the rival opinions of those who wanted to send every available man to France, and those who urged the advantages of striking the enemy at his weakest rather than at his strongest point of concentration. Avowedly and professedly a half-measure, it was not to escape a half-measure's inherent disadvantages. To undertake a big operation on the Western front might well be to gamble with pounds for a possible gain of pence. The pendulum had now swung back. Pence were to be wagered in the none too sanguine hope of winning pounds.

Yet, though all were agreed, none were satisfied, and from its very inception the operation was handicapped by lack of confidence in its success. One of the main objects was to bring in the Balkan states, and thereby to rescue Serbia from her plight. But on the very day the scheme was sanctioned, the Government were seeking an alternative and more certain method of helping the Serbs.

On the 23rd January the British minister in Athens was authorized to offer the Greek Government certain eventual concessions in Asia Minor if Greece would ally herself with Serbia. The Greek Government replied that they would march to the assistance of the Serbs only if one of the three following conditions could be fulfilled. Bulgaria must be induced to co-operate; or, if nothing better than friendly neutrality could be obtained from Sofia, Rumania must be persuaded to help; or, thirdly, if even the friendly neutrality of Bulgaria could not be assured, the Entente must send enough troops to Salonika to give a strong moral guarantee against possible fluctuations in King Ferdinand's attitude. For this purpose M. Venizelos suggested that two British or French army corps would suffice.

This was the situation when, on the 28th January, after the Admiralty had been charged with the task of forcing the Dardanelles without the help of troops, the Government considered the report of the committee which, a fortnight earlier, had been appointed to find an alternative theatre for the employment of the New Armies.

It was reported that the committee had voted for the Salonika theatre, as Salonika was considered to be the best port from which to assist the Serbs, and the plight of Serbia dominated the situation. The question now arose as to when troops could be sent. Undoubtedly there was danger in delay, but Lord Kitchener explained that no immediate Austro-German invasion was possible, for the northern passes were deep in snow. Moreover, he reiterated that at present there were no troops to spare, though some might be available later on.

In point of fact two recent events had increased the chance of troops being available for a diversion at an earlier date than was anticipated on the 13th January. The successful naval action off the Dogger Bank had dispelled some of the fears of a military raid by Germany on the East Coast. Secondly, the decision of General Joffre to withdraw 100,000 French troops from Flanders had necessitated the indefinite postponement of Sir John French's Zeebrugge offensive, for which he had been promised a reinforcement of the Canadians, the 29th, and two Territorial divisions. In these altered circumstances, it was generally considered unnecessary to send all four divisions to France. They had been promised solely for an offensive operation. As that operation had been postponed, it should suffice to give Sir John French one division, keeping three for a diversion elsewhere. But Lord Kitchener was still afraid of a new German attack on the Western front, and both he and Sir Edward Grey laid stress on the disfavour with which a military enterprise in the Mediterranean would be regarded in France.

So great was the influence exerted by the French High Command and British G.H.Q. in France, that, though the majority of the Government were in favour of a diversion, it was decided to give Sir John French the opportunity of expressing his views. Mr. Churchill consented to go to France and explain to Sir

John French that owing to the postponement of his advance it was "not desired" at present to send him any reinforcements except the Canadian Division. The First Lord was to "suggest" that the remaining three divisions should either be retained in England in readiness to meet any emergency, or sent to France only on the distinct understanding that they might be withdrawn in a month for service elsewhere. He was further to explain to the Commander-in-Chief the importance of a diversion in the Balkans, and to "consult" with him as to the best way of inducing the French to adopt a similar view.

On the 31st January Mr. Churchill returned with the news that Sir John French strongly urged that all four divisions should still be sent to France. Joffre would be greatly disappointed if this were not done; it would be useless for Sir John to address him on the subject; and if it were decided not to send this reinforcement as arranged, the matter would have to be settled between the two Governments. The Commander-in-Chief could recommend no weakening of the forces promised to him, even though the Zeebrugge advance was indefinitely postponed; nor did he favour on strategical grounds any diversion in the Mediterranean. Nevertheless, if all four divisions were sent to him, he would, if so desired, hold two of them at the Government's disposal from the middle of March, for service elsewhere.

Though this was not the answer wanted by the Government, it was now fairly certain that at least two divisions could be spared for the Mediterranean in six weeks' time. A few days later it seemed that this number might soon be increased by the addition of troops from Egypt, for early in February the news reached England that the Turkish attack on the Suez Canal had definitely failed.[1]

Feb. 1915.

On the 9th February the War Council heard the ominous news that Bulgaria had contracted a loan with Germany. There was now a real danger of her joining the Central Powers. King Ferdinand was spreading the rumour that Russia could do nothing for lack of ammunition, and, as a result, the sympathies of Rumania towards the Entente appeared to be cooling. Assistance for the Serbs seemed therefore more urgent than ever. The meeting was informed that, as a result of Mr. Lloyd George's visit to Paris to stress the importance of French co-operation, M. Delcassé had visited England to discuss the matter. There was a proposal that France and England should each offer to send one division to Salonika. Russia had been

[1] This news undoubtedly tended to depreciate still further the Government's opinion of the fighting value of Turkish troops.

asked to do the same, but had replied that the most she could spare was a contingent of 1,000 Cossacks.

A discussion then arose on the advantages of the Salonika project, some of which resembled very closely the advantages which, twelve days earlier, had been claimed for an attack on the Dardanelles. The Balkan states would be brought in, Serbia would be succoured, and the way would be opened for an eventual advance up the Danube. Even Sir John French, who was present at the meeting, agreed that a success of this nature might prove decisive.

It was therefore agreed, subject to French concurrence, to offer Greece one British and one French division to guard her communications, on condition that she should march to Serbia's assistance. It was the intention to increase these numbers as soon as troops became available, but the whole scheme of an Allied advance into Serbia obviously depended on Greek adherence to the cause of the Entente; otherwise Salonika would not be available.

Lord Kitchener observed that he would detail the 29th Division for Salonika. But as the French would only agree to our diverting troops to the Mediterranean on condition that Britain's promised strength in France was not immediately reduced, he would send a Territorial division to take its place in Sir John French's army.

Thus, twelve days after it had been thought that no troops could be spared for a subsidiary theatre for several months, and that the fleet must make an unaided attack on the Dardanelles, it was plain that a considerable military force would, after all, be available at an early date, and that France would agree to a diversion. Yet, owing to half-hearted confidence in the results of the Dardanelles enterprise, plans were now being made to employ these troops, not in a combined attack with the fleet, but in an entirely different theatre. An advantage claimed by Lord Kitchener for sending the 29th Division to Salonika was that it would be "very useful to the fleet at the Dardanelles " to have some good troops at that port". Lord Kitchener also agreed that if the fleet at the Dardanelles wanted military assistance at a later date, it should be forthcoming. This was the first hint of putting any more determination into the effort to force the Straits. But the supreme importance of surprise in a combined operation was overlooked, as also was the certainty that if troops were sent out only after the fleet had been held up for lack of them, their task on arrival would be peculiarly difficult.

The offer of one British and one French division to Greece

INITIATION OF DARDANELLES CAMPAIGN 67

was conveyed to Athens, but the proposal of so small a reinforcement did nothing to alleviate Greek anxiety with regard to their powerful neighbour. On the 15th February the Greek Government refused the offer unless Rumania could also be persuaded to come in; and owing to the recent retreat of the Russian right wing, and the Russian retirement from the Bukovina, it was for the moment useless to address Rumania again. So the Salonika project had to be dropped, and attention at last became focussed on the chances at the Dardanelles.

Admiralty opinion was meanwhile inclining more and more to the belief that no real success could be achieved at the Dardanelles without the aid of troops. Two battalions of marines belonging to the Royal Naval Division had already been sent out by Mr. Churchill on the 6th February to furnish small landing parties for destroying guns;[1] but now that considerable forces would be available in the near future, it was urged by the Admiralty Staff that they should be sent to the Dardanelles rather than to any alternative theatre. On 15th February an important memorandum on this subject was written by Admiral Sir H. B. Jackson. Not only, it observed, would landing parties be required to finish off the forts. If the channel was to be of any use for merchant vessels, both shores must be held after the fleet passed into the Marmara. The best plan of all would be to have a combined attack from the outset, and to occupy the whole peninsula.[2]

These expressions of Admiralty opinion were to have immediate effect. On the 16th February — the day after

[1] These troops, which had received their warning orders on 29th January, were proceeding to Mudros harbour (island of Lemnos), which had just been borrowed from Greece as a naval advanced base for the operations. The borrowing of the harbour created no international complications, for Turkey had not acknowledged Greek sovereignty over the island.

[2] Sir Henry Jackson's memorandum concluded as follows:
" The provision of the necessary military forces to enable the fruits
" of this heavy naval undertaking to be gathered must never be lost sight
" of. The transports carrying them should be ready to enter the Straits
" as soon as it is seen that the forts at the Narrows will be silenced. To
" complete their destruction, strong military landing parties with strong
" covering forces will be necessary. It is considered, however, that the full
" advantage of the undertaking would only be obtained by the occupation
" of the peninsula by a military force acting in conjunction with the naval
" operations, as the pressure of a strong Turkish field army on the peninsula
" would not only greatly harass the operations, but would render the
" passage of the Straits impracticable by any but powerfully armed vessels,
" even though all the permanent defences had been silenced. The naval
" bombardment is not recommended as a sound military operation, unless
" a strong military force is ready to assist in the operation, or at least to
" follow it up immediately the forts are silenced."
Compare Admiral Hornby's arguments in 1877-8, page 27.

Admiral Jackson's memorandum was written—the subject was discussed at an informal meeting of ministers. So important was the matter considered that other ministers were summoned; the meeting resolved itself into an impromptu session of the War Council; and it was there and then decided to prepare large military forces for the Dardanelles. The actual decisions were as follows:

1. The 29th Division to be despatched to Mudros at the earliest possible date. It was hoped that it would be able to sail in nine or ten days.
2. Arrangements to be made for a force to be despatched from Egypt if required.
3. All these forces to be available in case of necessity to support the naval attack on the Dardanelles.
4. Horse boats to be taken out with the 29th Division, and the Admiralty to collect small craft, tugs, and lighters in the Levant.[1]

This meeting marks the second great landmark of the campaign. It had not yet been finally determined to use troops on a large scale. But they were to be concentrated in the neighbourhood, in case their assistance should be required. The enterprise, in fact, was being placed on a new footing. The intention of breaking off the attack, if satisfactory progress were not made by the fleet, had begun to disappear.

But despite these signs of a vital change of policy, there was no request by the Admiralty for a change of plan, or even for a postponement of naval action till military forces could arrive. The bombardment of the outer forts was now due to begin in three days, whereas the troops could not be on the spot for at least another month. Yet the disadvantage of striking this warning blow a month before the arrival of the military help which the Admiralty were so sure would be needed, was apparently urged by no one. No one suggested the advisability, now that troops were to be sent, of avoiding the risk of a piecemeal attack, and of waiting for a combined operation with all the advantages of surprise.[2] Even the question of ordering the

---

[1] A fifth decision arrived at on this day was to build special transports and lighters for landing 50,000 men. This decision related, however, to projected operations in the Baltic at a later date, and had no relation to the Dardanelles enterprise; though, as a matter of fact, the motor lighters were afterwards sent to the Dardanelles in time for the Suvla landing.

[2] It was probably believed by the Government that, unless an immediate diversion were made, Bulgaria would join the Central Powers. It is certainly true that the opening of the naval attack made an enormous impression on all the Balkan states.

INITIATION OF DARDANELLES CAMPAIGN 69

General Staff to work out preliminary plans for the employment of the troops was not discussed.[1] In these omissions lay the root cause of future failure.

Up to this time the Government had no definite conviction that large numbers of troops would be required to assist the fleet in the actual attack on the Dardanelles. True, it had been agreed in September, and again in November, that the best way to force the Straits was for an army to capture the peninsula and admit the fleet into the Narrows. But this was to be a naval attack. Such confidence as ministers had in its success was based on a belief in the power of naval guns to silence the hostile forts; and the intention of abandoning the enterprise if this belief should prove fallacious had not as yet been definitely relinquished. It was for employment after the fleet had reached the Marmara, to hold the shores of the Straits, and possibly to occupy Constantinople, that a considerable force was to be concentrated, and even for these tasks the necessity of large numbers was not unanimously admitted. Up to the 16th February the First Lord of the Admiralty had not pressed for anything more than landing parties to complete the destruction of the enemy's guns at the Narrows. Both Lord Kitchener and Sir Edward Grey looked confidently, and apparently with good reason, to a revolution at the Turkish capital if the Dardanelles should fall. It was equally expected that the Turks would evacuate the peninsula if their sea-communications were cut.

Britain's hope of forcing the Dardanelles, and the possibility of the early arrival of British troops at Constantinople, was to lead to important developments in France. On the 18th February, two days after the British War Council had decided to send a military force to the Dardanelles, the French Government, which had already agreed to the co-operation of a French naval squadron, resolved to participate still further in the operation by the immediate despatch of an infantry division to the Eastern Mediterranean.[2] General Joffre, however, on being sounded by the French War Ministry on this subject, replied at once that he found it "absolutely impossible to "consent" to any levy on the troops under his command. The

---

[1] The Report of the Dardanelles Commission comments on the absence of any preliminary plan by the General Staff. The reason for the omission was that until 11th March the General Staff were not informed that any large military operations in the Dardanelles were contemplated. It is true that the C.I.G.S. (Lieut.-General Sir James Wolfe Murray) was present at all the meetings of the War Council, but he made no comment thereat, and issued no instructions to his subordinate officers.

[2] French Official Account, Tome viii. i. pp. 13, 18.

Staff at the French War Ministry were consequently ordered on the 22nd February to organize a new division from troops in the depots in France and North Africa, consisting of Europeans, French Colonials, Foreign Legionaries, and Senegalese. This division, to be commanded by General d'Amade, was designated "Corps Expéditionnaire d'Orient"; it was to come into being on the 1st March, and to be ready to sail a few days later.

General Joffre's attitude towards this decision can be inferred from a telegram which he addressed to the French military mission at British G.H.Q. in France on the 25th February. Asked by the mission to give Lord Kitchener some information regarding the 18,000 French troops which the Admiralty had that day told Kitchener were being sent to the Near East, he replied: "The Government has informed me " that it is organizing a division for the expedition with troops " from the interior. It will not comprise any unit serving on " or destined for the Western front."[1]

The new French division was formed with lightning speed,[2] and its first elements, together with General d'Amade and his staff, embarked on the 3rd March. General d'Amade's orders, issued to him on the 2nd, were to co-operate with the Allied fleet and the British troops in forcing the Dardanelles, in keeping the Straits open, and in any subsequent action by the Allied forces at Constantinople and the Bosporus. He was to take his instructions from Admiral Carden, who would be in supreme command of the operations in the Near East.[3]

In the absence of an unanimous ministerial conviction of its urgency, the Government's decision of the 16th February could scarcely be expected to escape a determined challenge from those imbued with the doctrines of the "Western school". Even when the Dardanelles operations had assumed an entirely military character it remained the tendency of the "Western school" to regard every reinforcement for Gallipoli as an unjustifiable theft from France.[4] In the earlier days, before the

[1] French Official Account, Tome viii. Annexes i. No. 9.
[2] See Appendix 2 for Order of Battle.
[3] This order was subsequently (10th March) altered, the French Government agreeing that, in the best interests of the operations, General d'Amade should be placed under the command of the British military C.-in-C. See French Official Account, Tome viii. Annexes No. 24.
[4] The situation has been wittily epitomized by an American writer: " The expedition remained to the end an illegitimate child, importunate " in its demands and annoying by the very fact of its existence." Major S. Miles, General Staff, U.S. Army, " Coast Artillery Journal," December 1924.

INITIATION OF DARDANELLES CAMPAIGN 71

necessity of giving strong military support to the fleet was recognized by the Government, this contention was very hard to combat. Thus it happened that the sudden decision of the 16th February to send the 29th Division to Gallipoli was as suddenly cancelled on the 19th, the date of the opening of the naval attack. And thus, while at the Dardanelles the British fleet was thundering a message of resolve, at home the prospects of this great adventure were still being handicapped by doubt and indecision.

It was at the War Council meeting on the 19th February that Lord Kitchener announced his change of mind with regard to the 29th Division.[1] He stated that the news from the Russian front was grave. At any moment the Germans might mass for a new attack in the West, and it was therefore imperative to keep this last remaining Regular division at Sir John French's disposal. But the Australian and New Zealand divisions in Egypt should be sent to the Dardanelles instead, and would be able to arrive more quickly than the 29th from home.[2] He added that these two divisions would give all the help the fleet needed. The most he would promise in addition was that the 29th should be sent to the Straits later, if its absence was found to be prejudicing the success of the operations.

All attempts to shake Lord Kitchener's decision were in vain. Neither the argument that new and untried troops should not be employed on so difficult a task without a stiffening of Regulars, nor the contention that the best way of relieving the Russian situation, and preventing a German onslaught in the West, was to open the Dardanelles, was of any avail. Mr. Churchill was now a strong advocate of having at least 50,000 men available to reach the Dardanelles at three days' notice. For the first time, he insisted that it would be impossible for the fleet to keep the Dardanelles open for merchant ships, and urged that ministers would never forgive themselves if this promising operation were to fail for lack of troops at the

[1] Lord Kitchener's change of mind was evidently prompted by very great pressure from the French High Command. This pressure was continued for a considerable time, and on 28th February the French Ambassador in London went so far as to call on Sir Edward Grey to beg that the 29th Division should not be sent elsewhere than to France without the concurrence of the French Commander-in-Chief. It would seem, indeed, that this last remaining Regular division was being regarded by French G.Q.G. as a symbol of Britain's future attitude with regard to the Western front.

[2] Here Lord Kitchener was mistaken. The Australian and New Zealand troops were still short of a good deal of equipment and ammunition which would have to be sent from England before they could take the field, and transports to take them to the peninsula would also have to be sent from England.

critical moment. So far as the 29th Division was concerned, Lord Kitchener remained obdurate. Not until the Russian situation had cleared up, or until there was some sign of a probable success at the Dardanelles, would he agree to override the claims of France to the services of these last remaining Regular troops. It was not until the 10th March that he finally consented to the division being sent to the Dardanelles.[1]

The protracted struggle for the services of the 29th Division, though in itself only a minor incident, throws a vivid light on the Government's need at that period of the advice of a trusted General Staff. Without a detailed study of the strategical situation on all fronts, and a careful balancing of the rival claims to the forces now becoming available, it was impossible for ministers to form a trustworthy judgment as to whether they would be justified in substituting a strenuous combined effort to reach the Marmara for the strictly limited commitments of their original plan. The Admiralty were calling for large and indefinite numbers of troops, without any definite opinion as to how, when, or where they would be required. British headquarters in France, whose views were necessarily narrowed by the limits of their immediate horizon, were urging that none could be spared. The General Staff in England, who alone could give an independent and unbiassed opinion, were not consulted. The first requirement of the Government was a reasoned statement of the numbers wanted to ensure success in the Dardanelles, and the date by which these numbers would be required. It was essential to know exactly what risks would be run in France by making this diversion. Then, and then only, could ministers be in a position to count the cost, and to decide whether or not the risks would be justified. To attempt a solution of the problem without the knowledge of these factors was to grope in the dark.

[1] The Dardanelles Commission attached the utmost importance to the three weeks' delay in the despatch of the 29th Division, and stated that it was owing to this delay that the favourable moment for action was allowed to lapse. In arriving at this conclusion they omitted to take into consideration the actual weather conditions at the Dardanelles in April 1915. Had combined operations been able to begin three weeks earlier the chances of success would undoubtedly have been better. But in point of fact the weather was so unsettled throughout this period that 25th April—the eventual day of the landings—was actually the first day in April on which the disembarkation of a large force on exposed beaches could have been safely undertaken. Regrettable, and infinitely serious, though the delay might have proved, it is not historically accurate to attribute to it any of the subsequent lack of success.

23rd April was the original date fixed for the landings, but the weather was still so boisterous on 21st April that the admiral insisted on a postponement for 48 hours.

INITIATION OF DARDANELLES CAMPAIGN 73

Lord Kitchener now took steps to place a small force from Egypt at the immediate disposal of the fleet, in addition to arranging for the early despatch of the Australian and New Zealand divisions. He also resolved to gauge for himself the military situation at the Dardanelles, and to gain some indication of the admiral's probable requirements. It was characteristic of his methods that he took upon his own shoulders the full weight of this new and in many respects unwelcome military burden, and the history of the preparations now set on foot is largely contained in a series of personal telegrams which passed between him and the British Commander-in-Chief in Egypt. On the 20th February Lord Kitchener informed General Maxwell[1] that the fleet had started an attack on the Dardanelles, and ordered him to warn a force of 30,000 Australian and New Zealand troops under Lieut.-General Sir W. R. Birdwood to be ready to embark about the 9th March, in transports sent from England,[2] "to assist the navy in their undertaking . . . to " give any co-operation that may be required, and to occupy " any captured forts ". As Carden might require a considerable force before that date, Maxwell was, in addition, to take up all the ships he could obtain locally, and to despatch them to Lemnos as quickly as possible with all the troops they would hold. Maxwell was also to get into immediate touch with Carden, find out exactly what he wanted, and endeavour to satisfy all his needs.

By the 23rd February Maxwell had collected transports for one brigade. In other respects the news from Egypt was not so encouraging. A great deal of material would be required from England before the remainder of Birdwood's force could take the field. There were only four horse-boats at Alexandria, and none at Malta. Carden's reply to Maxwell's telegram disclosed the disturbing fact that he regarded the Government as the authors of the enterprise, and himself only as its executant; and that he had no clearer views than ministers at home as to the nature of his probable military requirements. "I have " been directed", his message ran, "to make preparations for " landing a force of 10,000 men, if such a step is found " necessary ;[3] at present my instructions go no further. If

---

[1] Lieut.-General Sir John Maxwell, commanding the troops in Egypt.
[2] These transports had originally been ordered for the 29th Division, but were despatched to Egypt for the Australians as soon as the orders for the 29th were cancelled.
[3] The Admiralty had just ordered the remainder of the Royal Naval Division, less 3 battalions and a field company still too raw to leave England, to follow the two marine battalions to Mudros. The Naval Division, it must be remembered was still a division only in name: it

"such a force is sent, I would propose landing it at Sedd el Bahr with the object of occupying the Gallipoli peninsula as far east as the Soghanli Dere—Chanav Ova."[1]

Information in England pointed to the presence of 40,000 Turks on the peninsula, and the idea of occupying its southern end with a quarter of that number was frankly alarming. It seemed imperative to exercise some sort of control over the uses to be made of the troops. But before this could be done it was essential to gain a clearer knowledge of the situation. Lord Kitchener ordered General Birdwood[2] post-haste to the Dardanelles, sending him the following telegram, through General Maxwell, on the 23rd February:

Proceed to meet Admiral Carden at the earliest possible opportunity and consult him as to the nature of the combined operations which the forcing of the Dardanelles is to involve. Report the result to me. You should learn from local observation and information the numbers of the Turkish garrison on the peninsula, and whether the admiral thinks it will be necessary to land troops to take the forts in reverse; if so what force will be required, and generally in what manner it is proposed to use the troops. Will the Bulair lines have to be held, and will operations on the Asiatic side be necessary or advisable?

Lord Kitchener's own views on the matter can be gauged from a telegram which he addressed to General Maxwell the following day:

In concerting operations Birdwood should be guided by the following considerations. The object of forcing the Dardanelles is to gain possession of the Bosporus and overawe Constantinople. The forcing of the Straits is to be effected mainly by naval means, and, when successful it will doubtless be followed by the retirement of the Gallipoli garrison. So far as our information goes, it does not appear a sound military undertaking to attempt a landing in force on the Gallipoli peninsula, the garrison of which is reported to be 40,000, until the passage has been forced. The entry of the fleet into the Marmara would probably make the Turkish position untenable, and enable British troops to occupy the peninsula if

---

had no artillery, and though many of its men had already fought at Antwerp and all were of magnificent material, they were still short of training. The division left Avonmouth on 1st and 2nd March, and arrived at Mudros on the 12th. But they had been embarked without any reference to their tactical employment on arrival, and all their transports had to be sent to Port Said to be re-sorted before the troops could be landed on the peninsula.

[1] A general line across the peninsula at the foot of the south-western slopes of the Kilid Bahr plateau.

[2] General Birdwood had held many appointments on Lord Kitchener's personal staff, and was a trusted friend.

INITIATION OF DARDANELLES CAMPAIGN 75

considered necessary. But to land with 10,000 in the face of 40,000 seems extremely hazardous. If it can be done without seriously compromising the troops landed for the purpose, there would be no objection to the employment of troops to secure forts or positions already gained or dominated by naval fire, and to deny their reoccupation by the enemy. It therefore seems desirable as a first step that one Australian brigade should be sent to Lemnos, where it will be at hand if required. The rest of Birdwood's force should be held in readiness to embark at Alexandria at short notice.

General Birdwood should give me his own views as to the number of troops required for the above purposes. Further, in case it should prove possible to send more troops, he should report how he thinks they could be best utilized for a further enterprise after the Straits have been forced.

Birdwood should also inform me privately whether from the results of the bombardment up to date he considers that it will be necessary to land considerable numbers to take the forts in reverse before the Straits can be forced, or whether he thinks that the naval operations will succeed without having recourse to such a step.

Preparations had gone thus far when, on the 24th February, the Government reached a further stage on the unmapped road so soon to lead them, without adequate preparation, into the hazards of a great campaign on the peninsula. Ministers were rapidly realizing that the original idea of abandoning the operations if the task should prove too difficult for the fleet was no longer as simple as it had seemed. If a success at the Dardanelles could win the Balkans to the Entente, a failure must have the opposite effect. The opening of the bombardment had attracted such world-wide attention that, for the sake of British prestige, the enterprise must be carried through, no matter what the cost. At a meeting of the War Council on the 24th February Mr. Lloyd George was the only dissentient to this policy. He objected to the army being used "to pull the navy's chestnuts out of the fire". He insisted that though the bombardment had committed the Government to a campaign in the Near East, they were not necessarily committed to the Dardanelles. If the naval attack failed, it would be far wiser to let the army try somewhere else than to ask it to make good the naval failure. His advice was not followed. Mr. Churchill argued that the country was absolutely committed to seeing the Dardanelles attack through.[1] Lord Kitchener agreed that the

---

[1] It will be remembered that Mr. Churchill had anticipated this view when, on 19th January, he informed the Grand Duke Nicholas that it was the British Government's intention to "press the matter to a conclusion". See page 60.

army must help if the necessity should arise, and that there could be no going back now. Sir Edward Grey was certain that the acceptance of a naval failure would be equivalent to a great military defeat on land.

Thus, by the 24th February the Government found themselves committed, by force of circumstances rather than by choice, to the possibility of extensive military operations in the Dardanelles. The idea of half-measures and limited risks had finally disappeared. In their place there now stood a definite determination to see the matter through, and an indefinite resolve to support the fleet with all the troops that might, at a later date, be required to make the difference between success and failure. The size of the force likely to be wanted for this purpose, and the probable nature of its task, was not, however, discussed. The Government were awaiting guidance from Admiral Carden, while the admiral was expecting instructions from home. The extent to which the difficulties of an opposed landing were being daily increased by the reverberations of the naval attack was still but faintly realized.

Meanwhile from Egypt General Maxwell sounded a note of warning about the probable strength of the Turkish positions in Gallipoli. On the 24th February he telegraphed his belief that the peninsula was everywhere heavily fortified and was "practically a fort", advance against which without heavy guns would seem to be hazardous. Two days later he telegraphed the gist of a written report by Colonel Maucorps of the French military mission at Cairo, and lately military attaché at Constantinople, to the effect that a landing on the peninsula would be extremely hazardous. It had a garrison of 30,000 men, with another 30,000 on the Asiatic shore; the Bulair lines had been rearmed; and the Turkish commander of the peninsula was an excellent and energetic officer.

These telegrams, though we now know that they gave an exaggerated account of Turkish readiness at that time, naturally increased Lord Kitchener's anxiety to avoid serious military operations on the peninsula. With the situation on the Western front in an unsatisfactory state, and with Britain still lamentably short of men and ammunition, it was no time to embark upon a new and desperate military enterprise, the extent of which could not at present be foreseen. The peninsula, in fact, was apparently a hornets' nest, extremely dangerous to intruders. Lord Kitchener hoped to take it by first putting the hornets to flight. "The forcing of the Dardanelles", he wired to Birdwood on the evening of the 26th, "is being undertaken by the navy, " and as far as can be foreseen at present the task of your troops,

INITIATION OF DARDANELLES CAMPAIGN 77

" until the passage has been actually secured, will be limited to
" minor operations, such as final destruction of batteries, after
" they have been silenced, under the covering fire of ships.
" It is possible, however, that howitzer batteries may be con-
" cealed inland, with which ships cannot deal effectively. If
" called upon by the admiral you might have to undertake
" special minor operations from within the Straits for dealing
" with these. But large Turkish forces are stationed on both
" sides of the Straits, and you should not commit yourself to
" any operations of this class without aerial reconnaissance and
" assurance of ample covering fire from the fleet." At this
point in his telegram it apparently occurred to Lord Kitchener
that the troops already *en route* for the Dardanelles might not
after all suffice for these "minor operations", and that a force
of 40,000 men might possibly be required; for the message
continued: "at any time during the bombardment you can of
" course obtain any additional troops from your corps in Egypt
" that you may require, up to its total strength". "It is
" anticipated", Lord Kitchener added, "that when the forcing
" of the Narrows is practically assured, the Turks will probably
" evacuate the peninsula, and a small force at Bulair will then
" be able to hold it . . . it might be well to induce the enemy
" to believe that landings are under consideration at this point,
" threatening his retreat out of the peninsula. . . . As soon
" as you can get into touch with local information, send me an
" appreciation of what is likely to happen at Constantinople,
" and whether you think that more than 64,000 [1] troops will be
" required for operations there after the Straits have been
" forced."

Meanwhile at the Dardanelles the progress of the naval bombardment was being seriously impeded by bad weather. These adverse conditions would have made the co-operation of troops impracticable, even if a large force had already arrived on the spot.

The official account of the naval operations has already been written,[2] and all that will be attempted in this volume is to give a brief outline of events and to indicate the influence of the naval effort upon the subsequent military campaign. The attack began on the 19th February,[3] with the bombardment of

[1] Lord Kitchener had heard the previous day of the approaching despatch of a French division, and his numbers were apparently made up as follows: Naval Division, 10,000; Anzac corps, 36,000; one French division, 18,000—total 64,000.
[2] Corbett, "Naval Operations," ii.
[3] By a strange coincidence, the anniversary of Admiral Duckworth's exploit in 1807.

the outer forts. The Allied fleet mounted a total of 274 medium and heavy pieces, culminating in the *Queen Elizabeth's* eight 15-inch guns. The forts mounted nineteen guns, of which all but four were old-pattern short guns with a maximum range of 6,000-8,000 yards. The first day's bombardment, carried out by roughly half the available fleet, was inconclusive.

For the next five days no operations were possible, owing to bad weather. On the 25th February the bombardment was resumed. Keeping out of range of the forts, and mutually observing each other's fire at right angles, the ships developed a remarkable degree of accuracy, and all the four modern guns at the entrance were put out of action. In the afternoon the ships advanced to close range; and the Turks, deeming it useless, with their old-pattern guns, to persist in so one-sided a contest, ordered the evacuation of the outer forts. It was impossible to use seaplanes on this day, owing to adverse weather.

Next day the second phase of the operations was begun— the leisurely and piecemeal reduction of the Intermediate Defences by bombardment from inside the Straits. Only three ships took part in this bombardment, and for the first time trouble was experienced from the fire of mobile guns and howitzers which it was impossible to locate. Little was accomplished by the ships, and at 4 P.M. the admiral signalled the recall. Aerial reconnaissance had again proved impossible.

Meanwhile, two small parties of marines, landing at the mouth of the Straits to demolish guns in the outer forts, had achieved a flattering measure of success. It had been the original intention to employ detachments from one of the marine battalions of the Naval Division for this service, but the sea was so boisterous in the early morning that the operation was cancelled for the day. It was only when the deserted appearance of the two promontories was noticed that it was suddenly decided to take advantage of a calm interval by landing a few marines from the bombarding ships.

The first party to land was from the *Vengeance*, and consisted of 50 marines under Major G. M. Heriot, and a demolition party under Lieut.-Commander E. G. Robinson, R.N. Landing at 2.30 P.M. at Kum Kale pier, they met with no opposition until some little way inland, when their advance was checked by a brisk fire. About the same time their left flank guard, pushed out towards the Mendere river, was ambushed with the loss of one killed and two wounded. These were the only casualties of the day, and the demolition party, supported by fire from the *Dublin*, succeeded in reaching Fort 4 on Orkanie Mound, which they found deserted. The one remaining gun

SEDD EL BAHR AND MORTO BAY FROM THE AIR
From a photograph taken in 1922
The 'Camber' landing place is on the right of the picture

INITIATION OF DARDANELLES CAMPAIGN 79

and two anti-aircraft guns were blown up, and, despite the attentions of some snipers, the whole detachment re-embarked without further loss.

On the European side, the *Irresistible's* men, who landed at the Camber, a small jetty at the foot of a steep path leading up to Sedd el Bahr, had much the same experience. To begin with there was no opposition. The covering party of 45 marines took post near some windmills at the east end of the village, with a small piquet in the old castle to the north of it,[1] while the demolition party of 30 men got to work in four sections. The small piquet in the old castle was soon forced to retire by the approach of a party of Turks, but the enemy's further advance was stopped by some 6-inch common shell from the *Irresistible*. Four of the six heavy guns in Fort No. 1 were found undamaged, but were quickly destroyed. As there was now no sign of Turks, a start was made by the demolition party for Cape Tekke (Tekke Burnu); but it soon became evident that the local garrison, though consisting of only a few posts, was too strong for this part of the programme to be carried out by a mere handful of men. Nevertheless one section did succeed in destroying two 12-pdr. guns near Tekke battery, and the whole detachment was then withdrawn without a casualty. On this very spot, where a demolition party of 30 men had moved about with impunity on 26th February, the 29th Division exactly two months later lost 3,000 men before nightfall.[2]

It was intended to resume the operations next day, but again the weather changed, and again the landing of detachments from the marine battalions had to be abandoned. But with the wind dropping in the afternoon, a demolition party, with a covering force of 78 marines, was once more sent ashore at Sedd el Bahr, and again succeeded in carrying out some useful destruction without casualty. A Turkish outpost was still holding a position near the old castle, and kept up a desultory fire on the invaders; but the guns of the *Irresistible* deterred them from coming to close quarters during the re-embarkation.

On the 28th February a heavy gale blew all day, and again no progress was possible. Next day showed little improvement, and the arrangements made for landing two companies of the Plymouth Battalion, R.M.L.I., again had to be cancelled. The delay was all the more regrettable in that it was a handicap only to the attackers. The Turks were able to make good use

---

[1] Afterwards known as Fort Doughty-Wylie.
[2] See Chapter XIII.

of these days of grace. Trenches and entanglements were soon to appear, and it began to be realized that well-concealed infantry had little to fear from ships. At the outset of the naval bombardment the mere detonation of heavy shell had a paralysing effect on the Turkish troops; but once it was realized that their bark was worse than their bite, the moral effect of naval guns rapidly disappeared.

Mar. 1915.
About midday on the 1st March, while the weather was still too boisterous for the seaplanes, four battleships resumed the bombardment of the Intermediate Defences, but the fire from concealed batteries was so harassing that nothing was accomplished. Later in the day the wind moderated, and the opportunity was snatched to land a demolition party at Kum Kale, escorted by 50 marines from the *Irresistible*. No opposition of any kind was encountered. Proceeding to the fort, the party found that seven of its nine guns had not been touched by the bombardments, and that only one was unserviceable. After destroying these guns the party proceeded south and demolished an abandoned field battery, four Nordenfeldts, and a searchlight. They then returned to the boats without incident.

The experiences of the landing parties had been encouraging, but the progress of the naval bombardment was unsatisfactory. Moreover, it was obvious that the fire of the Turkish mobile armament would be even more effective against trawler minesweepers than it had been against armoured ships. And until the mines were swept, though it might be possible, at great loss, to "rush" the passage, the destruction of the Inner Defences by a deliberate bombardment at decisive range would be out of the question. During the night of the 1st March the unprotected trawlers, manned by fishermen, and terribly handicapped by lack of speed, endeavoured to sweep the Kephez minefield, but so slow was their progress against the swift current that they were unable to face the heavy fire which met them.

A few hours before this set-back, on the evening of the 1st March, Captain M. S. Fitzmaurice of the *Triumph*, who had lately witnessed the Japanese operations at Tsingtao, and of whose experience the admiral had been specially instructed to avail himself, forwarded an appreciation in which he urged that there was little hope of dealing with the hidden batteries from the sea, and that the best way of reducing the howitzers on the Asiatic shore was to land guns and howitzers on the European side of the Straits. Nevertheless, in England there were high hopes for the success of the naval enterprise, for on

INITIATION OF DARDANELLES CAMPAIGN

the 2nd March, in reply to an enquiry from Mr. Churchill, Admiral Carden telegraphed that he required only fourteen more fine days to reach the Marmara.

The morning of the 2nd March was as tempestuous as ever, and once more the projected landing of marines had to be postponed. Later in the day the bombardment of the Intermediate Defences was continued, again without the help of aircraft; and again the few ships engaged could claim but little success. Once or twice the forts appeared to be silenced; but they were only husbanding ammunition or removing débris from the guns, and renewed their activity when a favourable opportunity occurred. A second attempt to sweep the Kephez minefield that night ended in complete failure.

On the 3rd March the weather was so stormy that all operations had to be suspended, but late in the afternoon a small party was again landed at Sedd el Bahr Camber and destroyed a 15-pdr. battery, hidden in the arches under the old fort, without encountering opposition. No attempt was made on this occasion to push further inland.

The naval operations had now lasted a fortnight, and, though the destruction of the Outer Defences was practically complete, the second phase, the methodical destruction of the Intermediate Defences and the sweeping of the minefield, had made no progress.

On the 4th March the weather temporarily cleared, and it at last became possible to carry out the landing operations by detachments of the Plymouth Battalion which had been postponed from the 25th February. Much of the demolition work which these detachments were originally intended to cover had already been completed, but a certain number of guns were still intact; it was also desired to reconnoitre for a suitable aerodrome. Unfortunately, the stiffening of Turkish opposition as the result of a week's delay was not foreseen. The detachments originally detailed—one company for each side of the Straits—were not increased, and proved inadequate for the task. Moreover the troops were brought over from their transports at Imbros on the decks of four destroyers in broad daylight, and, their intentions being obvious, the enemy piquets were on the alert to frustrate them.

The scouts and advanced party of the Kum Kale company landed at the jetty to the north of Kum Kale fort about 9 A.M., accompanied by the commanding officer of the battalion, Lieut.-Colonel G. E. Matthews, and immediately came under the fire of snipers in the village. The fort was soon reached, and Colonel Matthews determined to clear the village, but he then discovered that the remainder of his company, who ought to have landed immediately after him, had not yet left the destroyers. On their arrival about 11.30 A.M. the enemy fire had slackened; so, leaving a platoon to guard the line of retreat, an attempt was made to advance southwards to Orkanie. But the party soon came under rifle fire from Yeni Shehr, and, finding the opposition too strong for the small force at his disposal, Colonel Matthews decided at 3.45 P.M. to retire. A retreat was made to Kum Kale fort, but enemy snipers in the village prevented the re-embarkation of the troops till after nightfall. The total casualties suffered by this company were 20 killed, 24 wounded, and 4 missing. These losses would doubtless have been heavier but for the fact that the captain of the *Irresistible* had furnished Colonel Matthews with a code for directing the fire of the ship's guns, with the result that during the day 400 rounds of 6-inch and 800 rounds of 12-pdr. ammunition were fired in his close support.

The Sedd el Bahr company, under Major H. D. Palmer, met with no better success. For the fourth time in succession the landing took place at the Camber. Thanks to the support of naval guns, the men got ashore without opposition. But this time the narrow path leading up to the village was strongly held by a Turkish piquet, and progress up it was barred. Eventually one platoon effected an entrance into the old fort on the left while another scaled the cliffs to the right, and by this means the village was made good. Beyond the village, however, a number of Turks were holding the old castle, and, on Major Palmer asking for a reinforcement of 200 men to turn them out, it was deemed wiser to cancel the programme and order him to withdraw. Helped by the favourable nature of the ground the retirement was made without difficulty, and, covered by fire from the ships, the whole company was re-embarked with a loss of only three killed and one wounded.

The failure of these two minor operations had a result out of all proportion to the numbers engaged. Enemy reports magnified the incident into a victory, with a consequent valuable gain to Turkish morale.

The effect produced throughout Europe by the fall of the outer forts had exceeded expectations. From a trustworthy source in Bucharest the news arrived that there was now great hope of Italy joining the Entente. Bulgaria was already visibly influenced. Russia offered to send an army corps of 40,000 men to co-operate at the Black Sea entrance to the Bosporus. Most important of all, Venizelos proposed on the

INITIATION OF DARDANELLES CAMPAIGN 83

1st March that three Greek divisions should be landed on the Gallipoli peninsula, and it was reported that the Greek king was now ready for war. But the latter hope was doomed to disappointment. On the 3rd March, the Greek General Staff declared that the moment for successful military action on the peninsula had passed, and the king refused to consent to Venizelos's proposal. It is possible, however, that the king was influenced by an even more potent argument than the objections of his General Staff. It is now known that on the 2nd March the Russian Government informed their Minister in Athens that they could not agree to Greek participation in the Dardanelles campaign.[1]

Shortsighted though Russia's objection must appear at first sight, its motives can be understood. Russia was insisting that Constantinople and the Straits should be assigned to her in the event of their falling to the Entente, but no guarantee to this effect had yet been given. On the other hand, it was the dearest dream of Greece to secure Constantinople as the capital of a Greek empire; and if the Greeks were to enter the city in triumph there might be endless difficulties in persuading them to surrender it to Russia. On the 12th March Russian fears were assuaged but not wholly appeased by a secret promise made to her by Britain and France. In accordance with this promise, provided Russia would prosecute the war to a vigorous conclusion, Constantinople was to be handed over to her as the prize of victory.

On the 4th March two telegrams arrived in London from General Birdwood, in which he reported the result of his visit to Admiral Carden and replied to Lord Kitchener's queries of the 23rd and 24th February. He estimated the number of Turks in the vicinity of the Straits at 40,000, with many reinforcements at Constantinople. Carden still intended to force the Straits with ships alone, if this were practicable. If he could not silence the hidden guns with naval fire, he would either try to get through in spite of them, or would wait until the army arrived to co-operate. The choice of alternatives would depend on the Government's view of the urgency of an early success, as the main force from Egypt could not be ready to disembark till the 18th March. Birdwood pointed out that if troops were required to assist the fleet, it would be impossible to restrict movements to minor operations. He felt sure that practically

[1] Telegram from Russian Minister of Foreign Affairs to Russian Minister in Athens, repeated to London and Paris: "2nd March 1915. In no "circumstances can we allow Greek forces to participate in the Allied "attack on Constantinople." "Constantinople and the Straits: Russian "Secret Documents," Moscow, 1926, p. 189.

the whole of his force would be wanted at the outset. The hidden guns and howitzers were certain to be protected by heavily entrenched infantry, and the sea defences were said to be strongly fortified on the land side. He and Carden agreed that if military aid were wanted, the best plan would be to make a feint at Bulair, and to land a strong force at Cape Helles to take the forts in reverse. He deprecated a landing on the Asiatic shore, as the country looked big and difficult; but it would be necessary to do this if the Asiatic guns could not be dominated from the European side. No local information about Constantinople feeling could be obtained, but he thought that the arrival of an Allied fleet at the capital might lead to the collapse of opposition.

These messages were followed by a third on the 5th March, in which Birdwood reported that he did not believe the fleet alone could force the Dardanelles. In any event the operation must take a considerable time. The outer forts had been an easy prey; the fleet could stand off and shoot from anywhere. Inside the Straits it was another story, and the ships were hampered by unlocated fire. The weather was atrocious, only one day in several being fine, and operations were continually delayed in consequence. "Before troops can be landed", he added, "it is absolutely necessary to have settled weather. The " landing sites are indifferent, and a small force cannot safely " be landed, for fear of being cut off by a gale."

Meanwhile, on the strength of Carden's estimate of fourteen more fine days being required for the fleet to reach the Marmara, Mr. Churchill was apparently no longer of opinion that more troops than those already on the spot would be wanted to assist in forcing the Straits. On the 4th March he wrote to Lord Kitchener [1] suggesting that as the fleet would probably be through soon after the 16th, the 40,000 British troops and the French division already detailed for the Dardanelles should be assembled at Mudros about that date, ready either to be landed at Bulair or, alternatively, if practicable, to be taken through the Straits to Constantinople.[2]

[1] Churchill, " The World Crisis, 1915 ", p. 195.
[2] On 5th March the French naval attaché in London telegraphed to the Ministry of Marine as follows:
"The War Office having asked the Admiralty to deal direct with the " French Government regarding the disposition of the troops before operat- " ing at the Dardanelles, the First Lord asks me to let you know that he " considers it essential that from the 18th instant the troops should be in " immediate readiness either to be landed at Bulair or sent through the " Straits to Constantinople, according to circumstances. The British " military forces will be on that date in their transports, close to the scene " of operations. It is therefore indispensable that the French force should

In view of this letter Lord Kitchener evidently felt it advisable to restrain Birdwood from any unnecessary landing operations on the peninsula. He accordingly telegraphed to him late on the 4th March, that from the admiral's estimate he expected the fleet to reach the Marmara by the 20th. The Anzac corps, the French division, and the Royal Naval Division would be assembled at Mudros by the 18th, but there was no intention of using these troops to take the Gallipoli peninsula unless the admiral subsequently found it impossible to get through without them. Their concentration was principally intended for operations in the neighbourhood of Constantinople. While the admiral continued to silence the forts successfully, he would require nothing but small bodies of troops for subsidiary operations, and Birdwood could find these from the brigade already at Mudros.[1] Extensive operations on the peninsula were not to be undertaken without further orders from home, and in this case more troops would probably be sent out from England. Lord Kitchener did not anticipate that any such large landing would be required. "It will most "probably only be necessary", he said, "to leave a force large "enough to hold the Bulair lines, as it is anticipated that the "Turks will evacuate the peninsula. . . . After sinking the "Turkish navy, the first duty of the fleet will be to open the "Bosporus to the Russian fleet, which will be accompanied by "a corps of 40,000 men, and the operations on land will take "place in co-operation with these forces."

Birdwood replied to this message in vigorous terms. "I have already informed you", he said, "that I consider the "admiral's forecast too sanguine, and I doubt his ability to force "the passage unaided. . . . I have no intention of rushing blindly "into the Gallipoli peninsula, and I quite realize that my move-"ments must depend entirely on the navy's progress." He added that even if the fleet did get through without the army's help, transports would be unable to follow without being exposed to fire from the hidden guns, which the navy could not destroy. It was this difficulty which had prompted his suggestion of a landing in force at Helles.

The War Council, however, were still hoping for the unaided

" be there too, so that if necessary the most powerful effort can be made. " It is of course not possible to predict the date on which the Straits will " be opened, for the weather and the degree of Turkish resistance are " uncertain factors, but as the War Office is making all its preparations for " the 18th, the date of the French embarkation should be calculated " accordingly. . . ." French Official Account, Tome viii. Annexes i. No. 20.

[1] This, the 3rd Australian Brigade, left Alexandria on 2nd March, and arrived at Mudros on 4th March.

success of the fleet, despite the contrary opinion of the soldier on the spot. Though large military forces were rapidly approaching the scene of action, they were only to be used on the Gallipoli peninsula as a last resource.

Mention must here be made of two other important points in Mr. Churchill's letter of the 4th March to Lord Kitchener. About the 20th February all available transports in England had been despatched to Alexandria for the conveyance of the Anzac corps to Gallipoli. Mr. Churchill informed Lord Kitchener on the 4th March that ships for any further reinforcements from home could not be ready till the 15th March, and that he therefore need not decide till the 10th whether he would allot the 29th Division or a Yeomanry division for this service.[1] In this letter, too, there appears the first mention of a senior officer being appointed to command the Allied forces at the Dardanelles. Mr. Churchill said that the Admiralty were strongly of opinion that a general of high rank and reputation should be nominated for this post; he had heard Lord Kitchener mention Sir Ian Hamilton's name, and no choice would give more satisfaction both to the Admiralty and the navy. At the same time he urged the importance of the selected officer reaching the Dardanelles as soon as possible. But he added that the naval operations could not be delayed for troop movements, "as we must get into the Marmara as soon as possible "in the normal course".

At the Dardanelles, after the abortive landings of the 4th March, no further minor enterprises were attempted. For the next three days the bombardment was continued in fine weather, the *Queen Elizabeth* co-operating with indirect fire across the peninsula from the neighbourhood of Gaba Tepe. Results were so uniformly disappointing that it was resolved to try more drastic measures on the 8th, with the *Queen Elizabeth* inside the Straits. But the weather now broke once more, and the operations of the 8th were barren of important results.

Three of the four weeks which Admiral Carden had calculated he would require for the whole task had now gone by. But the second phase was no nearer completion, and the expenditure of ammunition was causing him much anxiety. It was in these circumstances that he suddenly reported to the Admiralty, on the 9th March, that he could do no more till his air service was reinforced.[2] Meanwhile he would concentrate

[1] Churchill, "The World Crisis, 1915," p. 196.
[2] Though the Air Service was in its infancy in 1914 its growth during the war was so rapid that it is hard to realize that, until the end of March

INITIATION OF DARDANELLES CAMPAIGN 87

on clearing the minefield, for the Inner Defences could not be reduced by long-range fire, and he could not get to decisive range until the mines were swept.

At a War Council meeting on the 10th March (the first day of the battle of Neuve Chapelle) Lord Kitchener announced that he would now despatch the 29th Division to the Mediterranean. He stated that the Allied force available for operations against Constantinople was approximately 130,000 [1] men, against which the Turks could possibly muster 180,000. The Russian admiral's orders were to attack the Bosporus as soon as the British fleet reached the Marmara, but the troops were not to be landed till the Turkish fleet had been sunk and the two Allied fleets had joined hands.

Mr. Churchill informed the War Council that he still believed the navy could get through without the army's help, though he was glad that troops would be available if required.

The following day Lord Kitchener informed the General Staff that General Sir Ian Hamilton had been appointed to command the Allied troops in the Mediterranean, with Br.-General (temporary Major-General) W. P. Braithwaite as his Chief of the General Staff, and orders were issued for the immediate formation of a General Headquarters for the new Mediterranean Expeditionary Force. Orders were also issued to prepare the 29th Division for early embarkation for service in the Eastern Mediterranean, and here a minor incident will illustrate conditions in the War Office at that time. The 29th Division supply column was equipped with 3-ton lorries, in readiness for service in France. It was obviously useless to send out these vehicles if suitable roads did not exist in the areas in which they might have to operate. Provision had to be made for the possibility of operations in the Gallipoli peninsula, but the Intelligence Section of the General Staff, not having

---

1915, the British forces at the Dardanelles so far as aerial reconnaissance was concerned, were little better than blind. The only machines available in the first instance (six seaplanes and two aeroplanes) were quite unfitted for the work required of them. The aeroplanes could not be used owing to lack of suitable landing grounds; the seaplanes could not rise except from smooth water; and even in calm weather, which was exceptional, they had to fly at such a low altitude, owing to engine weakness, that they were constantly hit. Wireless gear was primitive, maps were inaccurate, and no up-to-date cameras were available. There were no trained observers, and naval officers (midshipmen for choice on account of their light weight) were asked to volunteer for this difficult and specialized duty. Throughout the month of March indeed, the one bright spot was the courage and self-sacrifice of the personnel.

[1] Actually, including 40,000 Russians, it was about 115,000.

been informed that military operations in that area were even contemplated, were unable to say whether the roads in the peninsula at that season were fit for mechanical transport, or whether there were any roads at all. In the absence of definite information it was decided, as a measure of safety, to withdraw the 3-ton lorries and substitute vehicles of half that size, and new war-establishments were hurriedly made out on this basis. Not till many months afterwards was it known that General Maxwell had informed Lord Kitchener on the 7th March that "all our information indicates that there are no roads . . . it "therefore seems that pack transport is necessary".

On the 12th March Lord Kitchener sent for Sir Ian Hamilton, at that time commanding the Central Force, and gave him the first official intimation of his new appointment. After detailing the composition of his force, Lord Kitchener explained that, though he personally believed that the 29th Division could be more useful in the Near East than anywhere else, this view was not held by G.H.Q. in France. The division was therefore to be regarded as a temporary loan, and to be returned as soon as its services could be spared.

The Director of Military Operations (General Callwell) then came in, and with the aid of a wall-map, gave Hamilton a rough outline of what he believed to be the Greek plan for capturing the Gallipoli peninsula. Callwell explained that the Greeks had meant to employ about 150,000 men,[1] but Lord Kitchener interposed that half that number would now suffice, as the Turks were busy elsewhere. He hoped, indeed, that it would be unnecessary to use Hamilton's troops in the Dardanelles at all. But if they did have to land, they must see the enterprise through at all costs. He further added that the Turkish garrison of the peninsula was estimated at 40,000 men, and that the Kilid Bahr plateau was probably well protected. South of Kilid Bahr, to the point at Cape Helles, he believed that the peninsula was open to a landing on very easy terms. The fire of the fleet from both sides would make the flat and open country south of Achi Baba untenable by the enemy.

The regrettable consequences of the delay in appointing a commander for the Allied military forces were quickly to disclose

---

[1] This was the number which Lord Kitchener had mentioned to the War Council on 8th January, as likely to be required for such an operation. (See page 56.) General Callwell told the Dardanelles Commission that he never saw any Greek plan for the capture of the peninsula. He tried to obtain details through the military attaché, but was unsuccessful. This evidence refutes the story, current in 1915–16, that the War Office had a copy of the Greek plan, but omitted to show it to Sir Ian Hamilton before he left England.

INITIATION OF DARDANELLES CAMPAIGN 89

themselves. It was arranged in the War Office on the 11th March that Sir Ian Hamilton and his headquarters should leave England as soon as a transport could be provided, probably in a week. Nothing of the War Council's plans was known by the War Office Staff, and the urgency of the situation was not realized. As soon, however, as General Hamilton's appointment was confirmed, Mr. Churchill rightly stressed the importance of his arriving at the Dardanelles at the earliest possible moment. In view of the critical decisions which might have to be taken in the course of the next few days, he had already ordered a fast cruiser to Marseilles to convey his party to the scene of action. He now urged that the Commander-in-Chief should leave London that very afternoon. General Hamilton was ready and anxious to agree, but other considerations made it impossible. The Staff had not yet been appointed, no information had been collected, and no single Staff preparation had yet been made for the expedition. In consequence of the immense urgency of the military commander's presence at the Dardanelles, it was now decided that he and as many of his Staff as could be collected, should proceed by special train the following afternoon, leaving the remainder of the headquarters to follow by transport as quickly as possible. Unfortunately, both the Adjutant-General and Quartermaster-General, who were respectively responsible for the appointment of the A. and Q. staffs, declared that they could not assemble any of their nominees in so short a time. As a result, none but General Staff officers were ready on the 13th. The Commander-in-Chief was obliged to leave England with only that branch of his Staff, and for over a fortnight was deprived of the services of any representative of the A. and Q. branches. Events were to prove that his arrival at the Dardanelles was not an hour too soon; but the separation of his Staff caused by this necessarily hurried departure was a misfortune from which the Expeditionary Force never quite recovered.

On the morning of the 13th Sir Ian Hamilton had a second interview with Lord Kitchener, and was given his final instructions.[1] In view of the uncertainty as to the task which would await him, these instructions were necessarily vague, but they clearly reveal the hope that extensive military operations in the Straits could be avoided. Lord Kitchener still clung to the belief that the army's help, except for minor enterprises, would not be needed till the Turkish capital was reached, and the whole tenour of his instructions was such as to rivet Sir Ian Hamilton's attention more firmly upon the gleaming minarets

[1] Appendix 1.

of Constantinople than on the rugged heights of Gallipoli. Yet on certain points the instructions were as peremptory as commands, and left little discretion in the hands of the Commander-in-Chief. The army was not to be used until the fleet had exhausted every effort to get through alone. No major operation was to be engaged in until the 29th Division had arrived. The occupation of the Asiatic side was strongly to be deprecated. Most important of all, as events were soon to prove, "having entered on the project of forcing the Straits, " there can be no idea of abandoning the scheme".

On the afternoon of Friday, 13th March, Sir Ian Hamilton left London by special train with a Staff of thirteen officers. Crossing from Dover in H.M.S. *Foresight*, another special conveyed him to Marseilles, where a 30-knot cruiser, the *Phaeton*, awaited his arrival. It was characteristic of the Admiralty that, despite the difficulties of wartime travel, they succeeded in conveying the new military commander from London to the Dardanelles more quickly than he could have completed the journey in times of peace by the Orient Express.

Once in the train the Commander-in-Chief had leisure to examine the information at his disposal. The catalogue was not a long one. Three Intelligence officers, who had left England a few days before, would, it was hoped, be able to furnish him with news of the enemy; but, for the moment, his store of knowledge consisted of Lord Kitchener's instructions, a handbook of the Turkish army, dated 1912, a pre-war report on the Dardanelles defences, and a map which subsequently proved inaccurate.[1] One other piece of information had, however, been given to the Chief of Staff just before he started. It was the custom at that time for troops proceeding on active service to be accompanied by a ten per cent reinforcement, to make good the first wastage in the ranks. But for this expedition, to be entered upon 3,000 miles from its home base, the first reinforcements were to remain in England.

[1] It is instructive to compare the meagre information placed at Sir Ian Hamilton's disposal with that which, in accordance with British Field Service Regulations, should be handed to a commander-in-chief on appointment:
"As soon as the C.-in-C of the forces in the field is appointed, he will
" be furnished by the C.I.G.S. with the approved plan of campaign,
" and with an appreciation of the military situation, including detailed
" information on the following points:

"1. The forces to be placed at his disposal and their state of
 "mobilization.
"2. The armed forces and military resources of allied and hostile
 "powers, with their special characteristics.
"3. The theatre of war.
"4. Any other information which may be of use to him."

INITIATION OF DARDANELLES CAMPAIGN 91

The absence of any detailed plan for the employment of the large force to be concentrated in the Eastern Mediterranean was meanwhile causing no little uneasiness in Paris. On the 11th March, M. Millerand, French Minister of War, wrote to the French Minister of Foreign Affairs, insisting on the importance of obtaining more information from Whitehall:

> Has the British Commander-in-Chief, under whose command, in the best interests of the operations, the French Government has agreed to place our troops, decided on a plan, and what is it? Does he propose to land at the north of the peninsula, to block the Bulair isthmus? What are his ideas about the landing of the French and British at Constantinople or in the neighbourhood? Does he foresee any previous or subsequent operations, and what are they?
>
> I need scarcely draw your attention to the difficult situation which is being created by the ignorance in which the French Minister of War is being kept, and to the consequences which may arise. The number of troops required depends upon the plan adopted. But you well know that, having regard to the general military situation as also to the views of Parliament and public opinion, we cannot agree to dissipate our strength by allotting to the Dardanelles operations, from which our political interests do not allow us to be absent, a much larger force than that which we have already collected.[1]

In reply to these enquiries, the French military attaché in London telegraphed to M. Millerand on the 15th March:

> Lord Kitchener has not yet formed any plan for the operations against Turkey. He considers that the action of the Allied forces has not yet gone far enough for any decision to be taken regarding future steps after the forcing of the Dardanelles.
>
> At the present moment Admiral Carden thinks that the Straits cannot be forced by the unaided effort of the fleet. The Turks have constructed numerous defences which cannot be destroyed by naval guns and which it will be necessary to take with the co-operation of the Expeditionary Force.
>
> For the moment, therefore, the thing is to seize the Gallipoli peninsula, to establish the force there strongly, and from there to bombard the defences on the Asiatic shore. As for the means to be employed for obtaining this end, it is for Admiral Carden, Sir Ian Hamilton, and General d'Amade to choose them.
>
> It will only be after opening the Straits to admit the fleet that it will be possible to think about subsequent operations, the nature and importance of which will depend above all on the attitude of the Ottoman Government and the movements of the Turkish army.

[1] French Official Account, Tome viii. Annexes i. No. 24.

Lord Kitchener will willingly discuss all these questions, as well as those concerning the operations in France, with you and General Joffre. He hopes, with the British Government's permission, to be able to go to Chantilly next Monday, 22nd March, or Tuesday 23rd. He could only be away for 24 hours, owing to pressing obligations here.

This reply, though it reflected a less optimistic view than that held by Lord Kitchener himself, and by the rest of the War Council, all of whom were still hoping that the fleet would reach the Marmara without the army's aid, appears to have restored confidence in Paris. Having agreed, for the sake of unity of command, and because of the superior strength of the British force, to place the French contingent under the supreme command of the British general, the French Government adhered most loyally to that arrangement. From first to last, too, the various commanders of the Corps Expéditionnaire d'Orient co-operated with the British Commander-in-Chief with unswerving loyalty; and it can here be acknowledged with warm gratitude that, thanks to their untiring efforts through the nine arduous months spent on the peninsula, there was never a single instance of friction.

CHAPTER V

The Initiation of the Dardanelles Campaign (*concluded*)

(Maps 1, 2 ; Sketches 1, 8A)

On the 11th March, the Admiralty telegraphed a reply to Admiral Carden's disheartening report.[1] They highly approved the skill and patience with which Carden had advanced hitherto without loss. But they pointed out that at a certain period in his operations he would have to press hard for a decision, and without wishing to hurry him or urge him beyond his judgment, they asked whether he did not think that point had now been reached. They would support him, even if heavy losses were entailed.[2]

Mar. 1915.

Admiral Carden's reply, dated the 14th March, bore no resemblance to his earlier message, though recent efforts to clear the minefields had met with disappointment. He entirely agreed that the moment for vigorous and sustained action had now arrived. He would attack the forts at the Narrows with his whole force, clearing the minefields (by daylight) under cover of this attack. He further advised that military operations on a large scale should begin immediately, to ensure the fleet's communications after it had reached the Marmara.

---

[1] See page 86.
[2] Admiral Sir H. B. Jackson suggested this day that the time had come to make use of the " ample military forces ready at short notice ", to occupy the Gallipoli peninsula. This suggestion was shown to Lord Kitchener, who replied that, unless his estimate of Turkish strength on the peninsula proved to be wrong, no large operations of so difficult a nature should be undertaken until the 29th Division arrived. It is important to notice that, in any case, large scale operations could not have taken place at this date: (i.) because of the unsettled weather; (ii.) because the only troops available at Mudros were one Australian brigade and two marine battalions. The Royal Naval Division had to go to Port Said to be re-sorted before it could be used in an opposed landing, and the same remark would have applied to the 29th Division had it been embarked three weeks earlier. When the troops left England the embarkation authorities were not informed that they might possibly be used in opposed landings, and they were shipped with a view to disembarkation in a friendly harbour.

94   GALLIPOLI

On the 15th the Admiralty agreed to Carden's proposal for a general fleet attack. As regards a landing in force, they would ask the War Office to accelerate the arrival of troops from Egypt, but the admiral must consult General Hamilton about military operations when that officer reached the Dardanelles. The admiral was warned that he must on no account attempt to rush the passage, without having previously cleared the mines and destroyed the primary armament of the forts, before consulting the Admiralty on this point. The capture of Kilid Bahr by the army might prove less costly than a naval rush.

Admiral Carden replied the same afternoon that all was ready for the attack, and that action would begin on the first fine day. Next morning he was placed on the sick list by order of his medical officer.

The command of the Allied fleet was now given to Vice-Admiral J. M. de Robeck, Carden's second-in-command. In informing him of his appointment on the 17th March, Mr. Churchill asked for an assurance that he agreed that the forthcoming attack was wise and practicable. The admiral replied in the affirmative, and added that, weather permitting, he would begin the attack next day.

Map 1. At 3 P.M. on the 17th March the *Phaeton* cast anchor at Tenedos, in the midst of the Allied fleet. General d'Amade, commanding the French division, arrived at the same moment,[1] and an immediate conference[2] was held on board the *Queen Elizabeth*. Admiral de Robeck informed the soldiers that his chief difficulty was the enemy's mobile artillery. He could silence the fortress guns, but the mobile artillery could not be located, and their fire was preventing the clearance of the minefield. Nevertheless he felt confident that the fleet would be able to force a passage without military assistance on a large scale, and he meant to try. If the army could then attack Bulair, the Turks on the peninsula would be caught in a trap. But if the army had to attack the peninsula before the fleet got through, their task would be difficult. The Turks were "working like beavers" every night, and every morning new trenches and wire could be seen. All possible landing places were rapidly being

Sketch 1.

---

[1] General d'Amade had reached Mudros with the French troops on 15th March, and was brought over to Tenedos by Admiral Wemyss to meet Sir Ian Hamilton.

[2] Present at the conference: Vice-Admiral J. M. de Robeck and his Chief of Staff, Commodore Roger Keyes; Rear-Admiral R. E. Wemyss, Governor of Mudros; Admiral Guépratte, commanding the French fleet; General Sir Ian Hamilton and his C.G.S. Major-General Braithwaite; General d'Amade, commanding the French division.

INITIATION OF DARDANELLES CAMPAIGN 95

prepared for defence, and the ships' guns would not be able to give the troops a great deal of help.

The result of the conference was to confirm, in General Hamilton's mind, the wisdom of Lord Kitchener's order that the army was not to be used till the navy had exhausted every effort to get through alone. That evening he wired to the War Minister that this was also the admiral's wish.

Another matter brought up at the conference was the unsuitability of Lemnos as a base for a large military force. Until a long pipe-line could bring water from the distant hills to Mudros harbour, there was only a precarious supply for a maximum of 10,000 men. For the present, therefore, all troops arriving at the island would have to remain on board their transports, to the great detriment of their health. Even if they could be landed, there were no piers or jetties, and the harbour was so big that even in a moderate breeze the sea rapidly became too rough for small boats. Disembarkation would be a long, and re-embarkation a still longer process. For all these reasons it seemed better to make Alexandria the base. It was only 50 hours distant from the Dardanelles, and troops could probably be concentrated more quickly from Alexandria, where every facility existed, than they could be embarked and sent the seven hours' journey from Mudros.

Very early on the 18th Sir Ian Hamilton proceeded to Mudros to see the situation for himself. Here it was reported by General Paris, commanding the Royal Naval Division, that before his troops could be disembarked in fighting order on an open beach, the transports must be completely discharged, and every vessel reloaded. At Mudros, with its lack of facilities, and its constant heavy gales, this might be a matter of weeks. It would be far quicker for the transports to proceed to Alexandria for this purpose. General Hamilton at once telegraphed to Lord Kitchener to this effect, and recommended that Alexandria should become the base for the whole force. This done, and while the fleet was beginning its momentous attack on the Narrows, he started off in the *Phaeton* to take his first look at the Ægean coast-line of the peninsula from Cape Helles to the isthmus of Bulair.

The rugged and inhospitable outline which now unfolded itself, with its tangled maze of hill and deep ravine, left the Commander-in-Chief and his Staff no illusions as to the difficulty of their probable task. "Here", he wrote to Lord Kitchener, "Gallipoli looks a much tougher nut to crack than it did over "the map in your office." Except at the southern end of the peninsula, and north of Gaba Tepe, newly turned earth could be seen wherever a break in the cliff disclosed a possible landing place, while newly erected wire glittered blue in the brilliant sun. To the neighbourhood of Bulair the Turks had devoted particular attention. The vital importance of this locality had evidently not escaped them, and here at least a landing was plainly impossible.

Hugging the coast more closely on their return journey, it was noticed that even in the south, where fewer preparations were visible, the path of an invading army would be strewn with difficulties. Owing to the spoon-shaped lie of the land, the southern plain, which looked so easy on the map, was hidden from the sea, and no direct support could be given to advancing troops by naval gun-fire, except on the extreme flanks. From a military point of view, indeed, the importance of an unaided naval success was abundantly clear, and it was with quickened interest and anxiety that Sir Ian Hamilton and his staff listened to the thunder of the sailors' guns on the other side of that fateful strip of land.

Already the Turks had been given a clear month's warning of a probable military attack. With every day's delay the hostile positions would increase in strength. Even the present necessary reconnaissance of the coast was a fresh warning of British interest in possible landing places, and a new incentive to the garrison to dig themselves in. And if the naval effort should fail, and the stage have to be reset for a military campaign, several more weeks must elapse before the army could be ready to land.

Sketch 8A.

18 Mar. Map 2. The plan of the great naval attack on the 18th March was to silence simultaneously the forts at the Narrows and the batteries protecting the Kephez minefield. As soon as the forts were dominated, the mine-sweepers were to clear a channel through that minefield, continuing the work throughout the night. Next morning, the fleet was to advance into Sari Sighlar Bay and destroy the Narrows forts at close range, after which the minefield at the Narrows was to be swept.

The foundation of the whole scheme was that battleships should only be employed in waters which were known to be free of mines. With this object the whole of the Straits from the entrance at Helles to within 8,000 yards of the Narrows had been carefully examined and swept, and was thought to be clear of obstructions. But by calamitous misfortune, one row of twenty mines had not been discovered. This line, which according to one Turkish report, was laid on the night of the 7th/8th March, and to another on the night of the 17th/18th,

INITIATION OF DARDANELLES CAMPAIGN 97

was placed, unlike the others, not across the Straits but lengthways down the channel, and well in advance of the main Kephez minefield. It thus extended right across the head of Eren Keui Bay, in which, as carefully noted by the Germans, the battleships had been accustomed to manœuvre during the earlier bombardments. Here this fatal row of mines lay unsuspected, when at ten o'clock on the morning of the 18th March the Allied fleet steamed proudly into battle.

Despite a heavy and accurate Turkish fire the attack at first made good progress. By 1.45 P.M., though the fire of the enemy's howitzers was still heavy, the forts were almost silent; their garrisons had been driven or withdrawn from the guns, and the interiors of the various works were choked with débris. Many of the ships had been repeatedly hit, but none of them except the *Gaulois*, badly holed by a big shell from one of the forts, were seriously crippled, and the casualties were so far trifling.[1]

The mine-sweepers were now ordered to go in, and British vessels moved forward to relieve the French squadron, which throughout the morning had been in the van of the attack. At this moment occurred the first disaster of the day. The French battleship *Bouvet*, retiring through Eren Keui Bay, was suddenly enveloped in the smoke of a gigantic explosion. Next moment she had heeled over, and in less than two minutes had sunk with nearly all her crew.[2] On the advance of the British relieving vessels the Turkish gun crews, encouraged by the fate of the *Bouvet*, returned to their batteries, and the forts once more became active. But the fire was no longer so heavy or so effective. It was evident that the garrisons were shaken, their communications damaged, and many guns temporarily out of action. All was therefore going well when, about 4 o'clock, the *Inflexible*, on the right of the second line of ships, reported that she had struck a mine. A few minutes later, the *Irresistible*, immediately ahead of her, on the right of the leading line, shared the same fate. Unaware of the new row of mines, Admiral de Robeck was forced to the conclusion

---

[1] A Turkish General Staff account of the situation at this moment is as follows:

"By 2 P.M. the situation had become very critical. All telephone "wires were cut, all communication with the forts was interrupted, "some of the guns had been knocked out, others were half buried, others "again were out of action with their breech mechanism jammed; in "consequence the artillery fire of the defence had slackened considerably."

[2] It was at first believed that a shell had exploded her magazine, but from the statements of survivors (48 officers and men were picked up) it is now certain that she struck one of that fatal row of mines. See French Official Account, Tome viii. Annexes i. No. 55.

that floating mines, or torpedoes from shore tubes, were responsible for these sudden disasters. Deeming it impossible to keep his fleet in the Straits in face of this new and unknown danger, he decided to interrupt the operations; and sending the *Ocean* to help the *Irresistible*, he ordered a general retirement. But the tale of disaster was not yet ended. An hour later, the *Ocean* struck another of that fatal row, and later in the evening it was reported that both she and the *Irresistible* had foundered.

Thanks to the extraordinary and shattering success of that single line of unsuspected mines, the day so auspiciously begun had ended in complete failure. Three battleships, the *Bouvet*, *Ocean*, and *Irresistible*, were lost on the 18th March. Three others, the *Inflexible*, *Gaulois*, and *Suffren* (the latter two as the result of gun-fire) were so badly damaged that they had to be docked. Thus the total strength of the battle fleet had been reduced by one-third as the result of the day's action. Of these six casualties four had been caused by the unknown row of mines.

The effect of those twenty mines on the fortunes of the campaign can scarcely be measured. Suffice to say that, from that day onwards, the fleet was allowed to make no further attempts, either single-handed or in co-operation with the army, to force the Dardanelles, and the great combined operation eventually decided upon was fated to develop into a land campaign supported by the guns of the fleet.

At first Admiral de Robeck had no thought of accepting defeat. Reporting the result of the day's action, he said that his squadron was ready for an immediate resumption of the attack, but that, in view of the new danger of floating mines, his plan of operations must first be reconsidered.

Nor was there any sign of wavering at home. At a meeting of the War Council on the 19th it was decided to allow the Admiral to renew the attack if he thought fit, and he was informed that five more battleships were being sent out to replace the vessels lost. But later in the day Lord Kitchener's hopes of a naval success were rudely shaken by a telegram from the military Commander-in-Chief. Sir Ian Hamilton, who had witnessed the latter half of the big attack from inside the Straits, and had seen the *Inflexible* and the *Gaulois* retiring in an almost sinking condition, reported that he no longer believed that the Straits could be forced by ships. If the army had to co-operate, it would mean, not a subsidiary operation, but a deliberate advance by his whole force, to open the passage for the fleet.

INITIATION OF DARDANELLES CAMPAIGN 99

Reluctant though Lord Kitchener was to embark upon so difficult an operation, it was now too late to demur. In view of the heavy losses of the previous day, the abandonment of the enterprise was more than ever unthinkable. Without hesitation, but with deep distress over this threatened collapse of the naval hopes which had for so long sustained him, he sent his firm reply. "You know my views," this fateful message ran, " that the passage of the Dardanelles must be forced, and that " if large military operations on the Gallipoli peninsula are " necessary to clear the way, they must be undertaken, and " must be carried through."[1]

For a few more days Lord Kitchener, Mr. Churchill, and the Government hoped against hope that a fresh attack by the fleet might relieve the army of this new and difficult task. It was not to be. On the 22nd March, at a naval and military conference[2] on board the *Queen Elizabeth*, Admiral de Robeck expressed his conviction that the fleet could not get through without the help of Sir Ian Hamilton's force. Admiral Wemyss concurred, and no voice was raised to question the decision. The following day General Hamilton informed Lord Kitchener that he and the admiral agreed that it would be necessary to use his whole force to enable the fleet to force the Dardanelles. The present unsettled weather introduced a dangerous and incalculable factor, but the weather in April should be better, and he was sanguine of the success then of a simple straightforward scheme. Everything would depend on the thoroughness of his preparations; hence his desire to organize the expedition at a convenient base like Alexandria.

At the same time Admiral de Robeck informed the Admiralty that the peninsula must be captured before he could count on safely taking into the Marmara sufficient ships and colliers to ensure the destruction of the Turkish fleet.[3] The army, he

---

[1] About this time Lord Kitchener had received the following telegram from General Sir A. Paget, on a special military mission to the Balkans:
" 17th March. The operations in the Dardanelles have made a deep " impression. The possibilities of Bulgaria attacking any Balkan state " that might side with the Entente are now over, and there is some reason " to think that shortly the Bulgarian army will move against Turkey to " co-operate in the Dardanelles operations."

[2] Present at the conference: Admirals de Robeck and Wemyss, Generals Hamilton, Birdwood, and Braithwaite. The naval Chief of Staff, Commodore Keyes, was away at Tenedos reorganizing the mine-sweepers in view of further operations.

[3] On 26th March he amplified this message by explaining that the assistance of all naval forces available would be needed to land the army in the teeth of strenuous opposition. From this message it was obvious that, once the troops had begun to land, no further full dress naval attack on the Narrows could begin till they were safely established ashore.

added, could not be ready to land until the middle of April, and by that time he hoped to have reorganized his means of dealing with fixed and floating mines.

Mr. Churchill was convinced of the vital importance of a further unaided effort by the fleet, and a number of telegrams on this subject passed between him and Admiral de Robeck. But naval opinion at the Admiralty had meanwhile hardened against unaided fleet action in the Dardanelles, and the professional members of the War Staff Group [1] were firm in their determination to rely on the opinion of the admiral and the general on the spot. These opinions remaining unshaken, the Government had no alternative but to agree,[2] and on the 27th March Mr. Churchill telegraphed to Admiral de Robeck that though he had hoped the result might be achieved without the army being involved, he now saw that a combined operation was essential. Official approval would therefore be given to all the admiral's proposals.

Thus was the die cast. The idea of naval operations with limited military assistance was finally abandoned. In its place there now stood the dreaded alternative of a landing on a large scale. Already on the 22nd March the first transports had left Mudros for Alexandria, and thither they were followed on the 24th by Sir Ian Hamilton and his Staff.

It must here be noticed that though this new and difficult military enterprise had now been decided upon, no estimate of the probable scope and duration of the operations had been drawn up for discussion by the War Council. Ministers had generally agreed on the 24th February [3] that the Straits must be forced at all costs, but owing to the persistent hope that the army would not be needed till the fleet had entered the Marmara, the question of large military operations on the peninsula had never been seriously considered in council, and the decision registered at the last meeting on the 19th March had been in favour of a renewed attack by the fleet. For everyone in authority at home, therefore, this new undertaking was an unmeasured leap in the dark.

[1] This body consisted of the First Lord, the First Sea Lord, the Chief of the Staff (Rear-Admiral H. F. Oliver), Admiral Sir A. Wilson, the Secretary to the Board (Sir Wm. Graham Greene) and the Naval Secretary (Commodore C. M. de Bartolomé).

[2] Mr. Churchill told the Dardanelles Commission: " Both the Prime " Minister and Mr. Balfour, with whom I discussed the matter, were " inclined to my view (*i.e.* to insist on another naval attack) but as our " professional advisers and the admiral on the spot were against it, it " was impossible to go further, and I bowed to their decision ".

[3] See page 75.

In Service circles, however, where the chances of an unaided naval success had been regarded less hopefully, there had for some time been a growing belief that the whole of Sir Ian Hamilton's force would be needed to co-operate; and many of the vital problems now calling for immediate solution had been brought to the notice of the Prime Minister on the 16th March, two days before the great naval attack on the Narrows, in a memorandum by the Secretary of the War Council (Lieut.-Colonel M. P. A. Hankey):

1. From the point of view of the War Council the situation as regards the attack on the Dardanelles is far from clear. As recently as the last meeting the War Council were informed by the First Lord that the navy still hoped and expected to get through the Dardanelles without the assistance of military forces. Now, however, as was anticipated by most naval officers who were acquainted with the locality, the fleet is held up by a combination of mines and howitzers. In order to overcome these obstacles, the employment of a considerable land force is contemplated.

2. It must be borne in mind that up to the present time the employment of military forces has been proposed only to clear up the situation *after* the Dardanelles have been forced. Now, therefore, so far as the War Council is concerned, we are faced with a new and possibly very formidable operation to be carried out by the land forces.

3. Is it not desirable that the War Council should ascertain definitely the scope of the operations contemplated, and the extent of the preparations made to carry out these operations? In this connection it must be remembered that combined operations require more careful preparation than any other class of military enterprise. All through our history such attacks have failed when the preparations have been inadequate, and the successes are in nearly every case due to the most careful preparation beforehand. It would appear to be the business of the War Council to assure themselves, in the present instance, that these preparations have been thoroughly thought out.

4. It must be remembered also that one of the greatest advantages to be obtained from this class of operation, namely, that of surprise, has been lost. If a large force of troops had been sent at the very outset, secretly and unobtrusively, and fully equipped with boats and everything they required, so as to be available the moment the outer forts had fallen, it is by no means unlikely that, assisted by judicious feints to confuse the enemy as to their intended objective, they might have captured the plateau overlooking the forts at the Narrows by a *coup-de-main*. Instead of being announced as a mere demonstration, as was contemplated by the War Council, even the first bombardment of the outer forts was announced as an attack, and at no time has any attempt

been made to conceal our intention to force the Dardanelles at any cost. Now that the fleet has been held up by the minefields, the enemy knows exactly the point at which our attack must be directed. He has had as much time as he requires to entrench this point, to emplace his artillery, to pour reinforcements on to the land on both sides of the Straits, and to make every sort of preparation. The military enterprise, therefore, will be of a most formidable nature. It is suggested that the War Council ought to cross-examine the naval and military authorities on the extent of the preparations, and particularly with regard to such points as the following:

(a) The number of troops it is proposed to employ?
(b) The arrangements made for the supply of boats and tugs?
(c) The preparations made for the provision of landing piers, pontoons, etc.?
(d) The arrangements for the supply of water and provisions?
(e) The hospital arrangements. Is it contemplated to use nothing but floating hospitals, or will there be field hospitals on shore?
(f) Is it expected that the Dardanelles will be carried by a *coup-de-main*, or is the possibility of siege operations contemplated?
(g) In the latter event, what siege guns will be available, and what arrangements have been made for landing them and their ammunition?
(h) Possibly, it is proposed that the men-of-war should supply the necessary heavy artillery to overcome the enemy's heavy movable artillery. If so, are the military authorities satisfied that the projectiles available in men-of-war are suitable for this purpose, and that they will be able to search the valleys in which the howitzers are likely to be found?
(i) What arrangements have been made for the supply of the very large amount of ammunition that may be required for the operation?
(j) What arrangements are contemplated for the transport from the landing place to the army, of supplies of ammunition, food, water, etc., over a rough country with very few roads in it, bearing in mind that these roads will probably be broken up by the enemy before evacuating them?

5. Unless details such as these, and there are probably others, are fully thought out before the landing takes place, it is conceivable that a serious disaster may occur.

The truth of this prophecy was soon to be demonstrated. On the 16th March, however, Mr. Asquith's principal advisers

INITIATION OF DARDANELLES CAMPAIGN 103

still expected the naval attack to succeed, and there can be little surprise if, in the circumstances existing at that moment, the Prime Minister was satisfied that the arrangements already made for any landing that might be required were amply sufficient. Lord Kitchener's exalted rank in the army, and his brilliant record of past achievements, gave him at that time unique power in the War Council. He enjoyed the full confidence of his colleagues, few of whom had ever studied warlike problems or dreamed of being plunged into war. Actually it was no part of his duty to be saddled with undivided responsibility for the arrangements for a combined operation. But everyone looked to him to take the lead; every burden was thrown upon his broad and willing back; and if he gave voice to no anxiety, there seemed no reason for a civilian to anticipate trouble. Even the Prime Minister was loth to question his views.

On the 19th March, however, Mr. Asquith did ask whether a scheme for a possible disembarkation had been worked out. Lord Kitchener replied that there was not enough information at home to prepare a detailed scheme, and that this would have to be done by the general and admiral on the spot. This answer closed the discussion, and none of the other points raised in the secretary's memorandum were pressed.

It was undoubtedly true that the plans for disembarkation could only be worked out by a joint naval and military Staff on the spot. But it will probably be agreed that the general outline of these plans should have been drawn up long in advance, and the operation explored in sufficient detail to ascertain, before its sanction, the probable inroad it would make on the Empire's resources in men and ammunition.

For want of this thorough exploration the strength of the force at Sir Ian Hamilton's disposal at the end of March[1] bore no relation to any reasoned estimate of the numbers that were now likely to be required. It consisted only of the troops— approximately 75,000—which, at an earlier date, and to meet a less serious situation, Lord Kitchener had been able to deflect from France or Egypt without offending the French High Command or endangering the Suez Canal. Even at that earlier date, moreover, it is doubtful whether 75,000 men would have sufficed.

On the 8th January, it will be remembered, Lord Kitchener had told the War Council that a combined operation to take the Gallipoli peninsula would require 150,000 men. On the 12th March, however, he told Sir Ian Hamilton that 75,000 men would be enough for the task, as the Turks were busy elsewhere.

[1] See Order of Battle (Appendix 2) and f.n. 1, page 127.

To some extent, this revision was justified; for the earlier figures were based on a pre-war estimate of the Greek General Staff, which made no allowance for the Turks being simultaneously engaged in an attack on the Suez Canal, in campaigns in the Caucasus, in Persia, and in Mesopotamia. Nevertheless, even on the 12th March, it would have been a fair assumption that, in consequence of the opening of the British naval attack in February, a landing on Gallipoli was already a more difficult instead of an easier problem than it had been two months earlier.[1] But 75,000 men was the largest force that Lord Kitchener had felt justified in allotting to the Dardanelles at that date, and his belief that the fleet would get through without calling upon the army's help had apparently fortified his opinion that this number would suffice for every need.

On the 27th March, when a military landing in force was finally agreed upon, there can have been little doubt that an extra month's delay would make the army's task more difficult than ever. But there was still no suggestion of increasing its strength; the General Staff at home was still not called upon for a forecast of the men and ammunition likely to be required in these increasingly arduous conditions, or for an expression of opinion as to whether the resources of the Empire could meet this new commitment in addition to prosecuting a spring offensive on the Western front. To some extent, no doubt, this omission may be traced to the confident telegrams received from the British Commander-in-Chief. But though Sir Ian Hamilton had expressed himself sanguine of success, he had stated at the same time that he would have to use the whole of his force, or, in other words, that there would be no margin for the reproof of chance. Sir Ian Hamilton, moreover, had only just arrived at the scene of action, and in his own published diary he has written that when informed of his appointment a week earlier, his "knowledge of the Turks and the Dardanelles "was nil".

It is now known that Sir Edward Grey's anticipations of the effect of the British fleet's arrival at the capital were justified.

---

[1] It is now known that the Turkish strength in the Dardanelles area in January was two divisions. By March it had risen to five divisions, and by the first week in April to six. The actual figures, of course, were not known to the Entente in 1915. But it is interesting to compare Lord Kitchener's estimate of the Turks in 1915 with a much earlier and more faithful appreciation of their fighting qualities which he wrote as a young man. After witnessing some of the fighting between the Russians and Turks in 1877 he described the Turkish soldier as "always ready "to fight and never conquered except by overwhelming numbers." Sir George Arthur, "Life of Lord Kitchener," i. p. 30.

INITIATION OF DARDANELLES CAMPAIGN 105

Liman von Sanders and the American Ambassador at Constantinople, as also the latter's special agent at his Embassy, have placed on record that the fall of the outer forts caused consternation in Turkey. Everyone in Constantinople believed that the success of the Allied fleets was inevitable. The Germans were apprehensive that a revolution would follow the fleet's arrival at the Golden Horn and that Turkey would sign a separate peace. The credit of the Turkish Government was at its lowest ebb. Their military plans had everywhere ended in failure; their treasury was empty; their country was on the brink of ruin; and another reverse was expected to change the prevailing dissatisfaction into open revolt. Liman von Sanders has stated that at the end of February the Turkish General Headquarters firmly believed that the Straits would be forced. Everything had been prepared for the departure of the Sultan and his court, as well as the civil and military authorities, to the interior of Asia Minor. These precautions, he significantly adds, were justified.[1]

On the evening of the 18th March the Turkish command at the Dardanelles was weighed down by the premonition of defeat. More than half the ammunition had been expended, and it could not be replaced.[2] The antiquated means of fire control had been seriously interrupted. The Turkish gun crews were demoralized and even the German officers present had, apparently, little hope of successful resistance if the fleet attacked next day. Of the nine rows of mines, many had been in position for six months, and a large proportion of these were believed either to have been carried away by the

---

[1] " Fünf Jahre Türkei," p. 72.
It is important to realize that had Constantinople been abandoned, the Turks would have been unable to continue the war. Their only arms and munition factories were at the capital and would have been destroyed by the fleet, and the supply of material from Germany would have been impossible.

[2] According to the German Official Account, written by a staff officer of Liman von Sanders:
" Most of the Turkish ammunition had been expended. The medium " howitzers and minefield batteries had fired half of their supply . . . " for the five 35·5-cm. guns there were only 271 rounds, say 50 each; " for the eleven 23-cm. between 30 to 50 rounds per gun. . . . Particularly " serious was the fact that the long range H.E. shell, which alone were " effective against armour, were nearly entirely used up. Fort Hamidieh " had only 17 of them; Kilid Bahr but 10. Also there was no reserve of " mines. What, then, was to happen if the battle was renewed on the 19th " and following days with undiminished violence? " Mühlmann, " Der " Kampf um die Dardanellen 1915," p. 74.
Details of the ammunition expended by the British fleet (irrespective of the French squadron) on 18th March are as follow: 15-inch, 170 rounds; 12-inch, 538; 10-inch, 85; 9·2-inch, 277; 7·5-inch, 516; 6-inch, 828; 4-inch, 132; 12-pdr., 254.

current, or to have sunk to such a depth that ships would not have touched them. For the rest, many were of old pattern, and not too trustworthy, and, owing to the shortage of numbers, they were, on an average, 90 yards apart, more than three times the beam of a ship. A German journalist describes the great astonishment of the defenders of the coast forts when the attack suddenly ceased. He records that the German naval gunners who were manning the batteries at Chanak told him later that they had made up their minds the fleet would win, and that they themselves could not have held out much longer.[1]

Turning to the military measures for the defence of the capital, Liman von Sanders roundly asserts that the orders issued by Turkish G.H.Q. between the 20th February and 1st March entailed the worst defensive dispositions imaginable, and placed the Dardanelles at the mercy of a hostile landing. "If the orders given at that moment had been carried out", he writes, "the course of the world war would have changed after " the spring of 1915, and Germany and Austria would have " been constrained to continue the fight alone."[2] But wiser counsels prevailed.

It has already been shown that the British estimate of 40,000 Turkish troops on the peninsula at the end of February was wildly wide of the mark. Up to that date there were only two divisions in the whole Dardanelles area, of which one was on the European side of the Straits, and it was not until 26 days after the opening of the British bombardment on the 19th February that the number of rifles on both sides of the waterway approximated to 40,000. After the fall of the outer forts on the 25th February there were still several days during which, if the weather had been favourable for a landing, and an army ready to land, the capture of the peninsula would have provided no great difficulty. But the breaking down of his outer gateway roused even the lethargic Turk to definite though somewhat sluggish activity. Two months more were to elapse before the defences of the area were placed on a thoroughly sound footing, but from the end of February reinforcements began to trickle towards the threatened area. Two

---

[1] Stuermer, " Zwei Kriegsjahre in Konstantinopel," p. 68.
The Turkish Official Account says: " In the attainment of such an " important objective, disregarding comparatively small losses, the enemy " should have repeated his attacks with great force, and in all probability " he would have succeeded in forcing the Straits by sea. . . . In Fort " Hamidieh there were but 5 to 10 rounds left, and the batteries on the " European side were equally low."

[2] " Fünf Jahre Türkei," p. 72.

INITIATION OF DARDANELLES CAMPAIGN 107

divisions and two gendarmerie battalions[1] were despatched from the capital in the early days of March, to be followed at the middle of the month by a fifth division (the *11th*) from Smyrna. Thus by the date of the great naval attack on the 18th March the defending garrison was already almost equal in numbers to Sir Ian Hamilton's force, and, as will be shown in a later chapter, during the five weeks which elapsed between that attack and the date of the military landing, these numbers were further increased and the Turkish scheme of defence improved out of all recognition.

[1] The *5th* and *19th Divisions*, and the *Stamboul* and *Pera Gendarmerie*.

CHAPTER VI

PRELIMINARY PREPARATIONS AT ALEXANDRIA

(Maps 2, 3; Sketches 4, 5, 8A)

Mar. 1915. WHEN the military Commander-in-Chief could at last begin to elaborate his plans for the landing, the situation that confronted him was remarkable.

An army had been embarked upon a great amphibious campaign without previous preparation or plan. Some of the troops had already arrived in enemy waters; others were on the way; but all alike were unready for action till they could be landed in a friendly port,[1] re-sorted, and re-embarked. The Turks, forewarned, were digging for their lives. Lack of preparation, and lack of secrecy, had converted a daring but legitimate operation into an adventure of extreme hazard. Yet Sir Ian Hamilton had been told that there could be no thought of abandoning the enterprise; the forcing of the Dardanelles was to be accomplished at all costs. It needs no rhetoric to describe the difficulties of the problem, and no special military training to understand them.

The well-known axiom—that it is hardly possible during the course of a campaign to repair errors committed in the original concentration—has seldom been better illustrated. In every sphere of human activity, and above all in war, the foundation of success may be said to lie in thoughtful preparation. Even in the case of minor enterprises a neglect of this precept is the most fruitful source of failure, whilst to embark upon the most difficult of all military operations—a descent on a hostile beach—before every detail of the plan has been carefully weighed, is to court, and to deserve, disaster.

Nor was this truth unrealized in the spring of 1915. Both the army and the navy were aware that to land troops in face of

[1] The orders issued to the Quartermaster-General's branch at the War Office were to embark the troops for Mudros. In the absence of any knowledge as to their probable employment they had been embarked as if for landing at a friendly port, irrespective of any tactical requirements, and with regard only to economizing tonnage.

PREPARATIONS AT ALEXANDRIA

an entrenched enemy is the most difficult operation of war, and the Staff Colleges at Camberley and Quetta had for years included in their curriculum a special study of the problems which this type of warfare entails. It was realized that even after a scheme has been deemed practicable, every step of the landing should be worked out in complete detail before a man is embarked. Above all was it laid down that the two considerations of paramount importance are the maintenance of secrecy, in order to secure surprise, and the choice of a favourable season for the campaign.

Yet in February and March 1915 not one of these precautions had been observed. Through causes already explained the British Government had drifted [1] almost unconsciously into the hazards of this great undertaking.

One of the disadvantages of reorganizing the military force at Alexandria was that it separated the naval and military Staffs at a moment when they should have been preparing every detail connected with the landing in the closest co-operation. This disadvantage was to some extent reduced by the attachment to General Headquarters of a naval officer [2] well acquainted with the naval Commander-in-Chief's views. But both naval and military ideas were naturally to undergo various changes and modifications in the light of a close study of the problem; and many important details decided upon in Egypt had subsequently to be revised when the transports reassembled in Mudros harbour a few days before the landing.

As regards the question of secrecy, it is true that when the practicability of a joint naval and military attack on the Dardanelles was examined in 1906, stress was laid on the difficulty of concealing the preparations for such an expedition. But difficult though this would have been in the case of a single-handed war between Britain and Turkey, the same disadvantages did not apply in 1915, when a rigid censorship had already been imposed, when large numbers of troops were constantly leaving British ports, and when the departure of ships for the Mediterranean might reasonably be supposed to have reference to the defence of Egypt. In effect, however, no expedition was ever more loudly heralded. In the early days of 1915, when nothing but a demonstration was intended, and there was no idea of using troops at the Dardanelles, the question of secrecy did not arise. The more the Turks knew about the pretended attack, and the more they feared it, the greater the chances of its object being effected and of the pressure against the Russians in the

---

[1] See "Dardanelles Commission. First Report. 1917." p. 30.
[2] Captain F. H. Mitchell, R.N.

Caucasus being relieved. When, therefore, it was subsequently decided to make a real attack, and to send British troops to assist the fleet, a certain amount of damage had already been done to their chances of success, and this was irretrievable. Had the publicity ceased at that early date, however, little harm would have resulted from it; but unfortunately this was only the beginning. There followed the warnings given by the naval attacks and the several landings of marines; and as soon as a large military expedition was decided upon, the pending arrival of troops was made still more clear by the necessarily hurried acquisition of small craft in every port in the Eastern Mediterranean.[1] The preparation of the Australian troops in Egypt was obviously difficult to conceal, but here again something might have been done to induce the belief that they were going to the Western front.

The disembarkation of the Expeditionary Force in Egypt dissipated the last hope of any form of secrecy, for it resulted in the whole composition of the force becoming known to the Turks.

News of the arrival and departure of transports was common property in Alexandria and Port Said; the names of units were freely mentioned in the Egyptian Press; and there were public reviews of the troops both at Alexandria and at Cairo. At this time, too, one of Sir Ian Hamilton's Staff received an official letter from London, sent through the ordinary post, and addressed to the "Constantinople Field Force".

Finally, in picturing the situation at the end of March 1915, it should be remembered that the army entrusted with the solution of this problem had been neither specially selected nor specially trained for the work. It is to cast no reflection either upon the commanders or the staffs, or upon the troops who gained such imperishable renown on the peninsula, to say that in March 1915 they were practically a scratch team. Added to this disadvantage, the British were heavily handicapped by a shortage of gun ammunition—a handicap never wholly removed during the course of the operations—and were even deficient of the normal complement of divisional artillery.[2]

[1] The difficulty of procuring enough tugs and lighters was extreme. No arrangements had been made at home, and the authorities on the spot were faced with the necessity of procuring these small craft locally. The only places where they could be purchased were neutral or friendly ports in the Mediterranean, and the material available for sale was very limited.

[2] According to "British War Establishments 1914," the normal complement of artillery for 4 divisions was 304 guns. The 4 British divisions of the Mediterranean Expeditionary Force had a total of only 118 guns. The only artillery sent out with the Royal Naval Division consisted of

PREPARATIONS AT ALEXANDRIA

In drawing up a military plan of campaign for the ensuing operations, two points demanded particular attention. First, the primary task of the army, on which every effort must be concentrated, was to assist the fleet to force the Dardanelles. Secondly the plan had to be not only within the capacity of the available troops, but so arranged, especially with regard to the various beaches to be used, that the successive stages of the disembarkation would be within the capacity of the available resources of the fleet.

With these points in view Sir Ian Hamilton and his General Staff had been engaged in a study of the problem from the date of his arrival at the Dardanelles, and on the 23rd March he approved in principle an outline plan completed on the previous day. Three Intelligence officers had joined the Staff at Mudros on the 18th March; but, judged by the appreciation which prefaced this plan, information regarding the Turkish forces was still very uncertain. The number of troops on the peninsula was placed at between 40,000 and 80,000 men—a wide margin. In addition there were said to be 30,000 on the Asiatic side of the Straits and 60,000 more within close call, a possible total of 170,000 men. This number made no allowance for the possible detention of troops at Constantinople by the threat of a Russian descent on the Bosporus. But whatever the nature of that threat, it was evident that the Turks would have enough men on the peninsula to make a stout defence.[1]

The primary object of the whole enterprise being the forcing of the Dardanelles, the essence of the operations was held to be the reduction of the batteries at the Narrows. To achieve this object two alternative courses had been considered:

Sketch 5.

(*a*) A landing on the Asiatic side of the Straits;
(*b*) A landing on, or to the north-west of, the peninsula.

The objections to the Asiatic shore were numerous. In the case of a landing at Besika Bay or three miles further south at Yukyeri Bay opposite Tenedos, the country to be traversed was big and difficult and would entail a continental campaign

---

two 12-pdr. guns, one 6-inch howitzer, and three 4·7-inch guns mounted on pontoons. These latter weapons had been provided on the understanding that, as soon as Constantinople fell, the Naval Division was to proceed to East Africa to tackle the German cruiser *Koenigsberg* at that time taking refuge in the Rufiji river.

The French contingent, which started the campaign with 40 guns, was, from the first, well supplied with ammunition. On the other hand, its infantry units only came into being a week before they sailed.

[1] See Chapter VIII. for the actual numbers obtained from Turkish information.

for which the forces available were insufficient. In addition, once a landing had been effected, the army would be unable to obtain further help from the guns of the fleet. In the case of an advance from near Kum Kale, at the mouth of the Straits, the Allied right would be in the air, while the left and centre would be faced by a broad marsh and a network of rivers. The principal defences of the Narrows were on the European shore, and it was improbable that they could be dominated from Asia. Finally, Lord Kitchener had impressed upon the Commander-in-Chief that the occupation of the Asiatic shore was strongly to be deprecated.

For these reasons the General Staff favoured operations on the European side, where the capture of the Kilid Bahr plateau would, it was believed, fulfil the main object of the landing.

Information pointed to the existence of five possible localities on, or to the north-west of the peninsula for the disembarkation of troops:

1. In the Gulf of Saros (Bakla Bay, Ibrije, or Enos);
2. Suvla Bay, and immediately south of it;
3. North of Gaba Tepe;
4. South of Gaba Tepe;
5. Cape Helles and Sedd el Bahr.

Of these, Bakla Bay, an inlet barely two miles north of Bulair, was ruled out by the fact that transports would have to lie about a mile out from the shore, that the beach and anchorage would be under fire from the main Turkish position, and that the enemy had made more extensive preparations here than anywhere else for opposing a disembarkation. A landing at Ibrije or Enos would not be open to these objections; but Enos was dangerously near the Bulgarian frontier in the event of that country joining the Turks, and from either Enos or Ibrije the march towards Bulair would be through difficult country, with the army's left flank exposed to attack from Thrace. Arrived at the isthmus it would be necessary to assault and capture the heavily fortified positions running across the neck of the peninsula near Bulair. Furthermore, as the main Turkish communications with the peninsula were by water, the mere investment of the Bulair lines would not involve the surrender of the Gallipoli garrison.[1]

---

[1] The possibility of attacking the Turkish sea-communications with submarines was not overlooked. But it was considered that light draft vessels, hugging the Asiatic coast at night, could not be prevented from supplying the garrison, and that even if a submarine base could be established on the eastern shore of the isthmus, an absolute blockade would be most difficult and would take a long time to make its effect felt.

Again, in the event of a protracted struggle, the rear of the besiegers would be exposed to attack by reinforcements from Thrace. Even after the fall of the Bulair lines, the Turks, it was believed, would still maintain their grip on the Narrows, and the army would then be forced to fight its way down the peninsula, through difficult country, and to attack the Kilid Bahr plateau, before it could fulfil its function of assisting the fleet.[1]

The beaches at Suvla Bay and south of Nibrunesi Point Map 3. were attractive, but the salt lake at this time of year was full of water and impassable, and the only available map[2] showed the road south from Suvla as a defile between the Sari Bair ridge and the sea. The alternative route east of Sari Bair involved a detour through difficult country, believed to be strongly held, where more troops than those available would be required, and where no assistance could be derived from the guns of the fleet.

For the beach between Fisherman's Hut and Gaba Tepe (where the Australian and New Zealand troops eventually landed), it was claimed that though the exits were bad, the actual landing would probably be immune from hostile artillery. Similarly, against the rugged difficulties of the Sari Bair range

---

[1] It is of interest to compare this appreciation, written in March 1915, with the German Official Account of the Dardanelles campaign. Discussing the courses open to Sir Ian Hamilton, the author writes:
"The most attractive spot at first sight seemed to be Bulair. There the peninsula was narrowest. If the enemy was fortunate in disembarking a large force it might push through quickly to the Sea of Marmara. The Turks on the peninsula would then be in a critical position. Their natural rearward communication would be broken, the road to Constantinople cut, and transport by sea made questionable. Success at Bulair would not, however, entail the collapse of resistance nor the fall of the Narrows. However heavy a blow on the rear of the Fifth Army it might be, it would not cut a vital artery; there was always the possibility of changing the line of communication, and of supplying the Army from the Asiatic side. The enemy, therefore, would have to reckon with the fact that the Turkish resistance would be continued unweakened, and that it would cost him much blood to traverse the thirty miles which separated Bulair from the fortress (the Narrows). Further, if the enemy landed at Bulair, he would expose himself to the danger of fire from two sides. Besides facing west, he must also face east against the main Turkish forces approaching from Thrace. Finally, the landing place lay east of Bulair forts and open to their fire; the difficulties of capturing this line were not to be over-rated. There were, therefore, many reasons against the choice of the Bulair sector as a landing place." Mühlmann, "Der Kampf um die Dardanellen 1915," pp. 82-3.

[2] This map was subsequently found to be inaccurate. Before the war there was no road along the coast here. Since the war a passable road has been constructed by the Imperial War Graves Commission.

were weighed the chances of fewer defensive preparations in this comparatively inaccessible locality.

The excellent landing places south of Gaba Tepe, giving direct access to the Kilid Bahr plateau, were dismissed as obviously impracticable. An elaborate network of trenches and wire was plainly visible from the sea; the beach was in easy reach of the Turkish batteries; and here, without doubt, the Turk was prepared to parry a thrust which, if successful, would pierce his very vitals.

With regard to the beaches at the southern end of the peninsula, destined so soon to become world-famous, the actual words of the General Staff appreciation, which undoubtedly influenced the Commander-in-Chief's choice, were as follows:

Map 2.
Sketch 8A.

The landing places[1] at this point are not so extensive as those previously referred to, but in other respects there are considerable advantages. During the landing, and in the subsequent advance, effective assistance could be afforded by the fleet on both flanks. As far as the Achi Baba ridge the ground is a more uniform and less accidented slope than in the case of the other landing places mentioned. Once ashore, the army would have both flanks and rear secured by the sea. The front available for deployment is narrow, but not so narrow as before the Bulair Lines. The Kilid Bahr position does not appear to be more formidable on its southern than on its northern face. The enemy may have organized a complete line of defence on the Achi Baba ridge, but at least this can hardly be as strong as the Bulair lines.

Based on the foregoing considerations, the draft plan accepted in principle by Sir Ian Hamilton on the 23rd March closely resembled the plan which was finally adopted for the landings on the 25th April. It included a landing at the south of the peninsula by the 29th Division, supported by the French, and a simultaneous landing by the Australian and New Zealand Corps to the north of Gaba Tepe. As the sea assured ready inter-communication, the objections to this comparatively wide dispersal of force were considered of little importance, while the advantages of a dual landing were expected to be far-reaching. By this means the numbers that could be landed in the first day would be more than doubled, and the presence of troops in the neighbourhood of Sari Bair would hinder and perhaps prevent the arrival of Turkish reinforcements at the

[1] These consisted of three tiny beaches, one on the western coast above Tekke Burnu, afterwards called X Beach, and two at the extreme southern end, afterwards named W and V. They are described in detail in Chapter XI., and it will suffice to notice here that W, the largest, was only 350 yards long by about 15 yards broad.

PREPARATIONS AT ALEXANDRIA 115

southern end of the peninsula. The plan further contemplated a feint near Bulair, to detain the Turkish garrison in that locality: this to be entrusted to troops who would otherwise be inactive while waiting their turn to land.[1]

By the time, therefore, that the transports began to assemble at Alexandria and Port Said, the plan of operations was already far enough advanced to enable the reorganization of the force and redistribution of the troops to be put in hand at once. Sir Ian Hamilton reached Port Said on the 26th March, and proceeded direct to Cairo for a consultation with Sir John Maxwell. The following day his General Headquarters was established at Alexandria;[2] but it was still a General Headquarters in name only. The transport *Arcadian* with the A. and Q. branches of the Staff was not due to reach Egypt from England till the 1st April, and until these officers arrived the General Staff were obliged to deal as best they could with the many important administrative questions pressing for decision.

Many of the arrangements made for the landing had subsequently to be revised in accordance with various modifications of the original scheme. It will suffice, therefore, to indicate the general system under which the preparations were carried out, and to give a brief outline of the detailed work accomplished.

Before the arrival of G.H.Q. in Egypt, and even before the appointment of Sir Ian Hamilton as Commander-in-Chief, a good deal of preliminary work in connection with the probable employment of the "Anzac" corps[3] in the Dardanelles had been completed by the corps Staff. It was decided that these arrangements, so far as they fitted in with Sir Ian Hamilton's

---

[1] This plan did not coincide with the views held in France. At first the French War Office advised General d'Amade to suggest a landing at Bulair. Later (on 23rd March), hearing that Bulair was now impracticable, they suggested the Asiatic coast near Besika. General d'Amade replied on 30th March that he had mentioned this project to Sir Ian Hamilton, but that Lord Kitchener's instructions forbade a landing in Asia (see French Official Account, Tome viii. Annexes i. Nos. 31, 43, 50). No further action was taken to press the French view.

[2] At No. 18 Rue el Caied Gohar. A few days later the Hotel Metropole was taken on a quarterly lease for the accommodation of the base offices.

[3] The name "Anzac" was given to the Australian and New Zealand Army Corps about this time as an official code word and short title. The origin of the word was the initials " A. & N.Z.A.C." which were stamped on all the stationery boxes of the corps. After the landing of 25th April at Ari Burnu, when this gallant corps so nearly succeeded in gaining its objective, the name Anzac Cove was given to the Ari Burnu beach as a special mark of honour to the troops concerned. Not until later was it realized that by a strange coincidence a very similar word—*anjac*—is Turkish for " almost ".

scheme, should be allowed to stand, and little but general instructions was issued by G.H.Q. with regard to the embarkation and disembarkation of the Anzac corps. This policy was maintained throughout the days of preparation; and after the general scheme had been drawn up by the naval and military Commanders-in-Chief, and the ships and small craft available to support and effect the northern landing had been allocated, all details regarding the disembarkation of General Birdwood's force were worked out by corps headquarters in consultation with the senior naval officer (Rear-Admiral C. F. Thursby) in charge of the operation. A similarly wide discretion was left to General d'Amade, commanding the French, whose task at that time was intended to be confined to landing in support of the 29th Division. He was told where his troops would be required to land, and what they would be required to do, but, subject to the Commander-in-Chief's final approval, all details were left for him to settle with his naval colleague, Admiral P. Guépratte, commanding the French squadron.

In the case of the 29th Division, chosen for the main operation, the matter was treated differently, and throughout the period of preparation, all arrangements as to the size of the covering force, its disembarkation, and the disembarkation of the main body, were worked out by General Headquarters in conference with the staff of the naval Commander-in-Chief; and detailed orders on all these subjects were issued by G.H.Q. to Major-General Hunter-Weston, commanding the 29th Division.

By the 27th March the fourteen transports of the Royal Naval Division had assembled at Port Said, and on the following day the armada of some fifty vessels bearing the 29th Division and the French contingent began to arrive at Alexandria. The first task was to disembark men and animals and send them into camp; and here it is fitting to notice the valuable assistance given to the Mediterranean Expeditionary Force by Sir John Maxwell and his Staff in this and in so many other directions throughout the duration of the Dardanelles campaign.

The course of this disembarkation proved that the moving of the base to Alexandria was fully justified. Even the available quay space of the Egyptian ports was barely sufficient to cope with the vast amount of unloading and reloading that had to be undertaken. In the resourceless harbour of Mudros, with its constantly rough water and its total absence of wharves or quays, the necessary rearrangement could never have been carried out. In the hurry of embarkation in England the contents of the transports had been even more intermixed than was at first realized, and there was no alternative to completely

PREPARATIONS AT ALEXANDRIA

unloading every ship. One of the infantry battalions of the 29th Division, for instance, had been embarked in four different vessels. Units had been separated from their first line transport, wagons from their horses. Guns had been loaded in one vessel, their ammunition in a second, and, in some cases, the necessary fuzes in a third. For a whole week the ammunition of the 29th Division's ammunition column could not be traced at all. A similar confusion existed in the supply ships, each of which had to be almost completely unloaded and its cargo re-sorted on the quays. These vessels were then reloaded in such a way that each of the various categories of supplies on board would be easily accessible.

The next step was to decide on the exact numbers and composition of the covering forces for the two main landings on the day of battle; the best tactical sequence for landing the main bodies; and the irreducible number of animals and vehicles required in the first instance. To solve these problems it was essential to arrive at the number of men that could be landed simultaneously on the selected beaches, and this depended on the exact size of the beaches and on the navy's resources in small craft for putting the troops ashore.

With regard to the number of animals and vehicles to be landed, it was essential to preserve the mobility of the force, for it was hoped that the first day's fighting would lead to a considerable advance. But the decision rested largely on questions of water-supply and of roads. As the roads were supposed to be unfit for mechanical transport, units would be obliged to depend on horses and mules. Yet to land a considerable number of animals, in view of the reported shortage of water, might well be worse than useless. Similarly it would be impossible to land animals in the first instance without a serious reduction in the rate of landing troops. To meet these difficulties the whole system of food and ammunition supply was temporarily reorganized; the number of animals to be landed was cut down to an absolute minimum; officers' kits and men's blankets were to be left behind; and, in the case of an advance, supply and ammunition vehicles or mules were to refill from specially loaded store-ships which would land ammunition and supplies at convenient points on the coast in rear of the fighting troops.

These matters decided upon, it was possible to issue orders for the re-allotment of troops to transports; to carry out the necessary alterations to the ships' fittings for the accommodation of their new freights; and to arrange for all surplus units, animals, and vehicles to be left in Egypt till their services were required. The admiral had stipulated that the covering force for the southern landing should be such that it could be carried in not more than three transports, and for the northern landing in not more than four, these being the maximum numbers that he would undertake to manœuvre into their respective beaches in the dark. For the main body, on the other hand, the number of ships to be unloaded simultaneously could be increased respectively to six and eight. Orders were drawn up to this effect, and special instructions were issued regarding the equipment to be taken ashore. All troops were to land with 200 rounds of ammunition and three days' food, and in addition, each transport was to land a reserve of seven days' food and 300 rounds of ammunition for every man put ashore. The covering force was to land without horses or vehicles of any kind; machine guns were to be man-handled; entrenching tools and all stores landed in the first instance were to be limited to what could be carried by hand.

The main body was to be embarked as far as possible in complete units, with all their first requirements in ammunition, transport, stores, water, and food. All transports were to start with full water tanks, and 30 days' ship's victuals, seven days' military rations, and two days' iron rations for all the troops on board.

During these days of preparation it was reported to General Headquarters that amongst the somewhat unusual equipment with which the Royal Naval Division had been provided, one transport contained an assortment of Rolls Royce armoured cars, Ford cars, motor cycles and side-cars, pack ponies, and a number of old and new pattern machine guns. Machine guns were a precious find in those days, and to make as much use as possible of this windfall, an improvised establishment was drawn up for a pack-cob machine-gun battery to accompany the division.

Finally, as soon as the allocation of troops to transports[1] had been finished, a detailed table of "tows"[2] was made out,

[1] Amongst other details, in order to simplify reference to the 96 transports taking part in the initial operations, and to show at a glance the duties on which each one was employed, the vessels of each corps or division were allotted a distinguishing index letter and numbered serially in their class from 1 upwards. The Anzac transports were numbered A1 to A35, the 29th Division's B1 to B15, the French F1 to F23, and the Naval Division's N1 to N12. Similarly the supply ships were numbered S1 to S10, and the ship to convey Sir Ian Hamilton and his headquarters was numbered H1.

[2] A "tow" was the term used for a string of four ship's cutters, or similar boats, towed by a steam launch, and carrying a total of 120-130 men. A "trip" was a "tow's" round journey—from ship to shore and back again to ship.

PREPARATIONS AT ALEXANDRIA

showing the exact sequence in which every man, gun, animal, and vehicle would be landed, and the approximate hour at which the various stages of the disembarkation might be expected to be complete. Owing to subsequent modifications of the plan and, still later, to Turkish opposition on the day of landing, this programme was considerably altered, and, as will be seen in a later chapter, certain stages of the disembarkation were very considerably delayed. But it is interesting to notice from these tables that, so constricted were the beaches at the south of the peninsula, that even with everything going strictly in accordance with plan it was calculated that the landing of the fighting troops of the 29th Division, with their very modified scale of horses, vehicles, and guns, could not be completed in less than two and a half days. It was this fact more than any other which necessitated the simultaneous landing of the Australians and New Zealanders at another place.

As no detailed consideration had been given to the requirements of an opposed landing before the troops left England, it was perhaps inevitable that during this period of last-minute preparation many serious deficiencies should be discovered in the organization and equipment of the Expeditionary Force; and the record of telegrams despatched from General Headquarters about this time discloses the wide range of the anxieties of the Commander-in-Chief. The only engineers allotted to the force were the divisional field companies; and additional skilled labour was urgently needed for the building of piers, the construction of roads, and the multifarious duties connected with the transformation of a barren beach into a large advanced base. The force was deficient of a General Headquarters signal company.[1] No provision had been made for lighting the headquarters offices at night. The ammunition allotted to the expedition was barely sufficient for one sustained battle, and no reserve was in sight. No provision had been made for the necessary materials for temporary and permanent piers and jetties, and this important matter was further complicated, and a considerable amount of effort wasted, by the fact that existing regulations and text-books paid little attention to the subject, and the responsible authority for controlling and organizing the work was imperfectly defined.

Equally serious was the almost complete deficiency of trench stores. With a month's respite given to the Turk to

[1] This signal company was got ready to leave England on 10th April, but an outbreak of measles subsequently delayed its departure, and a portion of the Anzac headquarters signal company had to be borrowed for G.H.Q.

improve his defences, there could plainly be no alternative to a runaway success but a period of trench warfare; but the expeditionary force had been equipped only for a mobile campaign, and was entirely deficient of all the special material which experience of position warfare in France was finding of first importance. Urgent messages were sent, not only to England but also to Cairo and Malta, asking for the hasty provision or improvisation of periscopes, hand-grenades, trench mortars, and mortar-bombs. In face of the urgent needs of the French front it was difficult for the War Office to meet this new and unexpected demand, but the promise of a few hand-grenades and twenty 3·7-inch trench mortars was obtained; and Sir Ian Hamilton was also informed that two Japanese mortars and 500 bombs, shortly due to leave Tokyo, would be diverted to the Dardanelles on arrival at Suez. It was from Malta and Egypt, however, that most assistance was forthcoming in this respect in the early days of the campaign. Thanks to the ingenuity of an assistant, named Garland, in the Cairo arsenal, a rough but fairly efficient bomb-thrower was designed, and a supply of some hundreds of bombs per week was guaranteed. In the early days of the campaign Mr. Garland's name became famous in the peninsula, and his weapons were eagerly sought after by the British troops in the line.

Ammunition supply was an unceasing anxiety, and in view of the improbability of an early improvement in the situation the War Office was asked at this time whether any new device had lately been discovered for dealing with wire entanglements. The reply to this message, that the best way was to destroy them with shrapnel and high explosive, cannot have been very encouraging. At that moment only 623 rounds per 18-pdr. gun were available in the Mediterranean, which was little enough for an operation to be entered upon at a distance of 3,000 miles from the home base.[1] Moreover, the whole of this ammunition was shrapnel, and the 18-pdr. batteries had not a single round of H.E. shell among them. The warships, too, had only their ordinary outfit of ammunition, which provides a very small proportion of suitable projectiles either for bombardment or for firing at troops or entrenchments. This shortage was a continual source of anxiety to Admiral de Robeck.

Rifle ammunition was equally scarce. Available stocks

[1] It must be remembered that the army in France was equally short of ammunition at this time, but it is interesting to notice that a little more than two years later, at the successful battle of Messines, 1152 18-pdrs. on a battle front of 16,000 yards, fired an average of 510 rounds per gun in 24 hours.

PREPARATIONS AT ALEXANDRIA

amounted to only 500 rounds per rifle for the 29th Division and 430 per rifle for the Royal Naval Division. The situation was moreover complicated by the fact that these two divisions, so soon to fight side by side, were armed with rifles of a different mark, and that though the 29th Division, with Mark VII. rifles, could use the Naval Division's Mark VI. ammunition, their Mark VII. ammunition was useless for the rifles of the R.N.D.

With regard to the provision of piers, 250 yards of trestle piering were made up by Malta dockyard and despatched to Mudros; nine barrel piers, constructed in Egypt, were placed on board the transports of the covering force; and some large lighters, to be used as floating piers, were purchased at Port Said, and towed to the scene of action by the transports of the Royal Naval Division. Four of these lighters were specially decked in and filled with fresh water, with a view to forming a reserve supply at the beaches, but in the rough weather encountered during the voyage three of them were lost.

Throughout this period of preparation the fear of a shortage of water on the peninsula was a haunting nightmare to the Commander-in-Chief; and the Intelligence service was unable to add in any way to the vague and indefinite information on this all-important subject. On the 3rd April the War Office telegraphed to Sir Ian Hamilton: "Have you any good and recent information as to the water supply on the Gallipoli peninsula? We have received a very bad account on this point." Hamilton replied next day that he anticipated difficulty everywhere on the peninsula, and that special arrangements were being made, but he asked the War Office to give him all particulars in their possession. In reply the War Office stated that their principal source of information was an official report on Eastern Turkey, dated 1905, and a report by Admiral Jeffrey (date not mentioned), that water in the villages was scanty and polluted, and that the streams dried up quickly after rain.

It may here be added that the report in the 1905 handbook stated that "water is generally plentiful in the valleys", and that this report turned out to be substantially correct. Except at Anzac,[1] indeed, where the water supply was always an anxious problem, the fears of an insufficient natural supply proved to be groundless. Nothing was left to chance, however, and throughout the month of April every conceivable precaution

---

[1] For some time at Anzac even the mules had the unaccustomed privilege of drinking, in Gallipoli, water brought from the Nile at an estimated cost of something like 4d. to 6d. per gallon.

was taken to guard against an initial shortage. A condensing steamer was chartered by the War Office, a large tank steamer was hired at Port Said, and the bazaars of Cairo and Alexandria were ransacked for skins, tanks, oil tins, and every conceivable receptacle either for storing water on the beaches or for sending it forward to the troops in the line. Many thousands of kerosene-oil tins, packed two in a box for attachment to pack-saddles, were filled with water and embarked in the transports. Amongst other precautions, special orders were issued against the wastage of ships' water during the voyage, and all units were warned that no biscuit tins, or other vessels useful for storing water, were to be thrown away. Towards the middle of April the transport difficulty was considerably reduced by the allotment to the expedition of an Indian mule corps from France (4,316 mules and 2,000 carts) [1] and by the formation in Egypt of the Zion Mule Corps (750 mules), an organization recruited from Russian Jews who had fled from Palestine on the outbreak of war. But before the arrival of these units the means of sending water forward to the troops was an anxious problem, and the measure of current anxiety can be gauged from a telegram to the Alexandria base on the 17th April, instructing them to buy 200 donkeys and 800 milk cans as quickly as possible and to embark them, together with 20 Egyptian donkey boys, at the earliest possible opportunity. A request was also made at this time for the Zion Mule Corps to be sent off immediately, even if they were not yet properly equipped. Anything that could be purchased locally in the way of water tins was to be shipped with them, and tied to their pack-saddles during the voyage.

The inadequate size of the Expeditionary Force for the heavy task entrusted to it has been noticed on a previous page.[2] At first Sir Ian Hamilton seems to have had no desire to ask for reinforcements, and the impression he gave to those around him was that of a man who is fully confident of success. But his position *vis-à-vis* Lord Kitchener—his former Commander-in-Chief—was in many respects peculiar, and his confidence was largely the reflection of the Secretary of State's views. During the last six months of the South African War, as Chief of the Staff, he had worked in the same room and lived under the same roof as Lord Kitchener, and to some extent he was still under the domination of that forceful personality. When told, therefore, that 75,000 men would suffice for an operation which he had never himself studied,

---

[1] The last contingent embarked at Marseilles on 22nd April.
[2] See page 103.

confidence in his old chief induced an almost unquestioning acceptance of his estimate. He had seen Lord Kitchener overcome other "impossibilities" by ignoring them; and as to the future, if further troops should be wanted, he had Lord Kitchener's written instructions that "having entered on " the project of forcing the Dardanelles there can be no idea " of abandoning the enterprise ".

But towards the end of March, though still sanguine of success, Sir Ian Hamilton began to feel that it would be well to be provided, before the operations began, with a margin of safety. A definite appeal for more troops at this moment, with a full emphasis on the risks of embarking on this unexpectedly difficult enterprise, 3,000 miles from England, without an adequate reserve on the spot, might have achieved its purpose. But it was here that Sir Ian felt unable to telegraph a clear expression of his views. Lord Kitchener, a soldier Secretary of State, was acting to all intents and purposes as his own Chief of the General Staff. All messages from commanders-in-chief in the field had to be addressed to him direct. Demands for reinforcements were adjudicated on by him alone. His position was pre-eminent, his power almost supreme. Sir Ian Hamilton had seen him, in South African days, reply to an officer's appeal for reinforcements by taking half his troops away from him; he himself had been warned before leaving England that there could be little hope of adding to his strength, and he had promised to be very moderate in any demands for help. Even the 29th Division, he had been told, was only a temporary loan, which he must send back to France as quickly as possible. He looked upon these warnings as an inviolable order, and with what was perhaps mistaken loyalty, he could not bring himself to make an unwelcome demand for troops which after all might never be needed. The most he would do was to ask for one Gurkha brigade from Egypt, and even this request was qualified by an offer to leave four mounted brigades[1] in Egypt in exchange.[2]

---

[1] This proposal was first made by General Birdwood on his return to Cairo from the Dardanelles early in March. Realizing that mounted units could not be used in Gallipoli in the first instance, he suggested exchanging them for an Indian infantry brigade belonging to the Egyptian garrison, in order to bring the N.Z. & A. Division up to the normal strength of three infantry brigades. Later these mounted brigades unanimously volunteered to serve in Gallipoli as infantry, and fought with great distinction at Anzac.

[2] Later, on 11th April, hearing from Admiral Guépratte that he believed that General d'Amade had been informed that French reinforcements, up to one division, would be sent out in case of necessity (see French Official Account, Tome viii. Annexes i. No. 43), he asked Lord Kitchener if the rumour was true that another French division was to be allotted to

It is nevertheless probable that this request for Gurkhas played an important part. Towards the end of March, with a growing consciousness of the dangers ahead, Lord Kitchener decided to send the 2nd Mounted Division [1] to Egypt, to be handy in case of emergencies, and on the 6th April, further prompted no doubt by Sir Ian Hamilton's request, he telegraphed to General Maxwell in Cairo with a view to increasing the strength of the Dardanelles force:

You should supply any troops in Egypt that can be spared, or even selected officers or men that Sir Ian Hamilton may want, for Gallipoli. You know that Peyton's Mounted Division is leaving for Egypt. This telegram should be communicated by you to Sir Ian Hamilton.

It will be seen from this telegram that the Gallipoli operations were still to suffer the disadvantages of a subsidiary enterprise. They were still to be given only such troops as could be spared from elsewhere. Nevertheless Lord Kitchener's telegram opened the door to a far greater reinforcement than one Indian brigade, and there can be little doubt that had Sir Ian Hamilton seen it, as Lord Kitchener intended, he would have seized his opportunity. But through some mischance no copy of the message was sent to him; he remained in ignorance of its existence, and the opportunity slipped away. He did, however, succeed in getting his Indian brigade. When in Cairo at the end of March he had told General Maxwell how much he wanted it. On the evening of the 6th April he sent him a parting telephone message, begging him "to jog K's elbow "about the Gurkhas", and two days later, just as he was sailing from Alexandria, an answer was received that General Maxwell "would do his best to meet his wishes". General Cox's Indian brigade[2] was detailed for the Dardanelles; but it could not be got ready for embarkation for over a fortnight and did not reach the peninsula till the 1st May.

April. Early in April the heartening news reached Alexandria that a complete Russian corps was in readiness at Odessa to come under British orders for the eventual attack on Constantinople,

---

his force. But though anxious to have the division, General Hamilton was also anxious to avoid the impression that he was asking for it. So he ended his message: "Just in case there is truth in the report you should know " that Mudros harbour is as full as it will hold."

[1] This division, commanded by Major-Gen. C. E. Peyton, was composed of Yeomanry. It began to leave England on 8th April.

[2] The 29th Indian Brigade (Major-Gen. H. V. Cox) consisted of the 14th Sikhs, the 69th and 89th Punjabis, and the 1/6th Gurkhas. No brigade composed entirely of Gurkhas was serving in Egypt at the time.

But interest in this reinforcement was minimized by the tantalizing reminder that until the Dardanelles were forced and the *Goeben* destroyed the sailing of Russian transports could not be sanctioned. Nevertheless the silent pressure exerted by the presence of this corps at Odessa was of material benefit to the Mediterranean force. Nervous of the implied threat, Admiral Souchon made a fruitless raid on Odessa harbour on the 5th April, and a Turkish battleship was lost by striking a mine during the return passage. Moreover, the fear of a Russian landing detained three Turkish divisions in the Bosporus till almost the end of June.

Despite his anxiety to procure a few more troops, Sir Ian Hamilton's reports to Lord Kitchener show that the inspections he carried out in Egypt at the beginning of April went far to increase his confidence in the future. Eleven of the twelve battalions of the 29th Division were thoroughly trained and seasoned Regular troops, and the twelfth was a specially selected battalion of Territorials. The Royal Naval Division, though short of training, showed great promise; the French contingent, which included many coloured troops, impressed him as being a "very keen and workmanlike body".

In a telegram to Lord Kitchener describing his inspection of the Australian and New Zealand Army Corps, General Hamilton remarked that they were "very fine troops". The wording of a telegram is usually laconic, but in point of fact no praise could well have been higher or, as events were soon to prove, more richly deserved. The prowess of Australian and New Zealand troops in the Great War has won a lasting fame. But it was in Gallipoli, above the beach that bears their name, that their first laurels were gained, and it was there that they set up a standard of bravery, tenacity, and resource which furnished an example for all who followed them. From the point of view of general physique these two divisions were the flower of Australian and New Zealand manhood, and all who saw them in the early days of the campaign agree that they were probably as fine a body of men as ever stood to arms.

Though the Turks had been fully warned, Sir Ian Hamilton argued that they could not hope to be strong everywhere. Seapower, and the mobility it conferred, still offered him the chance of tactical surprise; and if every man that could be carried in the small boats available could be landed in one simultaneous rush at selected points, while the remainder were employed in feints against other likely places, he felt that there was every prospect of breaking down local opposition and gaining his objectives before the enemy's reserves could intervene.

By the 3rd April the re-allotment of troops to transports had been completed, and from now onwards the despatch of the army from Alexandria[1] was pressed forward by the embarkation authorities with a speed that in view of the many obstacles to be surmounted can only be regarded as remarkable. The first units of the Anzac corps from Cairo were embarked on the 4th April, and from that moment work in the harbour continued night and day till the whole expedition had sailed. Amongst the many causes that combined to retard progress, it should be noticed that only six steamer berths were available, and for the first week at least half of these were still engaged in discharging the last ships of the 29th Division to arrive from England. Facilities for coaling were limited; and the inadequacy of the plant for filling water tanks caused much delay. More serious still, it was found necessary in the case of one transport to replace a recalcitrant captain and crew at the very moment of departure, thereby incurring a delay of three days in the sailing of that particular vessel. Despite these handicaps, 30 Australian transports, 15 of the 29th Division, and a few supply ships were got away by the 16th April; the 22 transports of the French contingent and some more supply ships followed in quick succession, and by the 22nd April a total of no less than 77 ships had been loaded and despatched from this one port in a period of 19 days.

It is instructive to compare this record with the embarkation of the original British Expeditionary Force for France in August 1914. For that operation Southampton, Liverpool, Avonmouth, Dublin, and Newhaven were the principal ports used, and during the time of greatest activity an average daily total of 20 transports[2] was despatched from these five ports. The plans and time-tables for that movement had all been carefully prepared in peace time, and the troops had only to be carried the short journey to France, where they would be disembarked under peace conditions at a quay. When, in comparing the above figures, it is remembered that in the case of the Mediterranean movement the troops might have to remain on board for three weeks or longer, and that men, animals, and stores had to be loaded in such a way as to meet

[1] At Port Said, where the ships of the Royal Naval Division required considerable structural alterations before the troops could be re-embarked in accordance with tactical requirements, re-embarkation could not begin till 16th April. The delay was turned to good account by attaching units to the Canal defences for a spell of training under service conditions.

[2] Exclusive of small steamers carrying stores and troop details.

EMBARKING MULES AT ALEXANDRIA, APRIL 1915

PREPARATIONS AT ALEXANDRIA

the tactical requirements of an opposed landing on an open beach, the work of the embarkation staff at Alexandria stands out as a remarkable achievement.[1]

During the last week in March and the first week in April, while the military staff offices and the docks at Alexandria and Port Said were humming with activity, seven hundred miles away at Mudros the fleet was no less busily employed. Not only had all naval preparations to be made for the biggest landing in history, but the fleet had also to prepare for a new attack on the Narrows as soon as the army was safely established on shore. Beach gear for this mighty disembarkation had to be improvised; tugs, steamboats, lighters, and other small craft to be collected, organized, and provided with crews. Land reconnaissance being out of the question, the various selected landing places had to be examined as closely as possible from the sea; shoal water had to be carefully measured, charts verified, and anchorages arranged for the large number of transports to be employed. The whole peninsula had to be kept under careful observation, and the Turkish defensive preparations interfered with by naval fire. Several hundred naval officers and men had to be told off for, and instructed in, such unaccustomed duties as those of naval transport officers, boat and hold parties for the transports, and beach personnel for the various landing places on the day of battle. The enormous strain placed on the resources of a fleet by finding this large number of men without impairing its own fighting efficiency was in the first instance scarcely realized either at home or on the spot. Early in April, at the urgent request of Admiral de Robeck, a number of special service officers were hurried out from England; but even with these, and with the personnel of the battleships lost on the 18th March, great difficulty was experienced in providing the necessary numbers, and towards the end of the preparatory period the Royal Naval Division, to the detriment of its own efficiency, was obliged to

[1] The total strength of the Mediterranean Expeditionary Force, as allotted to transports, was as follows:

	Ships.	Personnel.	Animals.	Vehicles.
29th Div. (Alexandria,	15	17,649	3,962	692
Anzac (Alexandria)	30	25,784	6,920	1,271
Anzac (at Mudros)	5	4,854	698	147
French Force (Alexandria)	22*	16,762	3,511	647
R.N.D. (Port Said)	12	10,007	1,390	347
	84	75,056	16,481	3,104

* Does not include the transport *Ceylan* which arrived at Lemnos on 20th April with 2 batteries of heavy artillery for the French contingent.

surrender three hundred naval reservists to meet the needs of the fleet. Amongst other activities, with a view to an early resumption of the naval attack, the whole mine-sweeping service had to be entirely reorganized, and finally, and most important of all, naval orders had to be written for the covering squadrons, for the transports, and for the actual disembarkation of troops. It was, however, impossible for any progress to be made in this final stage of the work till the return of General Headquarters to Mudros.

It was equally impossible for the army to complete its plans, and to issue detailed orders for the landing, till close touch with the sailors was resumed, and the necessity of getting these important matters settled at the earliest possible opportunity now led to a second and wholly regrettable separation of the various branches of General Headquarters. By the 6th April, all the preliminary arrangements for the landing were well forward, and there was nothing more to detain the General Staff in Alexandria. On the other hand many important administrative matters still claimed the presence of the Adjutant-General and Quartermaster-General at the base, and the Commander-in-Chief further considered that, out of courtesy to the French, his senior administrative Staff officers should be available in Egypt to render every assistance to General d'Amade till his troops were ready to embark. It was decided therefore that Sir Ian Hamilton and the General Staff, accompanied by a representative of the Director of Medical Services to advise on medical arrangements, should leave Egypt in the *Arcadian* on the 7th April, and that the remainder of General Headquarters should follow as soon as the progress of their work and the completion of the French preparations for embarkation permitted them to do so. This decision, which resulted in the separation of the various branches of the Staff from the 7th to the 18th April, was perhaps inevitable, but it would undoubtedly have led to the easier running of the Staff machine if senior representatives of the Adjutant-General and Quartermaster-General had sailed in the *Arcadian* to assist the General Staff, and to keep their own branches in close touch with the development of the military plan.

Going on board on the afternoon of the 7th April, and expecting to sail at once for Mudros, the Commander-in-Chief was forcibly reminded of the element of uncertainty that in combined operations so often intrudes to mar the simplest plan. Though orders had been issued overnight for his ship to sail that afternoon, it was now found that she was short of water and that her tanks could not be filled till next morning—a vexatious loss of sixteen precious hours. On the 8th April, however, all was ready for sea. Bent on a strangely different errand to the Norwegian pleasure cruises associated with her name, the once luxurious *Arcadian*, now shorn of her luxury and disguised as transport H1, slowly threaded her way through the maze of shipping in harbour; and under a sky of serene and cloudless blue Sir Ian Hamilton and his General Staff sailed north to join the fleet.

CHAPTER VII

FINAL PREPARATIONS AT MUDROS

(Maps 1, 2 ; Sketches 1, 4)

April 1915. THE return of General Headquarters to Mudros on the 10th April marks the beginning of the final preparations for the landing. Immediately after their arrival a conference was held in the *Queen Elizabeth*, to review the military plan of campaign in the light of the further knowledge of the peninsula gained by the navy in the last ten days. After examining every other alternative, it was agreed that the plan decided upon on the 23rd March[1] held the greatest chances of success; and the general outline of that scheme was finally approved.

The main objection to a landing on the toe of the peninsula lay in the fact that there, manifestly, a very complete preparation was being made to repel an invasion. But only in the south could the army count on the close co-operation of the fleet; there both its flanks would rest on a friendly element, and every mile of advance towards the main objective at Kilid Bahr would be of direct assistance to the seamen in their task of sweeping the minefields. It had to be remembered, too, that all other suitable points for a large landing were equally if not more strongly defended; while an attempt to land in force on an unsuitable beach, in the hope of avoiding initial opposition, might defeat its own object by making it impossible to supply the troops with ammunition, water, and stores. These views were fully shared by the admiral, who welcomed a landing in the south of the peninsula as the operation best calculated to assist the fleet in its next attack on the Narrows.

With the general plan of campaign thus decided upon, the next two days were spent in examining the detailed scheme for the landing. Naval opinion had considerably changed on this point during the absence of General Headquarters in

[1] See page 114.

FINAL PREPARATIONS AT MUDROS

Egypt, and as a result of these joint conferences, several important amendments were made to the existing scheme.

Owing partly to a shortage of small craft, but more especially to the limited size of the landing places, the military plan had contemplated the necessity of more or less dribbling the covering force ashore in successive trips of tows plying between the transports and the beach. To reduce the time occupied in this operation to the shortest limits it was obviously essential that the transports should anchor close to the shore. Sir Ian Hamilton was also anxious that at least the first trip of tows should be landed under cover of darkness.[1] After careful consideration Admiral de Robeck decided that this part of the scheme could not be allowed to stand. It would throw upon the masters of the transports the arduous responsibility of approaching an unknown shore, and anchoring in exactly the right position, at night. It would involve for the troops the difficult task of climbing down the high side of a transport in the dark in heavy marching order. There was, in addition, the haunting fear that shell fire from the beaches might prove too great a strain on the steadfastness of mercantile crews; and the still greater risk that some of the transports might actually be sunk. This last danger could be reduced by anchoring a long way out, but the remedy would be as dangerous as the disease. The tows would be exposed to artillery and machine-gun fire for a much longer period, and the time elapsing before the successive trips could be completed would be indefinitely prolonged.

The admiral considered that, though the main body might safely be landed direct from transports after the beaches had been cleared of the enemy, the initial landings should be made from men-of-war. Sir Ian Hamilton agreed; and it was now arranged that on the night before the landing the transports carrying the covering force for the northern and southern landings should assemble near Imbros and Tenedos respectively, and should there transfer the troops detailed to land in the first

[1] With this object, orders had already been issued for troops to be practised in climbing quickly and silently down "Jacob's ladders" into small boats at night in their full equipment, carrying 200 rounds of ammunition and three days' food. On the night of the landing eight exits would be used on each transport—four on each side of the ship—and in some cases seven of these might have to be Jacob's ladders. The men were to be made thoroughly conversant with the order in which they would have to disembark, and, as few naval ratings would be available for the boats, eight of the men told off for each boat were to be detailed to row her ashore from the point where the water became too shallow for towing. The men were also to be practised in lowering machine guns, bundles of entrenching tools, etc., noiselessly into small boats.

trip to battleships,[1] and those detailed for the following trips to destroyers or fleet sweepers. The battleships, each with her necessary complement of small craft in tow, would then approach their respective beaches under cover of darkness; their troops, safely under cover till the last moment, would be able to climb into the tows more quickly and easily than they could do from the high deck of a transport; and the risk of any untoward incident during that part of the operation would be reduced to a minimum. Meanwhile the fleet sweepers and destroyers carrying the remainder of the covering force would follow the battleships, and, after the first troops had been landed, would steam quickly inshore to meet the tows returning from the beach, thus ensuring the disembarkation of the second trip with a minimum of delay.

Map. 2.
Sketch 4.
The second important amendment adopted was the introduction into the plan of the now famous *River Clyde*. The number of troops that could be thrown ashore in the first rush for the beach was of vital importance, but for the main operation there was only room on the three southern beaches for eighteen tows to arrive simultaneously, namely, four at X, eight at W, and six at V;[2] making a total of not more than 2,200 men all told for the first attack. The new plan for carrying the remainder of the covering force on fleet sweepers would increase the speed at which the first troops could be reinforced; but even with this new method at least three-quarters of an hour would probably elapse before the second trip of tows could reach the shore.

To increase the number of men that could be landed practically simultaneously at Sedd el Bahr, and to produce at the same time an element of surprise, it was now suggested by Commander E. Unwin, R.N., commanding H.M.S. *Hussar*, that a stratagem should be borrowed from local history, and that, after the manner of the wooden horse of Troy, a harmless-looking collier, filled with all the troops she could carry, should be run ashore on V Beach immediately after the arrival of the first tows, whilst the attention of the defenders would be occupied in repelling the initial attack. This scheme, which promised to double the numbers thrown ashore in the south during the first few minutes of the attack, was accepted with enthusiasm. The collier *River Clyde*, capable of holding 2,000 men, was chosen for the task; and much ingenuity in preparing her for

[1] In the case of the Australians it was subsequently decided that the first 1,500 troops to be landed should be transferred to the three battleships allotted for this duty in Mudros harbour the day before the landing, and that the battleships should then proceed direct to their final rendezvous midway between Imbros and Gaba Tepe.

[2] Including one at the Camber at Sedd el Bahr.

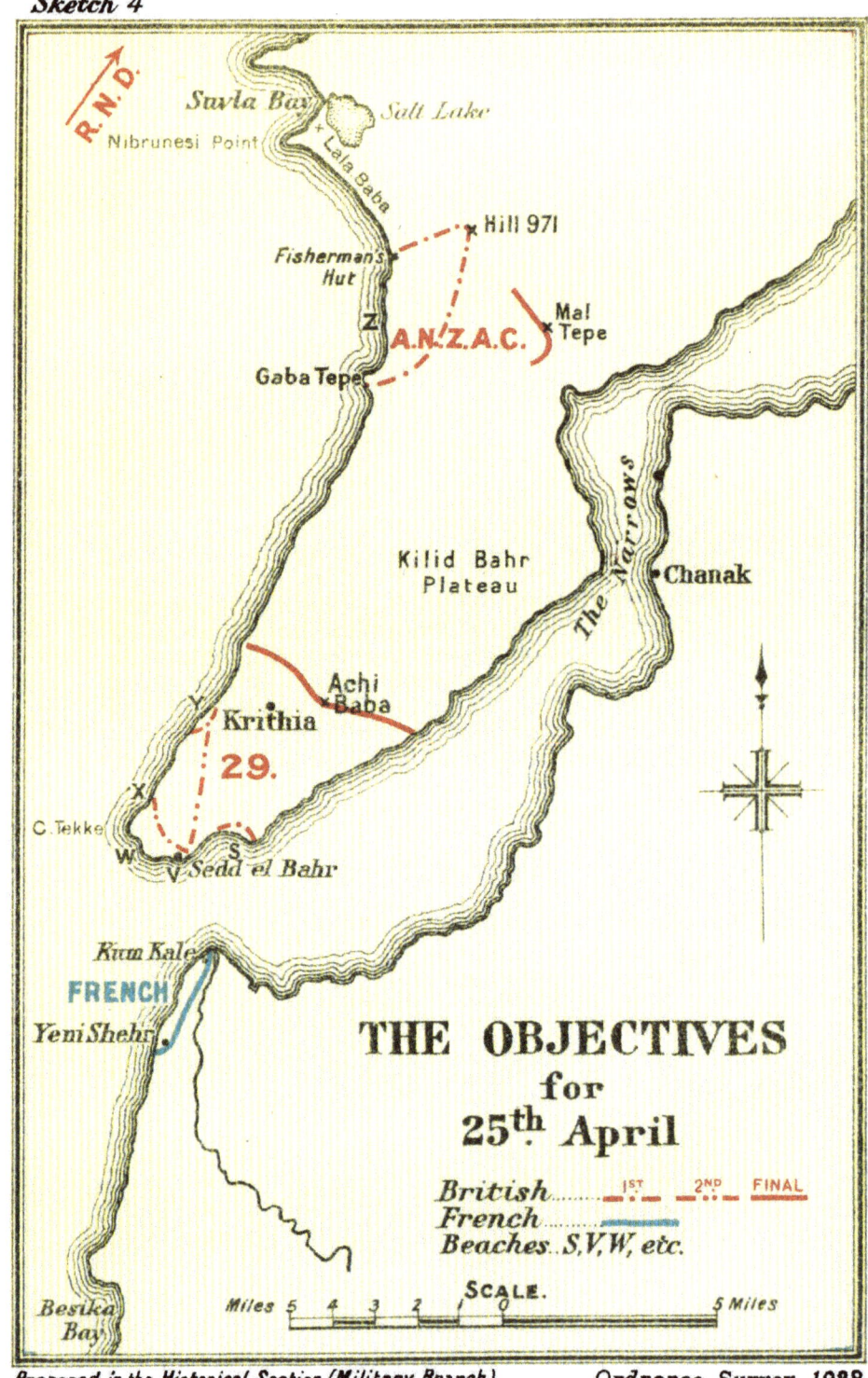

FINAL PREPARATIONS AT MUDROS 133

action was shown by Commander Unwin, who was placed in command of the ship. To enable the men to land with the utmost rapidity, large openings, giving access to wide gangplanks, were cut in the ship's sides, and it was arranged that she should tow a steam hopper[1] and three specially decked lighters, which, as soon as she took the ground, would be run forward to form a floating bridge connecting her with the shore.[2] To cover the advance of the infantry a battery of machine guns,[3] carefully protected with sandbags, was placed in the bows of the vessel, and these guns, as will be shown later, were probably the means of saving hundreds of lives.[4]

The third amendment to the original scheme was the decision to land a detachment of French troops on the Asiatic shore. Up to this time there had been no idea at G.H.Q. of trespassing in Asia, and the intention was to keep the whole of General d'Amade's force in reserve to support the southern attack. But there had always been some fear that the landing on V Beach would be harassed by fire from Asia, and with the acceptance of the *River Clyde* scheme it was more important than ever to guard against this eventuality. Furthermore, it was felt that a landing in Asia, even if only of a temporary nature, would help to confuse the Turkish command and to delay the despatch of the Asiatic garrison to reinforce the peninsula. The French would be able to supply the necessary small craft for their own disembarkation, and the use of an extra beach would materially increase the total numbers thrown ashore at the outset of the battle. It was consequently decided to land a regiment of French troops as a temporary measure at Kum Kale, simultaneously with the landing of the 29th Division. The time of their subsequent withdrawal would depend on the course of events.

[1] A hopper is a flat-bottomed vessel used for taking the spoil (or dredgings) from a dredger.

[2] The shore was known to be "steep-to", and it was hoped that by lightening the collier so that she drew only seven feet of water forward she would get near enough to the beach for the hopper alone to bridge the gap, and that the troops would be able to land practically dryshod by means of a brow from the hopper's bows. But it was obviously impossible to take soundings beforehand, so the three decked lighters were to be available to fill any gap between the collier's stem and the hopper's stern.

[3] This detachment, belonging to the Royal Naval Division, was under Commander Josiah Wedgwood.

[4] Further advantages to be gained from the employment of the *River Clyde* were that her tanks would supply an abundance of fresh water on the beach, which could be added to by her condensing plant; an unlimited supply of S.A.A. could be taken ashore in her; after the landing her holds would be available as temporary dressing-stations for the wounded; and subsequently she would be most useful as a breakwater or pier for light-draught vessels to run alongside when disembarking stores.

One other addition to the scheme was made at the personal instance of the military Commander-in-Chief. From the first, Sir Ian Hamilton had been impressed with the possible advantage of landing a small force of infantry at some apparently inaccessible and therefore undefended spot to the west of Krithia. Such a force, he was convinced, would greatly assist the southern landing by threatening the line of retreat of the defenders of Sedd el Bahr; and the navy had been asked to reconnoitre for a feasible landing place where the cliffs were not too steep for lightly laden troops. A suitable spot was now reported at a point afterwards known as "Y Beach", and Sir Ian Hamilton accordingly directed that the Plymouth Battalion R.M.L.I. of the Royal Naval Division, which had already gained some experience of the peninsula on the 4th March, should be held at his personal disposition on the day of landing, ready to disembark at this point should circumstances render such a step desirable.

Finally, to increase the uncertainty at Turkish headquarters as to the main point of attack, it was decided that, in addition to a feint by the Royal Naval Division near Bulair, a portion of the French squadron and all the French transports not engaged at Kum Kale, should make a feint of landing in Besika Bay.

As regards the date of attack, it was hoped that all would be ready by the 23rd April, but the actual date could not as yet be fixed, depending as it did on the progress of the embarkation in Egypt, and, more particularly, on the arrival of settled weather. Nor had it yet been definitely decided whether the landing should begin before daylight, in which case no preliminary bombardment of the beaches would be possible, or whether the advantages of a bombardment would outweigh the disadvantage of landing the covering force in the full light of day. The plans, however, were far enough advanced for a great deal of preparatory action to be started by subordinate commanders, and with this object in view Force Order No. 1, and special instructions to the various commanders concerned,[1] were completed by G.H.Q. on the 13th April, exactly one month from the date of Sir Ian Hamilton's departure from London.

During the next few days two small but important amendments were made to the arrangements for landing the 29th Division, and were incorporated in revised instructions issued to that division on the 19th April. In the first instance, a landing from a point inside the Straits had been considered out of the question, owing to the fear of artillery fire from the Asiatic shore. But with the French landing at Kum Kale, this objec-

[1] Appendices 3-5.

FINAL PREPARATIONS AT MUDROS 135

tion largely disappeared, and it was now decided that, to increase still further the number of men who could be landed simultaneously, and at the same time to threaten the defenders of the southern beaches with envelopment, two additional landings should be definitely included in the southern scheme, one on each side of the peninsula. On the Ægean coast, it was decided to develop the original idea of a landing at Y Beach, and to allocate two battalions to land at this point, under the orders of the G.O.C. 29th Division. These battalions would approach the shore in their transports, escorted by men-of-war, and four tows would be made available for landing them. On the eastern side it was arranged that one battalion should be taken to the mouth of the Straits in a battleship, whence the troops would be transferred to four trawlers, and landed in small boats at the northern extremity of Morto Bay, afterwards known as S Beach.

After going into details, it was found that the fleet was now at the end of its resources for small craft, and that boats for only three companies could be provided at this point. The fourth company of the S Beach battalion was accordingly added to the Y Beach landing, with the idea that it should rejoin its unit later. It was also found that no steam launches could be made available for S Beach; but as the distance would be short, and little opposition was expected at the actual landing, it was decided that the men could row themselves ashore.

In broad outline, therefore, the plan of operations as finally approved was that, early on the morning of the day of battle, aided by important demonstrations at such widely separated points as Bulair and Besika Bay, by a diversion on the Asiatic shore at Kum Kale, and by a strong thrust towards the Narrows from a point to the north of Gaba Tepe, the main attack should be developed at the southern end of the peninsula, with Achi Baba for its immediate and the Kilid Bahr plateau for its ultimate objective.[1]

On the five southern beaches a total of 4,900 [2] men would be

---

[1] A simple way of picturing the juxtaposition of the five southern beaches in relation to each other and to the Achi Baba ridge is to place the right hand flat on the table, palm downwards, fingers together, thumb extended, and elbow slightly raised. The top of the elbow is the Achi Baba peak. The wristbone marks the village of Krithia, with Y Beach below it on the right. The tip of the little finger is X Beach; W Beach is between the tips of the second and third fingers; V between the tips of the first and second; while the curve between forefinger and thumb marks Morto Bay, with S Beach at the end of the thumb.

[2] 2,000 at Y to begin landing when the bombardment opened at Helles, and 2,900 to land in the first trip of tows at S, V, W, and X half an hour later.

flung ashore almost simultaneously; these would be reinforced at once by 2,100 men in the *River Clyde*, and shortly afterwards by some 1,200 more in the second trip of tows. The task allotted to these troops, who comprised the fighting ranks of 7½ battalions,[1] was the capture of a covering position to protect the disembarkation of the main body.

In the north, at Z Beach,[2] the first troops to land would number 1,500, to be reinforced from eight destroyers by a further 2,500, bringing the total covering force for the Anzac landing to 4,000 men. The task assigned to this force was the capture of the southern spurs of the Sari Bair ridge overlooking the beach. As soon as this was accomplished the remainder of the 1st Australian Division, followed by the New Zealand and Australian Division, was to land, with its ultimate objective the high ground crossed by the Gallipoli—Maidos and the Boghali—Kojadere roads, and particularly the conical hill of Mal Tepe.[3] Though the main object of this landing by the Anzac corps was to assist the southern attack by preventing the reinforcement of the Kilid Bahr plateau, and by threatening and perhaps cutting the Turkish line of retreat from that position, it was pointed out to the corps commander that if he succeeded in gaining his whole objective, " the results should " be more vital and valuable than the capture of the Kilid Bahr " plateau itself ".[4]

The plan of operations also included a renewal of the naval attack on the Narrows. It was expected that once the army was established on shore, the cruiser squadron, reinforced by one or two battleships, would suffice for its support in the advance on Kilid Bahr, and orders now issued by the admiral included instructions for preliminary naval operations in the Straits on the second day of the landing, followed by a general bombardment of the forts at the Narrows to begin the following day.

The fact that the Allied troops never once succeeded throughout the campaign in capturing Achi Baba[5] has at times been

---

[1] With R.E. and R.A.M.C. units, and naval and military beach personnel.

[2] The six beaches on the peninsula to be used on 25th April were named in inverse alphabetical order, beginning at the Australians' landing place at Anzac, which was at first known as Z Beach. The letter T was omitted as sounding too like V, and the Morto Bay landing place thus became S Beach.

[3] Mal Tepe is supposed to be the hill from which Xerxes reviewed his fleet in the Hellespont.

[4] See Appendix 5.

[5] The story of marines picnicking on its summit during the naval operations in February and March has no foundation in fact.

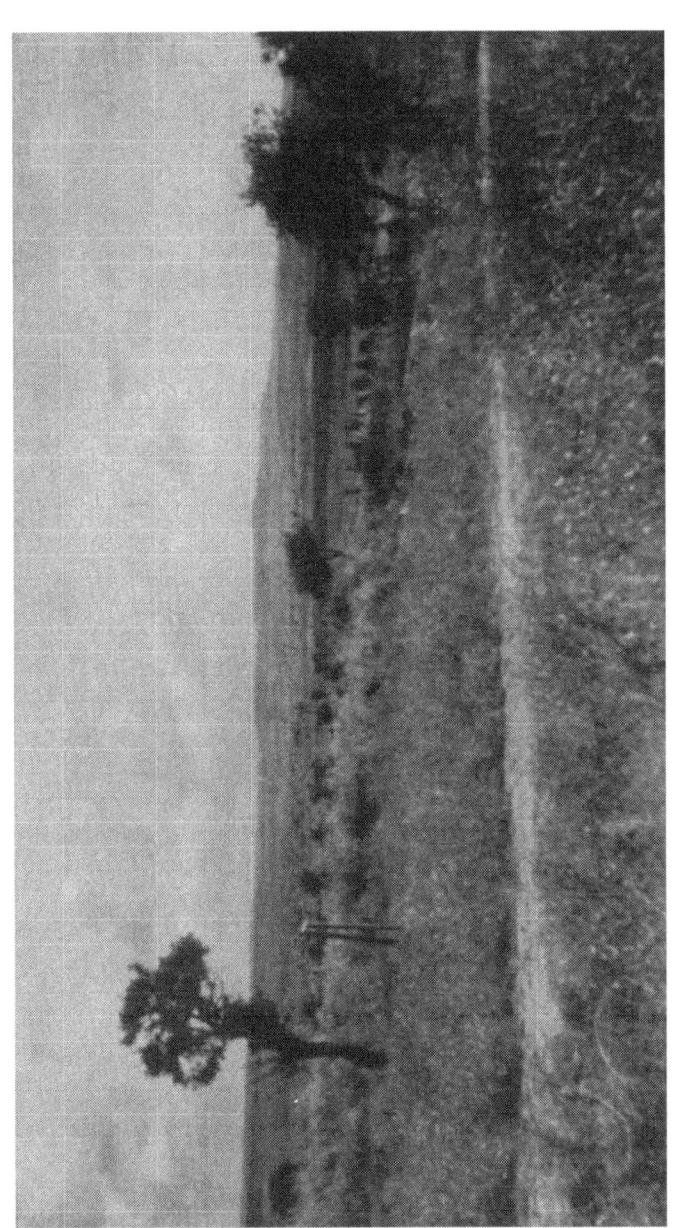

THE ACHI BABA RIDGE FROM THE HIGH GROUND ABOVE V BEACH

FINAL PREPARATIONS AT MUDROS 137

held to prove that the British plan for the 25th April was at fault in giving the 29th Division that distant objective for its first day's task. It will therefore be of interest to examine the reasons which induced G.H.Q. to hope for the capture of the ridge on the first day of the landing. In so doing it must be remembered that although the Achi Baba position eventually became impregnable except against a far more powerful artillery than was ever possessed by the Expeditionary Force, in April 1915 the Turks had done very little to improve its natural advantages for defence.[1]

Anyone who passes through the Dardanelles by daylight has only to glance at that rounded hill standing sentinel over the southern beaches, with its broad shoulders flung east and west across the peninsula, to realize that the British commander could scarcely have decided on a landing at Helles unless he had felt fairly confident of the early capture of that menacing feature, from the summit of which every exit from the beaches was in full view. Such was indeed the case. Sir Ian Hamilton and his Staff were under no illusions as to the bitter fighting that must be expected at the landing and afterwards. But it was believed that once the beaches were captured—and the plan was obviously framed with the expectation that they would be captured—the Turks would offer no serious resistance to the south of their main position on Kilid Bahr.

This belief was founded on three separate hypotheses. Although the reputation of the Turkish soldier as a stubborn fighter behind entrenchments was not overlooked, there was a distinct tendency to underestimate his capacity for open warfare and the general organization and efficiency of the Turkish army as a whole. Available maps showed the southern end of the peninsula as a gentle and even slope;[2] and, in view of the fact that it had not been heavily entrenched, there was a good deal of misplaced confidence as to the effect, in such open country, of the fire of some 200 naval guns. Each of these three

---

[1] Air reconnaissances on 14th and 15th April reported numerous trenches above Helles and Sedd el Bahr, and a strong defensive line on the Kilid Bahr plateau; but up to the day of the landing no air report or photograph showed more than isolated trenches and gun-pits on the slopes of Achi Baba. Owing to faulty equipment and lack of trained observers, air reports before the landing were not very trustworthy, and the first photographs—no cameras were available before 14th April—were unsatisfactory owing to the film being old. Nevertheless the information received on this point proved generally accurate.

[2] Owing to the impossibility of any ground reconnaissance before the landing, and to the lack of trained observers for air reconnaissance it was not fully realized till after the landing that the country was in reality deeply scarred by numerous water-courses and offered many natural advantages to the defence.

hypotheses was unfortunately incorrect. Yet, read in its true light, the story of the 25th April gives little ground for the view that the British plan was unduly optimistic. In many a hard-fought battle there is a moment when the ever-widening gap which finally separates failure from success is little broader than a thread; and it will be seen in a subsequent chapter that with a greater share of good fortune, and fewer casualties amongst their battalion commanders and brigadiers, it might not have proved impossible for the magnificent troops of the 29th Division to carry out the difficult task allotted to them on the 25th April.

The slight tendency at British headquarters before the landing to underestimate the efficiency of the Turkish military machine is capable of explanation. Up to the middle of April 1915 the record of the Turkish army in the war had been a record of failure; and to those who did not know of the vast improvements effected by the German military mission—as evidenced by the campaign in the Caucasus—there seemed little reason to think that its value had improved since the defeats of 1912. All that was known at Mediterranean G.H.Q. about the Caucasus was that a large Turkish army had surrendered almost *en masse* at Sarikamish in January.[1] The incident at Alexandretta in December 1914 suggested that the Turk had no great enthusiasm for a war against Britain.[2] The attack on Egypt had collapsed. In Mesopotamia the story seemed much the same. Basra had fallen to an Indian division in November, and Qurna had been occupied a few weeks later without serious difficulty.

On the 19th April Lord Kitchener telegraphed a very different story to Sir Ian Hamilton about recent fighting near Basra. There the Turks had displayed an admirable spirit. They were spoken of as well-disciplined, well-trained, and brave. They had handled their machine guns with great effect. They had only been turned out of their trenches by the bayonet; and nothing but skilful leadership and indomitable pluck had gained the day for the British. This telegram, however, did not extinguish the hopes of Mediterranean G.H.Q. that Achi Baba would be captured on the first day. It ended with the news that, after losing their trenches, the Turks had retired 19 miles in the night, and continued their retreat next morning. This was precisely what the Turks in Gallipoli were expected to do when driven from their trenches at Helles and Sedd el Bahr. But Lord Kitchener had read the right lesson from recent events in Mesopotamia. The impressions formed by

[1] See page 52.   [2] See page 53.

FINAL PREPARATIONS AT MUDROS 139

the earlier widely separated defeats were fundamentally wrong; and the Turk in 1915 was an efficient as well as a brave antagonist.

It had been decided by Lord Kitchener that any air requirements of the army must be met by the Royal Naval Air Service. The shortage of air equipment during the first stages of the campaign has already been mentioned; but at the end of March No. 3 Squadron R.N.A.S. arrived, and from that date, though no cameras were available for another fortnight, matters began to improve. Bombing flights were now undertaken, and a certain amount of information was collected. But the lack of observers was still a difficulty, and reliance had to be placed on volunteers, who learnt their work as they went along. The weather, too, was still unfavourable for flying, and between the 19th March and the 24th April there were nine days when no flying at all was possible, and twenty-four more when the full air programme could not be carried out.

Fortunately for the British cause, the Turkish army was equally short of aeroplanes. Nevertheless, from the 11th April onwards a hostile plane constantly flew over Mudros harbour, where there was unfortunately no suitable machine to set against it,[1] and Turkish headquarters was thus kept well aware of the growing size of the British armada.[2]

It will give some idea of the difficulties of the air situation at this time to notice that General Birdwood's request for two machines to be allotted to his front for the day of the landing could not be granted, owing to lack of landing grounds nearer than Tenedos, though that island was only thirty miles away from the Anzac front. Two planes, working from Tenedos, were allotted to the southern landing, which was nearer by ten miles to their base, but the Anzac landing could only be supported by a balloon ship with one kite balloon.

By the middle of April practically the whole of the Australian and New Zealand Corps and the 29th Division had assembled at Mudros. Even that immense harbour was now so crowded with vessels of every imaginable description, from the majestic *Queen Elizabeth* to the humble North Sea trawler, and from the proud Atlantic liner to the dirtiest of Thames tugs, that another

[1] " One of our lumbering seaplanes went up after it like an owl in " sunlight, but could rise no higher than the masts of the Fleet." Hamilton, " Gallipoli Diary," i. p. 102.
[2] The Turks had other means, too, of learning the course of events at Mudros. The island was under British governorship, but it was impossible to control the whole civilian population, or to guard against any leakage of information by means of the small local craft trading between the islands of the Ægean.

rendezvous for the thirty-four transports of the French and the Royal Naval Division had to be found at Trebuki Bay.[1] This unavoidable dispersion increased in an unexpected way the difficulties of inter-communication at a moment when the concentration of the whole force would have simplified the question of Staff conferences and the prompt receipt of naval and military orders. It added, moreover, to the difficulties of collecting the various transports at their allotted stations on the actual day of landing. Yet so carefully were all the arrangements worked out by the naval transport officers [2] and so close was the co-operation of the masters of the various transports, that no hitch of any kind occurred. The marshalling of nearly one hundred merchant ships without mishap or accident, and strictly in accordance with the time-table, is a feat that will appeal to every seafaring man.[3]

The question of a day or night disembarkation was finally decided at a joint naval and military conference. Sir Ian Hamilton personally favoured the night, as also did General Birdwood, arguing that though the support of naval guns would thus be lost, the troops would be spared the ordeal of sitting helpless in their boats under a well-directed fire from the shore. It was suggested by General Hunter-Weston, on the other hand, that in the absence of any previous land reconnaissance there would be great confusion and loss of direction in a night landing when once the troops were ashore. It was probable, too, that in bright starlight approaching boats would be seen from the shore while still a long way out, and that the fire from machine guns unshaken by naval bombardment might be so deadly that it would be wiser to trust to the guns of the fleet being able to subdue them by day. Finally,

---

[1] In the island of Skyros, about eighty miles from Mudros.

[2] Shortly after the return of Sir Ian Hamilton to Mudros, in order to simplify the co-ordination of all plans connected with the landing, Captain D. L. Dent, R.N., the principal naval transport officer, accompanied by an office staff consisting of his steward, cook, and coxswain, joined the G.H.Q. transport *Arcadian*, where his office was established in the only part of the ship still available—a portion of the saloon pantry. Captain F. H. Mitchell, R.N., who had been acting as naval adviser to G.H.Q. during their absence in Egypt, was appointed assistant to the P.N.T.O., and Commander H. V. Simpson R.N. (retired) and three other officers were added to his establishment a few days later. It was in this slenderly staffed office that all the transport arrangements for the landing were worked out.

[3] One transport, the *Manitou*, on passage from Alexandria to Mudros, had a narrow escape from being torpedoed by a Turkish torpedo-boat which had boldly slipped out from Smyrna, eluding the British blockade. Fortunately, however, all three torpedoes missed their target, and the *Manitou* reached port in safety. The torpedo-boat was subsequently chased by British destroyers and ran herself aground on Chios Island.

FINAL PREPARATIONS AT MUDROS

naval opinion decided the issue, so far as the southern landing was concerned, by stating that it would be impossible to guarantee that the tows could make their various beaches in the dark, as the strong current which sets out of the Dardanelles might carry them out of their course. There was also the danger of uncharted rocks. In these circumstances, it was decided that the southern landing should take place about 5.30 A.M.[1] after half an hour's bombardment beginning as soon as it was light enough to see. North of Gaba Tepe, where the beach was extensive, the current weaker,[2] and rocks less likely, it was determined to land the covering force in the dark, in the hope that it might reach the shore unopposed and gain a firm footing before daylight. It was also decided that the landing at Y Beach should begin simultaneously with the naval bombardment at Helles and Sedd el Bahr. At the same conference the date of the landing was definitely fixed, weather permitting, for the 23rd April.[3] All the preparations would be safely completed by that date, and there was the added advantage that on the 23rd April the moon would set about two hours before dawn, thus minimizing the risk of the battleships for General Birdwood's covering force being silhouetted against the moon in their passage from Imbros to the peninsula.

During the concentration of the army at Mudros and Trebuki Bay every chance was seized to exercise the troops in harbour in getting noiselessly into small boats, in rowing, and in landing silently and quickly. Whenever the water at Mudros was calm enough for these exercises, which unfortunately was not often, the harbour was alive with ships' boats crowded with laughing men, and this training did much to keep them healthy and in good spirits during their enforced idleness. Opportunity was also taken to practise the two thousand men detailed for the *River Clyde* in rapidly disembarking from that vessel in full marching order, carrying everything that they were to take ashore on the day of battle. A pamphlet was also issued to units, giving extracts from the various textbooks with regard to landings and combined work with the navy.

In order to give officers as good an idea as possible of the ground they were to fight over, it was arranged that parties of

---

[1] Eastern Mediterranean time was used by the army and navy, *i.e.* two hours in advance of G.M.T. The time was given daily to G.H.Q. Signal Coy. by the flagship, and communicated to all formations at 8 A.M. Hours were reckoned 0 to 24, one minute after midnight being written 00.01, and one minute before midnight, 23.59.

[2] Unfortunately the current off Gaba Tepe was to prove far stronger than anticipated.

[3] Owing to bad weather the date was subsequently altered to 25th.

staff and commanding officers should be sent up to Tenedos and taken for a cruise along the coast in patrolling destroyers. The Turk was already so well aware of the British preparations that there can have been little harm in these reconnaissance patrols. But to be on the safe side, special warnings were issued against appearing on deck in military uniform while near the peninsula.

Meanwhile the navy continued to keep the whole coast-line under observation, and to interfere as much as possible with the enemy's defensive work. It was as a result of this careful observation that two days before the landing the important news reached General Headquarters from the *Queen Elizabeth* that a length of sixty yards on the west side of W Beach was free of wire but was probably mined, and that in fine weather a few boats could land under the cliffs to the north-west of the beach without difficulty.[1]

The navy's plans to assist the army included a daring scheme for sending submarines up the Straits into the Marmara before the army landed, to prey upon the Turkish sea-communications with Constantinople. The Dardanelles garrison was known to be dependent on the capital for its ammunition and stores, for most of its supplies, and for all its reinforcements. These could be sent either by sea or land, but it was believed that the Turks were relying chiefly on the sea route, and this in fact was true. By sea the peninsula was less than 150 miles from the Golden Horn, and disembarkation in any of the quiet bays of the land-locked Dardanelles was a simple operation. The land route on the other hand was open to many objections. The journey by train to the nearest railhead, Uzun Keupri, was 150 miles from Constantinople, and thence by road to the Narrows was another 100 miles, or about seven days' march. The road was in a fair state of repair, but the Turks had no motor transport, and all stores and ammunition sent by this route had to be carried in bullock or buffalo carts with a maximum speed of about $2\frac{1}{2}$ miles an hour. The capacity of the road was therefore very limited, and it was plain to the Turks that without the free use of the Marmara route it would be difficult to maintain a large force in the peninsula and almost impossible to ensure an adequate supply of artillery ammunition. A further objection to the land route was that near Bulair the road could be kept under fire by warships in the Gulf of Saros, and that movement would probably be restricted to the hours

---

[1] This important information was repeated to the 29th Division on 23rd April, but unfortunately did not reach the brigade concerned.

FINAL PREPARATIONS AT MUDROS

of darkness, thus reducing still further the capacity of the road.

In these early days, when the fleet was expecting to reach the Marmara a few days after the army landed, and when there was no thought of a long military campaign on the peninsula, there was small expectation of the submarines being useful to the army unless they could get through the Straits some little time before the landing took place. But from what has been said above it will be clear that in the event of the army being held up and the navy being unable to force the Narrows, submarine action in the Marmara was likely to have an important influence on the fortunes of the campaign.

The passage of the closely watched and strongly defended Straits by submarine was a task of extreme peril, and though Lieut. Holbrook's exploit in December had shown that it was probably possible to complete the whole journey, it was almost certain that that warning had induced the Turks to strengthen their submarine defences. The result of the first attempt to get through was awaited, therefore, with keen anxiety.

The first attempt was made by Submarine *E15* (Lieut.-Commander T. S. Brodie) on the 17th April, and unfortunately ended in failure. Carried out of her course by the swift current, the vessel grounded near Kephez Point;[1] the commander and six of his men were killed by Turkish shell-fire, and the rest of the crew made prisoner. It now became imperative to prevent the submarine falling into German hands, and after several attempts to destroy her had failed, this hazardous task was at last accomplished by two picket boats under Lieut.-Commander E. G. Robinson[2] and Lieut. C. H. Godwin. Manned by volunteer crews, these two small boats, each towing a torpedo, crept up the Dardanelles at night till they were opposite Kephez. Here they were discovered by the Turkish searchlight and came under heavy fire. But the Turkish beam simultaneously disclosed the stranded submarine. Both torpedoes were fired at her, and though Lieut. Godwin's boat was immediately afterwards hit and began to sink, its occupants were rescued by the other boat and the whole party got safely out of the Straits with only one casualty. Next morning an aeroplane sent to examine the wreck reported that the torpedo attack had been successful.

[1] By a pathetic coincidence the observer in the aeroplane, which was accompanying the submarine up the Straits and saw her run aground, was Lieut.-Commander Brodie's twin brother.
[2] Lieut.-Commander Robinson had won the V.C. for his demolition work at Kum Kale on 26th February (see page 78), and for gallant service with the mine-sweepers.

After this disaster several days elapsed before the attempt to send a submarine up the Straits was repeated, and the Turkish sea-communications remained undisturbed till after the landing. But, as will be described in a later chapter, the Australian submarine *AE2* made the passage on the 25th April: from that date onwards there was always at least one submarine in the Marmara; and the activities of these vessels were so successful that from the middle of May the Sea of Marmara was practically closed to Turkish shipping.

The long distance separating the peninsula from the British overseas base in Egypt was to place an inevitable strain on the administrative services and departments and particularly on the medical service in their plans for the care of the wounded. Owing to the impracticability of opening large hospitals at Mudros till a better water supply could be secured, it was decided early in April that all casualties must at first be evacuated to Egypt or Malta.[1] For this purpose four general hospitals were established at Cairo and Alexandria, with room for 4,500 patients, and accommodation for at least 3,000 more cases was arranged in Malta. Though these numbers did not seem excessive, it is curious to notice that no exception was taken at that time to the inadequate allotment of only two hospital ships to the Expeditionary Force for the voyage between these widely separated hospitals and the Dardanelles.[2] It would appear that in the early stages of the preparations no attempt was made to predict the number of casualties likely to be suffered in the landing. After the return of G.H.Q. to Mudros, however, this subject was carefully examined, and though no figure could be more than guesswork, the losses incurred at the battle of Mons were taken as a basis of calculation. In that action the two divisions of the II. Corps had a total loss of 1,500 killed, wounded, and missing, or roughly 7·5 per cent of the 20,000 infantry engaged. In order to be on the safe side, it was determined to increase the Mons figures, and to anticipate that, in the fighting for the beaches, the three divisions to be first engaged would sustain a loss of 3,000, or 10 per cent of their infantry, in wounded alone, exclusive of missing and killed.

[1] Egypt was two to three days' and Malta four to five days' journey from the peninsula.
[2] On 6th April Lord Kitchener asked by telegram whether the Director of Medical Services was satisfied with the adequacy of the medical arrangements, and instructed him to make any further demands he considered necessary. On the 8th, with the concurrence of the Adjutant-General, General Birrell replied that the arrangements already made appeared sufficient.

FINAL PREPARATIONS AT MUDROS

It was obvious that if these figures were reached, the two hospital ships, with a total accommodation for only 700 serious cases, would be quite inadequate, and arrangements were now made for one transport for the northern and one for the southern landing to be equipped with medical personnel and stores sufficient for the care of 1,000 light cases each. The arrangement by which all casualties were to be evacuated to the base was adhered to; the wounded were to be embarked in specially equipped small craft from central collecting stations on each beach, and orders embracing these various points were issued on the 14th April. Four days later, however, on the arrival at Mudros of the Adjutant-General and the Director of Medical Services, these two officers urged that it would be unsafe to prepare for less than 10,000 casualties in the initial fighting, that the number of transports to be prepared for the accommodation of wounded should be increased from two to eight, and that two stationary hospitals should be ordered to sail forthwith from Egypt to supply the necessary medical personnel. These proposals were agreed to, the only stipulation being that in view of the possibility of a forced re-embarkation, so large a number of transports must not be despatched from the peninsula till at least 48 hours after the troops had established themselves ashore.

A few days later the situation was immensely improved by the allotment to the Expeditionary Force of two more hospital ships for the ferry service to the base.[1] In addition, a fifth hospital ship was sent from Egypt to clear the Australian hospital which had been established at Mudros since the middle of March and was now full to overflowing.

But no matter how many hospital ships and transports equipped as casualty carriers [2] were available off the peninsula, it was obvious that the weakest link in the chain of evacuation must be the actual embarkation of the wounded on an open beach while fighting was still in progress in the immediate neighbourhood. The dictates of humanity, apart from the necessity of preventing the tiny beaches becoming overcrowded with non-effective men, called for the prompt embarkation of every casualty. Yet it was even more important, and in fact vital, that the disembarkation of the fighting troops, their ammunition, food, and water, should not be interfered with; and all available small craft would be needed for this latter

[1] These vessels did not arrive until just after the landing had begun, and they were not included in the memorandum by the D.M.S. dated 24th April (Appendix 11).
[2] These vessels were subsequently known as the "black ships" by the force, to distinguish them from the white-painted hospital ships.

service. It was this question that offered the greatest obstacle to a satisfactory solution. It opened up a problem not only without precedent in modern war, but one which, before the inception of the Dardanelles campaign, had formed no part of the training either of the Staff or the medical services. Apart from the meagre instructions that "sanitary and medical officers " should be landed amongst the first troops of the main body", and that, in the event of a forced re-embarkation, "wounded " men, if they cannot be re-embarked during daylight, and " without interfering with the re-embarkation of the other " troops and material, must be left on shore and the best " arrangements possible made for their care", the pre-war textbooks can be searched in vain for any reference to this important and thorny subject.

In these difficult circumstances, Sir Ian Hamilton adhered to the principle that tactical requirements must be pre-eminent. He laid down that small craft engaged on disembarking troops must on no account be diverted to take wounded to the waiting ships, and that this work must be undertaken solely by specially equipped pulling launches which the navy would make available in the afternoon of the day of landing, as soon as steamboats to tow them could be spared. Unfortunately only six of these launches in all were available, and each launch could carry only twelve serious cases in cots, or treble that number of light cases. It was recognized that these arrangements could not fail to inflict hardship on the wounded, but this was looked upon as unavoidable in the peculiar circumstances of the case, as indeed it probably was. To do everything possible for the wounded on shore it had already been arranged that portions of a field ambulance should land with the covering force at each main landing, and that the remainder of these ambulances should be ashore by 2 P.M. on the first day. It was also hoped that special arrangements could be made to embark large numbers of wounded during the first night, and that a rapid advance by the troops would enable those casualties which could not be embarked to be looked after in comparative comfort and security in the neighbourhood of the beaches.

On the 19th April the detail of naval and military beach personnel for supervising the disembarkation at the various beaches was published by G.H.Q. At the three beaches at the south of the peninsula the military personnel consisted of a number of specially selected officers, the 2nd London Field Company R.E., and two and a half companies of the Anson Battalion, Royal Naval Division. The latter were to supply beach and working parties, while the field company was to work on

FINAL PREPARATIONS AT MUDROS 147

exits, piers, jetties, and water stations. The beaches at Anzac were equipped on a similar scale.[1]

As regards naval covering fire to support the landing and the subsequent advance of the troops, both the army and navy in these early days had everything to learn with regard to the best means of directing and controlling naval fire on shore targets. Careful arrangements were, however, co-ordinated between the 29th Division and Admiral Nicholson who was to command the covering squadron.

Artillery observation officers would, in all cases—except at Y Beach—land with the leading troops, and others would be present in the ships. Communication from ship to shore was to be both by visual signalling and wireless, the latter to be used as soon as stations could be established on V, W, and X Beaches. Arrangements were made for repeating shore signals from ship to ship as required, and it was hoped that aeroplanes, using wireless, would supplement the above means of observation. All located Turkish defences were plotted on a map which was issued to supporting ships; the ground was divided into areas, and each ship was allotted special areas to be kept under observation.

In the first instance a particular effort was to be made to demolish all defences and buildings commanding the beaches; and all located batteries, whose fire could reach the beaches and anchorages, were to be engaged with increasing intensity as the first tows went in to land. It was further arranged between the army and the fleet that, during the operations, naval searchlights should not be turned on to the land except at the direct request of the army.

Amongst the minor mishaps at this time, was the discovery on the 20th April that one of the Commander-in-Chief's clerks had contracted small-pox, with the result that everyone on board the headquarters ship *Arcadian* had to be hurriedly vaccinated next morning—a curiously unfortunate time for so fretful a proceeding. For the most part officers and men were lined up together in the big saloon; but an exception was made in favour of Sir Ian Hamilton and his Chief of the General Staff, who were visited in their cabins by a special operator. In some

---

[1] The actual numbers to be employed at the three southern beaches were as follows:

	X Beach.		W Beach.		V Beach.		Total.	
	Off.	O.R.	Off.	O.R.	Off.	O.R.	Off.	O.R.
Naval	6	30	14	80	10	50	30	160
Military	8	200	22	500	13	300	43	1000
Grand Total							73	1160

cases the vaccination "took" very severely, and the two senior officers carried their arms in slings for the next three weeks.

The disadvantage of assembling a large portion of the force at Trebuki has already been mentioned, but it soon turned out that even in Mudros it was impossible to keep up an efficient service of intercommunication between the vast number of transports in harbour. Naval wireless, except in the case of extreme urgency, was not available; visual signalling, with so large a crowd of vessels in port, was impossible except for adjacent ships. The water was often too rough, and the distances too great, for the use of rowing boats. The only means of inter-communication was therefore by sea-going steam launch, and there were never enough of these vessels for the amount of work to be done. Even in the case of headquarters transports it was often impossible for a third of their needs to be met;[1] and great difficulty was found in conveying commanding officers and their staffs to attend conferences or to visit the various units under their command. Battalion commanders, anxious to consult their brigadiers, were often virtually prisoners on board ship; while in some cases officers arriving unadvised in harbour on urgent business were marooned in their transports for days before they could report their arrival. To facilitate the despatch of signal messages endeavours were made by General Headquarters to establish a regular service of steamboats between the *Arcadian* and the assembled transports three times a day; but owing to lack of steamboats this service broke down. The most that could be attained was one round trip per day; and this service, in addition to being useless to individual officers wishing to go in an opposite direction, was often suspended owing to rough weather. Shortage of steamboats, and the constant rough seas in harbour, similarly added to the difficulty of carrying out the re-shuffling of units necessitated by changes in the landing scheme. The majority of these movements had to be deferred to a fine day, when the troops rowed themselves to their new quarters in ships' boats.

To a land force, accustomed to the use of telephones, motor cars, and cyclist orderlies for the prompt despatch of business, these very inadequate means of inter-communication were peculiarly irritating and were sometimes a positive danger. Numerous instances could be quoted, but one will suffice. On the afternoon of the 20th April a junior staff officer of the 29th Division started on a steam launch to deliver the

[1] It is recorded in the A.N.Z.A.C. war diary that on the Anzac H.Q. transport alone, on 21st April, 206 outward and 66 inward messages passed through the corps signal office.

FINAL PREPARATIONS AT MUDROS

orders for the landing. Heavy seas put out the fires of his launch, which drifted out to sea, to be picked up later by a man-of-war. Next morning the officer was able to return to his transport, but meanwhile most of the orders had not been delivered.

To allow all the warships, transports, tugs, lighters, and small craft to reach their respective beaches in the early hours of the 23rd April, it was necessary, owing to the large number of vessels to be passed out of Mudros Harbour, for the forward movement of the ships and lighters employed in the southern operations to begin on the afternoon of the 21st. These vessels were to rendezvous early on the 22nd to the north of Tenedos, where various final adjustments, such as transference of stores to the lighters, and embarkation of the covering force in the men-of-war and the *River Clyde*, would be undertaken. The force for the Anzac landing was to leave Mudros during the 22nd, and similar adjustments would be undertaken at a rendezvous off Imbros the same evening.

By the 20th April the last preparations for the forward movement had been completed; all the troops concerned in the initial operations had assembled at Mudros; and all that was now awaited was the prospect of fine weather. But at that moment so far as the elements were concerned, the prospect was alarming. The glass spoke only of danger; the wind was blowing hard, with driving showers from the north-east. Throughout the whole preparatory period the caprice of the weather had been a source of unending trouble and anxiety. From the time of Sir Ian Hamilton's arrival at Tenedos on the 17th March there had scarcely been two consecutive fine days, and at no moment since that date would it have been safe to begin the landing even if his whole force had accompanied him, with every plan ready. The months of March and April are normally unsettled in the Ægean, and continuous spells of fine weather can never be counted on till about the beginning of May. Yet a succession of fine days was essential for the success of the landing. Even a moderate wind from any other quarter than the north or north-east would suffice to bring the operation to a standstill.

Thus it will be seen that not the least serious of the odds to be accepted by the Expeditionary Force was the fact that the whole edifice of the naval and military plans was at the mercy of the weather. Only when this is remembered, and the fact that, whatever date was selected for the landing, the whole machine would have to be set in motion thirty-six hours beforehand, is it possible to gain some faint conception of the anxieties of the naval Commander-in-Chief, on whom rested the responsibility for choosing the moment for the operations to begin.

On the 21st April the morning broke with half a gale of wind. It was impossible for the small craft to start for Tenedos; and the admiral had to postpone the date of landing, first for 24 hours and then for 48. But on the morning of the 23rd the weather was at last fine and clear; and, though not without acute misgiving, Admiral de Robeck ordered the movement to begin. His choice was not mistaken. From that moment the weather set fair, and continued to be almost ideal throughout the period of the landing.

During these days of anxious tension for all ranks a Special Order was issued to the British and French troops by Sir Ian Hamilton, and a heartening telegram of good wishes was received from Lord Kitchener. Finally, on the 22nd April, the army was inspired by a gracious message from the King:

To Sir Ian Hamilton

The King wishes you and your army every success, and you are all constantly in His Majesty's thoughts and prayers.

On this day the ominous news reached Mudros that two German submarines had passed through the Straits of Gibraltar, heading east.

One final provision required to be made, and this was completed by the morning of the 24th April. In view of the distinct possibility of failure it was essential to consider the best line of action to be taken in such an emergency. At that time the likelihood of what may be termed a partial success was not considered. Though the serious opposition likely to be encountered in the fight for the Kilid Bahr plateau was well realized, it was believed that in the actual landing, the odds would be so much in favour of the defending force that the capture of the shore defences must be the supreme difficulty to be encountered by the troops. It was held that either the beaches would be captured and a substantial advance completed immediately afterwards; or that the troops would definitely fail to establish themselves ashore at one or both of the main points of landing. It was to meet the case of either of these latter alternatives that a General Staff memorandum was prepared.[1]

No details were included in this paper; for the possibility of making a new attempt to land elsewhere in the event of initial failure depended on the extent of the loss in boats at

[1] Appendix 13.

FINAL PREPARATIONS AT MUDROS

the original points of disembarkation, and it was impossible for more than the general outline of an alternative plan to be prepared beforehand.

The 23rd and 24th April were days of matchless beauty, and the glistening splendour of sea and sky was a picture such as can only be found in the Ægean, and there only in days of early spring. To all who watched, amid those exquisite surroundings, the crowded ships of the covering force steam slowly out of Mudros, that unforgettable pageant of British manhood moving into battle is engraved on heart and mind as a proud and poignant memory. The task in front of the troops was one that no other army had ever been called upon to face; and they were facing it as a long-expected holiday.[1] As each transport passed through the waiting fleet, cheer upon cheer broke out from her crowded decks and the watching bluejackets cheered and cheered again. The die was now cast. With the issue shrouded in uncertainty, one fact alone was clear. If the capture of the beaches was humanly possible, those gallant troops would do it.

Shortly after midday on the 24th Sir Ian Hamilton, accompanied by a few officers of his General Staff, proceeded on board the *Queen Elizabeth* in order to be in close touch with the naval Commander-in-Chief during the crucial hours of the landing. A few minutes later, attended by the *Arcadian* with the rest of General Headquarters on board, the flagship weighed anchor and shaped her course for Tenedos.

As the moon climbed slowly to her zenith on the night of the 24th April, lighting up the rugged coast of Imbros and the sombre outline of the peninsula, the sleeping waters of the northern Ægean were dotted with nearly two hundred vessels heading for their various rendezvous. Away to the north, led by the battleship *Canopus*, were the ships of the Royal Naval Division and their supporting squadron, bound for the Gulf of Saros. To the east of Imbros were the transports of the Anzac corps, their covering squadron, their numerous trawlers and small craft, and their attendant battleships and destroyers packed with eager troops. Further south, near Tenedos, were the vessels allotted to the Helles landing; and further south again the French squadrons heading for the Asiatic shore.

The period of preparation, with all its cares and anxieties, was at an end. The hour for action had arrived. Everything

[1] On one of the transports the name "Turkish Delight" had been surreptitiously painted by the troops: another bore the words "to "Constantinople and the Harems" in large white letters on her side.

that the naval and military commanders could think of to smooth the path of the troops had been done. The final issue, as always, lay with the infantry. It was they who must bear the brunt. It was they who must turn to best account the orders, good or bad, that had committed them to their various tasks. It was they who must answer whether even British and Australian troops could triumph in the face of such gigantic difficulties.

Small wonder that Enver Pasha, after two full months of warning, believed that the Gallipoli defences were unassailable and that no troops in the world could now succeed in landing. Yet in a few more hours those silent forms on board the battleships, snatching, so many of them, their last hours of sleep, were to win undying fame. They were to add another jewel to the setting of the British Army's renown, and, by the example of their heroism, to gain a priceless heritage for future generations.

CHAPTER VIII

Final Preparations by the Turks

(Sketches 5, 5A)

HERE let us leave for a moment the crowded transports as they steal towards the unknown, and examine in the light of after knowledge the use made by the Turks of the five weeks' respite so unexpectedly afforded them by the Allies.

It has been well said that the art of successful invasion is to strike before the defender is fully prepared, and to break down his power of resistance before he has time to restore the balance. No conquest can be completed too rapidly, for delay in the consummation of success gives time for a crop of difficulties to spring up in the face of the invader. The unfortunate but inevitable delay between the naval attack of the 18th March and the military landing on the 25th April was fated to re-affirm this century-old doctrine, and the invaders were to suffer dearly for the lack of earlier preparation.

On the 24th March Enver Pasha, the Turkish War Lord, had made a sudden and far-reaching decision. While the British and French troops already collected for the attack on the peninsula were steaming away from the scene of action to re-pack their transports in Egypt, he at last determined to combine the various Turkish formations at the Dardanelles into one Army command, and to place the fortunes of this new Army, and incidentally the destinies of the whole Empire, in the capable hands of Marshal[1] Liman von Sanders.

Mar. 1915.

Liman von Sanders at once accepted the proffered post, but fully conscious of the onerous nature of the task, he begged that not a moment should be lost in reinforcing to the utmost possible extent the garrison already assembled in the area. The hurried departure of the new Commander-in-Chief from Constantinople bears a curious resemblance to that of his British adversary from London eleven days earlier. There was

[1] General Liman van Sanders held the temporary rank of Marshal in the Turkish army.

no time to collect a Staff, and he sailed from the capital the following evening, accompanied only by his Turkish Chief of Staff, Kiasim Bey, and two German orderly officers, leaving the rest of the new Army headquarters to follow at the first opportunity. It may here be noticed that with the exception of one German captain, the whole of the *Fifth Army* Staff was to consist of Turkish officers.[1]

Disembarking at Gallipoli town on the 26th March, Liman at once set himself to remodel the existing defence scheme from top to bottom. "Quite contrary to my principles," he writes, "the troops were scattered all along the coast like the frontier "detachments of days gone by. Everywhere the enemy would "meet with a certain amount of opposition, but the absence of "reserves precluded the possibility of a sustained and vigorous "defence."[2] He accordingly gave orders that each division was to concentrate immediately, and that only the indispensable minimum of outpost troops were to be left to guard the coast.

It is impossible to trace the exact location of the Turkish forces in the Dardanelles area at the time of Liman's arrival, but their general distribution was roughly as follows: On the mainland, north of the peninsula, spread out along the coast of the Gulf of Saros, was the *5th Division*. The *7th Division* was holding the Bulair lines, and guarding likely landing places in the neighbourhood of the isthmus, while two gendarmerie battalions watched the coast between that point and the southern arm of Suvla Bay. The protection of the peninsula from Suvla to Sedd el Bahr was shared by the *9th* and *19th Divisions*, the latter a new formation commanded by Mustafa Kemal Bey. But half of the *9th Division* was detached to the Asiatic side of the Straits at Kum Kale and Yeni Shehr. The *11th Division* was on the Asiatic shore, one regiment at Chanak and the remainder at Besika Bay, while three gendarmerie battalions (there were by this time five in the area) were spread out along the Asiatic side. From a technical point of view the situation was further complicated by the fact that the troops at Sedd el Bahr, Kum Kale, and Yeni Shehr were under the immediate orders, not of their divisional commanders, but of the officer commanding the forts and batteries of the Straits.

No aircraft were allotted to the field troops. The few machines at Chanak belonged to the fortress command, and barely sufficed for its needs.

[1] Later, according to the report of a neutral military attaché, there were three German staff officers at *Fifth Army H.Q.*, and one at each divisional H.Q. The chief artillery officer was also a German.
[2] "Fünf Jahre Türkei," pp. 81-2.

FINAL PREPARATIONS BY THE TURKS 155

Including the troops for the Bosporus defences there were at this time nine divisions in and around Constantinople. But though one of these, the *3rd Division*, was ordered to the Dardanelles about the 25th March, the move was not completed till the end of the first week in April. This division was followed shortly afterwards by a cavalry brigade, and the Turkish official account states that after its arrival the total strength of the troops in the Dardanelles area amounted to 84,000 men.[1] This number obviously includes all ancillary services and departments, as also a certain number of unarmed labour companies, but the number of rifles in the area cannot have been less than 45,000.

In his memoirs of the campaign Liman von Sanders describes in some detail the problem that faced the defenders of the Straits in the spring of 1915, and though this appreciation[2] was written after the event, and with a more or less detailed knowledge of the ground, it is of interest to compare it with the British appreciation drawn up on the 23rd March.[3]

The German general considered that a landing on the Asiatic shore, in the neighbourhood of Besika Bay, was the invader's most likely plan of attack, for at that point, helped by the proximity of the island of Tenedos, a strong force could quickly be thrown ashore. There were other reasons, too, that seemed to favour an attack in this locality. High ground near the coast afforded excellent positions for artillery supporting an advance across the Mendere plain; the river and marshes in the neighbourhood offered no great obstacles to movement in the spring and summer; road communications were adequate; the most important defences of the Straits were on the Asiatic side, and as these defences were very vulnerable to land attack, an operation designed to take them in reverse offered real chance of success.[4]

---

[1] Liman von Sanders claims that his army at this time did not exceed 60,000, but he is probably referring to "fighting strength", for Turkish documents give a " fighting strength " of 62,077.
[2] " Fünf Jahre Türkei," pp. 80-1.   [3] See pages 111 *et seq.*
[4] Major Sherman Miles, General Staff U.S. Army, lately military attaché at Constantinople, in a series of illuminating articles on the campaign contributed to the American " Coast Artillery Journal " after four extended visits to the peninsula, suggests that Liman's appreciation smacks of a desire to justify his dispositions. " To one who has gone " over the ground from Chanak to Kum Kale ", he writes, " the ad- " vantages of this [Asiatic] plan are not apparent. The country which " an allied advance would have had to traverse is even more rugged and " difficult than that of the peninsula. . . . The route of march would " have been considerably longer. Both allied flanks would have been " exposed, the left to artillery fire from the peninsula, and the right to " attack by Turkish troops."

April. On the peninsula itself there seemed to Liman to be three specially favourable localities for a landing in force. First came the beaches at the southern end of the peninsula, which the British fleet could sweep with its fire on three sides at once. Should a landing take place here, he thought, "the enemy's "immediate objective, and one of decisive importance, would "be the heights of Achi Baba".[1]

The second favourable locality on the peninsula for obtaining a definite decision appeared to him to be a stretch of coast on either side of Gaba Tepe, where an open plain led straight to Maidos and to hills which would facilitate the reduction of the coast batteries. He noticed that the overhanging cliffs of the Sari Bair massif would afford the British a well-protected landing place to the north of Gaba Tepe, but he judged that the capture of the whole massif would have to be an essential part of any plan for an advance across the Maidos plain.

It was, however, to the neighbourhood of Bulair that the German commander looked with the greatest apprehension, for he considered that in the capture of the isthmus lay the strategic solution of the problem of the Dardanelles. With this narrow belt of country in the hands of the Allies, he was of opinion that all communication with Constantinople by sea as well as by land would be severed, for he counted that British long-range guns, helped by searchlights at night, could make it practically impossible for unarmoured vessels to enter the Straits, and that British submarines could effectually complete the blockade.[2]

To guard these various danger points Liman von Sanders had five divisions at his immediate disposal, while a sixth was to be sent from the capital as soon as shipping could be provided. It was impossible to be strong everywhere, and in accordance with his principle of concentration of force, he decided to divide his command into three combat groups, and to do everything possible to improve land and sea communications, so that reinforcements could be sent quickly to any threatened point. In the immediate neighbourhood of the isthmus of Bulair he concentrated the *5th* and *7th Divisions*, commanded by Colonel von Sodenstern and Colonel Remsi Bey respectively, to deal with any attempt at a landing in that locality. The *9th Division*, commanded by Lieut.-Colonel Khalil Sami Bey, was set to

[1] Though the Achi Baba peak would not have given the British any view of the Narrows defences, it was of immense importance to the Turks. It was their main observing station in the south, and their chief artillery command post.
[2] It is of interest to compare this opinion with the views expressed in the German Official Account (f.n. 1, page 113).

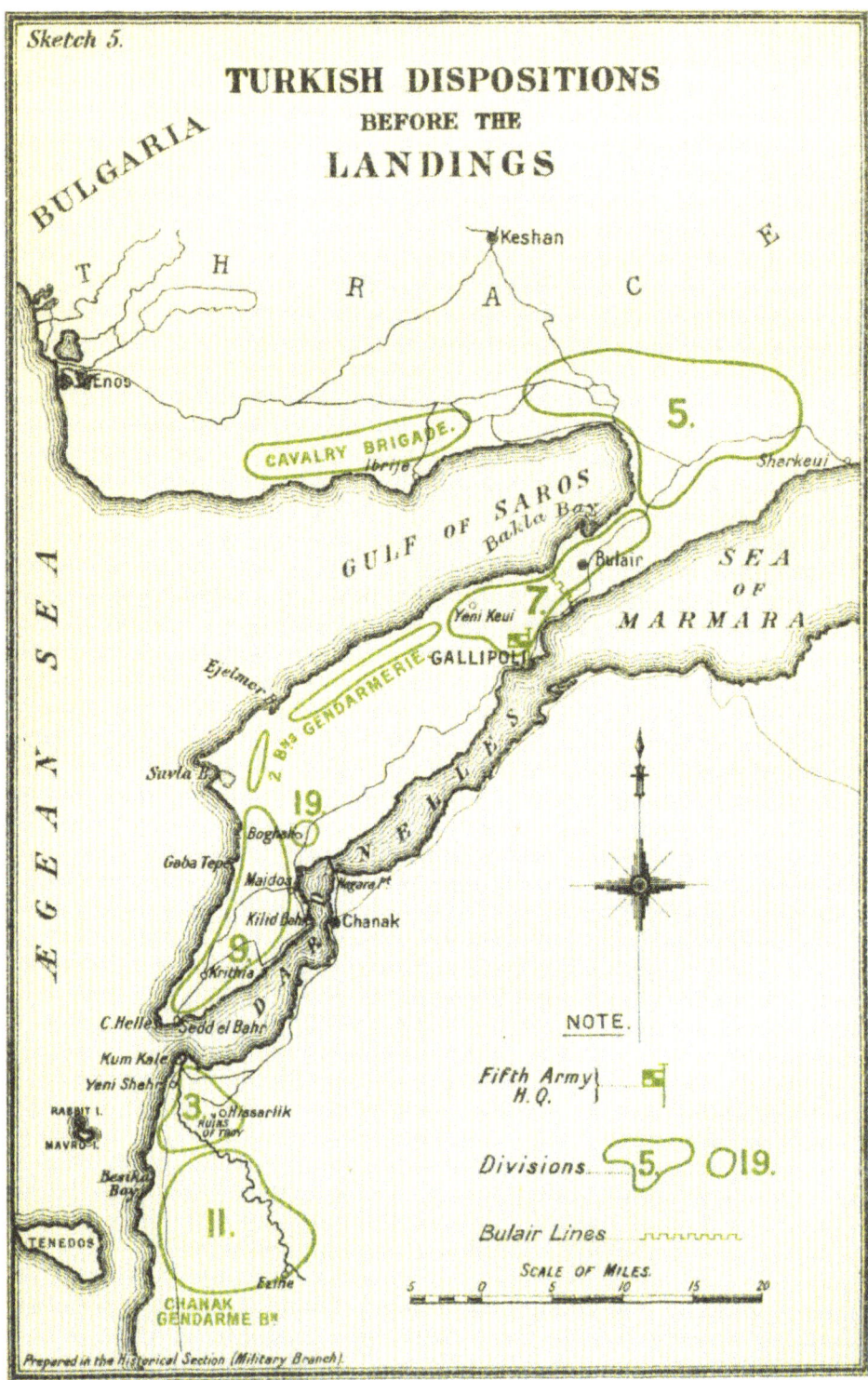

FINAL PREPARATIONS BY THE TURKS 157

guard the southern portion of the peninsula from Suvla Bay (exclusive) to Sedd el Bahr; and the *11th Division* (Lieut.-Colonel Refet Bey, an Arab officer), to be reinforced later by the *3rd Division* (Colonel Nicolai), was to hold the Asiatic shore.[1] The *19th Division* was concentrated near Boghali as a general reserve in the hands of the Commander-in-Chief, and was to be ready to move either to Bulair, to Gaba Tepe, or to the Asiatic side of the Straits as required.[2]

It was expressly pointed out to divisional commanders that the one hope of success lay in the mobility of the three groups, and not in the employment of a rigid system of defence.

To avoid detection by hostile aircraft the troop movements necessitated by the new scheme of defence were all carried out by night; and as, with one exception,[3] the dispositions now taken up remained unchanged till the day of the landing, it will be of interest to examine the distribution of troops from Ari Burnu to Sedd el Bahr in considerable detail.

The troops at the disposal of Colonel Sami Bey, commanding the *9th Division*, for the defence of this part of the peninsula amounted to three regiments (nine battalions) of infantry, three field batteries and two batteries of mountain guns. He divided his front into two defensive zones, the northern zone extending from the mouth of Aghyl Dere, north of Ari Burnu, to Semerly Tepe, and the southern zone from Semerly Tepe to Sedd el Bahr. He allotted the *27th Regiment* and two mountain batteries to the northern zone, and the *26th Regiment* and one field battery to the southern zone. The *25th Regiment* with his two remaining batteries of field artillery, he placed in divisional reserve at Serafim Farm, on the Kilid Bahr plateau, where it would be available to move either north or south, or, in the last resort to man the Kilid Bahr position.

Sketch 5A.

---
[1] These dispositions should be compared with the information available at British G.H.Q. at the time of the landing. G.H.Q. placed the number of Turkish troops on the peninsula at 34,000 men, and believed that one division was at Bulair, one or more distributed between the Anafarta villages and Kilid Bahr, and one south of Achi Baba. In his special instruction to Gen. Birdwood (Appendix 5) the Commander-in-Chief stated that there might be two Turkish divisions (20,000 men) between Anafarta and Maidos.
[2] This information is derived from a captured *19th Division* order, dated 7th April, and signed by Mustafa Kemal Bey.
[3] The one exception was the garrison of Suvla Bay. Up to 24th April this locality, from Ejelmer Bay to the mouth of Aghyl Dere, north of Ari Burnu, was guarded by the *Broussa Gendarmerie* battalion. On the 24th it was decided to strengthen the Sedd el Bahr garrison, and the gendarmerie battalion was ordered south, its place at Suvla being taken by a battalion of the *19th Division* in general reserve. The *Broussa Gendarmerie* were on the march when the British landing began.

In the northern zone the commander of the *27th Regiment*, Lieut.-Colonel Ali Chefik Bey, kept two of his battalions, the *1st* and *3rd*, and one mountain battery in reserve near Maidos,[1] and detailed the *2nd/27th* and one mountain battery to guard the coast. Of this battalion one company was deployed between Aghyl Dere and Ari Burnu; another from Ari Burnu to Gaba Tepe; and a third from Gaba Tepe to Semerly Tepe. The fourth company was in battalion reserve about one mile inland from Gaba Tepe. The mountain battery was placed on 400 Plateau. There were in addition two 12-cm. guns guarding the coast at Gaba Tepe, and two 15-cm. guns a little inland from that point.

It will thus be seen that for the defence of the beach selected for the landing of the Australian and New Zealand Corps only one company of infantry was immediately available, with a second company in comparatively close support. But two battalions, and another mountain battery were in local reserve, only four miles away, and the general reserve, consisting of eight battalions of the *19th Division* with one mountain and two field batteries, was in close proximity in the Boghali valley.

The commander of the *26th Regiment*, Lieut. - Colonel Kadri Bey, divided the southern zone into three battalion sectors. Of these the northern or Kum Tepe sector extended from Semerly Tepe to Sari Tepe (exclusive), and was held by the *1st/26th* with three companies and one field battery along the coast, and one company in reserve. In this sector there were also two 15-cm. guns guarding the coast south of Gaba Tepe.

The centre, or Krithia, sector was held by the *2nd/26th* and extended from Sari Tepe to the mouth of Gully Ravine, and, on the Dardanelles side, from Sedd el Bahr, exclusive, to the mouth of Tenkir Dere. The Ægean coast of this sector was considered so unsuitable for a landing that it was held by only one company. Of this company two platoons, with two old-pattern Nordenfeldt machine guns, were near the mouth of Gully Ravine, and the third platoon at Sari Tepe. Another company was distributed in the neighbourhood of Morto Bay; and the two remaining companies were in reserve in Kanli Dere, south-east of Krithia. Here also was situated the headquarters of the *26th Regiment*. In this sector on the western bank of Kereves Dere, was a coast defence battery of 10·5-cm.

---

[1] Up to 23rd April these battalions were at Maidos, but on that day they were bombed out of the village by a British air raid, and very unfortunately moved into bivouacs 1½ miles nearer Gaba Tepe.

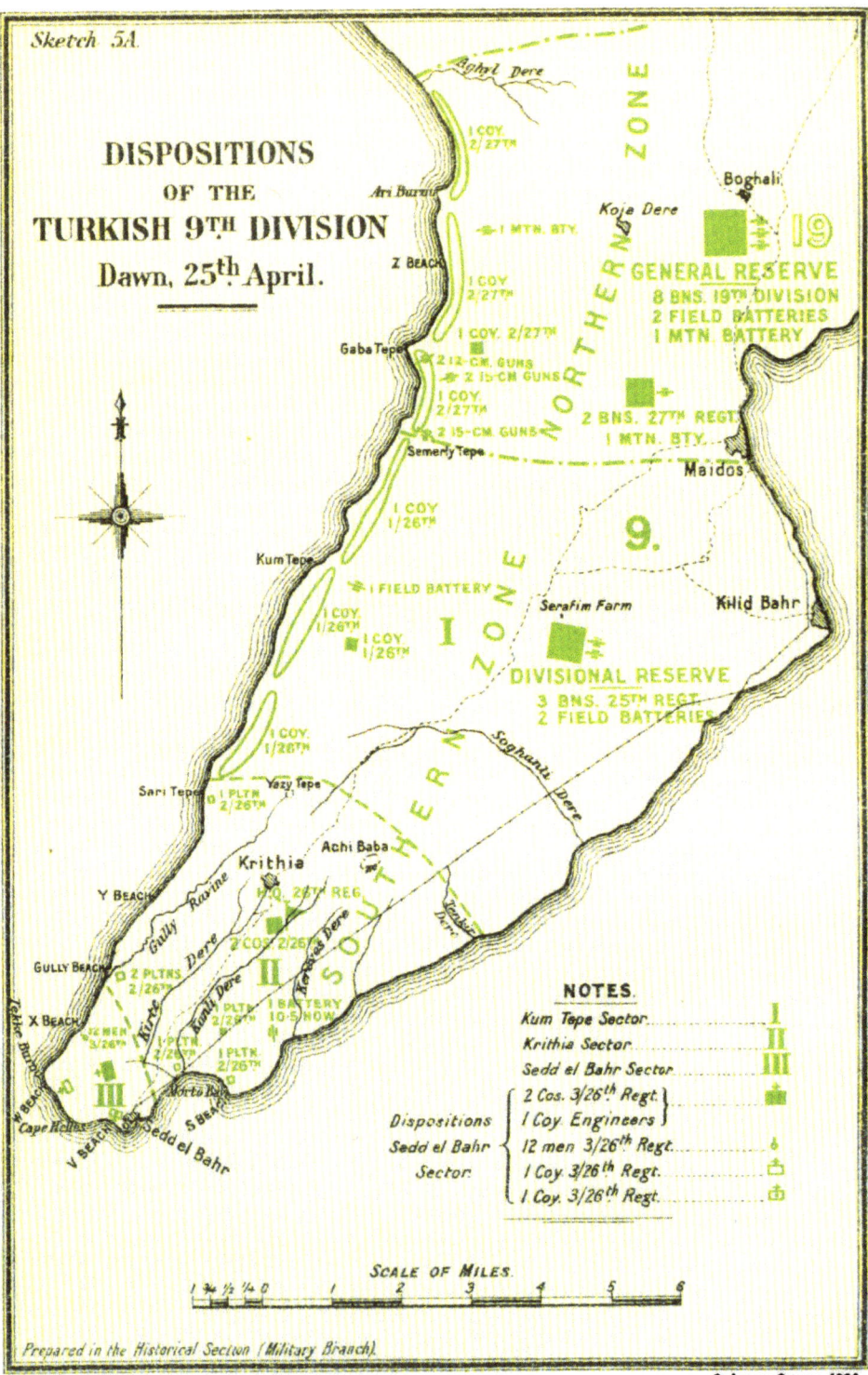

FINAL PREPARATIONS BY THE TURKS 159

howitzers charged with the duty of firing on any vessels that entered the Straits.

The southern, or Sedd el Bahr sector comprised the toe of the peninsula from Gully Beach (exclusive) to Sedd el Bahr (inclusive), and was held by the *3rd/26th Regiment*, with one company of engineers attached for work on the defences. This battalion had one company guarding W Beach; one company with four old-pattern Maxim guns [1] at Sedd el Bahr and above V Beach; and the remaining two companies in reserve on the low ground north-west of Morto Bay. A post of twelve men watched the coast at X. There was no artillery in this sector.

Thus, for the immediate defence of the three main beaches at V, W, and X there were only two companies and four (perhaps six) machine guns, with two more companies and a company of engineers in reserve.

On the Asiatic shore, the *3rd Division* kept two regiments in reserve near the ruins of Troy, with one regiment near the coast from Kum Kale to beyond Yeni Shehr. The *11th Division* similarly had the greater part of its strength in reserve near Ezine, with detachments watching the coast on both sides of Besika Bay.

The story of the landing on the 25th April will show how well these dispositions served. Owing partly to the fact that Sir Ian Hamilton launched his attacks where the defenders were least strong,[2] but mainly to the prowess of his infantry, the Turkish shores could not be kept inviolate. But bearing in mind the great length of coast to be defended, and remembering that the initiative lay with the invader, it is difficult to criticise Liman's scheme of defence, or to see how his initial dispositions could have been improved upon.

The regrouping effected, Liman's next step, in so far as time and circumstances permitted, was to work off the torpor into which the troops had sunk as the result of their sedentary outpost life on the coast. For the first time all units were practised in march and manœuvre; rifle ranges were constructed; and instruction was given in bombing—an accomplishment hitherto unknown to the Turkish soldier.

The amount of work required on communications and defences was found to be very great. As regards sea communications, pontoons and lighters were collected in the various small bays in the Straits, and a new landing stage was constructed at

---

[1] According to British reports there were also two maxims at W Beach.
[2] On 25th April only 17 Turkish battalions were available in the southern half of the peninsula to oppose 24 British and Anzac battalions who had landed by noon.

Nagara to facilitate the rapid transfer of troops from one side of the Straits to the other. Land communications were a far more difficult problem, as the peninsula was almost destitute of roads. Energetic measures were set on foot to remedy this serious defect, and the construction of roads for wheeled traffic between the chief strategic points was put in hand.

Finally, and this was of paramount importance, every available man was employed each night on the construction of defensive positions. The wiring of likely landing places was also actively continued, the obstacle at many points being placed at the edge of and sometimes under the water.[1] There appears at this time to have been a great shortage of engineer stores. Wire in particular was at first so difficult to procure that use had to be made of the wire fences of gardens at Sedd el Bahr. On the southern beaches this work met with considerable interruption from British naval fire, and the Turkish official account asserts that the close attention paid by the fleet to V and W Beaches inclined the Turks to anticipate a landing at those points.

By the 24th April the German commander appears to have become well satisfied with the progress of his defences. According to the Turkish General Staff, in addition to the trenches guarding the landing places, work was now well forward on no less than five lines of defence, of which only the two lines on the Kilid Bahr plateau had been in existence before the 25th March.[2]

"The English", wrote Liman, "allowed us four good weeks " of respite for all this work before their great disembarkation. " . . . This respite just sufficed for the most indispensable " measures to be taken."[3]

"A month earlier", wrote his German orderly officer,[4] "might have been fatal to the defenders."

---

[1] There is practically no tide in the Ægean and high-water mark does not vary.

[2]   i. Between the old Castle above Sedd el Bahr and a point to the north of Cape Helles.
   ii. Groups of unconnected shelter trenches in process of construction on a general line across the peninsula from the mouth of Gully Ravine to the mouth of Kereves Dere.
   iii. A number of unconnected trenches protecting Yazy Tepe (Hill 472) and Achi Baba from attacks from the west or south.
   iv. and v. A strong outer and inner line of defence on the Kilid Bahr plateau.

[3] " Fünf Jahre Türkei," p. 78.

[4] Major E. R. Prigge, " Der Kampf um die Dardanellen," p. 32.

PART II
THE BATTLES OF THE BEACHES

CHAPTER IX

THE LANDING AT ANZAC

THE NEWS AT TURKISH HEADQUARTERS

(Map 3 ; Sketches 5, 5A, 6, 7)

25 Apr. FROM six o'clock onwards on the morning of the 25th April a flood of urgent messages came pouring in to Turkish headquarters at Gallipoli, reporting that several hostile landings had already begun, and that others were imminent.

Sketch 5. At Gaba Tepe British warships and transports were disembarking troops in dangerous proximity to Maidos, and the cliffs at Ari Burnu were already in the hands of the invaders. At several points near Sedd el Bahr strong British forces were reported to be at grips with the outposts of the *9th Division*, and the whole of the southern end of the peninsula was being lacerated by heavy naval guns. Across the Straits, at Kum Kale, the *3rd Division* was said to be heavily engaged with French troops, whose landing had been supported by a galling fire from attendant men-of-war. Further south, where the *11th Division* was watching the coast, a considerable fleet of French warships and transports was entering Besika Bay. Finally, close at hand, in the Gulf of Saros, a number of British warships and a dozen large liners were approaching the shore. From that direction, too, there soon was heard the boom of naval guns. "I could tell," writes General Liman von Sanders, "by the pallor of the "officers who brought me the reports, that the long-awaited "landing was surprising them, and filling them with un-"easiness, by the fact of its taking place at so many points "at once."[1]

Convinced though the German general was that all these landings could not be serious, it was for the moment impossible to tell at which of them the invaders were seeking a decision. But it was the safety of the isthmus that caused him the greatest

[1] " Fünf Jahre Türkei," p. 84.

anxiety, and the measure of that anxiety can be gauged by the fact that here one-third of his whole force had been concentrated, and here he had kept his headquarters and the headquarters of the *III. Corps* in order to be as near as possible to what he considered the most likely point of attack. Nor was Liman von Sanders alone in expecting the Allied troops to land near Bulair. Everywhere critics of the campaign were sharing the same view, and Sir Ian Hamilton has placed on record that, apart from other weighty reasons, one of the influences that persuaded him to try elsewhere was a reluctance to throw his troops against just that point where it was probable that the greatest preparations had been made to receive them. But, to play upon the Turkish commander's fears, he had decided on a demonstration in that neighbourhood, and well was his ruse to succeed.

Serious as were the reports from the centre and south of the peninsula, and from the Asiatic shore, it was the isthmus that now claimed Liman's personal attention. Mounting his horse, and accompanied by two German orderly officers, he galloped to a position on the heights of Bulair, and there he remained till the events of the next day persuaded him of the real state of affairs. Despite the urgent calls for help from other sectors, it was not until the evening of the 25th that he would allow the Bulair garrison to be weakened even to the extent of five battalions; and though further units of the two northern divisions were permitted to embark for Maidos on the night of the 26th, another twenty-four hours were to elapse before the isthmus was denuded of troops. For more than forty-eight hours, indeed, the Turkish units at the main points of attack were denied reinforcements, which, had they arrived earlier, might well have turned the scale against the British in the hotly contested battle for the beaches.

THE DEMONSTRATION OFF BULAIR

Eleven transports of the Royal Naval Division, escorted by the warships *Canopus*, *Dartmouth*, and *Doris*, with two destroyers and some trawlers, sailed from Trebuki Bay on the evening of the 24th April for a rendezvous in the Gulf of Saros. Major-General A. Paris was on board the *Canopus*, while the commanders of the 2nd Royal Naval and Royal Marine brigades were in the *Dartmouth* and *Doris* respectively.

Arriving at the rendezvous soon after daybreak on the 25th, the warships began a slow bombardment of the Bulair lines which was to continue throughout the day, and shortly afterwards the divisional Staff carried out a close reconnaissance of three landing places on the northern side of the gulf from the deck of the destroyer *Kennet*. Later in the day ships' boats were ostentatiously swung out from the transports, and strings of tows, each consisting of eight cutters and a trawler, were got ready as if for a landing. Towards evening the boats were filled with men, and, shortly before darkness fell, the tows headed for the shore—to return to the transports as soon as their movements were shrouded by the dusk.

Up to this hour the demonstration had called for little effort on the part of the Royal Naval Division. But for the night of the 25th a more realistic enterprise had been planned, which, through the initiative of a junior officer, was to resolve itself into an individual exploit as gallant as it was picturesque. It had been arranged that towards midnight a platoon of the Hood Battalion should be thrown ashore on the westernmost of the three northern beaches to light flares and to simulate the landing of a large body of troops. During the afternoon, however, it was suggested by Lieut.-Commander B.C. Freyberg, the leader of the selected platoon, that, after the day's happenings, the approach of boats would certainly be noticed, and the attempt to land a small party frustrated with useless loss of life. This young officer pleaded that, as he was a strong swimmer, the actual landing should be entrusted to him alone, a ship's boat being used only to take him within a mile of the shore, whence he would complete the journey by swimming, light flares along the coast, and swim back to the boat. This change of plan was sanctioned, and the story of the adventure can best be told in the words of Freyberg's official report:

26 Apr. At 9 P.M. last night (25th April), as ordered we left H.M. Transport *Grantully Castle* for the western landing place to light flares. We were taken in tow by the steam pinnace of H.M.S. *Dartmouth*, and towed to within three miles of the shore, when we slipped and rowed in another mile. It now became evident that to proceed further without being seen from the shore would be impossible. At 12.40 this morning, therefore, I started swimming to cover the remaining distance, towing a waterproof canvas bag containing three oil flares and five calcium lights, a knife, signalling light, and a revolver. After an hour and a quarter's hard swimming in bitterly cold water I reached the shore and lighted my first flare, and again took to the water and swam towards the east, and landed about 300 yards away, where I lighted my second flare and hid among some bushes to await developments. Nothing happening, I crawled up a slope to where some trenches were

THE ANZAC PLAN

located the morning before. I discovered they were only dummies, consisting only of a pile of earth about two feet high and 100 yards long, and looked to be quite newly made. I crawled in about 350 yards and listened for some time, but could discover nothing. I now went to the beach, where I lighted my last flare, and left on a bearing due south. After swimming for a considerable distance I was picked up by Lieut. Nelson in our cutter some time after 3 A.M. Our cutter, in company with the pinnace and the destroyer *Kennet*, searched the shore with 12-pdr. and machine-gun fire, but could get no answer from the shore.

It is my opinion that the shore was not occupied, but from the appearance and lights on the tops of the hills during the early hours of the morning, I feel sure that numbers of the enemy were there, but owing to chance of being captured, and as I had cramp badly, I could not get further.

Early on the 26th, the Royal Naval Division and its escorting squadron were ordered south to take part in the main operations; but not till many hours after the last ship had sunk below the horizon were Turkish fears for the safety of the isthmus allayed.

THE ANZAC PLAN

The task allotted to the Australian and New Zealand Army Corps was to effect a landing north of Gaba Tepe, and, after securing its left flank, to push eastwards towards Maidos with a view to severing the Turkish north and south communications.

25 Apr.
Map 3.
Sketch 5A.

Available information at British headquarters pointed to the Gaba Tepe promontory being strongly held, but to the north of it, apart from some unconnected trenches on the spurs overlooking the shore, and a few gun emplacements, no other defences were known to exist,[1] and it was hoped from this lack of preparation that the covering force would encounter little opposition on the beach. Further inland resistance was expected to be severe, for the Anafarta villages and Maidos were reported to be crowded with soldiery, and the probable number of troops in the neighbourhood was placed at two complete divisions, or, roughly, 20,000 men.[2]

---

[1] The defences reported to G.H.Q. before the landing were: 7 emplacements and 3 occupied trenches, on Gaba Tepe; 4 emplacements half a mile inland; some disconnected trenches on the crest and forward slopes of the spurs overlooking "Brighton Beach"; and two gun emplacements on "400 Plateau", south-east of Ari Burnu. No guns were visible and the emplacements were reported as "empty or roofed over".

[2] In point of fact, the Turks in this area now appear to have numbered about 13,000 men. They consisted of the *27th Regiment*, which had one battalion on outpost duty along the coast on a five-mile front, and two

166   GALLIPOLI

The Anzac covering force consisted of the 3rd Australian Infantry Brigade, the 1st Field Company, and the bearer subdivisions of the 3rd Field Ambulance, the whole under command of Colonel E. G. Sinclair-MacLagan.[1] These were the troops who had been sent to Mudros from Egypt at the beginning of March, and for the last few weeks they had undergone a special course of training in landing operations.

A serious difficulty connected with an opposed landing on the coast of a little-known country is the impossibility of effecting any adequate reconnaissance of the ground over which the first battle must be fought. In the case of the Australian landing this difficulty was enhanced by the incredibly broken nature of the Sari Bair range, on the left flank of the intended landing place. Most of the senior officers concerned in the operation were given a view of the coast from the deck of a warship ten days before the landing, and one of the corps Staff flew over the area on the 14th April;[2] but, apart from these inadequate reconnaissances, reliance had to be placed on the only available map of the peninsula, and this was subsequently to prove inaccurate in many important particulars.[3]

The main Sari Bair range extends south-westwards in an unbroken chain from the Anafarta villages to a point about three-quarters of a mile north-east of Ari Burnu. There it divides into three long and tortuous spurs or ridges, which are in their turn split up by countless gullies and depressions and eventually reach the sea coast between Ari Burnu and Gaba Tepe. About its centre the range is crowned by three rounded hills of nearly identical height, namely—reading from north to south—Koja Chemen Tepe,[4] Hill Q,[5] and Chunuk

---

battalions in local reserve near Maidos, and the *19th Division* at Boghali. The *19th Division* was the general reserve for the whole Dardanelles zone. The Turkish artillery in position guarding the coast consisted of one mountain battery on 400 Plateau, and two 12-cm. guns at Gaba Tepe. There were, in addition, two 15-cm. guns a little inland from Gaba Tepe.

[1] Colonel Sinclair-MacLagan's substantive rank at this time was that of major (Yorkshire Regiment). The infantry brigade commanders of the Australian and New Zealand Corps were graded as colonels until July 1915, when they were granted the rank of brigadier-general, in accordance with the custom in vogue in the British service.

[2] The paucity of aircraft and trained observers has been referred to.

[3] The map was particularly misleading as regards the Anzac neighbourhood, and gave no idea of the extreme difficulties of the country.

[4] On the first map issued to the troops this hill was marked 971 (feet) and throughout this history it will be referred to as Hill 971. The Turkish map subsequently brought into use described it as Koja Chemen Tepe, and gave its height as 305 metres.

[5] Hill Q is actually crowned by twin summits, but this is not apparent from the south.

THE SEAWARD FACE OF FIRST RIDGE

FULL FACE VIEW OF THE SPHINX

THE ANZAC PLAN 167

Bair, all three of which command an extensive view of the Narrows above Chanak. These heights are guarded on the Ægean side by a maze of indescribably difficult underfeatures, but on their inland flank the slopes are more gradual, and there are fewer obstacles to the movement of troops. All three hills were destined to play an important part in the later stages of the campaign, but this present chapter is more particularly concerned with two lower eminences south of Chunuk Bair, and with the three long ridges, already alluded to, which extend south-west towards Gaba Tepe. None of these features were named in the original map (a point which added to the difficulty of writing orders for the troops); but so great was their influence on the operations that it is essential to study their general outline, and their relation to each other, before attempting to understand either the orders for the covering force or the subsequent course of events.

The two eminences at the southern end of the main ridge were soon to be known as "Battleship Hill" and "Baby 700",[1] and at this stage it will suffice to notice that both are overlooked by Chunuk Bair, that Battleship Hill affords a good though somewhat restricted view of the Narrows, and that Baby 700 cannot be approached under cover from the south.[2]

Sketches 6, 7.

The three long ridges which extend from Battleship Hill towards Gaba Tepe were on the day of the landing referred to as "First", "Second", and "Third" Ridges. Of these, "First", the westernmost ridge, was the scene of incessant fighting, and many of its features now bear immortal names. Starting immediately south-west of Baby 700 it consists at first of a narrow saddle-back known as "The Nek". Continuing south-west the ground rises to a commanding plateau, long and narrow, known as "Russell's Top", on the western side of which two steep and tortuous underfeatures give access to the seashore between Ari Burnu and Fisherman's Hut. South of "Walker's Ridge" (the southernmost of these two spurs) the seaward face of Russell's Top is practically unclimbable, and here is located the gravel-faced cliff some 300 feet high, called by the New Zealanders and Australians "The Sphinx". At the southern end of Russell's Top the ridge suddenly contracts for 200 yards into a veritable razor edge, impassable even by infantry, with a deep chasm on either side. It then opens

[1] In the original map issued to the troops both these heights were ringed with a 700-ft. contour; hence the name Baby 700 for the smaller one. In reality, Baby 700 was merely the southern shoulder of the main ridge, and was 50-100 feet lower than Battleship Hill, which overlooked it.
[2] A small portion of the Narrows is also visible from Baby 700, but not enough to make the hill of value for that reason.

out again to "Plugge's Plateau", with an underfeature, Ari Burnu, jutting out to the sea below it. Thence the ridge turns south, and its steep scrub-covered slopes fringe the coast of Anzac Cove, the southern arm of which is formed by another and smaller underfeature, subsequently known as "Hell Spit". This southern portion of First Ridge, which ends at the mouth of a deep ravine called "Shrapnel Gully",[1] was called "MacLagan's Ridge".

It is important to notice that whereas the original map indicated that troops could advance straight up First Ridge from its southern extremity to Baby 700, in point of fact the "Razor Edge" made this impossible, and to get from Plugge's Plateau to Russell's Top it was necessary to climb down into the gully and up the steep slope on the other side.

Second Ridge forms the eastern wall of Monash and Shrapnel Gullies, and then continues south to a point about one mile north-east of Gaba Tepe. This ridge, too, was for many months the scene of desperate fighting. It embraces such immortal names as "Quinn's", "Steele's", "Courtney's", and "Lone Pine"; and every yard of its length has been hallowed by brave deeds. For a thousand yards, from its starting-point on the southern slopes of Baby 700, it consists of a narrow crest-line, with a steep and sometimes precipitous fall towards Monash Gully and a less abrupt descent to "Mule Valley" on its eastern flank. It then widens into an important and conspicuous plateau, some 400 feet high, known as "400 Plateau", with an extreme length and breadth of about half a mile. It was on the eastern slopes of this plateau that two Turkish gun positions were reported before the landing.[2] From the southern end of the plateau five minor spurs fall south-westward towards the sea.

The easternmost of the three ridges, called Third Ridge on the day of the landing, was subsequently known throughout the campaign as "Gun Ridge", and to avoid confusion this name will be used for it from the outset. The longest and biggest of the three ridges, it starts due south of Chunuk Bair, and merges into the Maidos plain a little to the east of Gaba Tepe, to which it is joined by a low and narrow spur which conceals the plain from the sea. Two important features to be

---

[1] The upper half of this ravine was called " Monash Gully ".

[2] At the landing two or three positions for mountain guns, consisting of roughly made pits were found on the east and south-east edges of the plateau, one of them containing three mountain guns. Owing to the vigour of the Australian advance, these guns were overrun before they could open fire, but the Turks succeeded in withdrawing them to Third Ridge later in the morning.

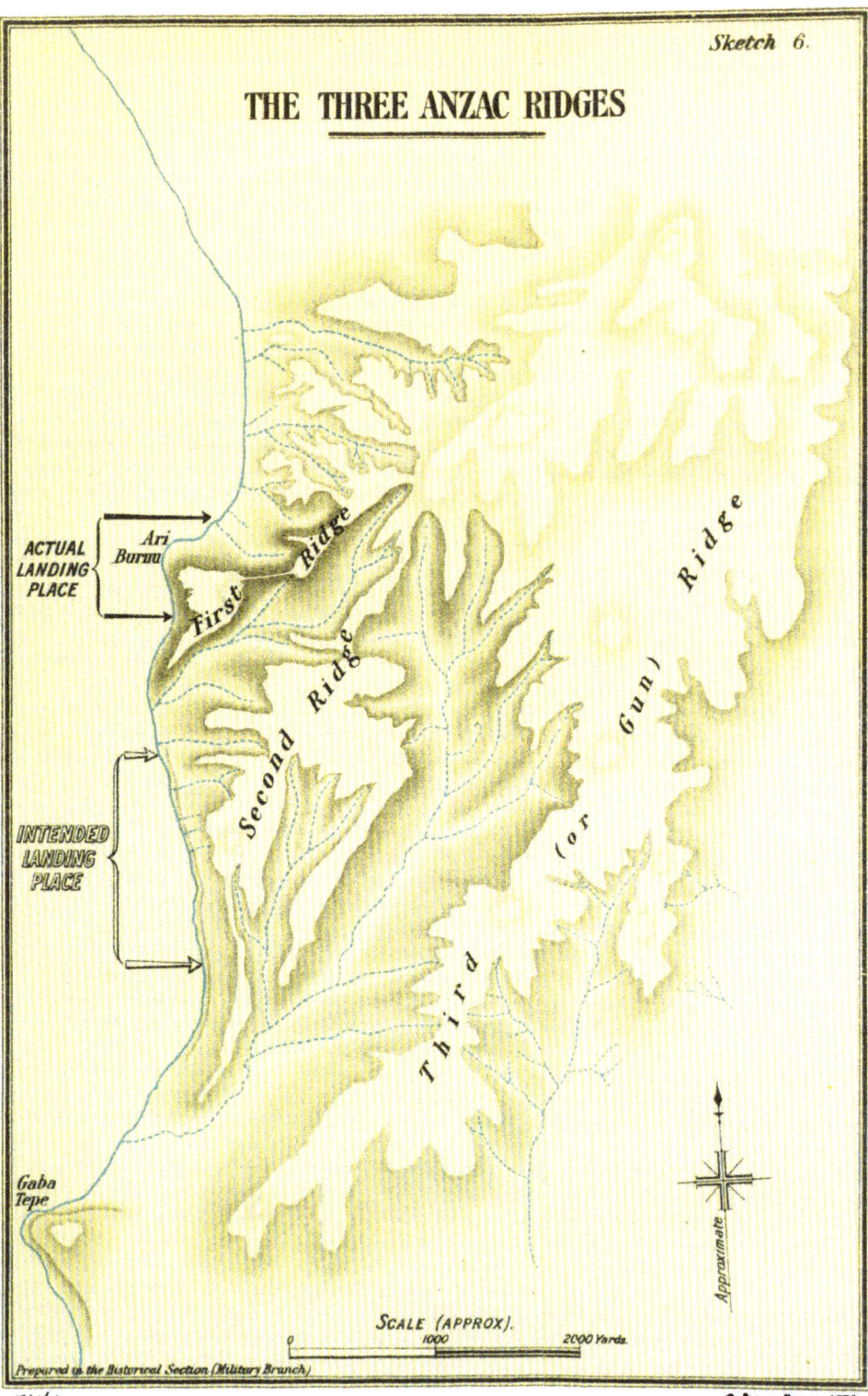

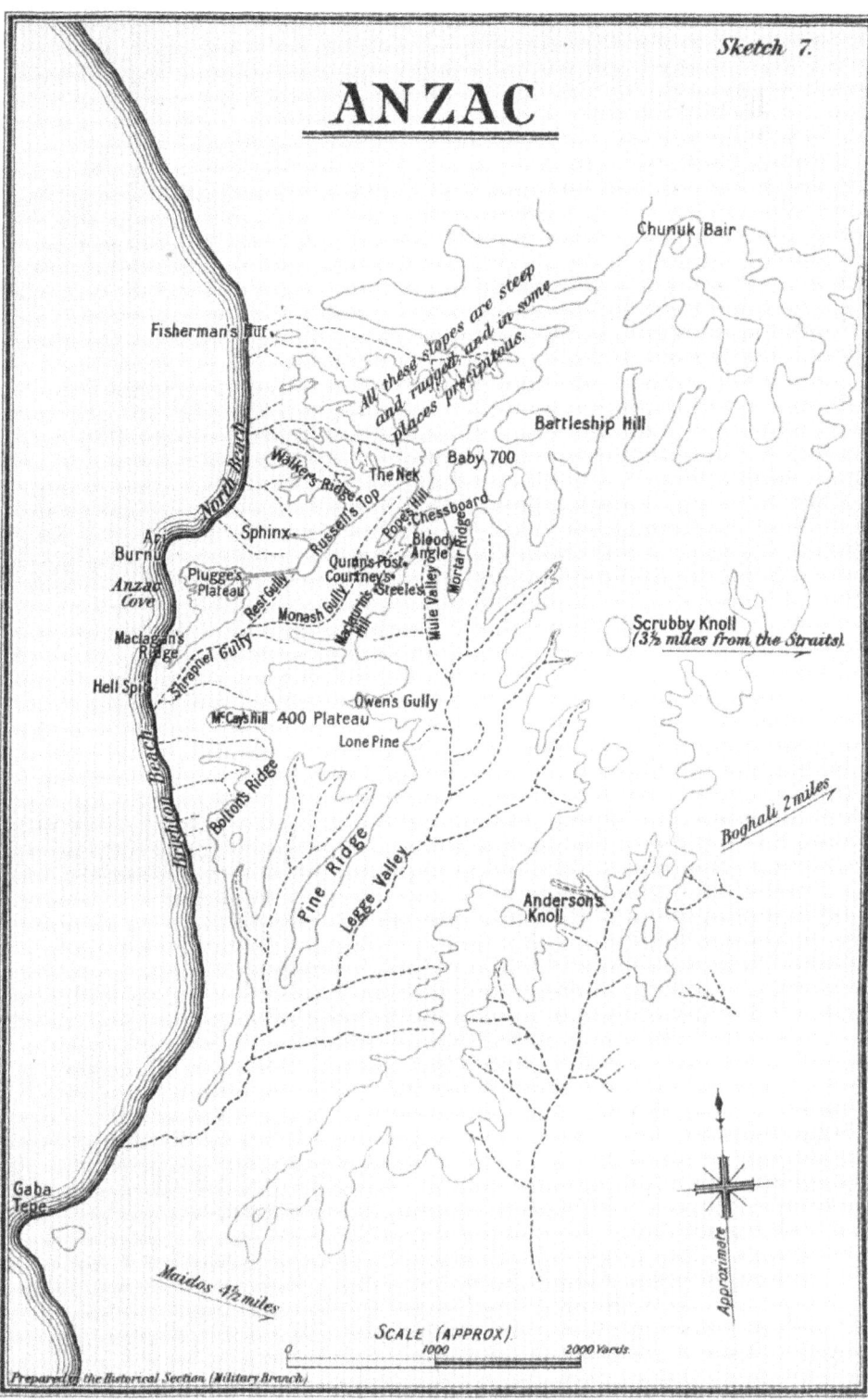

THE ANZAC PLAN

noticed on Gun Ridge are "Scrubby Knoll" in the north, and "Anderson's Knoll" towards the southern end.

All reports agreed that the Sari Bair country was for the most part covered with low scrub. This, indeed, could be seen from the sea, but the resisting nature of that scrub was never suspected before the operations began. Standing some three feet high and interspersed with prickly dwarf oak, its stubborn bushes are often so close together, and so thorny, that even a strong man has difficulty in forcing his way through. In the attack, therefore, it is a serious obstacle to movement; while it has the further disadvantage that men lying down in it are unable to see their neighbours on either flank. But for snipers, or for infantry delaying a hostile advance, the cover that it affords is almost ideal.

It will be noticed that 1,000 yards south of Anzac Cove the high ground recedes from the shore, and that troops landing between that point and Gaba Tepe would find a stretch of more or less level ground between themselves and the nearest hill. Also, if troops were advancing direct on Maidos from the beach north of Gaba Tepe, the nearer they had landed to that promontory the fewer and less abrupt would be the obstacles blocking their way. On the other hand, a few machine guns on Gaba Tepe could forbid a landing in its immediate vicinity.

The locality finally chosen for the landing of the covering force was the sandy beach between Gaba Tepe and Anzac Cove. The force was to land on a front of 1,600 yards, its right resting on a point one mile north of Gaba Tepe, and its left near the southern extremity of First Ridge. In his orders to Colonel Sinclair-MacLagan,[1] General Bridges, commanding the 1st Australian Division, instructed him to push forward across Second Ridge as rapidly as possible, and to take up a covering position on Gun Ridge. The troops were to advance on a broad front, so that if one portion of the line was held up by a hostile post, the portions on each flank would help it forward by threatening the enemy's flanks and rear. The left of the line was to establish itself on Chunuk Bair, while on the right a party was to be detached to clear Gaba Tepe and to disable any guns found there. It was also important that the guns reported on 400 Plateau should be quickly captured and disabled. Colonel Sinclair-MacLagan was informed that the 2nd Brigade, which was to land immediately after the covering force, would extend the front northwards to the summit of Hill 971, and protect the left flank by holding a line

[1] Appendix 16.

from that point to Fisherman's Hut; the 1st Brigade would in the first instance be held in reserve just clear of the beach. The 7th Indian Mountain Artillery Brigade would be landed as early as possible in the morning, and would be attached to the covering force on arrival.

In accordance with these orders, Colonel Sinclair-MacLagan detailed the 9th Battalion to land on the right, the 10th in the centre, and the 11th on the left. Two companies of the 9th were to clear Gaba Tepe as soon as they landed, while the remaining two companies were to make straight for Anderson's Knoll on Gun Ridge, a mile east of their landing place. The 10th Battalion, on their left, after capturing the guns on 400 Plateau, was to occupy Scrubby Knoll on Gun Ridge, while the 11th Battalion was to seize the northern end of the ridge and Chunuk Bair. The 12th Battalion would, in the first instance, form the reserve. The mountain guns, on arrival, were to proceed to 400 Plateau.

The first point to be noticed about the naval arrangements for the landing is that the exact time at which the leading troops were to reach the shore was eventually governed by the hour of the moon's setting. General Birdwood was convinced that his best chance of success lay in a night landing, and it was his wish that the covering force should be landed in time to reach its first positions before daybreak. But the selected beach faced due west; the moon was not due to set till 2.57 A.M. on the 25th April; and it was feared that, if ships were to approach within five miles of the shore before that hour, they would be seen by the enemy outposts and that all hopes of surprise would disappear. This was held to be the governing factor; and working from the basis that there must be no movement within five miles of the shore till 2.57 A.M., it was found that the first tows could not be beached till 4.30 A.M., or half an hour after the first streak of dawn. The hope of establishing the covering force ashore before daylight was therefore frustrated; but the corps commander agreed that this departure from the original intention was the lesser of two evils.[1]

As regards the actual plans for landing the troops,[2] the aim of the navy was to meet the army's wishes by landing as many of the covering force as possible simultaneously, to reinforce them with the utmost possible speed, and to be ready to disembark the main body as soon afterwards as the military

---

[1] Had the landing taken place on 23rd April, as originally arranged, the first troops were timed to arrive on the beach at 4 A.M., for the moon set half an hour earlier on that day. But even this was somewhat later than General Birdwood's original suggestion. [2] Appendix 12.

THE ANZAC PLAN

commander asked for this to be done. As the result of frequent conferences between General Birdwood, Admiral Thursby, and their respective Staffs, it was decided that the 4,000 men composing the covering force should be thrown ashore in three echelons. The first echelon of 1,500 would be taken to within two miles of the shore on board three battle-ships, whence they would be landed simultaneously in 12 tows. The second and third echelons, each of 1,250 men, would land immediately afterwards from seven destroyers, which would pass through the line of battleships and approach to within 100 yards of the shore, each towing a number of ships' lifeboats behind them. By this means, 2,750 men would be landed within a few minutes of each other, and the remaining 1,250 as quickly as the destroyers' boats could make a second journey to the shore.

The main body of the 1st Australian Division, if the situation ashore permitted, was to follow close on the heels of the covering force. With this object, eight transports carrying the 1st and 2nd Australian Infantry Brigades and a portion of the 7th Indian Mountain Artillery Brigade were to approach the shore at 5 A.M. Four of these transports were to anchor in allotted berths close to the beach, where they would be met by the battleships' twelve tows. The remaining four, while still under way, were to transfer their infantry to the seven destroyers as soon as the latter had disembarked their complement of the covering force. By this means, and with the aid of the horse-boats carried in one of the transports, it was calculated that all three infantry brigades and the mountain artillery would be ashore by 9 A.M. The landing of the remainder of the corps would follow as quickly as possible, and transports carrying freights not wanted in the first instance were to be called up from Mudros as required. The order in which these ships were to approach the anchorage was not laid down beforehand, and was to depend on the tactical necessities of the moment. In every case only a specified minimum of animals and vehicles was to be landed with the fighting troops in the first instance, and as soon as this had been done each transport was to proceed out of range of hostile artillery, and to wait in the offing until called upon to disembark the remainder of her complement.

Such, in brief, were the arrangements for the Anzac landing, but the foregoing summary does little more than touch the hem of the very elaborate details which had to be dealt with in the naval and military instructions. The naval orders alone, with their various tables and appendices, amounted to no less than twenty-seven typed pages of foolscap. Enough, however, has been said to explain the main intentions of the scheme, and to enable the reader to appreciate the many variations from it imposed by the course of events.

23/25 April. On the 23rd April General Birdwood and the principal officers of his corps headquarters moved from the transport *Minnewaska* to H.M.S. *Queen*, in order to be in close touch with Admiral Thursby in naval command of their landing. The headquarters of the 1st Australian Division transhipped to H.M.S. *Prince of Wales*. During the forenoon of the 24th April the 1,500 men who were to be the first to land were transferred in destroyers to the attendant battleships, about 500 of the 9th Battalion going to the *Queen*, 500 of the 10th to the *Prince of Wales*, and 500 of the 11th to the *London*. A detachment of the 1st Field Company Australian Engineers was included in the numbers sent to each battleship.

Later in the day these three battleships, accompanied by the *Triumph*, *Majestic*, and *Bacchante*, left Mudros for a sea rendezvous five miles west of Gaba Tepe, where the 1,500 men were to be transferred to the tows of boats in which they were to land. The transfer of the remainder of the covering force into seven destroyers was to take place at Imbros; and shortly after the battleships had sailed the four transports of the covering force left Mudros for that destination.

Steering on a light shown by the *Triumph*, which had gone forward to mark the sea rendezvous, the ships of Admiral Thursby's squadron crept noiselessly into their stations at 1 A.M. Dead astern, the moon was sinking to the western horizon. To the east the sombre mass of Gallipoli was faintly visible, its rugged summits now and again thrown into black relief by an upward sweep of the searchlights in the Dardanelles. The boats were lowered, and tows formed, and half an hour later, in absolute silence, the heavily laden troops[1] began to climb down the sides of the battleships and fill the waiting boats. By 2.35 A.M. all the tows were ready. Twenty minutes later, as the moon sank behind Imbros, the three battleships, followed by the twelve tows, and, further astern, by the seven destroyers which at that moment arrived from Imbros with the rest of the covering force, steamed slowly towards the peninsula.

[1] Every man, in addition to rifle and pack, was carrying 200 rounds of ammunition and three days' food—a total weight of 88 lbs.

THE LANDING OF THE COVERING FORCE

Sunrise at the Dardanelles on that unforgettable Sunday 25 Apr. morning—the first Anzac Day—was due at a quarter-past five, and the first streak of dawn at five minutes past four. During the hour of inky darkness that preceded the dawn the faint night breeze died suddenly, and the surface of the Ægean grew smooth and still as glass. In face of the coming drama, the very elements appeared to hold their breath.

At half-past three, when two and a half miles from the shore, now completely invisible, the three battleships again came to rest. The signal "land armed parties" was made, and the twelve tows moved slowly forward in line abreast. The 9th Battalion's boats were on the right, those of the 10th Battalion in the centre, and the 11th Battalion's on the left.

It is difficult to appreciate the intense strain of being towed in an open boat to a hostile beach that is likely to be defended by machine guns. But it is essential, in studying the problem of the Gallipoli landings, to try to gauge the feelings of the private soldier—on whose bearing so much depended—as he slowly approached the shore. For the Australians the ordeal was a particularly long one. It prefaced, moreover, not only their own but their army's baptism of fire. The loading of the boats had begun at 1.30 A.M. Thenceforward for three hours, till half-past four, the men sat motionless and silent, so tightly wedged together that they could scarcely move their limbs, heading towards the unknown. Whether the landing would be a surprise, or whether an army was awaiting them, was a question none could answer. But to the men in the tows, as the dark mass of the shore drew ever nearer, the hope of a surprise was dwindling, for the throb of their steamboats' engines seemed loud enough to wake the dead. Every breathless second a roar of Turkish fire was expected. Yet, till the shore was reached, they must remain motionless and silent—a helpless mark for the enemy.

The naval officer responsible for guiding the line of tows was Lieut. J. B. Waterlow, R.N., in No. 1 (the starboard) steamboat, and he steered by a compass bearing which was to land his own tow on the extreme right of the selected beach. To maintain their direction, and to cover the whole frontage correctly, the remaining eleven steamboats were to keep a lateral interval of 150 yards from, and to steer their course by, the tow on their immediate right. Commander C. Dix, in naval charge of the flotilla, was on the extreme left, in steamboat No. 12. There was a midshipman with every tow, and each boat carried five seamen to row it ashore when the ropes were cast off. In addition there was a commissioned naval officer in steamboats Nos. 3, 5, and 9.

In the black darkness it was so difficult for the tows to see each other that they insensibly bunched together, some of them even getting into their wrong positions in the line; and there now occurred one of those mischances, the fear of which had inclined the navy to favour a daylight landing. The northerly current that sets along the Gallipoli coast was stronger than the sailors had realized; the tows were imperceptibly carried a full mile to the north of the selected landing place; and when, shortly after 4 A.M., the shore became faintly visible, Lieut. Waterlow catching sight of Ari Burnu on his port bow, mistook it for Gaba Tepe. Jumping to the erroneous conclusion that he was a mile south of his course, he at once starboarded his helm, and made for a point actually north of Anzac Cove. Commander Dix, in No. 12 steamboat, at the same moment realized the true state of affairs, and saw that unless instant action was taken the covering force would be landed at least two miles to the north of the intended beach, with perhaps fatal results to the whole military plan. It was too late for the mistake to be entirely remedied, for the boats were nearing the shore. It might, however, be partially retrieved. With this object, Commander Dix instantly put his helm hard over, and, passing close under the stern of the tows that were now crossing his bows, he placed himself on the extreme starboard (right) flank, and headed for Ari Burnu. Seeing this manœuvre, the remaining steamboats steadied on a roughly parallel course, and all twelve tows made for the shore at a point approximately one mile to the north of the intended landing place.

Day was just breaking when at 4.25 A.M. while fifty yards from the beach, the tows were cast off. As yet no sign of life had come from the shore; but suddenly a warning light flared up from a neighbouring spur, and a scattered fire rang out from Ari Burnu.

The three left-hand tows, carrying men of the 11th Battalion, had fetched up some two hundred yards north of Ari Burnu. The remaining nine, including Dix's 11th Battalion tow, were clustered round the headland. Spattered by an erratic fire, all 48 boats were now rowed ashore by the bluejackets. There was little thought of maintaining their relative positions. Each boat landed where it could.[1] Some of the larger ones grounded

[1] The result was a serious intermixing of units from the very start. Added to this, the very small frontage on which the landing had taken place was a great disadvantage.

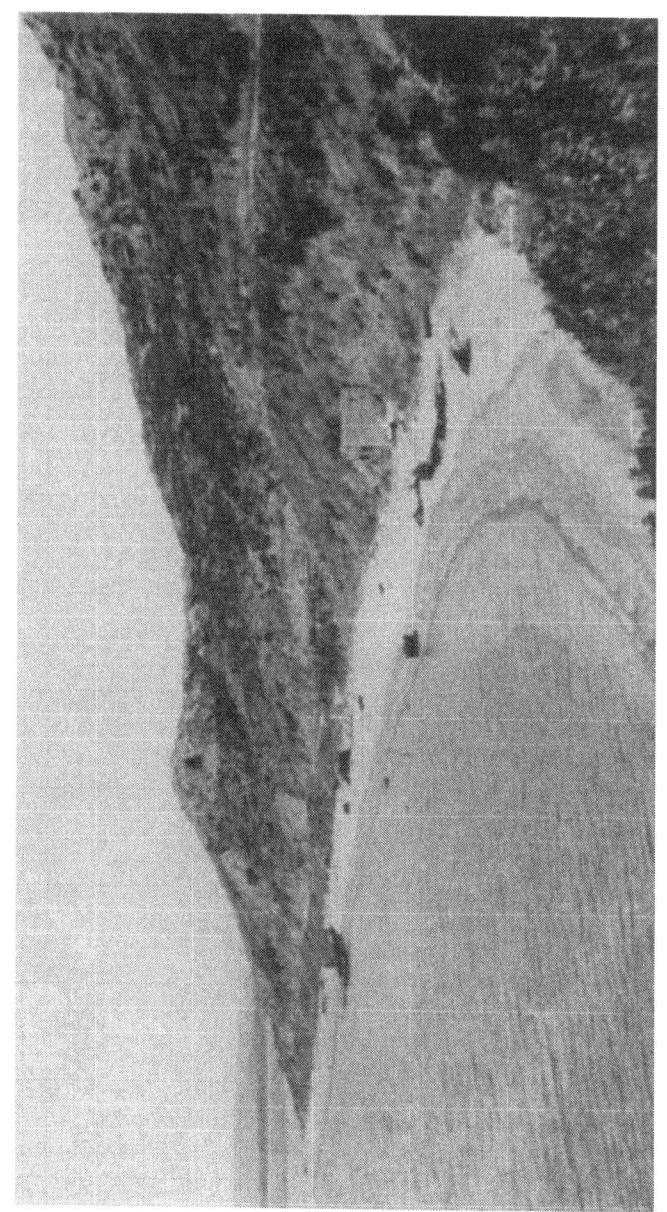

ANZAC COVE AND ARI BURNU FROM HELL SPIT

From a photograph taken in 1922

LANDING OF THE ANZAC COVERING FORCE 175

in three feet of water, and their inmates, scrambling over the sides, found themselves immersed to their waists. But in a few minutes every boat was emptied and the first echelon was ashore with very little loss.

The surprise had been complete. The battleships had not been seen, or had at least aroused no suspicion. The tows had escaped notice till within fifty yards of the shore. There had been no time for the Turkish outposts in the vicinity to call for assistance; and the only troops available to oppose the landing were a strong sentry group on Ari Burnu and a few small posts on the ridge overlooking the beach.[1] For the moment, therefore, the Australians were in a superiority of more than ten to one; but the Turks had the priceless advantage of concealment, and a thorough knowledge of the extraordinarily difficult ground.

The unfortunate swing of the tows, however, was to bear disastrous consequences. Though Commander Dix's prompt action had halved the error, and had saved the troops from landing at a still more unfavourable beach, the rugged hills immediately in front of them, especially those to the north of Ari Burnu, were to prove a bigger obstacle than any words can describe. Even in time of peace the precipitous ridges and tortuous ravines which formed the first Australian and New Zealand battlefield are an arduous climb for an active and unarmed man, while the steep, scrub-covered gullies are so confusing that it is easy to lose one's way. To preserve the cohesion of an attack across such country, immediately after an opposed landing in the dark, and without previous reconnaissance, would be an impossible task for the best-trained troops in the world.[2] This was the ordeal that faced the

[1] None of these positions were wired, and no wire was seen by the Australians throughout the day. Gaba Tepe was strongly wired; but the beach to the north of it was considered so unlikely a landing place, that its protection had been neglected.

[2] Had the landing taken place where originally planned, the task, though still difficult, would have been far less severe. The defences in that locality were no stronger than at Ari Burnu, and the natural obstacles, approached from that direction, are much easier to surmount. On the other hand, it is fair to remember that the chance which brought the Australians to Anzac Cove landed them at the only spot on that part of the coast in any way suitable as a permanent landing place. If they had in any case failed to gain their objectives, and had not extended their left to include that tiny bay, their whole position might well have proved untenable. The beach at Anzac Cove was throughout the campaign one of the most constantly shelled areas on the peninsula; but, unlike the coast on either side of it, it had at least the advantage of being almost entirely screened from direct observation by the Turks. Even so, the southern half of the cove could be seen from Nibrunesi Point, $4\frac{1}{2}$ miles away, while the tip of Ari Burnu was visible from Gaba Tepe.

Australian troops at the first moment of their baptism of fire.

For the Australians the forbidding slopes immediately in front of them were not only unknown, but entirely unexpected. The men had been told that they would find a low sandy bank skirting the beach, under cover of which they were to form up by companies before rushing across two hundred yards of level ground to the first low hill. The mistake in the landing place, coupled with the unfortunate intermixing of units as the boats approached the shore, caused, therefore, a certain confusion. But the necessity of pushing straight inland at all costs had been so impressed upon the men that in a remarkably short time eager parties of all three battalions, without waiting to sort themselves, had scrambled to the summit of Plugge's Plateau just in time to see some thirty or forty Turks disappear down the precipitous slopes of a vast scrub-covered ravine on the further side.

Up to this moment the casualties had been almost negligible, and the troops on the plateau were in high spirits. To many of them the campaign already seemed half over, and none can have dreamed of the bitter fighting that was to follow later in the day. The ease of their landing may, indeed, have been a positive disadvantage, by tending to create a false sense of security.

Day was now dawning rapidly, and from the top of Plugge's Plateau the full error of the landing was at last visible, for the easily recognized 400 Plateau, the first objective of the left and centre battalions, could be seen a thousand yards away to the right. Mixed groups of men belonging to all three battalions, flushed with success and thinking only of closing with the enemy, had already charged headlong down the almost precipitous face of Shrapnel Gully; but for the most part a halt was now wisely called, in an endeavour to collect units under their own leaders, and to wait for the men still coming up from the beach, before making a further advance.[1]

Shortly after 5 A.M. both companies of the 10th Battalion, now more or less complete, were moved down into Shrapnel Gully, heading for the steep path at the northern end of 400 Plateau, up which the Turks had retreated. The men of the 9th Battalion were already widely scattered, and one small

---

[1] This reorganization caused delay, but the dislocation of units on landing had been so complete that it was imperatively necessary. Even a longer delay than actually took place would probably have been well repaid, for the wide separation of the men from their accustomed leaders was one of the chief causes of subsequent confusion.

party, regardless of its allotted rôle, had dashed off to the extreme left in pursuit of a handful of Turks; but Major A. G. Salisbury collected about a hundred men on the right of Plugge's, and these he now led across the gully in the direction of Lone Pine. Of the 11th Battalion contingent, those who had reached the top of Plugge's were directed by Major E. A. Drake Brockman to the shelter of Rest Gully to reorganize. Another party, advancing from north of Ari Burnu, had meanwhile reached the same gully by climbing over the cliff-like sides of the Razor Edge.[1] Others were still on the northern beach, pinned to their position by newly opened machine-gun fire from the direction of Fisherman's Hut. Stray men of all three battalions, separated from their leaders and with no one to give them orders, were collecting in considerable numbers in Anzac Cove and in the small gullies which run down to it from the top of the ridge above.

Meanwhile the seven destroyers, carrying the second echelon of the covering force, with Colonel Sinclair-MacLagan and his Staff, had followed the battleship tows to Anzac Cove, and by 4.40 A.M. had begun to disembark their men on a somewhat broader front than that of the leading troops. The two right-hand destroyers, one of which was lying off Hell Spit and the other five hundred yards to the south of it, carried two companies of the 9th Battalion, one company of the 12th, and brigade headquarters. The three centre vessels, opposite Anzac Cove, held two companies of the 10th and two of the 12th. The two left-hand vessels carried two companies of the 11th, one of the 12th, and the field ambulance, and lay to the north of Ari Burnu. The 12th Battalion was supposed to concentrate after landing, and to remain in reserve on the western slopes of 400 Plateau; but its dispersion amongst all seven destroyers proved fatal to that plan. Landing under fire, amid great confusion and excitement, on a front of over a mile, its scattered companies were not unnaturally caught up in the advance of the units nearest to them, and the battalion was never able to fulfil its proper function, or to fight as a complete unit, throughout the 25th.

The troops from the starboard destroyers were ashore by

[1] In addition to the 11th Battalion, numbers of men belonging to other battalions of the brigade continued to filter into Rest Gully about this time, and were organized into a composite company. Owing to lack of officers, three of its platoons were commanded by non-commissioned officers. It is a clear indication of the difficulties which had faced the troops that so drastic a reorganization should have been necessary thus early in the day, before any serious fighting had taken place.

5 A.M. Heading straight up the comparatively easy slopes in front of them, they made short work of a small Turkish piquet guarding this part of the coast, and reached 400 Plateau in front of the battleship detachments who had landed twenty minutes earlier. One small party, dashing boldly across the plateau, surprised and temporarily captured three mountain guns on its eastern slopes. Another pushed down Pine Ridge and away across Legge Valley towards its final objective. Two of the companies landed on this flank had been ordered to capture Gaba Tepe, but the mistake in the landing made this task impossible from the first. Not only were they a mile further north than intended, but the Turks on the promontory were now wide awake, and the rattle of machine guns could be heard from that direction. Nevertheless, on reaching 400 Plateau, the two companies detailed for this task wheeled to the right, only to find themselves opposed by a party of Turks entrenched at the head of Bolton's Ridge. Several officers, including both company commanders, were wounded in the course of the fighting that ensued, and, though the enemy trench was captured, the troops were too scattered to make further organized progress. They succeeded, however, in occupying posts on Bolton's Ridge to guard the right flank of the landing.

In the centre, the four companies landing at Anzac Cove were somewhat badly shelled from Gaba Tepe at 4.45 A.M. But the leading troops pressed forward and one small party of the 10th, under Lieut. N. M. Loutit, advancing over the southern end of MacLagan's Ridge, outdistanced the first echelon and reached Owen's Gully slightly in front of the party that captured the guns.

North of Ari Burnu the troops landing on the left of the line were less fortunate, and it was here that the heaviest casualties occurred. By the time the destroyers neared the land, more Turks had assembled at Fisherman's Hut; the incoming boats were met by a hail of lead; and a large number of men were killed and wounded before they reached the shore. A few yards from the water's edge a stretch of broken ground afforded some little cover from this flanking fire, and here were still assembled a few of the 11th, who had landed twenty minutes earlier. But fifty yards beyond the broken ground the troops were confronted by a wall of almost precipitous cliff, some three hundred feet high, the central crag of which—later to be called the Sphinx—has already been referred to. Sending a small party to the north to tackle the post at Fisherman's Hut —a point they never succeeded in reaching—Colonel L. F.

THE SPHINX FROM THE NORTH

Showing the cliffs which faced the Australians who landed north of Anzac Cove

LANDING OF THE ANZAC COVERING FORCE 179

Clarke of the 12th Battalion now ordered an advance of all the troops near him to the top of the ridge, and he himself, accompanied by about fifty men, actually succeeded in climbing the steep side of the cliff to the north of the Sphinx. For a few minutes a Turkish post on Russell's Top continued to fire on the advancing troops, and several casualties were incurred; but, seeing their retreat threatened by another body of Australians advancing up Walker's Ridge,[1] they soon fled north across the Nek to Baby 700. Between 5.30 and 6 A.M. the whole of First Ridge was cleared of the enemy.[2]

Arriving off Hell Spit about 4.40 A.M. Colonel Sinclair-MacLagan quickly realized that his first echelon had landed too far north, and that there were no Australians ashore between Anzac Cove and Gaba Tepe. On reaching the beach some twenty minutes later he sent his brigade-major southwards to look after the right flank, and then climbed to the top of Mac-Lagan's Ridge to gain a first-hand knowledge of the situation. His main anxiety at this moment was for his right, for it was to the east of Gaba Tepe that large Turkish concentrations had been reported before the landing, and it was from that direction that he expected the inevitable counter-attack. At the summit of the ridge, however, he realized for the first time the extreme difficulty of the country to which the swing of the tows had committed him.

The tactical situation was unexpectedly obscure. The deep scrub-covered ravine in front, with its succession of rugged spurs, had swallowed up the troops who had moved inland. Even the men who had only just gone forward were out of sight, and the intervening crest of Russell's Top was concealing the fortunes of Clarke's and Tulloch's parties at the northern end of First Ridge, though heavy fire could be heard from that direction. Brockman reported that a number of the 11th Battalion and a composite company of all units were organizing in Rest Gully, but with this exception the only reinforcements available were a company of the 12th Battalion that had just reached the plateau. Nevertheless there was at the moment little cause for serious misgiving. The whole of the covering force was at least ashore, and some of its advanced elements were already on the crest of Second Ridge. The Turks had evidently been surprised and were in no great strength; the volume of their fire was negligible; and

[1] Captain E. W. Tulloch, 11th Battalion, with a mixed party of 11th and 12th.
[2] Colonel Clarke was killed in the act of writing a report.

there was no immediate sign of enemy reinforcements. These facts were all to the good; and though there was plainly a lot of disorganization amongst the units which had first landed, the transports of the 2nd Brigade were steaming in to the anchorage, and four more battalions would shortly be disembarking. It was clear, however, to Colonel Sinclair-MacLagan that owing to the mistake in the landing place, the rôle of the 2nd Brigade would have to be reversed; and that, instead of prolonging the left, it must be employed on the right to carry out the task originally allotted to the right of the covering force.

Meanwhile Sinclair-MacLagan set himself to strengthen the position on his left front at the head of Second Ridge, and particularly to safeguard his left flank by ensuring the occupation of Baby 700. With this object he despatched the company of the 12th Battalion straight across to Second Ridge, and ordered Major Brockman to send part of his detachment up Monash Gully to occupy the indentations on its eastern slopes, afterwards known as Quinn's, Courtney's, and Steele's Posts, and to proceed with the remainder to reinforce the advance on Baby 700.[1]

About this time Sir Ian Hamilton arrived off Anzac Cove in the *Queen Elizabeth*, and received the welcome news that the covering force had landed without serious opposition and was already a mile inland. The muffled sound of continuous rifle fire came floating out to sea, but, apart from some light shelling of the anchorage with shrapnel from Gaba Tepe, there seemed to be no hostile artillery in action; and it was with a feeling of hopeful confidence in the success of this portion of his plan that, soon after 6 A.M., the Commander-in-Chief headed south for the toe of the peninsula.

[1] The importance of Baby 700 was self-evident. It commanded Monash Gully throughout its length, and Monash Gully formed the only line of communication between the upper portion of Second Ridge and the coast. It was plain, too, that unless the head of First Ridge was firmly held, a Turkish force moving south from Baby 700 to Russell's Top could outflank a position on Second Ridge and take it in reverse.

CHAPTER X

THE LANDING AT ANZAC (concluded)

THE MAIN BODY

(Map 3 ; Sketches 6, 7, 11)

COLONEL J. W. M'CAY, commanding the 2nd Australian 25 Apr. Brigade, landed about 6 o'clock. On learning from Colonel Sinclair-MacLagan, whom he joined on First Ridge, that the right was in imminent danger and might be turned at any moment, whereas the left was comparatively secure, he agreed to place his brigade on the right flank. The two brigade commanders then proceeded independently to 400 Plateau, Sinclair-MacLagan going to its northern end, and M'Cay to the spur afterwards known as M'Cay's Hill, where he decided to establish his headquarters. From this point he examined the ground over which his brigade was to be employed, and, impressed by the importance of Bolton's Ridge as a position for guarding the right flank of the landing places, he issued orders for the few men already in that locality to be strongly reinforced as soon as troops became available. It was decided that the dividing line between the 2nd and 3rd Brigades should be a line running east and west across the centre of 400 Plateau, through Owen's Gully.

By this time—about 7 o'clock—the sun was high in the heavens, and it was a perfect spring day. With the exception of a few snipers all opposition on Second Ridge had ceased, and scattered groups of Australians were in undisputed possession of the crest, including the eastern slopes of 400 Plateau, and the long pine-covered spur—Pine Ridge—at its south-eastern extremity. A few small parties, led by very gallant officers, had even succeeded in reaching various points on the western slopes of Gun Ridge, the final objective of the covering force. In particular, Lieut. Loutit, of the 10th Battalion, had actually penetrated with a couple of scouts as far as Scrubby Knoll, whence he could see, only $3\frac{1}{2}$ miles away, the gleaming waters of the Narrows—the goal of the whole campaign.[1]

But these gallant advanced parties could progress no further till reinforced, and owing to the intricate country this urgently required support was not forthcoming for the moment. The disastrous swing of the tows had upset every carefully laid plan for the battle. Much time had already been lost, and the precious hours during which Gun Ridge was almost undefended were remorselessly ebbing away.

When Sinclair-MacLagan reached 400 Plateau he found a number of his troops on its western side in disconnected detachments and a few posts on its eastern edge; but the thick scrub and precipitous slopes had completely disrupted the organization of his battalions. In these circumstances, unaware that any troops had already penetrated to Gun Ridge, he decided that, with his brigade so dislocated, it would be unsafe at present to make any attempt to occupy the wide frontage allotted to him on that ridge, and that the line of Second Ridge must for the moment be held as a covering position. He accordingly issued orders for the western edge of 400 Plateau to be entrenched, and also the positions occupied by detachments further north, on the crest of MacLaurin's Hill.[2] The detachments on the eastern edge of the plateau were meanwhile to remain out in observation till the trenches behind them were complete.

On the extreme left at the same hour—7 A.M.—though, owing to the difficult nature of the ground, Colonel Sinclair-MacLagan was not aware of it, the situation was no less confused, and the consequent delay in reinforcing the advanced troops no less disastrous. The troops on Russell's Top and at the Nek still consisted only of scattered fragments of all four battalions of the 3rd Brigade. Casualties amongst their officers had been heavy, and though by this time a small party under Captain Tulloch had crossed the Nek and reached the lower slopes of Baby 700, so much confusion and uncertainty had been caused by the complete shipwreck of all the elaborate plans for each unit on reaching the shore, that supports were long in reaching him. Here, too, precious hours were slipping

---

[1] This was the nearest point to the Narrows reached by any Allied soldier during the campaign.

[2] At Steele's and Courtney's. The important post at Quinn's had not yet been occupied, and a wide gap existed between Courtney's and the troops on Baby 700. The approach to both these posts, which were situated at the head of narrow indentations in the western side of Monash Gully, was exceedingly steep—that to Steele's being a mere landslide up which men could barely scramble on hands and knees.

LANDING OF THE ANZAC MAIN BODY 183

away, and the attack was being held up by a small number of well-concealed marksmen.

The transports of the 2nd and 1st Brigades had arrived off the coast with clock-like precision, but the disembarkation of their troops was proving a troublesome matter. The shelling of the anchorage was increasing, and though the *Bacchante* stood close in to Gaba Tepe and raked the Turkish position with her broadsides, she was unable to silence its fire.

On the extreme left, the landing from the *Galeka* began disastrously. This transport, carrying the 6th and 7th Battalions, had been directed in its original orders to disembark on the left of the 3rd Brigade. Arriving off the shore at 4.45 A.M., the commander of the vessel steered to the north of Ari Burnu, and stood in to an anchorage some six hundred yards from the shore. Here for some time he awaited in vain the arrival of tows to disembark the troops. But none arrived, and as it was obviously impossible to remain for long in that exposed position, with shrapnel bursting above the crowded decks, it was decided to make a start by landing some troops in the ship's own boats. Six boats were filled with a company of the 7th Battalion, and the first four of these, steering for what appeared to be the left flank of the troops already ashore, headed straight for the Turkish post at Fisherman's Hut. For some time the Turks withheld their fire, but when the boats came within two hundred yards of the shore, so heavy a fusillade was poured into them that over a hundred of the 140 men they contained were killed or wounded before they reached the land. The survivors captured the post without difficulty, for the Turks bolted eastwards as soon as they jumped ashore. But these few men were eventually forced to retire on Ari Burnu, and only 18 out of the 140 succeeded in rejoining their battalion during the day.

After this unfortunate episode all the infantry of the 2nd and 1st Brigades were taken to Anzac Cove, which now became the main landing place for the whole corps. But the majority of the transports anchored a long way out to avoid the shelling from Gaba Tepe, and the consequent delay was considerable. It had been hoped that both brigades would be landed by 9 A.M., but, though most of the troops were ashore soon after that hour and some of them a great deal earlier, it was one o'clock before the last battalion [1] of the 1st Brigade had completed its disembarkation.

A contributory cause of this delay was a disregard of the

[1] The 4th Battalion.

orders for the evacuation of the wounded. The naval beach personnel had been instructed that the evacuation of wounded was to be carried out only in medical boats specially detailed for this purpose, and that the tows engaged in landing the fighting troops were on no account to be used for wounded men. In the event, however, not only were men who were killed or wounded on their way to the shore not unnaturally left in the tows, but, owing to lack of organization on the beach during the early hours of the morning,[1] the return of the boats was in many cases delayed while other wounded were embarked. As a result, still further delay occurred when the tows returned to the transports, for the troops for the next trip could not be transferred to the boats till the wounded had been lifted on board and the dead disposed of; and facilities for this work were in many cases non-existent.[2]

As each company of the 2nd Brigade and the leading companies of the 1st Brigade reached the shore, they were guided to a rendezvous at the southern end of Shrapnel Gully, but even here there was further cause for confusion. Owing to the change of plan there were at first no definite orders for any unit; many officers indeed were for some time unaware that the plans had been changed at all. Added to this, there were throughout the morning constant and often unauthorized calls for reinforcing companies to fill a gap in the line, which individual groups of high-spirited men would answer on their own initiative. As a result, and contrary to expectation, the leading battalions of both reinforcing brigades became scattered as soon as they arrived, and General Bridges' plan for keeping the 1st Brigade intact as divisional reserve was from the outset to prove impossible. To make matters worse, companies and platoons advancing independently up the main ravine frequently lost their way in one of its many branches, or found themselves called into an entirely different part of the line from that to which they had been despatched. Thus the units of the main body were soon almost as much intermixed as those of the covering force.

The serious results of landing at so difficult a portion of the coast, and of the consequent unexpected delay in getting up

[1] In accordance with naval and military orders, the naval and military beach personnel did not land till 10 A.M. This scheme differed from the procedure adopted at Helles where they landed with the second trip of tows.
[2] A cause of delay in the return of the boats for their second consignment of troops was, in some cases, the enthusiasm of the boats' crews. There were many instances of bluejackets rushing forward with the troops in the excitement of the moment when the boats first landed, and Colonel Sinclair-MacLagan reports that he himself sent several back to the shore.

LANDING OF THE ANZAC MAIN BODY 185

formed bodies of reinforcements to the points where they were most urgently required, can best be gauged by a study of the Turkish movements during the morning of the 25th. According to the information available from Turkish sources the first news of the Australian landing did not reach Colonel Sami Bey's headquarters at Maidos till 5.30 A.M., or an hour after the landing had begun. For the moment, believing that the main landing would be at Bulair, Sami Bey was inclined to think that nothing but a minor enterprise was intended at Ari Burnu, but he ordered his two reserve battalions of the *27th Regiment* and the machine-gun company to march at once towards Gaba Tepe to drive the invaders into the sea. It was 7.30 A.M., however, before these troops were ready to march, and 9 A.M. before they were seen by the advanced posts of the Australians, slowly filing up Gun Ridge from the south. Meanwhile the news of the Ari Burnu landing had been carried to Marshal Liman von Sanders about 6 A.M. But that officer, firm in his belief that the main attack would be made against the isthmus, had decided to remain at Bulair, and to allow, for the present, no weakening of his strength in that locality. Between 7 and 8 A.M., however, hearing of the further landings at Helles and Kum Kale, the Turkish Commander-in-Chief decided to send Essad Pasha, commanding the *III. Corps*, to take command in the south; and the commanders of the *9th* and *19th Divisions* were informed accordingly.

Shortly after the receipt of this message, and after the two battalions of the *27th* had marched towards Gaba Tepe, a second report reached Sami Bey to the effect that the invaders at Ari Burnu, strength about one battalion,[1] were advancing left-handed up the main ridge in the direction of Chunuk Bair. As the Helles area was by this time claiming his attention, he now asked the *19th Division*, which formed the general reserve for the whole Dardanelles area, to detach one battalion to the Chunuk Bair ridge to guard the right flank.

Fortunately for the Turks, the commander of the *19th Division* was none other than Mustafa Kemal Bey, the future President of the Republic; and that Man of Destiny was at once to show an outstanding genius for command. As soon as he heard that the enemy was making for Chunuk Bair he realized that this could be no feint, but was a serious attack in strength. Appreciating at once that it constituted a threat against the heart of the Turkish defence, he determined to examine the

---

[1] The landing beaches were invisible to the Turks, and the fact that they placed the Australian strength so low seems to indicate that few men had yet succeeded in reaching the high ground on the left.

situation for himself, and to throw not a battalion but a whole regiment into the fight. Accompanied by an advanced party of one company, he set off in the direction of Chunuk Bair, ordering the remainder of the *57th Regiment* to follow as quickly as possible. As already mentioned, the approaches to the main ridge were many times less abrupt on the inland than on the seaward side, and shortly after 10 A.M. this advanced party was in collision with Tulloch's small detachment in the neighbourhood of Battleship Hill. Mustafa Kemal remained on the spot long enough to issue orders for an attack by two battalions and a mountain battery as soon as they arrived. Then, having satisfied himself that the situation was temporarily in hand, he hurried back to Maidos to report to Essad Pasha.[1]

The time of the arrival of the main body of the *57th Regiment* has never been fully established, but their mountain battery, which took up a position near Chunuk Bair, did not open fire till 1 P.M., and the counter-attack down both sides of Battleship Hill did not develop till half-past four. It is probable, however, that, in addition to the detachment which arrived with Mustafa Kemal about 10 A.M., reinforcing companies began to trickle in to the Turkish position in that neighbourhood from midday onwards.

A study of these figures will show that for several hours the Turkish troops available to oppose the Australian advance to Gun Ridge consisted only of the outpost company in and around Ari Burnu at the time of the landing, supported by such portions of the remainder of the outpost battalion, spread out over a five-mile front, as were withdrawn from their own posts to meet the attack. The delaying power of well-armed and well-concealed marksmen, favoured by a perfect knowledge of the ground, is undoubtedly very great. Nevertheless there can be little doubt that the extreme difficulties of the country played an even greater part than the opposition of the enemy in frustrating the Australian plan, and that but for the unfortunate mistake in the landing place the 4,000 Australians who disembarked before 5 A.M. and the 4,000 who followed them between 6 and 8 A.M. could have pushed back the Turkish outposts and established themselves on Gun Ridge and Chunuk Bair before the arrival of enemy reinforcements.

[1] Essad Pasha arrived at Maidos about noon. When Mustafa Kemal returned Essad approved his dispositions and gave him permission to use the whole of the *19th Division* in the Anzac area. He then followed Sami Bey southward, to learn the situation in the Helles sector, leaving Mustafa Kemal in temporary command opposite the Australians.

It was about half-past nine when the leading troops of the Turkish *27th Regiment* began to advance westwards from the centre of Gun Ridge. The scattered detachments of Australians on the western slopes of the ridge were now forced to retire, and shortly afterwards a heavy and sustained rifle fire was poured by the Turks on to the summit of 400 Plateau and the crest of MacLaurin's Hill.

Fearing an immediate counter-attack on the eastern slopes of Lone Pine, Colonel Sinclair-MacLagan ordered the companies of the 9th Battalion, who were digging themselves in to the west of that locality, where the dense scrub prevented any field of fire, to hurry forward to meet it. Section by section the men were led forward through the scrub, but the volume of fire now being directed on the summit was much heavier than Sinclair-MacLagan had realized, and only a remnant of those who started succeeded in passing through it. Thus a gap was formed in the Australian front which throughout the rest of the day was a constant source of anxiety.

Colonel Sinclair-MacLagan had early decided to establish his headquarters on MacLaurin's Hill, and the brigade signallers had already chosen a position and connected it by telephone to the beach. When the brigade commander arrived there about 10 o'clock the Turks seemed to be threatening an immediate attack, and it was obvious that a break-through at this point would make 400 Plateau untenable. The decision not to advance beyond Second Ridge had had the effect of placing brigade headquarters in the firing line. But it was vitally important to hold MacLaurin's Hill, and the brigadier determined to stay in this exposed and in many ways unsuitable position in order to encourage his men.

Meanwhile, on the extreme left flank, Captain Tulloch with about sixty men had reached the south-eastern slopes of Battleship Hill between 9 and 10 o'clock, and had sent a small party under Lieut. S. H. Jackson to the seaward side of the hill to protect his left flank. Progress had been slow since passing the Nek, for though the Turks were few in numbers their shooting was deadly. In places it was nearly impossible to crawl through the prickly scrub; yet to show oneself above it for an instant was to attract a hot fire. Further in rear, on Baby 700, were other small parties under Captain J. P. Lalor and Lieut. I. S. Margetts of the 12th Battalion.

Shortly after 10 A.M. the leading troops of the *57th Regiment*, brought up by Mustafa, began to trickle into action on the seaward slopes of Battleship Hill, and first Jackson, and then the parties on Baby 700, were forced to give ground. A few minutes later a flanking fire was poured into Tulloch's party, and that officer, finding his left flank uncovered, was in turn compelled to withdraw. The retirement was only momentary, for shortly afterwards a company of the 1st Battalion [1] under Major B. I. Swannell, swept over the Nek and recaptured Baby 700. But, away to the right rear, Sinclair-MacLagan, who had hitherto looked upon his left flank as reasonably secure, had witnessed with alarm the withdrawal from Baby 700 of Margetts, who also had been outflanked. At 10.35 A.M., expecting the Turks at any moment to appear on Russell's Top behind him, he informed divisional headquarters [2] that unless the Nek could be held he would be unable to remain on Second Ridge. He urged that reinforcements should at once be sent to the left.

For Major-General Bridges the situation was an anxious one, for the whole plan of the landing had evidently fallen to pieces. G.H.Q. had expected a semicircular position, including Gun Ridge, to be seized by a covering force of one brigade, preparatory to an eastward advance by the main body of the corps. General Birdwood had modified this order to the extent of authorizing the employment of a second brigade to assist the covering force by extending its left flank.[3] But, despite this increase of strength, nothing but the unexpected had happened. The covering force had landed at the wrong place. The 2nd Brigade had been brought in on the right instead of on the left. Both brigades had become disintegrated. Since General Bridges' arrival on shore, eight of the sixteen companies of the 1st Brigade, which he had hoped to keep intact as divisional reserve, had already been rushed into the fight on Second Ridge. Of the remaining eight companies, six had not yet landed, and only two were available on shore to meet any further urgent calls for reinforcements. And now, at 10.35 A.M., the divisional commander was to learn that his left flank, which Sinclair-MacLagan had at first thought to be reasonably safe, was after all in imminent peril. Orders were at once issued for the two available companies to reinforce the Nek, and with their departure, except for the 4th Battalion and two companies of the 2nd which were still afloat, all the infantry of the division had been absorbed into the battle. Little progress had been made; only half of the covering force's task had been

---

[1] This battalion, landed at 7.40 A.M., had been ordered at 9.30 to reinforce 400 Plateau; but Swannell's company, becoming sandwiched in between companies of the 3rd Battalion, proceeded up Monash Gully to the left flank, lost its way, and at 10.15 found itself at the Nek.

[2] General Bridges landed at 7.30 A.M. and was now directing the battle from his headquarters in a gully on the seaward side of Plugge's.

[3] See Appendices 3, 5, 15, 16 for operation orders.

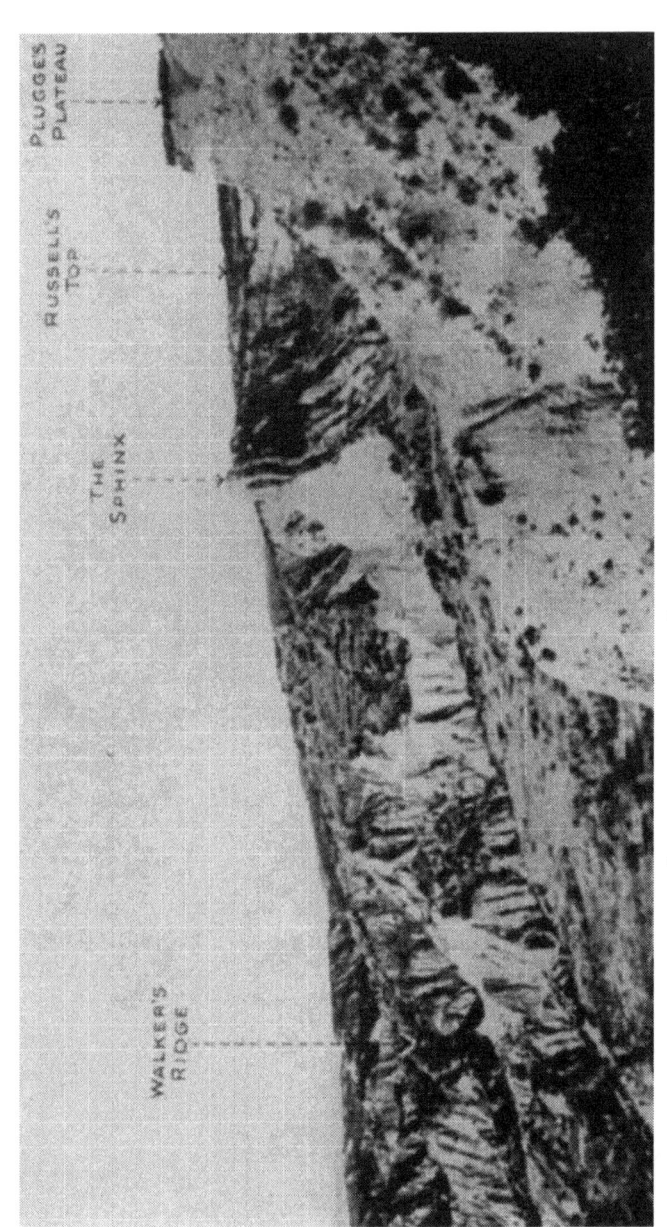

WALKER'S RIDGE AND RUSSELL'S TOP FROM ARI BURNU

LANDING OF THE ANZAC MAIN BODY 189

accomplished; the position was manifestly insecure; and the inevitable counter-attack had hardly yet begun.

At this critical juncture, about 10.45 A.M., General Birdwood signalled that he was landing one and a half battalions [1] of the New Zealand Infantry Brigade, which had arrived with divisional headquarters in the transport *Lutzow*, and that Br.-General H. B. Walker, B.G.G.S. Anzac corps, would take command of the brigade *vice* Colonel F. E. Johnston on the sick list. General Bridges at once decided to throw these troops in on his left flank, with orders to reinforce the line on Baby 700 by way of Walker's Ridge. A start was made by the Auckland Battalion (Lieut.-Colonel A. Plugge) in this direction, but after proceeding some distance the rugged slopes of the ridge appeared so difficult and so exposed that General Walker—unaware of the existence of the Razor Edge—passed the word for the troops to retire, and to proceed to Russell's Top by way of Plugge's Plateau. The change of plan was unfortunate. Many of the men could not be recalled; the remainder, like the earlier arrivals, lost their way. Companies and platoons became scattered and intermixed. Some of the men found themselves on 400 Plateau; others on MacLaurin's Hill; others again at the head of Monash Gully; and not more than one company appears to have reached the Nek [2] before 1.30 P.M.

Thus it was that throughout the day the Anzac fortunes on Baby 700 were jeopardized and eventually ruined by the extraordinary difficulties of the ground. Thanks to the gallantry and devotion of officers and men, the Turks were kept at bay on that dangerous left flank, but the invading reinforcements were invariably so disorganized by the time they reached the Nek, that it was never possible to develop their full power. By 3 P.M. the Australians and New Zealanders on the spot consisted of fragments of no less than seven battalions, all very intermixed, and all more or less worn out by a succession of spasmodic and disjointed attacks. There was no one in chief command of this section of the battlefield; the scattered companies had no knowledge of what was required of them; and unity of effort was impossible. For several hours the line

[1] The Auckland Battalion and two companies of the Canterbury Battalion. In the original plan no arrangements had been made to land this brigade till the disembarkation of the Australian infantry, with a proportion of artillery and ancillary services, had been completed. It is possible that the change of programme was to some extent responsible for the delay in landing the 1st Brigade already referred to.

[2] Lieut.-Colonel D. McB. Stewart, Canterbury Battalion, was killed in the fighting near the Nek during the afternoon, and Lieut.-Colonel Plugge was wounded.

had swayed backwards and forwards over Baby 700, each reinforcing detachment in turn succeeding in making a little headway, only to be driven back by Turkish rifle fire when it showed above the crest. The Turkish fire had sensibly increased since the morning; losses amongst officers had been heavy;[1] since 1 P.M. the troops had been subjected to considerable shelling from the direction of Chunuk Bair, to which there was no reply. To lie out in the thick scrub under this shrapnel fire, separated from and out of sight of their comrades, unsupported by friendly artillery, ignorant of the situation, and imagining that they were the sole survivors of their units, was a severe strain to young troops in their first day of battle. For many the breaking point had already been passed.

This was the situation when, about 4 o'clock, the long expected counter-attack developed on both sides of Baby 700. Shortly afterwards the hill was in the hands of the Turks, and the sorely tried Australians and New Zealanders were falling back, some to the beach, some to Pope's Hill and MacLaurin's Hill, where they formed the first garrison of Quinn's Post, and a few to a small trench at the southern end of the Nek. Except for these few men, commanded by a corporal,[2] and for two companies of the 2nd Battalion under Lieut.-Colonel G. F. Braund at the head of Walker's Ridge,[3] a clear road now lay open to the Turks across the Nek to the heart of the Anzac position. But the Turks, too, were scattered and disorganized, and for some hours they made no further progress.

Even now it was not too late for the situation to be restored. "If reinforced," wrote Braund to his brigadier at 5 P.M., "I can "advance." But General Bridges had just sent his last reserve to the right; the remainder of the New Zealand Brigade, and the 4th Australian Infantry Brigade, had not yet landed. Until these could arrive not another man was available.[4]

Simultaneously with the attack on Baby 700, a small body of Turks advanced against the seaward end of Walker's Ridge. A success at this point might well have had disastrous consequences, but the position was securely held by Captain A. C. B.

---

[1] The extraordinary difficulty of maintaining direction and keeping touch with the flanks in this tortuous scrub-covered country was mainly responsible for the heavy losses amongst officers. All leaders had to expose themselves very considerably to get their bearings, and thus formed an easy and conspicuous target for Turkish snipers.

[2] Afterwards Lieut. H. V. Howe, 11th Battalion.

[3] The last two companies of the 2nd Battalion, under Colonel Braund, landed about noon and were sent to the left flank. The 4th Battalion landed at 12.45 P.M. and was kept in divisional reserve till 5 P.M.

[4] The Otago Battalion began to land about 5 P.M. and was told to dig in on Plugge's Plateau.

LANDING OF THE ANZAC MAIN BODY 191

Critchley-Salmonson,[1] with a mixed detachment of 33 men belonging to five different battalions. Recognizing the importance of this flank, Critchley - Salmonson impressed upon his men the necessity of holding it at all costs, and the position remained intact till reinforcements arrived.

At 6 P.M. the situation at the Nek was still obscure, but a dangerous gap was known to exist between Second Ridge and Braund's troops on Walker's Ridge. Colonel Sinclair-MacLagan, still apprehensive of the Turks appearing in rear of him at any moment, asked that the 4th Australian Brigade should be sent up to fill this gap as soon as it arrived. At this moment the 16th Battalion, under Lieut.-Colonel H. Pope, was just landing, and Pope was ordered to push on with all available men to the head of Monash Gully. Starting soon afterwards with two companies of his own battalion, one of the 15th, and two platoons of New Zealanders, Pope eventually occupied the wedge-shaped hill afterwards known by his name. But, as in the case of all other parties which had advanced up Monash Gully, the tail of the column got separated from the head, and was finally used to reinforce the garrisons of Steele's and Courtney's Posts. At nightfall there was still a gap between Pope and Braund, and between Pope's right and the troops on Second Ridge.[2]

The Turks were fortunately too weary to profit by these opportunities or even to discover them; and, though a small party succeeded in pushing forward to Russell's Top, they did little damage, and were successfully accounted for next morning. There was, however, to be no rest for anyone on those rugged hill-sides that night. Worn out with fatigue, scattered and disorganized, it was impossible for either side to make further progress. But the noise of battle continued; and with only the flash of their assailants' rifles to guide them, invaders and invaded alike kept up a continuous fire.[3]

On Second Ridge, and particularly on 400 Plateau, where portions of no less than ten out of the twelve battalions of the 1st

[1] An officer of the Royal Munster Fusiliers temporarily serving with the Canterbury Battalion.

[2] This latter gap, at the head of the eastern fork of Monash Gully, was never bridged throughout the campaign. It was eventually securely held by cross-fire from either flank, but the ground at the head of this fork, known as the "Chessboard", remained in Turkish hands, and much of the gully was under constant observation by the enemy.

[3] Many times during the confused fighting that day, and especially after dark, men fired on their own friends in front or on the flank; and the story spread that the Turks had shouted out, "Don't shoot, we're "Australians". But the many assertions that the Turks employed this ruse were in no single instance substantiated.

Australian Division were now engaged, the battle raged all the afternoon with unabated fury. Having been definitely ordered to remain on the defensive, the Australians in that sector were somewhat better placed than those on the left flank to resist a counter-attack, and their position gave many advantages to the defence. On the other hand 400 Plateau was an easy target for the Turkish artillery. A mountain battery was brought into action against it about 11 A.M., and throughout the afternoon three Turkish batteries covered it with persistent and well-directed bursts of shrapnel fire. For the Australians, whose trenches on the 25th provided practically no cover,[1] and who for most of the day were without artillery support of any kind, this first experience of shrapnel was very trying. Nevertheless the advanced detachments on the eastern side of the plateau held their ground tenaciously, and kept up so steady a fire on the oncoming Turks that throughout the afternoon the enemy never once set foot on the plateau. The value of this plucky stand was enhanced by the fact that, in rear, where the 9th Battalion had made its costly advance in the morning, there was a wide gap in the Australian main line on the western edge of the plateau.

Colonel M'Cay, naturally anxious about this gap, repeatedly asked for reinforcements during the afternoon. But with the exception of the 4th Battalion, not another man would be available till the remainder of the New Zealand Brigade arrived in the evening, and General Bridges had determined to keep this battalion in hand to meet a sudden crisis. About 4.45 P.M., however, M'Cay again called for help, urging that the whole safety of the position would be jeopardized if another battalion could not be sent him at once. In face of this opinion General Bridges decided that he could refuse M'Cay's request no longer, and the 4th Battalion was ordered to the right. Scarcely had it started when news was received that the Australians on the left flank were retiring across the Nek, and Colonel Braund sent in the message that if reinforced he could restore the situation. But there was no longer a man to send.

With the assistance of the 4th Battalion the gap on the right front was filled about 6 o'clock, and M'Cay's line then consisted of a succession of irregular lengths of trench from the seaward end of Bolton's Ridge to a point on 400 Plateau north-east of M'Cay's Hill, a total frontage of rather less than 1,200 yards. As darkness fell the gallant but worn-out detachments who had

[1] Most of the heavy entrenching tools brought ashore were left behind on the beach, and the light entrenching implement was of little use against the stubborn roots of the scrub.

LANDING OF THE ANZAC MAIN BODY 193

so long withstood the Turkish attacks on the eastern slopes of the plateau at last fell back to the main line. The Turks at this stage were too disorganized to follow, and for the rest of the night the summit of the plateau was occupied only by the dead.

Further south, meanwhile, a small column of the *27th Regiment*, detached earlier in the afternoon to make a flank attack on M'Cay's extreme right, debouched from the southern end of Gun Ridge about 3 o'clock. Half an hour later, having overwhelmed a heroic handful of the 6th Battalion occupying an advanced position on the eastern slopes of Pine Ridge, it continued its advance towards Bolton's. To avoid exposure to the fire of Admiral Thursby's ships, a halt was then made in a gully till after dark. Eventually, between 8 and 10 P.M., the advance was resumed, and an attack was launched on the trenches of the 4th and 8th Battalions. But it was only a half-hearted effort, and a gallant sally by men of the 8th Battalion sufficed to drive it back.

This was the enemy's last attempt to penetrate the Australian positions on the 25th April. But throughout the whole length of Second Ridge, as on the extreme left, there was to be no rest for the weary troops, and all through the night thousands of rounds of ammunition were expended in ceaseless firing.

The absence of artillery support during the greater part of the day was a very severe handicap to the Australian and New Zealand troops, especially to those who were suffering from unanswered Turkish shrapnel. Before the landing it had been expected that two batteries of mountain guns would be ashore before 9 A.M. and in action immediately afterwards, and that several batteries of field artillery would be landed before noon. It was also expected that the fleet would be able to render considerable assistance with its guns.[1] In the event, however, practically none of this support was forthcoming. One mountain battery[2] was ashore by 9 A.M., but it was long before any suitable position could be found for it, and, though it eventually came into action soon after midday on the western slopes of 400 Plateau, its position was quickly enfiladed by a

---

[1] The following arrangements had been made for naval support:
  i. The O.C. covering force to ask for ships' fire by signal, the objective to be indicated by reference to map squares.
  ii. The fleet, on its own initiative, to open fire on any Turkish troops or guns clearly visible from the sea.
  iii. On each flank an artillery officer to act as an observer for the ships. Messages from these officers to be transmitted to the beach by telephone and thence by W/T to the flagship.

[2] The 26th Indian Mountain Battery commanded by Captain H. A. Kirby.

VOL. I   O

Turkish battery on the main (Chunuk Bair) ridge, and at 2.30 P.M., after sustaining heavy casualties, it had to withdraw. This battery, and one 18-pdr. gun which landed at 3.30 P.M., were the only guns disembarked before 6 P.M. To some extent this delay was due to the lighters being detained to evacuate wounded, and partly to disorganization caused by the shelling of the anchorage.[1]

General Godley had signalled to the flagship at 1.45 P.M. begging that his howitzers might be sent in quickly, but was told that no lighters were available. Later in the afternoon, however, definite orders delayed the arrival of the guns. General Bridges had come to the conclusion that the ground was almost impracticable for field artillery, and that in any case the situation was still too critical to admit of guns being landed. He seems to have expressed this view to the corps commander, who visited his headquarters during the afternoon; for at 3.45 P.M. General Birdwood signalled to Admiral Thursby: " Please " stop sending field artillery". The admiral thereupon ordered the transports to land no more guns,[2] and to re-embark any that had already been transferred to lighters, and thus it was that the troops were deprived that evening of the moral support of hearing their own artillery in action.

As for naval gun-fire, the ships were for most of the day compelled to remain idle. It was impossible for the warships, even with the help of balloon-ships and seaplanes, to pick out targets for themselves, nor could they search the approaches to the shore without knowing the whereabouts of the Australian line; and information on this point was particularly slow in reaching them. About 5 P.M., however, the fleet was at last given an opportunity of assisting the troops. Since 12 noon an officer on Pine Ridge had been trying to send back a report

---

[1] In addition to the two 12-cm. guns at Gaba Tepe, a Turkish battleship in the Narrows shelled the anchorage intermittently during the morning, and compelled the transports to move out to a safer position. At the time, those watching the landing were surprised that the Turkish battleship ceased firing just when her fire was causing most annoyance. From a neutral military attaché, however, who was present at Chanak on 25th April, it has been ascertained that this relief was directly due to the Australian submarine which passed up the Narrows on the 25th. The Turkish battleship caught sight of her periscope just above Chanak, and had to run for safety. Thus the Australian submarine was very appropriately of direct assistance to the Anzac landing.

[2] In one case Admiral Thursby's order miscarried, and two more field guns arrived at the beach late in the afternoon, but these were at once sent back to their transport. When the artillery officer, who had been reconnoitring for a position and who knew nothing about the order that had been issued, returned to the beach and found the guns gone he did his best to recall them, but found it impossible to get into touch with the ship.

LANDING OF THE ANZAC MAIN BODY 195

describing the position of two Turkish guns near Anderson's Knoll, but all his messages miscarried, and it was not till 5 P.M. that the report at last got through. A quarter of an hour later, to the intense delight of the harassed troops, naval gun-fire opened accurately on Anderson's Knoll, and the guns which had so long tormented them were silenced.

The transports bearing the 4th Australian Brigade and the remainder of the New Zealand Brigade arrived off Anzac Cove about 5 P.M., and it was then decided that General Godley's division should be allotted to the left flank. Some of the troops, including two companies of the Wellington Battalion (Lieut.-Colonel W. G. Malone) and the majority of the 16th Australian Battalion, were landed almost immediately. But the divisional Staffs were by this time considering the possibility of having to evacuate the whole position that night.[1] Vague rumours to this effect spread along the shore, and the doubts and uncertainties raised by this possibility, coupled with some lack of organization on the beach, were responsible for further delays. A study of the war diaries of some of the battalions of the 4th Australian Brigade throws a vivid light on this subject. Thus the 13th Battalion arrived at its anchorage at 4.30 P.M. Its disembarkation did not begin till 9.30 P.M., and did not finish till 3.30 A.M. on the 26th. The 14th anchored at 5 P.M., but its landing was not begun till next day. Numbers of lighters, filled with wounded, arrived alongside the transport during the hours of waiting, and many of the men spent the whole night in carrying the wounded below. Equally trying to the troops concerned was the experience of the 15th Battalion. Anchoring at 4 P.M., two companies of the battalion were crowded on board a destroyer half an hour later, but were not disembarked till 10.30. While awaiting disembarkation the destroyer came under shell fire, and some of the men were hit.

No story of the Anzac landing would be complete that did not mention the three field companies of the Australian Engineers. Some of the 1st Field Company, landing with the advanced echelon, for the moment forgot their allotted rôle. They dashed forward with the leading infantry to the top of Plugge's Plateau, and it was some little time before they could be re-assembled on the beach. Later in the morning the engineers were divided into three parties, one to make roads, another to search for water, and the third to construct piers for landing stores. Paths to the top of Plugge's Plateau, and a track for 18-pdr. guns to the top of Queensland Point[2] were

[1] See Chapter XV. [2] Above Hell Spit.

constructed during the day; and communications up Shrapnel Gully were greatly improved. A water-tank boat, provided with eleven galvanized tanks and pumps, was towed ashore, and early in the evening there was enough water available to supply the whole force. On the right flank, too, a certain amount of water was found in Shrapnel Gully. Pumps and water-troughs were erected there, and a fair amount of water was available from that source late in the afternoon. On the left flank no water could be found in the first instance, but water tins were landed and sent to the troops in the line. As regards piers, a barrel pier had arrived by noon and a pontoon equipment a little later; and despite the continuous shrapnel fire from Gaba Tepe, an excellent landing-stage was erected in Anzac Cove. This pier proved invaluable for evacuating the wounded, and 1,500 men were embarked from it before midnight on the 25th/26th.

The cessation of the enemy counter-attacks on the evening of the 25th April makes a convenient point at which to break the thread of the Anzac narrative, and to follow the fortunes of the landings further south. But, before doing this, it is of interest briefly to notice the general results of the Australians' and New Zealanders' first day of battle, and to study the situation, first as it must have appeared that evening to the commanders on the spot, and secondly as the information now available shows it to have been in reality.

The actual results of the day's fighting may be summarized briefly as follows: the initial landing in the early morning (the operation involving the greatest risk) had been accomplished with slight loss. Fifteen thousand men were ashore;[1] a comparatively favourable beach had been secured; the troops were in occupation of a position which, except at one point, where a dangerous gap existed, was practicable for defence; and, finally, they had succeeded in beating off a series of counter-attacks. The casualties, which amounted to two thousand, were undeniably heavy; yet they were no larger than might have been suffered by the 3rd Infantry Brigade in the first hour had its landing been strenuously opposed. Fresh troops would be arriving during the night, and by early morning the weak points in the line could be strongly reinforced.

On the other hand, to the commanders on the spot, there

---

[1] By 6 P.M. the force landed consisted of 3 Australian infantry brigades, half of the New Zealand Infantry Brigade, one 18-pdr. gun, 2 mountain batteries, casualty clearing station, bearer sub-divisions of three field ambulances, details of engineers and signallers—approximately 15,000 all ranks—and 42 mules.

LANDING OF THE ANZAC MAIN BODY 197

appeared to be many disturbing symptoms. The sanguine hopes of G.H.Q. had proved illusory, and it seemed clear that the higher Staffs had greatly underestimated the difficulties. Three Australian brigades and two battalions of New Zealanders, fighting with great gallantry throughout the day, had been unable to gain more than half the objectives which G.H.Q. had assigned to one infantry brigade as its initial operation. Owing to the fantastic configuration of the ground, and the extraordinarily thick scrub, every unit had become widely scattered from the start, and its normal organization broken. Every available man had been hurried into the battle, and, for the moment, there were no reserves. The Turks, on the other hand, were believed to have strong reinforcements in the immediate vicinity. So much small arms ammunition had been expended that its replacement was causing anxiety, and the difficulty of sending water to the troops on those precipitous hillsides presented a very anxious problem. The number of casualties could not yet be estimated, but was believed to be extremely heavy. Exaggerated reports as to the serious situation in front were arriving at the various headquarters;[1] and, most impressive feature of all, a disturbing number of leaderless men were filtering back to the beach. Though the officers who saw them did not realize it at the time,[2] hardly any of these men were stragglers in the ordinary sense of the word. Some of them had come back to the only centre of authority they knew in search of fresh orders. Others had returned in consequence of rumours that an order had been given to retire. Many of them, though desperately weary, were in high spirits, the reaction from the strain of the day. Elbowing and pushing their way about the crowded strip of beach, they were recounting their experiences, taking a "breather" after a hard day's work, searching for their packs (it was now turning cold), and sizing up the prospects of a meal. Hundreds of them were soon collected together, formed into companies, and pushed off to reinforce the left flank. But more and more kept drifting back to the beach. Few of them perhaps, had any idea that their return from the front might be misinterpreted, or was constituting an actual danger. But to the divisional Staffs in rear the scene on the beach was alarming.

Taking all these factors into consideration, the situation

Sketch 11,

[1] At 5.20 P.M. M'Cay reported to Bridges that a considerable number of unwounded men were leaving the firing line. Australian Official Account, i. p. 454.
[2] The Australian Official Account, i. p. 453 states: "Officers of the "various headquarters, being mostly behind the lines, were also deeply "impressed by the stragglers who, in ever-growing numbers, began to find "their way back into the valleys behind the firing line."

seemed gloomy indeed to General Bridges and his brigadiers; and the idea gradually began to take shape that in the event of a strong Turkish attack by fresh troops in the morning, the chances of preventing a disaster were remote.

At General Headquarters, though two telegrams despatched by General Birdwood had sounded a somewhat uncertain note,[1] the general tenour of the news had been encouraging, and not until midnight was the Commander-in-Chief to learn that the situation was considered grave.

In the peculiar circumstances of an opposed landing on a little known and mountainous coast it must always be more than usually difficult to pierce the fog of war. But, studied in the light of that knowledge which can only come after the event, the situation of the invaders at Anzac on the night of the 25th, so far from being unsatisfactory, would appear to have held many promises of success. Except at the head of Monash Gully, the position which the Australians and New Zealanders had occupied, and which at least 10,000 men were available to hold, was, despite many disadvantages, a strong one, and was only 6,000 yards long. With slight modifications it was destined to be the front line of the Anzac corps for more than three months, and, despite the yawning gaps between Russell's Top and Quinn's, all the efforts of the Turks in that period could never succeed in breaking it. The troops in front on the night of the 25th, though tired out with the immense strain of the day, were still in good heart. They knew that they held the measure of the Turks, and they asked only for reinforcements and artillery support to enable them to advance against the enemy next day. Most important

---

[1] The following messages were received from General Birdwood during the day:

"6.39 A.M. Australians reported capture of 400 Plateau and advancing, extending their right towards Gaba Tepe. Three Krupp guns captured. Disembarkation proceeding satisfactorily and 8,000 men landed."

"4.30 P.M. Have now about 13,000 men ashore, but only one mountain battery. Troops have been fighting hard all over Sari Bair since morning, and have been shelled from positions we are unable to reach. Shall be landing field guns shortly and will try to solidify position on hill. Trying to make water arrangements."

"8.45 P.M. Have visited Sari Bair position which I find not very satisfactory. Very difficult country and heavily entrenched. Australians pressed forward too far and had to retire. Bombarded for several hours by shrapnel and unable to reply. Casualties about 2,000. Hope to complete by night disembarkation of remaining infantry and howitzer battery. Enemy reported 9 battalions strong, with machine guns, and prepared for our landing."

LANDING OF THE ANZAC MAIN BODY 199

of all, though this could not be known at the time, the Turks were more disorganized than the Australians, and they, too, had suffered 2,000 casualties, which was an even higher percentage of loss.[1] At dusk on the 25th Mustafa Kemal was informed that the *2nd/57th Regiment* had completely disappeared, that the *1st/57th* was in dire straits, and that the commander of the *3rd/57th*, which had been ordered to fill the gap between the two, had only some eighty to ninety men present. The *27th Regiment* by the end of the day had suffered severe casualties, and was completely worn out. The condition of the *77th Regiment*, composed of Arabs, was even worse. This regiment had been ordered to attack at dusk at the head of MacLaurin's Hill. After meeting the Australian rifle fire, it broke and fled in panic to Gun Ridge, whence some of the men fired all night into the backs of their comrades of the *27th* and *57th*. By daylight the regiment was completely scattered. The *72nd Regiment* was the last regiment of the *19th Division* to leave camp, and apparently did not reach the battlefield till the morning of the 26th. Like the *77th* it was an Arab formation, and none too trustworthy. Yet it was the only reserve in Mustafa Kemal's hands.

It would appear indeed that by the evening of the 25th, despite the almost impossible task to which the mistake in the landing place had committed them, the Australian and New Zealand troops were within an ace of triumph. Yet such is War. The student of military history must ever remember that there is nothing more easy than wisdom after the event. To quote the words of Frederick the Great: "If we all knew " before a battle as much as we know after its conclusion, every " one of us would be a great general".

Seldom indeed has the mettle of inexperienced troops been subjected to a more severe test than was that of the citizen soldiers of Australia and New Zealand on their first day of active service. Hazardous as a landing on an unknown shore must always be, the task of the 3rd Australian Brigade was made still more arduous by the unfortunate chance which carried it to a landing place of unexpected and unexampled severity. The battle which then began cannot be judged by the standards of any ordinary attack, where the troops, carefully assembled beforehand, start from a definite line, at a definite zero hour. Arriving piecemeal in boats, landing

---

[1] From daybreak till 9.30 A.M. not more than five hundred Turks had been actually engaged, and from 9.30 A.M. till dusk a gradually increasing number which at no time exceeded six battalions.

under fire where best they could, wading ashore in the dark, finding themselves in many cases confronted by unclimbable cliffs, hunting for a practicable line of ascent, and then scrambling up a difficult hill-side covered with prickly scrub, it would have been hard indeed for units to avoid disintegration. The means of communicating orders and getting back information, always liable to interruption, were completely dislocated; the chain of command—none too strong at that time—was snapped. Individual groups of high-mettled men flung themselves forward on their own initiative; platoons and companies became fatally intermixed; and the plans for each battalion's special task fell hopelessly to bits.

Taking all these factors into consideration it may well be doubted whether even a division of veteran troops could have carried out a co-ordinated attack at Anzac on the 25th April. The predominant feeling, which that astounding battlefield must always arouse in the military student who visits it, will be a sense of unstinted admiration for those untried battalions who did so exceedingly well. The magnificent physique, the reckless daring, and the fine enthusiasm of the Dominion troops on their first day of trial went far to counteract anything they lacked in training and war experience. The story of their landing will remain for all time amongst the proudest traditions of the Australian and New Zealand Forces.

CHAPTER XI

THE LANDING AT Y BEACH

(Map 2 ; Sketches 5A, 8, 12, 13)

THE object of the Y Beach landing was to assist the main opera- **25 Apr.** tions at Helles and Sedd el Bahr by throwing a small force ashore at an unexpected spot where the Turkish communications with the toe of the peninsula could be threatened and perhaps interrupted. The locality selected for this landing was admirably suited for the purpose. The coast line consisted of steep, forbidding, scrub-covered cliffs about 150 feet high; but at the actual point chosen for the landing place two breaks in the cliff, caused by water-courses, offered a comparatively easy access to the summit, while a steep-to shore, devoid of rocks, enabled light-draught vessels to approach within a few yards of the narrow strip of beach. Better still, though this was unknown beforehand, no preparations of any kind had been made by the Turks to guard the locality. The nearest Turkish troops were two platoons of infantry more than a mile away to the south, near the mouth of Gully Ravine. **Sketch** Apart from this small detachment, no portion of which came **5A.** into action against the Y Beach troops till late in the afternoon, the only Turks in the neighbourhood were one platoon of the *2nd/26th Regiment* at Sari Tepe, and the *25th Regiment* at Serafim Farm, five miles distant. This regiment formed the divisional reserve for the whole front from Aghyl Dere to Sedd el Bahr. The *1st/26th Regiment* was distributed along the coast between Semerly Tepe and Sari Tepe, one and three-quarter miles north of Y Beach, but fear of a landing in that neighbourhood prevented this battalion from taking any part in the fighting on the 25th and 26th April.

Despite these almost unhoped-for advantages, the landing at Y Beach was perhaps the most disappointing of all the Gallipoli landings. As the following pages will show, 2,000 men were safely disembarked without a hitch, and without any opposition. For eleven hours they were left undisturbed by the enemy, and, throughout that period, they alone were equal in numbers to all the Turkish forces south of Achi Baba. Yet throughout the 25th the initial success remained unexploited. During the ensuing night the troops gallantly repulsed a succession of fierce attacks on their line. But the whole enterprise was suddenly abandoned next morning, and the men re-embarked, at the very moment when the enemy himself was in full retreat. The re-embarkation, like the landing, was completed without a shot being fired.

The troops for the Y Beach landing consisted of the 1/King's Own Scottish Borderers under Lieut.-Colonel A. S. Koe, one company 2/South Wales Borderers, and the Plymouth Battalion, R.M.L.I., under Lieut.-Colonel G. E. Matthews. The last-named unit consisted almost entirely of men specially enlisted for the war. Colonel Matthews, as senior combatant officer, was in command of the force.[1]

In the first instance the troops for Y Beach, as also those for S, had been regarded by G.H.Q. as part of the 29th Division's covering force, and in G.H.Q. instructions dated the 19th April [2] the operations at both these beaches had been placed under the control of the G.O.C. Covering Force, Br.-General S. W. Hare, whose own brigade, the 86th, was to land at the toe of the peninsula. These arrangements were repeated in the 29th Division's orders published the following day.[3] But at a conference held at divisional headquarters on the 21st April it was realized that it would be impossible for General Hare, who was himself landing at W, to exercise any adequate control over these distant detachments. His responsibilities were consequently limited to the landings at X, W, and V, and the local commanders at Y and S were placed under the direct orders of divisional headquarters.

In the original instructions issued by G.H.Q. the R.M.L.I. battalion was detailed as the first to land at Y; but at the divisional conference on the 21st April Colonel Matthews represented that more reliance could be placed on Regulars than on his own half-trained troops, and asked that these orders might be changed. It was also reported by Lieut.-Commander

---

[1] Through an omission to specify in any written order the name of the officer commanding this operation, the question of who was in local command was at first not clear even to some of the senior officers on the spot. Actually the point had been settled at a divisional conference on 21st April, when it was found that Colonel Matthews was senior to Colonel Koe. But Colonel Koe was in bad health at this time; he was too ill to attend the conference; and for some time after landing he imagined himself in command. It was also thought at G.H.Q. that Colonel Koe was in command.

[2] Appendix 4.   [3] Appendix 17.

A. St. V. Keyes R.N., who was to be in naval charge of the landing, and had been practising the troops in getting in and out of boats, that the Borderers were handier than the marines in boat work.[1] It was accordingly decided that the King's Own Scottish Borderers should land first, and to facilitate their rapid disembarkation it was arranged with the naval authorities that they should be transferred to warships on the day before the landing, as in the case of the leading units of the Anzac covering force.

On the evening of the 24th April, therefore, the Scottish Borderers and the company of South Wales Borderers were transferred to the cruisers *Amethyst* and *Sapphire*. Shortly afterwards these two vessels, accompanied by transport N2, carrying the Plymouth Battalion, and by eight trawlers, left Mudros for a sea rendezvous four miles west of Y Beach. Here they were joined by the cruiser *Dublin* and the battleship *Goliath* which were to assist in covering the disembarkation.

General Hunter-Weston's orders to Colonel Matthews [2] were to the effect that his first task was to advance some little distance inland, capture a Turkish gun thought to have been located in the vicinity, and, by attracting the Turkish reserves towards himself, to interfere with the reinforcement of Helles and Sedd el Bahr. He was at the same time to gain touch with the troops disembarking at X,[3] and, later in the day, when the main portion of the covering force drew level with his position, he was to join in the advance to the Achi Baba ridge. The action to be taken by Colonel Matthews in the event of this advance from the south not materializing was not mentioned, and does not appear to have been considered.

Map 2. Sketch 8.

About 2.30 A.M. on the 25th all the troops were transferred to the trawlers, and the whole flotilla steamed towards the shore. The *Goliath* took up her station at about 4,000 yards, and the cruisers their respective stations at 2,000 yards from the beach. At 4.15 A.M. four trawlers carrying the Regular troops, and each towing six cutters manned by naval ratings, steamed boldly in under the cliffs, their orders being to "hold on till they felt the bottom". A and B Companies, K.O.S.B., and the battalion machine guns were then embarked in the

25 Apr.

---

[1] The fact that the marine battalion contained few, if any, Regulars and consisted almost entirely of specially enlisted recruits was not realized by G.H.Q. when the original orders were written.
[2] Only verbal orders were given.
[3] It would appear that Colonel Matthews was uncertain whether actual contact was meant or only visual signalling communication. In the end he obtained neither.

boats, and when the naval bombardment opened at Helles the troops were thrown on the beach.

The surprise was complete. Not a shot was fired from the shore, and the scouts who quickly climbed the cliff reported no sign of the enemy. By 5.15 A.M. the whole of the Regular troops were ashore, and half an hour later they were joined by the marine battalion. Scouts were sent out to the front and to both flanks, but with the exception of four Turks, two of whom were killed and the others captured, no opposition of any kind was encountered.[1] At the same time two companies of the Scottish Borderers were pushed eastwards to the edge of Gully Ravine,[2] some 300 yards beyond the top of the cliff, and at 7.30 A.M. two companies of marines moved south-eastward across the ravine to search for the Turkish gun reported in the vicinity.

Sketches 12, 13.

The welcome news of the unopposed landing was signalled to Sir Ian Hamilton as he passed the beach in the *Queen Elizabeth* about an hour later, on his way to Helles from Anzac. Crowds of troops were at that time sitting about the edge of the cliff, while working parties were clearly visible carrying water in glittering kerosene tins up the steep path from the beach.

With the Anzac and Y Beach landings apparently proceeding without a hitch, hopes that the whole plan might work out successfully began to run high at G.H.Q., and there was at the moment no need for Sir Ian Hamilton to think of increasing the strength at Y. But a few hours later, in view of the serious check at V, the Commander-in-Chief began to consider the advantage of exploiting his success on the enemy's flank. Unfortunately the only troops readily available for this purpose had been placed under General Hunter-Weston's command, and as executive control of the southern battle-front had been delegated to that officer, General Hamilton felt that he could do no more than suggest a change of plan to his subordinate. The moment for such a change seemed propitious. The troops at V appeared to be held up, and some of the reinforcements for that beach had already been deflected to W. At 9.21 A.M., therefore, Sir Ian Hamilton signalled to General Hunter-Weston "Would you like to get some more men ashore on "Y Beach? If so, trawlers are available." No answer was

[1] About 6 A.M. a few heavy shells fell near the beach. These proved to be "overs" from the *Albion* firing at V. Fortunately they did no damage.
[2] The existing map gave no indication of the extreme importance of this feature. It was an immense ravine, with deep and confusing tributary gullies running into it, and with rugged banks in some places nearly 50 feet high.

GULLY RAVINE

received to this message,¹ so it was repeated at 10 A.M. Half an hour later General Hunter-Weston replied that he was advised by Admiral Wemyss that any alteration of present arrangements would delay the landing.² Nothing, therefore, was done, and a golden opportunity was allowed to escape. Had the suggestion been acted upon, or had Sir Ian Hamilton seen fit to issue a definite order on the subject, the whole story of the Gallipoli campaign might well have been different. But it is fair to remember that at this moment General Hunter-Weston still expected that the enemy's opposition in the south would shortly be broken down, and that the Commander-in-Chief did not know enough about the situation ashore to justify him in interfering with his subordinate's battle.

Throughout the morning, and till long after midday, the bulk of the Y Beach detachment remained in its initial position above the landing place, awaiting the advance from Helles. So quiet was the situation at Y that during the morning Colonel Matthews and his adjutant crossed Gully Ravine, and walked unaccompanied to within 500 yards of Krithia without seeing any sign of the enemy. The village itself seemed deserted, and it is now known that this was so, the two Turkish companies who were in local reserve in its vicinity at daybreak having been ordered south when the British bombardment opened.³

The two companies of marines, which left the beach at 7.30 A.M., penetrated to a point on the 200 contour about a mile south-east of the beach without finding any trace of the gun supposed to be in that locality,⁴ and about 11 A.M. they returned unmolested to their starting place.⁵ On their return Lieut.-Colonel Koe sent a helio message to X Beach, announcing that

Sketch 8.

---

¹ At the time of its receipt General Hunter-Weston, lying off W Beach, was still unaware that the V landing was definitely held up, and his reason for deflecting one battalion from V to W was to reinforce the Lancashire Fusiliers, whom he had seen suffering heavy casualties in the capture of W Beach.

² " 10.35 A.M. General Hunter-Weston to G.O.C.-in-C. Admiral Wemyss and principal transport officer state that to interfere with present arrangements and try and land men at Y Beach would delay disembarkation."

³ According to Turkish information one company was sent to Morto Bay at 5.15 A.M.; the other to Helles at 6.45 A.M. This latter company was seen on the march by the Y Beach troops, but it was out of rifle shot, and no steps were taken to arrest its progress.

⁴ According to Turkish accounts there was no gun there.

⁵ The fact that these troops found no trace of the Turks who were garrisoning the mouth of the ravine at daybreak suggests that that small detachment had vacated its position before 7.30 A.M. Some of it probably marched against X. The remainder apparently retired inland and eventually took part in the evening attack on Y.

his landing had been unopposed, and asking whether he was to remain at Y, or to march south to X. This message was somewhat curiously worded,[1] but it shows that even up to 11.45 A.M., Colonel Koe still fancied that he was in command at Y. This was the only message received at X from the Y Beach troops throughout the day, and it was not replied to.

About 9 A.M., and again about noon, considerable firing was heard from the direction of X, but throughout the day no news of the course of events at the main landing places was received by Colonel Matthews, and no fresh orders arrived from divisional headquarters. In these circumstances Colonel Matthews decided that his most important duty was to ensure the retention of Y Beach, and when, by 3 P.M., there was still no sign of the expected advance from the south, he determined to withdraw from the edge of the ravine and to entrench a position on the top of the cliff covering the landing place. In the endeavour to leave no dead ground unwatched the line taken up was longer than could be adequately defended with the available force, and was very thinly held. The Regular troops were placed in the centre, with two companies of marines on either flank. Unfortunately this retirement was not reported to the covering ships; and as the edge of the cliff was higher than the surrounding country, the navy could see nothing for themselves and remained in almost complete ignorance of the position of the troops on shore.[2]

---

[1] "O.C. K.O.S.B., to 86th Bde. X Beach: 11.45 A.M. K.O.S.B. are "established at Y. [Marines] have advanced to 200 ridge. Have stored "S.A.A. on top of cliff. Shall I guard it and join you, or remain where "I am? Have withdrawn (sic) from 200 ridge, as your advance would "prevent my remaining there."

[2] Message from *Goliath* to *Sapphire* 6.37 P.M. "What is the position "occupied by our troops?" Reply: "No news from the shore, but "northern limit appears to be Square 176 R3 [about 1¼ miles north of "beach] and southern limit Square 175 U4 [about 700 yards south of it]. "Our troops are also manning the 200 ridge."
This message, sent during the Turkish attack, was quite inaccurate, and illustrates the manner in which the fleet was hampered by lack of information in its endeavour to support the troops. It is noticeable indeed, that throughout the landing operations both at Y Beach and elsewhere, the navy's unavoidable difficulties in picking up shore targets were seriously increased both by inadequate signal arrangements ashore, and by an omission to provide the supporting ships, before the landing began, with full information regarding the composition and tasks of the various portions of the force. Shore signalling stations were opened punctually, but too often they were unable to get into touch with anyone in authority on land who could give the fleet the information that it most required. A reference to the signal logs of the supporting ships indicates that their captains were constantly asking each other such questions as "Are any of our troops dressed in blue?" or, "Have we landed any "cavalry?" At other times ships asked the shore in vain for a point of aim when called upon to "Open fire at once". In reply to a message

Sketch 8.

Y BEACH
(Reduced from the Turkish 1:5,000 Survey)

Attack by 1/R. 25th Regt.

Krithia

Achi Baba
1 mile

Gully Ravine

Y BEACH

SCALE.
Heights in feet.

Ordnance Survey, 1928

Prepared in the Historical Section (Military Branch).

The decision of Colonel Matthews to entrench his position had been arrived at many hours too late. Though no warning had yet come in from his patrols, the long respite given to him by the Turks was fast coming to an end, and the storm was already gathering.

At his command post at Serafim Farm, Colonel Sami Bey, commanding the Turkish *9th Division*, had been kept fully informed of the British movements, and the measure of his anxieties can be gauged by the fact that this one division was primarily responsible for the defence of the whole front of attack from Fisherman's Hut to Morto Bay. At 1 P.M., owing to the critical position in which his southern troops had been placed by the British landing at Y, Sami Bey resolved to send one of his three reserve battalions, one field battery, and a machine-gun section to that beach to "drive the English " into the sea". By the time the Y Beach detachment had begun to dig, these reinforcements were well on their way south.

Shortly after 4 P.M. a Turkish field gun was brought into action between Krithia and Gully Ravine, and at 5.40 P.M. there developed the first of a series of attacks which continued throughout the night.[1] The opening attack was made in no great strength,[2] and quickly melted away before the guns of the supporting ships. But as soon as the navy had ceased fire for the night,[3] the enemy came on again, and, though his numbers were at that time scarcely more than half those of the defence, his successive attacks were pressed with great determination. Time and again, favoured to some extent by a cloudy night with occasional showers of rain, he hurled himself against the British troops with bayonet and bomb, while other parts of the line were raked with machine-gun fire. At the beginning of the action the British trenches were little more than eighteen inches deep, and thereafter there was small chance of improving them. Heavy entrenching tools had been landed, but they had been left on the beach, and the ground was so thick with fibrous roots that the entrenching implement

---

from the *Sapphire* asking if her fire was doing any good during one of the Turkish attacks, the shore station replied, " Impossible to watch your " fire at present ". " Have you any idea how things have been going? " the *Amethyst* despairingly asked the *Sapphire*; and the *Sapphire* could only reply: " No news at all! "

[1] 5.40 P.M. O.C. Y to *Sapphire*: " Counter-attack is commencing " from north. Bring all guns to bear. Start firing at once."

[2] Probably only by the leading company of the battalion from Serafim Farm and a portion of the detachment from Gully Ravine.

[3] A signal from the flagship at 7.15 P.M. ordered all ships to cease fire.

was almost useless. About 11 P.M. two more companies of Turkish infantry, making 1½ battalions in all, arrived from Serafim Farm, and the British casualties now became so serious that Colonel Matthews signalled to divisional headquarters for reinforcements.[1] This message was not replied to, nor even acknowledged.

Thanks to a stubborn defence by all ranks the British line remained intact throughout the night, and by daylight the Turks had retired.[2] For the moment the crisis was over. But for the Y Beach force, and especially for the young recruits in the marine battalion, the night of ceaseless fighting had been a severe strain. Casualties had been very heavy;[3] the troops were dead tired; and many of them had fired away all their ammunition.[4] Plainly, unless reinforcements and ammunition could arrive, there would be small hope of withstanding another determined attack. But the number of Turkish dead showed that the enemy, too, had suffered heavily; and though the absence of any reply to his appeals for reinforcements caused Matthews keen anxiety, it would appear that at that time he had no idea of evacuating his position.

26 Apr.   Daybreak found the supporting ships still in ignorance of the position of the British trenches,[5] but as soon as it was light enough to open fire, they began a spasmodic bombardment of Krithia and the surrounding country. At 5.20 A.M. in reply to

[1] This message, transmitted by H.M.S. *Goliath* at 11.55 P.M., reached divisional headquarters at 12.15 A.M. and was as follows: "For G.O.C. " 29th Division. Following received from Y Beach. Situation serious. " One battalion to reinforce should arrive before dawn." After waiting in vain for a reply Matthews despatched a second message which arrived at 6 A.M.; but this, too, was not answered.

[2] The Turkish casualties at Y during 25th-26th April were estimated by the Turks at 50 per cent of the numbers engaged.

[3] The Plymouth Battalion's losses during the night amounted to 331 all ranks, killed and wounded; the K.O.S.B.'s to 296. Colonel Koe had been mortally wounded, and his adjutant killed. The company of S.W.B. lost 70, including its commander who was killed.

[4] The situation was complicated by the fact that the Regular troops were armed with the short Lee-Enfield, firing Mark VII ammunition, while the Plymouth Battalion had the old pattern long rifle, firing Mark VI. This latter ammunition could be used in the short rifle, but the Mark VII ammunition did not fit the magazine of the long rifle.

The K.O.S.B. were the first to run out of ammunition, and a message asking for more was despatched to 29th Division at 10.5 P.M. and reached the *Euryalus* at 12.25 A.M. No action was taken by 29th Division, but the message was picked up by the *Queen Elizabeth* and Admiral de Robeck ordered the *Goliath* to send some Mark VII ammunition ashore immediately.

[5] *Dublin* to *Sapphire*: " 5.25 A.M. Are any of our troops more than " 1,000 yards inland? " Reply: " No information from beach, but from " what I can see they do not extend beyond . . ." (here followed a map reference to a point on the coast 1½ miles north of the troops' actual position).

THE LANDING AT Y BEACH

a message from the *Sapphire*, asking whether he required any more assistance, Colonel Matthews replied: "Yes, have asked "twice for another battalion. Am running short of Mark VI "ammunition". Thirty thousand rounds were at once sent ashore in a steamboat.

But, as a result of the night's ordeal, their own lack of experience, and loss of touch with their units, a number of men were now finding their way down to the beach. About 6 A.M. the tension was increased by a salvo from one of the supporting war vessels bursting in the middle of the British position, and at 6.30 A.M. an alarming message to the *Dublin* gave the first hint to the navy of real trouble ashore. This message was despatched by a young officer of the K.O.S.B. from a point on the beach about 500 yards south of the main landing place. "Will you please send help," it ran, "as we are cut off, " and have no ammunition and also a number of wounded." Knowing nothing of the situation ashore, and ever ready to help the sister service, the navy at once sent boats to the beach, and the party was re-embarked. The sight of troops re-embarking gave the impression to many of those at the main landing place that a withdrawal had begun; and when boats arrived at that beach to fetch the wounded, a number of unwounded stragglers also climbed in. Thus, all unknown to Colonel Matthews, and to the troops still holding the top of the cliff, the evacuation began.

Meanwhile, at 6.32 A.M., noticing a party of Turks collecting as if for another attack, Colonel Matthews had signalled to the ships to concentrate their fire 1,000 yards over the edge of the cliff. Ten minutes later he asked for boats to be sent to embark the wounded, but it is clear that he still had no idea of evacuating his position, for the message ended with a request for two flash-lamps to be sent ashore.

At 7 A.M. the shore signal station sent "Open fire at once " 500 yards over ridge. Heavy fire. Tell all ships"[1] and a few minutes later the Turks attacked the centre of the British position. The line suddenly broke at this point, and some of the enemy penetrated through the gap. For a moment the situation looked ugly, for there were no British reserves. But the retreating men were rallied, and the position was restored with the bayonet. The Turks fled in disorder, and from that moment not another shot was fired at the Y Beach troops. The landing had been made good!

[1] At this moment the captain of the *Goliath*, knowing that Colonel Matthews had received no reply to his call for help, again signalled to *Euryalus* " Y force in desperate position and asking for reinforcements ".

But panic—that most contagious of military diseases—had by this time infected a large proportion of the Y Beach detachment, and the situation ashore can best be gauged by a study of the many alarmist messages which for the next hour continued to reach the supporting ships. To the *Dublin*, who asked whether her shots were falling correctly, the laconic reply came back: "Cannot possibly say". At 7.25 A.M., someone on the beach signalled "Send all boats at once. We are out-numbered. Hurry." This was immediately followed by a message saying "We are driven on to beach. I will give you the order when we are clear of the crest," and ten minutes later by another saying "Send boats to Y Beach. Position desperate."

After the Turks had been driven out of the British line, Colonel Matthews, still unaware of what was happening on the beach below him, started to walk round his position, and then for the first time he discovered that his right flank trenches were empty. Sending his adjutant to find out what had happened, he thereupon signalled to the 29th Division as follows: "7.45 A.M. Situation critical. Urgent need reinforcements and ammunition, without which cannot maintain ridge at Y. Alternative is to retire on to beach under cover ships' guns." He then collected all the men he could find, and took up a position at the head of the gully leading to the beach, to cover the removal of his wounded.

Meanwhile Colonel Matthews, finding that the re-embarkation of his detachment had proceeded thus far, decided to allow it to continue. By 11 A.M. all the men on the beach, wounded and unwounded, had been embarked; and as no message had arrived from divisional headquarters and there seemed no hope of reinforcements,[1] Colonel Matthews withdrew his rearguard from the top of the cliff. Half an hour later the last man had embarked, and the high hopes centred in the Y Beach landing had melted into thin air. Throughout the course of the re-embarkation the Turks gave no sign of life;[2] and late in the afternoon, when Lieut.-Commander Keyes went back with a few bluejackets to look for any wounded who might have escaped notice, he searched the battlefield for an hour without being fired on.

So many versions of the origin of this unfortunate with-

---

[1] Major W. H. S. McAlester, who had succeeded to the command of the K.O.S.B., at this time suggested that, failing other reinforcements, his battalion cyclists, still on board the transport, should be sent for, but this was not agreed to.

[2] In spite of this fact practically every man's kit was abandoned on the beach.

drawal have been given credence[1] that it is of interest to notice that Colonel Matthews accepted full responsibility for it in front of the Dardanelles Commission, arguing that in the absence of reinforcements no other course was open to him.

Whatever opportunities Colonel Matthews may have lost on the morning of the 25th, it is easy to sympathize with him in the predicament in which he found himself next day, for his superior commander's apparent lack of interest in his fortunes had been complete. Throughout the 29 hours' tenure of his position no word of any kind had reached him from divisional headquarters. No reply had been sent to his urgent appeals for reinforcements. Though Y Beach was only twenty minutes' distance in a destroyer from divisional headquarters, no officer of the divisional Staff had been sent to gain a personal knowledge of his position. Not even a situation report had been despatched to tell him what was happening at the southern end of the peninsula. To all intents and purposes he had been forgotten.

Such being the situation as it must have appeared from a regimental point of view, it is instructive to examine it from the point of view of divisional headquarters and G.H.Q., and to search for the reason for this apparent neglect by the Staff.

As regards divisional headquarters, the divisional commander's silence can only be explained by the fact that he was too fully occupied with the anxious problems on his immediate front to be able to devote any time to a distant detachment. It may be said, however, that up to the evening of the 25th April General Hunter-Weston had no reason for anxiety about the Y Beach force. News of its unopposed landing had reached him during the morning, and in the afternoon credence was for some time given to an erroneous report that the troops at X and Y had joined hands.[2] Even the report

---

[1] For many months after the landing persistent reports were current that the withdrawal was started by a naval officer giving the order to re-embark. This false impression was probably derived from the following message written by Colonel Matthews at 10.15 A.M. on 26th April: "To Commander Keyes, R.N. or Adjutant R.M.L.I. The only orders "received by me to retire reached me at 10 A.M. verbally from Commander "Keyes. Can you get volunteers from ships to come and help with "wounded? I shall hold on to top of gully till wounded removed."
There can be no doubt, however, that Colonel Matthews afterwards discovered that no such orders had been given by Commander Keyes, for in 1916, when definitely asked by the Dardanelles Commission whether a naval officer had given the order, he replied, " No, I never "understood that at all ". Further, it may be pointed out that a junior naval officer could not order a senior military officer to retire.

[2] This belief was founded on a message from the Royal Fusiliers on Hill 114, midway between X and W Beaches, that they were in touch with the Lancashire Fusiliers on the right and the " Borderers " on their left. In point of fact the word " Borderers " was a mistake. What the

of the Turkish counter-attack on the evening of the 25th gave no real cause for alarm, and up to 9 P.M. the divisional commander could fairly assume from the absence of any further news that the attack had been driven off.

At 9.5 P.M. a report announced heavy firing at Y, and the succession of messages which reached divisional headquarters after midnight can have left little doubt as to the serious situation at that beach.[1] But by that time the position at Helles and Sedd el Bahr was causing General Hunter-Weston increasing anxiety, and he apparently decided that the Y Beach detachment must be left to its fate. At daybreak on the 26th the village of Sedd el Bahr was still in the hands of the Turks, and at 6.25 A.M. General Hunter-Weston signalled to the Commander-in-Chief that he feared the 29th Division was not strong enough to take it, or to make good the landing at V, unless a regiment of French troops (three battalions) could be landed at W Beach to assist.[2] When, therefore, half an hour later, at 7 A.M., he received the *Goliath's* report of the desperate situation at Y, he merely repeated that message to G.H.Q., adding that he had no reinforcements to spare.[3]

Meanwhile, before receiving General Hunter-Weston's

---

writer of the message evidently meant was that the Royal Fusiliers on Hill 114 were in touch with the Border Regiment at X Beach. But the mistake was not discovered at the time, and for some hours it was believed that they were in touch with the K.O.S.B. and South Wales Borderers at Y.

[1] 9.5 P.M. Message from X Beach:—" Heavy firing at Y."
12.15 A.M. Message from Colonel Matthews:—" Situation serious. A reinforcing battalion should arrive before dawn."
12.20 A.M. Message from Colonel Matthews:—" Mark VII ammunition required urgently."
12.40 A.M. Message from W Beach:—" Heavy and continuous firing at Y."
6.0 A.M. Message from Colonel Matthews:—" A reinforcing battalion urgently required, also ammunition."
7.0 A.M. Message from *Goliath*:—" Y force in desperate position. Can you send reinforcements immediately."
7.45 A.M. Message from Y Beach (through *Goliath*). " Send boats at once. We are outnumbered."
8.20 A.M. Message from Y Beach:—" We are holding the ridge till wounded are embarked."
8.50 A.M. Message from Colonel Matthews:—" Situation critical. Urgent need reinforcements and ammunition, without which cannot maintain ridge at Y. Alternative is to retire on to beach under cover ships' guns."

The times given in the above messages are times of receipt at divisional headquarters.

[2] This message was delayed in transit and did not reach G.H.Q. till 8.15 A.M.

[3] He did, however, cause a signal to be made to the *Implacable* to send 50 boxes of ammunition to Y Beach.

request for the French troops to be landed at W Beach, Sir Ian Hamilton had signalled to offer him the help of a brigade (six battalions) of French infantry.¹ This message reached General Hunter-Weston at 7.45 A.M. and at first glance it may be thought to have given him the chance of promising Colonel Matthews some support. But the divisional commander's energies were now concentrated on securing his main landing places by the capture of Sedd el Bahr and the hill behind it. This was the main problem and the most pressing. It could be solved most quickly, he considered, by landing the French at W Beach; and the success of the main venture would compensate for a defeat at Y. Failure in the principal effort, on the other hand, might spell the ruin of the whole undertaking, no matter how brilliant the success of a minor enterprise. At 8.11 A.M. therefore, General Hunter-Weston replied to the Commander-in-Chief's message, repeating his request for three French battalions to be landed at W. Ten minutes later arrived the message from Y Beach " We are holding the ridge till " wounded are embarked ", and at 8.50 A.M. Colonel Matthews's final appeal for assistance. But General Hunter-Weston's mind was made up. The only action taken on these messages was to warn the troops at X Beach (three miles south of Y) to establish their left firmly, to guard against a probable attack from the north. To Colonel Matthews no reply was sent.

The first news of the serious situation at Y to reach General Headquarters was General Hunter-Weston's repetition of the message from H.M.S. *Goliath*. At the time of its arrival the *Queen Elizabeth* was supporting the Anzac troops with her fire, and there was keen anxiety lest, if the Turks should attack in force, General Birdwood's corps might be unable to maintain its position. The situation at Helles and Sedd el Bahr was also causing some anxiety, and as already mentioned, General Hamilton had just offered to send a French brigade to support the 29th Division. But Sir Ian Hamilton had from the first set great store on the advantages to be gained from the possession of Y Beach. As soon, therefore, as the *Goliath's* disturbing news arrived, and without waiting for General Hunter-Weston's reply to his earlier message, he decided to order a French brigade to X Beach, whence they could march to Colonel

¹ " From Sir Ian Hamilton to General Hunter-Weston:—7.15 A.M. " Would you like me to send you a brigade of French infantry. If so " your tows would have to land it. Please reply urgently."
    This offer was prompted by a report of the southern situation received at G.H.Q. from the G.H.Q. liaison officer on W Beach. The two French infantry brigades at Sir Ian Hamilton's disposal each consisted of 2 regiments each of 3 battalions.

Matthews's assistance. Orders were at once sent to General d'Amade to this effect, and Hunter-Weston was informed of the action taken.[1]

For another hour no further news was heard from the south, but about 9 A.M. the *Queen Elizabeth* picked up the ominous message from the *Goliath*: "From Y Beach to all ships. "We are holding the ridge till wounded are embarked." This left no further doubt as to the gravity of the situation at Y, and as the Anzac position now seemed more secure, Sir Ian Hamilton asked the admiral to proceed at once to Y Beach. On arrival the evacuation was found to be in full swing. For the next hour a vain attempt was made to get in touch with the troops still ashore, but there was apparently no one left to reply, and the *Queen Elizabeth* could get no answer from any of the supporting ships.[2] So, forming the conclusion that the evacuation had been sanctioned by General Hunter-Weston, and that, not knowing the situation, it would be dangerous to interfere, Sir Ian Hamilton steamed on to W Beach. At 10.30 A.M. the *Queen Elizabeth* reached Helles, and then to his astonishment the Commander-in-Chief learnt that General Hunter-Weston was unaware that the evacuation had begun. At 10.50 A.M. an urgent message was despatched to the *Dublin* to report the situation at Y Beach, and at 11.15 the reply was received: " Nearly all wounded embarked. Last ridge being " held by rearguard. Remainder of troops embarking."

As it did not for a moment enter anyone's calculations that there were no Turks at Y, it now seemed too late to arrest the withdrawal, or to retrieve the lost opportunity, except by a fresh landing under fire. No further action was taken, therefore, and the evacuation was allowed to proceed.

Cleverly conceived, happily opened, hesitatingly conducted, miserably ended—such is the story of the landing at Y Beach.

[1] " C - in - C to General Hunter - Weston:—7.43 A.M. Have asked " French to send you a brigade of infantry and to land it at X. With " that brigade you can support troops at Y which you report require " support."

Had this message been repeated to Colonel Matthews by divisional headquarters, it is possible that the promise of support might have sufficed to prevent the regrettable evacuation, even though, as events turned out, the leading French regiment was not ready to land till late in the evening. But though the message reached 29th Divisional headquarters at 8.20 A.M., it was not seen by General Hunter-Weston till two hours later, by which time the evacuation was almost completed. (The original copy of the message is endorsed in red pencil, in General Hunter-Weston's handwriting, " seen by me 10.14 A.H.W.")

[2] The flagship was so far out that she could only send messages by wireless, and it subsequently transpired that the wireless gear of the supporting ships was temporarily out of action while they were hoisting in the wounded.

THE LANDING AT Y BEACH

In deciding to throw a force ashore at that point Sir Ian Hamilton would seem to have hit upon the key of the whole situation. Favoured by an unopposed landing, and by the absence of any Turks in the neighbourhood for many hours, it is as certain as anything can be in war that a bold advance from Y on the morning of the 25th April must have freed the southern beaches that morning, and ensured a decisive victory for the 29th Division. But apart from its original conception, no other part of the operation was free from calamitous mistakes, and Fortune seldom smiles on a force that neglects its opportunities.

From the various incidents of the story, now set down for the first time in full detail, it will be seen that the inadequate orders which Colonel Matthews originally received from divisional headquarters, his own lack of initiative after landing, and the subsequent absence of that interest and attention which he had a right to expect from the Staff, all played their part in the squandered opportunity of the 25th and in the final and unnecessary withdrawal from a position of immense advantage. In one respect the operation was redeemed from complete failure, for the 29 hours' tenure of the position kept $1\frac{1}{2}$ battalions of Turks away from the southern beaches at a critical period of the battle. But the real value of Y Beach was appreciated by no one till the opportunity had passed. Compared with the advantages which must have accrued from a clearer grasp of the immense potentialities of this position on the enemy's flank, the results of the enterprise were heart-breaking.

CHAPTER XII

THE LANDINGS AT HELLES

THE PLAN

(Maps 2, 4; Sketches 4, 8A, 9; Diagram)

25 Apr.
Map 2.
To the 29th Division, which comprised the only Regular troops in the expedition, the post of honour at the landing belonged as if by right. The allotment of this division to the Helles beaches was therefore the natural corollary to Sir Ian Hamilton's decision to hurl his main attack against the southern end of the peninsula, with the Kilid Bahr plateau as its ultimate objective. The southern beaches promised to be more strongly defended than the other selected landing places, yet on their early capture depended the whole success of the Commander-in-Chief's plan.

For the purpose of the landing, two extra battalions, both of the Royal Naval Division, were attached to the 29th, namely, the Plymouth Battalion R.M.L.I. for Y beach,[1] and the Anson Battalion to furnish working parties at X, W, and V. Two companies of the 1/5th Royal Scots, the only non-Regular battalion in the division,[2] were detailed as hold-parties in the transports, and the fighting troops at General Hunter-Weston's disposal on the 25th consisted, therefore, of $12\frac{1}{2}$ battalions, of which $7\frac{1}{2}$ were allotted to the covering force and five retained in the main body.[3]

The military orders and instructions for the landings, and a précis of the orders by Rear-Admiral R. E. Wemyss, who was in naval charge of the operations, are included in the appendices to this volume,[4] but the following short summary will give a general idea of the necessarily elaborate plan.

Five beaches were to be utilized by the covering force,

[1] See Chapter XI.
[2] The divisional engineers and the ancillary units of the division were also furnished from the Territorial Force.
[3] To be reinforced as quickly as possible by the French troops under General d'Amade.
[4] Appendices 3, 4, 9, 17-19.

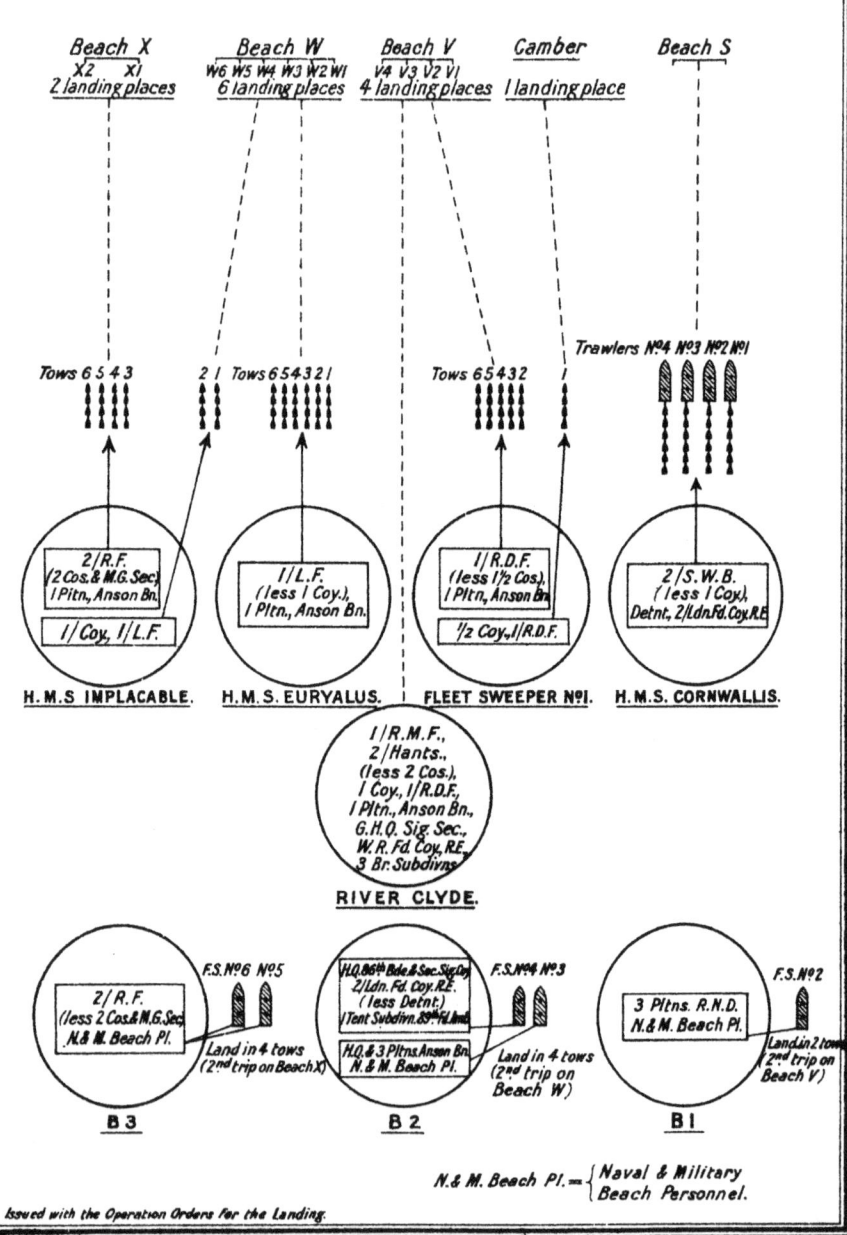

THE HELLES PLAN

namely Y (already described), X, W, V, and S.[1] But, as already noticed,[2] the responsibilities of Br.-General S. H. Hare, who was named in G.H.Q. instructions as the commander of the whole covering force, were subsequently limited by the 29th Division to co-ordinating the action of the 86th Brigade. This brigade, reinforced by two companies of the 2/Hampshire, was regarded as the covering force proper, and was to disembark at X, W, and V.[3]

Sketch 4.

Map 4.
Sketch 8A.

In an inspiring Special Order published on the eve of the landing, Br.-General Hare addressed the 86th Brigade as follows:

Fusiliers, our brigade is to have the honour to be the first to land and to cover the disembarkation of the rest of the division. Our task will be no easy one. Let us carry it through in a way worthy of the traditions of the distinguished regiments of which the Fusilier Brigade is composed . . . in such a way that future historians may say of us, as Napier said of the Fusilier Brigade at Albuhera—" Nothing could stop that astonishing infantry ".

Owing to the restricted size of the beaches, the strong current, and the fear of hidden reefs, the navy had vetoed a night operation at Helles, and the landings were to take place by day. The first troops to land at X, W and V were to be disembarked from the *Implacable*, *Euryalus*, and Fleet Sweeper No. 1[4] in eighteen tows,[5] and these three vessels were to be in

[1] In addition, a landing subsidiary to that at V was to be made at the Camber east of Sedd el Bahr.
[2] See page 202.
[3] It was recognized that to divide the 86th Brigade even among three beaches, was not an ideal arrangement, but this separation of force at the outset was dictated by the small size of the available landing places. It was hoped, moreover, that the objections would prove to be more apparent than real. W beach was only a mile from X, and a little less than that distance from V, and once the troops were ashore, and had linked up their flanks, the brigade would be on a front of about one and a half miles from X to Sedd el Bahr. The extension of its left by the landing at X, which was believed to be only lightly defended, would, it was hoped, be actually advantageous, for it would enable the Turkish defences on Hill 114 to be taken in reverse, while other portions of the X Beach force would be on the flank of the Turks retreating from W and V, and of any reinforcements arriving from the north.
It was further expected that until the three landings could be linked up ashore the covering ships off the coast would furnish an adequate means of inter-communication.
[4] The fleet sweepers were mostly cross-channel cargo boats.
[5] From *Implacable*: 2 coys. 2/Royal Fus. in 4 tows, to land at X.
   „   1 „ 1/Lancs. Fus. „ 2 „ „ W.
   „ *Euryalus*: 3 „ 1/Lancs. Fus. „ 6 „ „ W.
   „ F.S. No. 1: 2½ „ 1/R. Dub. Fus. „ 5 „ „ V.
                 ½ „ 1/R. Dub. Fus. „ 1 „ „ the Camber.

A tow consisted of one steamboat and 4 cutters or ship's lifeboats,

position off their respective beaches, with the troops ready in their tows beside them, at daybreak.

A heavy bombardment of the southern end of the peninsula was to be opened by the fleet [1] at 5 A.M., and half an hour later the fire was to be lifted and the tows to go ahead. The troops for the flank landing at S (three companies of the South Wales Borderers), transferred to four trawlers from the battleship *Cornwallis*, would meanwhile have entered the Straits with that vessel, ready to disembark on the northern point of Morto Bay at the same moment.

Immediately after the first tows had arrived at V the collier *River Clyde*, with over two thousand men on board,[2] was to be run aground on that beach, and about three-quarters of an hour later the remainder of the covering force was to land from three fleet sweepers at X, W, and V, in the second trip of tows.[3]

Thus, if all went well, the whole of the covering force would be ashore by 7 A.M., and according to a time table that had been worked out in every detail,[4] it was hoped that the landing of the main body would begin about half-past eight, and that the disembarkation of all the infantry and engineers of the division, two mountain batteries, a howitzer battery, and a section of 18-pdrs., with sufficient animals to move the guns, would be completed before noon. Of the five main body battalions, the two remaining units of the 87th Brigade [5] were to land at X, and form the divisional reserve, and the remainder of the 88th Brigade [6] at V. The beach at W was to be reserved for the disembarkation of guns, animals, and stores, partly because of its easier exits, and partly because its anchorage

---

and held approximately half a company, or 120 men, in addition to a naval coxswain and 6 seamen in each boat to row it ashore when the tow ropes were cast off.

[1] The actual beaches were to be bombarded as follows: V by *Albion*, W by *Swiftsure* and *Euryalus*, X by *Implacable*.

[2] 1/Royal Munster Fusiliers, two companies 2/Hampshire, one company 1/Royal Dublin Fusiliers, and other details.

[3] These sweepers, like the three "attendant" warships and Fleet Sweeper No. 1, were to take their troops on board at Tenedos overnight. They included the personnel of 86th Brigade headquarters, the naval and military beach personnel, working parties, and certain technical troops. The original intention was for Br.-General Hare to land at W Beach with his headquarters in the second trip.

[4] Commenting on the careful detail of the British orders General d'Amade wrote after the war: " Minute precision regulated every detail in " the orders . . . with the same care that characterizes a ceremonial parade " at Whitehall ".

[5] The 1/Border Regiment and the 1/R. Inniskilling Fusiliers.

[6] The 1/Essex, 4/Worcestershire, two companies 2/Hampshire and two companies 1/5th R. Scots.

THE HELLES PLAN

was expected to be more immune than V from Asiatic shell fire. No arrangements had been made for reinforcing the Lancashire Fusiliers at W, but it was expected that even if that battalion were held up by the Turkish defence, the garrison would quickly be "pinched out" by a successful advance from X and V.

The transports of the main body were to reach the outer anchorage, three miles south of Cape Helles, at 6.30 A.M., whence they would be ordered up to their respective beaches as soon as it was considered safe for them to approach. If this situation had not occurred by the time the main body infantry were required, the fleet sweepers would bring up units from their transports to the tows.

The nine vessels of Admiral Wemyss's squadron responsible for supporting the troops with their fire both at the landing and during the subsequent advance were styled the "covering ships", and were under the immediate command of Rear-Admiral Stuart Nicholson.[1] Arrangements had been co-ordinated between that officer and the 29th Division whereby all located Turkish guns and trenches as far north as Achi Baba were to be kept under constant fire, and as soon as the covering force had been landed the *Implacable*, *Euryalus*, and *Cornwallis* were to assist in this work. In addition, the cruisers *Sapphire* and *Amethyst* would be in position near Y Beach, and the total number of naval guns available to support the southern landings would thus amount to 345.[2]

The first task assigned to the troops disembarking at X, W, and V was to capture the high ground above the two southern

---

[1] The distribution of ships was as follows:
    Vengeance and *Lord Nelson* in the Straits;
    Prince George off the Asiatic coast;
    Albion off Sedd el Bahr;
    Swiftsure (Rear-Admiral Nicholson's flagship) off Tekke Burnu;
    Dublin, *Goliath*, *Talbot* and *Minerva* off Y Beach and north of it.

[2]
12-inch	28
10-inch	4
9·2-inch	12
7·5-inch	14
6-inch	126
4-inch	24
12-pdr.	137
	345

The *Queen Elizabeth*, with eight 15-inch and twelve 6-inch, would also be available during a portion of the day.

The southern end of the peninsula had been divided into areas, to each of which one or more ships were allotted, and all trenches and suspected gun emplacements that had been located by aircraft were shown on specially prepared area maps issued to the ships.

beaches, which were to form the principal landing places for the main portion of the Expeditionary Force. This accomplished, and touch between the three detachments being gained, Br.-General Hare was to throw forward his left flank to join up with the troops at Y, and to occupy as his second objective a line roughly north and south from Y to Sedd el Bahr.

To give effect to these orders Br.-General Hare allotted the Dublin Fusiliers for the capture of Sedd el Bahr village and Hill 141,[1] and the Munsters for the remaining defences of V Beach, including the gun emplacements north of Fort No. 1 on the left. Two companies of the 2/Hampshire were to be in local reserve. At X Beach the first task of the Royal Fusiliers was to form a defensive flank against attacks from the north-east and to capture Hill 114 above Cape Tekke (Tekke Burnu). In the centre, at W Beach, one company of the Lancashire Fusiliers was to link up with the Royal Fusiliers on Hill 114, and the rest of the battalion was to capture " the trenches and redoubt on "Hill 138" above Cape Helles and join hands with the Munsters near Fort No. 1. Brigade headquarters was in the first instance to be established near the ruined lighthouse.

Map 4. Sketch 8A.

After the attainment of the line Y Beach—Sedd el Bahr by the 86th Brigade, Major-General Hunter-Weston intended to take personal command of the action, and the remainder of the advance to the final objective of the day—the Achi Baba ridge—was to be made by all the infantry of the division. Br.-General H. E. Napier, with the equivalent of three battalions of the 88th Brigade was to be thrown in on the right from V Beach, while Br.-General W. R. Marshall, who was landing at X with the remaining two battalions of the 87th Brigade was to be in divisional reserve.

The reasons which prompted the selection of the Achi Baba ridge as the final objective for the first day have been discussed on an earlier page.[2] But General Hunter-Weston had set himself an even heavier task than that allotted him by G.H.Q., for whereas the Commander-in-Chief had named a point near Tener Chift Knoll as the right of the final position to be attained on the 25th, the G.O.C. 29th Division intended to try for all the high ground running due east from Achi Baba peak to the Dardanelles. This objective, though more ambitious than the one laid down by G.H.Q., was distinctly more desirable. The line mentioned in G.H.Q. orders was solely defensive in character. Its choice had been governed by the necessity of

---

[1] $3\frac{1}{2}$ companies were to attack from V Beach, and two platoons from the Camber on the right flank.

[2] See page 137.

THE TURKISH FORCES

freeing the southern end of the peninsula from enemy observation. Highly important though the Achi Baba peak was as a Turkish observing station, it promised to be of little direct value to the British from the point of view of assisting a naval attack. But the capture of Tenkir Tepe, included in General Hunter-Weston's objective, would afford valuable observation of the Narrows.

Before embarking on the narrative of the landings it must be noticed that British information greatly exaggerated the number of Turks likely to be met in the southern end of the peninsula. The total numbers of the enemy in the Dardanelles area had been gauged fairly accurately by G.H.Q., but no news of their defensive arrangements was obtainable, and Liman's orders against his troops exposing themselves by daylight had been so faithfully observed that it was impossible to gain any clue to their dispositions. Information from a hitherto reliable source did, however, point to the presence of one complete division south of Achi Baba, and this report was published by G.H.Q. to the troops.

In point of fact, as mentioned on a previous page, the Turkish strength south of Achi Baba at daybreak on the 25th amounted only to two battalions and one company of engineers. At Y Beach there were no defenders; at W and V there were two companies in all; at S one platoon; and at X a post of twelve men. Moreover, of the five selected landing places only two—W and V—were protected by wire and machine guns.[1]

This large overestimate of the Turkish strength on the morning of the landing was unfortunate, for the belief that strong reinforcements were in the immediate neighbourhood undoubtedly tended to delay the British advance from W and X beaches about midday on the 25th. This erroneous estimate, moreover, was thought to be confirmed by the statements of prisoners captured later in the day. The prisoners stated quite accurately that there were "only covering troops of one division southwest of Krithia"; but it was wrongly inferred that the rest of the division was between Krithia and Achi Baba. It must also be noticed that throughout the campaign it was firmly believed that the landing of the 29th Division had been opposed by at

---

[1] An article by a Turkish officer in the "Turkish Military Review", October 1926, admits that the Turks had four old-pattern maxim guns at V, but states that two of them were knocked out by the naval bombardment before the troops landed. They also had two pom-poms at V. The article does not admit that there were any machine guns at W; but Br.-General Hare is certain that two were firing on the beach from the right flank when he landed.

least one Turkish division, and that the true facts did not come to light till after the conclusion of peace.

The numerical weakness of the enemy forces holding the actual beaches at W and V affords, however, no criterion of the resistance that had to be overcome, nor does it dim the glory of the troops who made those beaches good on the 25th and 26th April. There is no analogy between the storming of trenches from open boats and any operation in land warfare. A bombardment of the beach defences by flat-trajectory guns—especially when the defences cannot be accurately located beforehand—can in no way be compared in effect with the preliminary bombardment and barrage fire of land operations. The naval shells are not man-killing projectiles. The stretch of sand over which the attackers must pass is devoid of all cover. In the case of a daylight landing, such as for naval reasons was necessary at Helles, the point of disembarkation can be gauged by the defenders to a nicety as the boats approach the shore. While the defenceless troops scramble out of their boats, and struggle waist-deep in water, they can be shot down as easily, and almost as safely, as bottles at a fair.

THE COVERING FORCE

By 8 A.M. on the 24th April all the ships of the southern covering force had assembled at Tenedos. Here were the attendant warships *Implacable*, *Euryalus*, and *Cornwallis*, and three Cunarders packed with eager troops. Here, too, were the collier *River Clyde*, newly camouflaged with broad patches of sand-coloured paint, six fleet sweepers, six trawlers, and a number of lighters and tugs. The anchorage was only a few miles from the Asiatic shore, but so accustomed were the Turks at this time to naval activity that the large concentration apparently passed unnoticed.

The weather was clear and bright, but a stiff breeze, strong enough to cause some anxiety, had again sprung up at daybreak, and continued to blow till late in the afternoon.

During the day all ranks were engaged in preparing for the morrow's operation. Final conferences were held by the various Staffs, last orders issued, and tasks explained to subordinate leaders. Lighters were brought alongside the transports and filled with beach equipment, stores, and ammunition. Naval and military beach personnel were mustered, instructed in their duties, and distributed to their various ships. Picket boats, steam pinnaces, and pulling boats, dancing like corks in the tumbling sea, were collected from

Sketch 8.

HELLES
The Beaches & the Turkish Defences
25th April 1915.

the warships and transports, and organized into eighteen tows, each with its crew. At midday General Hunter-Weston and his Staff took up their quarters in the flagship *Euryalus* to be in close touch with Rear-Admiral Wemyss. Towards evening, the sea having moderated, the troops were gradually transferred to the vessels from which they were to land. Here they were provided with a hot meal by the navy, all ranks and ratings doing everything possible for the comfort of their soldier guests. Br.-General Hare and his brigade-major [1] were so anxious to be ashore at the first possible moment that they obtained the somewhat unwilling permission of the divisional commander to land with the first trip of tows at W Beach.[2] They accordingly transferred to the *Implacable* during the afternoon, while the remainder of the 86th Brigade headquarters boarded the fleet sweeper *Whitby Abbey* to land in the second trip.

About 10 P.M. the unwieldy flotilla of warships, transports, lighters, and small craft moved slowly out from the anchorage, speed and course being so arranged as to bring the ships west of Tekke Burnu about an hour before daylight. There was a bright moon; the breeze had died away; the sea was a sheet of shining silver. Away to the south eleven transports carrying the main body of the 29th Division were approaching from Mudros, bound for the "outer anchorage" some three miles south of Cape Helles.

At 3.30 A.M., in inky darkness, for the moon had now set, the *Implacable*, *Euryalus*, and Fleet Sweeper No. 1 glided into their appointed stations about two miles from X, W, and V. The troops were roused, and after a breakfast provided by the sailors were quietly mustered on deck. Slightly ahead, barely visible in the darkness, were the covering ships under Rear-Admiral Nicholson, and away to the south the *Cornwallis* and her four trawlers making for S Beach. A mile astern, near the outer anchorage, were the troops for the second trip of tows, the collier *River Clyde* with her unaccustomed freight of 2,000 fighting men, and the lighters filled with ammunition and stores.

Half an hour later six tows were assembled alongside each of the three attendant vessels *Implacable*, *Euryalus*, and Fleet Sweeper No. 1, and just as day began to dawn the troops filed down the gangways and filled the waiting boats. The men

---

[1] Major T. H. C. Frankland, Royal Dublin Fusiliers.
[2] Owing to both these officers becoming casualties, this point was overlooked by the officer who wrote up the brigade war diary several days later, and it was not mentioned in the official despatch.

were heavily laden, carrying packs, three days' rations, and 200 rounds of ammunition;[1] yet they moved so silently that to the sailors who watched them embark the impression conveyed was that of a phantom force.[2] The morning was absolutely still. The garrison of the peninsula gave no sign of life. A thick veil of mist hung motionless over the beaches. The sea was smooth as glass.

About 5 A.M., in a somewhat baffling light, a thunderous bombardment was opened by the fleet, and the attendant ships with their crowded tows crept slowly towards the shore. It had been hoped to make all four landings simultaneously, after the beaches had been shelled for half an hour. But the trawlers for S, each towing six lifeboats, were making unexpectedly slow progress against the Dardanelles current, and by half-past five they had scarcely entered the Straits.[3] So the tows for the other beaches waited, whilst the thunder of the fleet continued, and the sun came up from Asia and blinded the gunners with its glow. Then, shortly before six o'clock, it was decided to wait no longer. The signal was made for the ships to lift their fire and for the tows to go ahead.

There was still no sign of life on the peninsula. Except for a few shells from the Asiatic shore the terrific pounding of the beaches had met with no response.

THE LANDING AT X BEACH

A few minutes before 6 A.M. the *Implacable* (Captain H. C. Lockyer) sent off her company of the Lancashire Fusiliers[4] to W Beach accompanied by the brigadier-general commanding the covering force, and then, continuing to fire on X with every gun that could be brought to bear, and keeping her four tows of Royal Fusiliers abeam, she held on to within 500 yards of the shore.[5]

Situated about one mile above Tekke Burnu, X Beach consisted of a narrow ribbon of sand, some 200 yards in length,

---

[1] Here, as at Anzac, the average weight carried by the soldier was 88 lbs.
[2] Wemyss, "The Navy in the Dardanelles Campaign," p. 71.
[3] Here their progress was still further impeded by the mine-sweeping flotilla which began to sweep the lower reaches of the Dardanelles at daybreak in preparation for a renewed attack on the Narrows when the army was safely ashore. When the delay was noticed, the flagship endeavoured to deflect the trawlers to V Beach instead of to S, but, fortunately as events proved, the signal miscarried.
[4] Actually these troops consisted of 2 platoons of D Company and the Headquarters Company.
[5] Captain Lockyer had his anchor suspended from a spar at the bows, and went ahead till it dragged.

THE LANDING AT X BEACH

at the foot of a low, crumbling cliff. The locality had been happily chosen, for though the cliff offered no real obstacle to infantry the Turks were not prepared for a landing at this point. No wire had been put up, and there was only a piquet of twelve men to guard this part of the coast. Stupefied by the *Implacable's* fire, the Turkish guard could do nothing to oppose the landing, and by 6.30 A.M. the two leading companies of the Royal Fusiliers, with battalion headquarters and the machine-gun section, had reached the top of the cliff without a casualty. The tows went back to the approaching fleet sweepers for the remaining two companies, and these, together with the naval and military beach personnel, the heavy entrenching tools, and reserve ammunition, were landed without mishap by half-past seven.

By this time the covering troops, pushing inland, had been checked by a hot fire,[1] and Lieut.-Colonel H. E. B. Newenham decided that in order to establish a defensive flank on his left it was essential to gain ground in a north-easterly direction. He accordingly detailed Captain F. K. Leslie's company for this duty, and, after leaving one company in reserve and pushing out two platoons straight to the front to take up a position about 500 yards from the beach, he himself moved off with one and a half companies to attack the Turkish trenches on Hill 114 and gain touch with the troops from W.

Starting about 8 A.M. Captain Leslie at first made steady progress, but after advancing some 800 yards strong opposition was encountered and he could make no further headway. On the right, Colonel Newenham's party carried all before it, and by 11 A.M. had gained the summit of the hill. This advance was carried out in full view of the *Implacable*, and when the troops reached the summit they were wildly cheered by the bluejackets, who had eagerly watched each stage of the advance.[2]

On the whole, therefore, the X Beach operation had started well. Thanks to the moral effect of 12-inch guns fired at point-blank range, the leading troops had landed without mishap; the first objective had been gained; and the beach was already available for the disembarkation of the main body. But the front of the Royal Fusiliers was a long one; there were several gaps in it; and the company on the left was heavily engaged.

---

[1] The Turkish local reserves for the southern landing places, two companies of infantry, were bivouacking in the locality. One company was at once sent to reinforce Sedd el Bahr. The other company was sent to W Beach, and it was this latter company which now came into action against the Royal Fusiliers at X.

[2] A fleet surgeon was killed on the quarter-deck of the *Implacable* by a rifle bullet from the shore.

A visit to X Beach discloses the fact that the view from the cliffs above the beach is extraordinarily valuable. But with previous reconnaissance out of the question, and only an inaccurate map available, this happy circumstance was not realized before the landing. Actually, from the cliffs above the beach the summit and inland slopes of hills 138 and 141, and the position of the two Turkish redoubts near Hill 138, are all plainly visible, and had stronger forces been detailed to land at X there can be little doubt that the disastrous delays at W and V could have been prevented by an advance from that point against the Turkish rear. From these cliffs, too, the ground slopes gently towards Morto Bay, giving an unbroken view of the foreshore of that bay, and, at only two miles' distance, of S Beach. Had the troops at X been warned of this beforehand they could have seen the South Wales Borderers landing at S at 7.30 A.M., and visual communication between the two detachments could have been maintained. As it was, the troops who first landed at X were probably too much engaged with carrying out the task allotted to them to give even a thought to the boats which must have been clearly visible in Morto Bay. It is even doubtful whether many of the officers at X had been told where S Beach was, even if they knew that a landing was to take place there. In any case no messages seem to have passed between the two detachments throughout the day.

Sketch 8A.

THE LANDING AT W BEACH

A mile to the south, the capture of W Beach was meanwhile proving a far more hazardous enterprise than the landing at X.

W Beach, situated immediately south of Tekke Burnu, where a small gully opens out a break in the cliffs, consists of a strip of deep powdery sand some 350 yards long, and from 15 to 40 yards wide. On either side the cliffs are almost precipitous, but in the centre a number of sand dunes offer an easy approach to the ridge overlooking the sea. Much ingenuity had been employed by the Turks in turning this beach into a death-trap. Close to the water's edge a deep belt of wire extended almost the whole length of the landing place. Trip wires had been laid in the water a few yards from the shore; and on the beach itself were a number of land mines. The slopes in front and the summits of the cliffs on each flank were defended by short lengths of trench; while at least two machine guns,[1] concealed in small holes in the cliffs, enfiladed the main entanglement.

[1] See f.n. 1, page 221.

W BEACH

From a photograph taken in 1922, showing the remains of the British piers and jetties

THE LANDING AT W BEACH

The low ridge overlooking the centre of the beach was in turn commanded by other trenches on the high ground to the north-east and south-west, and, at a range of 600 yards, by the nearer of two redoubts in the neighbourhood of Hill 138. Both these redoubts were protected by strong wire, and were approached by glacis-like slopes, devoid of cover. Another wide entanglement ran down from the southernmost redoubt to a point on the cliffs near the lighthouse, making an advance from W to V impossible till the redoubt itself had been captured. So strong were the defences at this beach that, even though the garrison was but one company of infantry, the Turks may well have considered them impregnable to an attack from open boats.

At 6 A.M., simultaneously with the attack on X Beach, the six tows from the *Euryalus* headed for the shore in line abreast, at about 50 yards interval, with the tows from the *Implacable* on their left and slightly astern. On the right A and B Companies (Captains R. Haworth and H. Shaw), with the battalion machine guns,[1] were to attack "the trenches and redoubt on "Hill 138" as soon as they got ashore. C Company (Captain R. R. Willis) on their left, was to capture the trenches guarding the centre and left of the beach, and to assist with its fire the Royal Fusiliers' attack on Hill 114. Two platoons of D Company (Major G. S. Adams) were to form the battalion reserve under Tekke Burnu,[2] where they would be joined by the two tows from the *Implacable*, carrying the remainder of D Company and the Headquarters Company.

Fifty yards from the shore the tow ropes were slipped, the bluejackets bent to their oars, and the thirty-two cutters toiled slowly in to the beach. Up to this moment no sound had come from the shore, but just before the first boat grounded a hurricane of lead swept over the battalion,[3] inflicting a heavy toll. Gallantly led by their officers, the Fusiliers jumped waist-deep into the sea and hurled themselves ashore, only to find the entanglement on the water's edge untouched by the naval bombardment. Fired at from three sides, the first arrivals suffered heavily as they hacked and tore at the obstacle. Nevertheless, scrambling underneath it, or tearing their way

[1] The boats carrying the machine guns eventually grounded in such deep water that the guns could not be landed. Some of the men swam ashore losing three of the guns in the process; others remained with the fourth gun and landed it later.

[2] Major H. O. Bishop, commanding the battalion, and Captain C. Bromley, his adjutant, accompanied this party. Captain Bromley showed the utmost gallantry throughout the day and was awarded the V.C.

[3] The *Euryalus* and *Swiftsure*, lying a mile out, had to lift their fire at least 10 minutes before the boats reached the shore, and the Turks could take advantage of this respite to man their fire-steps·

through, small parties soon reached the sand dunes on the further side of the beach;[1] and in a few minutes the trenches above its centre had been taken.

Meanwhile, approaching the shore slightly behind the tows from the *Euryalus*, Br.-General Hare noticed that the water was calm enough for boats to land safely on the ledge of rock just to the north of the bay, whence the Turkish flank defences might possibly be turned.[2] Urging his own boat's crew in that direction, and shouting to the remaining boats from the *Implacable* to follow, he reached the shore without opposition; and a few minutes later he and his brigade-major and a handful of Fusiliers had occupied an empty trench on the top of the cliff. Here the commander of the covering force found himself in rear of, and only a few yards from, the Turks holding the northern flank of the beach. Seizing an orderly's rifle, Major Frankland shot two of them, and the remainder took to flight.

The volume of fire on the beach was now diminishing. More passages were cut through the wire, and the troops on the right swept forward against the enemy on the low cliff overlooking the southern end of the beach. But fresh trouble awaited the remnants of A Company, for just as the summit was gained many of them were hurled to the beach by a violent explosion. This, at first thought to be a land-mine, was in reality a heavy naval shell which struck the top of the cliff. Elsewhere, after bitter fighting, the Turks were forced to give ground, and by 7.15 A.M. a line had been gained which shielded the actual landing place from all but stray shots.

To the north of the bay, as soon as the Turks on the cliff had been put to flight, Br.-General Hare and his brigade-major, with a small party of signallers, pushed on towards X Beach, to establish touch with the Royal Fusiliers. But this was no task for the commander of the covering force. Before his little party had gone 200 yards it was fired on from Hill 114, and Br.-General Hare was severely wounded. The covering force was thus deprived of its leader at the very outset of the battle.

Frankland sent word to tell Lieut.-Colonel Newenham[3] that he had succeeded to the command of the brigade. Then,

---

[1] Many stories are told of the unimaginative bravery that carried the men of Lancashire through their ordeal. 'Thou'st given me a bloody "job," laughed one man to his officer as he went on pulling up the stakes of the entanglement though spouting blood from seven different wounds.

[2] The navy had pointed this out on the 23rd, but the information had not reached Br.-General Hare.

[3] By signal through the *Implacable*. Colonel Newenham was commanding the Royal Fusiliers, at that time advancing against Hill 114, and could do nothing till that hill was captured. Shortly afterwards he too was badly wounded, before he could assume command of the brigade.

having assured himself that all was well on the left he returned to the beach about 7.30 A.M., to organize the attack on Hill 138 and establish headquarters at the lighthouse. The second trip of tows had just landed with trifling loss,[1] and Captain Shaw, B Company, had collected the remnants of his command, and was leading them to attack the redoubt on Hill 138 in accordance with his original instructions. Captain Haworth (A Company), was under the cliffs on the right, reorganizing his company, now only 50 strong. Taking Haworth's party with him, Major Frankland, accompanied by Captain H. M. Farmar, staff-captain of the brigade, led the way under the shelter of the cliff towards the lighthouse, with a view to attacking the same redoubt from the south.

Here, too, it must be noticed, a good deal of confusion was caused by an inaccuracy in the British map. This map showed the high ground above Cape Helles as culminating in a single mound, marked Hill 138, due north of the lighthouse, and General Hare's orders had spoken only of the "redoubt on "Hill 138". In reality there was a second and somewhat higher crest 400 yards to the south-east of Hill 138, and each of these mounds or hills was crowned with a redoubt, that on the unmarked one being the larger of the two.[2] It must also be remarked that the undulating high ground at the toe of the peninsula is very confusing to a newcomer, and that most of the officers' compasses and field glasses were temporarily useless from the wetting they received when landing, and most of their watches had stopped. *Map 4. Sketch 8A.*

Advancing south-east from the right of W Beach, and out of sight of the coast-line, Captain Shaw soon found himself held up by a redoubt which he rightly took for Hill 138. But seeing the crest beyond it, which was not marked on the map, he at first mistook it for Hill 141 to the north of Sedd el Bahr. This natural mistake was to cause a great deal of confusion.[3] On the other hand, when Major Frankland reached the top of the cliff a little north-west of the lighthouse, his small party came under fire from the larger of the two redoubts. This he at first mistook for the redoubt on Hill 138, and for some

---

[1] These tows brought the remainder of Bde. H.Q., a field company of engineers, 3 platoons of the Anson Battalion for work on the beach, the naval and military beach staff, and a tent sub-division of a field ambulance. Their arrival had been delayed by the necessity of disposing of the dead and wounded in the boats before the second echelon could embark.

[2] These two hills are clearly shown on Map 2, taken from the Turkish survey, as Point 42 and Point 47 respectively. As already noticed, both of them were in full view of the cliff above X Beach.

[3] On several different occasions after this second redoubt had fallen it was reported to the 29th Division that Hill 141 had been captured.

time the smaller work to the left, which was checking Captain Shaw's advance, does not appear to have been noticed.

As a result of these two small parties making independent attacks on the two redoubts, neither was able to make any further headway. This was the situation when about 8.30 A.M. the gallant Frankland was killed while making a reconnaissance beyond the lighthouse towards V Beach. Captain Farmar assumed the duties of brigade-major, but the covering force was still without a commander, and there was no one on shore to co-ordinate the operations.

On the left, meanwhile, C and D Companies, led by Captain Willis and Major Adams, were fighting their way to the head of W Beach gully, and to the summit of Hill 114, whither at the same time $1\frac{1}{2}$ companies of the Royal Fusiliers were slowly advancing from X. Twenty-seven Turkish prisoners had been captured near W. Beach.[1]

On the beach the naval and military beach personnel, assisted by two liaison officers from G.H.Q.[2] who had landed in the second trip of tows, were preparing for the disembarkation of the main body and the organization of an advanced base. Parties of the 1/2nd London Field Company, working under the C.R.E. 29th Division,[3] had begun the construction of exits from the beach, while others were collecting the wounded, and removing wire entanglements. Owing to the lack of working parties, the landing of stores, ammunition, and water could not be undertaken till later in the day, for the three platoons of the Anson Battalion, which arrived with the second trip for this purpose, had been rushed forward to strengthen the Lancashire Fusiliers.

THE LANDING AT V BEACH

Dominated on the west by Fort No. 1 and on the east by the old fort and the village of Sedd el Bahr, V Beach lies at the foot of a natural amphitheatre which rises by gentle slopes to

---

[1] The information elicited from these prisoners was in reality remarkably accurate. They reported four Turkish divisions on the peninsula; main position Kilid Bahr plateau; "only covering troops of one division south "of Krithia"; no Germans on the peninsula. This information was repeated to units soon after midday, but, as already mentioned, it was taken to confirm, and not to dissipate, the report that there was a complete Turkish division south of Achi Baba.

[2] Captain R. F. Phillimore, R.N., Principal Beach Master.
    Br.-General A. W. Roper (Chief Engineer, G.H.Q.), Principal Military Landing Officer.
    Lieut.-Colonel L. R. Beadon (A.Q.M.G., G.H.Q.), Q. Liaison Officer.
    Captain C. A. Bolton (G.S.O.3, G.H.Q.), General Staff Liaison Officer.

[3] Lieut.-Colonel G. B. Hingston.

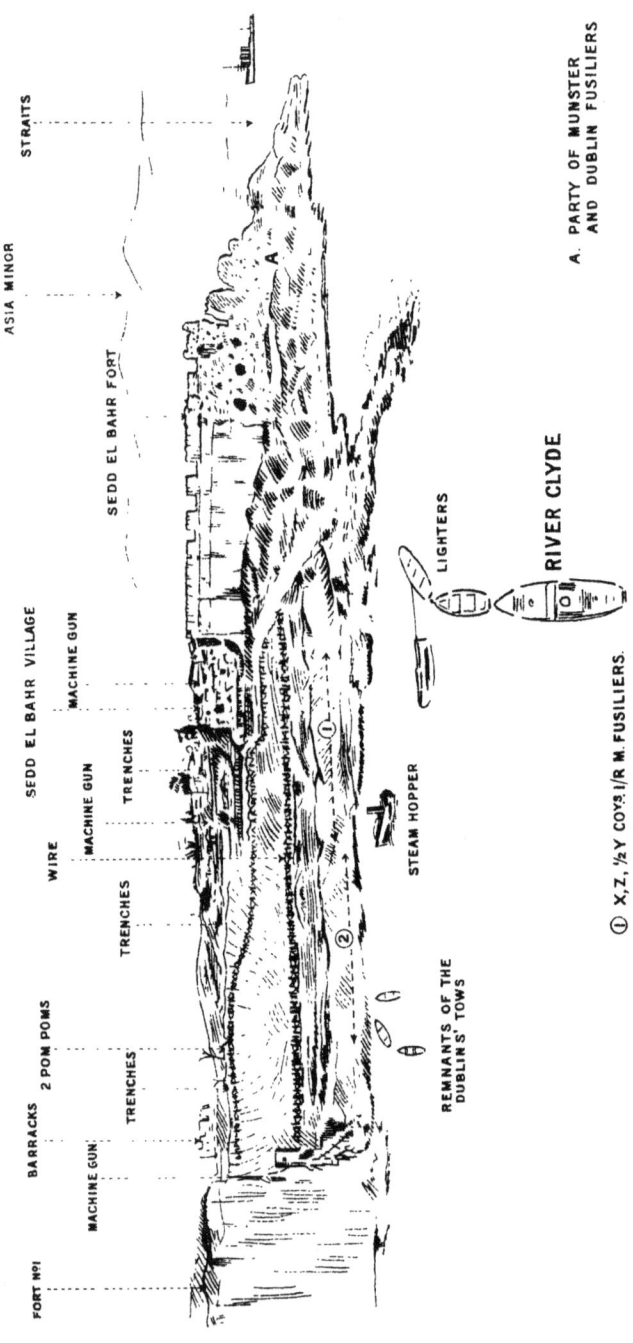

a height of a hundred feet. The actual beach is a sandy strip some 10 yards wide and 300 yards long, bordered in most places by a low bank about 5 feet high. The slight shelter afforded by this bank was to be of priceless value to the attackers during the first day of the landing. So far as V beach was concerned, it marked the limits of the first day's advance.

The old fort of Sedd el Bahr was a battered ruin with wide breaches in its walls. Above the left centre of the amphitheatre stood a ruined barrack. Both these buildings, as well as Fort No. 1, had for long been bombarded by the fleet, and the guns of the forts were out of action; but the battered walls, and the ruined outskirts of the village, afforded admirable cover for riflemen. From these points of vantage, and from narrow trenches on either flank, the beach was overlooked like a stage from the balconies of a theatre. About twenty yards from the shore a strong wire entanglement ran across from the old fort to the western headland. Two-thirds of the way up the amphitheatre was a similar obstacle, while a third, joining these two, ran up the hill from the eastern side of the beach. In one of the trenches on the left of the ridge were two pom-poms, while in the centre, and in the débris of the buildings on either flank, at least four machine guns had been posted to bring a cross-fire to bear upon the beach.[1]

Though the extraordinary strength of this position could not be gauged by a coastal reconnaissance, it had been obvious for some weeks that the Turks were fortifying the landing place. It would seem, therefore, that in selecting so strong a position as one of the principal points of disembarkation, both naval and military commanders must have overestimated the effect of naval gun-fire against field defences. Every part of the amphitheatre was visible from the sea; its garrison was believed to be small;[2] and it was hoped that half an hour's intense bombardment would crush the opposition. In addition, the troops making the frontal attack from the beach were expected to receive considerable support from an outflanking movement by the half-company which was to land under cover of the cliffs above the Camber. But though the *Albion* pounded the amphitheatre for nearly an hour, and did considerable damage to the buildings, the effect on the trenches was negligible.[3] Moreover,

---
[1] See f.n. 1, page 221.
[2] The total absence of movement by day had induced the belief that very few troops were garrisoning the actual beaches; and this surmise proved correct.
[3] So well concealed were these trenches that even from the bridge of the *River Clyde*, where officers were continually scouring the amphitheatre with strong glasses, they were not located till the afternoon.

in the delay which occurred between the lifting of the bombardment and the arrival of the boats, the Turkish infantry had time to recover from the deafening explosions around them, and to reoccupy points of vantage in the débris of the village and forts.

As at X and W, the five tows of the Dublin Fusiliers for V Beach and the one tow for the Camber were ordered to go ahead shortly before 6 A.M., the intention being that the *River Clyde* should be run ashore a few minutes later. But, owing to the strong current, the tows were late; the *River Clyde* had to alter her course to wait for them; and it was half-past six when tows and collier [1] approached the beach together. Up to the last moment it seemed that the Turkish defences had been abandoned; but just as the *River Clyde* grounded, and when the boats were only a few yards from the shore, Hell was suddenly let loose. A tornado of fire swept over the incoming boats, lashing the calm waters of the bay as with a thousand whips. Devastating casualties were suffered in the first few seconds. Some of the boats drifted helplessly away with every man in them killed.[2] Many more of the Dublins were killed as they waded ashore. Others, badly wounded, stumbling in the water, were drowned. Those who succeeded in landing safely,

---

[1] The captain of the *River Clyde* had temporarily to alter course at the last minute—a difficult manœuvre in such crowded water—to avoid landing before the tows. But he succeeded in grounding his vessel at the exact spot he had decided on beforehand.

[2] The following notes are extracts from the diary of Lieut.-Colonel (now Major-General) W. de L. Williams, General Staff, G.H.Q., who was on the bridge of the *River Clyde*, and jotted down incidents as they occurred:

6.10 A.M. Within ¼ mile of the shore. We are far ahead of the tows. No O.C. Troops on board. It must cause a mix-up if we, 2nd line, arrive before the 1st line. With difficulty I get Unwin (Captain of *River Clyde*) to swerve off and await the tows.

6.22 A.M. Ran smoothly ashore without a tremor. No opposition. We shall land unopposed.

6.25 A.M. Tows within a few yards of shore. Hell burst loose on them. One boat drifting to north, all killed. Others almost equally helpless. Our hopper gone away.

6.35 A.M. Connection with shore very bad. Only single file possible and not one man in ten gets across. Lighters blocked with dead and wounded. Very little fire on this ship. Wedgwood's maxims in bows firing full blast, but nothing to be seen excepting a maxim firing through a hole in the fort and a pom-pom near the skyline on our left front.

9.0 A.M. Fear we'll not land to-day.

10.0 A.M. ... Very little directed fire against us on the ship, but fire immediately concentrates on any attempt to land. The Turks' fire discipline is really wonderful. (N.B. In another place Colonel Williams writes: "Turkish fire was extraordinarily well-" handled, being almost entirely confined to movement. The " tows and lighters were subjected to very heavy and accurate " fire.")

and in crossing the strip of sand, managed to gain a precarious shelter under the bank on the further side. Few of the boats were able to get off again. Most of them, with their devoted crews, were destroyed on the beach.[1] The ripples placidly lapping the shore were tinged with blood.

On the right, the two platoons ordered to land at the Camber were able to get ashore in safety, and a few men succeeded in reaching the village, where they were eventually overpowered. But the greater number were held up by the galling fire that met them and all the officers were killed.

Meanwhile the stranded *River Clyde*, and the bullet-swept water around it, was the scene of unforgettable heroism. To enable the troops to land quickly from the collier, wide sally ports had been cut in both her sides. Issuing from these, the troops were to double along broad gang-planks to a platform rigged up under the vessel's bows, whence a floating bridge was to span the gap to the shore. To form this bridge, a steam hopper, towed ashore on the port side of the collier, was to go ahead when the collier grounded, and to beach herself in front of the collier's stem. In addition, the collier had three lighters on her starboard side, so that if she grounded further out than expected, one or more of these could be used to fill the gap between her bows and the hopper's stern.

Simple though this plan appeared on paper, in execution it collapsed. The hopper, instead of running forward when the *River Clyde* grounded, swung suddenly out to port; and there for some time she lay immovable, broadside on to the beach, and useless for her intended purpose. Faced with this unexpected failure of his scheme, and realizing the danger of delay, Commander E. Unwin at once decided to make a bridge of lighters to get the troops ashore. Rushing to the bows of the collier, where the lighters had now collected, he soon had two connected with a gang-plank. Seizing a line from one of them, he plunged into the sea, closely followed by Able Seaman W. C. Williams,[2] and swam ashore to pull them into position.

---

[1] The following extract from the naval despatch dated 1st July 1915 is typical of the work of the naval boats' crews on 25th April: " Able Seaman " Lewis Jacobs, H.M.S. *Lord Nelson*, took his boat in to V Beach unaided, " after all the remainder of the crew and the troops were killed or wounded. " When last seen Jacobs was standing up and endeavouring to pole the " cutter ashore. While thus employed, he was killed."

[2] Able Seaman Williams was a leading seaman in H.M.S. *Hussar*, but had volunteered to revert to able seaman to accompany Commander Unwin in the *River Clyde*. Having no definite task to give him, Unwin told him the night before to stay beside him on the 25th. Williams obeyed literally. His gallantry cost him his life, but won him a posthumous V.C.

In a few minutes the leading lighter had been dragged to within a few yards of the beach, where the sea was not more than three feet deep. There, standing waist-deep in the water, exposed to a murderous fire, and continuing to haul on his line to keep the bridge in position, Commander Unwin shouted to the *River Clyde* for the disembarkation to begin.

Covered by the fire of Wedgwood's machine-guns in the collier's bows, Captain E. L. H. Henderson's company of the Munsters streamed down the starboard gangway, and fell in heaps as they ran. Henderson was mortally wounded, and very few reached the cover of the sandy bank in front of them. On the port side, the jamming of the gangway caused another short delay; but here Captain G. W. Geddes's company was soon pouring out of the ship, the Irishmen cheering as they went. On this side the volume of fire was even more intense. The first 48 men behind Geddes all fell. The gangways and lighters were choked with dead and wounded. But those behind never faltered; and Lieut. Watts, lying on the gangway, wounded in five places, cheered them on with shouts of "Follow the Captain!"

At this moment Able Seaman Williams, who had been helping Commander Unwin to hold the lighters in position, was killed by a shell from the Asiatic shore. Trying to support him, Unwin momentarily dropped the line they had been holding, and the bridge drifted away into deeper water. Some of Geddes's men succeeded in swimming ashore; others, though the water was chest high, managed to struggle to the beach; but many were drowned by the weight of their equipment.

To the right of the *River Clyde*, a small rocky spit jutted out invitingly from the shore. The Turkish fire on this point was at first particularly severe, and few survived who attempted to land there. The sandy bank on the edge of the beach was highest to the left of the *River Clyde*, and here the remnants of both Dublins and Munsters collected. Of the Dublins nearly all the officers, and of the Munsters seven out of the ten who had attempted to land, were already casualties, and seventy per cent of the rank and file. To climb to the top of the bank was certain death, and all the gallant men who had crawled forward to cut the wire were lying dead in front of it.

Noticing that his right flank was exposed, and fearing that the Turks might counter-attack from the old fort, Captain Geddes now called for volunteers to occupy that end of the shore. The task was a dangerous one, for it entailed doubling across a part of the beach where there was no protecting ledge of sand. Every man in his neighbourhood volunteering to go, Geddes picked out five, and the little party rushed across the gap.

V BEACH FROM THE "RIVER CLYDE," 8 A.M. 25TH APRIL 1915

Short though the distance was, two of the six were killed, and Geddes and another wounded, in getting across. But another handful followed shortly afterwards, and a few minutes later the little party met fourteen Dublins from the Camber detachment, who, finding the direct route to the village impassable, had made a detour to the left.[1] With the assistance of these reinforcements, an endeavour was now made to gain a lodgment inside the old fort. This proving impossible, the little party dug themselves in as best they could with their entrenching implements. Geddes signalled to the *River Clyde* that he could make no further progress.

All this time gallant efforts were being made by officers and men of the fleet to complete a better bridge between the *River Clyde* and the shore. Commander Unwin remained in the water till he collapsed from cold and exhaustion an hour later.[2] The work was then continued by Lieut. J. A. V. Morse and Midshipmen G. L. Drewry and W. St. A. Malleson,[3] all of whom seemed to bear charmed lives. The third lighter was brought up to fill the gap between the hopper and the *River Clyde*; and after the two young midshipmen had repeatedly swum with lines from lighter to lighter, the task was eventually completed about 9 A.M.

Major C. H. B. Jarrett of the Munsters now led his company ashore, but so heavy were the casualties suffered by the first two platoons that he sent back Lieut. G. W. Nightingale to urge that no more troops should be landed from the collier till after nightfall. This suggestion was agreed to by Lieut.-Colonel H. Carington Smith, 2/Hampshire Regiment, senior officer in the *River Clyde*, and orders were issued accordingly.[4]

[1] As already mentioned, the attack on the village from the Camber, from which so much had been hoped, had entirely failed. Remnants of the two platoons who attempted this flank attack eventually returned to the Camber, where, all their officers being killed, they signalled to the flagship to be re-embarked. They were eventually rescued by a picket boat from the *Queen Elizabeth*, which volunteered to run in with two cutters to bring them off.

[2] Despite his 51 years, Unwin was in the water again after an hour's rest, superintending the work, and about noon he again left his ship in a lifeboat, alone, and continued to rescue wounded men lying on the beach until forced to stop through sheer physical exhaustion. Subsequently this gallant rescue work was continued by Sub-Lieut. Tisdall, Anson Bn., R.N.D., who took a boat five times from the *River Clyde* to the shore to succour the wounded.

[3] For their gallantry on this occasion Commander Unwin, Sub-Lieut. Tisdall, Midshipman Malleson and Midshipman Drewry were awarded the V.C., and Lieut. Morse the D.S.O. The V.C. was also awarded to Seaman G. M. Samson for " working all day on the hopper, attending the wounded " and getting out lines ".

[4] Owing to the almost total absence of shell-fire the men were comparatively safe in the collier's hold, though many were killed by snipers when they showed themselves on deck. Colonel Carington Smith was killed in this way in the afternoon.

Thus, shortly after 9 A.M. the landing on V Beach had been definitely held up. The survivors on the beach, sheltering behind that lucky ledge of sand, were powerless to move. The 1,000 men remaining in the collier were prisoners till nightfall, or till a successful advance from W could turn the Turkish defences.

THE LANDING AT S BEACH

Meanwhile, less than two miles in rear of Sedd el Bahr, where one company of Turks was frustrating the British plan, three companies of the 2/South Wales Borderers [1] had landed successfully at S Beach at 7.30 A.M., and were now in firm possession of that point.

Map 2. Sketch 8A.

S Beach consists of a small break in the cliff on the northern arm of Morto Bay, at the end of which, on the top of the cliff, was a disused work known as de Tott's Battery. A less likely spot for a landing could scarcely be imagined, and the Turks had made few preparations to defend it. There was no wire, and the garrison consisted of only one platoon with a second platoon in support about half a mile inland.

The four trawlers for this beach, each towing six lifeboats, could make little headway against the Dardanelles current, and their progress was further hampered by the presence of the mine-sweeping flotilla in the Straits. But the Asiatic batteries were too much occupied elsewhere to fire at the trawlers, and the small flotilla crossed Morto Bay without accident. Here the soldiers were transferred to the lifeboats; and when the water became too shallow for further towing, they proceeded to row themselves ashore, covered by the guns of the *Cornwallis*. Colonel Casson had ordered two companies to land at the actual beach, while the third (in shirt sleeves, and without packs) were to scramble ashore on the rocks at the extreme point, and scale the cliffs to de Tott's.

This plan was entirely successful. As the boats were pulled slowly ashore by their unaccustomed crews those approaching the beach came under a hot fire from the outpost platoon in a trench half-way up the cliff. But the flanking company met with no opposition, and, scrambling to the top of the cliff, the men soon held the Turks below at their mercy.

[1] This force, commanded by Lieut.-Colonel H. G. Casson, consisted of the 2/South Wales Borderers (less one company detached to Y Beach), a small detachment of engineers, a party of R.A.M.C., an artillery liaison officer and signallers, and a party of marines and bluejackets provided by H.M.S. *Cornwallis* and led by the captain of that vessel (Captain A. P. Davidson), who insisted on landing personally.

THE LANDING AT S BEACH

The rest of the force now landed in safety; the trench and 15 prisoners were taken; and by 8 A.M. the whole position was safely in British hands.[1]

From this commanding point it soon became clear that the landing at V was making no progress. But Colonel Casson's orders had conveyed no hint of what he was to do in such an emergency. He had been instructed that, his landing made good, he was to await the advance from the south. In these circumstances, hearing from a Turkish prisoner that there were 2,000 Turks in the neighbourhood, he apparently decided that it would be an unjustifiable departure from orders to endeavour to attack, with his own small force, the rear of the Turkish position at Sedd el Bahr. The rest of the day was consequently spent in consolidating his position;[2] the Turks were too much occupied with the main landings to make any serious attempt to eject him; and except for some Asiatic shelling, which did little damage, the S Beach detachment was left in comparative peace till the advance of the French on the 27th April linked it up once more with the rest of the 29th Division. During the interval naval picket boats were able to keep up communication with Colonel Casson, to evacuate the wounded, and to bring up water, ammunition, and supplies. A certain amount of useful information regarding Turkish batteries was transmitted to headquarters; but in other respects, as in the case of Y Beach, no advantage was taken of the important opportunities which this flank landing had created.[3]

[1] During their 48 hours' stay at S Beach the total casualties of the S.W.B., including those sustained at the landing, amounted to 2 officers and 13 men killed; 3 officers and 45 men wounded.

[2] This action was approved by G.O.C. 29th Division, who signalled to Col. Casson at 7.15 P.M. to consolidate his position for the night and report situation. Again on the 26th, at 3.15 P.M., General Hunter-Weston signalled "Well done, South Wales Borderers. Can you maintain your position "for another 48 hours? Am sending you rations to-night. Send report of "situation twice daily."

[3] "I fear the S.W.B. are hardly strong enough alone to move across "and threaten Sedd el Bahr. Big flanking attacks at Y and S might have "converged on Sedd el Bahr, and carried it from the rear, when none of "the garrison would have escaped. But until we tried, we were afraid fire "from Asia might defeat the de Tott's Battery attack, and that the Y "party might not scale the cliffs."—Hamilton, "Gallipoli Diary," i. p. 134.

When he wrote this, the Commander-in-Chief was unaware that the troops at Y and S alone were stronger than the whole Turkish force south of Achi Baba at the time of the landing.

It is now known that the only Turks near S Beach on the 25th consisted of one company (one platoon of which was killed or captured by the S.W.B. on landing). Another company was despatched as a reinforcement from Krithia to Morto Bay after the opening of the British bombardment, but was diverted to Sedd el Bahr.

CHAPTER XIII

THE LANDINGS AT HELLES (*concluded*)

THE MAIN BODY

(Map 4 ; Sketches 8A, 11)

25 Apr.
Map 4.
Sketch
8A.

FROM his post in the *Euryalus*, lying some 1,000 yards off W Beach, Major-General Hunter-Weston had been an eye-witness of the landing of the Lancashire Fusiliers,[1] and encouraging news had reached him of the successes at Y, X, and S. In addition, very heartening, but entirely misleading reports had arrived about the situation at V. A message received at 7.30 A.M. read "Troops from collier appear to be getting "ashore well", and, twenty minutes later, the *Lord Nelson* signalled that British troops could be seen in Sedd el Bahr village.[2]

At 8.30 A.M., therefore, General Hunter-Weston gave orders for the landing of the main body. But realizing that more infantry were required at W to confirm the success of the Lancashire Fusiliers, he directed the 1/Essex Regiment to be disembarked at that beach instead of at V. Signals were now made for the main body transports to approach from the outer anchorages; and fleet sweepers rushed back to meet them and take their troops on board.[3] Half an hour later, or little more than 30 minutes after schedule time, the 1/Border Regiment began to land at X and the 1/Essex at W, while, unaware of the true position at V, a fleet sweeper approached that tragic beach with Br.-General H. E. Napier and the 88th Brigade Staff, two platoons of the 4/Worcestershire, and two companies of the 2/Hampshire.

[1] W Beach was subsequently christened "Lancashire Landing" in honour of that battalion's exploit.

[2] These were evidently a few of the Dublin Fusiliers from the Camber, whose dead bodies were found in the village next day.

[3] There was at this time some promiscuous shelling of the inner anchorage from Asia, and the admiral deemed it unsafe for transports to lie at anchor near the shore.

LANDING OF THE HELLES MAIN BODY 239

Some distance from the shore Br.-General Napier's little vessel awaited the return of the tows which, according to the original plan, were to land his troops, and it was only the melancholy destruction of these boats a few hours earlier which now prevented a repetition of the disaster that had befallen the Dublin Fusiliers.[1] Soon after 9 A.M. some of the few remaining boats from that disastrous landing arrived alongside the fleet sweeper, battered but undismayed. The sailors who manned them were well aware of the hopelessness of any further attempt to land on that tragic beach. But if the army wanted to try, it was not for the navy to say "impossible"; and without a murmur they were ready to face for a second time an ordeal which they knew to be almost certain death. Willing hands quickly emptied the boats of the wounded and dead with which they were crowded, and a few minutes later General Napier and his Staff, and two platoons of the Worcestershire, were heading for the beach, followed by a small party of the 2/Hampshire.

General Hunter-Weston in the *Euryalus* was still unaware of the desperate situation at V;[2] and about 9 A.M. he had signalled to the *River Clyde*, urging the troops to move left-handed to join up with the Lancashire Fusiliers. About 9.30 A.M., in answer to this message, Lieut.-Colonel Carington Smith ordered one of the two companies of his own battalion (2/Hampshire) in the collier to try to succeed where the Irish troops had failed. But only a few men reached the lighters alive.[3] A minute later the hopper again swung out into deep water, and as it was now impossible to reach the shore the order was countermanded.

At this moment General Napier's tow was seen to be heading for the beach. Realizing the futility of trying to land, Carington Smith hailed it to come alongside the collier. The naval officer in charge complied; but General Napier, seeing the lighters choked with men, and not realizing that they were

---

[1] The paucity of boats similarly saved the troops detailed to land at V in the second trip of tows. These troops—3 platoons of the Anson Battalion, and the naval and military beach personnel—lay off V Beach in Fleet Sweeper No. 2, waiting for the tows, till 10.30 A.M. when an order reached them to land at W.

[2] A message received from Captain Farmar at the lighthouse at 9.30 spoke of the troops at V being held up, but a study of existing records shows that for another hour and a half divisional H.Q. did not realize that the hold-up was complete. During that time they believed that it was only our own shell-fire which was preventing the V Beach troops from moving left-handed to join up with the Lancashire Fusiliers.

[3] Captain C. L. Boxall, who led this party ashore, was mortally wounded on gaining the beach.

dead, sprung on board the nearest lighter, meaning to lead them ashore. A warning voice from the collier shouted "You can't "possibly land!" but Napier shouted back: "I'll have a "damned good try!"

At once there was a renewed burst of Turkish fire. General Napier and his Staff reached the hopper, but could get no further, and there, a quarter of an hour later, he and his brigade-major (Captain J. H. D. Costeker) were killed. Thus died the very man who by his rank, his nerve, and his knowledge, would have been of priceless value to the troops in the southern area during the rest of that vital day.

At 10.21 A.M. Sir Ian Hamilton had signalled to General Hunter-Weston: "Not advisable to send more men to V Beach. "We have 200 on shore unable to progress." The remaining infantry intended for V were then diverted to W.[1]

The first troops of the main body to land at W Beach were two companies of the 1/Essex Regiment. These suffered a good many casualties in their boats from long-range rifle fire; but once under cover of the cliffs they were able to wade ashore in safety, and a few minutes later were rushing up the W Beach gully to fill a gap between the right and left flanks of the Lancashire Fusiliers. Helped by this reinforcement the troops on the left were able to make better progress; by half-past eleven they had joined up with the Royal Fusiliers from X, and the whole of Hill 114 was at last in British hands.

The remaining two companies of the Essex arrived about 10 A.M., and after some delay, due to no senior officer being left alive on shore to issue orders,[2] tasks were eventually allotted to them by their own battalion commander, Lieut.-Colonel O. G. Godfrey-Faussett. One company was directed to the high ground south of the gully. The fourth company was sent right-handed towards Hill 138, and almost at once

---

[1] These included the Worcestershire Regiment and 2 companies 2/Hampshire, less the small party under Captains H. J. de C. Wymer and R. O. Spencer-Smith which succeeded in getting ashore on the starboard side of the *River Clyde* just about the time that General Napier was killed.

[2] At 11.20 A.M. Captain C. A. Bolton, G.H.Q. liaison officer on the beach, signalled to 29th Division H.Q.: " Send someone ashore to order " advance. Essex Regiment hung up on ridge north-east of W Beach. No " brigade H.Q. here and no divisional staff. Still hung up as nothing has " come ashore for last hour and half." Colonel O. C. Wolley-Dod, G.S.O.1 of the division was then sent ashore and landed soon after 12.30 P.M.

Captain Bolton's remark about nothing coming ashore for $1\frac{1}{2}$ hours was prompted by the fact that, in the original programme, guns, stores, animals, and ammunition were to begin landing about 9 A.M. But the transports conveying these had not been allowed to approach the beach owing to shelling of the anchorage.

LANDING OF THE HELLES MAIN BODY

came under fire from the small redoubt which had brought the advance of Captain Shaw's party to a standstill earlier in the day. Half-way up the slope its progress was stopped by wire.

Meanwhile Captain Farmar had crawled from the lighthouse to a point on the cliff whence he could see the *River Clyde*, and at 12.25 P.M. he sent by runner to W Beach a valuable message which he had already signalled to divisional headquarters on board the *Euryalus*. This message gave the first clear picture of the actual situation at V. "Two hundred men", it said, "have "landed on V Beach. These cannot get forward. Connection "between *River Clyde* and shore is very bad and casualties "occur as soon as men move from the ship. . . . Landing is "easy near lighthouse and cliff accessible. If redoubts 1 and "2 are taken it would facilitate capture of village."

Had this message arrived at divisional headquarters in time to be acted upon, and had the Worcestershire landed near the lighthouse instead of at W Beach, the situation at V must almost certainly have been relieved early in the afternoon. But Colonel Wolley-Dod, who arrived soon after 12.30 to direct the operations at W, did not receive it till 1.10 P.M., and by that time most of the Worcestershire had already landed.

Col. Wolley-Dod does not seem to have gauged from this message the full extent of the hold-up at V. He realized, however, that Hill 138, which the Lancashire Fusiliers had hoped to take on first landing, must still be in Turkish hands, and he decided to send the Worcestershire to reinforce the troops in front of it as soon as that battalion was complete.[1] Shortly after 2 o'clock, therefore, the Worcestershire moved up on the right of the fourth company of the Essex Regiment, and after the first redoubt had been bombarded by *Swiftsure* and *Euryalus* for twenty minutes, it was successfully carried by the left of the line about 3 P.M. The Worcestershire then continued their advance towards the larger redoubt to the southeast, and after being held up for some time longer by another belt of wire, they succeeded in capturing the position with little loss, the small Turkish garrison beating a hasty retreat from the overwhelming numbers opposed to them.

A detachment of Haworth's[2] company of the Lancashire Fusiliers, which had been lying out near the lighthouse all day, unable to show a head, reinforced by some of the Worcestershire, now found it possible to advance in an easterly direction

---

[1] Telegram from Colonel Wolley-Dod to H.Q. 29th Division, 1.22 P.M., 25th April: "Balance of Worcestershire now arriving. I will send whole "battalion against Hill 138. Will ships look out and support by fire."

[2] Captain Haworth was severely wounded at 11.30 A.M. but refused to leave his company till the redoubt had fallen.

towards V Beach; but this party too was soon held up by a stout entanglement. This obstacle, which consisted of a broad belt of new wire running down towards the edge of the cliff, was plainly visible to the *Queen Elizabeth* and *Albion* at a range of less than a mile, but neither vessel knew enough of the position ashore to be able to open fire. For the next hour, therefore, the sailors were obliged to stand idly by, while in full view of them brave men continued to lose their lives in cutting the obstacle by hand. Time after time, plainly silhouetted against the sky-line, a man would be seen rushing up to that glistening belt, only to fall lifeless across it a few minutes later, when his place would at once be taken by another volunteer.

Finally, to the admiration of the navy, these brave efforts were crowned with success, and the attacking troops went streaming through the gap. But heavy fire again checked them on the other side, and they could make no further progress.

Meanwhile the urgency of pushing right on to succour the troops at V was still unrecognized on W Beach, and at 4.35 P.M., on hearing of the capture of the second redoubt, Colonel Wolley-Dod signalled to the reserve company of the Worcestershire to reverse the trenches in the position gained and to bury the dead. At five o'clock, however, a message from divisional headquarters told Colonel Wolley-Dod that the landing at V was definitely held up, and that the Irishmen could make no headway till an advance from W had cleared the trenches on their western flank. A revised order was consequently sent to the Worcestershire, telling them to continue their attack to the edge of the cliff above V. But Colonel Cayley had already learnt the situation from Captain Farmar, who had walked over from the lighthouse to see him, and he was now advancing on Fort No. 1. To the watchers in the ships it seemed that the worst was over, and that the Turks at V would be obliged to release their grasp.[1] But these hopes were not realized. Considerable fire was again encountered, and the Worcestershire were again held up. Finding that his men were making little headway, Colonel Cayley now decided to consolidate the ground won. His battalion was very scattered; the day

---

[1] Captain Farmar signalled to *Euryalus* at 5.40 P.M. that " Hill 138 has " been captured ", and General Hunter-Weston, with a clear grasp of the requirements of the situation, replied at 6.12 P.M.: " Leaving troops to " consolidate 138, and a detachment to take in reverse the enemy trenches " to the east of lighthouse overlooking V Beach, push on all remainder " rapidly to take Hill 141." He also signalled to *River Clyde* that an attack on 141 was imminent, and that the V Beach troops should co-operate. But these orders were not acted on, and it is indeed doubtful whether they ever reached the troops.

Imperial War Museum Photo. *Crown Copyright.*

TURKISH WIRE ENTANGLEMENT RUNNING DOWN TO THE CLIFF EAST OF CAPE HELLES LIGHTHOUSE

LANDING OF THE HELLES MAIN BODY 243

was closing in; and there was every chance of a determined counter-attack at night. This decision marked the end of the first day's fighting on the right of W Beach. All hope of retrieving the situation at V was now postponed till the morrow.[1]

On the remainder of the W Beach front, and on Hill 114, the position had remained unchanged since 11.30 A.M. Since early in the afternoon all opposition had practically ceased. But in contrast to the gallant exploits of the morning a certain inertia seems to have overtaken the troops on this part of the front, who now amounted to at least 2,000 men.[2]

This inertia, perhaps, was largely due to the loss of the commander of the covering force. Owing to the hold-up at V, and the delay in capturing the redoubts near Hill 138, the scheme of a united advance to the second objective had fallen to pieces, and there was no one in chief command on shore to initiate a fresh plan. But to some extent the lack of further progress was also due to an absence of initiative amongst subordinate commanders. For most of the 29th Division, it must be remembered, as for the Australian and New Zealand troops, this was their first experience of modern war, and they had been suddenly hurled into an unparalleled situation after four enervating weeks on board ship.

Faced with a definite task—the capture of the beaches—the 29th Division had put an indelible mark on history. But once that task was done, platoon, company, and even battalion commanders, each in their own sphere, were awaiting fresh and definite orders, and on their own initiative did little to exploit the morning's success or to keep in touch with the enemy by means of fighting patrols. With victory within their grasp, the twelve companies between Hills 114 and 138 continued to maintain a passive attitude against an enemy whom they had already driven from his trenches, and whom, though unaware of the fact, they outnumbered by at least six to one.

It will be remembered that the troops of the main body detailed to land at X were the 1/Border Regiment, and the 1/Inniskilling Fusiliers, and that their brigadier, General

---

[1] At 6.30 P.M. W Beach erroneously reported to General Hunter-Weston that the Worcestershire had captured Hill 141, and this was believed until a message arrived from Colonel Cayley at 9.15 P.M. saying that he had been held up by wire and that his line ran from Hill 138 southwards to a point on the cliff east of Helles lighthouse.

[2] From left to right: 2 coys. 2/R.F.; 2 coys. 1/L.F.; 1 coy. 1/5th R. Scots; 2 coys. 1/Essex; 1½ coys. 2/Hampshire; the remaining 2 coys. 1/Essex. One company 1/5th R. Scots was in reserve on the beach.

W. R. Marshall, had been instructed that these two battalions were to form the divisional reserve.

When the first tows of the Border Regiment began to land about 9 A.M., a certain amount of firing could be heard on the left, but the beach itself and the cliffs above it were very peaceful, and for some time the disembarkation proceeded smoothly and without interruption. A detachment of the Anson Battalion was making a road up the cliff, other working parties, including some Royal Fusiliers, were unloading water and ammunition, and a wireless station was being erected on the beach.

Br.-General Marshall's position on arrival about 9 A.M. was in many respects peculiar. Two of his battalions, the Scottish Borderers and the South Wales Borderers, had been withdrawn from his command to land at Y and S. The other two were in divisional reserve and, except in an emergency, could not be seriously committed without divisional sanction. The Royal Fusiliers in front were not under his orders, but formed part of the covering force under Br.-General Hare, and it was no part of his allotted task to co-operate in the advance of that force to its second objective, the line Y Beach—Sedd el Bahr. No news had yet reached him regarding events at the other landings, and not until the afternoon was he to learn that Br.-General Hare had been wounded and Br.-General Napier killed. The comparative peacefulness at X, the ease of his own landing, and the fact that it had taken place almost at schedule time, all tended at first to persuade him that everything was going well, and that the advance of the three Fusilier battalions from W and V might be expected at any minute.

Climbing to the top of the cliff, Br.-General Marshall was learning the dispositions of the Royal Fusiliers from the officer commanding the reserve company, when a message arrived from Captain Leslie on the left, to say that he was being heavily attacked and to ask for assistance.[1] The reserve company at once moved forward, and General Marshall, in order to be ready for emergencies, ordered as many of the Border Regiment as had yet landed to man the top of the cliff.

About 10.30 A.M. a message was received from Colonel Newenham, asking for reinforcements to prolong the left of the Royal Fusiliers on Hill 114, and one company of the Border Regiment with two machine guns was detailed for this duty. Soon after these troops had gone forward parties of the Royal

---

[1] Captain Leslie was killed in this attack and his company suffered so many casualties that no authentic details of the action have ever been obtained.

LANDING OF THE HELLES MAIN BODY 245

Fusiliers were seen retiring from the left front, closely followed by Turks. Br.-General Marshall called up Major C. D. Vaughan, second in command of the Border Regiment, and was pointing out the situation, and ordering the Borders to get ready to charge, when a ragged Turkish volley swept the top of the cliff, killing Vaughan and wounding the brigadier.[1]

By this time the Turks were within a few hundred yards of the shore, and with the hurried order "Fix bayonets, charge!" two companies of the Border Regiment, cheering loudly, went over the top of the cliff. About forty casualties, including three officers killed, were suffered during their advance, but the Turks refused to wait for cold steel, and after firing heavily for a moment they turned and fled. There was no pursuit, and no attempt was made to keep in touch with the retreating enemy.

It was now about 1 P.M., and the Inniskilling Fusiliers had arrived. But General Marshall was still hampered by lack of information. A helio message received from Y Beach at noon had informed him that the Y landing had been unopposed;[2] but no news had reached him from W, and not a single message had yet arrived from divisional headquarters.[3] He knew, however, that the advance from W and V was held up, for from his position above X Beach he could see that Hill 141 and the two redoubts on Hill 138 were still in enemy occupation. But he had no knowledge of the strength of the enemy holding them. In these circumstances, remembering that his two battalions were the only divisional reserve, he decided that it would be wrong to commit them without orders, and that his only course was to keep them as intact as possible and to ensure

---

[1] Happily Br.-General Marshall's wound was not severe, and he was able to remain at duty, but it will not escape notice, when the incidents of this remarkable day are considered, that all three of the 29th Division's brigade commanders, and two of its brigade-majors, had become casualties on the first morning of active operations. In addition, Colonel Newenham, who succeeded to the command of the 86th Brigade, was himself wounded at noon, and Colonel Carington Smith, who succeeded General Napier at 10.30 A.M., was killed a few hours later. The brigade-major, divisional artillery, was killed next morning.

[2] See f.n. 1, page 206.

[3] General Hunter-Weston personally sent him a situation message at 2.15 P.M. (most of the messages issued to the signals by divisional headquarters on the 25th are in General Hunter-Weston's handwriting). In this message he told him to "keep touch with troops from Y"—at this time it was believed that touch had been established, see f.n. 2, page 211—and at the same time asked if he could attack Hill 138 from the north. Very unfortunately this message, which gave Br.-Gen. Marshall the right to use the divisional reserve, does not appear to have arrived, for at 3.43 P.M. Marshall reported to divisional headquarters that he was digging in and awaiting the advance from V Beach.

the protection of the beach. The Border Regiment was ordered to dig in on the ground it already held, and one company of the Inniskillings was sent up on the right to complete a semi-circular position, with a radius of some 600-800 yards from the landing place. The remainder of the Inniskillings were held in reserve.[1]

Thus at X, as at W, the attacking force, though in greatly superior numbers, remained on the defensive throughout the afternoon and evening of the 25th. By the use of a bold counter-offensive, the Turks had succeeded in paralysing the initiative of the landing force, and had gained for themselves the one advantage of which they were in most need—time to organize a position in rear and to bring up reinforcements.

At 6 P.M. Br.-General Marshall at last gave up hope of any advance from W and V that day, and asked General Hunter-Weston whether he was to remain in his present position, or to endeavour single-handed to link up with the troops at Y. He pointed out, however, that such an advance would leave X Beach very weakly held, with an extended and weak line between X and Y. In reply he was told, about two hours later, to remain at X, and to make preparations for an advance next morning, when the programme for the 25th would be continued without alteration.[2]

About the same time another divisional order, written by Colonel Wolley-Dod at W Beach,[3] reached General Marshall, telling him to direct the Y Beach troops to extend their right until they gained "actual touch" with the left of the troops at X. But it was now too late to carry out this order, for the Turkish attack on Y had already begun.[4]

At V Beach, throughout the remaining hours of daylight, the troops on shore continued to cling to their scanty strip of

---

[1] At 5 P.M. Br.-General Marshall reported to divisional headquarters: "Am digging in on 800 yards semi-circle. Have only three companies "Inniskillings left in reserve, as covering force was driven back towards "beach and we had to counter-attack to restore situation. As soon as I see "88th Brigade moving forward to clear hollow ground [in front of Sedd el "Bahr] I will push forward on their left towards Krithia."

[2] When sending this message General Hunter-Weston believed that Hill 141 had fallen and that the V Beach situation would be cleared up during the night without difficulty.

[3] Col. Wolley-Dod, when sent ashore at noon, was given authority to issue orders where necessary in the divisional commander's name. Thus it happened that on some occasions contradictory orders were issued by the G.O.C. and his G.S.O.1.

[4] General Marshall to 29th Division. "9.5 P.M. Colonel Matthews "appears to be heavily attacked at Y. All quiet on rest of front. Have "sent patrols along beach to gain touch with Y." These patrols failed to establish communication.

cover, while their comrades of the navy, watching the tragedy from the supporting battleships, were practically powerless to help. All afternoon the *Queen Elizabeth*, *Albion*, and *Cornwallis* searched the defences with their guns, but the naval shells could accomplish little,[1] and the Turkish fire burst out afresh at the least movement on the beach.

General Hunter-Weston, not realizing the impossibility of movement by daylight on that exposed shore, had continued to urge the capture of the western defences of the beach, to assist the troops from W in their advance on Hill 138. At 2.30 P.M., therefore, Lieut. Morse R.N., who had already distinguished himself in helping to build the bridge to the shore, went off to the flagship with a note from Colonel Carington Smith:

> Your first two proposals I have already considered, but each attempt to disembark troops has ended in many casualties. Enemy's position round Beach V very strong, and tremendous lot of wire. Every attempt to reconnoitre ground has so far failed. My casualties are very heavy, including General Napier and his brigade-major, both killed. Unless in the meantime the high ground to the N.W. of me is taken by other troops, I intend to wait till dark and then attack position 141.
>
> To carry this out, can you send me a barrel pier, as I am very short of boats and our pontoon pier does not reach the shore. I have a great number of wounded on the beach. I have 900 infantry still on ship. Of the half company Dublins landed at Camber only 25 remain. O.C. Munsters roughly estimates his casualties at 200. Mark VI ammunition for R.N.A.S. machine guns is required.
>
> 2.25 P.M.

Within half an hour of writing this message, Colonel Carington Smith was killed on the bridge of the collier.

About 4 P.M. the bridge to the shore had again been repaired by the sailors; and the Turks were so quiet that another attempt was made to land troops, Lieut. Nightingale of the Munsters leading the remaining platoons of his company ashore, with orders to gain the high ground on the western side of the bay. But again a terrific fire broke out at the first sign of movement. Those who succeeded in getting across the lighters could do no more than reach the sandy bank in front of them;[2] and divisional headquarters was again informed

---

[1] " The shots from our naval guns, smashing as their impact appears, " might as well be confetti for all the effect they have upon the Turkish " trenches." Hamilton, " Gallipoli Diary," i. p. 135.

[2] Those on board the *River Clyde* at the time speak of the unconquerable spirit of the men ashore, who, from their position behind that ledge of sand, light-heartedly cheered the new arrivals as they rushed across the lighters and ran the gauntlet of the fire-swept beach.

that no advance could be made from V till the high ground on the left was captured by an advance from W.[1]

From 5.30 P.M. onwards the three battleships again bombarded the village, the crest of the ridge, and the upper part of the old fort. The village broke into flames, and the whole amphitheatre was wrapped in a cloud of blinding dust and smoke.[2] About 7 P.M., profiting by this bombardment, the remnants of the Munsters and a few Hampshires, about 120 men in all, were led by Major Jarrett to the right of the beach, and a fresh attempt was made to effect a lodgment in the old fort.[3] But despite the battleships' fire a number of Turks and a machine gun had been able to maintain their position in the lower part of the fort; the attempt to enter it was frustrated; and the invading troops once more took cover on the seaward face of the battlements.

So the long day ended. Night closed in on that unforgettable scene with the thin line of tired troops still clinging to their precarious position, the sombre silhouette of ridge and fort still barring their advance, and the burning village reddening sea and sky. And it was here that two months earlier a handful of marines had landed without a casualty.

As soon as it was dark Major A. T. Beckwith, senior surviving officer of the 2/Hampshire, was sent ashore to arrange for a renewal of the attack, and a start was then made to disembark the remaining fighting troops from the *River Clyde*, and to clear the gangways and beach of wounded. This work was carried out with little interference from the enemy, but it was nearly 3 A.M. before it was finished.[4]

---

[1] This information was repeated to Colonel Wolley-Dod at 5 P.M. See page 242.
[2] The naval ammunition fired at V Beach during the day was:

Albion.	12 rounds 12-inch: 898 rounds 6-inch: 1225 rounds 12-pdr. (6-inch and 12-pdr. guns fired two rounds of common to one round of shrapnel).
Cornwallis.	Approximately the same as *Albion*.
Queen Elizabeth.	9 rounds 15-inch; 370 rounds 6-inch (high explosive).

The small amount of heavy ammunition expended was due to the necessity of husbanding this class of ammunition for the renewed attack on the Narrows and for meeting the Turkish fleet. The ammunition situation was causing the admiral much uneasiness at this time.

[3] Major Jarrett was killed by a sniper a few minutes later.
[4] Great difficulty was experienced in carrying the wounded on board. The bridge of boats was still incomplete: it consisted in places of only single planks, and did not reach the shore. It was eventually linked up to a temporary jetty made out of dead men's packs.

As a collecting and dressing station for the wounded the collier proved invaluable. The work of Surgeon P. B. Kelly on board was particularly noteworthy. Though wounded on the morning of the 25th he remained on duty till the 27th, during which time he attended 750 men. He received the D.S.O.

LANDING OF THE HELLES MAIN BODY 249

Owing to the death of Br.-General Napier and Colonel Carington Smith, the command of the troops at V had devolved on Lieut.-Colonel H. E. Tizard,[1] Royal Munster Fusiliers, and just before midnight General Hunter-Weston sent Captain G. N. Walford, brigade-major 29th Division artillery, to act as his staff officer, with orders to push on at once and capture Hill 141. But meanwhile two officers of Sir Ian Hamilton's Staff,[2] who had accompanied the *River Clyde*, had been ashore to reconnoitre the situation, and had reported that an advance before daylight was out of the question. The night was pitch dark, and most of the troops, other than those recently landed, were badly shaken by the events of the day. Major Beckwith had moreover explained to Colonel Doughty-Wylie that his preparations for an advance could not be completed before daybreak. He was organizing the troops ashore into three parties for an early morning attack, and if the *Albion* could be asked to bombard the fort and village for half an hour at daybreak he would get his men into motion at 5.30 A.M. This plan was accordingly agreed to, and for the rest of the night the overwrought troops on the beach were left to get such rest as the Turks would allow them.

Elsewhere on the southern battle-front as daylight died away efforts were being made by unit commanders to establish some sort of connected line from X Beach on the left to the vicinity of Fort No. 1.

Sketch 11.

Apart from occasional sniping, all opposition on this front had disappeared. But the inertia of the afternoon still paralysed the British line; there had been little or no patrolling, and touch with the enemy was lost. As a result of this ignorance of the real state of affairs, many exaggerated reports were current regarding the strength of the Turks, and heavy counter-attacks by fresh troops, supported by a numerous artillery, were looked upon as certain.[3] To meet such attacks there were practically

---

[1] The other battalion commander at V Beach, Lt.-Col. R. A. Rooth, Dublin Fusiliers, was killed while landing with the tows.

[2] Lieut.-Colonel W. de L. Williams and Lieut.-Colonel C. H. M. Doughty-Wylie. The former was in the Operations section and the latter in the Intelligence section of the General Staff at G.H.Q., and they had accompanied the V Beach force as liaison officers.

[3] According to Turkish information available since the war the only reinforcements received by the *3rd/26th Regiment* during 25th April were two companies of the *2nd/26th*. About 2 A.M. on 26th two companies of the *1st/25th* reached Sedd el Bahr from Serafim Farm. Thus, 24 hours after the landing began the Turkish forces opposing the British at X, W, and V apparently amounted to eight companies of infantry and one engineer company.

no reserves, for though the British position from X Beach to a point just short of Fort No. 1 was less than two miles long, nearly every available man of the troops ashore had been pushed into the front line. The guns of the fleet would not be available at night; scarcely any artillery had been landed, and none of it was yet in a position to open fire.[1] Casualties, except in the case of the Lancashire Fusiliers and the Royal Fusiliers, had been singularly small,[2] but the unparalleled incidents of the day had been a severe strain. Few of the men had had any sleep since the night of the 23rd/24th; and all were dead tired. As an additional anxiety no water had yet been found ashore, few transport animals had been landed, and water and ammunition required by units had to be man-handled from the beach.

After midnight a few bold parties of Turks pushed up to the British lines, but nothing in the nature of a counter-attack was attempted. Nevertheless the night was spent by some of the British units in heavy and continuous firing, and frequent messages were received at W Beach to the effect that ammunition had run out, or that units were being heavily attacked and could not hold on without reinforcements.[3] As a result all ranks spent a sleepless and anxious night,[4] and not till morning, when it transpired that the night casualties had not exceeded half a dozen, was it realized that most of the disturbance had been due to overwrought nerves.

Thus in the southern zone, as at Anzac, the morning's promise of victory had not been fulfilled. The actual "coup" of the landing had come off. Three out of the five selected beaches had been captured soon after daybreak. A fourth had been taken without opposition. Throughout the day the Turks had been unable to array more than two battalions against $12\frac{1}{2}$

---

[1] The landing of artillery had fallen behind the programme, and by nightfall the only guns ashore were one field battery, 4 mountain guns, and one section of howitzers. Three reasons in particular had accounted for the delay: transports had not been allowed to anchor near the shore till evening; three extra battalions had landed at W; working parties at W had constantly been employed to fill gaps in the firing line, thereby bringing work on the beach to a standstill. Captain Bolton on W Beach reported at 12.45 P.M. on 25th—"Transports very slow off loading. Can they be "hastened? Cannot make progress with W Beach as nothing has come "ashore except infantry."

[2] The Border Regiment had lost only 50 men, the Essex only 70, and the Worcestershire only 40 by daybreak on the 26th, while the losses of the remaining units on this front had been trifling.

[3] Twice during the night news reached divisional H.Q. and G.H.Q. that the Turks were attacking " in German mass formation ".

[4] During the night, when every available fighting man had been sent into the line, midshipmen and even captains R.N. were carrying boxes of ammunition up to the troops.

battalions of British troops ashore. Yet at nightfall the 29th Division held only the fringe of the peninsula.

REVIEW OF THE OPERATION

At first glance, as already noticed, the fact that the Expeditionary Force, throughout the whole course of the campaign, never succeeded in attaining the position assigned to the 29th Division as its first day's objective may seem to indicate that this objective was born of a too-great optimism. But a careful study of the events of that memorable day dispels this first impression and leads to the conclusion that the plan for capturing Achi Baba on the 25th April had a reasonable prospect of success. It is essential, therefore, if any value is to be gained from the study of past events, to analyse very carefully the various causes of failure.

First amongst these causes, no doubt, was the quite abnormal number of casualties amongst the senior officers on shore. At the very outset of the action the 29th Division lost two out of its three brigadiers, two of its three brigade-majors, and the majority of its senior infantry officers in the four and a half battalions of the covering force that landed at X, W, and V.

This was an unavoidable misfortune; but there were other causes that exerted almost as important an influence on the events of the day, such as a certain lack of flexibility in the orders for the operation; the absence of any immediately available reserves in the hands of the Commander-in-Chief; the failure of the arrangements for intercommunication; and the great difficulty experienced by 29th Division headquarters in exercising adequate control over the operations from the deck of a man-of-war.

In the case of a landing on an open beach from ship's boats, especially when the size of the beaches and the number of available boats are both very small, the actual landing can only be carried out in accordance with detailed and rigid instructions worked out beforehand by the military and naval Staffs. For this part of the battle the orders and instructions issued by G.H.Q. and the 29th Division left little to be desired, but it was with regard to subsequent events that they suffered from too great a rigidity. They entered into so much detail as to what was to be done if all went well that they left little margin for the unexpected. The commanders for the Y and S landings, for instance, were definitely told beforehand that after the beaches had been captured they were to await the advance from the south, and then to join in the attack on Achi Baba; and the very rigidity of these instructions was probably responsible for damping the initiative of the commanders concerned and preventing them from utilizing their success to help the troops at X, W, and V. Before the landing there was no idea that the small forces landed at Y and S would be able to lend direct assistance to the main landings further south, or even that such assistance would be required. Yet, in the event, the troops at those two flank landings, who found themselves unmolested throughout the morning of the 25th April, were alone stronger than all the Turks at the southern end of the peninsula.

The failure to exploit the successes at Y and S also brings into prominence the advisability in operations of this nature of retaining a readily available reserve in the hands of the Commander-in-Chief. The difficulty of gauging beforehand with any accuracy the enemy's strength and dispositions is even greater in the case of the invasion of a hostile coast than in the case of a normal land attack; but if Sir Ian Hamilton had been able to land a couple of reserve battalions at the two points where the enemy proved to be weakest there can be little doubt that the Turkish resistance at Helles and Sedd el Bahr must have collapsed before midday.

The ability to use a general reserve rapidly, and with telling effect, implies, however, an adequate system for the passage of information and orders; and on the 25th April the difficulties of this problem were enhanced by the number of separate beaches on which the landing had to be made. It proved far harder to maintain communication between ship and shore than had been anticipated. Thus there was a serious lack of information at divisional headquarters and G.H.Q. regarding the situation on the beaches, and at the various beaches of the situation at the other landings. Previous to the landing it was believed that the presence of the supporting ships would afford ample means of communication. But this hope was not realized, and it is clear that a more certain means of forwarding orders and information should have been evolved beforehand. The neglect to do so was partly due to the unfounded expectation that communication by land would be opened at an early hour of the day.

During the days of preparation the actual storming of the beaches by daylight was looked upon at G.H.Q. as the most hazardous task that faced the Expeditionary Force. The subsequent advance to Achi Baba, it was felt, would offer no extraordinary difficulties; but in view of the possibility that every beach might be defended by wire and machine guns, the landing from open boats was regarded with keen anxiety. Despite the faith of the naval authorities in a preliminary bombardment, to many in authority the thought of those defenceless moments while the troops waded ashore, or struggled with the wire entanglements, had constituted an ever-haunting nightmare.

To a great extent these anxieties were justified. The landing at V was probably only saved from complete disaster by the machine guns in the *River Clyde*. If the Lancashire Fusiliers had failed to turn the enemy's right flank, the landing at W would in all probability have shared a similar fate. But the events of the forenoon proved that the actual getting ashore is by no means the hardest problem in an attack from open boats, and that after the beaches have been captured it may be equally hard to rally scattered units and press forward into the unknown. Had this been more fully realised beforehand; had it been thoroughly driven into the consciousness of all ranks that even if their landing were unopposed the respite allowed them by the enemy would be short, and that it would be of vital importance to exploit every success, and to act above all with swiftness, there can be little doubt that the paralysis which seized the troops after their first landing would have been materially reduced.

It is at moments like this, when the original plan for one reason or another is found to be hanging fire, that the continued exercise of control by higher headquarters can make itself most felt; and the means for enabling the higher commanders to assume this control as soon as the actual landing has been effected is an important and difficult problem. On the 25th April, in view of the supreme importance of close personal touch between the various naval and military commanders during the early stages of the landing, there was perhaps no better alternative than to establish the headquarters of the 29th Division on board the *Euryalus* and General Headquarters in the flagship of the naval Commander-in-Chief. But a study of the day's events goes far to prove that there can be few less satisfactory positions for the conduct of land operations than the deck of a man-of-war. In the case of the 29th Division, despite the utmost endeavours of the navy, the difficulties of intercommunication were so great that the divisional commander remained largely out of touch with the course of events, even though in actual distance he was at no time more than a mile from his front line. In the case of General Headquarters, even the mighty *Queen Elizabeth* could accommodate only a limited number of military staff officers in addition to the admiral's Staff. As a result, for the third time since the inception of the campaign, the administrative branches of General Headquarters were again separated from the Commander-in-Chief, and for several critical days they were unable to keep in close touch with the situation or to issue administrative orders.

An additional and unexpected disadvantage existing out of the location of General Headquarters on board the *Queen Elizabeth* was that, owing to the guns of that vessel being urgently needed to assist the troops at V Beach, Sir Ian Hamilton was chained to that locality throughout the afternoon and evening of the 25th, instead of being free to exercise a general supervision over the whole front of attack. From a strictly military point of view, indeed, it would probably have been better if, for the first few days of the landing, both the admiral and the military Commander-in-Chief, with all their respective Staffs, could have been accommodated on a specially equipped unarmed vessel, fitted with all the signalling apparatus necessary for the control of the fleet and for issuing orders and receiving messages from the shore.

Tired by their efforts in the early morning, and overwrought by the tension of the landing, the strangeness of the situation, and the heavy losses in officers, some of the units of the 29th Division who landed early in the day were in sore straits during the first afternoon.[1] Had they but known it, the enemy in front of them were equally distressed,[2] and this must be so in every hard-fought battle. Each side is prone to imagine that further progress is impossible, and the side with the more resolute leader, who insists on one further effort, will generally prove the victor. On the 25th April the Turks in the southern zone were too weak to win a victory, but the resolution of their leader was to gain them important advantages.

[1] Some of the hesitation which undoubtedly occurred at this time may have been due to a printed " Personal Note " issued by the G.O.C. 29th Division a few days before the landing to every soldier under his command. In this note, with the idea that to forewarn is to forearm, the divisional commander drew attention to the " Heavy losses by bullets, by shells, by "mines, and by drowning " to which the men would be exposed. As an example of the state of mind which this order induced, a man on X Beach went up to Br.-General Marshall with a dead tortoise which he had found, and said " I've found one of these here land mines, sir".

[2] The following Turkish message was captured next day:
" My Captain, either you must send up reinforcements and drive the " enemy into the sea or let us evacuate this place (Sedd el Bahr) because it " is absolutely certain that they will land more troops to-night. Send the " doctors to carry off my wounded. Alas! alas my captain, for God's sake " send me reinforcements because hundreds of soldiers are landing. Hurry " up. What on earth will happen my Captain."

"I am sending you a battalion," wrote Colonel Sami Bey, the commander of the Turkish *9th Division*, to the officer in command of the *26th Regiment*. "It is quite clear that the "enemy is weak; drive him into the sea, and do not let me "find an Englishman in the south when I arrive." With this inspiriting message he encouraged his troops. Throughout the night the weak Turkish detachments at W and X prevented any advance by the British, while by 8 A.M. on the 26th the regrettable evacuation of Y Beach was in full swing.

The small Turkish garrison of Sedd el Bahr, who, despite the terrifying effect of their first experience of naval gun-fire, clung doggedly to their position throughout the 25th, rendered a service to the defence which it would be difficult to exaggerate. The one company there in the morning was apparently reinforced during the day by two more companies, one belonging to its own battalion, and the other, from Krithia, to the *2/26th Regiment*. There can be little doubt that the failure to capture V Beach till the 26th was the main cause of the collapse of the British plan.

The gallantry of the British and Australian troops who stormed the beaches, and the heroism and self-sacrifice of the sailors who put them ashore, have added a new lustre to the glory of the Empire's fighting services; but viewed in its broader aspect the result of the first day's fighting was more favourable to the Turks than to the British. Despite the unparalleled publicity that heralded the British attack, one advantage remained in Sir Ian Hamilton's hand up to the morning of the 25th—the liberty to effect a tactical surprise, and to strike with his masses against the enemy detachments. General Hamilton made as full use of this advantage as the restricted size of the available beaches would permit. In the south he threw $12\frac{1}{2}$ battalions ashore by 1 P.M., and throughout the day they were opposed by only 2 battalions. At Anzac 4,000 men were landed by 5 A.M., 8,000 by 8 A.M., and 15,000 by the late afternoon, and against these the Turks could only place 500 troops up to 9.30 A.M., and from that hour till dusk a gradually increasing number which at no time exceeded 5,000 men. Yet so strong is the power of the defence against maritime invasion that the detachments had held their ground. By the evening of the 25th the sea had surrendered her secret. The British plan was now exposed. Liman von Sanders could in full confidence direct his reserves to each of the threatened points.

Fortunate indeed must it be considered that Sir Ian Hamilton had decided against a landing near Bulair. If the 29th Division, using five landing places, three of which were practically unprepared for defence, could effect so little against a total force of two battalions, an attempt to land at the northern isthmus, where only one small beach was available, where an attack was confidently expected, and where two divisions were waiting to oppose it, must surely have ended in failure.

THE OLD FORT, SEDD EL BAHR, AND THE ASIATIC SHORE

From the summit of Hill 141

CHAPTER XIV

THE FRENCH DIVERSION AT KUM KALE

(Map 2 ; Sketch 10)

IMMEDIATELY opposite Sedd el Bahr, two Turkish villages on the Asiatic coast stare into the V Beach landing place at a range of some 4,000 to 5,000 yards. The presence of mobile guns in the vicinity of these villages during the first days of the landing would have constituted so serious a menace to the 29th Division that Sir Ian Hamilton's plan of operations included the landing of a small force at Kum Kale with the object of temporarily denying that dangerous strip of coast to the enemy. This task was allotted to a detachment of French troops.

In the special instructions for the operation issued to General d'Amade,[1] the scope of his task was expressly limited to "clearing the region between Kum Kale and Yeni Shehr " and west of the Mendere river". The number of troops to be employed in the operation was also strictly limited by Sir Ian Hamilton, General d'Amade being informed that his landing was unlikely to be strongly opposed, and that one infantry regiment and one battery of field guns should suffice for the task in hand. It was undesirable, the special instructions added, to land a larger number of troops, because as soon as the 29th Division had gained a secure footing on the peninsula the Kum Kale detachment would be re-embarked and the whole of General d'Amade's force landed at Helles to join in the advance on the Kilid Bahr plateau.

The region thus assigned to General d'Amade for his initial operations consisted of a narrow tongue of land about two miles long by 500 yards wide lying between the sea and the Mendere river, which here flows parallel to the Ægean coast before emptying itself into the Dardanelles just inside

---
[1] Appendix 6. These instructions were not issued till 20th April, but their purport was explained in detail to General d'Amade by the Commander-in-Chief at a conference on the 19th.

the entrance to the Straits. Kum Kale village, then in ruins as the result of earlier bombardments, spread half-way across the tongue of land, with a bastioned fort, also partly in ruins, between it and the sea. Just south of the village was a large Turkish cemetery, and a wooden bridge across the river. Around Kum Kale the land is flat and sandy, with occasional patches of marsh; further south it rises gently towards a hillock known as Orkanie Mound,[1] where British marines destroyed a battery in March 1915, and then more steeply to the village of Yeni Shehr. Yeni Shehr stands on a high bluff, and the battery on its summit had long since been put out of action by the guns of the fleet.

Colonel Ruef, commanding the Brigade Coloniale, was chosen by General d'Amade to command the detachment, and the troops allotted to him consisted of the 6th Régiment mixte Coloniale (one battalion of Colonial infantry and two of Senegalese) commanded by Lieut.-Colonel Noguès, one battery of 75's, a section of engineers, a field ambulance, and a few signallers.

21 Apr. Following a coastal reconnaissance carried out by French staff officers on the 21st April, it was decided that a small wooden pier north of Kum Kale was too dilapidated, and too exposed to artillery fire from In Tepe ($2\frac{1}{2}$ miles inside the Straits), to be used by the detachment, and it was resolved to carry out the landing on a small beach immediately under the fort, where a break in the walls offered easy access to the battlements. The landing was to be supported by the French squadron (Contre-Amiral Guépratte) consisting of the battleships *Jauréguiberry* (flagship) and *Henri IV*, the cruisers *Jeanne d'Arc* and *Latouche-Tréville,* and a flotilla of light craft, reinforced by the British battleship *Prince George* and the small Russian cruiser *Askold*. This squadron was in addition to engage any Turkish guns on the Asiatic shore which might try to interfere with the landing operations at V Beach and Morto Bay.

The British belief that the Kum Kale landing would not be strongly opposed was founded on the fact that the neighbourhood of Kum Kale was flat and offered scant cover from the fire of the supporting ships. This surmise proved substantially correct. The Turks had done nothing to protect the beach at Kum Kale, and there was no wire. Nevertheless the Turkish higher command was so apprehensive of a main landing on the Asiatic shore that there were many more troops near Kum Kale and Yeni Shehr than between Achi Baba and the toe of the

[1] Claimed by local tradition as the tomb of Achilles.

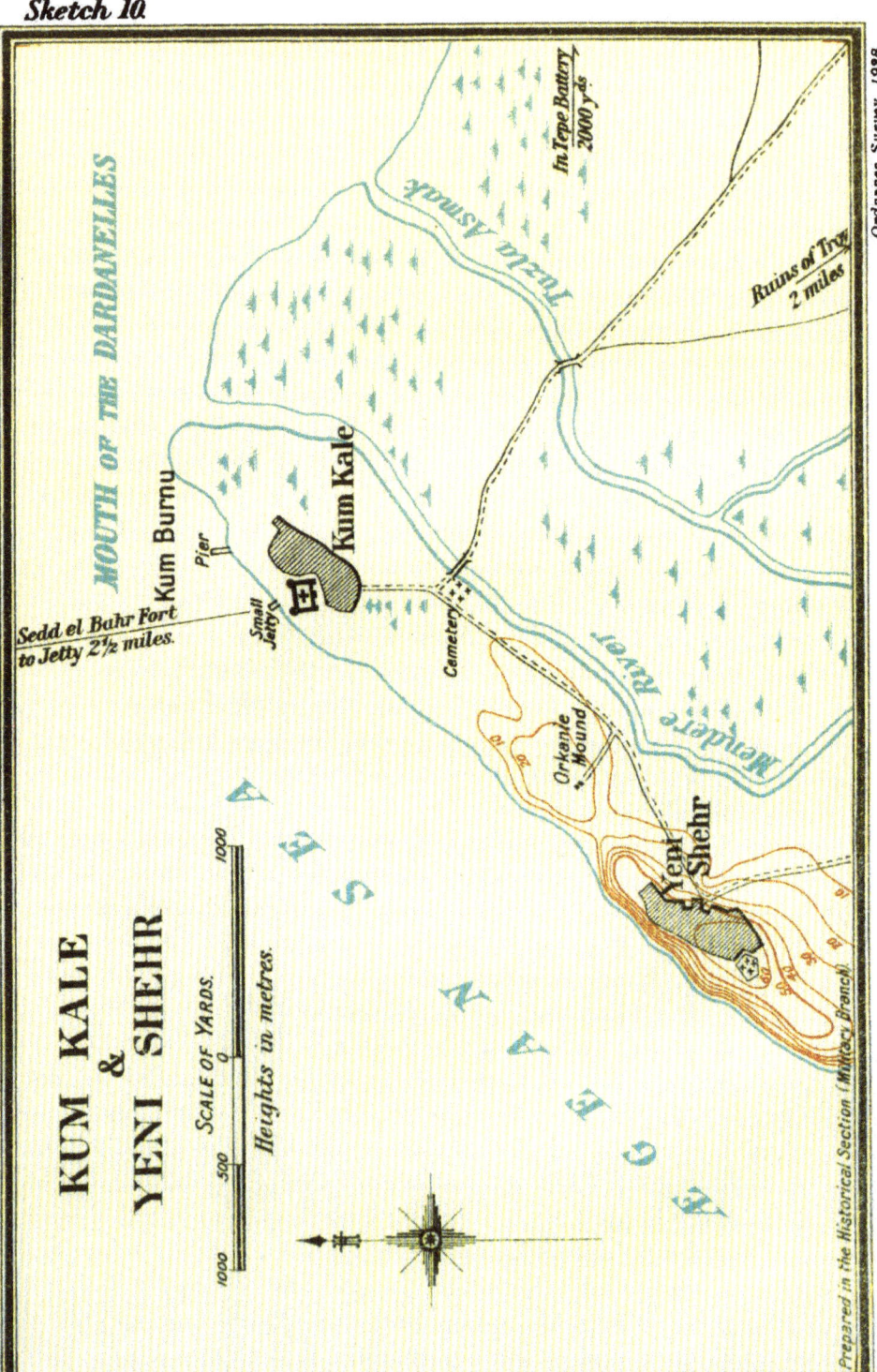

THE FRENCH DIVERSION AT KUM KALE

peninsula. According to the Turkish official account two regiments of the *3rd Division* (Colonel Nicolai) were concentrated near the ruins of ancient Troy, only three miles inland from Kum Kale, while the third regiment was holding the line of the Mendere river with detachments pushed out to Kum Kale cemetery, Orkanie, Yeni Shehr, and other points on the coast. It would seem, indeed, that Marshal Liman von Sanders was well prepared to deal with a landing in force in this vicinity, but that owing to the exposed nature of the tongue of land between the Mendere river and the sea, the first line of Turkish resistance was to be the right bank of the river and the high ground immediately to the east of it.

On the 21st April the French transports carrying the troops for the Kum Kale diversion were brought from Skyros to the outer harbour at Mudros, and here the necessary transhipments were made to assemble the whole force in four ships.[1] While at Mudros the opportunity was taken to rehearse the landing, and to give the Senegalese some much-needed practice in boat work.

Leaving Mudros at 10 P.M. on the 24th April the French squadron, followed by the transports, reached the mouth of the Straits about 4.30 A.M. Three-quarters of an hour later they began to open fire on the two villages of Kum Kale and Yeni Shehr. The Turkish reply was feeble and did no harm.

25 Apr.

At 6.20 A.M. Admiral Guépratte ordered the disembarkation to begin, and the *Vinh-Long*, carrying a battalion of Senegalese, moved in to about 4,000 yards from Kum Kale, with the other transports in a group rather astern of her. After some little delay the first tows started for the shore, but the small French steamboats could make no headway against the rapid current setting out from the Dardanelles. Torpedo boats and tugs had to be sent to their assistance, and owing to this unforeseen delay it was nearly 10 A.M. before the tows approached the beach.

This episode, which robbed the troops of the last hope of

---

[1] After this transhipment the troops were accommodated as follows:
  Savoie (auxiliary cruiser)—H.Q. Staff. 1 battalion Colonials, 1 section engineers, 1 ambulance.
  Carthage—1 battalion Senegalese, 1 section machine guns.
  Vinh-Long—1 battalion Senegalese.
  Th. Mante—1 field battery.
  Ceylan—disembarkation material.
The hospital ship *Duguay Trouin* accompanied these vessels. General d'Amade established his H.Q. on board the flagship *Jauréguiberry* on 24th April.

effecting a surprise, might well have had disastrous results, but actually it was a distinct advantage to the French. Owing to the long delay, the covering war vessels were able to bombard the villages and the low-lying strip of country for several hours; by 8 A.M. Yeni Shehr was in flames, and, by the time the Senegalese landed, the majority of the Turks near Kum Kale, badly shaken by the bombardment, had retreated to the opposite side of the river. One of the French cutters was struck by a shell from In Tepe, with the loss of all its occupants, and further casualties were suffered from a machine gun on the northern flank,[1] but with these exceptions the landing met with little resistance.

Led by Captain Brison, the 10th Company of the 6th Regiment was quickly in possession of the fort, and with the 11th Company landing shortly afterwards, the whole village was captured by 11.15 A.M. with surprisingly little loss. A small detachment was at the same time pushed southward along the coast. About this time the *Henri IV*, from a position inside the Straits, reported that she was shelling two Turkish columns advancing westwards towards the Mendere River. At 1.15 P.M. a signal was received from Sir Ian Hamilton: "I hope "you are getting on well," and the reply was at once sent: "Très "bien. Nous occupons Kum Kale et nous attaquons Yeni "Shehr. L'infanterie débarque. L'artillerie suit."

Throughout the afternoon the landing of the French detachment continued, but the work was unexpectedly slow, and though the battery of field guns[2] was ashore by 4 P.M., it was nearly 5.30 P.M. before the disembarkation of the three infantry battalions was complete. Pending their arrival, no further attempt was made to advance beyond Kum Kale, but under the direction of Colonel Noguès the village was put into a state of defence, and trenches were dug on its eastern and south-eastern flanks. Meanwhile Turkish reinforcements reoccupied various points vacated in the morning.

Soon after 5.30 P.M., covered by the fire of the warships and the 75's, an advance was at last made in the direction of Yeni Shehr, two companies moving on the cemetery, where the Turks were entrenched, and three companies moving along the coast towards Orkanie Mound. Both these movements were met by a heavy fire; at 6 P.M. practically no progress had been made; and when an aeroplane reported that strong

[1] This machine gun was destroyed a few minutes later by a shell from the *Henri IV*.
[2] The French system was to land a complete section of guns and limbers on two rafts towed by a tug, 2 guns and limbers on the first raft, and 24 horses on the second.

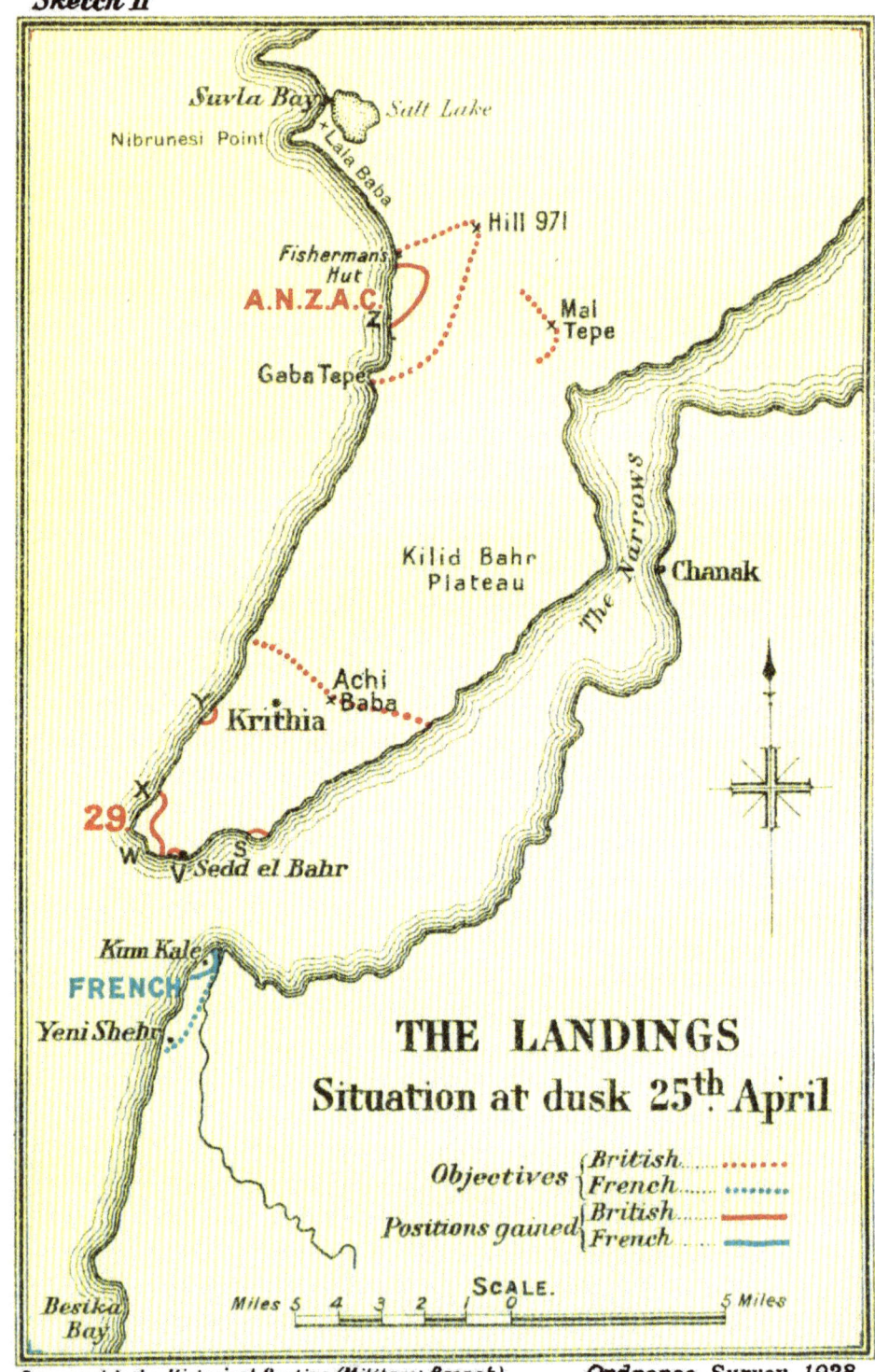

THE FRENCH DIVERSION AT KUM KALE 261

hostile columns were arriving at Yeni Shehr, all idea of a further advance that day was abandoned. The right flank of the French now rested on the coast about midway between Kum Kale and Orkanie; thence their line stretched north-east to the village and continued round its eastern flank to a point on the seashore just above the wooden pier.

The ground to the south of the French position was illuminated by searchlights during the night, and the *Jauréguiberry* continued to keep this area under a spasmodic fire. Nevertheless, the Turks managed to bring up strong reinforcements after nightfall, and between 8.30 P.M. and daybreak they made four determined attacks on the eastern side of the village, but all of these were driven off with heavy loss. In the hand-to-hand fighting which took place during these attacks, apparently made by at least three battalions,[1] the conduct of the Colonial and Senegalese infantry was most gallant, and when morning broke the ground in front of their trenches was strewn with Turkish dead.

Overnight Colonel Ruef had been ordered to resume his **26 Apr.** attack on Yeni Shehr next morning, covered by the guns of a French man-of-war. But, while the troops were waiting for the warships to open fire, an incident occurred which Colonel Ruef described in his official report as follows :

The enemy began to wave flags and showed a wish to give themselves up. Eighty Turkish soldiers approached unarmed and were conducted inside our lines. Immediately afterwards many more Turks (several hundred) arrived in succession but refused to lay down their arms. A parley took place, and Captain Rockel, a very courageous officer, pushed into the middle of the Turks to persuade them to give up their rifles. This officer was surrounded and was not seen again. General d'Amade had now come ashore, and, when the incident was reported to him, he at once gave orders for fire to be opened on the Turks.

Unfortunately, during the parley, a number of Turks had succeeded in slipping into the village and occupying several houses. Others, jostling our men, succeeded in seizing and making off with two machine guns. Our men did not dare to open fire for fear of wounding their own comrades. The Turks in the houses defended themselves energetically, killing several of our troops, amongst them the captain of engineers and his lieutenant, and it was only in the afternoon that we were able to drive these men out by bombarding the houses they occupied. About sixty men were captured. The officer in command, and eight of his men, were then shot.

[1] The Turkish Official Account admits that 3 battalions were engaged. The French estimated the Turkish numbers at $4\frac{1}{2}$ battalions.

The undue confidence of our troops, which caused this deplorable incident, can be accounted for by the arrival of the first deserters, who had shown no evil intentions. I am half inclined to believe, and so is Colonel Noguès, that the whole thing was a misunderstanding, and that the intention was really to surrender, but that our interpreters did not succeed in explaining things properly. The numerous surrenders during the afternoon (about 500) seem to confirm this opinion.[1]

Meanwhile, as already described, the position of the 29th Division on the toe of the peninsula was far from satisfactory. The troops at X and W were still holding only the fringe of the coast; Sedd el Bahr village was still in the hands of the enemy; and Colonel Matthews at Y was reporting that unless reinforcements could reach him he would be obliged to evacuate his position. In these circumstances Sir Ian Hamilton signalled to General d'Amade at 7.40 A.M., ordering him to call up his Metropolitan Brigade from Tenedos and to land it as quickly as possible at X Beach. This message reached the French commander at Kum Kale at 9.20 A.M., and the necessary executive orders were at once issued. But in acknowledging Sir Ian Hamilton's order, General d'Amade, evidently somewhat disturbed by the lack of progress on the peninsula, added that his Kum Kale troops had now fulfilled their limited mission and could make no further advance towards Yeni Shehr without reinforcements. An hour later a second order from the Commander-in-Chief reached the French headquarters. In accordance with General Hunter-Weston's wishes, Sir Ian Hamilton now required the Metropolitan Brigade to be landed at W instead of at X, and as the 29th Division was in need of artillery as well as infantry reinforcements, the whole of the remaining French units were to be brought up to Helles as soon as possible. The Commander-in-Chief was on his way to W Beach, and wished General d'Amade to visit him in the flagship as soon as he arrived. This message would appear to have increased General d'Amade's anxiety to withdraw his Kum Kale detachment before Turkish reinforcements arrived, for it was now plain that in no event would further French troops be available for the Asiatic shore.

About 11.30 A.M., therefore, General d'Amade set off to confer with Sir Ian Hamilton. He reported that he hoped to be able to begin landing his first three battalions from Tenedos at W Beach early in the afternoon; but since all his available troops had now been directed to the peninsula he asked

[1] French Official Account, Tome viii. Annexes i. No. 99.

THE FRENCH DIVERSION AT KUM KALE 263

permission to withdraw the Kum Kale detachment at nightfall, explaining that the village of Yeni Shehr had been strongly reinforced overnight, and that the capture of that position could not be attempted without the employment of the whole French division. In these circumstances, in view of the serious situation at Helles and Sedd el Bahr, and having regard to Lord Kitchener's clear order that the occupation of the Asiatic coast was strongly to be deprecated, Sir Ian Hamilton agreed that the Kum Kale detachment should be withdrawn at nightfall, and General d'Amade at once returned to his headquarters to make the necessary arrangements.

Soon after this decision was reached in the flagship, the situation at Kum Kale underwent a complete change. Early in the afternoon the slopes of Orkanie were subjected to a heavy bombardment, and about 3 P.M. a whole Turkish battalion in that neighbourhood suddenly took to flight, and about 450 men of the Turkish *31st* and *39th Regiments* came into the French lines and surrendered. But by this time orders for the withdrawal of the French detachment had been received at Kum Kale, so nothing could be done to exploit the situation.

Under cover of darkness every available boat was concentrated at Kum Kale by the French squadron; the re-embarkation was carried out smoothly and expeditiously; and by daybreak the whole detachment, with the wounded and 450 Turkish prisoners, were safely on board ship. No attack was made by the Turks during the night, but a few shells were fired from In Tepe, one of which killed some horses and wounded Colonel Noguès.

The total French casualties at Kum Kale were 778. The Turkish account admits the loss of 1,730 officers and men, including 500 missing.

One further incident in connection with this diversion remains to be noticed. During the evening of the 26th April, after the situation on the toe of the peninsula had been improved by the capture of Sedd el Bahr and the freeing of V Beach, Admiral de Robeck and General Braithwaite (Chief of the General Staff) urged Sir Ian Hamilton to reconsider his decision to evacuate Kum Kale, and to leave the French troops there for at least another 24 hours. Nothing was known at General Headquarters at that time about the large surrenders to the French that afternoon, but it was felt that every hour that Colonel Ruef remained on the Asiatic shore would be of value in confusing the Turkish command as to the main point of attack, and in delaying the transfer of Turkish troops to the western side of the Straits. In the middle of these deliberations Admiral Guépratte arrived on board the *Queen Elizabeth* about 7 P.M., and then for the first time Sir Ian Hamilton heard of the encouraging situation at Kum Kale and of the surrender of 500 Turks. This news determined the British commander to vary the orders already issued to General d'Amade, and, with Admiral Guépratte's full concurrence in the change of plan, a signal was made to the French general to maintain the Kum Kale position for another 24 hours. But at 2 A.M. a message arrived from the French flagship that the withdrawal was already in full swing and that it was now too late to stop it.

The Demonstration at Besika Bay

It will be remembered that, in addition to the Kum Kale landing, Sir Ian Hamilton's plans for the 25th April included a demonstration by French vessels at Besika Bay in order to confuse the Turkish command and to detain any Turkish troops in that neighbourhood.

Early on the morning of the 26th, therefore, a flotilla of six French transports, escorted by two destroyers and a torpedo boat, arrived off Besika Bay. The destroyers, and two of the transports equipped as auxiliary cruisers, at once began to bombard the surrounding beaches, and boats were lowered to simulate preparations for disembarking troops. At 8.30 A.M. the cruiser *Jeanne d'Arc* arrived to join in the bombardment, but at 10 A.M. the whole squadron was recalled to the Tenedos anchorage. Despite the shortness of this demonstration it would seem to have had some effect on the Turkish dispositions, for the Turkish division garrisoning that locality was not withdrawn till the 27th. On the other hand, the Turkish official account claims that it was early recognized that nothing serious was intended near Kum Kale or Besika Bay and that the delay in moving troops across the Straits was caused by the presence of submarines, and the shortage of small craft. Whatever the cause, no troops from the Asiatic shore were encountered on the Helles front until the 29th April.

PART III
THE STRUGGLE FOR ACHI BABA

CHAPTER XV

THE DAY AFTER THE LANDING

EVENTS AT ANZAC

(Maps 3, 4; Sketches 7, 8A)

25/26 Apr. AFTER nightfall on the 25th the *Queen Elizabeth* was at last free to leave the neighbourhood of Sedd el Bahr, and as soon as General Hunter-Weston had visited Sir Ian Hamilton to report on the situation ashore, the flagship weighed and sailed for Anzac Cove. Up to this moment all was believed to be going well with the Australians and New Zealanders, and the hopeful messages received from General Birdwood had gone far to counteract the anxiety caused by the slow progress in the south. Plainly, if the northern corps could gain even half its objective, it would constitute so serious a threat to the enemy's vitals, that there would be little fear of Turkish reinforcements being available for the southern end of the peninsula. Nevertheless, with the picture of the V Beach tragedy fresh in front of his eyes, the whole situation must have been charged with anxiety for the Commander-in-Chief, and it speaks well for his nerve and resolution that at this critical juncture he was able to retire to his cabin and snatch a hasty sleep.

Meanwhile at Anzac, though, judged in the light of subsequent knowledge, General Birdwood's earlier messages had conveyed a very faithful impression of the actual state of affairs, the evident exhaustion of some of the troops on shore was filling their commanders with anxiety, and unfounded rumours were hurrying the situation to the very brink of disaster.

Throughout the evening, General Bridges and his senior staff officer[1] became more and more convinced, by all they heard and saw, that the Anzac operation had failed, and that the position of the troops was desperate. Units were gravely disorganized; the men were reported to be utterly worn out; and there were no available reserves. A heavy counter-attack

[1] Lieut.-Colonel C. B. B. White.

in the morning by fresh troops, with largely increased artillery, was looked upon as certain; and there was the definite risk that in this event the exhausted invaders might be driven from their positions and annihilated on the beach. In all the circumstances it appeared to these officers that the best course would be to accept failure in this sector and immediately to re-embark the troops with a view to their subsequent and more useful employment on another part of the front. Towards nightfall Major-General Godley was called into conference,[1] and after a reference to Br.-General Walker, commanding the New Zealand Brigade, had drawn the reply that the situation of his troops was "most "serious", it was decided about 9.15 P.M. to ask the corps commander to come ashore again at once, and to put the position before him.[2]

About the same time the following unsigned and probably mutilated signal was received on board the flagship:

From officer on shore to *Queen*. All available boats are required on shore.

General Birdwood landed about 10 P.M., and a conference was at once held at General Bridges' headquarters in one of the narrow gullies which run down to the cove from the top of Plugge's Plateau. In addition to the two divisional commanders, their senior staff officers were present and one or two of the brigadiers.

No notes were taken at this conference. It is plain, however, from the message sent to the Commander-in-Chief at its termination, that the divisional commanders informed General Birdwood that their overstrained troops would be unable to withstand a heavy attack in the morning, and urged him to contemplate an immediate evacuation.

General Birdwood had hitherto believed that all was going comparatively well at Anzac. He was astounded to hear of this rapid change for the worse, and at first he refused to entertain the idea of a withdrawal. Eventually, however, he seems to have been persuaded by those in closer touch than himself with the situation that the chances of avoiding a disaster in the event of a counter-attack were very slender, and that,

---

[1] General Godley, commanding the New Zealand and Australian Division, was senior to General Bridges in date of army rank, but he had not yet assumed any executive command on shore, as those of his units which had already landed had been hurried into the line to reinforce General Bridges' brigades.

[2] General Birdwood had been ashore all the afternoon inspecting the position, but had returned at dark to the *Queen*, where his headquarters were still established.

at least from a local point of view, an immediate re-embarkation would be the best military course. He realized, however, that larger issues were at stake, and that only the Commander-in-Chief could decide whether as many as possible of the Anzac troops should be extricated, or whether the retention of their position was so vital to the success of the main plan as to justify the risk of the annihilation of the whole corps by trying to hold on. He resolved therefore to inform Sir Ian Hamilton of the views of his divisional commanders and to refer the decision to him, warning him at the same time of the possibilities of a "fiasco" if the troops were left on shore.

Thereupon, at General Birdwood's dictation, by the light of a guttering candle, General Godley took down the following message for despatch to the Commander-in-Chief:

Both my divisional generals and brigadiers have represented to me that they fear their men are thoroughly demoralized by shrapnel fire to which they have been subjected all day after exhaustion and gallant work in the morning. Numbers have dribbled back from firing line and cannot be collected in this difficult country. Even the New Zealand Brigade, which has only recently been engaged, lost heavily, and is to some extent demoralized. If troops are subjected to shell fire again to-morrow morning there is likely to be a fiasco, as I have no fresh troops with which to replace those in firing line. I know my representation is most serious, but if we are to re-embark it must be at once.

Meanwhile it became known that a request had been made for all available boats, and the crowded beach was alive with rumours of immediate evacuation.

Hearing these rumours, the naval beach-master, Captain A. V. Vyvyan, R.N., decided to go off to the flagship to discuss the problem with the admiral; and it was into his hands that General Birdwood's message was thrust, for conveyance to the *Queen*, just as he left the shore.

It was presumably intended that the message should be signalled to Sir Ian Hamilton from the *Queen*, for the *Queen Elizabeth* was believed to be still at Cape Helles. But in the hurry of its despatch, it was not addressed to anyone. When it was handed to Admiral Thursby, therefore, the admiral imagined that it was intended for him; and only by mere chance did this all-important message, fraught with such vital issues, eventually reach its proper destination.

By this time the night had turned dark and wet, and in the grave circumstances reported by General Birdwood Admiral Thursby felt convinced that an attempt to re-embark would be hazardous and could not be completed before dawn. As a precautionary measure, however, he ordered the following signal to be made to all transports:

From Rear-Admiral, *Queen*, to transports. Lower all boats and stand by to send them in to beach.

He then decided to go ashore to confer with General Birdwood, and he was on the point of starting when the *Queen Elizabeth* unexpectedly arrived at the anchorage with Sir Ian Hamilton on board. Taking Br.-Generals Carruthers and Cunliffe-Owen of the corps Staff with him, Admiral Thursby now made straight for the flagship, to report the situation.

Sir Ian Hamilton was still asleep when the little party arrived on board shortly after midnight, but he was quickly aroused by General Braithwaite, and in the admiral's dining-room, round the historic table where three and a half years later Admiral Beatty was to receive the surrender of the German fleet, there now took place one of the most momentous conferences of the Dardanelles campaign.

Seldom has a commander in the field been faced with a more difficult decision than that which General Birdwood's message called upon his Chief to make. An incorrect decision might spell the ruin of the campaign. Yet the matter must be decided at once; there was no time to call for further information; no use, at midnight, in landing to see the position for himself. Apart from Birdwood's brief report there was nothing to guide him but his knowledge of his subordinate commanders and his opinion of the Anzac troops. But Sir Ian Hamilton was now to show himself in possession of quick judgment and unflinching resolution. After reading General Birdwood's note aloud, he asked the officers of the corps Staff one or two questions about the tactical position ashore, but they were unable to add anything to Birdwood's general statement. Admiral Thursby was then asked for an opinion. He answered that it would take at least two days to re-embark the troops, and that he felt sure they would " stick it out " if only it were put to them that they must. This exactly corresponded with Sir Ian Hamilton's views, and without another word, he wrote the following reply:

Your news is indeed serious. But there is nothing for it but to dig yourselves right in and stick it out. It would take at least two days to re-embark you, as Admiral Thursby will explain to you. Meanwhile the Australian submarine has got up through the Narrows and has torpedoed a gunboat at Chanak. Hunter-Weston, despite his heavy losses, will be advancing to-morrow which should divert pressure from you. Make a personal appeal to your men and Godley's to make a supreme effort to hold their ground.

P.S.—You have got through the difficult business. Now you have only to dig, dig, dig, until you are safe.

The effect of this resolute and definite order, quickly taken ashore by Admiral Thursby, was electrical. All the vague doubts which had spread around the beach were settled. From that moment there was no further talk of evacuation at Anzac, and all ranks were soon filled with the same determination as the men in front line, none of whom had had any idea that a retirement was under discussion.

But though the position was to be held at all costs, prudence dictated that everything possible should be done by the navy to prepare for the worst. All available trawlers were called up from Mudros, and Captain H. S. Grant, commanding the Bulair squadron, was ordered to leave the transports of the Royal Naval Division in charge of the *Dartmouth*, and to hurry south with the *Canopus*, *Doris*, and his two destroyers. He was at the same time to have every available boat collected by his trawlers, and towed to Anzac Cove. Meanwhile the warships already at Anzac were allotted targets for the morning, and were to give the troops the utmost possible support.

The Anzac beach during the night of the 25th/26th April was a grim sight. The narrow fringe of sand between the water's edge and the cliffs was so crowded with wounded that it was difficult to find room for the ever-growing quantities of ammunition, stores, and supplies arriving from the transports. The Anzac medical officers were doing everything possible for the most serious cases; but no reasonable establishment of surgeons could have coped on that open beach with the very large numbers that needed immediate attention. The sight of the long rows of wounded, many of them in terrible pain, was, moreover, very trying to the arriving troops. In these circumstances, despite the order that the disembarkation of troops was not to be delayed by evacuating wounded in the boats allotted to fighting men, the naval beach-master took the law into his own hands, and gave express orders that no boat was to leave the shore without its full complement of wounded. Casualties were accordingly evacuated to all the transports indiscriminately. In some cases they were taken on board and cared for to such extent as the total lack of medical appliances or personnel would allow.[1] In other cases, the masters of the

---

[1] The medical personnel attached to units had naturally accompanied the troops ashore.

EVENTS AT ANZAC

transports, knowing that they had no means of dealing with serious cases, refused to take them on board, and ordered the boats to find another ship. In both cases the sufferings of the wounded were often indescribable; and even from a humane point of view little was gained by this departure from the original orders. From a tactical point of view the beachmaster's action, though it reduced the congestion on the beach, added to the already serious delay in disembarkation.[1] Often it would be several hours before boats could dispose of their wounded and return to the shore with a new trip of fighting men. As a result the last battalion of the New Zealand Brigade was not ashore till after midnight, and though three battalions of the 4th Australian Brigade, and a section of howitzers, were landed by 6 A.M., it was nearly midday on the 26th before the 14th Australian Battalion had completed its disembarkation.

Up in the front line, despite a great deal of useless firing, the Anzac troops, taught by their bitter experiences of the previous day, succeeded in digging themselves fairly well in, and water and ammunition were sent to most parts of the line from the beach. During the night, too, an inner line of defence, covering the beach, was dug on Plugge's Plateau and MacLagan's Ridge, and four mountain guns were dug in on the crest of the plateau.

Whether the fears of the divisional commanders would have been realized in the event of a strong Turkish attack next morning was happily not put to the test. Mustafa Kemal's troops, as we now know, were completely disorganized on the night of the 25th, and for another 24 hours he had no available reserves to renew the battle. When the morning of the 26th April, awaited with so much anxiety, broke fine and clear, there was no sign of a Turkish attack in force; and though the enemy batteries re-opened shortly after daybreak, there was little increase in the number of guns since the previous day. Up in the front the Australian and New Zealand troops were heartened by finding that their newly dug trenches gave cover from shrapnel fire, while even more heartening was the great array of warships off the coast, and the sight and sound of their thunderous cannonade. For some time after daybreak the light was very baffling for the naval gunners, for they were looking straight into the sun. But they searched the back areas with an effect on the nerves of the already demoralized Turkish troops which prisoners afterwards described as appalling; and when it was at last possible to locate some of the

26 Apr.

[1] See also page 184.

Turkish batteries, these were mostly silenced.[1] Later in the day cable communication was established between the beach and the flank observation officers, and the direction of the ships' fire was further improved.

Map 3.
Sketch 7.

In the general line held by the Anzac troops on the morning of the 26th, practically every battalion was very much split up. But speaking in general terms, the 2nd Australian Brigade was on the right of the line from Bolton's Ridge, running north-eastward from the sea, to the middle of 400 Plateau. Next came the 1st and 3rd Australian Brigades, very intermixed, stretching to Quinn's Post,[2] the most northerly point on Second Ridge at that time held by the corps. From Quinn's the general line bent sharply back across the head of Monash Gully to the centre of Russell's Top, and was then continued down the spur known as Walker's Ridge to the sea. There was a mixed party of men of the 4th Australian Brigade, under Lieut.-Colonel H. Pope of the 16th Battalion, on Pope's Hill, the spur which juts into the head of Monash Gully from Baby 700. But with this exception the head of the gully, and all the northern portion of Russell's Top, lay open to the enemy, and the Turks on Baby 700 had an almost uninterrupted view of the gully bed, which formed the only means of communication between Second Ridge and the sea. At the head of Walker's Ridge was Lieut.-Colonel G. F. Braund with two depleted companies of the 2nd Australian Battalion, while a little lower down were two companies of the Canterbury Battalion whose commanding officer, Lieut.-Colonel D. McB. Stewart, had been killed the previous day.

Apart from sniping and a few local encounters, the 26th April passed quietly at Anzac, and but for a misfortune which occurred on 400 Plateau during the afternoon, the total number of casualties would have been small. About 3 P.M., however, some detachments in front line near M'Cay's Hill were being pushed slightly forward, to straighten the general alignment, when a garbled verbal order was passed down the line to the 4th Australian Battalion to "join in a general advance".

[1] Two Turkish guns were in one instance knocked out by one of the *Queen Elizabeth's* 15-inch H.E. shells.

The material damage inflicted by the naval artillery during the landing certainly fell short of expectations, but Turkish official documents all agree as to its shattering moral effect during the first days. "The effect of the "ships' guns", writes Liman von Sanders, "was to give a support to their " land forces which was quite out of the ordinary."

[2] During the 26th an attempt was made to withdraw all the men of the 3rd Brigade to the beach for rest and reorganization. Owing to difficulties of movement by daylight, this proved impossible, but Col. MacLagan and his staff were relieved by Col. MacLaurin, and the staff of the 1st Brigade.

Without questioning the source of this order, three parts of the battalion, led by their commanding officer,[1] leapt from their trenches, and, swinging left-handed, started to advance northwards along the summit of the plateau. No one in authority knew of this bold but unfortunate movement, which was in reality an advance up No Man's Land between the Australian and Turkish lines. But it was soon noticed by the Turkish gunners near Chunuk Bair and on Gun Ridge, and very heavy casualties were suffered, including the commanding officer killed, before the remnants of the battalion were at last stopped on Johnston's Jolly.[2]

During the day it was decided that Major-General Godley should take over the left of the Anzac position, and from that time Walker's Ridge, Russell's Top, and the head of Monash Gully became the special province of the New Zealand and Australian Division. But communications in rear of the firing line were so exposed that it was several days before the intermixing of units that had taken place on the 25th could be rectified, and before all the various battalions in the corps could be concentrated on their own portion of the front.

THE 26TH APRIL AT HELLES AND SEDD EL BAHR

Lying off Cape Helles in the flagship *Euryalus* during the night of the 25th/26th, listening to the intense rifle fire ashore, General Hunter-Weston could only believe that his troops were being heavily attacked. This belief was soon confirmed by a disturbing message from W Beach that the Turks were advancing in mass formation. Soon after midnight the firing died down, and at daybreak it was found that the report was untrue. But the idea still persisted that the Turks were in considerable strength.

25/26 Apr.

When reporting to G.H.Q. on the evening of the 25th, General Hunter-Weston still imagined that his troops had captured Hill 141,[3] and his decision to resume the advance on Achi Baba next morning was based on the belief that there would be little difficulty in completing the capture of V Beach and Sedd el Bahr village during the night.

Towards midnight, however, it became clear that Hill 141 was still in Turkish hands; and when, a little later, a lull in the firing seemed to show that the Turkish counter-attack had been driven off, an order was issued to the troops on the right flank

---

[1] Lt.-Col. A. J. Onslow Thompson.
[2] The portion of 400 Plateau north of Owen's Gully.
[3] See f.n. 1, page 243.

of W Beach to attack the hill from the west at daybreak, in conjunction with an attack by the V Beach troops from the south. In his message, timed 1.12 A.M. on the 26th, informing Sir Ian Hamilton of this plan, General Hunter-Weston added that French reinforcements would certainly be needed to carry the attack to Achi Baba, but that he hoped to secure V Beach first, so that the French might have a separate landing place.

26 Apr. Soon after daybreak, however, General Hunter-Weston decided that he was not strong enough to take Hill 141 and make good the beach at V without considerable reinforcements. At 6.25 A.M., therefore, he asked the Commander-in-Chief for a reinforcement of three French battalions and a battery, to be landed at W, with orders to operate on the British right and secure V Beach for the disembarkation of the remainder of the French contingent. This message was delayed in transit, and did not reach G.H.Q. till 8.15 A.M. Nevertheless, in view of a somewhat disquieting report received from the G.H.Q. liaison officer on W Beach,[1] Sir Ian Hamilton had already realized that the 29th Division might need reinforcement, and at 7.15 he anticipated his subordinate's request by offering to land a French brigade (six battalions) at the southern end of the peninsula.[2]

This was the situation when at 7.35 A.M. another message reached G.H.Q. from General Hunter-Weston to the effect that the troops at Y Beach were in desperate straits and needed immediate reinforcement, but that he had no men to spare.

To the Commander-in-Chief the situation must now have seemed grave indeed. General Birdwood had reported that if the Turks attacked his position in strength, it would probably lead to a catastrophe; and though up to the present no attack had developed, the Anzac situation could not be regarded as secure. In the south General Hunter-Weston had not yet captured V Beach and Sedd el Bahr; and now from Y, the most successful of all the landings, came rumours of unexpected disaster.

Sir Ian Hamilton had throughout set great store on the possession of Y Beach. So without waiting for a reply to his earlier message to General Hunter-Weston, he immediately ordered a French brigade to X Beach, whence they could march to Colonel Matthews's support, and he informed General Hunter-Weston accordingly. Hunter-Weston, on the other hand, was of opinion that the matter of most urgent importance

---

[1] Message from Capt. Bolton (G.H.Q. liaison officer W Beach) to G.H.Q.: "4.15 A.M. Essential that more infantry be landed here to-day if progress is to be made." [2] See also page 213.

was to clear up the situation at Sedd el Bahr by a direct attack from the direction of W Beach. Before receiving this latter message from the Commander-in-Chief,[1] he had already replied to the offer of French reinforcements by repeating his request that they might be sent to W.

Meanwhile at X Beach the two battalions under Br.-General Marshall, which formed the divisional reserve, continued to await the long-expected advance from the south. Br.-General Marshall reported at daylight that he had maintained his position during the night with only two casualties, and that there was no sign of the enemy. But at 7.23 A.M., when again asking for news of the situation, he added that he could do nothing to assist the Y Beach troops until the hollow ground in front of Hills 138 and 141 was cleared.[2]

At 10.10 A.M., after hearing that the situation at Y was desperate, General Hunter-Weston signalled an order to the commanders at X and W to consolidate their positions, adding that there would be no forward movement from those beaches till the arrival of the French.

The situation on V Beach at daybreak on the 26th was little different from that of the previous evening, except that the sorely tried troops who had first landed were by this time on the verge of physical collapse. The majority of these survivors were on the left of the beach, with orders to attack in the direction of Fort No. 1 and to gain touch with the troops from W. But there is a limit to human endurance; this limit had in many cases been overpassed; and the few remaining officers, themselves almost completely worn out, for some time found it impossible to rouse their men to action. On the right of the beach, under the walls of the old fort, Major A. T. Beckwith had assembled the fresher troops, who had landed during the night. These, after a preliminary bombardment by the fleet, were to attack the fort and village, and the old castle on the summit of Hill 141. In the centre of the amphitheatre the wire was still intact, except for a small gap cut by the troops during the night. One company was to attack by the west of the old fort through this gap; the remainder were to clear the fort and then to attack the village from the fort's eastern side, issuing through a small gate which gave on to the steep path leading up from the Camber beach. As the result of a night reconnaissance, this

Map 4. Sketch 8A.

[1] Though this message reached the *Euryalus* (H.Q. of 29th Division) at 8.20 A.M., it was not seen by the divisional commander till two hours later. See f.n. 1, page 214.
[2] Though the summit and inland slopes of Hills 138 and 141 can be seen from the cliff above X Beach, the hollow ground at their foot is hidden by a spur of Hill 114.

route was thought to be the best line of approach to the village, for the main gate had been blocked by the Turks, and was moreover under point-blank fire from the village itself. But the smaller gate, too, was afterwards found to be under direct fire from a small Turkish trench on the edge of the cliff, and troops emerging from it were to prove an easy target.

The Turks on the morning of the 26th still held the village and Hill 141, a number of determined snipers were occupying points of vantage in the fort, and a machine gun was firing from a hole in one of its bastions. The Turkish strength in the immediate neighbourhood of Sedd el Bahr was still only three companies, each of which had already suffered heavily.

Just before dawn the British troops on the right were withdrawn from before the walls of the fort to enable the fleet to shell it. But the fire of the ships was directed only against the further side of the village. Obviously there had been some misunderstanding, for after waiting in vain for the ships to shorten their range, Major Beckwith received a message from the *River Clyde* asking why he did not advance. Thereupon he at once set his troops in motion; but scarcely had they started when he received another message from the *River Clyde* telling him to "look out", as the ships were about to fire on the fort. With difficulty the troops were again withdrawn, but the ships continued to direct their fire inland; so after another delay Beckwith decided to chance it, and the advance was again resumed. The fort itself was cleared without much difficulty, but as soon as the troops reached the gate they were met by an accurate fire, and for some time there was little progress. Realizing the importance of every minute the three staff officers on board the *River Clyde*—Colonel C. H. M. Doughty-Wylie, Colonel W. de L. Williams, and Captain G. N. Walford—threw themselves into the fight, Doughty-Wylie and Walford going to the right and Williams to the extreme left of the beach. Placing himself at the head of the troops emerging from the fort gateway, Captain Walford, ably assisted by Captain A. C. Addison, Hampshire Regiment, led them up into the village, and here, after being the life and soul of the house-to-house fighting that ensued, both he and Captain Addison were killed.[1]

From 10 A.M. till 1 P.M., though the Hampshires under Major Beckwith were straining every nerve to get forward, progress in the village was necessarily slow. The Turks, fighting with great bravery, disputed every inch of the advance. Many of them, hidden in cellars or upper stories or in the débris of

---

[1] For his gallant leadership on this occasion Captain Walford was awarded a posthumous V.C.

THE POSTERN GATE, SEDD EL BAHR
through which the British troops advanced on 26th April to storm the village

AT HELLES AND SEDD EL BAHR 277

ruined houses, were firing into the backs of the troops after they had passed.

Meanwhile throughout the forenoon the attack on Hill 141 from the north of Fort No. 1, and from the left and centre of V Beach, had made no progress.[1] Bold leadership and personal example was what the tired troops required, and this was now supplied by Colonel Doughty-Wylie. About noon that gallant officer, who had hitherto been helping Major Beckwith on the right, and had just led up a reinforcement of 50 men to that flank, placed himself at the head of the Munster and Dublin Fusiliers on the left of the old fort. The advance now began to make definite progress. Further breaches were made in the Turkish wire,[2] the houses on the left of the fort were carried with the bayonet, and about 2.30 P.M.[3] the old castle on Hill 141 was taken by assault. But Doughty-Wylie, leading the charge, fell mortally wounded just as he reached the summit.[4]

The Turks streamed away from hill and village and from Fort No. 1 towards Krithia, many of them being caught by the machine guns of the Hampshire. By 3 P.M. the V Beach landing had been made good.

Now was the moment for the troops at Sedd el Bahr to join hands with the South Wales Borderers at S Beach, and for the whole British line, reinforced by a fresh brigade, to press the fleeing Turk. But the troops on the left and centre had been told that there would be no advance till French reinforcements arrived; there was no fresh brigade available; and Major Beckwith, senior officer at Sedd el Bahr, was unaware that

---

[1] The following messages seem to show that General Hunter-Weston's orders for a daybreak attack on Hill 141 from the right of W Beach (see page 274) never reached the troops:
Capt. Walford to 29th Division, timed 8.45 A.M.:
"Advance through Sedd el Bahr is very slow. Am receiving no support on my left."
O.C. Worcestershire to 29th Division timed 8.33 A.M.:
"Situation unchanged since this morning. Fairly hot fire maintained against my trenches from direction of Sedd el Bahr."

[2] Corporal W. Cosgrave, 1/R. Munster Fusiliers, was awarded the V.C. for conspicuous bravery in leading his section on this occasion, and for pulling down the posts of the enemy's barbed wire single-handed under heavy fire from front and flank. Major C. T. W. Grimshaw, R. Dublin Fusiliers (killed), and Lieut. G. W. Nightingale, R. Munster Fusiliers, also distinguished themselves greatly in this advance.

[3] Message from General Hunter-Weston to W Beach timed 2.35 P.M.: "Our men swarming into old castle. Push forward your right to join hands, and consolidate your position."

[4] Colonel Doughty-Wylie's gallant leadership and inspiring example were rewarded by a posthumous V.C., and the hill was subsequently called by his name.

Colonel Casson was in possession of S Beach.¹ In view of the exhaustion of his men, therefore, and of their shortage of water and ammunition, he decided to consolidate a position at the eastern end of the village, and this decision was confirmed half an hour later by an order from the divisional commander. General Hunter-Weston realized the importance of exploiting his success at the earliest possible moment. But his men were done. They had suffered heavy casualties; many of them had had no sleep for three nights; water and ammunition supply was an anxious problem; and behind his front line there were not more than two companies of infantry in reserve. On the other hand, the Turks were believed to be in considerable strength, and it was looked upon as certain that further reinforcements would reach them during the night.

In all these circumstances, General Hunter-Weston's thoughts were turned to an even more pressing problem than pursuit—the ability of his tired troops to cling to the ground they had won till fresh units could arrive. There was no mention, therefore, in his orders of any attempt to advance. The troops were to "dig in on the captured position and to make all prepara-"tions for repelling a Turkish attack". "There must be no "retiring," the order ran. "Every man will die at his post rather "than retire." For the moment, and until reinforcements could arrive, all idea of an offensive battle had been abandoned.

On the right of the British line, therefore, the afternoon was spent in consolidating the captured position. The troops on Hill 141 were joined by the right flank of the Worcestershire from near Fort No. 1; and by the evening of the 26th a con-

Map 4. Sketch 8A. tinuous line was held from X Beach to Sedd el Bahr. But the line still bent back to Hills 114 and 138, so that at the end of the second day the invaders still held only the fringe of the coast.

As for the French reinforcements, General d'Amade had reported about midday, in reply to a revised order from G.H.Q., that he hoped to land his leading companies at W Beach early in the afternoon. But his transports were late in arriving; the engines of one of them broke down; and after Sedd el Bahr had fallen, it was arranged that they should disembark at V.² Eventually the transports began to arrive about 7 P.M. and the first troops landed about half-past ten. But owing to the Kum Kale operations the French could provide no steamboats for the disembarkation; during the first night only two were

¹ It must be remembered that the brigadier and brigade-major ordered to land at V, as also the commander of Beckwith's battalion, had been killed. The company officers, even if they knew beforehand that a landing was being attempted at S, had had no opportunity of learning its fate.

² On the 27th V Beach was handed over to the French.

lent them by the British; and as a result only two battalions of infantry had been landed by daylight on the 27th.

As regards the Turks, on the 26th April the commander of the *9th Division* was faced with the same problems of severe casualties, intense fatigue, and lack of reserves, as had delayed the British advance. The arrival of Turkish reinforcements was a far slower process than the British command realized. Up to the morning of the 27th April the Ottoman forces south of Achi Baba amounted to only five battalions,[1] and by the night of the 27th, they amounted only to nine. According to Turkish official accounts the whole Turkish line fell back on the afternoon of the 26th, leaving only a few posts in touch with the British, and that night and the next day were spent in organizing a new defensive position running roughly north-west and south-east in front of Krithia, with its left on the high ground west of Kereves Dere.[2] Units were much disorganized; an average of 400 casualties had been suffered by each battalion;[3] and even the troops in support had been badly shaken by the fire of the British fleet.

Thus, as so often happens after a hard-fought action, the opposing forces spent the night of the 26th/27th in mutual expectation of an attack which their opponents were physically incapable of delivering. Physical fatigue, uncertainty, and chance had proved themselves the elements of war.

Meanwhile at X and W, as also at Anzac, the landing of guns, stores, ammunition, water, and supplies continued day and night. This work, particularly at Anzac, was a trying service, and the seamanship displayed by all ranks of the navy and mercantile marine concerned was deserving of high praise. The Turks kept up an incessant shrapnel fire on the anchorages, and at Anzac the work was occasionally brought to a standstill by bursts of fire from the Turkish war vessels in the Narrows. But these were only of short duration, and a few rounds from the British battleships always succeeded in driving the Turkish ships away. By the evening of the 26th April, Anzac and W Beaches had already assumed the appearance of large supply depots, and the landing of iron tanks, fed from water-lighters,

[1] The *2nd* and *3rd Battalions 26th Regiment* (the *1st Battalion* was still holding the coast from Semerly Tepe to Sari Tepe) and three battalions *25th Regiment* from Serafim Farm. The *Broussa Gendarmerie Battalion*, which had been on the march south from Suvla Bay when the British landing began, had been detained near Semerly Tepe throughout the 25th and 26th in case a landing should be attempted in that neighbourhood.

[2] Four Turkish field batteries were in position near Krithia by the evening of 26th April.

[3] The Turkish official account admits 1,898 casualties south of Achi Baba in the first two days' fighting.

had considerably improved the water supply on shore. Nevertheless, the many serious impediments with which the naval and military beach personnel had to contend—such as hostile shelling, insufficiency of steamboats off the beach,[1] deep powdery sand to the water's edge, cramped spaces, indifferent exits from the shore, and shortage of labour—were proving far greater than anticipated;[2] and despite the hardest work by all concerned the rate of disembarkation of guns, ammunition, and stores was almost incredibly slow. It had been expected, according to the carefully prepared time-table, that the whole of the 29th Division would be landed in 60 hours. But the number of guns ashore at the end of the second day was still very small, and owing to the complete change of the programme of disembarkation necessitated by the march of events, the landing of the non-combatant units of the division was not completed for nearly ten days.

[1] On 27th April, the Principal Beach Master reported: "Delay in "unloading is due to there being no steamboats whatever on W Beach. "All we have are two cutters, which are constantly employed unloading "lighters. There is work for 4 steamboats and 4 cutters at W." On the same day Rear-Admiral Wemyss reported to the naval C.-in-C.: "Want of "steamboats much felt. I could do with twice as many." Throughout the campaign it was always the same story. Casualties amongst steamboats were always severe, as their work was never-ceasing. There was no shelter either from bad weather or hostile shelling; and despite the efforts of the authorities responsible for the provision of these little vessels, the supply rarely equalled the demand.

[2] On 25th April beach working parties had to be sent up to reinforce the firing line. Next morning these men were tired out, but it was found impossible to relieve them till the afternoon. For hauling guns from the beach manual labour proved better than horse-draught, the horses being very soft after their long stay on board ship, and many of their drivers inexperienced.

CHAPTER XVI

OPERATIONS 27TH–30TH APRIL

THE ADVANCE AT HELLES, 27TH APRIL

(Maps 2, 3 ; Sketches 12, 13, 14, 15)

ON the left and centre of the 29th Division front the compara- 26/27
tive quiet of the 26th April was followed by an undisturbed **Apr.**
night, and patrols sent out a mile to the front could find no
trace of the enemy. On the right, especially amongst the
exhausted troops from V Beach, there was less sleep for officers
and men. Too weary to patrol, the troops remained in ignorance of the Turkish withdrawal, and throughout the night
overwrought nerves were responsible for prolonged bursts of
firing. One officer relates that before nightfall he made his
men count the headstones and cypresses in a cemetery in front,
so that they should not mistake them for advancing Turks
during the night. But after dark, hearing that strong Turkish
reinforcements were advancing to attack, he himself imagined
that he saw large masses of infantry moving towards his position.
Next morning these proved to be nothing but patches of scrub.

Learning overnight that the French brigade would be
ready about noon, General Hunter-Weston had decided to
wait till that hour to resume his advance on Achi Baba. But
at daybreak on the 27th it became plain that a still longer **27 Apr.**
postponement was inevitable, for only two French battalions
had landed and the remainder could not be ready till late in the
afternoon. In these circumstances, General Hunter-Weston
resolved that the capture of Achi Baba must be postponed yet
another 24 hours, and that his action on the 27th must be
confined to throwing forward his centre and right to join hands
with the troops at S, and thus to secure a good jumping-off line
for his advance on the following day. Meanwhile he arranged
for the tired troops on his right to be relieved by the French.

About 8 A.M., General Vandenberg, commanding the
French Metropolitan Brigade, visited General Hunter-Weston

on board the *Euryalus*, and later in the morning, Br.-General Marshall and Colonel Wolley-Dod arrived to report on the situation at X and W and to receive their orders for the day.

General d'Amade had agreed that until his headquarters could be established ashore, the French battalions in the line should be under the tactical control of the 29th Division, and General Hunter-Weston now decided that it would facilitate the issue of orders and the receipt of information if he remained in the *Euryalus* for another 24 hours. Br.-General Marshall was consequently ordered to assume temporary command of the division and to open a divisional command post near the lighthouse. Lieut.-Colonel R. O. C. Hume, Border Regiment, was to be in temporary command of the 87th Brigade, Lieut.-Colonel Godfrey-Faussett, Essex Regiment, was to command the 88th, while Lieut.-Colonel Cayley, Worcestershire Regiment, was to command the 86th.

Map 2. At 10 A.M., divisional orders were issued. The division was to advance at 4 P.M. to take up a line across the peninsula from the high ground above S Beach to the mouth of Gully Ravine.[1] The operation was thus to be in the nature of a "left wheel", pivoting on the extreme left at X Beach. The distance to be covered was about two miles for the troops on the right and in the centre, and rather less than half a mile for those at the pivotal point.

During the morning it was possible to move about without interruption by the Turks, and the opportunity was taken to collect scattered units and to withdraw the depleted 86th Brigade into reserve. The supporting warships searched Krithia and the Achi Baba ridge with their fire, but the arrangements for ranging quickly on a definite target in response to an appeal from the shore were not yet satisfactory, and in one case over $1\frac{1}{2}$ hours elapsed before fire could be opened on an area in which large numbers of Turks were reported to be advancing.[2] Nevertheless even in these early days there were many instances of remarkable naval shooting. On the morning

[1] This was roughly the position which the Turks had originally intended to hold as a second line of defence for the troops defending the southern beaches. But, as already noted, they had now fallen back to a line from the mouth of Kereves Dere to the neighbourhood of Y Beach.

It is noteworthy that in describing the objective for the British left flank the actual words of the 29th Divisional order were " the mouth of the "stream in 168. c.". The available maps were so inaccurate, and available information so incomplete, that nothing was yet known at headquarters regarding the nature of this rugged and tortuous ravine, whose banks were in places over 100 feet high. The " stream " was shown on the map by a straight blue line. See Sketches 12 and 13.

[2] See Appendix 21. Happily this report of Turks advancing proved to be inaccurate.

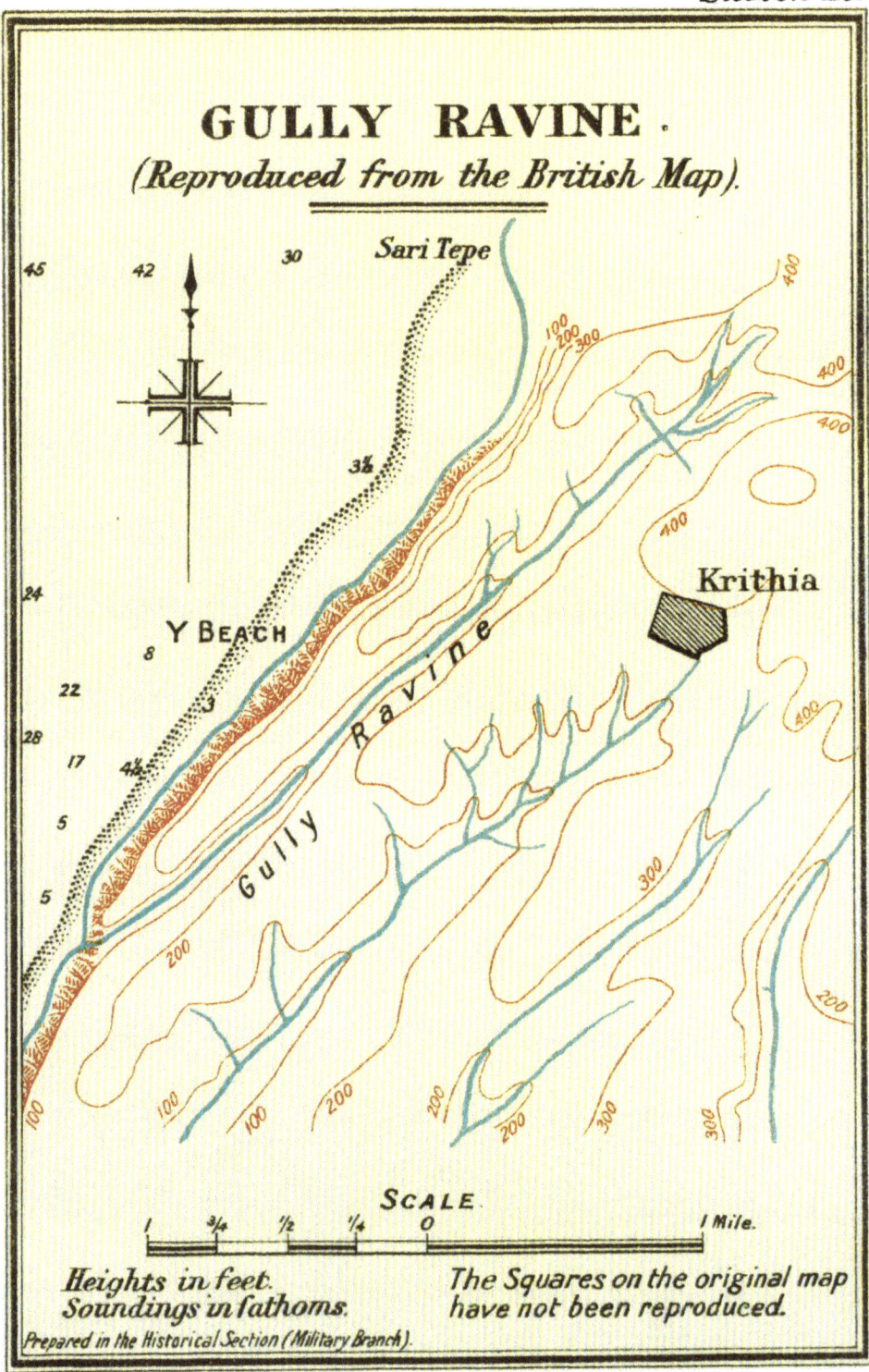

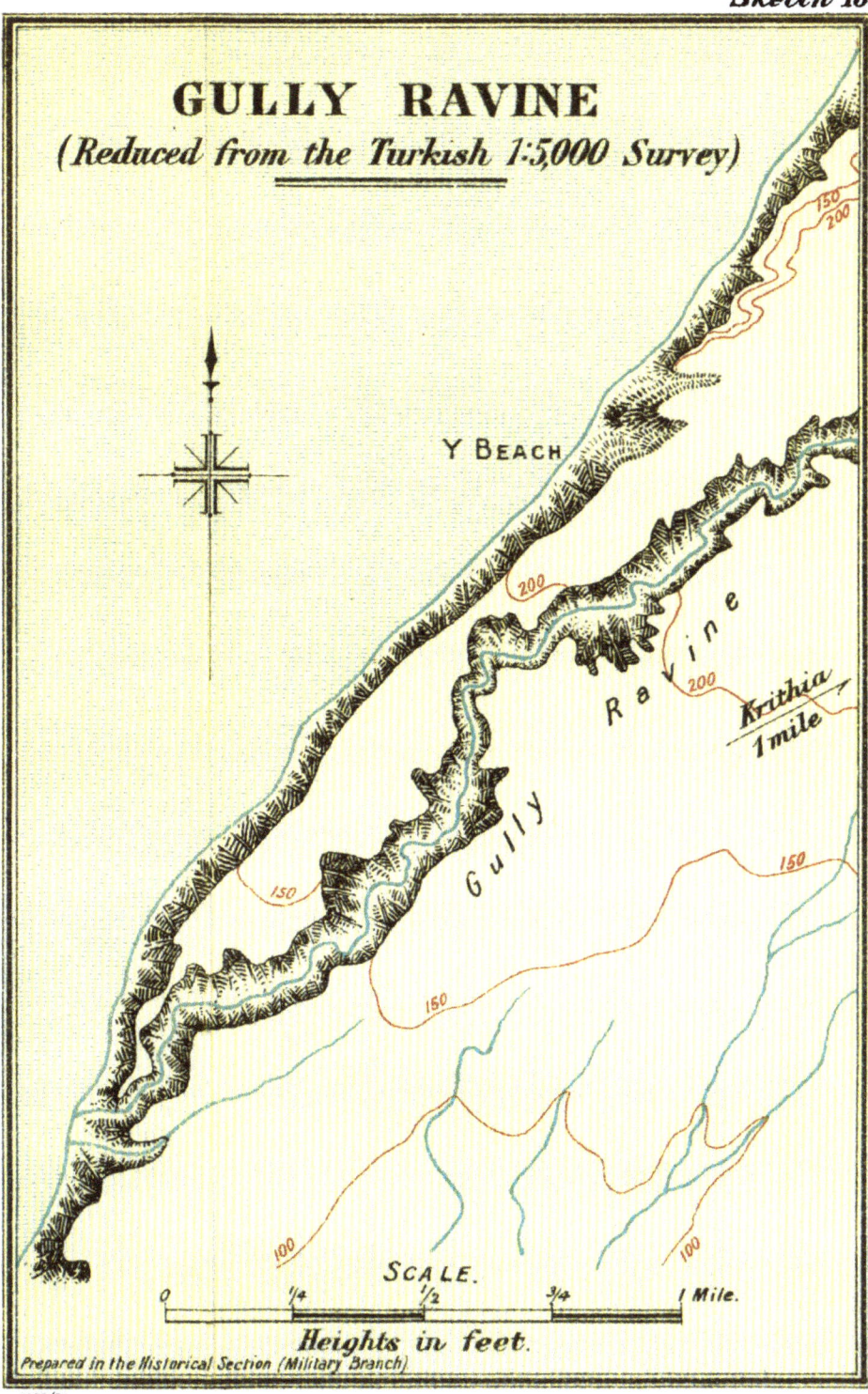

THE ADVANCE AT HELLES, 27TH APRIL

of the 27th, for instance, a balloon ship, spotting for the *Queen Elizabeth* off Gaba Tepe, noticed a Turkish transport in the Narrows. The flagship at once opened on the invisible enemy with her 15-inch guns, firing across the waist of the peninsula at a range of 16,500 yards. After her third shot the message "O.K." was telephoned down from the balloon. The message seemed too good to be true. "What does he mean?" shouted Admiral de Robeck, who, with Sir Ian Hamilton, and some of his staff, was on the compass platform. "Have we hit her?" "Yes", came back the observer's reply, "and she is sinking by the stern. Stand by while I put you on another."

By 3.30 P.M. on the 27th April all preparations for the southern advance had been made. Half an hour later, in brilliant sunlight, the 29th Division moved forward in long lines of platoons, the two battalions of the French 175th Regiment (Lieut.-Colonel Philippe) on the right keeping pace in a similar formation. The ground in front was shaped like a gigantic saucer, with its eastern lip submerged in the blue waters of Morto Bay. The troops in the centre and on the right were starting from the southern lip, and their route led down into the valley and then up towards the long slope that culminates in Achi Baba. The country was dotted with cypress and olive, clumps of stunted oak, and some patches of cultivation; but for the most part the whole line of advance was under direct observation from the north.

It soon became evident that not only had the Turkish infantry fallen back, but that some Turkish field guns in action the previous day had been withdrawn out of range. A few snipers were encountered, some of them feigning dead till the advancing lines had passed,[1] and two Turkish guns from the direction of Achi Baba fired a few rounds. But otherwise not a shot was fired, and by 5.30 P.M. the new line had been taken up and the French had joined hands with the South Wales Borderers above S Beach.[2] On the left the 87th Brigade had not advanced as far as intended. Its left flank company, in order to make use of a good field of fire, had remained in its original trenches on the coast some 500 yards short of Gully Ravine, and the rest of the brigade, and the Essex Regiment on their right, had merely swung into line. As a result the

Sketch 14.

---
[1] Battalion records contain frequent allusions to the fanatical bravery of the Turkish snipers, who seemed to have no fear of death provided they could kill a number of Christians first.
[2] The South Wales Borderers marched across the peninsula to join the 87th Brigade early on the 28th and Lieut.-Colonel Casson then assumed command of the brigade.

centre of the British front had to be bent back sharply, facing west, to link up with the left. This bend in the line had somewhat serious consequences.

There was again little sleep for the 29th Division during the night of the 27th/28th. From 6 P.M. till midnight the troops were engaged in digging. Thereafter two platoons in each company were made to stand to arms till daybreak; and though the Turks made no attack the activity of their patrols led to great expenditure of British and French ammunition.

PREPARATIONS FOR THE FIRST BATTLE OF KRITHIA

In framing plans for the morrow General Hunter-Weston was faced on the night of the 27th with many unpalatable facts. Though he could count on the services of at least three, and perhaps four, French battalions, all of which would be comparatively fresh, his own division was only a shadow of what it had been three days earlier. All three brigades were in charge of inexperienced brigadiers. Only one of the three brigade-majors was left alive, and of the twelve original battalion commanders only three remained at duty. As for company officers and men, the 86th Brigade had suffered crippling losses. Of its four battalions, the Dublin Fusiliers had lost all but four of their officers and over 550 men; the other three battalions had lost half their officers and a third of their rank and file. The 87th and 88th Brigades had been more fortunate, for, with the exception of the troops from Y Beach, none of their units had yet suffered more than 10 per cent of casualties, and in most cases their losses did not exceed 50 of all ranks. But the 87th Brigade consisted of only $2\frac{3}{4}$ battalions,[1] for the units from Y Beach had not yet rejoined. Most important of all, practically the whole division was physically spent, and a large proportion of officers and men would be starting the attack after four consecutive nights without sleep.

Some good wells had been found in the low ground north of Morto Bay, but rationing the troops, and keeping them supplied with ammunition, was an anxious problem, the difficulty of which would be aggravated by the new advance. Owing to the accidental stranding at Mudros of a ship carrying the Zion Mule Corps, very few transport animals had yet been landed,[2] and the ponies of the mountain battery, as well

[1] The Drake Battalion, R.N.D., was landed on the evening of the 26th and attached to the 87th Brigade for work on the beach.

[2] The Zion Mule Corps began to land on the evening of the 27th, but was not ready for duty till after the advance had begun on the 28th. Some of its mules were then employed in taking ammunition to the troops.

Sketch 14.

FIRST BATTLE OF KRITHIA,
Allied Objectives for 28th April.

THE FIRST BATTLE OF KRITHIA 285

as some of the 18-pdr. gun-teams, had been working almost without rest for 24 hours carrying water and ammunition from the beach.

The small amount of artillery ashore was also a source of uneasiness. A few more 18-pdrs. and a battery of French 75's had landed during the day, but the number of available guns amounted to only 28.[1] Moreover, owing to the shortage of gun-teams, it would be impossible for even this small number to move forward with the infantry. No horses had yet been landed by the French, and their valuable 75's were for the moment immobile on the beach. But considerable help was expected from the navy; special areas had been allotted to the supporting ships, and a forward observation post was established on the left flank to assist the direction of fire.

There was no shortage of small-arm ammunition on shore, despite its reckless expenditure since the landing; but many of the men in front line had thrown away their packs, and had neither reserve ammunition nor food.[2] As for artillery ammunition, it promised to become an even graver question than in France, for the expedition had been sent out from England with only 750 rounds per gun available or in sight, and only 600 rounds per howitzer. But till more batteries were disembarked, anxiety on this score would be confined to the problem of getting the available ammunition to the guns.

Weighing all these disadvantages General Hunter-Weston was again obliged to curb his impatience and to give up all idea of reaching Achi Baba on the 28th. In his plans for the capture of the ridge, however, he had from the first intended to advance against it with his left flank leading, and to deliver his main attack from the west, starting from the line of the Krithia road between Krithia and Hill 472, an eminence about 1½ miles due north of the village. He now resolved to adhere to this plan, but to confine his operations on the 28th to throwing forward his left and centre to gain the desired position on the Krithia road. The Allied advance, to begin at 8 A.M., would this time be in the nature of a right wheel, pivoting on the right of the French line above S Beach. The left and left centre of the 29th Division were to capture Sari Tepe on the Ægean coast, Hill 472, and Krithia, and at the end of the day would be facing due east with the northern flank bent back and facing north. The right of the

---

[1] Sixteen 18-pdrs., four 75's, four 4·5-in. hows., and four mountain guns.
[2] Every man had landed with extra ammunition and rations in his pack.

French line was to remain stationary on Hill 236, but its left was to swing forward with the right of the 29th Division.

Divisional orders in accordance with this plan were issued soon after 10 P.M. The 87th Brigade was to advance due north astride Gully Ravine and to occupy Sari Tepe and Hill 472. The 88th Brigade on its right was to seize Krithia and to take up a line running north and south on the eastern side of the village. The French, pivoting on Hill 236, were to link up with the right of the 88th at a point on Kanli Dere about half a mile south of Krithia. The 86th Brigade was to be in reserve. The orders contained no reference to the enemy or to probable opposition, and made no mention of artillery support.

It will be seen that the operation, involving as it did a complete change of front in face of the enemy, promised to be an unusually difficult manœuvre. Moreover, though the frontage of the Allied line at the starting point was only two miles, the frontage of the final objective was $5\frac{1}{2}$ miles. The orders were undoubtedly meagre, but at the time they were issued the divisional staff had little information to give. They had as yet received no detailed report of the actual line attained by the Allied troops that evening. They were ignorant of the nature of the country in front and of the extraordinary tactical importance of the harmless-looking water-courses marked on their maps. They knew nothing of the enemy's strength or of the position of his defences; they were even uncertain whether any opposition would be encountered within the limits of the day's advance.

As regards administrative details, the troops were warned that the "iron rations"[1] which they had taken ashore in their packs might have to last for two days instead of one, since there was a possibility that no further supplies could reach the troops till the evening of the 28th. This warning was necessary, but its effect on tired troops, many of whom had already thrown away their iron rations, must have been very disheartening.

The task of the 87th Brigade, the only one left with its original brigade-major,[2] was less complicated than that of the 88th, for its objective lay straight to its front, whereas that of the 88th, some of whose troops would still be facing west when their advance began, necessitated a complete wheel to the right till they eventually faced due east. Brigade orders were issued

---

[1] An "iron ration" was an emergency ration and consisted of a canvas bag of biscuit, a tin of beef, and a tin of tea and sugar, sufficient for one man for one day. The men had landed with 2 days' rations for the 25th and 26th, and one iron ration for the 27th.

[2] Captain C. H. T. Lucas.

by the 87th Brigade at 1.15 A.M., and the day's operations were further explained to battalion commanders at a conference held at daybreak. Similar action seems to have been taken in the case of the 88th Brigade, though no record of its orders has been preserved. Nevertheless, in the case of all the battalions engaged, company officers and the rank and file appear to have been too dead with fatigue to understand their orders or to have much idea of what was required of them when the time to advance arrived.[1]

The G.O.C. divisional artillery issued his orders at 10.30 P.M., and the gunners spent a busy night reconnoitring routes and getting guns forward to suitable positions. Two batteries of 18-pdrs. and one howitzer battery were taken two miles up the Krithia road to support the 88th Brigade. Another battery of 18-pdrs. and one section of mountain guns were placed on the left of the road to support the 87th. A section of the Ross Mountain Battery remained on Hill 141 to support the French. Thus, when the advance began the two-mile front of attack was covered by 20 guns.

Meanwhile, according to Turkish reports now available, Colonel Sami Bey, commanding the Turkish *9th Division*, had been preparing a defensive position covering the approach to Krithia. The troops of the *25th* and *26th Regiments* had had time to recover some of their equilibrium; by the evening of the 27th they had been reinforced by four fresh battalions,[2] and on the morning of the 28th the Turks were holding a number of mutually supporting points, on a line running generally south-east from near Y Beach to the mouth of Kereves Dere.

---

[1] The records of one of the battalions engaged afford a valuable sidelight on this point, for they fix the time at which the orders were (i.) received from brigade headquarters and (ii.) issued to company commanders, and reflect the intense weariness and strain from which many of the officers engaged were suffering. The adjutant of this battalion, in a letter written a few days later, wrote: " We had a fairly quiet night as far as the enemy " was concerned, but to my horror and surprise I received orders (from " my brigade) at 2 A.M. to the effect that the brigade would advance at " 8 A.M. Of course I had to go round and explain things to company " officers, and they, poor fellows, being dead with lack of sleep and ex-" haustion, were in no condition to take much interest. . . . It was not " till 7.40 A.M. that I got battalion orders out." Another officer of this battalion wrote: " We did not receive our orders till just before the time " for the advance to commence, and it was practically impossible for every-" one to understand in a hurry from the map the exact position we were to " reach."

[2] One battalion *15th Regiment*, two battalions *20th Regiment*, and the *Broussa Gendarmerie*. There were thus nine Turkish battalions available on the morning of the 28th (exclusive of the *1st/26th Regiment* still at Semerly Tepe) and further reinforcements were arriving. Turkish information shows no increase of artillery since 26th April.

There was as yet nothing in the nature of connected trenches, and the defenders were relying chiefly on the natural cover afforded by broken ground, while the ravines running southwest offered useful lines of approach. In front of the general line was a screen of advanced posts. Some of these, on the crest of the spur on the right bank of Kereves Dere, were in small trenches dug before the landing, the existence of which was not yet known to the Allies.

The Turkish position appears to have been held in depth by seven (or eight) battalions, with two battalions in reserve near Krithia. The bulk of this strength was on the Turkish left and left centre, while the right (Ægean) flank appears in the first instance to have been lightly held. From a tactical point of view the most interesting feature of the position is that it lay at an angle to, and intersected, the line of the British advance.

THE FIRST BATTLE OF KRITHIA

28 Apr. Sketch 14. About 8 A.M. on the 28th the covering warships began a desultory bombardment of Krithia and the forward slopes of Achi Baba. The 20 guns on shore joined in with a scattered fire, and the weary troops of the 29th Division climbed out of their trenches and plodded forward in the general direction of Krithia. On the left, the 87th Brigade had the Border Regiment between the Ægean coast and Gully Ravine, the Inniskilling Fusiliers on the eastern side of that ravine, and the South Wales Borderers in brigade reserve. Some of the Anson Battalion, who had formed a working party on X Beach, were also advancing with this brigade, attached to the Border Regiment.[1] In the centre of the line, from left to right, the 88th Brigade had the Essex Regiment, the Hampshire, and the Worcestershire in front line, with the 1/5th Royal Scots (not yet complete) in support. On the right of the Worcestershire, stretching southwards to the Dardanelles, were the three battalions of the French 175th Regiment, supported by two more battalions of the Metropolitan Brigade,[2] the whole under General Vandenberg.

The 86th Brigade formed the general reserve, and by 8 A.M.

---

[1] These men, and 1½ coys. Drake Battalion who went forward later, were apparently taken from the beach without the knowledge of the Military Landing Officer. The sequel was unfortunate. Orders arrived for them to return to the beach when they were in the firing line at a critical period of the battle, and some confusion was caused by the troops on either flank thinking that a general retirement had been ordered.

[2] One battalion of Zouaves and one of the Foreign Legion.

THE FIRST BATTLE OF KRITHIA 289

had assembled south-east of X Beach. Further in rear, at W Beach, the King's Own Scottish Borderers were landing, and were afterwards sent up to rejoin the 87th.

At first all went well on the 29th Division front. No opposition was encountered, there was little or no Turkish shelling, and by 9 A.M. the capture of Krithia seemed imminent. According to Turkish accounts some of their forward troops began to give ground directly the British advanced, and one battalion bolted. At 9.15 A.M. General Hunter-Weston arrived at Hill 138[1] to resume executive command of the division, and sent forward Br.-General Marshall with a more or less roving commission to superintend the advance. General Marshall took with him a few officers to act as a temporary staff; but having no fixed headquarters and no telephone, it was impossible for him to exercise adequate control over a two-mile front, and this delegation of divisional authority led to some delay and confusion in the issue and despatch of messages, orders, and reports.

The disadvantages of attempting a complete change of front, starting from an irregular line, in the face of an enemy whose strength and dispositions were unknown, were soon to assert themselves. In the centre the leading companies of the Hampshire Regiment had been at least 600 yards in front of the troops on their left when the forward movement began. Advancing straight to their front without waiting for these troops to come up into line, and not realizing that the whole division was to swing right-handed, or that the units on the right were not intended to advance so far or so fast as those in the centre, these leading companies soon found themselves with both flanks in the air. Eventually the Worcestershire Regiment, which had been waiting for the French, made a fine advance on the Hampshires' right, and some of the Essex Regiment and a company of the Royal Scots came up on their left. But once they were in touch with the Turks, the Turkish positions rather than an arbitrary line on a map became the true objective, and by every unit of the brigade all previous instructions were forgotten. With practically each company commander fighting an independent battle, all cohesion vanished, and by 11 A.M. the centre of the British line was in considerable confusion. Meanwhile the Turks began to dribble up reinforcements;[2] the British advance

[1] Afterwards known as " Hunter-Weston Hill '.
[2] Earlier, according to the Turkish official account, the Turkish centre had appeared to be broken, and an order for a general retirement to Achi Baba was given. The opportune arrival of a fresh battalion is said to have restored the battle about 11 A.M.

began to flag and ammunition to run out; and by 11.30 A.M. the advance of the 88th Brigade had stopped.

On the left the situation of the 87th Brigade was equally unsatisfactory, while on the extreme right the French were in an even worse predicament. Up to 10.30 A.M., the Border Regiment on the western side of Gully Ravine, and the Inniskilling Fusiliers to the east of it, had made steady progress. But though there had been no opposition on this flank except for a little shrapnel, the strain of the last three days was beginning to tell. Tired out before the advance began, none of the invading troops were really in a fit state to carry out an attack. Their vitality was at a low ebb, and the heat of the sun, combined with great shortage of water, was provoking an intolerable thirst. When, therefore, about 11 A.M., after reaching a point about half a mile short of Y Beach, the Border Regiment came under heavy rifle fire from its right front, the battalion was brought to a standstill. The Inniskillings were at the same time checked by another body of Turks, and for about two hours there was no further movement in this sector.

As for the French, it will be remembered that their right was to be the pivotal point of the whole advance and to remain stationary on Hill 236. It would appear, however, that the French commander, learning during the night that the Turks were holding the high ground on the right (western) bank of Kereves Dere, decided to vary his instructions, and to start the day by pushing forward a small column on his right to occupy a plateau near the mouth of that ravine. From this point he apparently hoped to enfilade the Turkish posts on the crest of the spur, and thus to assist the advance of his left, which was not to move till the right flanking column was in position.[1]

Shortly after 8 A.M., therefore, a small French column started off in single file from de Tott's battery, and, keeping well below the top of the cliffs, advanced towards the mouth of Kereves Dere without opposition.

Before reaching the mouth of the ravine the French troops —their blue uniforms terribly conspicuous against the khaki-coloured earth—filed to the top of the sloping cliffs, and continuing their advance to the summit of a plateau about 500 yards inland, took up a position facing north. A few moments later a Turkish field battery opened on them in enfilade with deadly effect. The position was obviously untenable, and after enduring this fire for a few minutes the

---

[1] It was the repercussion of this order which delayed the advance of the Worcestershire Regiment and led to the right of the Hampshires becoming exposed.

remnants of the party doubled back to the shelter of the cliffs. They were at once pursued by a number of Turks from the ravine, and though the *Albion's* [1] guns effectively stopped this counter-attack, the incident undoubtedly had much to do with the delay on the remainder of the French front. When, about 10 A.M., the centre and left of the 175th Regiment began to move forward, they soon came under a considerable rifle fire from the advanced posts which the column on the right had been expected to neutralize; and though a good deal of ground was gained, nearly the whole of it was lost a little later. All accounts agree that the gay French uniforms and white cork helmets were a severe handicap to their wearers, making them an easy mark for the enemy.

Meanwhile the British were unaware of the French effort on the right, or that the Turks held a position of great advantage on the western side of the Kereves Dere. Throughout the morning the difficulties of the 175th Regiment were misunderstood, and their slow rate of progress somewhat unjustly criticized.

When Br.-General Marshall reached the neighbourhood of the front about 11.30 A.M., the general situation was far from reassuring. He gauged, however, that it was the exhaustion of the troops, rather than the enemy's opposition, that was delaying the advance.[2] Thinking that the units of the 88th Brigade were almost at the end of their tether, he decided to throw the 86th—his only reserve—into the fight, with orders to take up ammunition to the 88th[3] and then, carrying the whole line forward, to capture Krithia. At the same time he sent Lieut.-Colonel Casson, commanding the 87th Brigade, to urge forward the left flank. At this moment the French on the right were seen to be falling back, taking with them the right of the 88th.

Lieut.-Colonel Cayley lost no time in issuing orders for the advance of the 86th Brigade. The Lancashire Fusiliers on the right and the Royal Fusiliers on the left were to lead the attack, with the Munster and Dublin Fusiliers in support. The two leading battalions were soon ready, but the others could not be found. Later it transpired that an officer of the 88th had met

---

[1] The *Albion* was in the Straits, supporting the French right, and this account is taken from the diary of an eye-witness on board.

[2] It subsequently transpired that lack of small-arm ammunition was the main factor in checking the 88th Brigade's advance. The men were dead tired, but were still full of heart; but many of them had scarcely a round of ammunition left.

[3] Lieut.-Commander A. Keyes, R.N., who had asked to go forward with Br.-General Marshall, had brought up several mule-loads of ammunition with him.

them moving up, and had rushed all but a handful to the right, saying that it was a matter of life and death to his brigade. Thus, for the rest of that day the 86th was deprived of half its strength, and only two battalions were available for reinforcing the attack on Krithia. Both these battalions, moreover, were very weak; the majority of their officers had already become casualties; and the men were almost as weary as those of the 88th.

Seeing that the new attack was making little progress, Captain Farmar, brigade-major of the 86th, went forward about 2 P.M. Accompanied by Captain C. Bromley, Adjutant of the Lancashire Fusiliers, and Lieut. M. J. A. O'Connell of the Royal Fusiliers, he led a mixed party of both battalions in the direction of a straggling copse afterwards known as Fir Tree Wood.[1] This example was followed by the men on either flank; and Fir Tree Wood was occupied with very little loss. Farmar, Bromley, 2/Lieut. G. G. Needham, and a few men then pushed on to reconnoitre, and got to within three-quarters of a mile of Krithia. By this time the Turks in the neighbourhood were in full retreat. But very unfortunately the senior officer in Fir Tree Wood, unaware that Farmar was in front, and judging the position insecure, had meanwhile ordered not an advance but a retirement. Thus, the little party in front was soon isolated, and the chance of capturing Krithia slipped away. Captain Bromley started back to call up reinforcements, but was immediately hit. A few minutes later the Turks came trickling back, and Farmar was forced to retire.

On the left, astride Gully Ravine, the 87th Brigade succeeded about 1 P.M. in resuming its advance, though only at the expense of considerable casualties.[2] But the Turks on the extreme left had meanwhile been reinforced; and when the Border Regiment approached the gully that leads down to Y Beach, it again came under a heavy fire and a few minutes later was counter-attacked with the bayonet. This was the last straw. The overstrained troops wavered, and, to the consternation of the Commander-in-Chief, who was watching from the deck of the *Queen Elizabeth*, the left-hand company retired down the steep cliffs and a few minutes later was withdrawing along the beach towards Helles. For a moment the situation looked critical, for the extreme left flank was now completely open; but a well-directed 15-inch shell from the flagship, bursting its 24,000 shrapnel bullets right in the middle

---

[1] About a mile south-west of Krithia.
[2] In the Border Regiment alone four officers were killed and three wounded during the morning.

of the Turks,[1] brought instantaneous relief. A staff officer was sent ashore from the *Queen Elizabeth* by Sir Ian Hamilton to intercept the retreating men and lead them back to the front; and though the right of the 87th Brigade (Inniskillings and S.W.B.) could gain no further ground during the day, the position already attained was safely held for the rest of the afternoon.

On the right, where the French had been driven back about midday, General Vandenberg made another effort during the afternoon to get his men forward, and threw his last remaining battalion into the fight. A little progress was made in some parts of the line, but the Turks counter-attacked with another fresh battalion which had just arrived from Bulair. The French fell back to their original line, and throughout the rest of the day no further advance was attempted.

As a result of the French retirement the 88th Brigade again found itself enfiladed, and some of its right flank companies began to withdraw. About the same time a number of men began to fall back from the left of the brigade, and the troops astride the Krithia road were again isolated. Fired at from three sides their casualties mounted rapidly, and, though the Turks made no attempt to counter-attack, these leading companies were at last ordered to give up the ground won.

Noticing this retirement Br.-General Marshall signalled to General Hunter-Weston:

5.15 P.M. Both brigades and battalions are very much mixed up and the men are thoroughly done. The French and 88th Brigade have both fallen back. On the left the Border Regiment and odds and ends of other units are held up by a redoubt. Unless you decide otherwise I propose to hold our ground till dusk, and then take up a line ... [here followed map co-ordinates indicating a line somewhat in rear of his present front]. Can the French hold our right? Owing to most of the men having discarded their packs there will be a shortage of rations, and I think of ammunition.

This report was sufficiently serious, but compared with the alarmist and unauthenticated messages that had been reaching divisional headquarters, and even General Headquarters, all the afternoon, it came as a welcome relief. So many unsigned reports that the whole division was being cut up had been signalled to the *Queen Elizabeth* from various points on the coast, that about half-past three Sir Ian Hamilton had referred

[1] The Turks, about one company strong, were rushing forward in a dense mass led by an officer with drawn sword. When the dust of the explosion cleared away not a single Turk was visible.

the matter to General Hunter-Weston, and two hours later the following reply was received:

> Alarmist messages have been sent to me all day, but there is nothing yet to justify them. There have been local successes and local reverses, and since my first report we have made no progress. There is no doubt that in present exhausted state of the troops a Turkish counter-attack would have serious effects. The French have just sent me a request for reinforcements and inform me they have used up all the French battalions already disembarked.

No clearer epitome could be given of the situation as night closed in on the 28th April; and the anxieties of the divisional commander and of the Commander-in-Chief, with no reserves immediately available and very few in sight, need little further emphasis. At times like this a commander has need of all his resolution.

At 6 P.M., Br.-General Marshall received orders to break off the action and entrench for the night; but he was now to learn that the British retirement in the centre had been carried much further than he expected. The right of the 87th Brigade had withdrawn at dusk, apparently without much trouble, to the line indicated by the division, but on its right was a yawning gap where the 86th and 88th Brigades had fallen back to their starting point.

Once again there was no sleep for officers and men, for the whole night was spent in re-sorting units and in a vain effort to fill the gaps in the line. The day's casualties had been heavy. The 29th Division started the day with between 8,000 and 9,000 infantry, and their casualties were 2,000, including a high proportion of officers. The French, out of some 5,000 men engaged, had lost 27 officers and 974 men.

The Turks made no attempt to counter-attack during the night, and it is now known that their losses had been as heavy as those of the Allies. The Turkish official account admits that throughout the day the situation was looked upon as critical.

So, on a note of failure, the first battle of Krithia came to an end. The advantages expected from postponing the attack till the 28th had been counterbalanced by the increased strength of the Turks. Up to midday on the 28th only five Allied battalions had reinforced the $12\frac{1}{2}$ which landed on the first day. In the same period the Turkish strength in the south had risen from two battalions to ten, with further reinforcements arriving in a steady stream. On the 25th, Krithia had lain open to Colonel Matthews at Y Beach. On the 26th, and even on the morning of the 27th, the door to Achi Baba was still ajar. But now it was bolted and barred.

At first the gravity of the situation was scarcely recognized at G.H.Q. When telegraphing to Lord Kitchener next morning Sir Ian Hamilton still believed that the battle had resulted in a gain of over a mile. But to the troops themselves there was little on the night of the 28th to lighten the surrounding gloom. Back again in their original trenches, it was plain that the day's operation had failed. Units were badly intermixed; casualties had been heavy; all ranks were dead tired: yet there was no chance of being withdrawn from the line to rest and re-fit. Food and ammunition were running out; few of the men had greatcoats; and a cold night with a steady drizzle of rain was adding the last drop to a brimming cup of misery.

But though the 29th Division was badly bent, it was to prove that night, as on countless future occasions, that its spirit could not be broken. By daybreak next morning the worst gaps in the line had been filled, and units sorted out. The next two days were spent in strengthening the position; and on the night of the 1st/2nd May, though still without reinforcements, the attenuated division was able to defeat a determined night attack by at least sixteen battalions.

OPERATIONS AT ANZAC

26 Apr. The heavy casualties suffered by the Australians and New Zealanders on the 25th April, the strength of the Turks now opposed to them, and the extraordinary difficulties of the Anzac country, all tended to show on the 26th April that no further advance inland could be made in the northern zone till General Birdwood was reinforced. For the moment, therefore, the principal task allotted to the Anzac corps by Sir Ian Hamilton was to reorganize its units and make its position impregnable. But at the same time, in order to assist the main operations in the south, it was to do all in its power to attract as many Turks as possible to its own front. This decision relieved the Australian and New Zealand troops of the strain of an immediate resumption of the offensive. Nevertheless, in other ways they were called upon for exertions as severe as those of the 29th Division, and for many days after the landing there was little rest for anybody.

27 Apr. At daybreak on the 27th the situation on the left and left centre of the corps front—on Russell's Top and at the head of Monash Gully—was still confused and gravely insecure. Wide gaps still existed between the troops at the head of

Map 3. Walker's Ridge and those on Pope's Hill, and between Pope's Hill and Quinn's Post. The northern half of Russell's Top was alive with Turkish snipers, who were firing straight into the backs of the troops at Pope's and on Second Ridge,[1] and a strong party of Turks had entrenched themselves near the head of Walker's Ridge, where the remnants of the 2nd Australian Battalion, under Lieut.-Colonel Braund, were holding on with praiseworthy tenacity.

About 8 A.M. Colonel Braund organized an attack on this trench, and it was captured by a bayonet charge. But more Turks kept filtering over the Nek; the trench was retaken by the enemy; and, though it was again captured by Braund's troops, bitter fighting continued in its neighbourhood. Towards midday the 2nd Battalion was reinforced by two companies of the Wellington Battalion. With this New Zealand reinforcement the Australians succeeded in retaining most of the ground gained, and by the evening of the 27th touch with Pope's Hill was at last established.

On Second Ridge, meanwhile, the Australian posts and trenches were subjected to a good deal of shrapnel fire,[2] and there were several disconnected attacks by Turkish infantry on various parts of the line. Though it was not realized at the time,[3] these half-hearted and ill-synchronized attacks represented an attempt by Mustafa Kemal to launch a simultaneous assault on all sections of the position.[4]

Rightly appreciating that Sir Ian Hamilton was making his main attack in the Krithia sector, the Turkish higher command

---

[1] Colonel H. N. MacLaurin, commanding 1st Brigade, and his brigade-major were both killed on MacLaurin's Hill by these snipers on 27th April.

[2] According to Turkish information there were now five mountain batteries opposite the Anzac front.

[3] The Anzac corps war diary for 27th April states: "The day was devoted chiefly to reorganization".

[4] The following is a translation of Mustafa Kemal's order, captured a few days later:

"Of the forces which the enemy brought in his ships only a remnant is "left. I presume he intends to bring others. Therefore we must drive "those now in front of us into the sea. . . . There is no need to scheme "much to make the enemy run. I do not expect that any of us would not "rather die than repeat the shameful story of the Balkan War. But if there "are such men among us, we should at once lay hands upon them, and set "them up in line to be shot. In order to complete the victory we have "already gained two new regiments have been placed under my orders. "The enemy cannot have received similar reinforcements. Therefore, "with the help of God, I intend to attack the enemy to-morrow. Prepara-"tions should be made as follows. Our artillery should keep up a continuous "fire on the fronts which I personally indicated to batteries, and should "cover the infantry advance and silence the enemy's machine guns. The "commanders of sectors should come to me at 2 P.M. to take further "instructions."

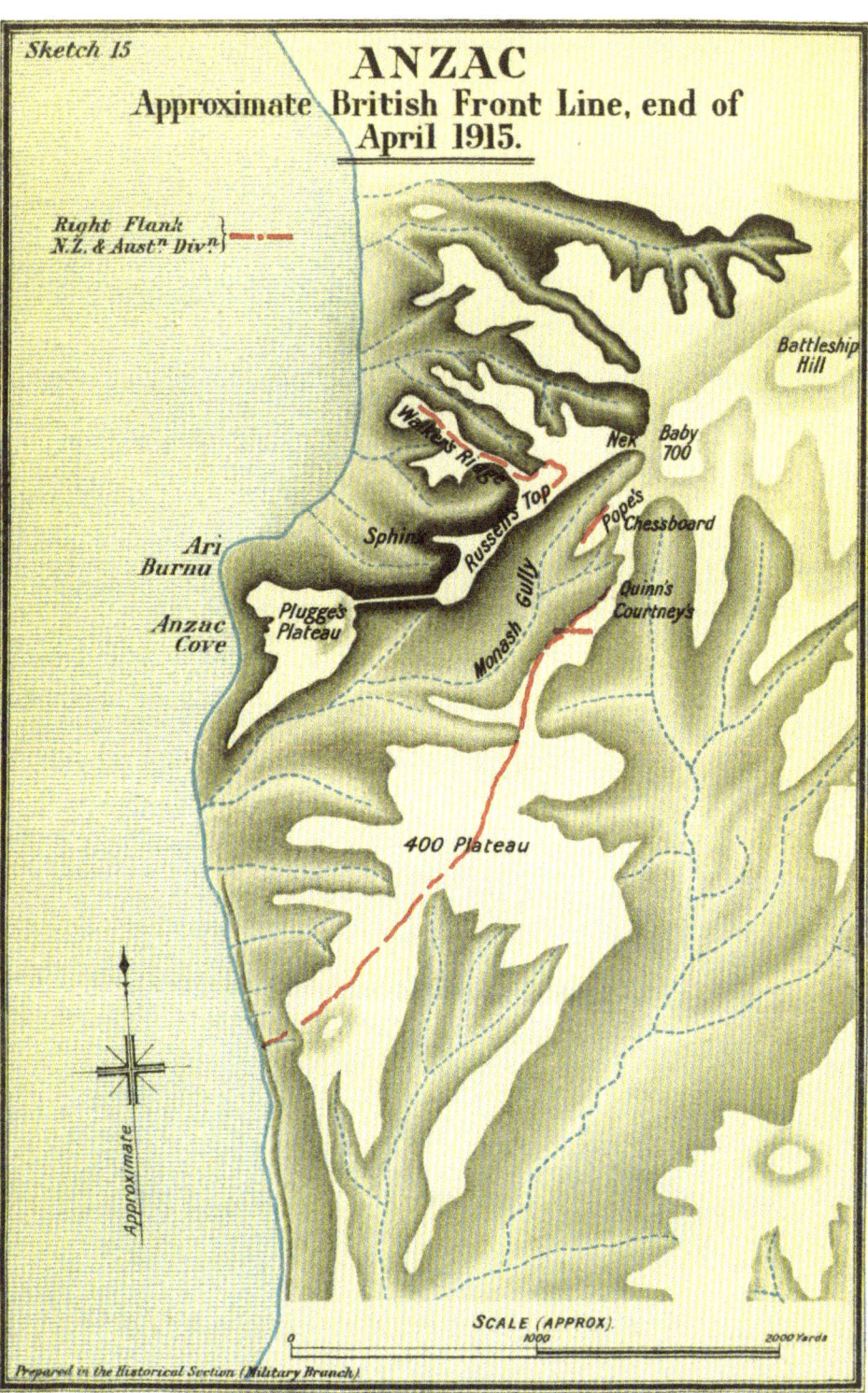

had on the 26th April hurried the first troops arriving from Bulair to that quarter, but on the evening of the 26th Kemal was reinforced with two regiments and some additional mountain batteries. These units were moved forward during the night, and it was arranged that they and the *72nd* (Arab) *Regiment*, which had not yet been actively engaged, should lead a general attack next day on General Birdwood's corps. The total number of troops to take part in this attack amounted to sixteen battalions.[1] But, fortunately for the Anzac troops, the ground was as trying and confusing to the newly arrived Turks as to themselves. Units lost their way and were late in reaching their destinations; their morale was badly shaken by the warships' searching fire; and further delay was caused by the demoralized condition of the troops already in the line. As a result, the general assault dwindled down to a number of weak and disconnected attacks, all of which were crushed by rifle and machine-gun fire before the attacking infantry arrived within assaulting distance. Only on the extreme left, where, early in the afternoon, large numbers of Turks were seen pouring over Battleship Hill towards the Nek, did the situation ever seem dangerous, and this attack was immediately crushed by the watchful guns of the fleet. The advancing troops offered an unrivalled target to the navy; and in a few moments they were retiring in confusion.[2]

The Anzac front was now divided into four sectors, the two on the left being allotted to General Godley's division, and the two on the right to General Bridges. The New Zealand Brigade (Br.-General Walker) was to hold Walker's Ridge to its summit on Russell's Top. Thence across the head of Monash Gully to Courtney's on Second Ridge, the line was allotted to the 4th Australian Brigade under Colonel Monash. From Courtney's to a point midway across 400 Plateau, was assigned to the 1st and 3rd Australian Brigades, temporarily commanded by Colonel R. H. Owen; while the southern sector to the sea was given to the 2nd Australian Brigade under Colonel M'Cay.

Several days were to elapse before the many widely scattered portions of all units could be collected in their right sectors. But on the morning of the 28th it was at last possible to relieve Lieut.-Colonel Braund and the remnants of the 2nd Australian

28 Apr.

---

[1] Apparently eighteen battalions were now in the northern sector.
[2] This incident, plainly visible to the Turks in other portions of the line, had a marked effect. For over three months, the Turks made no further attempt at Anzac to attack by daylight over ground that was in direct view of the supporting ships.

Battalion on Russell's Top, where for three days and three nights, at a cost of 450 casualties, their defence of this vital position had been of immense service to the corps. Colonel Braund's conduct of the defence during this period, his quick grasp of the situation, his fine leadership, and his great personal courage were beyond praise, and had marked him out for rapid promotion. But by cruel mischance, a few nights later, this exceptional officer was accidentally killed. Walking back to his battalion bivouac, he failed to hear a sentry's challenge, and the unfortunate sentry shot him.

After their failure on the 27th April the Turks in the northern theatre were too disorganized to carry out another big attack. Every available reserve was urgently needed in the south, and Essad Pasha, who had assumed command of the northern battle, was for several days to get no reinforcements.[1] Nevertheless, the eighteen Turkish battalions on the Anzac front continued to fight stubbornly, and General Birdwood's depleted units had all they could do to retain their foothold on the ground already won. Every unit in the corps had by this time lost at least a quarter of its effectives, and the casualties suffered on the first day of the landing had already been nearly doubled. For three days and nights, except where the steepness of the hill-sides offered some precarious cover, every corner of the Anzac position had been swept by a storm of bullets, and the supports and reserves, the stretcher-bearers and ration parties, had often suffered as heavily as the men in front line. The beach, too, had been subjected to heavy bursts of artillery fire, probably directed from observation posts at Gaba Tepe and Nibrunesi Point; and the number of wounded, already in excess of expectations, had outstripped the arrangements for their care.

28-30 Apr. During the 28th and 29th April, owing to the exhaustion of some of Birdwood's troops, Sir Ian Hamilton sent four battalions of the Royal Naval Division to Anzac to take over a portion of the line.[2] The arrival of these battalions gave a much-needed rest to some of the Australian and New Zealand units, and by the end of the month the defensive organization of the Anzac position was nearly complete. But

---

[1] Two more Turkish regiments were attached to the northern sector during the night 27th/28th, but were withdrawn next morning to the Krithia front.

[2] The Portsmouth, Chatham, and Deal Battalions, R.M.L.I., and the Nelson Battalion. Two days after the arrival of his battalion at Anzac, Lance-Corporal W. R. Parker, Portsmouth Battalion, was awarded the V.C. for conspicuous gallantry in carrying water, ammunition, and medical stores to an isolated trench on 400 Plateau.

the left flank, overlooked at point-blank range by the high ground at the head of Monash Gully, was still insecure, and it was decided that an early effort must be made to incorporate Baby 700 in the line. The Turks, however, were digging hard. In a few days General Birdwood's troops were to find themselves hemmed in by a broad girdle of trenches; and for the rest of the campaign Baby 700 defied every attempt at capture.

The minute scrap of territory which the Anzac corps had captured, and which was to be its home for the next three months, had a total length of rather less than $1\frac{1}{2}$ miles. Its greatest depth from the front line to the sea-coast was only 1,000 yards. Its perimeter was open to almost every objection as a position for defence. Its sea-base, only a thousand yards from the trenches, was the open beach, exposed to north-west and south-west winds. Its anchorage was under direct hostile observation from the coast on either flank. These details, and a moment's consideration of all they imply, will give some idea of the difficulties which faced the Anzac corps. But only those who visit the actual ground, and look at the incredible position from the old Turkish front line can fully appreciate the spirit of the troops who held it.

The moral and material advantages enjoyed by the Turks were those of a man looking down from the top of a cliff at his adversary clinging to a precarious ledge below him. The Turks had all the country in rear to rest in, or to fall back on if forced to retire. The invaders had nothing behind them but the open beach and the sea. That the Australian and New Zealand troops never relinquished their grasp; that they made this apparently hopeless position impregnable; that after waiting three months for reinforcements they attacked, and attacked again, and very nearly won, is a story that will live for ever.

CHAPTER XVII

REINFORCEMENTS

(Maps 2, 1)

30 Apr. THE position on the peninsula at the end of April, with the invading force held up everywhere for lack of fresh troops, is a convenient point from which to examine the results of the first four days' fighting, and the steps being taken, both at home and on the spot, for the further prosecution of the campaign.

A landing on a hostile beach has always been counted as one of the most arduous operations of war, and one that can hope for success only as the result of surprise or of overwhelming numerical superiority. But in the present instance the benefits of surprise had been renounced, and Sir Ian Hamilton had been sent to capture the peninsula with a force scarcely equal in numbers to the defending garrison. For lack of sufficient strength he had been unable either to retain his hold on Kum Kale or seriously to deceive the Turkish command by his threats at Bulair and Besika Bay. Obliged to concentrate almost his whole force from the outset where his main blows were to be struck, he now found himself held up by superior numbers, with his own men exhausted, and with no available reserves to renew the battle.

Throughout the days of preparation Sir Ian Hamilton had recognized that Time would be a vitally important factor. Though the advantages of strategical surprise had been denied him, Britain's command of the sea would give him the chance of effecting a tactical surprise, and he had been able to count on a brief period at the beginning of the campaign during which he could develop superior force against the enemy's necessarily scattered detachments. But in the five weeks that elapsed between the naval attack on the 18th March and the military landing on the 25th April the advantage of tactical surprise was counterbalanced by a reorganization of the defending garrison, whereby Turkish reinforcements could be hurried to any threatened point almost more quickly than the British reserves could disembark.

To gain the greatest possible advantages from tactical surprise the British aim on the 25th April was to land simultaneously the largest number of men that the size of the beaches and the numbers of small craft would allow. At four out of the five selected landing places, the beaches were made good, and it is now known that the day's operations came far nearer to complete success than anyone at the time realized. But the opportunities created by the flank landings were not made use of; the losses at the main beaches, the difficulties of the Anzac country, and the intense physical strain suffered by all ranks, led to unexpected delays; and the employment of 37 out of his 53 battalions in the initial effort left the British commander too small a reserve to overcome the increasing Turkish resistance.

For four days the issue remained uncertain, but by the evening of the 28th April the British plan had collapsed. With a little rest and with the help of the few fresh units still available, it might be possible to free the beaches from shell fire, perhaps even to capture Achi Baba. But Kilid Bahr plateau and the Map 2. Narrows were, in existing circumstances, definitely out of reach, and unless strong reinforcements could soon arrive on the scene, the chances of final success would be in jeopardy.

Yet, apart from one brigade of Indian infantry, there was no hope of any immediate addition to the Allied strength. Up to the 28th April not even a reinforcing draft had been despatched from England to replace the wastage in battle.[1]

Meanwhile the Turkish forces on the peninsula were accumulating, and their defences gaining in strength, and every day's delay in resuming the advance was increasing the numbers required by the Allies to win a decisive victory. What a single division could do to-day might need a corps to-morrow, and within a month the army might find itself faced by a system of trenches as formidable as those in France which it had travelled 3,000 miles to outflank.

In view of the possibility that the help of one fresh division, or perhaps even another fresh brigade, at Helles on the 28th April might have turned the scale in favour of the Allies, it can be no matter for surprise if the wisdom of landing General Birdwood's corps at Anzac on the 25th April is often searchingly criticized. To the military student the advantages which might

[1] Sir Ian Hamilton wired to the War Office on 3rd April stressing the urgency of the despatch of his " first reinforcements ", *i.e.* the 10 per cent drafts of officers and men which, according to usual custom, should have accompanied units overseas to replace the first wastage in battle. Eventually 1 officer and 46 men for each of the Regular battalions of the 29th Division (approximately a 5 per cent draft) sailed from England on 30th April.

have accrued from keeping that corps in reserve to reinforce the 29th Division at Helles, or alternatively, the advantages which might have been gained by landing the 29th Division beside the Australians and New Zealanders on the 25th April and neglecting the southern beaches, will always be an interesting study. But in weighing the various solutions of the problem which confronted Sir Ian Hamilton before the landing, it must be remembered that the Australians and New Zealanders at Anzac prevented a very large number of Turks from reinforcing the Krithia front during the first four critical days. On the 27th April General Birdwood's twenty battalions were detaining eighteen battalions of Turks, and on the evening of that day their presence at Anzac delayed the southward march of an additional six battalions for at least twelve hours. As a result, the seventeen British and French battalions engaged in the First Battle of Krithia were opposed by not more than eleven battalions of the enemy.

A consideration of these figures, when examined in the light of what actually occurred, will tend to show that whatever plan of attack had been decided on by Sir Ian Hamilton, the strength of his force was not in fact sufficient for its allotted task.

The reasons which dictated the original strength of the Expeditionary Force have been discussed on a previous page.[1] The Gallipoli operations were at the outset regarded as an entirely subsidiary enterprise, and the number of troops allotted to it was only such as could be spared from other theatres of war. Even the decision that "the Dardanelles must be forced " no matter what the cost" was registered without any Staff appreciation as to whether the resources of the Empire could meet this new commitment in addition to prosecuting a spring offensive in France.

The effects of this absence of a preliminary study of the problem asserted themselves from the outset of the Gallipoli campaign. The landings on the peninsula were fated to clash with the German introduction of poison gas at the Second Battle of Ypres. Had there been no immediate intention of assuming the offensive in France, Sir John French would have had more than enough men to ensure the safety of his whole line. But in the circumstances of the case as he knew it, he was, at an anxious moment, naturally opposed to the deflection of any more troops from France for what was still looked upon as a subsidiary effort in the Eastern Mediterranean.

The point of view of Sir John French at that time and of

---

[1] See page 103.

current public opinion, was reflected in a leading article in *The Times* newspaper published on the 27th April:

> The news that the fierce battle in Flanders which began on Thursday [22nd April] is being continued with unabated fury is coupled this morning with the news that the Allied troops have landed in Gallipoli. But the novel interests of that enterprise cannot be allowed to distract us from what is, and will remain, the decisive theatre of operations. Our first thoughts must be for the bent but unbroken line of battle in the West.

For the moment the warning was unnecessary. There was as yet no thought of sending large reinforcements to the East. Sir Ian Hamilton's need had not yet been realized. But when it is remembered that nearly every officer whose opinion counted was now on the Western front, and that there was scarcely an influential person in England who had not some friend or relation fighting in Sir John French's army, it is easy to gauge the tremendous opposition that was likely to be roused by any attempt to strengthen the Mediterranean force at the expense of the B.E.F. in France. Far different was the view expressed by the German Admiral von Tirpitz about this time. "The forcing of the Dardanelles", he wrote on the 21st March, "would be a severe blow to us. . . . We "have no trumps left." Nor did the passage of time alter his opinion. Four months later he was writing: "The situation "is obviously very critical. Should the Dardanelles fall, the "world war has been decided against us."[1]

Even in Gallipoli there was some delay in calling for reinforcements. Sir Ian Hamilton's diffidence about asking for additional help was not confined to the days before the landing, and it was only when a detailed account of the army's difficulties reached the Admiralty from Admiral de Robeck on the 27th April and was taken across to the War Office by Mr. Churchill and Lord Fisher, that Lord Kitchener began to realize the need for more men. At once (2.20 P.M.) he telegraphed to Hamilton: "If you want more troops from Egypt Maxwell will give you "any support from Egyptian garrison you may require", and a quarter of an hour later, on returning to the Admiralty, Mr. Churchill wired to Admiral de Robeck:

> Lord Kitchener has telegraphed to General Hamilton reminding him[2] that he is free to draw on Egypt for more troops if needed.

---

[1] "Erinnerungen," pp. 456 and 491.
[2] The words "reminding him" are of importance. Neither Mr. Churchill nor Lord Kitchener knew that Sir Ian Hamilton had never seen Lord Kitchener's telegram of 6th April to General Maxwell. See page 124.

First Sea Lord and I both think that as a matter of precaution it will be well to have more at hand. We are accordingly concentrating additional transports for 20,000 at Alexandria.

But it was from the French admiral at the Dardanelles that Lord Kitchener first learnt of the desperate need for help. On the evening of the 26th, while the British Commander-in-Chief was asking only for small-arm ammunition, Admiral Guépratte sent the following cable to his superior at Malta, whence it was repeated next day to London:

All goes well, but in order to ensure continued success it is of utmost importance to reinforce immediately the Expeditionary Force which is insufficient for such extensive operations.

On receipt of this definite message on the 28th April Lord Kitchener at once telegraphed to Sir John Maxwell at Cairo:

I see the French admiral considers that reinforcements are needed for the forces landed on the Gallipoli peninsula. Hamilton has not made any mention of this to me; nevertheless I told him yesterday that if he wants more troops from Egypt you will give him any support from the Egyptian garrison he may require . . . I hope all your troops are being kept quite ready to embark, and I would suggest that you should send the Territorial division [1] if Hamilton wants them. I presume you are keeping in close touch with Hamilton on such matters. Please ask him now if you should send reinforcements, and let me know the result.

Not until the night of the 27th did Sir Ian Hamilton himself make even a conditional request for more men:

Thanks to the weather and wonderfully fine spirit of our troops all continues to go well . . . 2,500 Australian and New Zealand wounded left for Alexandria to-day. Still no details of 29th Division casualties, but fear they cannot be less than those of Anzac corps . . . May I have a call on 42nd East Lancs. Territorial Division in case I should need them? You may be sure I shall not call up a man unless I really need him.

This message crossed Lord Kitchener's telegram of the same afternoon, and when it arrived Lord Kitchener had already seen the more definite report from Admiral Guépratte and had sent off his warning cable to Sir John Maxwell. He now sent a second message to Sir John Maxwell, instructing him to embark the 42nd Division at once. To Sir Ian Hamilton he replied laconically: "I feel sure you had better have the

---

[1] This was the 42nd (East Lancashire) Division, T.F., which had been in Egypt since September 1914.

"42nd Division, and I have instructed Maxwell to embark
"them."

Two days later, the French Government decided to send another division to Gallipoli, and the 156th Division (General Bailloud) was detailed for service under the title of the 2nd Division of the Corps Expéditionnaire d'Orient.[1] On the next day (30th April) General d'Amade ordered two 14-cm. guns of the French auxiliary cruiser *Provence* to be landed at Sedd el Bahr for counter-battery work against the enemy artillery on the Asiatic shore, which was already becoming troublesome.

Whether or not Sir Ian Hamilton could have succeeded in getting the 42nd Division allotted to his force in the early days of April is problematical. Sir John Maxwell had been told to give him any troops or individual officers from the Egyptian garrison that he could spare; but it may well be that, in view of the possibility of another attack on the Suez Canal, the G.O.C. Egypt would at that time have resisted any attempt to deprive him of his only British division. The question of sea transport would also have offered a difficulty. Nevertheless, from the moment of receiving Lord Kitchener's telegram on the 28th April Sir John Maxwell did all in his power to assist, and was ready to pare his own garrison to the bone to reinforce the Dardanelles. On the 30th April he sent off large reinforcing drafts for General Birdwood's corps; the next day he was collecting all available individual officers to replace casualties in the 29th Division; and on the 3rd May he suggested that the Australian Light Horse and the New Zealand Mounted Rifles should, in accordance with their own request, be sent to the peninsula as infantry. Lord Kitchener was at first surprised that Maxwell should be prepared to accept this risk. But Maxwell rightly replied that in his opinion the greatest of all risks was that of a failure in Gallipoli. "Any failure on the part "of Hamilton", he added, "would bring about a critical "situation all over the Moslem world, and I think we should "take all legitimate risks to avoid this."

Working with the utmost despatch, and making use of the transports which had just brought the 2nd Mounted Division from England, as well as some of the vessels that had arrived with wounded from Gallipoli,[2] Sir John Maxwell's Staff suc-

[1] This division, the first units of which began to leave Marseilles on 2nd May, had the same composition as the 1st Division, except that it had no battalion of the Foreign Legion, and no mountain artillery, and that one of its Colonial regiments had two European battalions instead of one.

[2] Some of the transports from Gallipoli had landed their wounded only a few hours before the Territorials went on board, and the blood-stained stretchers and clothing which still littered their holds were a stern reminder to the young troops of the realities of war.

ceeded in embarking the first brigade of the 42nd Division on the 1st May, and the whole division had sailed by the morning of the 5th. But it was not until the morning of the 6th May that the leading brigade landed on the peninsula, and the moment when one extra division had any chance of influencing the situation had by that time disappeared.

From the 27th April the growth of the Turkish forces in the southern half of the peninsula was rapid and continuous. On the night before the landing, while Sir Ian Hamilton was approaching the peninsula with 53 battalions,[1] the Dardanelles garrison consisted of 57 battalions, of which twenty-one were at the northern end of the peninsula, nineteen on the Asiatic side of the Straits, and only seventeen between Suvla and Sedd el Bahr. By the evening of the 27th the neighbourhood of Bulair had been denuded of troops, and the transfer of the Asiatic garrison to the European shore was already in full swing. In addition, the *15th* and *16th Divisions* were being hurried by sea from Constantinople, and by the 30th all their eighteen battalions had reached the peninsula.

By the 30th April, therefore, while Sir Ian Hamilton had still only 53 battalions available, with one Indian brigade (four battalions) on the point of arriving, Liman's strength had increased to 75 battalions, of which not more than twenty-eight had yet been engaged. Other energetic measures had also been taken to grapple with the situation. Despite the fear of Bulgaria joining the Entente, Adrianople was being denuded of guns, and some of its garrison was being sent to the peninsula. The *12th Division* at Smyrna had been ordered to march to Chanak, where its leading battalions were due on the 5th May, and throughout the country a general mobilization had been ordered of all categories hitherto excused military service.

Map 1.

On the 29th April Marshal Liman von Sanders divided the Turkish forces in the Dardanelles into two main groups. The northern group, opposed to the Anzac corps, he placed under Essad Pasha, commanding the *III. Corps*, while the southern, or Sedd el Bahr group was allotted to Colonel von Sodenstern, a German officer who had lately been in command of the Turkish *5th Division*. Captain Mühlmann, one of Liman's German orderly officers, was appointed Chief Staff

---

[1] British, French, and Turkish divisions on the peninsula differed so materially in size and composition, and all were so deficient of the normal complement of divisional artillery that in any comparison of the strengths of the opponents the best unit of measurement is the infantry battalion. At the outset of the campaign all the battalions engaged appear to have consisted of between 800 and 900 rifles.

Officer of the southern group, and its front was divided into two sectors, divided by the Krithia road. The Turkish *9th Division* was on the northern side of the road, the *7th Division* on the southern side. Turkish General Headquarters was established near Mal Tepe, about a mile from Kilia Liman.

It will be seen, therefore, that though by the end of April Sir Ian Hamilton had been promised all the reinforcements he had asked for, this number was already inadequate for the task in hand. One Indian infantry brigade was on the point of arriving; a British Territorial division would follow between the 6th and 9th May; and another French division and two Australian and New Zealand dismounted brigades a few days later. Till some of these new formations arrived he could do little but remain on the defensive, resting his battered battalions, consolidating the ground already won, beating back hostile attacks, and seizing every opportunity for local offensive action to improve his existing positions.

The enforced delay was to have disastrous consequences and to prove fatal to the Gallipoli campaign. But the fog of war hung thickly over the peninsula. On the night of the 29th/30th April Sir Ian Hamilton telegraphed to Lord Kitchener that he hoped to move forward again in a couple of days when the Indian brigade had landed; and in his anxiety to spare the overburdened War Secretary by not anticipating troubles which might never arise, none of his messages at this time gave serious cause for uneasiness.

CHAPTER XVIII

OPERATIONS 1ST–5TH MAY

BRITISH SUBMARINES IN THE MARMARA

(Maps 2, 3 ; Sketches 7, 16, 17, 18)

Apr./ May. THROUGHOUT these anxious days British and Australian submarines were straining every nerve to help the army by cutting the Marmara communications,[1] and though too late to interrupt the first flow of enemy reinforcements, they achieved by the middle of May an astonishing measure of success. It would be difficult to exaggerate the extreme hazards which attached Map 2. to this service, including a double journey through the closely guarded Narrows, with their ten rows of mines, their watchful batteries, and their submarine defences and nets. The imagination of all ranks of the Expeditionary Force was stirred by the risks involved, and the gallant exploits of the submarines won the army's admiration.

The first successful attempt to get through was made by the Australian *AE2* on the 25th April; but after sinking a Turkish gunboat above Nagara, she was herself destroyed by a torpedo boat a few days later. Meanwhile *E14* (Lt.-Commander E. C. Boyle) had also passed the Narrows on the 27th April. Handled with consummate skill by her commander this vessel remained in the Marmara for 22 days, in the course of which she sank two gunboats and two large transports heading for the Dardanelles. May. Her activity, and that of the *E11*[2] who followed her on the 18th May, was of immense value to the Expeditionary Force, and towards the end of the month the Turkish sea-communications

---

[1] See page 142.
[2] The exploits of *E11* (Lt.-Commander M. E. Nasmith) were even more remarkable than those of *E14*. On her first trip, during 19 days spent in the Marmara, she sank one large gunboat, three transports, and four other large vessels. She caused a panic at Constantinople by suddenly appearing off the capital and sinking a transport lying alongside the arsenal quay. For their gallant services Commanders Nasmith and Boyle were both awarded the V.C.

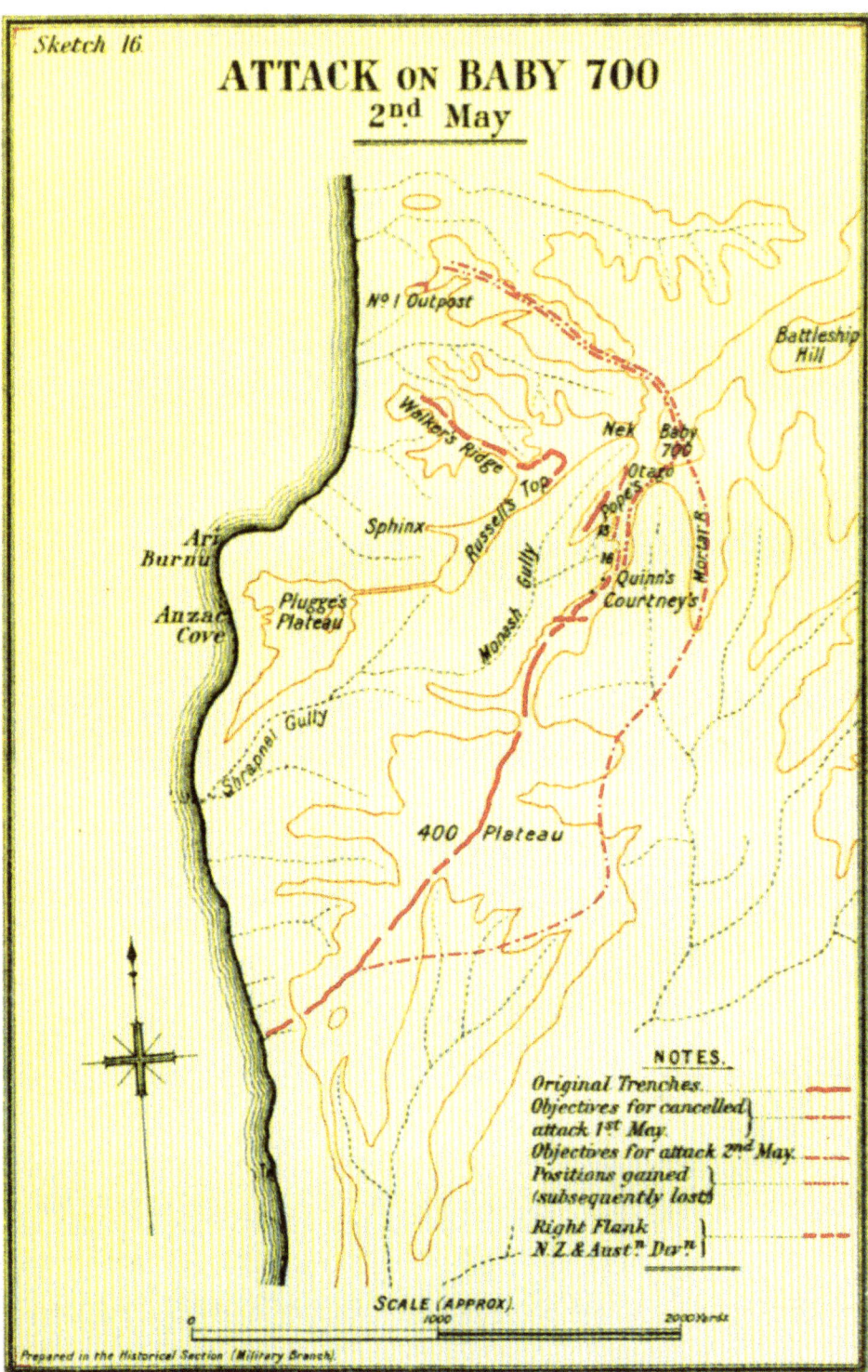

THE ATTACK ON BABY 700, 2ND MAY

had been completely interrupted. After that date, thanks to the continued activity of the submarine service, no more reinforcements were sent from Constantinople by sea, and though the enemy continued to despatch food and stores in small vessels which hugged the coast and moved only at night, all Turkish writers agree that the maintenance of their army on the peninsula remained throughout the campaign an acutely anxious problem.[1] After the middle of May practically the whole of the stores and ammunition, and all the reinforcing troops, were sent by the land route and it was some time before the necessary bullock and buffalo transport could be collected for this service. Turkish reports state that in consequence of this shortage the *Fifth Army* at one period in June had only 160 rounds of rifle ammunition per man left.

THE ATTACK ON BABY 700, 2ND MAY

One crowning mercy enjoyed by the Expeditionary Force in the early days of the campaign was the perfect spring weather. Later in the year the climate was to prove a remorseless enemy to the troops. But at the beginning of May climatic conditions were almost ideal for campaigning, and an unbroken series of brilliant days went far to hearten the troops in their otherwise depressing surroundings. This circumstance must not be overlooked when studying the events of April and May. Ideal weather was one of the two main factors—the other being the Turkish shortage of gun ammunition—which enabled the invaders to maintain their precarious foothold on the peninsula till further help could reach them.

At Anzac the chief problem facing General Birdwood's

---

[1] Between 25th April and the end of the year the passage of the Straits by submarine was made 27 times, and submarines remained in the Marmara for periods varying from 19 to 47 consecutive days. Almost all of them had narrow escapes of being destroyed at the Nagara net, and on many occasions by gun fire. Yet the total British losses were only four. In addition the French submarine *Turquoise*, the only French submarine that succeeded in making the passage, was captured by the Turks, after her periscope had been struck by shore gun-fire, on 30th October. She had then been 10 days in the Marmara.

Exclusive of vessels sunk by E20 (herself destroyed by a German submarine after 20 days in the Marmara) and the *Turquoise*, the Turkish losses from submarines during the campaign were:

Battleships	1
Destroyers	1
Gunboats	5
Transports	11
Steamers	44
Sailing Vessels	148

corps at the beginning of May was the improvement of the position at the head of Monash Gully, where the Turks on Baby 700 still overlooked the greater part of that valley, as well as the trenches on Russell's Top and MacLaurin's Hill. For a day or two, according to the war diary of General Godley's division, the enemy's artillery fire practically ceased; and the erroneous impression prevailed that the majority of the Turks had been withdrawn to oppose the 29th Division, so that the Anzac corps was being actively contained by only a small force. In those circumstances, orders were issued by the corps for an operation to be carried out on the evening of the 1st May with the object of capturing Baby 700 and of incorporating in the eastern front of the Anzac position the whole of Mortar Ridge and 400 Plateau. Later in the day these divergent objectives were considered too ambitious, and that part of the operation affecting Mortar Ridge and 400 Plateau was cancelled. It was decided to postpone the attack till the evening of the 2nd May, and to confine it to an attempt on Baby 700 by three battalions of General Godley's division.

The general plan was as follows:

At 7 P.M. on the 2nd May Baby 700 was to be bombarded by naval and military guns for a quarter of an hour. At 7.15 P.M. the fire was to lift to Battleship Hill and Chunuk Bair, and the infantry to advance to the assault, the Otago Battalion (Lt.-Col. A. Moore) of the New Zealand Brigade[1] moving by the western fork of Monash Gully and the 16th and 13th Battalions of Colonel J. Monash's 4th Australian Brigade by the eastern fork. The 16th Battalion (Lt.-Col. H. Pope) was to file up the narrow valley bed till the whole battalion was north of the foot of Quinn's Post, and was then to turn right-handed, climb the steep, scrub-covered hill-side, and seize and hold the crest from Quinn's Post to the northern end of Second Ridge. The 13th Battalion (Col. G. J. Burnage), following behind the 16th, was to continue the line from the head of Second Ridge to the summit of Baby 700. The Otago Battalion was to turn right-handed at the head of the western fork, and carry out the attack with its right flank directed on the summit of Baby 700, where it would join up with the left of the 13th Battalion, and its left on the seaward slopes of the hill. As soon as it had reached its objective, one company of the Canterbury Battalion from Walker's Ridge was to move forward across the Nek, and continue the line to the seashore near No. 1 Outpost. The

---

[1] Colonel Johnston had now resumed command of the New Zealand Brigade, and Br.-Gen. Walker had been transferred to the 1st Australian Brigade.

Nelson Battalion (Royal Naval Division) was to be at Colonel Johnston's disposal as a support for the operation, and the Portsmouth and Chatham R.M.L.I. battalions were subsequently sent to reinforce the 4th Australian Brigade.

This carefully prepared but difficult scheme was unsuccessful, and its failure was due partly to the difficulties of the ground, partly to the troops' inexperience of night operations, and partly to the Otago Battalion being 1½ hours late at the rendezvous in Monash Gully. On the afternoon of the 2nd the battalion was near the foot of Walker's Ridge. From this point to the rendezvous, *via* Russell's Top, was only a few hundred yards, but the Top was so exposed that Colonel Moore decided to move round *via* Anzac Cove and Shrapnel Gully, a distance of more than two miles. Unfortunately this route was very congested with traffic. Interminable delays occurred, and instead of reaching the rendezvous before seven o'clock the battalion did not arrive till 8.30 P.M.

The bombardment opened at 7 P.M., and with the 16th and 13th Battalions moving off punctually, a considerable advance was made on the right flank. But as soon as these troops reached the crest of Second Ridge they came under a heavy fire from their flank and rear, which led to some confusion. On the left the Otago Battalion eventually started its attack about 8.45 P.M.; but by this time the Turks were well prepared, and the New Zealand troops could do no more than occupy a line very slightly to the north of the existing position on Pope's Hill. Here they tried to entrench, but their right was out of touch with the left of the 13th, and their left, completely in the air, was badly enfiladed from the Nek.

Meanwhile on Walker's Ridge it was reported that the Otago Battalion had reached its objective, and a company of the Canterbury Battalion was pushed forward to support it *via* the Nek. Meeting with strenuous opposition this party was forced to retire, and after a second attempt had shared a similar fate, it was decided to send the rest of the battalion across Russell's Top into Monash Gully, with the object of reinforcing the Otago *via* the western fork of the gully. So difficult was the country that few of the battalion found their way by this route, but eventually a small party came up on the left of the Otago and continued the line of that battalion in the direction of the Nek. At the same time Colonel Monash sent forward a party of the 15th Battalion to fill the gap between the right of the Otago and the 13th.

About 1.30 A.M., believing that all was going well, General Godley placed the Portsmouth and Chatham Battalions R.M.L.I.

at Colonel Monash's disposal to confirm the success; but these two battalions, which were bivouacking in Shrapnel Gully, did not reach the foot of Pope's Hill till day was breaking. Colonel Monash ordered them up the eastern fork of the gully to support the 16th Battalion, but by this time there was a good deal of confusion in that sector. Streams of wounded were pouring down the valley; the marine battalions, strung out in an attenuated line, had lost all cohesion; and though heavy firing could be heard at the top of the scrub-covered heights above them, where the ridge rose like a wall on their right, there was great difficulty in learning the situation. After considerable delay the leading platoons of the Portsmouth Battalion began to climb the steep hill-side, but a moment later a few shells from Australian guns, falling short, dropped on the summit of the ridge. The troops in the neighbourhood came pouring back into the valley, the marines came back with them, and the whole line broke. After a fresh delay another effort was made to reinforce a small body of the 16th which still clung to the ridge, but it was too late. By midday all the gains in this part of the field had been lost.

3 May.

Soon afterwards the troops on the left were also forced to retire. The Otago and Canterbury Battalions fell back into the gully, and a little later the 13th and 15th Battalions were obliged to conform. By the afternoon of the 3rd May not a man remained in advance of the positions held the day before, and the attempt to capture Baby 700 had resulted only in some six hundred casualties. Fortunately the Turks failed to take advantage of the resulting confusion, and there was no counter-attack.[1]

For some time the failure of this attack was not realized at corps headquarters, where early in the morning it had been reported that all was going well. At 9 A.M. on the 3rd General Birdwood visited the Commander-in-Chief on board the *Arcadian*,[2] and reported that the operation had enabled him to straighten out the left of his line, and that he now felt comparatively secure.

RAIDS AT SUVLA AND GABA TEPE

It will be remembered that the accuracy of Turkish gun-fire against the beach and anchorage at Anzac Cove pointed to

[1] The Turks were still very disorganized as a result of their heavy casualties since the landing. The Turkish official account admits the loss at Anzac between 25th April and 4th May of 13,955 men.
[2] Sir Ian Hamilton and his General Staff rejoined the H.Q. transport *Arcadian* on 30th April, and all branches of G.H.Q. were at last in permanent close touch.

RAIDS AT SUVLA AND GABA TEPE 313

the presence of artillery observers at Gaba Tepe and Nibrunesi **Map 3.** Point. In an effort to deal with this menace at the latter point, where strong opposition seemed unlikely, the navy landed a few men from a destroyer on the southern beach of Suvla Bay on the evening of the 30th April. Doubling to the top of Lala **30 Apr.** Baba, these men found and destroyed a telephone wire in a small trench on its summit, but the Turkish piquet escaped.

Two days later this raid was repeated on a somewhat larger scale, and at daybreak on the 2nd May 50 men of the Canterbury **2 May.** Battalion, under Capt. C. Cribb, left for Suvla in the destroyer *Colne* (Commander C. Seymour). This attack met with more success. A landing was effected inside the bay, at the foot of Lala Baba, and the raiders, advancing in three parties, found the trench at the top of the hill occupied by seventeen sleeping Turks. On the alarm being given the Turks fired a few shots, but it was too late to put up an organized resistance, and after two of them had been killed and two had bolted, the remainder of the party, consisting of an officer and twelve men, surrendered. The New Zealanders searched the neighbourhood, discovering a spring of drinking water on the western side of the hill and two other small trenches overlooking the beach to the south of Nibrunesi Point. But the telephone wire destroyed by the sailors had not been repaired, and no instruments were found. About noon the whole party re-embarked without interference from the enemy.

Encouraged by this success General Birdwood now decided to carry out a similar enterprise against Gaba Tepe, though the obvious strength of its wire entanglements made it unlikely that the position could be surprised.

The Gaba Tepe promontory is about a quarter of a mile long by 300 yards wide, and rises, towards its western end, to a height of about 100 feet above the sea. Its extremity is a sheer cliff, but elsewhere the slopes, though generally steep, are not a serious obstacle. On its northern flank the sea is very shallow, and towards the shore end of the promontory the narrow beach is bordered by a sandy cliff about ten to twelve feet high. The whole promontory was girdled by a continuous belt of trenches, somewhat high up, protected by a strong belt of wire.

The raiding of this stronghold was entrusted to a party of two officers and 100 men of the 11th Australian Battalion, commanded by Capt. R. L. Leane.[1] The party was to embark an hour before dawn on the 4th May, and land on the northern

[1] An engineer officer and 10 sappers, with explosives, were also attached to the party.

side of the promontory. Its orders were to raid the fort, destroy any communications found there, and then to return to the Anzac position by way of the beach. To assist the return journey twelve men of the 10th Battalion, under Lieut. C. Rumball, were to leave Anzac Cove an hour before dawn and proceed along the beach to the mouth of Legge Valley, to cut two heavy belts of wire which the Turks had erected across the shore near that point. Both parties were to carry red and yellow flags to enable the supporting ships to locate their positions. Capt. Leane was expressly told that he was free to vary his orders, and to act as he thought best in any emergency that might arise.

Sketch 7.

4 May. At 3.30 A.M. on the 4th May the raiding party was taken out to the destroyer *Colne* in four cutters. The destroyer took the boats in tow and steamed slowly towards Gaba Tepe. To give full naval support to the soldiers, three other destroyers (*Chelmer*, *Usk*, and *Ribble*) accompanied the *Colne*, with the cruisers *Bacchante* and *Dartmouth* a little further astern.

Day was just breaking when, at 500 yards from the beach, the four boats were cast off and headed for the shore, covered by fire from the destroyers. For a few minutes, as on the 25th April, the enemy remained silent. But as soon as the boats got within forty yards of the shore, a brisk fire was opened on them from several points in the trench overlooking the beach. About a dozen men, and both Capt. Leane's subalterns, were hit while still in the boats; the remainder succeeded in reaching the cover of the sandy cliff, though several more were wounded as they doubled across the beach. Three enemy machine guns and a one-inch Q.F. gun had by this time come into action, but all four destroyers were firing at the headland at point-blank range and the Turkish fire was weak and ill-directed. Nevertheless, though the raiders were for the moment under cover, and though the destroyers were protecting them from counter-attack, it was obvious to Capt. Leane that his operation could no longer hope to succeed, and that his only course was to retire as quickly as possible. His first idea was to follow out the original plan of retiring along the beach, and he detailed ten men to creep along under the bank towards the coast to cover the withdrawal of the remainder. At the same time, as the wounded could not be carried so long a distance under fire, he signalled to the *Colne* to send in a boat to re-embark them. Throughout the Gallipoli operations the army never appealed to the navy in vain. At once a picket boat dashed out from the nearest destroyer, towing a cutter. She was met by a heavy fire from the enemy's trenches; but to the great credit

SITUATION AT HELLES, 1ST MAY

of the Turks, as soon as they saw the stretcher-bearers carrying the wounded across the beach, they ceased fire and not another shot was fired till all the wounded were embarked.

Meanwhile four of the small advanced party sent along the shore had joined Rumball's men at the mouth of Legge Valley,[1] wading through the sea to avoid an uncut belt of wire en route. But they had been exposed to heavy fire, and it was clearly inadvisable for the rest of the force to follow them, even though the only alternative was a hazardous re-embarkation. About 6.30 A.M., therefore, Capt. Leane again appealed to the navy for boats. The sailors again rose manfully to the occasion, and five minutes later two picket boats, each towing two cutters, came dashing towards the beach. The boats were rowed to the shore, and covered by a heavy bombardment from every available naval gun, the whole force was taken off with a loss of only three men wounded.[2] The raid had failed, but thanks to the coolness of Capt. Leane and to the gallant support of the navy, disaster had been averted and the enterprise had resulted in a loss of only six killed and eighteen wounded. No subsequent attempt was made to seize or raid the promontory, and for the rest of the campaign, though incessantly shelled by the fleet, it continued to be the main observation station for the enemy artillery at Anzac.

SITUATION AT HELLES, 1ST MAY

At Helles on the 1st May, after two days of comparative inactivity, the British and French troops were again in good fettle. The Turks had been strangely quiet since the battle of the 28th April, and the Allies were now holding a practically continuous line of trenches from a point about a quarter of a mile south of Y Beach to Hill 236 on the Dardanelles side of the peninsula.[3] The losses of the 29th Division were proving to have been somewhat lighter than at first imagined,[4] and the

1 May.

Sketch 17.

---

[1] Lieut. Rumball's men reached this point, and cut a passage through two broad belts of wire, with only one casualty.

[2] It was subsequently discovered that two soldiers had been left behind. Sub-Lieut. L. G. Addington and two seamen returned in the *Usk's* dinghy and brought them off under heavy fire.

[3] The 87th and 86th Brigades each had three battalions in front line and one in support. The 88th, on a narrow front, had one battalion in front and three in support.

[4] The British casualties at Helles and Anzac between 25th-30th April were returned as:

Helles	. .	187 officers, 4,266 other ranks.
Anzac	. .	208 ,, 4,478 ,,

effective strength of the infantry of the division was nearly 7,000 men.[1]

The British front-line trenches were fairly deep, and a support line was being made a few hundred yards in rear. Work on the French trenches was not so far advanced, and in one place, where the French were being supported by British artillery, one shallow ditch manned by Senegalese troops was the only obstacle between the guns and the enemy.

All the infantry of the French division, and practically all the guns of both the 29th Division and the French, were ashore, but most of the transport animals and artillery wagons were still on board ship. The Indian brigade had just arrived from Egypt and was landing at Helles. The Howe and Hood Battalions of the Royal Naval Division had already been landed, and, with the Anson Battalion, were in reserve near Hill 138. Five of the nine battalions of the Naval Division were therefore in the southern theatre, and four at Anzac.[2]

Sir Ian Hamilton was anxious to give the Turks as little time as possible to strengthen their positions, and he intended

---

[1] The strength by brigades on 1st May was:

	86th Brigade			
	Off.	O.R.	Off.	Total. O.R.
2/Royal Fusiliers	11	494		
1/Lancashire Fus.	11	398		
1/R. Muns. Fus.	12	588		
1/R. Dublin Fus.	1	344	35	1,824
	87th Brigade			
2/S. Wales Borderers	17	636		
1/K.O.S.B.	11	523		
1/R. Inniskilling Fus.	17	758		
1/Border Regt.	12	564	57	2,481
	88th Brigade			
2/Hampshire Regt.	11	494		
4/Worcestershire Regt.	12	623		
1/Essex Regt.	15	659		
1/5th R. Scots	19	665	57	2,441
TOTAL			149	6,746

[2] The Royal Naval Division at this time was a division only in name. It comprised nine infantry battalions instead of twelve, and had no artillery.

Portsmouth, Deal, and Chatham Battalions, R.M.L.I., and the Nelson Battalion were at Anzac, and Howe, Hood, Anson, Drake Battalions, and Plymouth Battalion, R.M.L.I., at Helles. This separation of the division, caused by the necessity of relieving some of General Birdwood's tired troops on 28th April, was unfortunate, but the divisional commander (Major-General Paris) had been assured that all nine battalions should be concentrated at Helles at the earliest opportunity.

Sketch 17.

TURKISH NIGHT ATTACK
1st/2nd May

British Red. French Blue. Turks Green.
Heights in metres

Prepared in the Historical Section (Military Branch)
Ordnance Survey. 1928.

THE TURKISH NIGHT ATTACKS 317

to renew his attack on Achi Baba as soon as the landing of the French division and the Indian brigade was complete. On the 1st May, therefore, after spending two days in visiting the Helles and Anzac fronts, he ordered General d'Amade, as a first step, to push his line forward at daybreak next morning to the summit of the spur overlooking Kereves Dere. This preliminary move was not expected to meet with much opposition, for since the action of the 28th the enemy was believed to have kept only a few outpost troops on the western side of that ravine.

Meanwhile the Turks were busily preparing a general attack to be launched against the invaders that very night, hoping by one prodigious effort to make an end of them altogether. But though their artillery had been registering the Allied trenches during the day, this desultory fire had attracted little attention.

THE TURKISH NIGHT ATTACKS, 1ST–3RD MAY

On the 30th April Marshal Liman von Sanders received a peremptory order from Enver Pasha to "drive the invaders " into the sea". This was just what he was trying to do, but the task was beyond him. "The British fleet was sweeping " the southern end of the peninsula from three sides . . ., " and the Turks had only field guns to oppose to this fire, and " a very limited supply of ammunition." [1]

30 Apr.

In these circumstances the only action open to the Turkish marshal was a night attack, and on the evening of the 30th April he ordered Colonel von Sodenstern to assault the Helles positions the following night with every man he could muster.

Sodenstern's available strength amounted to some twenty-one battalions of infantry with 56 guns,[2] and orders for the attack were issued from his headquarters at Kuchuk Mehmed Bey Tepe[3] on the morning of the 1st May. Rifles were not to be loaded and bayonets only were to be used. It was to be a bloody business, and according to a copy of his order, subsequently captured, the German commander did not hesitate to stir up the religious enthusiasm of his troops against the infidel invader. The order ran: "Attack the enemy with the bayonet " and utterly destroy him! We shall not retire one step; for if " we do our religion, our country, and our nation will perish."

---

[1] "Funf Jähre Türkei," p. 93.
[2] Ten batteries field artillery, one battery 12-cm. guns, three batteries 15-cm. howitzers.
[3] Two miles S.E. of Krithia.

Lest any of the "infidels" should escape destruction, special parties of troops were to carry inflammable material to burn their boats on the beach.

1 May. The early hours of the night of the 1st May were quiet, but at 10 P.M. the Turkish artillery opened with a crash. A few minutes afterwards, with cries of "Allah!" dense masses of Turks assaulted the Allied line. The first point in the British front to be attacked was the trench astride Kirte Dere, where one of the assaulting columns had outdistanced the troops on either flank. Here the attack met with momentary success. The Munster and Dublin Fusiliers[1] were driven from a portion of their trench and a number of Turks poured through the gap. But the success was short-lived. A company of the Royal Fusiliers under Captain North Bomford regained the lost trench, and the 1/5th R. Scots, who were in reserve, succeeded in driving back the Turks who had penetrated the British line. Elsewhere on the British front the garrison stood like rocks and mowed down the attacking masses with their fire.

But it was on the French front that the Turks made their principal effort, and there for some time the situation was critical. Heavy fighting continued till daybreak, and about 2 A.M. General Masnou asked the 29th Division for two British battalions to support him. With his own situation still obscure, General Hunter-Weston was at first unable to comply with this demand. But he sent the Howe Battalion along the Krithia road to be ready to assist the French if help was actually required; and a few hours later he sent the Anson Battalion to the French sector where it was at once pressed into service on the extreme right of the line.

On the French left the situation had meanwhile been saved only by the prompt action of some British gunners and a company of the Worcestershire, for here a Senegalese battalion, undergoing its first experience of shell fire, was driven from its trenches by the Turkish bombardment.

The XV Brigade R.H.A. was in rear of this part of the line, and, on the withdrawal of the troops in front, a party of gunners under Major P. Wheatley doubled forward to hold the trench till a company of the Worcestershire arrived to fill the gap.[2]

---

[1] As the Dublins had only one officer left these two battalions had been temporarily amalgamated on 30th April.
[2] Three gunner signallers with a telephone were in a shallow pit behind the front line. After the Senegalese retired two of these men (one of them wounded) came back to call for reinforcements. The third man (Gunner Allpress) stayed behind, alone, to "mind the telephone". He was awarded the D.C.M.

THE TURKISH NIGHT ATTACKS 319

At daylight the Allied line was everywhere intact, and the ground in front was strewn with Turkish dead. One final effort was now made by a party of Turks opposite the French front, but they were met and driven back in a spirited counter-attack by a portion of the Colonial Brigade. Seeing this local success the G.O.C. 87th Brigade at once ordered a counter-attack by portions of the Inniskillings and K.O.S.B., and two companies of these battalions made a successful advance of about 500 yards on the eastern side of Gully Ravine, capturing a Turkish trench and 123 prisoners.

2 May.

Deeming the moment ripe for a general counter-attack General d'Amade now decided to advance to the high ground above Kereves Dere in accordance with the Commander-in-Chief's instructions of the day before. General Hunter-Weston agreed to support him by throwing forward the 29th Division, and about 10 A.M. the British advance began. But there had been no time for co-ordination; there was little artillery support; and except on the extreme right, where the French had made some headway, the attack resulted in no appreciable gain. Here and there on the 29th Division front an advance of a few hundred yards was made, and a further number of Turks were taken prisoner.[1] But the companies who succeeded in getting forward were invariably held up by cross-fire from invisible machine-gun posts; and by 11 A.M. the whole force, except the extreme right of the French, was back in its old positions. This left the two companies of the 87th Brigade, which had advanced earlier in the morning, in a very exposed position, but they were eventually withdrawn in good order to the line of the previous day.

The French losses during the night attack and the subsequent advance amounted to over 2,000 killed and wounded. The British casualties were only a third of that number,[2] but the 29th Division had again lost a disproportionate number of senior officers, including five battalion commanders, four adjutants, and the commander of an artillery brigade. Turkish accounts confess to cruel losses.

The rest of the day passed quietly, but soon after nightfall heavy firing again broke out all along the line and lasted till after midnight. No Turkish infantry attack developed, but the situation on the French front caused some anxiety to General d'Amade, and he again asked for two or three British battalions to be held at his disposal.

[1] Up to 5th May the total number of Turkish prisoners captured on the Peninsula was 531. In addition, the French had captured 450 at Kum Kale.
[2] French losses . . 58 officers, 2,064 other ranks.
British „ . . 37 „ 641 „

320   GALLIPOLI

3 May.   The examination of prisoners had proved that the Turks
       were receiving heavy reinforcements, and by the morning of
       the 3rd May it was more obvious than ever that if the objects
       of the campaign were to be accomplished an early advance was
       imperative. The disorganization and loss resulting from the
       Turkish night attack had caused another short delay, but Sir
       Ian Hamilton decided to make his attack not later than the
       6th, by which time the 125th Brigade of the 42nd Division
       would have arrived. He also determined to bring down some
       troops from Anzac to assist in the southern battle, including
       all the field batteries for which no suitable positions had yet
       been found in that mountainous country. General Birdwood,
       when he visited the G.H.Q. transport *Arcadian* on the morning
       of the 3rd, said that he considered his line comparatively secure,
       and he was thereupon ordered to abstain from offensive action
       for the present, and to hold two of his best infantry brigades
       in readiness for transfer to Helles [1] on the 5th May. The five
       Australian and New Zealand field batteries still on board their
       transports were to be sent to W Beach forthwith.
            But the Turks had not yet given up hope of breaking the
       Allied line. On the night of the 3rd/4th May they launched
       yet another determined attack against the French sector. On
       the left the Senegalese were again unable to hold their trenches
       and withdrew towards Morto Bay. But energetic counter-
       attacks, in which the cooks and orderlies from the reserve lines
       took part, restored this dangerous situation, and at daybreak the
       retreating Turks, caught in the open by the French 75's, were
       literally blown to pieces.[2]

                    PREPARATIONS FOR AN ALLIED ADVANCE

4 May.   The Allied line was again intact, but the repeated Turkish
       attacks had sensibly reduced the fighting value of the French
       division, and soon after 10 A.M. on 4th May a disturbing report
       was received at G.H.Q. from General d'Amade. The French
       commander reported that his situation was serious. He had
       now used up all his reserves; his men had had no sleep for
       several nights; their trenches were under a continuous and
       very intense artillery fire; and their losses, especially amongst

       [1] Cable communication was established between Anzac and G.H.Q.
       (transport *Arcadian*) on 4th May.
       [2] Subsequently it transpired that eight battalions of the Turkish
       15th Division, which landed at Kilia Liman on the morning of 3rd May,
       were thrown straight into this action after a march of 20 miles. They all
       suffered severely, and it was more than a week before they could be collected
       and reorganized.

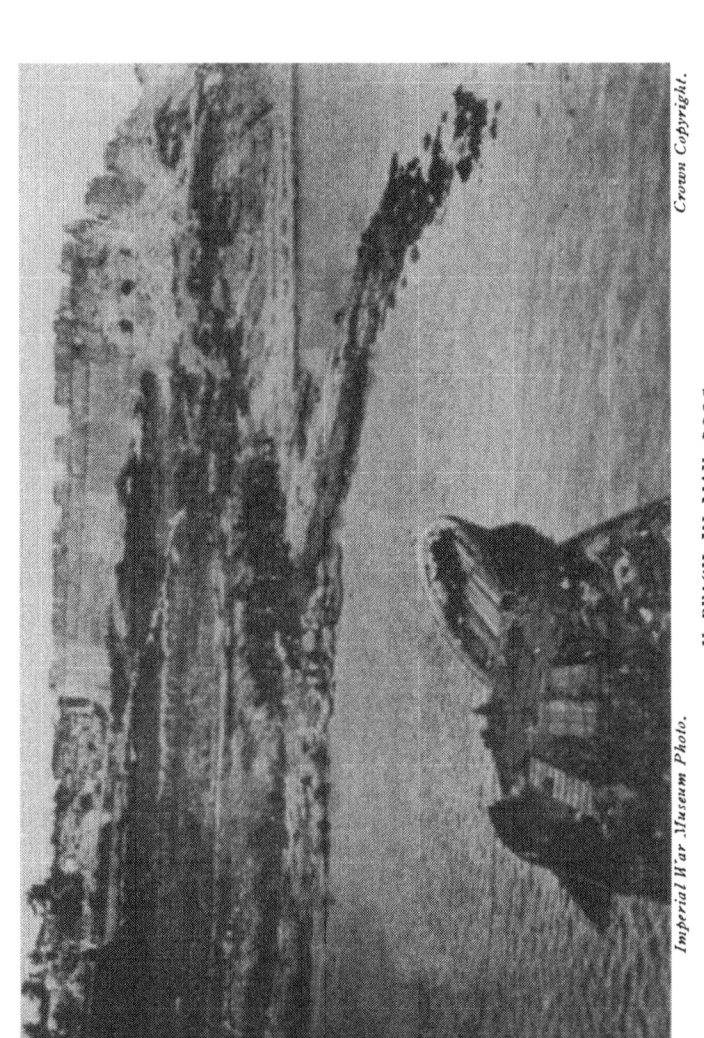

Imperial War Museum Photo. *Crown Copyright.*

V BEACH IN MAY 1915

PREPARATIONS FOR AN ALLIED ADVANCE

officers, had been very heavy. The Zouaves and Foreign Legion were at the end of their tether and really ought to be relieved, and he added that the Senegalese had become so unsteady that it was no longer safe to leave them in front line. In these circumstances, as he had no troops to take their place, he asked that they might be relieved by two battalions of the Royal Naval Division. This request was granted, and later in the day the Hood and Howe Battalions of the 2nd Naval Brigade (Commodore Oliver Backhouse) took over the French front from the Krithia road to the permanent telegraph line running north-east from Sedd el Bahr.¹

Sketch 18.

The news from General d'Amade was disheartening, but Sir Ian Hamilton would not allow it to deflect him from his purpose of attacking on the 6th. The Turks had apparently suffered even more than the French in the recent counter-attacks; they had as yet, so far as G.H.Q. could ascertain, no strong defensive line in front of Achi Baba; and there seemed little doubt that they stood to gain more than the Allies by any postponement of the attack. Lord Kitchener, too, was repeatedly applying the spur from England, and urging the dangers of delay.² It was possible, moreover, that with the help of their next reinforcements the Turks might be able to hem in the Allies still more closely, in which case there would be no room at the southern end of the peninsula for any increase in the size of the British force. For all these reasons the date of the next attack remained unchanged.

During these days of preparation the navy continued to do all in its power to assist the troops, both by gun-fire on the enemy's territory, and by energetic co-operation in landing stores and organizing the various beaches which had to serve as ports. On the French front, after the Turkish night attack on the 3rd/4th May, Admiral Guépratte sent ashore some seamen to assist in holding the line, and the arrival of this reinforcement did much to steady the French Colonial troops. Four more French naval guns (two 14-cm. and two 10-cm.) and their detachments were also landed at Sedd el Bahr to harass the Asiatic

---

¹ Next day the Anson Battalion was released from the extreme right, and rejoined its brigade on this front. The whole brigade was then placed temporarily under the tactical command of French headquarters. The behaviour of the 2nd Naval Brigade in action won the warm praise of General d'Amade.

² Telegram from Lord Kitchener, received 4th May: " I hope the 5th " will see you strong enough to press on to Achi Baba. Any delay will " allow the Turks to bring up more reinforcements and to make unpleasant " preparations for your reception."

batteries, and though the only available position for these guns was very exposed, they rendered valuable service.

The various bombarding ships were allotted positions round the coast from Morto Bay to Anzac to support the army, while at least one battleship, protected from possible torpedo attack by a screen of destroyers, used to lie off the French right at night time, charged with the duty of keeping her searchlights on Turkish lines of approach. Other vessels, assisted by balloon ships or aeroplanes, were employed in firing on Chanak and Maidos and on Turkish transports and shipping anchored in the Narrows, or in counter-battery work against the Asiatic guns. This latter task, which necessitated lying at anchor in the mouth of the Straits, was accompanied by no little risk. The *Albion* was holed twice and had to be sent to Mudros for repairs, while the *Prince George*, holed by a 6-inch shell below the water-line, was obliged to be docked at Malta.

Unfortunately in these early days no one knew the exact positions of the enemy's trenches and batteries, and the material effect of the naval bombardments was consequently very small. Even when targets could be accurately located the means of communication between ship and shore left much to be desired. It was so difficult to pick up a target from the sea that ships often had to content themselves with almost random fire, while at other times they were obliged to abstain altogether from firing for fear of danger to their own troops. Aeroplanes were not always available, and even when they were, their wireless gear was often at fault; and an attempt to signal by means of Very lights was not attended by success. On some occasions ships would even have to wait for their corrections from a spotting aeroplane till a destroyer could bring the message from the landing ground at Tenedos, a course which led to interminable delays and no little confusion.

In preparing for the new advance the first step was the reorganization of the British forces, for with the arrival of the 125th Brigade from Egypt and two brigades from Anzac, there would be no less than four infantry brigades at Helles unallotted to any divisional headquarters. Owing to the heavy losses in the 29th Division it had already been necessary to break up the 86th Brigade, and to divide its units amongst the 87th and 88th. It was now decided to attach the 125th Brigade and the Indian brigade to the 29th Division for the battle, thereby bringing up its strength to four infantry brigades. It was further decided to form a composite division, commanded by Major-General Paris with the headquarters of the Royal Naval Division, the troops to consist of

G.H.Q.

29th Division (Hunter-Weston)

87th Bde.	88th Bde.	125th Bde.	29th Indian Bde.
2/S.W.B.	4/Worcs.	1/5th L.F.	14th Sikhs.
1/K.O.S.B.	2/Hants.	1/6th L.F.	69th Punjabis.
1/R. Innis. Fus.	1/Essex.	1/7th L.F.	89th Punjabis.
1/Border	2/R.F.	1/8th L.F.	1/6th Gurkhas.
R. Munster Fus.	1/5th R. Scots.		
R. Dublin Fus.	1/L.F.		

Divisional Troops including:

14 batteries 18-pdrs.	56
1 battery 4·5-in. hows.	4
1 ,, 60-pdr. guns	4
1 ,, 6-in. hows.	4
1 ,, mountain artillery.	4
	72

2 Field Companies R.E.
29th Divl. Cyclist Coy.
29th Divl. Signal Coy.
Motor Machine Gun Squad. R.N.D.

French Exp. Force (d'Amade)

1st (French) Divn. (Masnou)

Colonial Bde.	Metropolitan Bde.
6 Bns.	6 Bns.

Divisional Troops including:

Field guns 75-mm.	21
Mountain guns 65-mm. also	8
155-mm. long guns	2
120- ,, ,,	2
	33

2nd Aust. Bde.

5th Bn.
6th Bn.
7th Bn.
8th Bn.

N.Z. Bde.

Auckland Bn.
Canterbury Bn.
Otago Bn.
Wellington Bn.

Divisional Troops including:

R.N.D. Cyclist Coy.
2 Field Coys. R.N.D.
R.N.D. Signal Coy.
Machine Gun Detachment.

Composite Divn. (Paris)

2nd Naval Bde.

Hood Bn.
Howe ,,
Anson ,,

Comp. Naval Bde. R.M.L.I.

Plymouth Bn.
Drake Bn.

the Australian and New Zealand brigades from Anzac and one two-battalion brigade, made up of the only two battalions of the R.N.D. still remaining under General Paris's command. All the available artillery, including the five reinforcing batteries from Anzac, were to be under the orders of the G.O.C. 29th Divisional artillery, and divided into groups covering the British front of attack, each with its own zone of fire. The revised order of battle was therefore as shown overleaf. The Allied strength amounted to about 25,000 bayonets.[1]

It was no easy matter to gauge the enemy's strength, for Turkish reinforcements had been rushed to Krithia irrespective of their normal organization. Nevertheless the deductions made by G.H.Q. were remarkably accurate. On the 5th May they estimated the Turkish strength south of Achi Baba at about 20,000 infantry, and this figure was very near the truth.[2]

The shortage of aircraft[3] and the lack of trained military observers made it hard to locate the Turkish positions from the air, and hostile outposts were defeating the activity of British infantry patrols. Even the general locality of the enemy's main line of defence was therefore a matter of surmise. Up to the morning of the 5th May air reconnaissances had reported a few scattered trenches in front of Krithia, and a long single line running south-east from a point on the Krithia road about half a mile south of the village. At G.H.Q. and at 29th Division headquarters, however, it was believed that these were merely advanced positions, and that the main defensive area was further in rear, in front of the Achi Baba ridge. But apart from a girdle of deep trench round the actual peak, no trenches had been located in that vicinity either.[4]

---

[1] The 69th and 89th Punjabis each had 2 Mahommedan coys, and as General Cox, in view of the critical situation, was not prepared to guarantee the steadfastness of Mahommedan troops fighting against the Turks, it was decided to detail these for work on the beach. The fighting strength of the Indian brigade was thus reduced by one quarter.

[2] Turkish reports state that on 6th May their southern group consisted of 31 battalions. The strength was probably 20,000, though some Turkish accounts put it as low as 15,000.

[3] Of the 10–12 daily flights carried out by the Naval Air Service at this time, an average of 8 were devoted to bombing, or to spotting for naval guns, and only one or two were military reconnaissances. There was only one camera available for taking photographs, and the difficulty of distinguishing small trenches in a country covered with scrub and scored by numerous ditches and dry water-courses was very great.

[4] In point of fact the Turks had completed nothing in the way of a connected system of trenches in the southern theatre before the opening of the Second Battle of Krithia on 6th May, and owing to the activity of the naval guns little had been added to the work done before the landing on 25th April. According to Turkish accounts their main line, which consisted only of disconnected trenches on 6th May, ran in a south-

PREPARATIONS FOR AN ALLIED ADVANCE

The increasing shortage of gun ammunition both for field artillery and for the guns of the fleet was already an anxious problem, and the accidental sinking of a lighter with 150 precious cases of 18-pdr. shells on the 4th May added emphasis to the hazards of amphibious operations. In these early days of 1915 the idea of a creeping barrage had not as yet been evolved, but the casualties already suffered in Gallipoli were beginning to teach the same lesson that the army had just learnt in France—that a plentiful supply of ammunition, and especially of high explosive shell, is a vital adjunct to a successful daylight advance in the face of hidden machine guns.[1] But the Allied artillery had already fired away more than half its ammunition, and it was plain that available resources would permit of but little in the way of a preliminary bombardment. The British and Anzac 18-pdrs., moreover, were only equipped with shrapnel. In these circumstances, Sir Ian Hamilton wanted to launch his attack at least an hour before daybreak. He was dissuaded from this course, however, by the argument of General Hunter-Weston that owing to the heavy losses in company commanders it would no longer be wise to expect the 29th Division to carry out an opposed advance in the dark. A daylight attack was therefore decided on.

The amount of naval ammunition available for the battle was governed by the fact that the fleet had to keep enough in hand for its future task of forcing the Straits, sinking the Turco-German fleet, and dominating Constantinople. The expenditure during the landing had been unexpectedly heavy,[2] and on the 30th April the stock remaining with the fleet amounted to only 400 rounds 12-inch, 400 7.5-inch, 4,000 6-inch, 1,000 4-inch, and 12,000 12-pdr. At a naval and military conference held on the 1st May it had been agreed that not more

---

easterly direction across the peninsula about ¼ mile in front of Krithia (the trenches located by British planes evidently formed part of it), with a number of advanced posts, held by rifles and machine guns, pushed out in front. There were several trenches on the western side of Kereves ravine, opposite the French left and centre.

[1] Compare "Military Operations, France and Belgium, 1915," i. p. 240: "Sunday the 25th April . . . was overcast and cloudy . . . when the battalions of the 10th Brigade . . . were called on to attempt the impossible. Without adequate artillery preparation and support, on ground unknown and unreconnoitred, they were sent to turn an enemy well provided with machine guns out of a position which had ready-made cover. . . ." [N.B.—This attack was intended to begin before daylight, but the brigade was unable to reach its starting point in time.]

[2] The amounts expended to 28th April were as follows:

	Over 6-in.	6-in.	4-in. & 12-pdr.
25th April	327	4,903	2,780
26th–28th April	1,722	7,263	5,459

than one-third of these totals could be expended on the military operations up to and including the capture of Achi Baba; and this slender amount had already been considerably reduced.

The 125th Brigade arrived from Egypt on the 5th May. The first battalion to land—the 1/6th Lancashire Fusiliers under Lieut.-Colonel Lord Rochdale—was sent up into the line at dusk to take over the trenches of the King's Own Scottish Borderers on the extreme left. But the guides lost their way, and it was 2 A.M. before the battalion reached its new quarters. Its officers had no idea as yet that an attack was impending, and, to quote a report by a company commander, they "were "as ignorant of their position as if they had been dropped from "a balloon". The remainder of the brigade marched during the night, and bivouacked above Gully Beach at daybreak next morning.

5 May. Of the remaining reinforcements for the battle, the 2nd Australian Brigade (strength 2,300, commanded by Colonel M'Cay) and the New Zealand Brigade (2,700 strong, commanded by Colonel Johnston) were embarked at Anzac Cove in destroyers and fleet-sweepers during the night of the 5th/6th May, and, landing at W Beach early on the 6th, were moved to reserve positions north of Morto Bay.

The five Anzac batteries were landed at W on the 4th, and had a complete day in which to get their bearings before the battle began.

The country to be traversed in the new advance was far more intricate than it looked. South-west of Hill 472 and the Achi Baba ridge the ground falls towards the Helles end of the peninsula in a gentle and gradual slope, but though from the direction of Sedd el Bahr it appears to be little broken, it is in reality deeply furrowed by four important water-courses, one of which falls into the Ægean and the other three into the Dardanelles. Taking these four water-courses from north to south, the rugged Gully Ravine, which empties into the Ægean, has already been described. To the south of it, springing from the neighbourhood of Krithia, two much smaller nullahs known as Kirte Dere, or Krithia nullah, and Kanli Dere, or Achi Baba nullah, trace a roughly parallel course, and then turn southwards to Morto Bay. The fourth, and the most important from a tactical point of view, is the immense Kereves Dere, which lay in front of the French. Starting below the peak of Achi Baba this forbidding ravine heads first south-west and then due south to the Dardanelles about $1\frac{1}{2}$ miles north of S Beach.

The four long spurs or fingers into which the country is

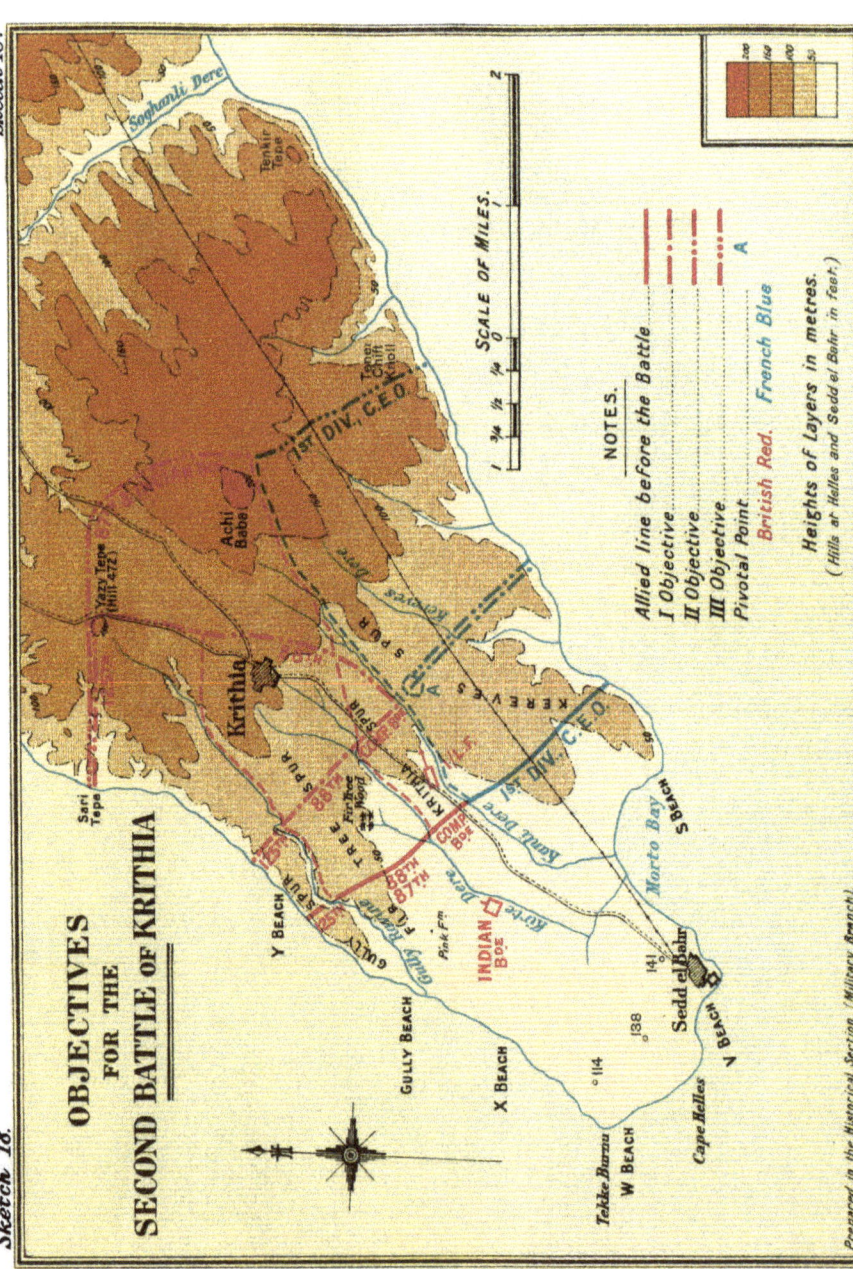

PREPARATIONS FOR AN ALLIED ADVANCE 327

divided by these nullahs and ravines bore no particular names during the course of the campaign, but to facilitate a description of the Second Battle of Krithia it will be convenient to call the high ground between the Ægean and Gully Ravine Gully Spur; that between Gully Ravine and Kirte Dere Fir Tree Spur, and the next two Krithia Spur and Kereves Spur respectively.[1] Gully Spur, the narrowest of the four, varies in breadth from a quarter of a mile to less than 100 yards. It was for the most part bare and open, and immediately south of Y Beach was devoid of all cover. Fir Tree Spur is intersected by a succession of tiny transverse nullahs running into Kirte Dere, offering excellent cover for riflemen barring an advance from the south. On this spur, which is over 1,000 yards wide, were several straggling fir copses. Krithia Spur, which nowhere has a width of more than half a mile, was more open and less broken, and along its eastern side, close to Kanli Dere, ran the straight ribbon of road from Krithia to Sedd el Bahr. Kereves Spur was the highest and most important of the four, as well as the most irregular in shape. Curving to the south in front of the position at that time occupied by the French, some of whose trenches were on its lower slopes, it effectually shut out all view of the Kereves ravine.

After several conferences with General Hunter-Weston and General d'Amade, orders for the battle of the 6th May were issued by G.H.Q. at 1.45 P.M. on the 5th.[2] The enemy was described as having suffered very severe losses, and as "occupy-" ing a position on and in front of the Achi Baba ridge, running " roughly south-east and north-west, with an advanced line " along the Kereves Dere and in front of Krithia." The object of the operations was the capture of the enemy's main position on Achi Baba, and the principal attack on this position was to be developed from the west and south-west by the 29th Division.

The advance was to begin at 11 A.M. The dividing line between British and French troops was to be the left (eastern) bank of Kanli Dere and thence a straight line to the eastern point of Achi Baba peak. The first stage of the battle was to consist of an advance of about a mile straight to the front, which would bring the French to a position astride Kereves Dere, with their left on the top of Kereves Spur[3] and their right on

---

[1] In the Australian official account the four spurs have been named, from the Ægean to the Dardanelles, as follows : Ravine Spur, Krithia Spur, Central Spur, and Kereves Spur.

[2] Appendix 24.

[3] On the evening of 5th May the Naval Air Service reported that a reconnaissance flight carried out at midday had discovered three lines of

the Dardanelles coast on the opposite (left) bank of Kereves Dere. This position the French were to entrench and to hold at all costs throughout the operation, special attention being paid to their left flank, which would form the pivotal point for the further advance of the 29th Division. As soon as this position had been made good, the 29th Division was to swing right-handed, pivoting on the French left, capture Krithia, and advance to a line running approximately north and south on the eastern side of the village.[1] This line would form the second objective. The third and final stage of the operation was to consist of a main attack on the Achi Baba ridge from the west and south-west by the 29th Division, coupled with a subsidiary attack by the French against a spur running south-east from Achi Baba peak to the Straits.

Special emphasis was laid on the importance of maintaining close touch between the French left and the British right throughout the operation, and it was expressly ordered that one battalion of the 88th Brigade was to move along Kanli Dere parallel with the French, and that General d'Amade was to keep the 2nd Naval Brigade (attached to his force for the battle) echeloned in rear of his left to guard against the risk of that part of his line being driven back by a counter-attack. Owing to the exposed nature of Krithia Spur, no attempt was to be made by the 29th Division to advance along this portion of its front. Apart from the one battalion moving along Kanli Dere, Kirte Dere was to mark the right of the 29th Division's initial attack. To fill up the gap created by this divergent advance the existing British front-line trench across Krithia Spur was to be held, during the first stage of the attack, by the Composite Brigade of General Paris's division. The remainder of this division was to form G.H.Q. reserve, but here it should be noticed that by a subsequent order issued before the attack General Hunter-Weston was given permission to use this reserve without further reference to G.H.Q.

No time was laid down by G.H.Q. for the successive stages of the attack, but it was hoped to capture Achi Baba before nightfall on the 6th.

Naval orders for the support of the army were issued on the evening of the 5th. The warships to take part in the operations

---

Turkish trenches near the very point (A in Sketch 18) where the French left was to rest. The report was forwarded to General d'Amade and arrangements made to give him extra artillery support in this area.

[1] There was no reference in the G.H.Q. order to the point to be reached by the left of the 29th Division, but in divisional orders the left flank brigade was ordered to capture Hill 472, and thence to bend back its left to the sea at Sari Tepe.

PREPARATIONS FOR AN ALLIED ADVANCE 329

were divided into "bombarding ships" and "ships on the flanks". The bombarding ships were the four battleships *Swiftsure*, *Cornwallis*, *Implacable*, and *Lord Nelson*, and their orders "to attend to the requirements of the situation by direct signal "from the G.O.C. R.A., on Hill 138".[1] A fifth battleship, the *Agamemnon*, with an aeroplane to spot for her, was to keep down the fire of the Asiatic batteries. The "ships on the "flanks" were to consist of one battleship in the Dardanelles[2] to support the French right, and four cruisers on the Ægean side of the peninsula. Of these, one (*Dublin*) was to fire on the southern slopes of Hill 472 and "any adjacent batteries", and was subsequently to move further north to deal with batteries on the north-west slopes of Achi Baba. Another (*Sapphire*) was to lie close in on the left flank and assist the advance of the left flank brigade with her 4-inch guns. The other two (*Talbot* and *Minerva*) were to lie north of Sari Tepe, to deal with the northern and north-western slopes of Achi Baba and any troops or guns moving across the open plain north-west of the main ridge.

General d'Amade's orders, issued at 8 P.M. on the 5th, dealt only with the first objective allotted to him by G.H.Q. Special emphasis was laid on the importance of gaining and retaining the pivotal point on Kereves Spur, where the Turks were now known to be entrenched, and as the enemy was believed to be in considerable strength in the upper reaches of the ravine, every effort was to be made to cross it as close to its mouth as possible.[3]

The 29th Division orders were necessarily long and elaborate, and were not ready for issue to brigades till 4 A.M. on the morning of the battle.[4] At that time the dispositions of the troops to take part in the attack were as follows: on the extreme left, on Gully Spur, the 1/6th Lancashire Fusiliers had

6 May.

---

[1] By the military orders subsequently issued these ships were to open fire at 10.30 A.M. on "such of the enemy's batteries as have been located, "and on localities in which bodies of the enemy have been reported to "have assembled".

[2] Three ships were detailed to relieve each other on this trying duty.

[3] General d'Amade also issued special instructions to the 2nd Naval Brigade detailing it to form the left flank of the French advance and directing it against the point where the three lines of trenches had been discovered that day. Subsequently it was noticed that these instructions were at variance with the G.H.Q. order (that the Naval Brigade was to be echeloned in rear of the French flank) and they were cancelled. The final orders were that the Colonial Brigade should be on the French left, and the Metropolitan Brigade on the right, but this change of plan caused half an hour's delay in the French advance, and the matter ended after all by the 2nd Naval Brigade attacking on the left of the French line.

[4] Appendix 25.

just taken over the front line trenches; the other three battalions of the 125th Brigade were marching to their bivouacs near the mouth of Gully Ravine. The trenches across Fir Tree Spur were held by three battalions[1] of the 87th Brigade, with its other two battalions in support. Across Krithia Spur lay the 88th Brigade, with three battalions in front line and three in support. The Indian brigade was in reserve about a mile south-east of the mouth of Gully Ravine.

General Hunter-Weston's orders divided the forthcoming operation into three distinct phases, but in the first instance only the details of the first two were communicated to subordinate commands. Phase 1 was to begin at 11 A.M. with the advance of the 125th and 88th Brigades along Gully and Fir Tree Spurs,[2] and the 1/Lancashire Fusiliers (temporarily attached to the Composite Brigade) along Kanli Dere in touch with the French left. This advance was to be carried to a line about one mile from Krithia, where the troops were to establish themselves and entrench. The Drake and Plymouth Battalions of the Composite Brigade were then to move forward and fill the gap across Krithia Spur between the right of the 88th and the left of the 1/Lancashire Fusiliers. Throughout this phase the 87th Brigade and Indian brigade were to stand fast in their original positions. The divisional artillery was to open fire with its howitzers[3] at 10.30 A.M. "on objectives in front of the two leading brigades", and at 11 A.M. it was to support the infantry advance with shrapnel and to cover the troops entrenching on the first objective.

Phase 2 would begin at a time to be notified later, and not before the French were firmly established on their first objective. During this phase the 88th Brigade, pivoting on the left of the Composite Brigade, was to swing right-handed, capture Krithia, and take up a position on its eastern side from the French left to a point midway between the village and Hill 472. The 125th Brigade on the left was to push straight forward to a line Sari Tepe—Hill 472, establish itself firmly on that hill, and extend its right flank to link up with the left of the 88th Brigade. This position, from Sari Tepe to the left of the 88th Brigade, a frontage of roughly two miles, was to be the final objective of the 125th Brigade. During this phase the 87th Brigade was to move forward and hold the line of the first objective, whilst the

[1] The Inniskillings, the Border Regiment, and the composite battalion of Munster and Dublin Fusiliers.
[2] The 88th Brigade was to be relieved in its trenches across Krithia Spur by the Composite Brigade before daylight. and was to advance through the 87th Brigade along Fir Tree Spur.
[3] Only eight howitzers were available, four 6-inch and four 4·5's.

PREPARATIONS FOR AN ALLIED ADVANCE 331

Indian brigade—still in general reserve—occupied the old front on Fir Tree Spur.

Phase 3,[1] like Phase 2, would begin at a time to be notified by divisional headquarters. In this phase the 87th Brigade, moving north of Krithia, and the Indian brigade moving south of the village, would advance through the 88th and attack the Achi Baba ridge from the west and south-west, the inner flank of each brigade being directed on the highest point of the peak.

Artillery orders were issued by Br.-General R. W. Breeks, commanding 29th Division artillery, at 7.15 A.M. on the morning of the battle.[2] The available guns had already been divided into four groups covering the British and part of the French front of attack, and during the battle each group was to be in observation of a definite portion of the front from Achi Baba peak to the Ægean. Three of the groups were in addition to be prepared to support the French attack on the Turkish trenches near the pivotal point. The arrangements for a preliminary bombardment were necessarily meagre. The 6-inch howitzer battery was to open slow fire at 10.30 A.M. on two groups of Turkish trenches west and south-west of Krithia, and the field batteries were at the same time "to take the " opportunity of firing a few registering rounds at objectives in " their zones hitherto unregistered".[3] After 11 A.M. batteries were to fire "on any objectives which may from time to time hinder " the advance of the infantry", and each group commander was to allot one battery for engaging "any hostile battery " that opened fire". For the second phase of the operations one field battery and the mountain battery were to move forward in close support of the troops; and three artillery brigades were to go forward for the final attack on Achi Baba. In addition to the normal method of ammunition supply, two advanced dumps had been formed to serve as reserve refilling depots, one on each flank.

Such in broad outline were the plans and preparations for the new advance on Achi Baba. The events of the battle will be described in the next chapter.

It remains to be noticed that, with the Composite Division placed under his orders for the battle, General Hunter-Weston

---

[1] The detailed orders for Phase 3 were not to be issued to brigades till everything was seen to be going well with Phase 1. Actually they were never issued.

[2] Preliminary orders had enabled any necessary movements to be completed the night before.

[3] So slight was this fire that a report of the battle by a Turkish staff officer stated that the Allies attacked without any artillery preparation.

on the morning of the 6th May had at his disposition all the British troops in the southern theatre. In these circumstances he again directed Br.-General Marshall, in addition to commanding his own brigade, to exercise a general control over the advance of the other three brigades of the 29th Division.

General Headquarters was to remain on board the *Arcadian*, lying off W Beach, and the fact that that vessel was now connected by cable with the shore would facilitate the prompt receipt of messages from both General Hunter-Weston and General d'Amade. But it was plain that Sir Ian Hamilton would be able to exercise little or no influence on the coming battle. His last remaining reserve had been handed over in advance to his subordinate commander on shore, and all that was left to him of the high office of Commander-in-Chief was its load of responsibility.

CHAPTER XIX

THE SECOND BATTLE OF KRITHIA
6TH–8TH MAY 1915

(Sketches 18, 19)

EVEN the Great War furnishes few examples of a series of offensive operations being entered upon with troops so worn out by continuous fighting and lack of sleep as those who took part in the Second Battle of Krithia. Only the 125th Brigade on the extreme left of the line was fresh, and its units were entirely new to their surroundings and had no knowledge of the ground to be traversed. In the centre, the 88th Brigade, made up of five very weak battalions, was but a skeleton of its former self; it had lost all but one of its battalion commanders and the majority of its company, platoon, and section leaders; and not a man in the brigade had had a real night's rest for a fortnight. On the right the French division, equally short of sleep, was still suffering from the effects of the Turkish night attacks, and its coloured battalions had lost so many of their European officers that their own commander reported he could no longer rely on them.

6 May.
Sketch 18.

The battle opened slowly. In the centre, on Fir Tree Spur, after the slight sprinkling of artillery fire which was all that could be afforded in place of a preliminary bombardment, the action began by the advance of the 88th Brigade with three battalions in front and two in support, the whole covered by a screen of scouts, feeling for the enemy. Moving forward very slowly, the advance was at first unopposed, but after covering a few hundred yards the scouts began to be held up by rifle and machine-gun fire from a screen of advanced posts. At the same time Turkish artillery opened on the advancing lines with shrapnel, and about noon, seeing that no progress was being made either by the 125th Brigade or by the French, and that both its flanks were exposed, the 88th Brigade came to a standstill.[1]

[1] The advance of the 1/Lancashire Fusiliers up Kanli Dere, to maintain touch between the 88th Brigade and the French, had been delayed by the French start being 40 minutes late.

Later in the afternoon further progress was made on both sides of Fir Tree Wood, but the wood itself, held by two unlocated machine guns, could not be entered, and about 4 P.M. the brigade began to dig in on a general line about 400 yards in front of its starting point. Its left flank, on Gully Ravine, was still in the air, owing to the 125th Brigade being unable to make headway. Its right, on Kirte Dere, was protected towards evening by the advance of the Composite Brigade to fill the gap between that nullah and the 1/Lancashire Fusiliers in Kanli Dere. At 8.30 P.M. Lieut.-Colonel Williams, commanding the 88th, reported that he had only been in contact with the enemy's covering troops throughout the day, and that the Turkish main body had not as yet been engaged. He placed his total casualties at not more than 50 men per battalion.

On the left flank, the fighting was more severe, and less progress was made. In this sector it was 11.30 A.M., half an hour behind time,[1] when the advance began, the 1/6th Lancashire Fusiliers moving off with its left flank on the edge of the cliffs, the 1/7th Battalion following in support. Men began to fall as soon as they started, and when the leading companies neared the bare plateau above Y Beach—that key position so unluckily abandoned on the 26th April—they came under accurate and galling machine-gun fire from the further side of the small gully leading down to the sea. Reinforcements were dribbled up, but the storm could not be breasted. Every attempt to make headway was met by a hail of lead; the cruiser on the flank was unable to help, as the hostile post was apparently defiladed from the sea. Throughout the day no further progress was made in this locality, which was to have been the scene of a rapid outflanking movement. By nightfall the losses of the brigade amounted to about 350 in the three battalions engaged.

About 1 P.M., coincident with the news that the British advance was being everywhere held up by unlocated machine guns, a telegram about ammunition supply arrived at G.H.Q.

---

[1] According to battalion records this was due to some mistake, for the orders received by telephone by the officer whose company was to lead the attack were: first, at 9.30 A.M., that the 88th Brigade on his right was to start at 10.30, but that he was not to move till 11 A.M.; and secondly, "some time afterwards", that "if the attack on his right had not developed by 11.30 A.M., he was to move forward at that hour". The movements of the 88th Brigade could not be seen by this officer, so he eventually started his advance at 11.30 A.M. Further information and orders given to him before he started were: (a) the position of battalion H.Q. and the battalion dressing station; (b) an objective which he could not locate on his map; (c) an order that his left flank man was to carry a blue and white flag. The object of the flag was to assist the warship on the flank to watch the progress of the advance.

THE SECOND BATTLE OF KRITHIA

from the War Office. Sir Ian Hamilton had telegraphed on the 4th May that, owing to the continuous fighting since the landing, the supply of ammunition had become a very serious matter and that 18-pdr. ammunition in particular was urgently required. The War Office reply was as follows: "The am-"munition supply for your force was never calculated on the "basis of a prolonged occupation of the peninsula. It is im-"portant to push on."

Like the British on the left, the French on the right had been late in starting, and it was 11.40 A.M. before their advance began. On their extreme right little opposition was encountered at first, and the Metropolitan Brigade was able to reach some high ground overlooking the mouth of Kereves Dere before it was checked by heavy fire from the opposite bank. Elsewhere, on the extreme left of the French line, and in the centre, where more Turkish trenches were now for the first time located,[1] little progress was made. A strong firing line was eventually built up at the foot of the long slope leading to the "pivotal point", but though the trenches in that locality were shelled by the Allied artillery, the Senegalese battalions were unable to make further headway,[2] and by the end of the day the French gains amounted nowhere to more than 400 yards. Even on the French right the situation was causing the commander of the Metropolitan Brigade some anxiety, and at 5.30 P.M. he reported: "Par suite extrême fatigue du 4ᵉ Zouaves, moral "médiocre, feu violent ennemi, suis obligé garder bataillon du "175ᵉ que voulais prêter brigade coloniale il y a un instant. "Il me parvient des nouvelles très pessimistes de ma "droite. . . ."[3] Two battalions of the French 2nd Division (General Bailloud) had landed on the morning of the 6th, and were hurried straight into the fight.

As already mentioned, the 2nd Naval Brigade had been ordered to remain echeloned in rear of the French left, but about midday, noticing a wide gap between the French flank and Kanli Dere, Commodore Backhouse ordered the Hood,

---

[1] When the front line of this group of trenches was subsequently captured it was converted into a strong point known as La Redoute Bouchet.

[2] Messages from O.C. Composite Brigade to 29th Division:

2.20 P.M. "French are building up their firing line. They should be in a "position soon to deliver a successful assault."

2.45 P.M. "French show no desire to assault position on their left and Turks "are showing increasing boldness, small parties coming forward "to the low ground on our right front."

3.20 P.M. "On our right cannot observe French making progress although "enemy fire appears weak and our artillery fire appears to have "been effective."

[3] French Official Account, Tome viii. (i), Annexes i. No. 144.

supported by the Anson, to fill it by joining in the advance. Good work was done by these battalions, and by a small party of the Howe attached to them, and at one time the Hood had made substantial progress towards the left of the French objective. But considerable casualties were suffered, including the commanding officer killed;[1] and, finding its right flank completely exposed, the battalion had to withdraw.

Sketch 19.

By the evening of the 6th, therefore, Achi Baba was almost as far away as ever. Only an average distance of 400 yards had been gained, while on the extreme left progress had been negligible. Through lack of adequate artillery support the Allied troops had been unable even to brush aside the enemy's advanced posts. The Turkish main force had not been engaged, and its positions were still unlocated.[2] But the Allied casualties as a whole had been comparatively slight, and at 7.30 P.M. Sir Ian Hamilton, who had visited Generals Hunter-Weston and d'Amade at their headquarters during the afternoon, and had found them in entire agreement with his view as to the necessity of a further effort, issued orders for the battle to be resumed at 10 o'clock next morning. The 127th Brigade of the 42nd Division, then disembarking, was to be attached to the Composite Division.[3]

Though the smallness of the Allied achievement was in vivid contrast to the wide objectives allotted to the troops, a perusal of the Turkish official account, and of Liman's memoir, suffices to show that the Turkish position at this time was far from impregnable, and that a reinforcement of another British division on the 6th May, supported by a reasonable amount of high-explosive shell, might well have secured success. It would appear that after the failure of the Turkish night attacks, Colonel von Sodenstern was removed from the command of the southern group (Liman states that he had been slightly wounded), and was replaced by Weber Pasha, another German hitherto in command of the troops on the Asiatic shore. The position, on Weber Pasha's arrival on the 5th May, is reported to have been very unsatisfactory. Owing to constant fighting and to lack of

[1] Lieut.-Colonel A. Quilter, Grenadier Guards.
[2] Turkish accounts of the battle this day are very meagre. The official account claims that no progress was made by the Allies throughout the day, though repeated attempts were made to get forward. A Turkish officer, present at the engagement, states that the British gained a little ground after nightfall. There is no record of Turkish casualties, and there is no doubt that only their advanced troops were engaged.
[3] Only two battalions disembarked before nightfall. The remainder landed at 10 A.M. on the 7th.

THE SECOND BATTLE OF KRITHIA

entrenching tools, little progress had been made in the construction of a defensive line, and casualties had been so heavy that, according to one account, the 31 battalions in the southern group amounted to only some 15,000 rifles.[1] Losses amongst senior officers had been particularly severe, and the continual shelling by the fleet had caused so much demoralization that the new commander was strongly urged to order a general retirement behind the Achi Baba ridge, where better cover could be obtained. Impressed by these arguments Weber Pasha recommended a retirement to *Fifth Army* Headquarters, but such a step was firmly vetoed by Liman von Sanders, who replied that every foot of the ground must be stubbornly contested, and that there must be no thought of a voluntary retirement, which would only result in doubling the length of the Turkish front line. He added that the best way to get cover from the British ships was to advance rather than to retire, and to establish a line as close as possible to the Allied trenches.

The 29th Division order for the advance on 7th May was issued at 10 P.M. on the 6th. Following a preliminary bombardment lasting fifteen minutes, the infantry were to advance at 10 A.M. The general scope of the attack was to be the same as laid down for the 6th, except that Phases 1 and 2 of the previous day's order were now rolled into one, and instead of waiting on the line of the first objective, when it was reached, until the French had secured the "pivotal point",[2] the 29th Division was to go straight through to the second objective.

[1] According to Turkish information the Turkish dispositions were: opposite the British front, the *9th Division* with four battalions and two machine-gun companies in front line and five battalions in support; opposite the French front the *7th Division* with seven battalions and one machine-gun company in front line and seven battalions and one machine-gun company in support. Six or eight battalions formed the general reserve.

The total force thus consisted of from 29 to 31 battalions, and their actual effective strength was probably not far short of 20,000. Both divisions were very mixed and contained units belonging to no fewer than six other divisions. The artillery comprised ten field batteries, one mountain battery, and three batteries of heavy calibre—total 56 guns. It will be noticed from these figures that whereas the British were opposed by nine battalions there were no less than fourteen battalions opposite the French sector, which being nearer the Dardanelles coast was regarded by the Turks as the more vitally necessary to defend.

[2] It was believed at 29th Divisional headquarters at this time that the French had gained most of their first objective except on the extreme left, where they were 800 yards short of the pivotal point. After the issue of the order an erroneous report was received that the French had after all reached the pivotal point at nightfall; but this mistake was subsequently corrected.

The actual wording of the order was "Phase 2, indicated in "Operation Order No. 4 of 5th May, will commence at 10 A.M. "to-morrow, at which hour the advance of the infantry as laid "down in paras. 18 to 22 of that order will commence".[1]

7 May. General d'Amade, on receiving a copy of the British orders, was apparently anxious about the success of the 88th Brigade's operation unless his own troops could first seize the vital pivotal point. At 4.50 A.M. on the 7th, therefore, he ordered General Masnou (commanding the French 1st Division) to utilize two battalions of Colonel Simonin's Colonial brigade, which had completed its disembarkation the previous evening, to capture this important position on the crest at 6 A.M., "to serve as a "pivot for the 29th Division, which is advancing on Krithia at 10 A.M." Later, however, this order seems to have been cancelled, and at 7.15 A.M. fresh instructions were issued to the French troops. The attack on the pivotal point was to begin at 10 A.M.; on the rest of the French front the task of the troops was to be confined to securing possession of the western bank of Kereves Dere, facing east, without crossing the ravine.

Before the battle began General Hunter-Weston did all he could to inspire his troops to vigorous action, and to prevent a repetition of the previous day's stalemate. He spoke personally on the telephone to each of his brigadiers, and sent a special message of encouragement and exhortation to the 125th Brigade.[2] But it was shells that the troops needed to help them forward, and shells were sadly lacking. The spirit of these raw battalions was high; but the ammunition situation was now more serious than ever, and to advance in daylight against unshaken machine guns was to prove an impossibility.

The story of the 7th May, therefore, can be told in a few words. The preliminary bombardment, which started at 9.45 A.M., accomplished little. Though the admiral did all in his power to obliterate the Turkish post near Y Beach by sending the *Swiftsure* and *Talbot* with the balloon ship *Manica*, to blow the top off the cliff, the kite balloon could find no trace of an enemy trench. The post remained undiscovered and therefore undismayed by the fire of the ships' guns. Elsewhere along the front, owing to the growing shortage of ammunition, the bombardment was weaker than ever. Unaware of the enemy's

[1] Appendix 26.
[2] "To the 125th Brigade is allotted the glorious task of seizing Hill 472 "and the slopes west and south of it, safeguarding the British left. The "eyes of Lancashire and the world are on you, and the honour of your "country and the welfare of your own folk at home depend on your deeds "to-day. The Major-General knows that no fire and no losses will stop "you, and that you will win through to a glorious victory."

positions, the gunners had to search the whole front and depth of the objective—an area of 10½ square miles—and the result was ineffective.

On the extreme left the orders of the 1/5th Lancashire Fusiliers, which had suffered a good many casualties in moving up to the front line, were to charge the unlocated post above Y Beach as soon as the bombardment ceased, after which the whole brigade was to advance with fixed bayonets to the capture of Hill 472. But the machine guns, at least five in number, had not been touched by the warships' fire, and the Fusiliers could make no headway. Repeated efforts were made to get them forward during the morning, but it was all of no avail. A party of the K.O.S.B. was ordered up to help the Territorials by moving under the cliffs. A party of Inniskilling Fusiliers was pushed up Gully Ravine on their right. The *Queen Elizabeth* arrived off Y Beach, and joined in the flank bombardment till the whole cliff seemed to crumble under the blast of her heavy guns. But the rattle of the machine guns broke out afresh on the least sign of movement. The Territorials could make no further effort; and at nightfall the situation on Gully Spur was unchanged.

With the 125th Brigade making no progress, the task of the 88th on Fir Tree Spur was doubly difficult, for any attempt to wheel right-handed would expose its left to enfilade fire. At the outset some progress was made, but battalions were not in touch, and each in turn reported that its flanks were exposed. The Essex Regiment appears at one time to have pushed beyond Fir Tree Wood, and the Worcestershire, sent up in support, also claim to have entered that locality; but both units were eventually forced to retire. By 12.30 P.M. the advance had come to a definite standstill nowhere more than 300 yards from the starting point, while many of the troops were back in their old line. At 1 P.M. the brigade commander reported that he could do no more till supported by an advance on the left.[1]

Finding inertia along his whole front, General Hunter-Weston determined on one more effort to retrieve the situation before nightfall. The 87th Brigade was moved forward, and orders were issued for a renewed bombardment at 4.30 P.M. for fifteen minutes, followed by a concerted attack along Fir Tree Spur by the 87th and 88th Brigades. The New Zealanders were at the same time ordered to the neighbourhood of Pink

[1] " Brigade on left have made no advance. Am ready to move forward " as soon as they do. If I move before, my left will be enfiladed and in the " air."

Farm in support. Here and there slight gains were made as the result of this fresh endeavour; but progress on the whole was negligible. At sunset the British line was practically unchanged from that of the day before.

On the French front progress was equally disappointing, for the Turks had strengthened their defences overnight and were now holding a strong position all along Kereves Spur. On the right no ground was gained during the day,[1] the Metropolitan Brigade reporting that it was impossible to make headway against the trenches on its front, and that they must be taken by a flank attack from the left. In the centre some of the newly arrived troops succeeded during the afternoon in getting to within 150 yards of the summit of the ridge which marked their objective. Here they captured a small Turkish trench, but reported that they could get no further till helped by an advance from the right, and they were eventually forced to retire by a spirited counter-attack. On the left progress had been negligible. At 11 A.M. the 2nd Naval Brigade reported to the 29th Division: "Up to date no sign of any " French movement beyond last night's line", and even as late as 3 P.M. another message from the same source reported " the French 2nd Division, allotted the task of seizing the " pivot indicated yesterday, is not moving yet, as its advance " depends on the success of the right".

Apart from the Asiatic shelling on the right flank, Turkish artillery fire during the action had again been very slight, and casualties, mostly from rifle and machine-gun bullets, had again been confined to the leading troops and were not inordinately severe. On the left the 1/5th Lancashire Fusiliers lost five officers and 183 men, but the rest of the brigade lost only 100 all told,[2] while the total casualties of the 87th and 88th Brigades were 15 officers and 498 other ranks. The 2nd Naval Brigade and the Composite Brigade took no part in the fighting.[3] The total British losses for the 7th amounted, therefore, to not more than 800. No record of the French casualties is available.

Studying the problem that now faced the invaders in the

---

[1] General d'Amade to G.H.Q.: " French 1st Division reports for 7th " as follows: ' Quiet day, but impossible to leave trenches owing to intensity " of enemy's fire ' ".

[2] The total casualties of the 125th Brigade on 6th and 7th May—its first experience of warfare—were 23 officers and 626 other ranks. The brigade was withdrawn into reserve on the evening of 7th May, its place being taken by the 87th Brigade.

[3] As the progress on Fir Tree and Kereves Spurs had been so slight there was no necessity for these troops to move forward to maintain touch between the 88th Brigade and the French.

THE SECOND BATTLE OF KRITHIA

clear light of after-knowledge, it would appear that after two days of failure there could have been little chance of a third attack of the same nature succeeding. It is now known that the enemy's casualties had not been heavy; and that his reserves had not been engaged.[1] He had, moreover, been allowed two extra nights in which to improve his defences and bring up more troops. But the Allied casualties during the two days' fighting had not been very severe; a little ground had been gained; there were still three infantry brigades that had as yet taken no part in the battle; and on the evening of the 7th May no one could tell the state of the enemy's morale or how he was feeling the strain. True, the British ammunition supply was almost down to zero. But with the Turks receiving daily reinforcements, and with barely standing room for his own troops at the southern end of the peninsula, the British commander was in very truth between the devil and the deep sea. In these circumstances, he now decided on one more effort to break the Turkish line. Orders were consequently issued by G.H.Q. at 10.25 P.M. for a resumption of the battle next morning.[2]

With the opposing forces in close touch, there was small scope for any radical change of plan, except by attempting a night attack, and this course was still considered impracticable. Accordingly for the third day in succession a start was to be made at almost the same hour, after the same period of preliminary bombardment, in the full blaze of day. The attack was to be pressed "with the utmost possible vigour", but this time British troops alone were to bear the brunt of it, and the French were allotted a comparatively small rôle. The 29th Division, reinforced by the New Zealand Brigade,[3] was to advance at 10.30 A.M. The left flank of the French was to "continue to consolidate" the pivotal point on Kereves

[1] As in the case of the operations on the 6th Turkish accounts make little of the fighting on 7th May. An assault by the French is reported to have begun at noon, but to have been repulsed with artillery and rifle fire. It is claimed that this attack was renewed in the afternoon, after an intense bombardment and resulted in the capture of a Turkish trench which was subsequently recaptured by counter-attack. There is mention of an unsuccessful attack on the (Turkish) right flank, and of heavy fire near Y Beach from naval guns, but no serious engagement is mentioned, and the Turkish High Command does not appear to have realized that anything in the nature of a general attack was attempted this day by the Allies. The Turkish general reserve had been withdrawn behind Hill 472, apparently to get cover from the naval guns, and was not called into action.
[2] Appendix 27.
[3] The New Zealanders had already been moved forward to the old British front line across Fir Tree Spur, to support the 88th Brigade in case of a counter-attack.

Spur,[1] while their right was to "endeavour to cross" Kereves Dere and reach the first objective assigned to it for the battle of the 6th. The Commander-in-Chief would come ashore for the battle and would establish a command post on Hill 114.

8 May.   General d'Amade's orders were issued on the morning of the 8th. His left flank (Colonel Simonin's brigade) was "to "continue to reinforce its position in the zone of the pivotal point", which was to be held by three battalions. The 1st Division was to cross Kereves Dere at whatever point the Turkish resistance should prove to be weakest.

General Hunter-Weston had sent out the following warning order to brigades at 11.25 P.M. on the 7th:

> The advance will be resumed at 10.30 to-morrow. The New Zealand Brigade will be prepared to move through the 88th Brigade at that hour. 87th Brigade will be left of the advance. 88th Brigade will be in reserve in their present position. The Indian Brigade and Composite Naval Brigade will maintain their present positions.

Detailed orders for the attack were not issued by divisional headquarters till 8.30 next morning, and did not reach brigades till 8.55 A.M. But, as a result of the warning order sent overnight, the commander of the New Zealand Brigade was able to hold a conference with his battalion commanders and to describe the tasks that would be required of them, and the brigade orders eventually issued at 10.10 A.M. were practically a written confirmation of the instructions given at that conference.

The orders issued by the New Zealand Brigade were that the objective was Krithia village, and that the attack was to be carried out by the Wellington on the left, the Auckland in the centre, and the Canterbury on the right. The Otago Battalion, which had suffered heavily in the fighting for Baby 700 on the 2nd May, was to be in reserve.

Units of the 87th Brigade on Gully Spur received their detailed orders at 10 A.M. There was to be no immediate advance by the whole brigade at zero hour, but the South Wales Borderers and the Inniskillings were to push out small parties on both sides of the spur—under the cliff and up Gully Ravine —with orders to locate the Turkish post near Y Beach, dig in as close to it as possible, and report on the best line of advance to attack it. The Inniskillings were in addition to establish a series of connecting posts on the eastern bank of Gully Ravine

---

[1] We now know that the French had never yet reached the "pivotal "point", but it is clear from this order that this was not known at G.H.Q. on 7th May.

THE SECOND BATTLE OF KRITHIA 343

to protect the left flank of the New Zealand Brigade as it advanced up Fir Tree Spur.

It will be seen, therefore, that the Commander-in-Chief's orders for the 29th Division to attack with the utmost possible vigour had been very considerably modified. The attack by the 29th Division was being confined to the isolated advance of one brigade up Fir Tree Spur. Four weak battalions of New Zealanders were to attack, in full daylight, a position held by at least nine battalions of Turks.

As on the previous evening, there was little or no firing during the night of the 7th/8th May—the enemy was busy digging—and when the Commander-in-Chief landed next morning, an exquisite spring day, and moved to his command post on Hill 114, it was hard to realize that the solitude in front of him was packed with armed men. Not a shot disturbed the serene silence of the morning, and to those who at this moment of tension had any eyes for the lavish beauty of their surroundings, there was an added and almost unendurable poignancy in the approach of zero hour.

The scene that unfolded itself from the forward slopes of Hill 114 still lives in many memories. The grassy slopes that crown the cliffs are carpeted with flowers. The azure sky is cloudless; the air is fragrant with the scent of wild thyme. In front, beyond a smiling valley studded with cypress and olive and patches of young corn, the ground rises gently to the village of Krithia, standing amidst clumps of mulberry and oak; and thence more steeply to a frowning ridge beyond, its highest point like the hump of a camel's back. Away to the right, edged with a ribbon of silvery sand, lie the sapphire arc of Morto Bay, the glistening Dardanelles, and the golden fields of Troy. On the left, a mile out in the Ægean, a few warships lie motionless, like giants asleep, their gaunt outlines mirrored in a satin sea; while behind them, in the tender haze of the horizon, is the delicately pencilled outline of snow-capped Samothrace. As far as the eye can reach there is no sign of movement; the world seems bathed in sleep. Only high on the shoulder of Achi Baba—the goal of the British troops—a field of scarlet poppies intrudes a restless note. Yet in half an hour that peaceful landscape will again be overrun by waves of flashing bayonets; and these are the last moments of hundreds of precious lives.

At 10.15 A.M. the storm broke. For a quarter of an hour the ships and the shore artillery made a further heavy inroad on their slender stocks of ammunition,[1] and soon afterwards the long waves of New Zealanders began to move steadily forward from the line of the 88th Brigade. But again the artillery had been able to accomplish little. On the right, the Canterbury gained some 300 yards, but could get no further. In the centre, parties of the Auckland reached the far side of Fir Tree Wood, only to be driven out of it with heavy loss. On the left, after advancing 250 yards, the Wellington was checked by galling fire from the direction of Y Beach and forced to take cover. On Gully Spur, meanwhile, though a few scouts succeeded in gaining a little ground on each flank, they could not locate the enemy's hidden post, and throughout the morning the enemy machine guns killed all movement on the crest. By midday the British attack had collapsed. At half-past three, the situation was still unchanged.

Meantime, on the right, not an infantryman had stirred in the French sector, though the French 75's, better supplied than the British with ammunition, were pounding the ridge in front of them with high-explosive shell. It is now clear that the task of the French on Kereves Spur was much more severe than was realized in the British lines. Ordered by Liman von Sanders to dispute every foot of the ground, the Turks had succeeded during the last few days in completing a formidable position on the high ground to the west of the Kereves ravine, and here they were resolved to stay. The ravine itself offered the Turks a covered way for their supports, while their left flank was well protected by batteries of heavy guns on the Asiatic shore. The French, therefore, unknown to the British, were already at grips with what was in effect a main Turkish position. Bearing this in mind, it is less difficult to understand the influences which caused General d'Amade to report to Sir Ian Hamilton that it was impossible for his left to make headway till the British had captured Krithia, and that his right was chained to its trenches by heavy fire from the Asiatic shore.

But to Sir Ian Hamilton, who knew little of the French

---

[1] During the period 26th-28th April inclusive the naval guns, including those firing on the Asiatic shore, expended 14,444 rounds in the army's support. For the five days 5th-9th May, which included the Second Battle of Krithia, the figures dropped to 3,489. During the actual three days of battle *Swiftsure* fired only 16 rounds of 10-inch ammunition and 207 rounds of 7·5, and the other ships in proportion. The Turks, moreover, had now begun to realize the limitations of naval guns, and, though material damage was sometimes caused, the moral effect of a naval bombardment was beginning to disappear. But, in view of the small number of rounds fired, and the inadequate aeroplane observation and arrangements for signalling, the results obtained cannot be taken as any criterion of the possibilities of modern naval artillery support.

THE SECOND BATTLE OF KRITHIA 345

difficulties and was aware that three brigades of the British force were still in reserve,[1] the acceptance of failure was unthinkable. He resolved on one final effort to retrieve the fortunes of the day, and at 4 P.M., after hearing that General Hunter-Weston was already organizing a fresh advance, he ordered the whole Allied line, reinforced by the Australian Brigade, to "fix bayonets, slope arms, and move on Krithia "precisely at 5.30 P.M."[2] The attack was again to be preceded by fifteen minutes' bombardment by every available gun.

Executive orders by Generals Hunter-Weston[3] and Paris (to the Australians) were issued half an hour later. As for the French commander, on receipt of this definite order, the word "impossible" faded from his vocabulary. No further mention was made of his difficulties, and at 5 P.M. he replied: "Your " message received. I have ordered a general advance with " the bayonet at 5.30 P.M."[4]

For this new attack the 87th Brigade, regardless of previous failures, was to charge the Turkish machine guns above Y Beach, and then to push on to the trenches west of Krithia. The New Zealanders, supported by the 88th Brigade, were to renew their attack along Fir Tree Spur and capture the village. The Australians were to do what hitherto had not been attempted: attack along the bare Krithia Spur on the right of the New Zealand Brigade. General d'Amade personally went forward to inspire the French troops, and, keeping only a small reserve under his own hand, ordered the rest of the force to co-operate by attacking all along its front.

Orders for the Australians reached their brigadier (Colonel M'Cay) a little after 5 P.M., and were quite unexpected. The brigade was at that time in reserve only about a thousand yards in rear of the British front line on Krithia Spur, then held by the Composite Naval Brigade. At 5.20 P.M. M'Cay was hurrying forward with the 6th and 7th Australian Battalions, followed a few minutes later by the 5th and 8th.

For this final effort the gunners were to be prodigal of

[1] 2nd Australian, 127th Brigade of the 42nd Division, and the 29th Indian Brigade.
[2] Despatches, " London Gazette," 20th September 1915.
[3] Appendix 28.
[4] General d'Amade's order, issued at 4.50 P.M., was as follows: " The " whole British line will make a general advance to-day, precisely at " 5.30 P.M. The Commander-in-Chief, Sir Ian Hamilton, expresses his " conviction that the French troops are ready to take part in this forward " movement. In consequence the general commanding the C.E.O. directs " that, at 5.35 P.M., all along the French front the troops will advance and " break down all opposition in front of them. The drums and trumpets " will sound the charge." French Official Account, Tome viii. (1), Annexes i. No. 166.

ammunition, and the preliminary bombardment was the heaviest yet seen on the peninsula. But so little was still known about the position of the Turks [1] that most of the fire was wasted. The defenders were quite unshaken; and from shore to shore of the peninsula, as soon as the advance started, the Allied troops were lashed and scourged by a hurricane of lead.

On the extreme left, on Gully Spur, the South Wales Borderers were shot down in rows as soon as they left their trenches, and in this sector not a single yard was ultimately gained. On Fir Tree Spur, the left of the Wellington was unable to move. Its right, together with the Auckland, staggered gallantly forward for about four hundred yards against an unseen enemy, but, after suffering very heavy casualties, the survivors fell back to their starting point. The Canterbury Battalion, also suffering heavily, made some three hundred yards on the right, but could nowhere get to grips with the Turk.

On the open Krithia Spur, in full view of the Turkish batteries during their approach march, the Australians came under artillery fire long before they reached the British front line. By this time the New Zealand attack had already been brought to a standstill, and when M'Cay's troops flung themselves forward from the Composite Brigade's trench with a shout of "Come on, Australians", they at once encountered the full fury of the storm. Pressing on with great dash and boldness, they succeeded in gaining some five hundred yards, but were at last beaten to the ground by converging fire from both flanks, from the low scrub in front of them, and from a Turkish trench now for the first time visible some five hundred yards ahead. The 5th and 8th Battalions rushed up to fill the gaps in the line, but further headway was impossible. In half an hour the gallant charge of this brigade—an unrecognized Balaklava—had ended with a loss of over a thousand men out of the 2,000 engaged, including the brigadier and both staff officers wounded.[2]

On the right the French, too, were late in starting,[3] but about 6 P.M., with drums beating and bugles sounding the charge, the whole French line surged forward in a frenzy of enthusiasm. The red and blue uniforms of the French troops showed up with terrible clearness, and for a moment, to those

---

[1] No aeroplane reports had been received since the opening of the battle on 6th May.
[2] The charge of the Light Brigade at Balaklava lasted 20 minutes, and resulted in the loss of 247 men out of 673 engaged.
[3] General Masnou's orders to his brigade commanders were only issued at 5.30 P.M.

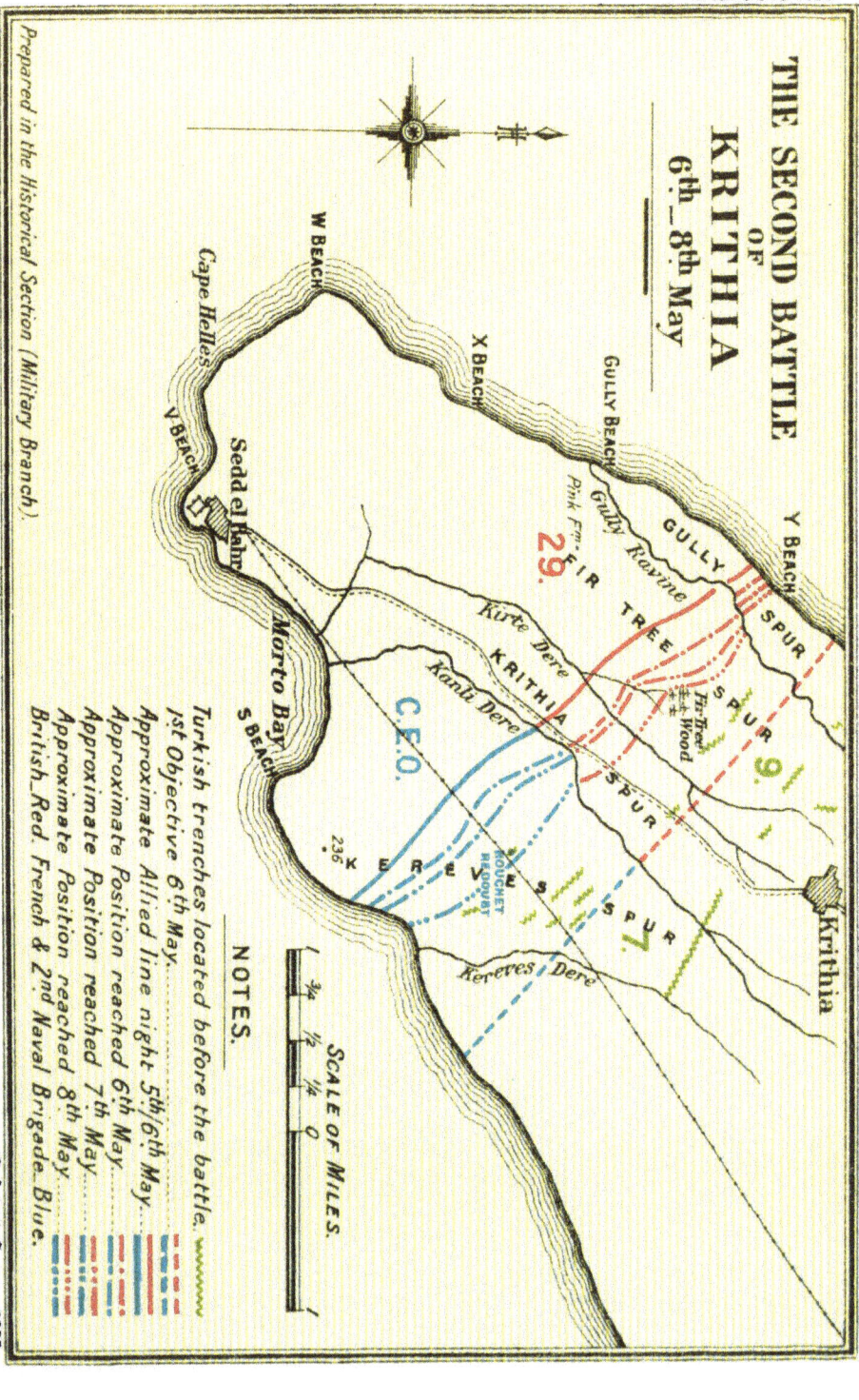

THE SECOND BATTLE OF KRITHIA

watching in rear, it seemed as if the whole spur, including the pivotal point on the left flank, had at last been captured. But a minute later the Turks covered the ridge with high-explosive shell. The trial was too severe. The left and centre recoiled; and though it subsequently transpired that a French counter-attack had regained the Bouchet redoubt, a position never again relinquished till the end of the campaign, the last thing seen from the Commander-in-Chief's post as night closed over the battlefield was a general withdrawal to the foot of Kereves Spur.

All along the front the fire died down at nightfall, and at 7 P.M. orders were sent out for units to dig in on the best positions they could find. The New Zealanders had at that time linked up with the Australian left flank, but the Australians' right was still in the air. The 1/Lancashire Fusiliers and the Drake Battalion now moved up to connect it with the 2nd Naval Brigade on the right. Advancing after nightfall, these troops were able to cross, without a casualty, a belt of country as wide as that which had cost the Australians a thousand men to capture. The Turks made no attempt to counter-attack, and the rest of the night passed quietly.[1]

So ended the Second Battle of Krithia. On the morning of the 6th May it had been hoped to reach Achi Baba before nightfall. On the evening of the 8th, after three days' fighting, the Allied line had nowhere advanced more than six hundred yards. Except on the French front, the attack had been unable even to press back the enemy's advanced troops, or to locate his main line, and apart from some forward trenches on Kereves Spur, the Turkish main position was everywhere intact. The Allied casualties during the three days' action had amounted to about 6,500, or nearly 30 per cent of the numbers actually engaged.

[1] The Turkish official account of the fighting on 8th May makes no mention of any Allied attack before 5.10 P.M., when, it relates, the land and sea artillery opened an intense bombardment, followed by an infantry attack all along the line. " The attack on the *9th Division* " [*i.e.* opposite the British sector], it says, " was in some cases checked and in others completely " repulsed. The French attack on the *7th Division* was more violent and " the first wave succeeded in penetrating a portion of our line. Thanks, " however, to counter-attacks, these trenches were recovered."

CHAPTER XX

THE END OF THE FIRST PHASE

May 1915.
THE close of the Second Battle of Krithia marks the end of the first phase of the Gallipoli campaign. The hope of reaching the Narrows with a comparatively small force and a limited amount of ammunition had finally disappeared.

On the night of the 8th May Sir Ian Hamilton was faced with a grave situation. The six hundred yards gained in the past three days' fighting were certainly valuable, for they gave much-needed elbow room in the crowded southern zone. But the Expeditionary Force had again shot its bolt. It had staked its little all upon the fight for Achi Baba, and was now at the end of its resources. Its battalions had dwindled to companies, and its divisions to brigades. Apart from eight Territorial Force battalions and General Cox's Indian brigade, there were no fresh troops left. Every unit of the original force was in need of rest and reorganization. The field ambulances were choked with wounded. The supply of ammunition was at its last ebb.[1] If the campaign was to be continued there was now no alternative for the Commander-in-Chief, despite his promise to Lord Kitchener, but to ask for large reinforcements. Yet,

[1] Helles ammunition situation, evening of 8th May:

	In Reserve on Beach. Rounds.	In Ships. Rounds.
18-pdr.	nil [a]	13,505 [b]
4·5-inch howitzer	106	800
10-pdr.	nil	1,440
60-pdr.	nil [c]	1,400
6-inch howitzer	nil [d]	nil

[a] After completing batteries and B.A.C.'s. [b] In process of being landed.
[c] 186 rounds with battery. [d] 537 rounds with battery.

Though Sir Ian Hamilton was unaware of it, his appeals for more ammunition had at last met with success, and on 9th May Sir John French was ordered to send 20,000 rounds of 18-pdr. and 2,000 rounds of 4·5-inch howitzer from his own inadequate reserves by special train to Marseilles, whence they were to be rushed by fast ship to the peninsula. Sir John was at that moment engaged in the Battle of Aubers Ridge and in the desperate fighting on Frezenberg ridge at Ypres (8th-13th May).

THE END OF THE FIRST PHASE

even if these could be spared, at least a month must elapse before they could begin to arrive. Throughout that period the Allies, except for local efforts to improve their existing positions, would be compelled to remain on the defensive; and in another month, even if nothing worse happened in the interval, they would undoubtedly be committed to the conditions of trench warfare.

There was no room for optimism that night. For the first time the pendulum swung in the opposite direction. "The "result of the operation", wired Sir Ian Hamilton to Lord Kitchener, "has been failure, as my object remains unachieved. "The fortifications and their machine guns were too scientific "and too strongly held to be rushed, although I had every "available man in to-day. Our troops have done all that "flesh and blood can do against semi-permanent works and "they are not able to carry them. More and more munitions "will be needed to do so. I fear that this is a very unpalatable "conclusion, but I can see no way out of it." Next day, however, his answer to a message from Lord Kitchener[1] shows that some of his old confidence had returned. He again laid stress on the strength of the Turkish positions, explaining that Achi Baba was really a fortress, and he suggested that the only sound course was to hammer away till the enemy became demoralized. But he added that everyone was in good spirits and confident, and he still held out some hopes of capturing the Achi Baba ridge, even without further reinforcements. His wish for more troops, however, was evidently battling with his promise not to ask for them, for the message ended with the remark that, if two fresh divisions could be spared him, he could push on both from Helles and Gaba Tepe with good prospects of success.[2]

[1] Lord Kitchener's message of 9th May:
"I should be glad if you would give me your views as to the future "operations that will be necessary. I presume that you have consulted with "the admiral on the subject. I had hoped that the naval artillery would "have been more effective than is apparently the case on the enemy's fixed "positions. . . . The whole situation naturally gives me some anxiety, "particularly as our transport service is much hampered by want of ships. "More ammunition is being pushed out to you via Marseilles. I hope you "and the admiral will be able to devise some means of clearing the way "through."

[2] The actual words of Sir Ian Hamilton's telegram were:
"With regard to future operations the admiral agrees with me in thinking "that the only sound procedure is to hammer away until the enemy gets "demoralized. Meanwhile grand attacks are impracticable and we must "make short advances during the night and dig in for the day until we get "Achi Baba. I then hope to be able to make progress without this trench "method, but Achi Baba is really a fortress. If two fresh divisions organized "as a corps could be spared me I could push on from this end and from Gaba

Lord Kitchener replied next day that he would send him one division.[1]

The Commander-in-Chief's tribute to his troops was abundantly deserved. Throughout the three days' fighting the conduct of the infantry had been superb, and their gallant and self-sacrificing response to every exacting call is at once the brightest and most poignant spot in the sombre picture of the battle. But Sir Ian Hamilton's impression of the enemy's defences was not in accordance with the facts. It is now known that the Turkish positions at that time could in no sense be described as semi-permanent works. They did not even consist of a connected line of trenches. They were nowhere protected by wire; and, except on the French front, the attacking units had as yet been engaged only against advanced troops lying out behind natural cover. The attack had failed, but the principal reason for its failure was the fact —not at that time fully realized either in Gallipoli or in France —that an advance by daylight, without adequate artillery support, against unlocated machine-gun positions, is in nine cases out of ten a sheer impossibility.

To a minor extent other causes, already mentioned in the narrative, such as inadequate air reports,[2] insufficient time allowed for the issue of brigade and battalion orders, and the fact that attacks meant to be simultaneous were often delivered piecemeal, all had their influence on the course of the battle.[3] But, looking at the picture in the light of that knowledge which comes only long after the event, it would seem that, notwithstanding its many disadvantages, Sir Ian Hamilton's original intention of a night advance was, in all

---

" Tepe with good prospects of success, otherwise I am afraid it will de-
" generate into trench warfare with its resultant slowness. Everyone is in
" good spirits and fully confident."

[1] The 52nd (Lowland) Division.

[2] In the early days, arguing that the operations were to be primarily naval, Lord Kitchener had refused to allot any military aeroplanes to the expedition, and this decision had never been rescinded. The Royal Naval Air Service did all it could to help the army, but the number of aeroplanes and trained observers available fell very short of requirements. During the three days' battle, the R.N.A.S. carried out 23 flights, but the majority of them were devoted to spotting for naval guns firing on Asiatic batteries, and none of them added to the army's knowledge of the whereabouts of the enemy's infantry.

[3] It has sometimes been suggested that a greater chance of success could have been secured by delaying the attack till the whole of the 42nd Division had arrived from Egypt. But it must be remembered that every day's delay was of great value to the Turks, and that there were ample grounds for deciding that one extra brigade to-day would be of more value to the British than a whole division in three days' time.

THE END OF THE FIRST PHASE

the circumstances of the case, the only plan with a reasonable prospect of success.

The anxieties of both the military and naval Commanders-in-Chief at Gallipoli in the early days of May were many-sided. Every day's experience of the peninsula was throwing into greater relief the extraordinary physical difficulties with which the campaign was hedged. Though many of these difficulties had been realized before the landing, all were now being accentuated by the failure of the initial plan.

First to be noticed, in view of the need for more men, was the distance of the peninsula from the home ports. Whereas the Turks were only 150 miles from Constantinople, and, until their sea communications were interrupted by British submarines in the month of May, could reach the front line in twenty-four hours from their capital, the distance from England to Helles was over 3,000 miles, or twenty times as far. The Australians were 7,000 miles and the New Zealanders 10,000 miles from their home ports and 600 miles from their first reinforcements in Egypt. Normally it would take a month for a British soldier from England to reach the fighting line. For ammunition, stores, and foodstuffs the period would be longer, for bulk would generally have to be broken at the base at Alexandria, and often a second time in the wind-swept harbour of Mudros. Even if ammunition was sent by train to Marseilles the sea voyage from that port to the peninsula was 1,400 miles.

More serious still was the absence of any sheltered landing places on the Ægean coast of the peninsula. With its exposed beaches and fragile piers, the Allied army was at the mercy of the elements. Happily the weather since the landing had been almost ideal, but already there had been more than one warning of future trouble.[1] Nor were the beaches even secure from hostile shelling. Every pier was exposed to artillery fire, and it was only the enemy's shortage of gun ammunition that permitted the daylight working of the beaches to continue. Particularly serious, in the event of more Turkish ammunition

---

[1] " The evening of 28th April ", wrote Rear-Admiral Wemyss, " did " not lessen our difficulties nor allay our anxieties, for it came on to blow " sufficiently hard to render the landing of our stores . . . impossible. The " abandonment of this work awoke gloomy forebodings as to the result of " two or three days of bad weather. Such an eventuality was improbable at " this time of year, but even the remote possibility of the Army being " imprisoned on the Peninsula with but little ammunition and no reserves of " rations caused me grave preoccupation. . . ." " The Navy in the Dardanelles Campaign," p. 114.

arriving, was the danger from the Asiatic batteries, for these commanded not only the right flank but also the reserve areas of the French.[1]

Above all, there was the haunting fear of German submarines, two of which were already believed to have passed the Straits of Gibraltar. For the moment—so long as the weather remained calm and the enemy artillery comparatively inactive—the feeding of the army and the landing of ammunition was causing little anxiety, for storeships were lying off the coast and their cargoes were being landed as required. The warships, too, could remain off the beaches to support the army with their fire, and troop transports could lie at the outer anchorages in almost complete security. But with the arrival of submarines the whole situation would change. Large vessels would be obliged to seek shelter in Mudros; the disadvantages of an advanced base without any conveniences, and 70 miles from the seat of operations, would at once become accentuated; and, until other arrangements could be made by the Admiralty, the problem of supporting the army with heavy naval guns would be increasingly difficult to solve.

The deplorable and even critical position of the Mediterranean Expeditionary Force at the middle of May must be ascribed partly to the two months' warning given to the Turks by the opening of the naval bombardment, and partly to the fact that, after the abandonment of the naval attack in March, the strength of the military force was not readjusted to meet the steadily mounting numbers and preparations of the enemy.

It is impossible to study the events of the 18th March, when the fleet did so well, and those of 25th-26th April, when the army for a short time had victory almost within its grasp, without realizing that, had the fleet attack been delayed till the army was ready and the weather favourable, a simultaneous and combined operation, launched, as it could have been in 1915,[2] with all the advantages of surprise, would probably have achieved an instantaneous and overwhelming success. " Up to 25th February ",[3] says the Turkish official account, "it " would have been possible to effect a landing successfully at " any point on the peninsula, and the capture of the Straits by " land troops would have been comparatively easy." But the

[1] Fortunately for the Allies, these batteries were short of ammunition, and a large proportion of their shell did not explode.
[2] See page 30, and Colonel Hankey's memorandum, page 101.
[3] That is, six days after the opening of the naval attack which had convinced the Turks of the necessity of putting their house in order.

THE END OF THE FIRST PHASE

two months' delay between the appearance of the fleet and the landing of the army transformed that "comparatively easy" operation into a task of superlative difficulty. Sir Ian Hamilton, to quote a remark by Enver Pasha, had been set to thread a needle with his toes.

But it was not so much the results of the two months' warning as the failure both at home and on the spot to appreciate the probable importance of those results which first prejudiced and then jeopardized the army's chances of success.

It would be hard to exaggerate the anxieties of the War Council at the beginning of 1915. Ministers had to assess as best they could the relative advantages claimed for alternative theatres of war, the views and needs of the Allies, the local outlooks of the various commanders already in the field, the number of reserves which should be kept in hand for home defence and for unforeseen contingencies. Decisions had to be made, at moments of supreme anxiety, on information which was always incomplete, often incorrect, and which varied from day to day. In the case of distant campaigns, the despatch of troops had to be undertaken many weeks before the operations contemplated could begin, and in a situation which might entirely change in every particular while the troops were still on passage.

But the difficulties which faced the War Council in 1915 can now be examined in the clear light of day, and it is permissible to notice the manner in which some of the decisions arrived at in moments of stress and strain adversely affected the fortunes of the army in Gallipoli.

The circumstances in which the military landing was finally sanctioned have already been described. The opening of the naval bombardment had created such a feeling among the Balkan states in favour of the Entente, and the immense advantages of a success in the Dardanelles were becoming so plain, that the original idea of abandoning the operations if the navy failed to get through unaided had become "unthinkable" to British ministers. Lord Kitchener informed Sir Ian Hamilton that if large military operations were necessary to clear the way for the fleet they must be undertaken, and must be carried through, and this definite order received the tacit approval of the Government. But there was no careful review of the altered situation, and no careful counting of the cost.

Thus, though the Government had decided that the peninsula must be captured, there had been no consideration of what was to be done if, as had now happened, Sir Ian Hamilton's force should prove too weak for its task. Sir Ian Hamilton, it is true, for reasons already explained, had given little indication that he thought his force too weak. He had, however, explained that the operations would require the whole of his force. Yet no steps had been taken while time was still available, to provide him with a margin of safety, nor any preparations made to keep his units up to strength. Most important of all, there had been no attempt to decide whether the Dardanelles operations were for the moment to be held as more important than Sir John French's approaching offensive on the Western front, and whether, in the case of necessity, Sir Ian Hamilton was to be given a prior claim to available men and ammunition.

Here undoubtedly was the crux of the whole situation. Whether or not it was right to embark on military operations in Gallipoli after the naval attack had failed must remain a matter of controversy. But there can be little question that, in view of the shortage of men and ammunition it was wrong to embark on them, and to proclaim that they must be carried through, unless it was first decided that they were of such supreme importance, that, till success was achieved, the peninsula must be regarded as the decisive theatre of war. This was the acid test. There could be only one decisive theatre. Either it lay in the Dardanelles, in which case, owing to the limited means available, the strategical defensive should have been temporarily imposed upon the army in France; or, if a spring offensive on the Western front, as urged by the French High Command, was held to be of greater importance, or, if the obligations to the French were considered paramount, every available man and gun should have been concentrated in France, and the landing in Gallipoli should not have been undertaken.

But neither of these courses had been adopted. For lack of a careful Staff study beforehand, Sir Ian Hamilton was ordered to enter upon a new campaign without a sufficient reserve. Sir John French, with a strength even less adequate for his task, was permitted to persevere with his plans for a spring offensive in France. With barely enough ammunition for one theatre, an offensive campaign was sanctioned in two, and both ended in failure.

In Gallipoli on the 6th, 7th, and 8th May, Sir Ian Hamilton attacked with 20,000 troops on a three-mile front. He was supported during the course of those three days with a total of some 18,500 rounds of ammunition, including those fired by the ships and the French artillery, or an average of about 6,000 rounds a day, principally field-gun shrapnel. His force

THE END OF THE FIRST PHASE 355

advanced 600 yards at an expense of 6,500 casualties. The enemy's trench system was not yet complete, and was nowhere protected by wire, and the main obstacle to progress had been unlocated machine guns concealed in natural cover.

On the following day, at Aubers Ridge in France, three divisions of Sir Douglas Haig's First Army (30,000 infantry) with eight more brigades (25,000 infantry) waiting in reserve, attacked two sectors of the German heavily wired and fortified line on a frontage of two miles.[1] They were supported by 500 guns, which fired 80,000 rounds in the course of the day, mostly in a forty-minute preliminary bombardment. These three divisions suffered 11,000 casualties. They were unable to gain a yard of ground. They did not attract a single company from the German reserves to the British battle front; and at nightfall the attack was abandoned on the score that its continuance would be useless waste of life.

The 18,500 rounds of all calibres expended during the three previous days in Gallipoli could not have made the difference between success and failure on this French battlefield. But the 80,000 rounds fired against Aubers ridge, and even two out of the three divisions launched that day against the German trenches, had they been available for the Second Battle of Krithia, might well have carried Sir Ian Hamilton to the Narrows and the fleet to Constantinople.

The moral and material effect of such a success on Turkey, on Russia, on the neutral Balkan states, and on the whole course of the war, must remain a matter of conjecture. But certain points stand out. First, as regards the Turkish Army on the peninsula. With British ships on each side of the Bulair isthmus, communication between the capital and the peninsula would have been finally severed, and Liman von Sanders, with his stocks of ammunition and supplies daily diminishing, would have been faced with the alternatives of retreat or surrender. Secondly, as regards the forts on the Asiatic shore, and the remaining Turkish armies wherever situated, it is known that Turkey was at that time short of ammunition, and that, apart from the small amounts which could be smuggled from Bulgaria or through the Balkans from Germany, her only source of supply was the factory at Zeitun Burnu. This factory was on the European shore, just south-west of Constantinople, and at the mercy of a hostile fleet in the Marmara. Even, therefore, if we discount the idea that the arrival of the fleet in the Marmara would have caused a revolution at Constantinople and brought

[1] Two divisions attacked on a front of 2,400 yards, and one on a front of 800 yards, with a gap of roughly four miles between the two attacks.

the wavering Balkans to the side of the Entente, Turkey's position would still have been untenable. Liman von Sanders has placed on record that if the Straits had fallen the Turkish military authorities would have retired across the Bosporus, and it has been argued from this that the Turks would have continued to fight in Asia Minor. But in this case they would have been fighting without ammunition, for neither by land nor sea could another round have reached them. For a short time, perhaps, till their ammunition was expended, they could have prevented unarmoured ships from passing the Dardanelles; but even this need have caused no great inconvenience to a fleet in the Marmara. With the retreat or surrender of the Turkish troops in Gallipoli, and the occupation of the Bulair isthmus by the Allies, the construction of a Decauville railway, brought by fast ships from France, across the isthmus from the Gulf of Saros to the Straits, could have been completed in a few days after its arrival, and would have formed a practicable line for supplying urgent stores to the fleet.

Upon the Allied squadrons at the Dardanelles the undreamed-of losses of the army, landed on the peninsula with the sole object of assisting the fleet, were creating a profound and painful impression, and amongst all ranks and ratings there was an urgent and chivalrous longing to come to the soldiers' aid. Ever since the abandonment of the unaided naval attack in March it had been intended that the fleet should resume its methodical reduction of the Dardanelles defences as soon as the army was in a position to engage the hostile forts and batteries from the land side.[1] The reasons that had delayed the opening of this second attack were that the soldiers had hitherto required the co-operation of the whole fleet to establish themselves ashore, and that they had not yet reached a position from which they could be of any help to the ships.

But now that it was clear that the army was definitely checked, and that naval guns could do little to help it forward in the face of hidden machine guns, there arose in some of the naval Staff on the spot a strong feeling that the fleet should make another unaided effort to force the Straits. These officers rejected the idea that the check on the 18th March had proved

---

[1] Telegram from Admiral de Robeck to Admiralty, dated 29th March 1915:
"... Directly the army is landed on the peninsula the fleet will renew "its attacks on the Narrows. ... No matter where the army effects its "landings, the extreme objective of both Services must be the forts at the "Narrows, and the intention is to attack them simultaneously with all our "forces."

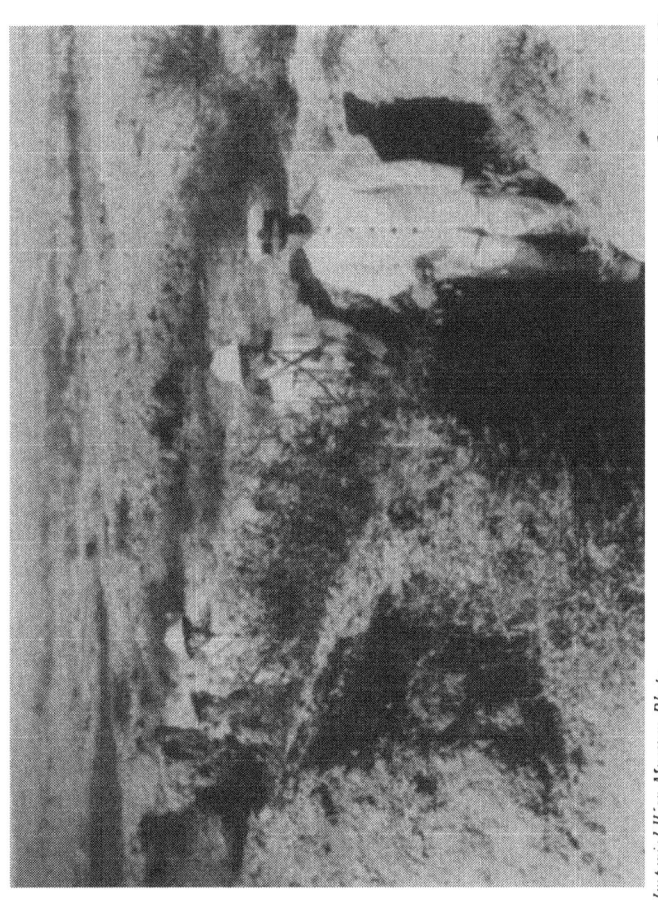

Imperial War Museum Photo. *Crown Copyright.*

NAVAL OFFICERS COMING FROM NAVAL OBSERVATION STATION ON FORWARD SLOPES OF HILL 114, KRITHIA RIDGE IN THE DISTANCE

THE END OF THE FIRST PHASE 357

the impossibility of forcing the Straits, and the French Admiral Guépratte shared their opinion whole-heartedly. They maintained that the fleet was now in a better position to make the attempt than it had been on the 18th March. The losses of that day had been made good; instead of old trawlers, whose engines could make no headway against the Dardanelles current, and untrained fishermen crews, there was now an efficient force of destroyers capable of rapid mine-sweeping at night; and the naval air force, though still very weak in numbers, was at least more numerous and better equipped for its work than it had been six weeks earlier. There was reason also for the belief that many of the mobile guns and howitzers which hindered naval operations in March had now been moved inland to oppose the army, and that all the Turkish heavy guns were short of ammunition. In favour of a renewal of the naval attack it was urged that, in addition to the moral effect of reaching the Marmara, which it was generally admitted might be great, the presence of ships on both sides of the Bulair isthmus would be of direct and material advantage to the Expeditionary Force, in that the communications between the peninsula and the rest of Turkey, both by land and sea, would then be cut, and that in these circumstances the Gallipoli garrison would be unable to hold out.[1]

But it must always be easier for a staff officer to recommend than for his commander, on whom the ultimate responsibility rests, to decide on a hazardous enterprise; and in this case, the naval Commander-in-Chief was responsible not only for the safety of the Allied fleet, but, indirectly, since the fleet was the army's life-line, for the safety of the army as well. Admiral de Robeck, moreover, was far from sharing the optimism of his subordinates. Though agreeing that the fleet, or a substantial portion of it, would probably reach the Marmara, he was doubtful if it could thereby achieve any decisive result; and there was the obvious risk of further heavy losses if it was eventually forced to return with its mission unfulfilled. He was not prepared, therefore, to order on his own responsibility,

[1] After the war the Turkish War Office, questioned on the probable effect of British ships reaching the Marmara, said: " It is impossible to " estimate the situation which would have arisen. But if the British fleet " had attacked land transport from both sides of the isthmus of Bulair a " very difficult situation would undoubtedly have arisen. But even in these " circumstances the Turkish situation would not have been essentially " changed during a fortnight. The Fifth Army could have held every " attack which could take place during the fortnight by using its ammunition " supplies with great care." (A fortnight was presumably looked upon as the limit of time that the fleet would be able to stay in the Marmara without running short of food and ammunition.)

or even to advise, a resumption of the naval attack, but, after a conference on board the *Queen Elizabeth* on the evening of the 9th May, he resolved to put the whole case before the Admiralty, and to leave the decision to higher authority. He accordingly telegraphed to the Admiralty on the morning of the 10th May:

The position in the Gallipoli peninsula. General Hamilton informs me that the army is checked; its advance on Achi Baba can only be carried out by a few yards at a time, and a condition of affairs is threatened approximating to that in northern France. The situation therefore arises as indicated in my telegram of the 29th March:[1]

" If the army is checked in its advance on Kilid Bahr, the
" question whether the navy should not force the Narrows, leaving
" the forts intact, will depend entirely on whether the fleet could
" assist the army in their advance to the Narrows best from below
" Chanak with communications intact, or from above cut off from
" its base."

The help which the navy has been able to give the army in its advance has not been as great as was anticipated. Though effective in keeping down the fire of the enemy's batteries, when it is a question of trenches and machine guns the navy is of small assistance. It is these latter that have checked the army.

From the vigour of the enemy's resistance it is improbable that the passage of the fleet into the Marmara will be decisive, and therefore it is equally probable that the Straits will be closed behind the fleet. This will be of slight importance if the resistance of the enemy could be overcome in time to prevent the enforced withdrawal of the fleet owing to lack of supplies.

The supporting of the attack of the army, should the fleet penetrate to the Sea of Marmara, will be entrusted to the cruisers and certain older battleships, including some of the French, whose ships are not fitted for a serious bombardment of the Narrows; this support will obviously be much less than is now given by the whole of the fleet. The temper of the Turkish army in the peninsula indicates that the forcing of the Dardanelles and subsequent appearance of the fleet off Constantinople will not, of itself, prove decisive.

The points for decision appear to be:

1. Can the navy, by forcing the Dardanelles, ensure the success of the operations?

2. If the navy were to suffer a reverse, which of necessity could only be a severe one, would the position of the army be so critical as to jeopardize the whole of the operations?

This message, it will be seen, held out no promise of success. Nevertheless, those at the Dardanelles who knew of

---

[1] Another paragraph of that telegram has been quoted in f.n. p. 356.

its despatch felt confident that it would result in orders to renew the naval attack. Admiral Guépratte, commanding the French squadron, telegraphed to the French Minister of Marine asking for the early return of three French battleships to take part in the coming operations.[1]

The Board of Admiralty, however, were not in favour of a second attempt. Quite apart from the inherent risks of the enterprise, two other weighty reasons were now urged against it. It was certain that at least one and probably two German submarines were nearing the Ægean, and, as it was considered most undesirable to expose England's newest and finest battleship to this fresh risk, the *Queen Elizabeth* was on the point of being recalled to home waters.[2] Secondly, Italy had just renounced the Triple Alliance and was about to declare war on Austria; but this welcome addition to the strength of the Entente was increasing rather than diminishing the British Navy's burden in the Mediterranean. In accordance with a convention signed at Paris on the 10th May, four battleships and four light cruisers were to be sent at once to reinforce the Italian fleet in the Adriatic, and as there was some difficulty about French ships serving under an Italian admiral, these reinforcements could only be found from the British ships at the Dardanelles. For the moment, therefore, though it would subsequently be strengthened by the inclusion of more French vessels, the Dardanelles fleet would be reduced, at least temporarily, by five battleships and four light cruisers. There was, moreover, the fear that even if the fleet reached the Marmara, its activities would be seriously curtailed by the action of German submarines. Finally, the army on the peninsula was held to be in urgent need of all the naval support it could get, both for the protection of its flanks and for ensuring the arrival of storeships and reinforcements; and both these services would be jeopardized by an unsuccessful attack on the Narrows.

The French Minister of Marine was equally opposed to

---

[1] Admiral Guépratte's message, " A fin d'assister l'Armée dans son " action énergique et rude, nous méditons vive action flotte dans détroite " avec attaque des forts. Dans ces conditions il me faut mes cuirassés, " *Suffren, Charlemagne, Gaulois* dans le plus bref délai possible." " La " Guerre navale aux Dardanelles," p. 147.

[2] Orders for her return were telegraphed on the evening of 12th May. Admiral de Robeck was informed that she would be replaced by the *Exmouth* and *Venerable* and that he should also have the first two new monitors, with two 14-inch guns apiece, as soon as they were ready. He was further informed in this telegram that two infantry divisions would leave for Gallipoli about 17th and 30th May. Actually, only one division was sent.

the resumption of the naval attack. On receipt of Admiral Guépratte's message, he telegraphed to London as follows:

If success is not absolutely certain, if the conditions are not different to those of 18th March, it seems to me imprudent to engage the fleet in this enterprise. In addition to the losses to be feared, a check would have a deplorable moral effect. From a practical point of view, far from being of service to the troops on shore in an already difficult situation, an unsuccessful intervention by the fleet would aggravate their position dangerously. I should be glad to know your views and intentions on this subject.[1]

After receiving Admiral de Robeck's telegram of 10th May, Mr. Churchill asked Admiral Sir H. B. Jackson for a Staff study on the probable losses by mine and gun-fire that a squadron might suffer if forced to return from the Marmara with the Turks still in possession of the Narrows. Next morning Admiral Jackson replied that if sixteen ships in two squadrons rushed the Straits, a total of eight might reach the Marmara, but only with depleted magazines. If these eight tried to return they would probably lose four on the way down by gun-fire alone; the loss from mine and torpedo could not be estimated. The memorandum ended: "Thus of the sixteen "ships that attempted to rush the Straits into the Sea of Mar- "mara to carry out operations therein and then rush back, it "appears probable that four badly injured ones might with "luck return." On the same day Lord Fisher informed Mr. Churchill and the Prime Minister in writing that he could not, in any circumstances, be a party to any further attempt to pass the Narrows until the shores were effectively occupied.

While these deliberations were still proceeding, the news reached England that the British battleship *Goliath* had been sunk in the Dardanelles by a Turkish torpedo boat in the early hours of the 13th.[2] That same evening the Admiralty informed Admiral de Robeck that they considered that the moment for an independent naval attempt on the Narrows had passed and would not arise again under present conditions. The army had now landed, it was to be largely reinforced, and there was no doubt that with time and patience the Kilid Bahr plateau would be taken. The rôle of the fleet should therefore be confined to supporting the army in its advance, and six new

---

[1] "La Guerre navale aux Dardanelles," p. 147.
[2] The *Goliath* was lying at anchor off the French right flank. With consummate gallantry, a Turkish torpedo boat, commanded by a German lieutenant, was taken down the Straits stern first to attack her; and was mistaken in the dark for a British vessel. She fired three torpedoes at the *Goliath* at short range, all of which took effect, and then made good her escape. The *Goliath* sank in two minutes.

THE END OF THE FIRST PHASE

monitors would be sent out to assist in this task as soon as they were delivered by the shipbuilders.

The gist of this decision was explained to Lord Kitchener at an Admiralty conference earlier in the day, and though he at first protested strongly against the recall of the *Queen Elizabeth*, in the belief that this order signified some weakening of the naval support to the troops, he withdrew his objections on a definite Admiralty assurance that the army should continue to be sustained by every means in the navy's power.

As for the French squadron, in view of its approaching increase of size to counterbalance the number of British ships going to the Adriatic, Vice-Admiral Nicol was nominated to its command on the 14th May in place of Rear-Admiral Guépratte, who clearly thought that his forward policy had been an important factor in his supersession.[1]

Nor was this the only change made in the French Dardanelles forces at this time. On the 14th May General Gouraud arrived at Sedd el Bahr to replace General d'Amade in command of the French corps. When General d'Amade left the peninsula two days later he received an ovation from the troops, his constant presence in the front line and his determination to share the life of his men having endeared him to all ranks.

The Admiralty telegram to Admiral de Robeck did more than veto a second naval attack on the Narrows; it foreshadowed a further change in the whole policy of the Dardanelles expedition. Conceived in January as an independent naval enterprise, which could be broken off at will if unsuccessful, it had been changed in February to a naval attack supported by a few troops. In April it had undergone another metamorphosis and had been converted into a combined naval and military attack on the Narrows. Now, according to this telegram, after one more month's delay, it was to develop in June into a great military campaign against what, by that time, would certainly be a veritable fortress.

This was the position when, for the first time since the 19th March, the War Council met again on the 14th May to review the situation on all fronts, and in particular the menacing problem of the Gallipoli peninsula.

The last resolution of the War Council with regard to the Dardanelles, arrived at on the day after the action of the 18th

---

[1] In a preface to "La Guerre navale aux Dardanelles," Admiral Guépratte, after discussing this naval plan, writes: " Hélas! Ce beau rêve n'eut " pas de lendemain! Peu de jours après, l'Amirauté britannique répondait, " . . . 'Non, trop tard!' Quant à moi, j'étais purement et simplement " relevé de mon commandement, comme casse-cou dangereux! "

March, had been "to inform Vice-Admiral de Robeck that he "could continue the operations against the Dardanelles if he "thought fit". But since that date the whole situation had fundamentally changed. The army had landed on the peninsula and had been definitely checked on both fronts with a loss of some 14,000 casualties, exclusive of the French. The troops held little more than the fringe of the coast; their beaches were under hostile shell-fire; and there was no space for rest behind the line.

The difficulties of advancing had proved far greater than anticipated; there was no chance of any material gain of ground without large reinforcements in men and ammunition; and no reinforcements could arrive in less than a month.

The Russian army corps, which was to have co-operated in the vicinity of Constantinople in the event of the British fleet reaching the Sea of Marmara, could no longer be counted on; for the Russian front in Galicia was being rolled up by the strong Austro-German offensive begun on the 2nd May, and owing to lack of arms and ammunition the situation of the Russian troops in that theatre was apparently desperate.

Little help could be expected from the navy. Ships' guns had proved of no avail against trenches and machine guns, and the Admiralty had definitely refused to be responsible for any further attempt to pass the Narrows till the army had effectively occupied its shores. The Admiralty view was that the Allied attack had now become primarily a military rather than a naval operation. There was some confidence that with patience and perseverance the army would get through, and the First Lord was urging that such arrangements should now be made as would secure finality to the enterprise within three months. But the problem of sea-transport—even if troops could be spared for the Dardanelles—was serious. There was a great scarcity of ships, and this scarcity was being aggravated by the detention of many large vessels at Mudros till the stores they carried were wanted on the peninsula. The recent sinking of the *Lusitania* had again concentrated attention on the German submarine menace; and there was the fear that even the maritime strength of Britain might be unable to meet all the requirements of a great campaign in Gallipoli.

Nor could the Dardanelles expedition be considered by itself. It was looked upon as subsidiary to the main operations in France; and from France, too, the news was grave and depressing. From Sir John French as well as from Gallipoli there was an insistent demand for more and more munitions.

Finally, in view of the lack of success on all fronts, and of

THE END OF THE FIRST PHASE 363

the attack on the Government that very morning in *The Times* newspaper on account of the shortage of gun ammunition,[1] there could be little doubt that a political crisis at home was imminent.

On the 13th May an appreciation of the military situation on the Western front, coupled with an account of the severe reverse lately inflicted on the Russians in Galicia, had been drawn up for the War Council by Lord Kitchener. This appreciation advanced a new argument against any further strengthening of Sir Ian Hamilton's force, namely, the fear of an invasion of England.

Lord Kitchener's view was that, although Sir John French now had more than half a million British troops on the flank of the French armies, recent experiences had proved that the German line in the West could not at present be broken. In these circumstances, he considered that the only course for the Allies in France and Flanders was to maintain a defensive rôle, and prepare for a gigantic concentration and attack by German forces, such as the Russians had recently been unable to withstand. In such an emergency France would need every available man that could be spared from England, and then would be the moment for Germany to attempt a landing on the east coast. Lord Kitchener looked upon such a landing as probable, and the danger from it as very serious. For this reason he did not consider it safe at the moment to send any more of the new divisions overseas.[2]

An important minute written by Lord Kitchener on the 13th May is also on record, in which he defined his own connection with the Dardanelles enterprise. In this minute Lord Kitchener stated that when the Admiralty first proposed to force the Dardanelles by means of the fleet alone, he had doubted whether the attempt would succeed, but was led to think it possible by the First Lord's belief in the power of the *Queen Elizabeth's* guns, and by the Admiralty staff paper showing how the operation was to be conducted. He mentioned that neither Lord Fisher nor Sir Arthur Wilson had raised any protest against the operation either at the Council or in the staff paper issued by the Admiralty, and that they both apparently agreed

---

[1] " British soldiers died in vain on the Aubers Ridge on Sunday because " more shells were needed. The Government, who have so seriously failed " to organize adequately our national resources, must bear their share of the " grave responsibility. Even now they will not fully face the situation." Leading article in *The Times*, Friday, 14th May 1915.

[2] One of the first six new divisions had already gone to France. The Second and Third New Armies would not be trained or equipped for several more weeks.

in the feasibility of carrying out the projects of the admiral on the spot. "I considered", he continued, "that though there " was a risk, the political advantages to be gained by forcing the " Straits were commensurate with that risk. I realized that if " the fleet failed the army would have to help the navy through." He added that, owing to the unexpected difficulties, and the grave situation elsewhere, he would now like to abandon the Dardanelles enterprise, but he realized that that was impossible.

Lord Kitchener's fears of an invasion, or even of a hostile raid on the east coast, were not shared by the Admiralty. The sea service held that with the British fleet able to reach any part of the east coast in from fifteen to twenty hours, and with so large a number of British destroyers and submarines in the North Sea, there was no need for anxiety. Even if a small German force did succeed in landing, it could not be maintained, and its sea communications would immediately be cut. The Admiralty, in fact, held to their old opinion that so long as there were enough men in England to meet 70,000 Germans, no hostile landing would be attempted.[1]

From a study of the foregoing considerations it will be seen that on the 14th May there were three alternative methods of dealing with the Dardanelles problem for discussion by the War Council: to abandon the operations and withdraw from the peninsula; to make a determined assault on the Turkish positions with large forces; or to hold the existing lines, to keep Sir Ian Hamilton's forces up to strength, send him the one division already promised, and trust to his being able to make slow and steady progress towards the Narrows.

The first of these alternatives was objectionable for political reasons. It was felt that such an admission of failure would not only turn the Balkan scale against the Entente but would almost certainly lead to risings all over the Moslem world. The second course, which might lead to an early and successful termination of the campaign, was obviously attractive; but against it there had to be weighed Lord Kitchener's view that for the moment not another man could be spared from England. The third alternative avoided both the abandonment of the enterprise and any excessive inroads into Britain's slender military resources. But it had the inherent disadvantages of a compromise, and would immobilize a large army and a considerable fleet for many months.

[1] No great consolation could be drawn from these figures at the time. No one at home yet knew, nor was it to be known for several years, that two Turkish battalions and four machine guns, without artillery, had held up the landing of the 29th Division.

THE END OF THE FIRST PHASE 365

The difficulty of reaching a decision was increased by the absence of any military estimate of the numbers required to ensure a rapid decision in Gallipoli. Lord Kitchener's note had made no mention of this point. In view of Sir Ian Hamilton's statement that he was opposed by semi-permanent works and would need more and more men and munitions to carry them—in view, too, of the shortage of munitions in France, and of the fears of a German invasion of England—the War Secretary had felt that even the most moderate requirements for a big offensive in the Dardanelles would be far in excess of Britain's available resources.

Despite Lord Kitchener's opinion, the general tendency of the War Council was towards sending out sufficient reinforcements for another military effort, but no final decision was reached. It was agreed, however, that the first step was to ascertain the dimensions of the problem, and then to decide whether the means for its solution existed. That night, at the request of the War Council, Lord Kitchener telegraphed to Sir Ian Hamilton:

The War Council would like to know what force you consider would be necessary to carry through the operations upon which you are engaged. You should base this estimate on the supposition that I have adequate forces to be placed at your disposal.

Heartened beyond measure by this encouraging enquiry, Sir Ian Hamilton replied three days later, placing his requirements at three more divisions in addition to the one already promised, or a total of four in all. But in the interval the Government had fallen. A Coalition Ministry was about to take its place, and for the next three weeks no further action was taken with regard to the Dardanelles. The one Territorial Force division already promised was despatched, and a number of reinforcing drafts, but all other decisions were adjourned. For another three weeks Sir Ian Hamilton had no material for making his new plans, and the Turkish positions in front of him grew daily stronger.

GENERAL INDEX

Achi Baba (Alchi Tepe), 37, 156; as objective on 25th Apr., 136, 220, 251; advance towards, 27th Apr., 283
Achi Baba nullah. *See* Kanli Dere
Adams, Major G. S., 227, 230
Addington, Sub-Lieut. L. G., 315
Addison, Captain A. C., 276
Adjutant-General's Staff. *See* Staff
Administrative Staffs. *See* Staff
Admiralty. Views on forcing Dardanelles, 1906, 28, 29; in 1914-15, 38; plan for Greek co-operation, 42; prefer combined operation, 57, 67; urge naval attack, 93; urge combined operation, 100; oppose fresh naval attack, 359; conference, 13th May, 361
AE2, Austr. S/M, 144, 194, 269, 308
Agamemnon, H.M.S., 329
Air service, British. Weather hampers work with fleet, 78, 80, 81, 139; deficiencies of, 86, 139, 322, 324, 346, 350; raid on Maidos, 158; reconnaissance before Second Krithia, 327
——, Turkish. State of, 19, 139; aeroplane over Mudros, 139
Albion, H.M.S., 204, 218, 219, 231, 242, 247, 248, 249, 291, 322
Alexandretta, 53, 56, 60, 138
Alexandria, suggested base, 95; preparations at, 108; hospital accommodation at, 144
Ali Chefik Bey, Lieut.-Col., 158
Allpress, Gunner, 318
Alternative theatre, reasons for seeking, 44, 48; Sir J. French's views, 51
Amanus tunnel, 21
Amethyst, H.M.S., 203, 207, 219
Ammunition, British, military. Shortage of, 110, 119, 120, 325, 338, 341, 354, 363; expenditure in France, 120, 355; original allotment, M.E.F., 285; W.O. reply to request for, 335; expenditure, Helles, 8th May, 348; sent from France, 348; expenditure, Second Krithia, 354
Ammunition, British, naval. Expenditure serious, 86; on 18th Mar., 105; 25th-28th Apr., 325; shortage, 325; rounds available 30th Apr., 325; expenditure, 5th-9th May, 344
——, —— (S.A.A.). Shortage, 120, 291, 293, 295; Mk. VI and Mk. VII, 121, 208; heavy expenditure, 197, 208
——, French, 344
——, Turkish. Shortage, 10, 33, 34, 309, 317, 351, 355, 357; arrival of, for *Goeben*, 14; expenditure, 105, 106
Anderson's Knoll, 169, 195
Anglo-Russian agreement (1907), 3
Anzac Cove, 168, 169, 174, 175, 177, 178, 179; becomes Anzac main landing place, 183; 195, 196, 270, 312, 314
——, derivation of name, 115
——, landing at. No aeroplanes available, 139; Turkish defences and strength, 165; ground, 166; plan, 169; naval arrangements, 170; preliminary movements, 172; covering force, 173; loss of direction, 173; delay in landing guns, 181; naval support, 194; engineer work, 195; evacuation considered, 195, 266; water supply, 196; piers and jetties, 196; situation in evening, 196, 255; A.N.Z.A.C. casualties, 196; Turkish casualties, 199; Turkish strength, 255; situation at night, 270; plight of wounded, 271; delay in disembarkation, 271
——, 26th Apr. Naval support, 270, 271, 272; situation in morning, 271; dispositions, 272; mishap to 4th Bn., 272

367

Anzac, 27th-30th Apr. Turkish counter-attack, 297; reorganization, 297; arrival of R.N.D. troops, 298; position described, 299; effect of operations, 302
Arab regiments, 199, 297
Arcadian, S.S., 115; as G.H.Q. transport, 128, 140, 147, 148, 151, 312, 320, 332
Ari Burnu, 174, 183
Army, British, at end of 1914, 45
Artillery, British. M.E.F. deficient in, 110, 306; delay in landing at Anzac, 194; delay at Helles, 250; strength, First Krithia, 285; flag signals from infantry, 314, 334; howitzers, Second Krithia, 330
——, French. Method of landing, 260; deficient, 306
——, Turkish. Deficiency, 10, 306; batteries destroyed, 80, 81, 272; strength, Second Krithia, 337
Asiatic shore, 155, 157. *See also* Kum Kale *and* Besika Bay
Asir, Turkish forces in (1914), 20
Askold, Russian L. Cr., 258
Asquith, Rt. Hon. H. H., 59, 61, 62, 100, 101, 102, 360
Aubers Ridge, Battle of, 355, 363
Australian official account, 197, 327

Baby 700, 167, 179, 180, 182, 187, 188, 189, 190, 299; attack on, 309
Bacchante, H.M.S., 172, 183; raid, 314
Backhouse, Commodore O., 321, 335
Baghdad railway, 21
Bailloud, Gen., 305, 335
Balfour, Rt. Hon. A. J., 61, 100
Balkan states, 21, 39, 68, 355
Balkan war (1912), 5, 18, 22, 296
Baltic coast project, 49, 60, 68
Battleship Hill, 167, 186, 187, 297, 310
Beach parties, 146, 184, 229, 230, 239, 280
Beaches, description of, 112, 135; nomenclature, 136. *See also* S, V, W, etc. Beaches
Beadon, Lieut.-Col. L. R., 230
Beckwith, Major A. T., 248, 249, 275, 276, 277
Belgian coast project, 49, 51, 56, 57, 60, 64
Berlin, Treaty of, 1
Besika Bay, 134, 300; demonstration at, 264
Bethmann Hollweg, Herr, 8
Bieberstein, Baron Marschall von, 4

Birdwood, Lieut.-Gen. Sir W., sent to Dardanelles, 74; his reports, 83; asks for Indian infantry, 123; asks for aeroplanes, 139; urges night landing, 140, 170; lands at Anzac, 194; reports to G.H.Q., 25th Apr., 198; night conference, 267; message to C.-in-C., 268; 313
Birrell, Surg.-Gen. W. G., 144
Bishop, Major H. O., 227
Black Sea, ports bombarded, 17, 43; raid in, 125
Bolton, Captain C. A., 230, 240, 250, 274
Bolton's Ridge, 178, 181, 272
Bombardments, naval, Black Sea ports, 17, 43
——, ——, Dardanelles, 3rd Nov. 1914, 34, 43; 19th Feb., 1915, 77; 25th-26th Feb., 78; 1st Mar., 80; 2nd Mar., 81; 5th-8th Mar., 86; 18th Mar., 96. *See also* Gunfire, naval
Bomford, Captain North, 318
Bosporus, 2, 10, 33
Bouchet, Redoute, 335, 347
Bouvet, Fr. B., 97, 98
Boxall, Captain C. L., 239
Boyle, Lieut.-Commr. E. C., V.C., 308
Braithwaite, Major-Gen. W. P., 87, 94, 99, 263, 269
Braund, Lieut.-Col. G. F., 190, 192, 272, 296, 297, 298
Breeks, Br.-Gen. R. W., 331
Breslau, Ger. L. Cr., 9, 12, 15, 21
Bridges, Major-Gen. W. T., 169, 184; lands at Anzac, 188; 189, 190, 192, 194, 198, 266, 267, 297
Brison, Captain, 260
Brockman, Major E. A. Drake, 177, 179, 180
Brodie, Lieut.-Commr. T. S., 143
Bromley, Captain C., 227, 292
Bucharest, Treaty of, 22
Bulair, question of landing at, 94, 96, 112, 255; German view, 113; Liman's view, 156
Bulgaria, attitude of, 10, 22, 40, 42, 45, 54, 55, 58, 65, 68, 82, 99, 306; military strength, 23
Burnage, Col. G. J., 310

Cairo, hospital accommodation at, 144
Callwell, Major-Gen. C. E., 41, 43, 88
Camber, The. *See* Sedd el Bahr
Canopus, H.M.S., 151, 163, 270

GENERAL INDEX 369

Carden, Vice-Admiral S. H., to command at Dardanelles, 55; asked if fleet can force Straits, 55; his scheme, 57; Government approval, 59; message to Gen. Maxwell, 73; his optimism, 81; wants stronger air service, 86; suggests immediate combined operation, 93; on sick list, 94

Carruthers, Br.-Gen. R.A., 69

Casson, Lieut.-Col. H. G., 236, 237, 278, 283, 291

Casualties, Allied, Second Krithia, 347

——, British military. Number anticipated, 144; Anzac, 25th Apr., 196, 198; Y Beach, 208; S Beach, 237; First Krithia, 294; Baby 700 attack, 312; Gaba Tepe raid, 315; total to 30th Apr., 315; Helles, night 1st/2nd May, 319; total to 14th May, 362

——, —— naval. Landing parties, 78, 82

——, French. Kum Kale, 263; First Krithia, 294; night 1st/2nd May, 319

——, Turkish. Anzac, 25th Apr., 199; Kum Kale, 263; Helles, 25th-26th Apr., 279; First Krithia, 294

Caucasus, operations in, 20, 51. 104, 138

Cayley, Col. D. E., 242, 282, 291

Charlemagne, Fr. B., 359

Chelmer, H.M.S., 314

Chessboard, 191

Chunuk Bair, 167, 194, 273, 310

Churchill, Rt. Hon. Winston S. Discusses Greek offer with Kitchener, 40; visualizes military operation, 41; raises subject at War Council, 44; Belgian coast operation, 49; 52, 53; asks Carden's view, 55; explains plan to War Council, 58; message to Grand Duke, 59; suggests Alexandretta, 60; 61; visits Sir J. French, 64; sends marines to Mudros, 67; asks for 50,000 men, 71; 75, 81; discusses military concentration, 84, 86; believes in naval success, 87; 89, 94, 99; favours fresh naval attack, 100; concurs in combined operation, 100; 303, 360; urges military reinforcements, 362; 363

Clarke, Col. L. F., 179

Colne, H.M.S., 313, 314

Command, Turkish, at Dardanelles, 37

Command, unity of, 91, 92

Communication, lines of, British, 351

——, ——, Turkish, 142, 159, 351; raided by submarines, 308

Constantine, King, of Greece, 23, 38, 42, 43, 83

Constantinople, strategic importance of, 1; 19, 36; promised to Russia, 83; Turkish Government prepare to evacuate, 105; 106

Cornwallis, H.M.S., 218, 219, 222, 223, 236, 247, 248, 329

Cosgrave, Corpl. W., V.C., 277

Costeker, Captain J. H. D., 240

Counter-attacks, Allied, 319, 320

——, Turkish. Anzac, 186, 190, 193, 296; Kum Kale, 261; Helles, 291, 293

Courtney's Post, 169, 180, 182, 191, 297

Cox, Major-Gen. H. V., 124, 324, 348

Cribb, Captain C., 313

Critchley-Salmonson, Captain A. C. B., 191

Cunliffe-Owen, Br.-Gen. C., 269

d'Amade, Gen., 70, 91, 94, 115, 116, 123, 128, 133, 214, 218; at Kum Kale, 257, 258, 262, 263, 264; 278, 282, 305, 317, 319; reports on condition of troops, 320; at Second Krithia, 327, 328, 329, 332; succeeded by Gen. Gouraud, 361

Dardanelles, strategic importance of, 1. 8, 17; *Goeben* and *Breslau* enter, 13; closed, 16; problem of forcing, 25; 1906 memorandum, 28, 41, 109; description of, 31; naval attacks, 34, 43, 77, 78, 80, 81, 86, 96; Greek plan for forcing, 42, 88; plan of naval attack, 57, 59; decision to attack, 61; decision to use troops, 68, 87; further naval attack vetoed, 356. *See also* Bombardments *and* Gallipoli

Dardanelles Commission, evidence before, 53, 60, 61, 88, 100, 211; report of, 58, 59, 69, 72

Dardanelles Defences, 14, 32. *See also* Bombardments *and* Mines in Dardanelles

Dardanos. *See* Forts

Dartmouth, H.M.S., 163, 164, 270, 314

Davidson, Captain A. P., R.N., 236

Day or night landing, question of, 140

de Bartolomé, Commodore C. M., 100

VOL. I   2 B

Deficiencies of M.E.F., 119 *See also* Ammunition, Reinforcements, Small craft
Delcassé, M., 65
Dent, Captain D. L., R.N., 140
Derby, Lord (1877), 27
de Robeck, Vice-Admiral J. M., 94, 97, 98, 99, 127; and landing scheme, 131; orders landing movement, 150; 208, 263, 283, 303, 356, 357, 360
de Tott's battery, 236, 290
Dix, Commr. C. C., 173, 175
Donkey transport, 122
Doris, H.M.S., 53, 163, 270
Doughty-Wylie, Lieut.-Col. C. H. M., V.C., 249, 276, 277
Drewry, Midshipman G. L., V.C., 235
Dublin, H.M.S., 78, 203, 208, 209, 210, 214, 219, 329
Duckworth, Admiral Sir John (1807), 25, 26, 77

E11, Brit. S/M., 308
E14, Brit. S/M., 308
E15, Brit. S/M., 143
E20, Brit. S/M., 309
Egypt, defence of, 44, 60; forces in, 46; troops from, 65, 68, 71, 73, 83, 94, 123, 124, 303, 305, 326; equipment and munitions from, 120, 121; collapse of attack on, 138
Egyptian expeditionary force, Turkish, 20
—— press, 110
Elliot, Sir Francis, 40, 63
Engineer work, 119, 121; at Anzac, 195; at W Beach, 230; at X Beach, 244. *See also* Water Supply *and* Piers
Enver Pasha, 5, 7, 8, 9, 11; admits *Goeben* and *Breslau* to Straits, 13; 16, 17, 18, 40; in Caucasus, 52; 152, 153, 317
Essad Pasha, 37, 185, 186, 298, 306
Euryalus, H.M.S., 208, 209, 217, 218, 219, 222, 223, 227, 228, 238, 239, 241, 242, 253, 273, 275, 282
Exmouth, H.M.S., 359

Farmar, Captain H. M., 229, 230, 239, 241, 242, 292
Ferdinand, Tzar, 22, 23, 43, 64, 65
First Ridge, 167, 179, 180
Fir Tree Spur, 327, 333, 339, 340, 341, 343, 345, 346
Fir Tree Wood, 292, 334, 339, 344
Fisher, Admiral of the Fleet, Lord, 27, 54, 58, 60, 61, 360, 363; and Baltic project, 49, 60

Fisherman's Hut, 177, 178, 183
FitzMaurice, Captain M. S., R.N., 80
Flags, infantry distinguishing, 314, 334
Foreign Legion, 70, 288, 321
Foresight, H.M.S., 90
Fort No. 1, 79, 220, 230, 249, 250, 277. *See also* Sedd el Bahr
—— No. 4, 78
—— Dardanos, 32
—— Doughty-Wylie, 79
—— Hamidieh, 105, 106
——, Kum Kale, 81, 82, 258, 260
—— at Sedd el Bahr, 35, 230, 231, 276
France, and Turkish neutrality, 39; her war policy, 48; her naval co-operation, 59; approves naval attack, 63; her military co-operation, 69; and destination of 29th Division, 71; asks for British plan, 91
Frankland, Major T. H. C., 223, 228, 229, 230
French, Field-Marshal Sir J. D. P., 47, 48; Belgian coast project, 49, 51, 56, 64; views on alternative theatre, 51, 65; 302, 348, 354, 362, 363
French official account, 69, 70, 84, 85, 91; on naval attack, 97; on plan of campaign, 115; on Kum Kale landing, 261; on Second Krithia, 335, 345
Freyberg, Lieut.-Commr. B. C., 164, 165

Gaba Tepe, 158, 165, 298; raid on, 313
Galeka, S.S., 183
Gallipoli peninsula. Problem of attack on, 41; estimate of troops required, 56, 88, 103, 122; Turkish strength on, 74, 76, 83, 88, 104, 106, 111, 155, 157, 306; Gen. Hamilton's first impression of, 95; communications with Constantinople, 142
Garland, Mr., 120
Gaulois, Fr. B., 97, 98, 359
Geddes, Captain G. W., 234, 235
General Staff, memoranda on forcing Straits, 28, 29; 46, 69, 72
German official account, ix, 113, 156
—— personnel, 14, 33, 34
Germany, relations with Turkey, 3; Eastern ambitions of, 3, 9; to supply Turks with munitions, 10, 20
Godfrey-Faussett, Lieut.-Col. O. G., 240, 282

GENERAL INDEX 371

Godley, Major-Gen. Sir A., 194, 195, 267, 268, 270, 273, 297, 310, 311
Godwin, Lieut. C. H., R.N., 143
Goeben, Ger. B. Cr., visits Constantinople before war, 6; 9, 10, 12; arrives in Straits, 13; 14, 15; Black Sea raid, 17; 58, 125
Goliath, H.M.S., 203, 206, 208, 209, 212, 213, 214, 219, 360
Goltz, Gen. von der, 5
Gouraud, Gen., 361
Grant, Captain H. S., R.N., 270
Grantully Castle, S.S., 164
Great Britain. Pre-war relations with Turkey, 2, 7; takes over Turkish battleships, 11; events leading to war, 13; Dardanelles problem, 1807–1914, 25; offers to Greece, 63, 65. *See also* War Council
Greece. Military strength, 23; her offers of assistance, 23, 39; her plan for forcing Straits, 42; 58; British offers of assistance, 63, 65; Russia forbids co-operation, 83
Greene, Sir W. Graham, 100
Grey, Sir Edward, 41, 53, 59, 61, 64, 69, 71, 76, 104
Grimshaw, Major C. T. W., 277
Guépratte, Rear-Admiral P. F. A. H., 94, 116, 123, 258, 259, 264, 304, 321, 357, 359, 360, 361
Gully Beach, 326
Gully Ravine, 204, 282, 283, 290, 292, 319, 326, 334, 339, 342
Gully Spur, 327, 339, 342, 344, 346
Gun-fire, naval. Government's belief in, 58; value in support of troops, 95, 222, 231, 247, 255, 272, 291, 292, 297, 339, 344, 358, 362; direction and control against shore targets, 147, 193, 282. *See also* Bombardments
Gun Ridge, 68, 181, 182, 185, 187, 188, 199, 273

Haig, General Sir D., 355
Hamilton, General Sir Ian. Appointed to command M.E.F., 86, 87; Lord Kitchener's instructions to, 89; leaves London, 90; arrives Tenedos, 94; conferences with admiral, 94, 99; views peninsula, 95; present at naval attack, 98; reports to Lord Kitchener, 98; goes to Egypt, 100; situation end of March, 108; initial plans for landing, 111; demands trench stores, 120; influence of Lord Kitchener on, 122; inspections in Egypt, 125; asks for Gurkhas, 123; returns to Mudros, 130; amends landing plan, 131; favours night operation, 140; on evacuation of wounded, 146; embarks in flagship, 151; arrives off Anzac, 180; off Y Beach, 204, 214; on landings at S and Y Beaches, 237; his instructions for Kum Kale landing, 257; consents to French withdrawal, 263; his message to Gen. Birdwood *re* evacuation, 269; his difficulties, 300; asks for reinforcements, 304, 365; decides on fresh advance, 316; at Second Krithia, 325, 336, 341, 343, 345; situation, night 8th May, 348; reports to Lord Kitchener, 349; anxieties, early May, 351
Hand grenades, supply of, 120
Hankey, Lieut.-Col. M. P. A., memoranda by, 49, 101
Hare, Br.-Gen. S. W., 202, 217, 218, 220, 221, 223, 228
Haworth, Captain R., 227, 229, 241
Hejaz, Turkish force in (1914), 20
Hejaz railway, 21
Helles, landings at. Forces available, 216; night operation vetoed, 217; naval support, 218; time-table, 218; plan, 219; Turkish strength and defences, 221; covering force, 222; main body, 238; situation at night, 249; the operation reviewed, 251. *See also* S, V, W and X Beaches
———, 26th Apr. Reinforcements wanted, 274; capture of Sedd el Bahr, 277; Turkish movements, 279. *See also* V Beach
Hell Spit, 168
Henderson, Captain E. L. H., 234
Henri IV, Fr. B., 258, 260
Heriot, Major G. M., R.M., 78
H.E. shell, importance of, 325; shortage of, 336
Hill Q, 166
Hill 114, 217, 220, 225, 227, 228; capture of, 240; 244, 275, 278, 342, 343
Hill 138 (Hunter-Weston Hill), 220, 226, 227, 240, 241; capture of, 242; 275, 278, 316
Hill 141, 220, 226, 229, 243, 246, 273, 274, 275; capture of, 277; 278, 287
Hill 236, 286, 290, 315
Hill 472, 285, 286, 326, 338, 339, 341
Hill 971, 37, 166, 169

Hingston, Lieut.-Col. G. B., 230
Holbrook, Lieut. N. D., R.N., V.C., 36, 143
Hopper, 133
Hornby, Admiral Sir Geoffrey Phipps (1877), 26, 27, 67
Horse-boats, 68, 73
Hospital ships, 145
Hospitals, base, 144
Howe, Lieut. H. V., 190
Hume, Lieut.-Col. R. O. C., 282
Hunter-Weston Hill. *See* Hill 138
Hunter-Weston, Major-Gen. A. G., 116; favours daylight landing, 140; Y Beach, 204, 211; his objective for 25th Apr., 220; 223, 237; lands main body, 238; 254, 274; at First Krithia, 282, 284, 286, 289, 294; assists the French, 318; at Second Krithia, 325, 328, 329, 337, 338, 339, 342, 345

Implacable, H.M.S., 212, 217, 218, 219, 222, 223, 224, 225, 329
Inflexible, H.M.S., 97, 98
Inner Defences. *See* Dardanelles Defences
Intelligence, British, 111, 221, 230, 320, 324
———, Turkish, 110, 139
Intermediate Defences. *See* Dardanelles Defences
In Tepe, 258, 260, 263
Irresistible, H.M.S., 79, 80, 82, 97, 98
Italy, and the Dardanelles, 58, 82; 359

Jackson, Admiral Sir H. B., 57, 67, 93, 360
Jackson, Lieut. S. H., 187
Jacobs, Able Seaman L., 233
"Jacob's ladders," 131
Jägow, Herr von, 9
Jarrett, Major C. H. B., 235, 248
Jauréguiberry, Fr. B., 258, 259, 261
Jeanne d'Arc, Fr. Cr., 258, 264
Jemal Pasha, 10, 14, 20
Jevad Bey, Col., 16, 35, 37
Joffre, General, 47, 51, 56, 64, 65, 69, 70, 92
Johnston, Col. F. E., 189, 310, 311, 326
Johnston's Jolly, 273

Kadri Bey, Lieut.-Col., 158
Kaiser Wilhelm II., 12, 16
Kanli Dere, 286, 333, 334, 335
Kelly, Surgeon P. B., 248
Kennet, H.M.S., 164, 165
Kephez minefield. *See* Mines in Dardanelles

Kereves Dere, 290, 291, 326, 335, 342, 344
Kereves Spur, 327, 340, 341, 342, 344, 347
Kerr, Rear-Admiral Mark, 42
Keyes, Lieut.-Commr. A. St. V., 203, 210, 211, 291
Keyes, Commodore R. J. B., 94, 99
Khalil Sami Bey, Col., 156, 157, 185, 207, 255, 287
Kiasim Bey, 154
Kilia Liman, 320
Kilid Bahr plateau, 37, 216
King, H.M. The, message to M.E.F., 150
Kirby, Captain H. A., 193
Kirte Dere, 318, 326, 334
Kitchener, Earl. On Turkey (1908), 4; on action against Turkey, 44; relations with Gen. Staff, 47; on Alexandretta, 48, 53, 60; 50; on help for Russia, 52; favours naval demonstration, 53; on combined operation, 56; on defence of Egypt, 60; 61, 64; disposal of 29th Div., 66, 68, 71, 87; 69; orders to A.N.Z.A.C., 71, 73; pressure of French Govt., 71; sends Birdwood to Dardanelles, 74, 76, 83; instructions to Hamilton, 88, 89; message to M. Millerand, 91; personality, 103; relations with Hamilton, 123; on reinforcements from Egypt, 124, 303, 304; on Turkish morale, 138; orders *re* aeroplanes, 139; urges Hamilton to push on, 321; promises another division from England, 350; fears of invasion, 363; minute of 13th May, 363; asks what reinforcements are required, 365
Koe, Lieut.-Col. A. S., 202, 205, 206, 208
Koja Chemen Tepe. *See* Hill 971
Krithia, First Battle of. Preparations, 284; artillery and ammunition available, 285; objectives, 285; orders, 286; Turkish strength and dispositions, 287; advance of 29th Div., 288; advance of French, 290; renewed advance, 291; withdrawal, 293; Allied casualties, 294; results, 295
———, Second Battle of. Preparations, 320; ignorance of Turkish dispositions, 322, 324; reorganization of Allied forces, 322, 323; Turkish strength, 324; ammunition shortage, 325; ground, 326;

GENERAL INDEX

orders, 327, 329; naval support, 328; attack, 6th May, 333; situation at night, 336; Turkish situation, 336; orders, 7th May, 337; attack, 7th May, 338; British casualties, 340; situation at night, 341; orders, 8th May, 343; results, 347; Allied casualties, 347 Krithia nullah. *See* Kirte Dere
Krithia Spur, 327, 345, 346
Kuchuk Mehmed Bey Tepe, 317
Kum Kale, landing parties at, 78, 80, 81
——, French diversion at. Object of, 133; ground, 257; force allotted, 258; Turkish strength at, 259; landing, 259; naval support, 259, 260, 261; situation at night, 261; "incident" of 26th Apr., 261; withdrawal, 262; French and Turkish casualties, 263

Lala Baba, raid on, 313
Lalor, Captain J. P., 187
Lancashire Landing. *See* W Beach
Latouche-Tréville, Fr. Cr., 258
Leane, Captain R. L., 313, 314, 315
Legge Valley, 178, 314, 315
Lemnos. *See* Mudros
Leontev, Gen., 11
Leslie, Captain F. K., 225, 244
Lighters, 110, 121. *See also* Small craft
Liman von Sanders, Marshal, 17, 18, 20; his measures to defend Constantinople, 36, 106; on effect of naval bombardments, 105; preparations for defence of peninsula, 153; on courses open to invader, 155; his dispositions, 156; on value of British delay, 160; receives reports of landings, 162; his anxiety for Bulair, 163; 255; on value of naval gun-fire, 272; receives reinforcements, 306; his orders from Enver Pasha, 317; 336; forbids retirement at Helles, 337, 344; 355, 356
Limpus, Vice-Admiral A. H., 14, 15
Lloyd George, Rt. Hon. D., memorandum by, 50; 65, 75
Lockyer, Captain H. C., R.N., 224
London, H.M.S., 172
London, Treaty of, 22
Lone Pine, 168, 177, 187
Lord Nelson, H.M.S., 219, 238, 329
Loutit, Lieut. N. M., 178, 181
Lucas, Captain C. H. T., 286
Ludendorff, Gen., vii

Lusitania, S.S., 362
Lutzow, S.S., 189

McAlester, Major W. H. S., 210
M'Cay, Col. J. W., 181, 192, 297, 326, 345, 346
M'Cay's Hill, 181, 272
Machine guns, R.N.D., 118, 133
—— ——, Turkish, at V Beach, 159, 231; at W Beach, 159, 221, 226; at Second Krithia, 338, 339, 345
MacLagan's Ridge, 168, 178, 179, 271
MacLaurin, Col. H. N., 272, 296
MacLaurin's Hill, 182, 187, 190, 199, 296, 310
Majestic, H.M.S., 172
Malleson, Midshipman W. St. A., V.C., 235
Mallett, Sir Louis, 14, 39
Malone, Lieut.-Col. W. G., 195
Malta, assistance from, 120, 121; hospital accommodation at, 144
Mal Tepe, 136, 307
Manica, balloon ship, 338
Manitou, S.S., 140
Maps, British, inaccuracy of, 37, 87, 90, 113, 137, 166, 167, 204, 226, 229, 282
Margetts, Lieut. I. S., 188
Marshall, Br.-Gen. W. R., 220, 244, 245, 246, 275; in temporary command of 29th Div., 282, 332; at First Krithia, 289, 291, 294
Masnou, Gen., 318, 338, 346
Matthews, Lieut.-Col. G. E., R.M., at Kum Kale, 81, 82; at Y Beach, 202, 203, 205, 206, 207, 208, 209, 210, 211, 246
Maucorps, Col., 76
Maxwell, Lieut.-Gen. Sir J., 73, 74, 115; report on Turkish strength, 76; help of, 116; reinforcements from Egypt, 124, 303
Medical service, 144
M.E.F. Separation of G. from A. & Q. staffs, 89, 128, 253; strength of, 103, 127, 302; absence of plan, 108; lack of secrecy, 109; arrival in Egypt, 115; reorganization of supply and transport, 117; general deficiencies, 119; ammunition shortage, 120; provision of beach gear, 121; water supply problem, 121; reinforcements for, 122, 301, 303, 307, 348; quality of troops, 125; deficiency of aeroplanes, 139; training, 131, 141, 166, 259; assembly at Mudros and Trebuki, 139; medical arrangements, 144;

the King's message, 150; first movement for landings, 151; result of first day's fighting, 255; situation, end of April, 300; strength at end of April, 306; situation after Second Krithia, 348; length of communications, 351; dependence on fine weather, 351; German submarine menace, 352
Mercantile marine, work of, 279
Merten, Vice-Admiral, 16, 33
Mesopotamia, Turkish force in (1914), 20; effect of operations in, 104; Turkish defeats in, 138
Messudieh, Turkish B., 21
Millerand, M., 91
Minerva, H.M.S., 219, 329
Mines in Dardanelles 8, 14, 16, 32, 34, 96, 97, 103
Mine-sweeping, 80, 81, 87, 97, 128, 224, 236
Minnewaska, S.S., 172
Mission, British naval, 6, 9, 14, 15
Missions, German military, 3, 5, 16, 17, 18, 52, 138
Mitchell, Captain F. H., R.N., 109, 140
Monash, Col. J., 297, 310, 311, 312
Monash Gully, 168, 180, 182, 188, 191, 198, 272, 295, 297, 299, 310, 311
Monitors, 359, 361
Moore, Lieut.-Col. A., 310, 311
Moore, Sir John (1807), 25
Morale, Turkish, 80, 105, 138, 271, 297
Morse, Lieut. J. A. V., R.N., 235, 247
Mortar Ridge, 310
Morto Bay. *See* S Beach
Mudros, arrival of troops at, 67, 73, 85, 94, 93; port facilities at, 95, 116, 351, 352; naval preparations at, 127; concentration of M.E.F. at, 139, 149, 259; Turkish aeroplane over, 139; inter-ship communication at, 148; 151, 203
Mühlmann, Captain, 306
Mule Valley, 168
Munitions, Turkish, deficiency, 10, 355; factories, 19, 20, 355; dependence on Germany, 20
Murray, Lieut.-Gen. Sir J. W., 69
Mustafa Kemal Bey, 154, 157; at Anzac, 185, 186, 199, 271, 296, 297

Napier, Br.-Gen. H. E., 220, 238, 239, 244, 245, 247, 249
Narrows, The. *See* Dardanelles Defences

Nasmith, Lieut.-Commr. M. E., V.C., 308
Naval operations, 25. *See also* Bombardments, Mine-sweeping, *and* Submarines
Needham, 2/Lieut., G. G., 292
Nek, The, 167, 182, 187, 188, 190, 296, 297, 310, 311
Nelson, Lieut. R. W., 165
Neutrality, Turkish breaches of, 14
Newenham, Lieut.-Col. H. E. B., 225, 228, 244, 245
Nibrunesi Point, 298; raids on, 313
Nicholas, Grand Duke, 52, 59, 60, 75
Nicholson, Rear-Admiral S., 147, 219, 223
Nicol, Vice-Admiral, 361
Nicolai, Col., 157, 259
Nightingale, Lieut. G. W., 235, 247, 277
Night operations. Decision for landings, 140, 217; Turkish, 207, 261, 317; at Baby 700, 310; rejected for Second Krithia, 325, 350; advance on 8th May, 347
Noguès, Lieut.-Col., 258, 260, 262, 263

Ocean, H.M.S., 98
O'Connell, Lieut. M. J. A., 292
Odessa, 17, 125
Oliver, Rear-Admiral H. F., 100
Oppenheim, Baron, 12
Orkanie. *See* Fort No. 4
Outer Defences. *See* Dardanelles Defences
Outpost No. 1, 310
Owen, Col. R. H., 297
Owen's Gully, 178, 181

Paget, Gen. Sir A., 99
Palmer, Major H. D., R.M., 82
Pan-Turkish movement, 6
Paris Convention, 359
——, Treaty of, 1
Paris, Major-Gen. A., 95, 163, 316, 322, 324, 328, 345
Parker, Lce.-Corpl. W. R., V.C., 298
Periscopes, 120
Peyton, Major-Gen. C. E., 124
Phaeton, H.M.S., 90, 94, 95
Philippe, Lieut.-Col., 283
Phillimore, Captain R. F., R.N., 230
Piers and jetties. Deficiencies at Mudros, 95; construction in Egypt and Malta, 119, 121; at Anzac, 195, 196; at V Beach, 233, 248; 351
Pine Ridge, 178, 181, 193
Pink Farm, 339

GENERAL INDEX 375

Plateau 400, 165, 166, 168, 169, 177, 178, 181, 182, 187, 188, 191, 192, 193, 198, 272, 297, 310
Plugge, Lieut.-Col. A., 189
Plugge's Plateau, 167, 176, 177, 188, 190, 195, 271
Point 42. *See* Hill 138
—— 47, 229, 241
Pope, Lieut.-Col. H., 191, 272, 310
Pope's Hill, 190, 191, 272, 296, 311, 312
Port Said, 115, 116, 126
Prince George, H.M.S., 219, 258, 322
Prince of Wales, H.M.S., 172
Propaganda, German, in Turkey, 12
Provence, Fr. Cr., 305
Prut, Russian minelayer, 17

Queen, H.M.S., 172, 267, 268, 269
Queen Elizabeth, H.M.S., 78, 86, 94, 99, 130, 142; G.H.Q. in, 151, 180, 204, 213, 253, 264, 266, 268, 269, 292; 208, 219, 235, 242, 247, 248, 272, 283, 339; recall of, 359, 361; 363
Queensland Point, 195
Quilter, Lieut.-Col. A., 336
Quinn's Post, 168, 180, 182, 190, 272, 296, 310

Railhead, Turkish, 142
Reconnaissance before landing, 137, 142, 166
——, aerial. *See* Air service
Refet Bey, Lieut.-Col., 157
Reinforcements, M.E.F., 122, 301, 303, 307, 363, 364
——, Turkish, 306
Remsi Bey, Col., 156
Rest Gully, 177, 179
Ribble, H.M.S., 314
River Clyde, S.S., function of, 132, 136, 218; preparation of, 133; 141, 149, 222, 223; at V Beach, 231, 232, 233, 239, 240, 241, 247, 248, 253, 276
Roads on peninsula, 88, 113, 142; Turkish work on, 160
Robinson, Lieut.-Commr. E. G., V.C., 78, 143
Rochdale, Lieut.-Col. Lord, 326
Rockel, Captain, 261
Rooth, Lieut.-Col. R.A., 249
Roper, Br.-Gen. R.A., 249
Ruef, Col., 258, 261
Rumania, 23, 58, 65, 67
Rumball, Lieut. C., 314, 315
Russell's Top, 167, 168, 179, 180, 182, 188, 272, 295, 296, 297, 298, 310, 311

Russia. Relations with Turkey, 3, 39; 44, 58; co-operation of, 59, 82, 87, 124, 362; 67, 71; objects to Greek co-operation, 83; 355.
See also Nicholas, Grand Duke
Russo-Turkish war (1877), 26

Salisbury, Major A. G., 177
Salonika, 64, 65
Sami Bey. *See* Khalil Sami Bey
Samson, Seaman G. M., V.C., 235
San Stefano, Treaty of, 1
Sapphire, H.M.S., 203, 206, 207, 208, 209, 219, 329
Sari Bair, 37
Sarikamish, Battle of, 52, 138
Sari Sighlar bay, 36, 96
Sari Tepe, 285, 286
Savoie, Fr. Cr., 259
S Beach. Decision to land at, 135; troops for, 135, 236; chain of command, 202; 217, 218; Turkish strength at, 221, 237; 226; description of, 236; landing at, 236; casualties at, 237; 238, 251, 277, 283
Scrubby Knoll, 169, 181
Seaplanes. *See* Air service
Searchlights, Turkish, 33, 34, 80
Second Ridge, 167, 179, 180, 181, 182, 187, 188, 191, 193, 272, 296, 297, 310, 311
Secrecy and surprise, importance of, 28, 68, 96, 108, 110, 301
Sedd el Bahr. Landing parties at, 79, 81, 82; 217, 220, 263; landing at the Camber, 231, 232, 233, 235, 238, 247; capture of, 276; French naval guns landed at, 321. *See also* Bombardments *and* V Beach
Senegalese troops, 70, 258, 259, 261, 318, 320, 321, 335
Serafim Farm, 207, 249
Serbia, 23, 45, 58, 63
Sevastopol bombarded, 17
Seymour, Commr. C., 313
Shaw, Captain H., 227, 229, 230, 241
Shrapnel Gully, 168, 176, 184, 196, 311, 312
Signal communications, ship to shore, 147, 193, 194, 206, 214, 252, 320, 322
Simonin, Col., 338, 342
Simpson, Commr. H. V., 140
Sinclair-MacLagan, Br.-Gen. E. G., 166, 169, 170, 177, 179, 180, 181, 182, 184, 187, 188, 191, 272
Skyros, 140, 259

Small craft, deficiency of, 135, 280.
    See also Horse-boats and Lighters.
Smith, Lieut.-Col. H. Carington, 235, 239, 245, 247, 249
Sodenstern, Col. von, 156, 317, 336
Souchon, Rear-Admiral, 9, 12, 13, 14, 17, 43, 125
Spee, Vice-Admiral Graf von, 57
Spencer - Smith, Captain R. O., 240
Sphinx, The, 167
Staff, separation of G. from A. & Q., 89, 128, 253
Steele's Post, 168, 180, 182, 191
Stewart, Lieut.-Col. D. McB., 189, 272
Strength, Allied, estimated for campaign, 56, 88, 103, 122
—— of M.E.F., 87, 103, 122, 127; at end Apr., 306; at Second Krithia, 324
——, Turkish. At Dardanelles, 41, 104, 106; Allied estimates of, 74, 76, 83, 87, 88, 111; at landings, 155; S. of Achi Baba, 25th Apr., 221; on Helles front, 27th Apr., 279; at end Apr., 306; at Second Krithia, 324
Sturdee, Vice-Admiral Sir F. D., 54
Submarines, operations of British, 35, 112, 142, 264, 308
——, German, 150, 352
Suez Canal, menace to, 14; Turkish force for attack on, 20; protection of, 44, 60; failure of attack on, 65; 104
Suffren, Fr. B., 359
Sultan of Turkey, 7, 105
Supply and transport of M.E.F., 87, 117, 122; after Helles landings, 250, 280, 284, 316
—— ——, Turkish, 19, 142, 309
Suvla, raids at, 312
Swannell, Major B. I., 188
Swiftsure, H.M.S., 218, 219, 227, 241, 329, 338, 344

Talaat Bey, 5, 7, 9, 24
Talbot, H.M.S., 219, 329, 338
Taurus tunnel, 21
Tekke Burnu, 32
Tenedos, 94, 139, 222
Tenkir Tepe, 221
Third Ridge. See Gun Ridge
Thompson, Lieut.-Col. A. J. Onslow, 273
Thursby, Rear-Admiral C. F., 116, 171, 172, 194, 268, 269, 270
Time (E.M.T.), 141

Time-table for Landings. General, 135; at Anzac, 170, 171; at Helles, 218, 219; delayed, 250, 280
Tirpitz, Admiral von, on Dardanelles, 9, 203; 12
Tisdall, Sub-Lieut. A. W., V.C., 235
Tizard, Lieut.-Col. H. E., 249
Tow, meaning of, 118
Tows, distribution of troops to, 171, 217
Transport. See Supply and transport
Trebuki Bay, 140, 141, 148, 163
Trench mortars, 120
—— warfare equipment, 120
Trip, meaning of, 118
Triumph, H.M.S., 172
Tugs. See Small craft, deficiency of
Tulloch, Captain E. W., 179, 182, 186, 187, 188
Turkey. Dardanelles problem, 1; relations with Britain, 2; with Russia, 3, 11; growth of German influence, 3; treaty with Germany, 7; situation in, Aug. 1914, 10; breaches of neutrality, 14, 17, 40; enters war, 17; situation in, Mar. 1915, 105
Turkish army. German mission to, 5, 17; mobilized, 18; state of, 18; strength and organization, 19; distribution, 20; quality of troops, 137, 138
—— navy. British mission to, 6; battleships detained by Britain, 11; German domination of, 14; Black Sea raids, 17, 43, 125; composition (1914), 21; in Dardanelles defence, 37
—— official account. On Turkish unreadiness, 33, 352; on preparations to meet land attack, 36, 38, 155; on naval attack, 97, 106; on Kum Kale, 259, 261, 263, 264; on First Krithia, 289, 294; losses at Anzac, 312; on Second Krithia, 336, 347
Turquoise, Fr. S/M., 309

Unwin, Commr. E., V.C., 132, 133, 233, 234, 235
Usedom, Vice-Admiral von, 33, 34, 36, 62
Usk, H.M.S., 314
Uzun Keupri, 142

Vandenberg, Gen., 281, 288, 293
Vaughan, Major C. D., 245

GENERAL INDEX

V Beach, 114; capacity of, 132; 133; beach party for, 147; Turkish strength at, 159, 221; Turks expect landing at, 160; covering force for, 217, 218; description of, 230; defences of, 231; landing at, 232, 239, 246; events at, 26th Apr., 275; French take over, 278
Venerable, H.M.S., 359
Vengeance, H.M.S., 78, 219
Venizelos, M., 23, 39, 64, 82, 83
Very lights, 322
Vyvyan, Captain A. V., R.N., 268

Walford, Captain G. N., V.C., 249, 276, 277
Walker, Br.-Gen. H. B., 189, 267, 297, 310
Walker's Ridge, 167, 179, 190, 191, 272, 296, 297, 310, 311
Wangenheim, Baron von, 5, 6, 7, 9, 10, 11, 12, 13, 16
War Council. Consider forcing Straits, 44; seek alternative to Western theatre, 46; decision of 8th Jan., 56; decide on naval demonstration, 58; decide on naval attack, 61; offer to Greece, 66; decide on troops to support fleet, 68; contemplate land campaign, 76; decision *re* fresh naval attack, 98; decide on combined operation, 100; anxieties of, 353; telegram to Hamilton, 365
War Office. Gen. Staff not consulted at, 46, 72; conditions at, Mar. 1915, 87; formation of M.E.F. staffs, 89; equipment of M.E.F., 120; action *re* water supply, 121, 122; and " first reinforcements ", 301
Waterlow, Lieut. J. B., R.N., 173
Water supply. At Lemnos, 95; on peninsula, 121; measures taken, 122; at Anzac, 196, 279; at Helles, 250, 279, 284
Watts, Lieut. J., 234
W Beach (Lancashire Landing), 114; capacity of, 132; 142; beach party for, 147; Turkish strength at, 159, 221; Turks expect landing at, 160; covering force for, 217, 218; description of, 226; defences of, 226; landing at, 227, 240, 250, 279, 280
Weather, influence of, 72, 78, 79, 80, 81, 84, 99, 109, 121, 139; delays landings, 149; 290, 295; Admiral Wemyss on, 351
Weber, Gen. (Weber Pasha), 33, 336, 337
Wedgwood, Commr. J., 133, 232, 234
Wemyss, Rear-Admiral R. E., 94, 99, 205, 216, 223, 280, 351
Western front as main theatre, 48, 63, 64, 66, 302, 354, 362
Wheatley, Major P., 318
White, Lieut.-Col. C. B. B., 266
Whitby Abbey, fleet sweeper, 223
Williams, Able Seaman W. C., V.C., 233, 234
Williams, Lieut.-Col. W. de L., 232, 249, 276, 334
Willis, Captain R. R., 227, 230
Wilson, Admiral of the Fleet Sir A., 59, 100, 363
Wilson, Major-Gen. H. H., 41
Wolley-Dod, Col. O. C., 240, 241, 242, 246, 248, 282
Wounded. Medical arrangements for, 144; evacuation at Anzac, 184, 195, 196, 270, 298; on *River Clyde*, 248
Wymer, Captain H. J. de C., 240

X Beach, 114; capacity of, 132; beach party for, 147; Turkish strength at, 159; covering force for, 217; description of, 224; landing at, 225, 238, 243

Y Beach. Decision to land at, 134, 135, 141; landing at, 201; 290, 334, 339, 345
Yemen, Turkish forces in (1914), 20
Yeni Shehr, 258, 259, 260

Z Beach, 136
Zeitun Burnu, 20, 355
Zouaves, 288, 321, 335

INDEX TO ARMS, FORMATIONS AND UNITS

Ambulance, 3rd Australian Field, 166, 177
Artillery—
  Batteries, Mountain—Ross, 287; 26th Indian, 193
  Brigade, Horse—XV., 318
  ——, Mountain—7th Indian, 170, 171
Cavalry (Yeomanry) Division—2nd Mounted, 124, 305
Corps—
  Australian and New Zealand—strengths, 77, 127; 85, 114, 115; inspected, 125; 132, 136, 139; orders of, 165; lands at Anzac, 173; casualties, 196; reorganization of line, 297; its achievement, 299
  French (C.E.O.). *See* Divisions—1st French
Divisions—
  29th—formation of, 45; disposal of, 46, 64, 66, 68, 71, 72, 86, 87, 88, 90, 93; 114, 116, 121, 123; inspection of, 125; strengths, 127, 294, 316; 133, 134, 135; orders of, 137, 219; 138, 139, 142, 147, 213, 216, 221; lands at Helles, 223; operation reviewed, 251; 262, 274, 280; advance of 27th Apr., 281; at First Krithia, 288; casualties, 28th Apr., 294; Turkish attack, 1st/2nd May, 318; casualties, 319; reorganization of, 322; at Second Krithia, 329
  42nd (1/1st East Lancs.)—304, 305, 306, 350
  52nd (1/1st Lowland)—350
  1st Australian—46, 71, 73, 136, 171, 188
  Composite—formation of, 322; at Second Krithia, 345
  New Zealand and Australian—71, 73, 136, 273

Royal Naval—45, 73; strengths, 77, 127; 85, 93, 110, 116, 118, 121; inspection of, 125; at Bulair demonstration, 163; 316
  1st French (C.E.O.)—formation, 69; strengths, 77, 127; 85, 92, 94, 114, 116; inspection of, 125; at Kum Kale, 257; casualties, 25th-26th Apr., 263; at First Krithia, 290, 293; casualties, 28th Apr., 294; Turkish attack, 1st/2nd May, 318; casualties, 319; at Second Krithia, 328, 329, 335, 338, 340, 342, 344, 345, 346
  2nd French (C.E.O.)—305, 335, 340
  156th. *See* 2nd French (C.E.O.)
Engineers—
  Field Company R.E.—1/2nd London, 146, 230
  —— ——, 1st Australian — 166, 172, 195
Infantry Battalions—
  Border Regt., 1st Bn., 212, 218, 238, 243, 244, 245, 246; casualties, 25th Apr., 250; 288, 290, 292, 316
  Dublin Fusiliers, Royal, 1st Bn., 217, 218, 220, 232, 234, 235, 238, 239, 247, 277; casualties by 27th Apr., 284; 291, 316, 318
  Essex Regt., 1st Bn., 218, 238, 240, 241, 243; casualties, 25th Apr., 250; 283, 288, 289, 316, 339
  Hampshire Regt., 2nd Bn., 217, 218, 220, 238, 239, 240, 243, 248, 277, 288, 289, 316
  Inniskilling Fusiliers, Royal, 1st Bn., 218, 243, 245, 246, 288, 290, 293, 316, 319, 339, 342
  King's Own Scottish Borderers, 1st Bn., 202, 203; casualties at Y Beach landing, 208; 210, 211, 212, 244, 289, 316, 319, 326, 339

Infantry Battalions (*continued*)—
Lancashire Fusiliers, 1st Bn., 205, 211, 217, 219, 220, 224, 230, 238, 239, 240, 241, 243, 250, 253, 291, 292, 330, 316, 334, 347
—— ——, 1/5th Bn., 339, 340; casualties, 7th May, 340
—— ——, 1/6th Bn., 334
—— ——, 1/7th Bn., 334
Munster Fusiliers, Royal, 1st Bn., 218, 220, 234, 235, 247, 248, 277, 291, 316, 318
Royal Fusiliers, 2nd Bn., 211, 217, 220, 224, 230, 240, 243, 244, 245, 291, 292, 316, 318
Royal Scots, 1/5th Bn., 216, 218, 243, 288, 289, 316, 318
South Wales Borderers, 2nd Bn., 202; casualties at Y Beach landing, 208; 218, 226, 236; casualties at S Beach, 237; 244, 277, 283, 288, 293, 316, 342, 346
Worcestershire Regt., 4th Bn., 218, 238, 239, 240, 241, 242; casualties, 25th Apr., 250; 278, 288, 289, 316, 318, 339
R.M.L.I., Chatham, 298, 311, 312, 316
——, Deal, 298, 316
——, Plymouth, 79, 81, 134, 202; casualties at Y Beach landing, 208; 216, 316
——, Portsmouth, 298, 311, 312, 316
Anson, 146, 216, 229, 239, 244, 288, 318, 321, 336
Drake, 284, 288, 316, 347
Hood, 136, 321, 335
Howe, 316, 318, 321, 336
Nelson, 298, 311, 312, 316
Australian, 1st, 188
——, 2nd, 188, 190, 272, 296, 297; casualties at Russell's Top, 298
——, 3rd, 188
——, 4th, 183, 188, 190, 192, 193, 272
——, 5th, 345, 346
——, 6th, 183, 193, 345, 346
——, 7th, 183, 345, 346
——, 8th, 193, 345, 346
——, 9th, 170, 172, 173, 176, 177, 187, 192
——, 10th, 170, 172, 173, 176, 177, 178, 314
——, 11th, 170, 172, 173, 174, 177, 178, 179, 313
——, 12th, 170, 177, 179, 180

Australian, 13th, 195, 310, 311, 312
——, 14th, 195, 271
——, 15th, 191, 195, 311, 312
——, 16th, 191, 195, 310, 311, 312
Auckland, 189, 342, 344, 346
Canterbury, 189, 272, 310, 311, 312, 313, 342, 344, 346
Otago, 190, 310, 311, 312, 342
Wellington, 195, 296, 342, 344, 346
14th Sikhs, 124
69th Punjabis, 124, 324
89th Punjabis, 124, 324
1/6th Gurkha Rifles, 124
Infantry Brigades—
86th—202, 206, 217, 220, 282, 284, 286, 288, 291, 294, 315, 316; broken up, 322
87th—220, 282, 283, 284, 286, 288, 290, 291, 292, 315, 316, 319, 339, 340, 342, 345
88th—218, 220, 282, 284, 286, 288, 290, 291, 293, 294, 315, 316, 322, 333; casualties, 6th May, 334; 339, 340
125th—320, 322, 326, 333; casualties, 6th May, 334; 338, 339; casualties, 6th and 7th May, 340
127th—336
2nd (Naval)—163, 321, 335, 340
3rd (R.M.)—163
Composite Naval, 322, 328, 334, 340
1st Australian—170, 171, 183, 184, 188, 272, 297
2nd Australian—169, 171, 180, 181, 183, 184, 188, 272, 297, 326, 345, 346; casualties, Second Krithia, 346; 347
3rd Australian—85, 93, 166, 169, 180, 181, 182, 188, 199, 272, 297
4th Australian—190, 191, 195, 271, 272, 297, 310
New Zealand—46, 189, 190, 192, 195, 271, 272, 297, 310, 326, 339, 341, 342, 344, 345, 346, 347
29th Indian—124, 316, 322, 331, 342, 348
Infantry Brigades (French)—
Colonial—258, 319
Metropolitan—262, 278, 281, 288, 335, 340
Infantry Regiments (French)—
175th—283, 288, 291, 335
6th Colonial—258, 260
Royal Naval Air Service—
No. 3 Squadron, 139
Zion Mule Corps, 122, 284

HISTORY OF THE GREAT WAR

BASED ON OFFICIAL DOCUMENTS
BY DIRECTION OF THE HISTORICAL SECTION
COMMITTEE OF IMPERIAL DEFENCE

MILITARY OPERATIONS

GALLIPOLI

VOL. I

APPENDICES

APPENDICES

		PAGE
1.	Lord Kitchener's Instructions to Sir Ian Hamilton	1
2.	Order of Battle, Mediterranean Expeditionary Force	4
3.	Sir I. Hamilton's Order for Landing, 25th April 1915	7
4.	Instructions for Helles Covering Force	12
5.	Instructions to G.O.C. A. & N.Z.A.C.	16
6.	Instructions for Kum Kale Landing	19
7.	Epitome of Orders issued by Vice-Admiral de Robeck	21
8.	Composition of Naval Squadrons	24
9.	Epitome of Orders issued by Rear-Admiral Wemyss	25
10.	General Orders to Masters of Transports	28
11.	Medical Arrangements for the Landings	29
12.	Epitome of Orders issued by Rear-Admiral Thursby	31
13.	Suggested Action in event of Failure	34
14.	Gen. Birdwood's Order for Anzac Landing	37
15.	Gen. Birdwood's Instructions to 1st Australian Division	42
16.	1st Australian Division Order for Landing	44
17.	29th Division Order for Landing	49
18.	29th Division Instructions for Covering Force	53
19.	86th Brigade Operation Order No. 1	54
20.	Instructions to G.O.C. C.E.O.	56
21.	Extracts from Signal Log, H.M.S. *Euryalus*	58
22.	29th Division Order, First Battle of Krithia	60
23.	87th Brigade Order, First Battle of Krithia	61
24.	G.H.Q. Order, Second Battle of Krithia	62
25.	29th Division Order, Second Battle of Krithia	66
26.	29th Division Order, Second Battle of Krithia (2nd Day)	71
27.	G.H.Q. Order, Second Battle of Krithia (3rd Day)	72
28.	29th Division Order, Second Battle of Krithia (Final Phase)	73
29.	Notes on Signal Arrangements	74

ABBREVIATIONS

Captain S. = Captain commanding submarines.
D.A.S. = Director of Army Signals.
F.A. = Field Artillery (Australian and New Zealand forces).
G.M.T. = Greenwich mean time.
N.T.O. = Naval Transport Officer.
P.M.L.O. = Principal Military Landing Officer.
P.N.T.O. = Principal Naval Transport Officer.
R.N.A.S. = Royal Naval Air Service.
S.N.O. = Senior Naval Officer.
t.b.d. = Torpedo boat destroyer.

APPENDIX I

LORD KITCHENER'S INSTRUCTIONS TO
SIR IAN HAMILTON

1. THE Fleet have undertaken to force the passage of the Maps 1, 2.
Dardanelles. The employment of military forces on any large Sketches
scale for land operations at this juncture is only contemplated 1, 3.
in the event of the Fleet failing to get through after every effort
has been exhausted.

2. Before any serious undertaking is carried out in the
Gallipoli Peninsula all the British Military forces detailed for
the expedition should be assembled, so that their full weight
can be thrown in.

3. Having entered on the project of forcing the Straits
there can be no idea of abandoning the scheme. It will require
time, patience, and methodical plans of co-operation between
the naval and military commanders. The essential point is to
avoid a check, which will jeopardise our chances of strategical
and political success.

4. This does not preclude the probability of minor operations being engaged upon to clear areas occupied by the Turks
with guns annoying the Fleet, or for the demolition of forts
already silenced by the Fleet. But such minor operations
should be as much as possible restricted to the forces necessary
to achieve the object in view, and should as far as practicable
not entail permanent occupation of positions on the Gallipoli
Peninsula.

5. Owing to the lack of any definite information we must
presume that the Gallipoli Peninsula is held in strength and
that the Kilid Bahr plateau has been fortified and armed for a
determined resistance. In fact, we must presuppose that the
Turks have taken every measure for the defence of the plateau,
which is the key to the Western front at the Narrows, until
such time as reconnaissance has proved otherwise.

6. Under present conditions it seems undesirable to land

any permanent garrison or hold any lines on the Gallipoli Peninsula. Probably an entrenched force will be required to retain the Turkish forces in the Peninsula and prevent reinforcements arriving at Bulair, and this force would naturally be supported on both flanks by gun-fire from the Fleet. Troops employed on the minor operations mentioned above (paragraph 4) should be withdrawn as soon as their mission is fulfilled.

7. In order not to reduce forces advancing on Constantinople, the security of the Dardanelles passage, once it has been forced, is a matter for the Fleet, except as in paragraph 6 with regard to Bulair.

The occupation of the Asiatic side by military forces is to be strongly deprecated.

8. When the advance through the Sea of Marmora is undertaken, and the Turkish Fleet has been destroyed, the opening of the Bosphorus for the passage of Russian forces will be proceeded with. During this period, the employment of the British and French troops, which will probably have been brought up to the neighbourhood of Constantinople, should be conducted with caution. As soon as the Russian corps has joined up with our troops, combined plans of operations against the Turkish Army (if it still remains in European Turkey) will be undertaken with a view to obtaining its defeat or surrender. Until this is achieved, landing in the town of Constantinople, which may entail street fighting, should be avoided.

9. As it is impossible now to foretell what action the Turkish military authorities may decide upon as regards holding their European territories, the plan of operations for the landing of the troops and their employment must be left for subsequent decision. It is, however, important that as soon as possible after the arrival of the Fleet at Constantinople, all communication from the West to the East across the Bosphorus, including telegraph cables, should be stopped. Assuming that the main portion of the Turkish Army is prepared to defend European Turkish territory, it may be necessary to land parties to hold entrenched positions on the East side of the Bosphorus, and thus assist the Fleet in preventing all communication across the Bosphorus.

10. Should the Turkish Army have retired to the East side of the Bosphorus, the occupation of Constantinople and the Western territories of Turkey may be proceeded with.

11. As, in certain contingencies, it may be important to be able to withdraw our troops from this theatre at an early date,

APPENDIX 1

the Allied troops working in conjunction with us should be placed in those positions which need to be garrisoned, and our troops might with advantage be employed principally in holding the railway line until a decision is come to as to future operations.

12. You will send all communications to the Secretary of State for War, and keep him fully informed of the operations and your anticipations as to future developments.

KITCHENER.

March 13th, 1915.

Appendix 2

ORDER OF BATTLE
MEDITERRANEAN EXPEDITIONARY FORCE

APRIL 1915[1]

Commander-in-Chief . . Gen. Sir Ian Hamilton, G.C.B.
Chief of the General Staff . Maj.-Gen. W. P. Braithwaite, C.B.
Deputy Adjutant-General . Br.-Gen. E. M. Woodward.
Deputy Quartermaster-General Br.-Gen. S. H. Winter.

29TH DIVISION:
Major-Gen. A. G. Hunter-Weston, C.B.

86th Brigade:
    2/Royal Fusiliers   1/R. Munster Fusiliers
    1/Lancashire Fusiliers   1/R. Dublin Fusiliers

87th Brigade:
    2/S. Wales Borderers   1/R. Inniskilling Fus.
    1/K.O.S.B.   1/Border Regt.

88th Brigade:
    4/Worcestershire Regt.   1/Essex Regt.
    2/Hampshire Regt.   1/5th Royal Scots (T.F.)

XV. Bde. R.H.A. (B, L & Y Btys.).
XVII. Bde. R.F.A. (13th, 26th & 92nd Btys.).
CXLVII. Bde. R.F.A. (10th, 97th & 368th Btys.).
460th (Howitzer) Bty. R.F.A.
4th (Highland) Mountain Bde. R.G.A. (T.F.).[2]
90th Heavy Bty. R.G.A.
14th Siege Bty. R.G.A.
1/2nd London, 1/2nd Lowland & 1/1st W. Riding Field Coys. R.E. (T.F.).
Divisional Cyclist Coy.

[1] Only fighting troops embarked for the first landing are shown.
[2] Argyllshire Battery and Ross & Cromarty Battery.

APPENDIX 2

Royal Naval Division:
Major-Gen. A. Paris, C.B.

1st (Naval) Brigade:
  Drake Bn. Deal Bn. R.M.L.I.
  Nelson Bn.

2nd (Naval) Brigade:
  Howe Bn. Anson Bn.
  Hood Bn.

3rd (R.M.) Brigade:
  Chatham Bn. R.M.L.I. Plymouth Bn. R.M.L.I.
  Portsmouth Bn. R.M.L.I.

Motor Maxim Squadron (R.N.A.S.).
1st & 2nd Field Coys. Engineers.
Divisional Cyclist Coy.

Australian & New Zealand Army Corps
G.O.C. . . . Lieut.-Gen. Sir W. Birdwood, K.C.S.I.

1st Australian Division:
Major-Gen. W. T. Bridges, C.M.G.

1st Australian Brigade:
  1st (N.S.W.) Bn. 3rd (N.S.W.) Bn.
  2nd (N.S.W.) Bn. 4th (N.S.W.) Bn.

2nd Australian Brigade:
  5th (Victoria) Bn. 7th (Victoria) Bn.
  6th (Victoria) Bn. 8th (Victoria) Bn.

3rd Australian Brigade:
  9th (Queensland) Bn. 11th (W. Australia) Bn.
  10th (S. Australia) Bn. 12th (S. & W. Austr. and Tasmania) Bn.

I. (N.S.W.) F.A. Bde. (1st, 2nd & 3rd Btys.).
II. (Victoria) F.A. Bde. (4th, 5th & 6th Btys.).
III. (Queensland) F.A. Bde. (7th, 8th & 9th Btys.).
1st, 2nd & 3rd Field Coys. Engineers.

New Zealand & Australian Division:
Major-Gen. Sir A. Godley, K.C.M.G.

New Zealand Brigade:
  Auckland Bn. Otago Bn.
  Canterbury Bn. Wellington Bn.

4th Australian Brigade:
    13th (N.S.W.) Bn.
    14th (Victoria) Bn.
    15th (Queensland and Tasmania) Bn.
    16th (S. & W. Australia) Bn.

New Zealand F.A. Bde. (1st, 2nd & 3rd Btys.).
New Zealand Field Howitzer Bty.
Field Coy. New Zealand Engineers.

Corps Troops

7th Indian Mountain Artillery Bde.[1]
Ceylon Planters Rifle Corps.

Corps Expéditionnaire d'Orient

Commander . . . . . . General d'Amade.

1st Division: Gen. Masnou.

Metropolitan Brigade:
    175th Regiment.
    Régt. de marche d'Afrique (2 Bns. Zouaves, 1 Bn. Foreign Legion).

Colonial Brigade:
    4th Colonial Regt. (2 Bns. Senegalese, 1 Bn. Colonial).
    6th Colonial Regt. (2 Bns. Senegalese, 1 Bn. Colonial).

6 Batteries of artillery (75-mm.).
2 Batteries of artillery (65-mm.).

---

[1] 21st (Kohat) Battery and 26th (Jacob's) Battery.

APPENDIX 3

SIR IAN HAMILTON'S ORDER FOR LANDING, 25TH APRIL 1915

FORCE ORDER No. 1

GENERAL HEADQUARTERS,
13th April[1] 1915.

1. Information.	The strength of the enemy in the Gallipoli Peninsula is estimated at 34,000 men made up of 3 Divisions of *Nizam* and one of *Redif*. Of these Divisions one is believed to be at Bulair and one or more in the neighbourhood of Anafarta and Kilid Bahr, and one between the Achi Baba ridge and Cape Helles.	Maps 2, 3. Sketches 4, 5.
	Information points to a landing being opposed.	
2. Object of the Expedition.	The object of the expedition is to assist the fleet to force the Dardanelles by capturing the Kilid Bahr plateau, and dominating the forts at the Narrows.	
3. General Plan.	The general plan to achieve this object is:—	

(i) A bombardment of the Bulair lines at daybreak on the —th,[2] followed by a feint of landing on the mainland N. of Bulair by the transport fleet of the Royal Naval Division.

(ii) Simultaneously with the above a bombardment of the heights commanding the beach Gaba Tepe—Nibrunesi Point, accompanied by a landing by the A. & N.Z. Army Corps.

(iii) Simultaneously with the above a bombardment of the southern extremity of the Peninsula, accompanied by a landing by the 29th Division in the neighbourhood of Cape Helles.

[1] Issued 14th April.
[2] Date to be divulged later.—Note by C.G.S.

(iv) Simultaneously with the foregoing, the French fleet will make a demonstration at Besika Bay, in combination with which a landing will be effected by a portion of the French Expeditionary Force near Kum Kale. Special instructions will be issued to General d'Amade.

4. Composition and general objective of the covering forces.

(i) *Gulf of Saros*
No covering force will be required. Special instructions as to his action have been issued to G.O.C. Royal Naval Division.

Gaba Tepe Landing:
1 Bde. A. & N.Z.A.C.,
1 Fd. Coy. R.E.
3 Bearer sub-divs. (less all animals and vehicles).

Cape Helles Landing:[1]
1 Bde. 29th Div.
1 Bn. do.
1 Fd. Coy. R.E.
3 Bearer sub-divs. (less all animals and vehicles)

Sketch 4.

(ii) *Gaba Tepe and Cape Helles*
The covering forces detailed in the margin will be moved in their transports on the evening of —th[1] to separate rendezvous fixed by the naval authorities. Special instructions regarding their disembarkation have been issued to G.O.C. A. & N.Z. Army Corps and to G.O.C. 29th Division respectively. The timing of the tows will be so arranged that the first troops reach the shore at — A.M.[1] The beaches to be used are shown in sketch "A" attached.[3]

Objectives of the covering forces:—
At Gaba Tepe a covering position on the south-western spurs of the hill in squares 224-237-238 (W.O. Map Sari Bair). At Cape Helles the Achi Baba ridge.

5. Disembarkation of the main bodies.

The disembarkation of the main bodies at Gaba Tepe and Cape Helles will commence directly the respective covering forces have landed, unless orders to the contrary are received from the G.O.C. A. & N.Z. Army Corps, or the G.O.C. 29th Division, as the case may be. The disembarkation of the A. & N.Z. Army Corps will be carried out under the orders of the G.O.C. Army Corps. That of the 29th Division will be carried out in accordance with diagram "B",[4] which also shows the beaches to be used by each transport.

The Plymouth Battalion R.M.L.I. will be held at the disposal of the General Commanding the Expeditionary Force, ready to land on Beach "Y"

---

[1] Date and times to be divulged later.—Note by C.G.S.
[2] Amended by Instructions to Covering Force issued 19th April. [3] Not reproduced.
[4] Not reproduced. It shows the berth of each transport.

APPENDIX 3

should circumstances render such a course advisable. Transport N. 2 carrying this battalion will form part of the transport fleet of the 29th Division.[1]

6. General instructions for landing.

Special attention is directed to the pamphlet of instructions on landings issued by General Headquarters.

A hot meal will be issued to all troops before leaving their transports, and troops will land in marching order with pack and one day's rations and 2 iron rations (or 3 iron rations in the case of units for which this number is available on their ships).

Infantry will carry 200 rounds of ammunition.

Horses will be harnessed before disembarkation.

Poles of G.S. wagons will be removed before slinging and made fast to the body of the wagon. Poles of carts, limbers, and limbered wagons will not be removed; these vehicles should be so placed in the boats that they can be landed pole leading.

Two staff officers of G.H.Q. will be landed with the covering force of the 29th Division, and G.O.C. A. & N.Z. Army Corps will detail two staff officers to land with the covering force of his corps, to select and mark out forming up places and rendezvous. Pending the completion of this work, troops will be formed up by their commanders in the most convenient localities close to, but clear of, the beach. Every endeavour must be made to prevent confusion on the beaches.

7. Naval & Military Beach Control Personnel.

The names of the officers appointed for duty as Naval & Military Beach Control Personnel will be notified later.

8. Military beach parties and fatigue parties.

G.O.C. A. & N.Z. Army Corps will detail beach parties for eight landing places, and the necessary fatigue parties for work on Beach "Z".

G.O.C. 29th Division will detail beach parties for twelve landing places. Two companies Anson Bn. R.N.D. are attached to the 29th Division for this duty, including reliefs. The Anson R.N.D. (less the two companies above mentioned) will be available for such other working and fatigue parties as may be detailed by G.O.C. 29th Division on the Cape Helles beaches.

[1] This paragraph was subsequently amended. See Appendix 4.

Beach, working and fatigue parties will, in all cases act under the orders of the P.M.L.O. concerned.

9. Piers and Jetties.
Two floating piers, one for Beach "Z" and one for Beach "W" will be available for use on the afternoon of the first day, and the construction of trestle piers will be commenced at the first opportunity. At Beach "Z" the G.O.C. A. & N.Z. Army Corps will make arrangements for their construction. At Cape Helles one Field Company R.E. to be detailed by G.O.C. 29th Division, will be landed for this work, and for improving exits from and communications on the beach.

10. Intercommunication.
The G.O.C. A. & N.Z. Army Corps will arrange for a central signal office to be established on Beach "Z", to be responsible for all signal communications forward from the beach. He will also arrange for telephonic communication on the beach.

Communications to escorting ships and to transports will be made through a Royal Naval base signal station to be established on Beach "Z". Pending its disembarkation 6 naval ratings, to be landed with the covering force, will form a temporary naval station.

At Cape Helles a central signal office, found by General Headquarters Signal Company, for working the beach ends of cables laid from it, and a Royal Naval base signal station for communications with the escorting ships and transports, will be established on Beach "W". Six naval ratings will be landed with the covering force to carry out the latter duty until the arrival of the Royal Naval base signal station.

As the General Headquarters Signal Company has not enough cable to maintain communication with all formations, each formation in turn will be responsible for maintaining communication with the central signal office.

Special telephones, to be landed with the beach equipment embarked in the transports of the 29th Division, for communication along the beaches and to the forming up places and rendezvous, will be set up by the Field Company R.E. landed for work on the beach.

Instructions for intercommunication with the fleet regarding support by naval guns have been

APPENDIX 3

issued in pamphlet form. Communication will usually be sent through the Royal Naval base signal stations, but two military W/T stations on the flanks will be provided both at Gaba Tepe and Cape Helles which can be used for this purpose if required.

11. Water.

A water station will be established at the earliest opportunity in the neighbourhood of Cape Helles and its locality communicated. G.O.'s C. will ensure that any springs or wells captured are carefully guarded. No one should be allowed to drink well-water until it has been tested.

Owing to the great scarcity of water on the Peninsula, all ranks must be cautioned against waste.

12. Medical.

Casualty Clearing Stations will be located on Beaches "W" and "Z" by the afternoon of the first day.

Men and animals unfit for duty on the day of disembarkation will remain on their transports.

13. Baggage left on Transports.

A small party from each battalion will be left on each transport to take charge of regimental baggage and stores remaining on board.

14. Reserve ammunition and supplies.

150 rounds S.A.A. per rifle landed;
150 rounds gun ammunition per gun landed;
1000 rounds S.A.A. per machine gun landed;
7 days' rations and forage per man and horse landed;

will be put on shore during the first day, and will be stored in convenient localities near the beaches under arrangements made by the P.M.L.O.'s. Guards for these stores will be found from the beach fatigue parties.

15. Position of G.O.C.

General Headquarters will, in the first instance, be established on board H.M.S. *Queen Elizabeth*.

W. P. BRAITHWAITE,
Major-General, C.G.S. Med. E.F.

APPENDIX 4

INSTRUCTIONS FOR HELLES COVERING FORCE[1]

G.H.Q.,
19th April, 1915.

1. COMPOSITION OF THE COVERING FORCE.

Map 2.
Sketch 4.
Diagram.

    O.C. Br.-General W. S. Hare.
    One Field Company R.E.
    86th Infantry Brigade.
    2 Battalions 87th Infantry Brigade.
    ½ Battalion 88th Infantry Brigade.
    Plymouth Battalion, Royal Naval Division.
    3 Bearer Sub-Divns., 89th Field Ambulance.

2. The objective of this force is the ridge across the Peninsula, point 344 (Sq. 170.d.)—Achi Baba peak—472—coast line (Sq. 184).[2]

3. NAVAL ARRANGEMENTS FOR LANDING.

(i) The covering force will be landed at 5 beaches as follows:—

Beach.	Locality.
S	Eski Hissarlik Point.
V	Sedd el Bahr—Cape Helles.
W	Cape Helles—Tekke Burnu.
X	Sq. 168Q.8.[3]
Y	At a point to be selected between Square 175.P. and Square 175.X.[3]

(ii) The landing will be carried out in four stages:—

1st Stage. Landing in 4 trips of 2¼ battalions on Beach Y, and a bombardment of the Helles beaches by the fleet.

2nd Stage. Landing in one trip of 2,900 troops at beaches S, V, W and X, as shewn in diagram attached.

---
[1] These Instructions cancelled those of 13th April which are not reproduced.
[2] Tener Chift Knoll—Achi Baba—Yazy Tepe—Ægean coast.
[3] The map co-ordinates refer to the 1/40,000 Map in use at the time.

APPENDIX 4

3rd Stage.   Landing of 2,100 troops in the collier *River Clyde*, which will be run ashore at beach V.

4th Stage.   Landing in one trip of remainder of the covering force on beaches V, W, and X—vide diagram.

(iii) At 8 A.M. on the day before the landing is to take place, transports B1, B2, B3 and collier *River Clyde* will arrive at Tenedos.

Three lighters will be brought alongside each transport and will be loaded with the reserve ammunition, reserve supplies, and beach equipment respectively, carried by these transports. These lighters will subsequently be towed to beaches V, W, and X.

The following re-arrangement of the troops on B1, B2, and B3 will then be carried out:—

2nd South Wales Borderers (less 1 Company)
Detachment 2nd London Field Co. R.E.
    } from B3 to 4 trawlers.*

1st R. Dublin Fus. (less 1 Coy.)
1 Platoon Anson Battalion
    } from B1 to Fleet Sweeper No. 1.

1st Lancashire Fus. (less 1 Coy.)
1 Platoon Anson Battalion
    } from B2 to H.M.S. *Euryalus*.

1 Co. Lancashire Fus.   from B2
2 Coys. & M. Gun Section
2nd R. Fusiliers
1 Platoon Anson Bn.   from B3
    } to H.M.S. *Implacable*.

West Riding Field Co., R.E.
1 Co. 1st Royal Dublin Fusiliers
3 Bearer Sub-divs. 89th Fd. Amb.   from B1
1st R. Munster Fus.
G.H.Q. Signal Section   from B2
2nd Hampshire Regt. (less 2 Coys.)
1 Platoon Anson Bn.   from B3
    } to *River Clyde*.

H.Q. 86th Inf. Bde. and Section Divl. Signal Co.
2nd London Field Co. R.E. (less detachment)
    } from B3 to B2.

* These trawlers will be alongside H.M.S. *Cornwallis* and the troops will be accommodated on that battleship until it is time to leave Tenedos. (Actually the troops were not transferred to the trawlers until the flotilla arrived at the mouth of the Straits on the morning of 25th April.)

(Before the above movements take place, one company 2nd South Wales Borderers will have been transferred at Mudros from B3 to B11, and the 2nd Hampshire Regiment (less 2 companies) from B7 to B3 under divisional arrangements.)

Troops moving from one ship to another, in accordance with the above orders, will take their full fighting equipment (Force Order No. 1, para. 6), including such additional tools, R.E. and medical stores as can be carried, but all baggage and kits will be left on their present ships.

(iv) Before dawn on the day of landing, the remaining troops on B1, B2, and B3, will be transferred to five fleet sweepers as shewn on diagram.[1]

(v) The three men-of-war, with six fleet sweepers, transports B1, B2, B3, the *River Clyde*, and four trawlers will then sail for Cape Helles, arriving there before dawn.

(vi) The covering ships will bombard the southern end of the Peninsula at daybreak.

H.M.S. *Cornwallis* will then escort the four trawlers, each accompanied by 6 cutters, to Morto Bay.

H.M.S. *Euryalus*, H.M.S. *Implacable* and Fleet Sweeper No. 1 will each be joined by 6 tows, each made up of a pinnace and four cutters—capacity of each tow about 125 men.

The troops detailed for these tows (vide diagram [1]) will be held ready to embark on the order of the S.N.O. The tows will then proceed to the beach in line abreast, covered by the guns of the fleet.

(vii) As soon as the tows for Beach "V" have landed their men and started on their return journey, the collier will be run aground on that beach, and the troops disembarked.

(viii) Fleet sweepers Nos. 2 to 6 will then approach the shore and will each be met by two tows returning from their first trip. The troops will be transferred to these tows and landed on the beaches shown on diagram.[1]

(ix) While the movement in paras (v) to (vii) above are in progress, transports N2 with the Plymouth Battalion, and B11 with the K.O. Scottish Borderers and one company South Wales Borderers will have reached the rendezvous off beach Y, and will have begun to transfer their infantry to four trawlers

---

[1] See "Diagram of the Helles Landing".

APPENDIX 4

to be disembarked in four trips of 20 cutters, commencing at dawn, the Plymouth Battalion being the first to disembark.[1]

4. There has been no opportunity to reconnoitre for forming up places and rendezvous; it will be necessary to move troops forward as soon as they land, taking advantage of any cover to get units together. Until the beach control personnel is disembarked, special arrangements must be made to organize the forming up and control of the troops as they come ashore.

W. P. BRAITHWAITE,
Major-General, C.G.S., Med. Ex. Force.

---

[1] Subsequently the K.O.S.B. and S.W.B. were ordered to land first, and to facilitate their rapid disembarkation they were transferred to the cruisers *Amethyst* and *Sapphire* on the night before the landing.

APPENDIX 5

INSTRUCTIONS TO
G.O.C. A. & N.Z. ARMY CORPS

Map 3.
Sketch 4.

G.H.Q.,
13th April[1] 1915.

1. Information regarding the enemy.

1. The enemy holds the Kilid Bahr plateau in strength and is believed to have a number of troops concentrated in the neighbourhood of the Anafarta villages and Maidos. There may be two divisions (20,000 men) distributed in these areas. Gun emplacements have been located at Gaba Tepe and Nibrunesi Point, but repeated air reconnaissances have failed, as yet, to disclose any guns.

2. Objective.

2. A landing in force is to be made by the A. & N.Z. Army Corps on the beach between Gaba Tepe and Fisherman's Hut. The objective assigned to the Army Corps is the ridge over which the Gallipoli—Maidos and Boghali—Kojadere roads run, especially Mal Tepe. Gaining such a position the Army Corps will threaten, and perhaps cut, the line of retreat of the enemy's forces on the Kilid Bahr plateau, and must, even by their preliminary operations, prevent the said plateau being reinforced, during the attack of the 29th Division, from Maidos, Gallipoli or Bulair.

3. Naval arrangements for landing covering force.

3. Four transports can be worked simultaneously on the beach selected (Beach "Z"). Three steam pinnaces, or picket boats, with 12 cutters or lifeboats, will be available for each transport of the covering force. These boats will be formed into three tows, each with a carrying capacity of 120-130

[1] Issued on 14th April.

APPENDIX 5

men. There will therefore be 12 tows available in all, with a total capacity of 1450 to 1500 men.

On the afternoon before the landing is to take place the troops detailed for the first trip of the tows will be transferred, under naval arrangements to be notified later, from their respective transports to H.M. Ships *Queen*, *London*, and *Prince of Wales*, which will steam during the night to a position off Gaba Tepe. The 12 tows will be brought alongside H.M. ships, under naval arrangements, in time to admit of the landing taking place on Beach "Z" at — A.M.[1]

Transports A1, A2, A3 and A4 carrying the remainder of the covering force will also rendezvous off Gaba Tepe during the night, attended by eight t.b. destroyers, two of which will be ready to stand by each transport to take off the remaining troops.[2]

The landing of the covering force will be effected in three stages as follows:—

1st Stage. Landing of 1450-1500 men from H.M. ships in the first trip of the tows.

2nd Stage. Embarkation of remainder of covering force into eight t.b.d. which will follow in to shore immediately after the despatch of the first tows.

3rd Stage. Landing of remainder of covering force from t.b.d. in successive trips of tows. Three tows will be allotted to each pair of destroyers.

In order to enable the t.b.d. to be emptied in three trips of the tows, it may be necessary to effect some redistribution of the troops left in the transports before the latter start for the rendezvous off Beach "Z".

4. Naval arrangements for landing main body.
4. Subsequently when the covering force is ashore, the transports of the Army Corps will come in and anchor, and the disembarkation will proceed in accordance with instructions given by you. Four transports can be worked out simultaneously—three steam pinnaces or picket boats, four lighters, four horseboats and eight cutters or lifeboats being available for each transport.

[1] Time to be divulged later.
[2] This arrangement was subsequently amended. See account of landing in Chapter IX.

5. Artillery support by the fleet.	5. During the disembarkation of the Army Corps the guns of the fleet will be available to support it by their fire.
6. Topography.	6. The first essential for the covering force will be to establish itself on the hill in Squares 224, 237 and 238 (Sari Bair on War Office map)[1] in order to protect the landing of the remainder of the Army Corps. From the ridge between squares 237.Z and 224.F spurs run north-west and south-west to the sea. This semicircular system of ridges seems to lend itself to the establishment of a strong covering position.[1] Whether it will be necessary or not to include the crest of the mountain must be left to your discretion.
7. General plan of operation of the Army Corps.	7. As soon as the first division is landed with an irreducible minimum of animals and vehicles, the disembarkation of the second division will commence.

By the time the second division begins to land, sufficient troops should be available to admit of a further advance. Leaving the covering force to protect the northern flank of the landing place and line of communication, an effort will be made to storm Mal Tepe which is the centre and key to the ridge over which the Gallipoli—Maidos and Boghali—Kojadere roads run. Should the A. & N.Z. Army Corps succeed in securing this ridge the results should be more vital and valuable than the capture of the Kilid Bahr plateau itself.

Times and dates have purposely been omitted in these instructions, and will be telegraphed later.

W. P. BRAITHWAITE,
Major-General, C.G.S.,
Med. Ex. Force.

---

[1] Position shown on Sketch 4. The map co-ordinates refer to the 1/40,000 Map in use at the time.

Appendix 6

INSTRUCTIONS TO GENERAL D'AMADE FOR THE KUM KALE LANDING

GENERAL HEADQUARTERS,
18th April[1] 1915.

Sir,

1. In order to assist the preliminary operations of the troops landing in the Gallipoli Peninsula, I have assigned to the force under your command the task of effecting a landing near Kum Kale, with the object of engaging the attention of any hostile troops which may be near the entrance to the Dardanelles on the Asiatic shore. Map 2. Sketch 4.

2. Admiral Guépratte, with whom I have been in consultation, has been asked to assist by making a demonstration simultaneously in Besika Bay.

3. The information received does not point to any considerable numbers of the enemy being met with by your landing party. With a view, however, to safeguarding the landing of the troops in Morto Bay, it is important to prevent the enemy from placing field batteries in the neighbourhood of Kum Kale, whence they could bring fire to bear on transports anchored in the bay.

4. The landing near Kum Kale is intended to be in the nature of a diversion, and it is not desirable to extend the scope of the operations further than is necessary for clearing the region between Kum Kale and Yeni Shehr and west of the Mendere river. For this purpose it should not be necessary to land more than one infantry regiment, without animals or vehicles, and one battery of 75 mm. guns.

5. It is desirable that you should not land any larger number of troops for the further reason that it is intended, as soon as a secure footing is gained on the Gallipoli Peninsula, to re-embark your landing party, and to transfer the force under

[1] Despatched 20th April.

your command to the European side of the Straits, where it will be landed at Cape Helles preparatory to the general advance of the Allied forces against the enemy's army in the Gallipoli Peninsula.

6. I regret that it will not be possible to provide boats for the purpose of your landing at Kum Kale, owing to the fact that all those available will be taking part in the landing on the Gallipoli Peninsula. Since, however, you will be disembarking no large number of troops, the boats carried on your transports will doubtless be sufficient for your purpose. Subsequently, when the force under your command is landed on the Peninsula the necessary arrangements for its disembarkation (including the provision of boats, etc.) will be made by me in conjunction with Vice-Admiral de Robeck.

I have the honour to be,
Sir,
Your obedient Servant,
IAN HAMILTON,
General,
Commanding Mediterranean Expeditionary Force.

Appendix 7

EPITOME OF ORDERS ISSUED BY THE NAVAL COMMANDER-IN-CHIEF, 12TH APRIL

TOGETHER WITH SUBSEQUENT ADDITIONS AND AMENDMENTS

I.—General Plan of Operations

"To ensure the destruction of the forts at the Narrows
" and secure command of the Dardanelles, a combined attack
" by Navy and Army will be delivered on the Gallipoli Penin-
" sula.

"The efforts of the Navy will primarily be directed to
" landing the Army and supporting it till its position is secure,
" after which the Navy will attack the forts at the Narrows,
" assisted by the Army."

II.—Disembarkation of the Army

General Instructions

The 29th Division landing to be conducted by the 1st Squadron under Rear-Admiral R. E. Wemyss, in *Euryalus*.

The landing at Y Beach to be conducted by the 4th Squadron also under the orders of Rear-Admiral Wemyss.

The Anzac landing to be conducted by the 2nd Squadron under Rear-Admiral C. F. Thursby, in *Queen*.

The 3rd Squadron, under Captain H. S. Grant, in *Canopus*, to make a feint to land troops at the same time near Bulair.

The 5th Squadron, under Captain H. A. S. Fyler, in *Agamemnon*, accompanied by Captain A. W. Heneage (Capt. S.), to clear certain areas inside the Straits of mines under special instructions, and lay a net defence against floating mines.

The 6th Squadron, under Contre-Amiral E. P. A. Guépratte, to convoy and cover the French Division.

The 7th Squadron to watch the port of Smyrna and certain enemy craft in that harbour.

[The hour of landing and directions as to routes, rendezvous, etc., were to be issued 24 hours before operations began.]

Fire of Covering Ships

In assisting the troops, the first objective of naval fire was to be the hostile artillery, and, except when targets were exceptionally good, ships were advised to confine their efforts to attacking the Turkish artillery personnel. Secondary objective, hostile troops. "The shelling of hostile trenches except to " cover an infantry attack, or for other specific object, is, as a " rule, a waste of ammunition."

"Ships will generally open fire whenever the enemy troops " are observed or for a definite tactical object; they are always " to open fire when requested to do so on any object indicated " by the military; if they are unable themselves to engage the " target, the request is to be at once passed on to another ship " in a favourable position. Ships will always cease fire when " asked to do so by troops ashore."

Searchlights

"Searchlights are not to be thrown on to the land except at " the expressed wish of the military. Their requests as to " areas to be illuminated or searched are to be carried out with " the least possible delay."

Ammunition Supply and Expenditure

"It is not desirable for me to definitely limit the expenditure " of ammunition of covering ships, during the landing and " subsequent advance of the troops, but the following figures " are issued as a guide of what I consider to be the maximum " expenditure, allowable on the first day without prejudice to " future operations":—

12-in. to 9·2-in. inclusive	20 rounds per gun
7·5-in.	80 ,, ,, ,,
6-in. Q.F. or B.L.	100 ,, ,, ,,
4-in. Q.F.	100 ,, ,, ,,
12-pdr. Q.F.	100 ,, ,, ,,

"This allowance should not be exceeded without urgent " military necessity."

APPENDIX 7

Special Instructions

All the officers in command of squadrons to issue necessary orders to their commands, and all concerned to understand that for a successful landing of the army it is necessary to have most precise and clearly defined instructions.

[Then followed instructions regarding inspecting all boats, exercising boats' crews, and visits by officers to vicinity of beaches on which they would have to land. The allocation of tugs, lighters, boats, and material was placed in the hands of Admiral Wemyss.]

"Instructions for hospital ships will be given by the Vice-"Admiral, but the conveyance of wounded from the shore to "the ship is to be arranged for by officers in command of "squadrons."

A covering force to seaward during the landing operations to be found by three special service ships and a number of trawler mine-sweepers.

Secret orders to be issued to submarines.

Aircraft

(a) Aeroplanes from Tenedos to work:—
   Some under Rear-Admiral S. Nicholson spotting for Covering Ships.[1]
   Others under orders of G.O.C. 29th Division.
(b) *Ark Royal* with seaplanes to be attached to 2nd Squadron.
(c) French air-craft to support the French landing.
(d) *Manica* with kite balloon to work under 2nd Squadron unless required by Vice-Admiral.

Detailed instructions were also issued on the following subjects:—

Naval Signal Parties landed with military.

W/T. Organization.

Naval Ranks and Ratings for duty in transports. One naval officer and about 10 petty officers and men accompanied each transport carrying the covering force.

Beach Parties. A total of 23 naval officers, 10 warrant officers, 17 midshipmen, and 232 petty officers and men were detailed for this duty.

---

[1] Part of 1st Squadron. See Appendix 8.

APPENDIX 8

COMPOSITION OF SQUADRONS SHOWING PRINCIPAL ARMAMENTS

	15"	12"	10"	9·2"	7·5"	6"	12pr.
Fleet Flagship:							
Queen Elizabeth	8	—	—	—	—	12	12
Helles. 1st Squadron:							
Attendant Ships.							
Euryalus	—	—	—	2	—	12	12
Implacable	—	4	—	—	—	12	16
Cornwallis	—	4	—	—	—	12	10
Covering Ships.							
Swiftsure	—	—	4	—	14	—	—
Albion	—	4	—	—	—	12	10
Vengeance	—	4	—	—	—	12	10
Lord Nelson	—	4	—	10	—	—	24
Prince George	—	4	—	—	—	12	16
Goliath	—	4	—	—	—	12	10
Talbot	—	—	—	—	—	11	8
Dublin	—	—	—	—	—	8	1
Minerva	—	—	—	—	—	11	8
Total 1st Sqdn.	—	28	4	12	14	114	125
Y Beach. 4th Squadron							
Amethyst	—	—	—	—	—	—	12 } 4"
Sapphire	—	—	—	—	—	—	12
Total 4th Sqdn.	—	—	—	—	—	—	24—4"
Anzac. 2nd Squadron							
Attendant Ships.							
Queen	—	4	—	—	—	12	16
London	—	4	—	—	—	12	16
Prince of Wales	—	4	—	—	—	12	16
Covering Ships.							
Triumph	—	—	4	—	14	—	—
Majestic	—	4	—	—	—	12	16
Bacchante	—	—	—	2	—	12	12
8 t.b.d.'s							
Total 2nd Sqdn. (excl. T.B.D. armament)	—	16	4	2	14	60	76
Gulf of Saros. 3rd Squadron							
Canopus	—	4	—	—	—	12	10
Dartmouth	—	—	—	—	—	8	—
Doris	—	—	—	—	—	11	8
2 t.b.d.'s							
Total 3rd Sqdn. (excl. T.B.D. armament)	—	4	—	—	—	31	18
Sweeping in Straits. 5th Sqdn.							
Agamemnon	—	4	10	—	—	—	24
12 t.b.d.'s							

Asiatic Coast. 6th Sqdn.	12"	10·8"	7·6"	6"	5·5"	4"	12pr.
French.							
Jauréguiberry	2	2	—	—	8	—	—
Charlemagne	4	—	—	—	10	8	—
Henri IV	—	2	—	—	7	—	—
Jeanne d'Arc	—	—	2	—	14	—	—
Askold (Russ.)	—	—	—	12	—	—	12
t.b.d.'s							
Total 6th Sqdn. (excl. t.b.d. armaments.)	6	4	2	12	39	8	12

Appendix 9

EPITOME OF ORDERS
BY REAR-ADMIRAL R. E. WEMYSS

FOR THE MOVEMENTS OF TRANSPORTS AND SHIPS OF THE 1ST AND 2ND SQUADRONS DURING THE TWO DAYS PREVIOUS TO LANDING; AND FOR THE 1ST SQUADRON AND 29TH DIVISION TRANSPORTS ON DAY OF LANDING

At Mudros—Two Days before Landing

Transports A18, A19, A9, A25, to leave harbour and anchor outside boom.

Following ships to proceed to anchorages on N. side of Tenedos, leaving Mudros at hours named:

Collier *River Clyde* at noon.
Transports B1, B2, B3, at half-hour intervals beginning at 5 P.M.
Euryalus, Cornwallis, Implacable at 6.30 P.M.
Fauvette (carrying buoys, &c.) at 7.0 P.M.

At Mudros—Day before Landing

Transports A10, A11, A13, A15, to leave at 10 minute intervals beginning at 5 A.M. for rendezvous appointed by Rear-Admiral 2nd Squadron.

Transports A17, A30, A32, S1, S2, to leave at 10 minute intervals beginning at 6.30 A.M. for rendezvous 20 miles S. of Kestra Island.[1] To remain there till sunset, then shape course and regulate speed in order to reach rendezvous 3 miles S.W. of Cape Helles at 6 A.M. next morning. Then to hoist out their horse boats required for southern landing and proceed to join 2nd Squadron.

[1] Off entrance to Mudros Bay.

Transport N2 to leave at 9.30 A.M. for rendezvous 20 miles S. of Kestra Island; thence, at 1 hr. before sunset, to proceed to rendezvous 3 miles W. of Tekke Burnu. To arrive at 1 A.M.

Transports A5, A6, A7, A8, A12, A14, A16, A21, to leave at 20 minute intervals, beginning at 11 A.M., to rendezvous off Imbros as directed by Rear-Admiral 2nd Squadron.

Transports A1, A2, A3, A4, to same rendezvous, but first ship leaving at 2 P.M.

2nd Squadron to leave Mudros for same rendezvous at an hour to be named by its Rear-Admiral.

Transports B4, B5, B6, B7, B8, B9, towing 14 lighters, to leave at 3.30 P.M. onwards. All to rendezvous 3 miles S.W. of Cape Helles at 6.30 A.M. next morning.

Arcadian (G.H.Q. transport) to leave at 6 P.M. and proceed to rendezvous as directed by Vice-Admiral.

At Tenedos—Day before Landing

Transports B1, B2, B3, and *River Clyde* to arrive by 8 A.M. Transports at once to load 3 lighters each with supplies and beach equipment for covering force: tugs to take charge of loaded lighters ready to tow them inshore next day.

Euryalus, *Cornwallis*, and *Implacable* to collect and organize boats and boats' crews in 18 tows—each of one steamboat and 4 pulling boats.

Naval beach parties to be mustered and sent to ships from which they land.

Buoys and moorings to be transferred to trawlers detailed to lay them.

Troops to land from warships, *River Clyde* and Fleet Sweeper No. 1 to be transferred from the transports by fleet sweepers.

Day of Landing

Troops on B1, B2, B3, detailed to land in second trip of tows to embark in five fleet sweepers just before sailing from Tenedos.

Euryalus, *Cornwallis*, *Implacable*, all 6 fleet sweepers, and tows of boats to leave anchorage at Tenedos in time for warships and Fleet Sweeper No. 1 to be anchored in assigned positions, with troops disembarked in boats, as day breaks.

APPENDIX 9

River Clyde to leave in time to arrive 1½ miles S.W. of Cape Helles one hour before dawn.

Transports B1, B2, B3 to sail at daybreak and proceed off beaches V, W, X respectively.

Covering ships to be in their allotted positions at dawn ready to open bombardment on signal from Rear-Admiral.

Rear-Admiral to give signal to land. The 18 tows then to proceed inshore and land troops: 10 of them to return to fleet sweepers Nos. 2-6 to embark remainder of covering force.

As soon as V Beach is clear of tows making first trip *River Clyde* to take up her position on V Beach.

When the 6 fleet sweepers are clear of troops they go to transports B6, B7, B9, embark their infantry, return to beaches and tranship troops to tows which will land them in 4 trips.

As soon as G.O.C. considers situation on shore satisfactory, transports B4 to B9 to be anchored in allotted positions off beaches and disembarkation of main body to begin in accordance with a detailed distribution of tugs, trawlers, horseboats and lighters. Transports B10, B12, B13, B14, B15, to leave Mudros at 6 A.M. and proceed to Helles.

Orders also provided for the laying of mark buoys and moorings, towing of supply lighters to peninsula, &c.

Landing at Y Beach [1]

Transports B11 and N2 to rendezvous with *Amethyst* and *Sapphire* and 4 trawlers as ordered by Vice-Admiral.

Trawlers to embark marine battalion from N2; warships to send crews to man 20 boats which will be taken in tow by trawlers. Latter, with warships, then remain off Cape Kephalo ready to disembark when ordered by military Commander-in-Chief. Battalion from B11 then to be landed.

Amethyst and *Sapphire* to be prepared to cover landing.

Everything to be ready for re-embarkation until orders are received from *Queen Elizabeth* that, this battalion being established, boats can be withdrawn from beach.

---

[1] These orders were subsequently amended. See Chapters VII. & XI.

Appendix 10

GENERAL ORDERS TO MASTERS OF TRANSPORTS
Issued by Principal Naval Transport Officer

Masters and crews of all craft and boats plying to and from transports, or lying alongside are subject to the authority of N.T.O. or his representative.

Written sailing orders not always possible. Orders by signal to be repeated back by signal and acted on.

Eastern Mediterranean time, *i.e.* 2 hrs. fast of G.M.T., to be kept. Day begins midnight, hours reckoned 0-24.

Ships to proceed to a rendezvous in complete darkness and silence; no navigation lights to be shown in vicinity of peninsula before operations commence.

Important to be under weigh and pointed to sea at time ordered to sail. Equally important to keep time at rendezvous and to anchor as accurately as possible in assigned position.

Masters to exercise personal supervision of condition of derricks, winches, lifeboats, gangways, ladders, &c.

Preparations to be made to use oil in case there is a sea while discharging. In all cases, ships to be ready to slip cable at short notice.

At scene of operations steam to be always ready to move engines and to be kept on windlass. Transports may be required to anchor in 50 fathoms.

After the landing, wireless signals may be made *en clair*, but signalling to be reduced to absolute minimum. Continuous wireless watch to be kept from sunset, after leaving Mudros, till operations begin.

APPENDIX 11

MEDICAL ARRANGEMENTS FOR THE LANDINGS OF THE M.E.F.

Issued by the Director of Medical Services, M.E.F.

1. With each covering force the bearer sub-divisions of a Field Ambulance and one tent sub-division will be landed with as much medical and surgical material as can be man-handled by the personnel, giving a total of 150 medical personnel with each covering force.
2. At 2 P.M. on day of landing the personnel of the Casualty Clearing Stations (one for the 29th Division and one for the Australian and New Zealand Army Corps) will be landed with as much surgical and medical material as can be man-handled.
3. When the remainder of the division lands the rest of the Field Ambulances and the equipment of the Casualty Clearing Stations will be put on shore as soon as it can be disembarked.
4. 2 hospital ships will be available
   With the 29th Division   *Sicilia* Accommodation
                                       serious cases   400
   With the A.N.Z. Army Corps *Gascon*   ,,   500
5. I understand from the Senior Naval Transport Officer that the Navy will commence the transport of wounded from the shore to the ships about 2 P.M.

The means of evacuation are as follows:—

3 launches each capable of holding 12 cots are available for the 29th Division and the same number for the A. & N.Z. Army Corps. These launches are to be towed to the hospital ships and other ships in which the men are to be accommodated.

The following transports are allotted to the 29th Division for accommodation of casualties:—

(a) B2 *Caledonia*   400 serious cases 1200-1500 slight.
    B7 *Aragon*   400   ,,   ,, 1200-1500 ,,
    B9 *Dongola*   400   ,,   ,, 1200-1500 ,,

(b) Allotted to the A. & N.Z. Army Corps:—

A25 *Lutzow*	200 serious cases	1000 slight cases.
A1 *Ionian*	100	,,	,,	1000	,,	,,
A15 *Clan McGillivray*	100	,,	,,	600	,,	,,
A31 *Seang-Chun*	100	,,	,,	600	,,	,,

Medical personnel and medical and surgical equipment for the *Caledonia*, *Aragon* and *Dongola* have been provided by No. 15 Stationary Hospital and for the *Clan McGillivray* and *Seang-Chun* by the A. & N.Z. Corps field ambulances at present, and later by No. 2 Australian Hospital. The *Lutzow* and *Ionian* to be supplied later with medical and surgical equipment from No. 2 Australian Hospital.

The personnel and equipment of No. 16 Stationary Hospital is kept in reserve.

6. No. 4 Advance Depot Medical Stores in *Anglo-Egyptian* is placed at disposal of A. & N.Z. A. Corps, and No. 5 Advance Depot Medical Stores at disposal of 29th Division.

7. It is proposed to evacuate ships with casualties direct to Alexandria and Malta.

8. No. 1 Australian Hospital at Mudros to be used for sick from shipping at Lemnos.

W. G. BIRRELL,
Surgeon-General.

GENERAL HEADQUARTERS,
S.S. *Arcadian*,
24/4/15.

Appendix 12

EPITOME OF ORDERS
ISSUED BY REAR-ADMIRAL C. F. THURSBY
FOR ANZAC LANDING

1. The first echelon of covering force to be transferred from transports A1, A2, A4 to *Queen*, *Prince of Wales*, and *London* at Mudros on morning before landing (500 to each ship).
2. Transports A1, A2, A3, A4 with second echelon of covering force (2,500 men) and accompanied by 7 destroyers to leave Mudros at 2 P.M. day before landing and anchor at rendezvous E. of Imbros at 10 P.M. There to hoist out boats, distribute boat and hold parties, make up tows.[1] Destroyers then to go alongside transports and second echelon of covering force to be transferred to them.
3. Battleships of 2nd Squadron to proceed direct from Mudros to rendezvous 5 miles W. of Gaba Tepe, there to stop, hoist out and lower boats, make up 12 tows. *Queen*, *Prince of Wales*, and *London* each to have 4 tows assembled alongside.
4. Destroyers, towing transports' tows, to sail so as to join battleships by 1.30 A.M., remaining outside and clear of them till ordered to proceed.
5. At hour to be notified battleships to steam due E. at 5 knots, *Queen*, *Prince of Wales*, and *London* in line abreast, each ship followed by her tows.
6. Signals "Stop engines", "Disembark troops", and "Anchor instantly" to be made by flagship[1] as necessary. On "Disembark troops" boats to be brought alongside and troops transferred to them as quickly as possible. On signal "Land armed parties" boats will shove off.

[1] All signals by wireless.

> *Queen's* boats to land on beach about 1 mile N. of Gaba Tepe.
> *Prince of Wales's* boats 4 cables[1] N. of *Queen's*.
> *London's* boats 4 cables[1] N. of *Prince of Wales's*.

7. When boats are well on their way, flagship to signal destroyers to proceed with their tows as close as possible inshore and land their troops in 2 trips, the southernmost landing place being about 1 mile N. of Gaba Tepe.
8. All destroyers and tows then to be used to disembark troops from other transports in accordance with a detailed programme.
9. Absolute silence. No smoking. No lights. Special precautions to prevent flaming from funnels. All oars to be muffled. All ships to be at action stations on leaving rendezvous. Both turrets and all guns on shore side to be manned.
10. Stations of covering ships (to work with and be at disposal of military):
    Triumph. R. flank. Spotted for by kite balloon *Manica*, visual signalling.
    Bacchante. Centre.
    Majestic. L. flank. Spotted for by *Ark Royal* (seaplane carrier), wireless signalling.

Orders for Boats Landing First Echelon.

Midshipmen, if available, in charge of each steamboat.
An additional officer, not below rank of sub-lieut. R.N.R. to go in No's 3, 5, and 9 steamboats (see below).
Each pulling boat to have 4 hands and coxswain.
When ordered to shove off flotilla to assume formation:—

Direction of advance ↑ 12 11 10 9 8 7 6 5 4 3 2 1

Lieut.-Cdr. Waterlow in No. 1 Boat to be guide and all boats to regulate their course and speed by No. 1 Boat, distance apart of tows being about 150 yards.
Commander Dix, in No. 12 Boat, Senior Naval Officer in charge.
Should the landing be opposed picket boats to follow the motions of the senior military officer of the tow as to opening fire with maxims. Picket boats on no account to fire after first man is ashore.

---

[1] 4 cables = 800 yards.

APPENDIX 12

When approaching beach boat hooks to be used for sounding; directly the water shoals, picket boats to cast off their tows, boats astern shearing off to port.

When troops are landed pulling boats to assist in landing troops from destroyers. Then to reform their normal tows, proceed to first four transports to anchor, and clear them of troops.

General Arrangements regarding Wounded.

Serious cases to hospital ship *Gascon*. Other cases to transports A13 and A 31.

As soon as covering force is ashore each battleship to equip a pinnace as hospital boat with 1 sick-berth rating and crew of 6 hands and coxswain. Ships to be prepared to equip a second pinnace at short notice.

An officer of *London* to be in charge of naval embarkation; senior medical officer of *London* to be Senior Medical Officer.

Trawler No. 705 to tow pinnaces from shore to transports.

The following were dealt with in other appendices:
Detail and Tasks of Boat and Hold Parties.
Detail of Beach Parties.
Detail of Crews for Horseboats, Tugs, and Lighters.
Rough Order of Arrival of Transports, their Berths, &c.[1]

[1] Every effort to be made to work first 8 transports of main body simultaneously; afterwards 4 at a time to be worked.

APPENDIX 13

SUGGESTED ACTION IN THE EVENT OF THE
29TH DIVISION, OR THE AUSTRALIANS FAILING
TO ESTABLISH THEMSELVES ASHORE

GENERAL HEADQUARTERS,
24th April, 1915.

C.G.S.

Maps 1, 2, 3.
Sketches 1, 4.

The following suggestions are put forward for your consideration.

1. In the event of the enemy preventing the 29th Division establishing itself on the Cape Helles beaches, though the Australian Division succeeds in landing at Gaba Tepe, the 29th Division should be re-embarked under cover of the guns of the fleet, and a landing at once attempted between Nibrunesi Point and Fisherman's Hut, or south of Gaba Tepe, by the French Expeditionary Force.

2. Conversely if the 29th Division succeeds in getting ashore, and the Australian Division fails, the Australians should re-embark under cover of the fleet, which must close in to render every possible assistance. In this case the question of landing extra troops simultaneously with the 29th and French divisions in the south must depend on whether Morto Bay is being shelled from the Asiatic shore, and whether it would be possible to land any considerable force on or near Beach Y.

3. If neither the 29th nor the Australian Divisions succeed in obtaining a footing on the peninsula at their first attempt, no second attempt at the same beaches will succeed, and we must go elsewhere. We must be prepared to put our new plan into execution immediately, and to strike at once. Political as well as military considerations will demand that the Gallipoli landings should be made to appear a feint, and it will be of the utmost importance to give the impression that our main

APPENDIX 13

effort was intended from the first to be made in another quarter. At the same time it will assist our new landing if the Turks are temporarily allowed to think that we have failed, and have no alternative plan.

The alternatives open to us are few. Besika Bay will be as strongly held as the Peninsula. Adramyti Bay is far from the objective; our advance would be unaided by the fleet, and we should be exposed to attack from three directions. A landing near Bulair entails a fight on two fronts in a cramped area, and we could be attacked by largely superior numbers before our main body was ashore.

There remain two possible landing places. Ibrije and its neighbourhood, 20 miles from Bulair, and Enos, 40 miles from that place. Of these, Ibrije has a very restricted beach (only 150 yards) and is perhaps too close to Bulair to be safe.

Enos possesses many advantages:—

(a) The beach is 2 miles long by 50 yards broad, sandy, with deep water for transports within half a mile of the shore.
(b) The garrison is small, and the opposition is likely to be slight.
(c) The left flank of the landing would be protected by the Maritsa river and a big lagoon.
(d) Hills in the neighbourhood, together with the lagoon, would form a bridgehead in which we could await reinforcements if necessary.
(e) Our eventual advance would have its right flank protected by the sea and the guns of the fleet.
(f) The supply question would be comparatively simple.

It is therefore recommended that, in the event of failure at Gallipoli, we immediately make a landing at Enos, and prepare for an advance against the Turkish army.

The suggested plan for carrying out this operation is as follows:—

(i) Navy to cover re-embarkation.
(ii) Royal Naval Division to continue demonstration during night and on second day.
(iii) New Zealand Division and French Division to rendezvous at Tenedos, followed by 29th, and Australian Divisions, and all tugs, lighters and horseboats.

4. French detachment to re-embark at Kum Kale and rendezvous at Rabbit Island.

5. Following afternoon, French Division and New Zealanders, with naval escort, to proceed south, in view of the shore, turning towards Enos by night. Horseboats and lighters to be towed direct from Tenedos to Enos after dark.

6. French Division and New Zealanders to land simultaneously next morning at dawn, without previous bombardment, and take up covering position. These troops to be followed by R.N.D., Australians and 29th Division, the covering position being enlarged as required.

7. Send for 2nd Mounted Division and East Lancs. Territorial Division.

8. In order to put this plan into execution, it would only be necessary to give the signal to re-embark and rendezvous on the south side of Tenedos. On arrival at Tenedos sailing orders would be issued for the southward movement of the transport fleet and attendant ships, and at the same time the position of the rendezvous X off Enos should be notified to all concerned. This would enable orders for assembly at rendezvous X to be signalled at the required time according to circumstances.

As regards a covering force for the landing at Enos, the French are already conveniently disposed on their transports; and either the Metropolitan Brigade or the Colonial Brigade (preferably the latter unless it had been roughly handled at Kum Kale) could be detailed for this duty without delay being involved.

C. F. ASPINALL, Captain,
General Staff,
Mediterranean Expeditionary Force.

APPENDIX 14

GENERAL BIRDWOOD'S ORDER FOR THE ANZAC LANDING

OPERATION ORDER No. 1

S.S. *Minnewaska*,
17th April, 1915.

Information.	(1) Information, intention, and detailed plan is transmitted to divisional commanders under a secret cover. The intention, generally, is to assist the fleet in forcing the passage of the Dardanelles by the capture of important land positions in the Gallipoli Peninsula. (Map 3.)
Intention.	(2) The Australian and New Zealand Army Corps is to land North of Gaba Tepe, and occupy the heights covering the beach there as a preliminary to further operations. This operation will probably be opposed.
Distribution.	(3) The "Covering Force" for the Army Corps will consist of:—

    One Infantry Brigade
    One Field Company Engineers } of the Australian Division.
    Bearer sub-divisions of Field Ambulance

No animals or vehicles will accompany the covering force.

Sequence of disembarkation Main Body.	(4) The general sequence of disembarkation of the main body of the Army Corps will be:—

    Indian Mountain Artillery Brigade
  (attached to Australian Division for the operation).
    Australian Division—
        One Infantry Brigade.

One Company Engineers.
Casualty Clearing Station.
Bearer Sub-division one Field Ambulance.
The remaining Infantry Brigade, Australian Division.
Two F.A. Brigades less Brigade Ammunition Columns.
Ceylon Planters Rifle Corps.
An advanced Supply and Ordnance Depôt.
Remainder of Divisional Engineers.
Bearer Sub-divisions, remaining Australian Field Ambulance.
Remaining F.A. Brigade, Australian Division, less Brigade Ammunition Columns.

New Zealand and Australian Division—
Two Infantry Brigades.
New Zealand Field Ambulance bearer Sub-divisions
Divisional Engineers.
Howitzer Battery and Ammunition Column.
Field Artillery Brigade less Brigade Ammunition Column.

The only animals landed will be:—
48 gun horses per F.A. Brigade (16 for New Zealand Howitzer Battery).
56 Ordnance Mules per Mountain Battery.
112 pack mules, per Mountain Artillery Brigade with saddles.
Donkeys.

Method of Disembarkation. (5) The method of disembarkation is given in Appendix I.[1]

Clearing Beach. (6) The duties laid down in "Manual of Combined Operations" Para. 52, iv., will be arranged for by the General Officer Commanding Australian Division, until the Army Corps Commander has landed to assume command ashore.

Order of dress. (7) Troops will land with packs, one day's rations, and two iron rations. Machine guns and belt boxes are to be carried by hand; also equipment usually carried on 1st line transport at discretion of divisional commanders.

[1] Not reproduced. It repeated the naval arrangements for berthing of transports, etc.

APPENDIX 14

Ammunition.	(8) Infantry will carry 200 rounds on the person, and 3,500 rounds per machine gun in belt boxes; other arms as in War Establishments. A reserve of ammunition is being formed close to the beach, the position of which will be notified when selected.
Hot meal.	(9) A hot meal will be issued for all troops as late as possible before leaving their ships.
Care of rations.	(10) All troops are to be warned to be very careful of their rations, as those taken on shore may have to be spread over more than three days.
Harness.	(11) Horses will be harnessed before disembarkation. Pack saddles will be loaded in the boats which carry the animals they equip.
Vehicles.	(12) All vehicles will be so placed in the boats that they can be landed pole leading.
Detail of Beach Control Personnel.	(13) The detail of beach control personnel and of fatigue parties allotted for the operation is given in Appendix II.[1]
Hold Parties.	(14) Hold parties have been allotted to transports as required. Where they have not been detailed the work is to be carried out by parties drawn from the echelon last to land, which will disembark on completion of their duty.
Inter-Communication.	(15) The arrangements for intercommunication during landing are given in Appendix III.[2]
Fire support and Aerial Observation.	(16) Arrangements made for fire support and for aerial observation will be issued as a supplement to this order.
Water.	(17) A party of engineers has been detailed from the Field Company on Transport A13 with well-sinking appliances. In addition, naval arrangements have been made to land as much water as possible by pumping from boats into receptacles on the beach. Water will be pushed up from the shore under Army Corps arrangements. Divisions will arrange for receptacles for the water, and will take steps that any transport, bringing water, will at once be emptied and returned without delay to the beach

[1] Not reproduced.
[2] Not reproduced. Its substance is contained in Appendix 16, paras. 7 & 8.

for replenishment. As soon as the position for the receptacles is decided upon, guides should be sent by the Engineers to the beach to accompany the water to the receptacles.

All commanders will take immediate steps for guarding and conserving any water supply. As there is a danger of the water being poisoned, water from wells should be tested before use.

Medical Arrangements.

(18) A casualty clearing station, found by No. 1 Australian Casualty Clearing Station, attached to the Australian and New Zealand Army Corps for the period of the operation, is being established on the beach in the vicinity of the northernmost landing place. This station will take the place of the Tent sub-divisions of Field Ambulances till such time as these are landed.

Naval arrangements for removing casualties are:—

Hospital ship *Gascon* for serious cases.

Transport *Clan McGillivray* } for slight cases.
  „ *Seeang Chun*

For transport from shore to ship, navy launches equipped as hospital boats for transport of wounded will ply from shore to ship under timings arranged as the medical situation develops. This work cannot, however, commence till the infantry of the Australian Division is ashore.

Disposal of men unfit.

(19) All men unfit for disembarkation will be transferred to the Stationary Hospital before leaving Mudros; any becoming unfit while at sea will be transferred to the Hospital ship *Clan McGillivray*, Australian units, or *Seeang Chun*, New Zealand units, as opportunity offers, under arrangements made by the Military Transport Officer of the transport.

Disposal of animals unfit.
Baggage Guards—
Disposal of Hold Parties.

(20) No animals unfit for duty will be landed.

(21) A small party from each unit will be left on each transport to take charge of regimental baggage and stores remaining on board. Men unfit to land will naturally be selected for this duty.

Hold parties, Military Transport Officers and their signal party remain on board till the last of

APPENDIX 14

Echelon "C" have landed. They will then be transferred under naval arrangements:

Australian Division to *Derfflinger* under command of Lieut.-Colonel McVea;

New Zealand and Australian Division to *Seeang Bee* under command of Captain Houlker;

taking with them the sick remaining in their transports.

Position of Army Corps Headquarters.

(22) Army Corps Headquarters will, in the first instance, be on board H.M.S. *Queen*.

H. B. WALKER,
Br.-General,
General Staff.

APPENDIX 15

GENERAL BIRDWOOD'S INSTRUCTIONS TO G.O.C. 1st AUSTRALIAN DIVISION

Map 3.
Sketches
4, 6, 7.

1. The attached extracts from Force Order No. 1 and Instructions for G.O.C. Australian and New Zealand Army Corps are for your information.

2. The objective of the covering force (which is detailed from your Division) and the subsequent action of the Army Corps is defined in these extracts, that is:—to secure a position covering the Gaba Tepe—Fisherman's Hut landing place; the landing of the Army Corps; and an advance to cover the enemy's North and South communications in the vicinity of Mal Tepe.

3. In your instructions to the covering force, you should keep in mind the advantage of landing on a broad front and the necessity for occupying as rapidly as possible the covering position laid down as objective in Force Orders.

4. In view of the reported presence of guns in Square 212, l and m,[1] and of troops and guns in the Peren Ovasi valley,[2] the covering force will have to advance and occupy the ridge running first East from Gaba Tepe and then North East in Square 212, towards the crest in Square 238—q—v.[3]

5. To assist it in this task, the rest of your Division is being landed immediately after the covering force, and should be disposed with a view to securing the above line and the Northern Flank in the direction of Fisherman's Hut.

6. When this line has been secured, you will be guided by the situation as to whether you make a further advance, or consolidate your position until the landing of the bulk of the Army Corps permits the development of an advance towards its objective—Mal Tepe. You should, however, watch the

---

[1] S.E. of Gaba Tepe.
[2] Maidos plain S.E. of Gaba Tepe.
[3] Gun Ridge with left on Chunuk Bair.

The map co-ordinates refer to the 1/40,000 Map in use at the time.

APPENDIX 15

approaches from the South, from Eski Keui, Koja Dere and Biyuk Anafarta, and you may find it possible to send detachments to the three places mentioned, to turn the enemy out of them.

H. B. WALKER,
Br.-General, General Staff,
Australian and New Zealand Army Corps.

H.M.T. *Minnewaska*,
18.4.15.

APPENDIX 16

1ST AUSTRALIAN DIVISION ORDER FOR THE LANDING

OPERATION ORDER No. 1
BY
MAJOR-GENERAL W. T. BRIDGES, C.M.G.,
COMMANDING 1ST AUSTRALIAN DIVISION

TRANSPORT A11. *Minnewaska*,
18th April, 1915.

Map 3.
Sketches 4, 6, 7.

1. Information of the disposition of the Turkish forces in the Gallipoli Peninsula is being issued separately to brigade commanders.

The general object of the Mediterranean Expeditionary Force is to assist the Fleet in forcing the passage of the Dardanelles by the occupation of important positions in the Gallipoli Peninsula. The 29th Division will operate from Cape Helles and the Naval Division near Bulair.

The Australian and New Zealand Army Corps will land north of Gaba Tepe—the landing will probably be opposed.

2. The Division will land between Gaba Tepe and Fisherman's Hut. Its first objective will be the occupation of the ridge extending from Sq. 212 (i) to point 971 in Sq. 238 (m).[1]

Covering Force.
Commander: Colonel E. G. Sinclair-MacLagan, D.S.O.
3rd Infantry Brigade fighting troops less all animals and vehicles.
1st Field Company less mounted branch and all horses and vehicles.
Bearer sub-divisions of 3rd Field Ambulance less all horses and vehicles.

3. The covering force, as shown in the margin, will occupy the ridge between square 212 (i) and 238 (v).[2] Special instructions have been issued to Colonel MacLagan.

[1] Gun Ridge with left on Hill 971.
[2] Gun Ridge with left on Chunuk Bair.

The map co-ordinates refer to the 1/40,000 Map in use at the time.

44

APPENDIX 16

4. The following unit is attached to the Division:—
No. 7 Indian Mountain Artillery Brigade.
5. General lines of disembarkation:—
   (i) The troops on each transport will be disembarked in echelons.
   All the "A" echelons will be landed before the remainder.
   The only animals and vehicles included in the "A" echelon are:—
   (a) 48 gun horses per field artillery brigade (these will be landed from the ships containing artillery brigade headquarters);
   56 ordnance mules per mountain battery;
   112 pack mules from the mountain artillery brigade.
   (b) Guns, firing battery and first line wagons, 2 water carts from the *Karroo* and 2 from the *Cardiganshire*.
   (ii) *Covering Force.* 1500 men of the covering force will be landed from H.M.S.'s *Queen, Prince of Wales*, and *London*, followed by the remainder which will be landed from seven destroyers.
   (iii) *Main Body.*
   (a) Transports will be anchored in four berths. The beach will be divided into eight landing places. After the disembarkation of the covering force, headquarters and three battalions (less 1 company) of the 2nd Infantry Brigade, headquarters and one battalion of the 1st Infantry Brigade, and the 26th Mountain Battery will be landed from:—

4	3	2	1
Galeka	*Novian*	*Hessen*	*Lake Michigan.*

   (b) When the *Hessen* is unloaded the *Pera* will move into berth 2 and the 21st Mountain Battery will disembark.
   The following four ships will move up opposite berths 1 to 4 and 400 troops will be transferred while under way to each of seven torpedo boat destroyers from which they will be landed:—*Clan McGillivray, Minnewaska, Mashobra, Derfflinger*. Naval conditions will then determine whether they will move into anchorage berths or continue to tranship into destroyers while under way.

This will complete the disembarkation of the "A" echelons of Divisional Headquarters, No. 7 Indian Mountain Artillery Brigade, 1st and 2nd Infantry Brigades, 2nd Field Company, and the three bearer sub-divisions of the 2nd Field Ambulance.

(c) Ships carrying artillery and other units will subsequently be brought up as berths become vacant. Batteries on the *Karroo* and *Cardiganshire* will disembark first.

The 3rd Battery, Field Artillery, will remain attached to 3rd Field Artillery Brigade until the Headquarters, 1st F.A. Brigade are landed.

6. Until the issue of orders upon the disembarkation of Divisional Headquarters:—

   (i) That portion of the objective between Sq. 224 (f) inclusive to 238 (m) inclusive,[1] and the protection of the left flank in the direction of Fisherman's Hut, is assigned to 2nd Infantry Brigade.

   (ii) That portion of the 1st Infantry Brigade disembarked will be in reserve near the rendezvous.

   (iii) The 7th Indian Mountain Artillery Brigade will be placed at the disposal of the Officer Commanding Covering Force.

   (iv) The 2nd Field Company will:—

   (a) improve exits from the beach and begin the construction of road communications from the centre of the beach up the spur in Sq. 224 (q) to (d) [2] and towards 212 (c).[3]

   (b) Search and sink for water.

7. (i) Communications between ships and shore will be made through a Royal Navy base signal station which will be established on the beach. Pending the establishment of this station a temporary naval station will be formed from naval ratings landed with the first tows of the covering force.

(ii) Close to this R.N. base signal station a central signal office will be established by a special detachment from Army Headquarters Signal Company. All communications inland from the beach will be sent through this office. The Divisional Signal Company is responsible for maintaining communication with this office.

(iii) Telephonic communication from the beach to the rendezvous will be organized by the military landing officer.

[1] S.W. of Chunuk Bair to Hill 971.
[2] S.E. side of Shrapnel Gulley.
[3] From beach across to Legge Valley.
} The map co-ordinates refer to the 1/40,000 Map in use at the time.

APPENDIX 16

(iv) On matters relating to disembarkation, military transport officers will communicate direct with the Naval Transport Officer (Captain Loring, R.N.) on H.M.S. *Queen*. Officers commanding troops on transports will provide a signal detail for this purpose.

8. (i) In addition to the above means of communication, the following special arrangements have been made for observing and directing fire from ships.

   (*a*) Two observation officers will be detailed by the Officer Commanding Divisional Artillery to observe fire from ships only. Special instructions have been issued to these officers by the Brigadier-General R.A., A. & N.Z. Army Corps. The observation officers will be allotted zones by the Officer Commanding Divisional Artillery, who will inform Army Corps Headquarters of the areas allotted.

   A pamphlet has been issued containing instructions for intercommunication respecting support by naval guns.

   (*b*) Communications will be sent through the R.N. base station until special flank signal stations are established when all communications regarding the fire of ships' guns will be sent through them.

   One cable section, Army Headquarters Signal Company, has been detailed to maintain communication between these observation officers and the flank signal stations on the shore.

   The observation officers and the cable section will land after the second portion of the covering force.

   (ii) A supply of red and yellow flags is being issued to units to indicate their positions to the Navy. Flags will be waved to and fro when ships' fire is to cease; at other times the flags will be carried or planted.

9. (i) Officer Commanding, Divisional Engineers, will, upon landing, detail a party from the 2nd Field Company, with well-sinking apparatus, to search for water. Major Stokes will accompany this party and will test all water before it is used.

   (ii) Naval arrangements have been made to land water by pumping from boats into receptacles on the beach. The removal of this water to areas close to the troops will be provided by Army Corps Headquarters. The O.C. Divisional Engineers will provide receptacles for taking over water so pushed forward. He will also furnish guides from the beach to the receptacles.

10. (i) A casualty clearing station found by No 1 Australian Casualty Clearing Station will be established on the beach and taken over by the A.D.M.S. till such time as the tent subdivisions of field ambulances are landed.

(ii) Casualties will be removed from the beach under naval arrangements:—

(a) serious cases to Hospital ship *Gascon*.
(b) slight cases to Transport *Clan McGillivray*.

The A.D.M.S. will detail a medical personnel of 2 non-commissioned officers and 20 men to the *Clan McGillivray*.

The navy launches equipped as hospital boats will begin to ply from shore to ship after the infantry of the division is landed.

11. Until Divisional Headquarters land, reports will be sent to H.M.S. *Prince of Wales*.

C. B. B. WHITE, Lieut.-Colonel,
General Staff, 1st Australian Division.

APPENDIX 17

29TH DIVISION ORDER FOR THE LANDING

OPERATION ORDER No. 1

29TH DIVISION H.Q.,
20th April, 1915.

Information.	1. Information points to any landing, in Turkish territory, being opposed.	Map 4.
Object of the Expedition.	2. The object of the Expedition, and the methods to be employed to attain that object are given in enclosed instructions.[1]	
Covering Force.	3. The covering force will be composed as under:—	

O.C. Br.-General W. S. Hare.
    86th Infantry Brigade.
    2nd South Wales Borderers.
    1st K.O.S. Borderers.
    2nd Hampshire Regiment (less two companies).
    Plymouth Battalion, R. Naval Division.
    West Riding Field Company, R.E.
    1 Section 2nd London Field Coy. R.E.
    The personnel of one Tent sub-division 87th Field Ambulance.
    A portion of the personnel of one tent Sub-division 88th Field Ambulance.
    Three bearer sub-divisions 89th Field Ambulance.

Landing of Covering Force.	4. The special instructions regarding the landing of the covering force are being issued to O.C. that force.[2]
Landing of Main Body.	5. The disembarkation of the main body will commence directly the covering force has landed.
General Instructions. Main Body.	6. A hot meal will be issued to all troops before leaving their transports.

[1] See below.   [2] Appendices 4, 18.

Infantry will carry 200 rounds of ammunition.

3500 rounds, in belt boxes, will be landed with each machine gun, and all carried by hand.

No transport will accompany the covering force.

Horses will be harnessed before disembarkation.

Poles of G.S. wagons will be removed before slinging and made fast to the bodies of the wagons.

Poles of carts, limbers, and limbered wagons will not be moved; these vehicles should be so placed in the boats that they can be landed pole leading.

Till the forming up places and rendezvous have been marked out companies, etc., will be formed up by their commanders close to, but clear of, the beach.

Every endeavour must be made to prevent confusion on the beaches.

The detachments of the Anson Battalion R.N.D. landing on each beach will report to the Military Landing Officer in charge of that beach and will be by him utilized for beach parties, guards, working parties, etc.

R.E. A floating pier and a trestle pier will be constructed on beach W by the Lowland Field Coy. R.E.

The 2nd London Field Company R.E. (less 1 Section) will improve the exits from beaches V, W, & X. It will set up the beach telephones and do any other work near the beaches that may be necessary.

Intercommunication. 7. Instructions for communication with the fleet, regarding support by naval guns, have been issued in pamphlet form.

The Central Military Base Signal Office (found by G.H.Q. Signal Company) and the Royal Naval Base Signal Station will be established on Beach W.

Flank signal stations will be established on or near hills 141 and 114.

Water &c. 8. A water station will be established at the earliest opportunity in the neighbourhood of W beach.

The O.C. a force which captures any springs or wells will arrange for them to be carefully guarded. No one should be allowed to drink any water till it has been tested, as there is a possibility of it being poisoned.

Water will be very scarce and must be carefully husbanded.

APPENDIX 17

Rations.
As it may be some time before supplies can be brought up to the force, rations must be carefully conserved. The three days' rations on the man may have to last 4 or 5 days.

Medical.
9. No men or animals unfit for duty are to leave their transports.

Baggage on Transports.
10. On each transport a Military Transport Officer will be appointed. He will remain on board till the ship is fully unloaded.

After that only one N.C.O. and the storeman laid down in War Establishments will remain on board and will take charge of all stores left on board.

Divl. H.Q.
11. Divisional H.Q. will, in the first instance, be in H.M.S. *Euryalus* and will afterwards move to Beach W.

O. W. Dod,
Colonel G.S., 29th Division.

ENCLOSURE TO 29TH DIVISION O.O. No. 1

1. The object of the Expedition is to assist the fleet to force the Dardanelles by capturing the Kilid Bahr plateau and dominating the forts of the Narrows.

2. The general plan to achieve this object includes the following operations taking place simultaneously.

   (a) A bombardment of the Bulair lines followed by a feint landing by the R. Naval Division on the mainland N. of the Saros Islands.

   (b) A bombardment of the heights commanding the beach between Gaba Tepe and Nibrunesi Pt. and the landing of the Australian and New Zealand Army Corps.

   (c) A bombardment of the Southern extremity of the Peninsula and the landing of the 29th Division.

   (d) A demonstration by the French fleet at Besika Bay and the landing of a portion of the French Expeditionary Force in the neighbourhood of Kum Kale.

Maps 2, 4.
3. The task of the 29th Division is the attack of the Kilid Bahr plateau from the South.

4. The general plan to carry out this task is to land under cover of the bombardment of the fleet:—
   (a) A force on the coast West of Krithia.
   (b) A force near Eski Hissarlik.
   (c) The remainder on three beaches on the south end of the Peninsula.
5. The lines to be gained successively are:—
   (a) the hills 141, 138, and 114.
   (b) a line running from the hills at the E of Old Castle to join hands on the left with the force landing at Y beach.
   (c) a line from Eski Hissarlik—about ½ a mile east of Krithia—hill 472 [1]—to the sea.
   (d) the capture of Achi Baba and the spur running south from it.
   (e) the occupation and fortification of a line running east from Achi Baba to the sea about level 300,[2] and west from Achi Baba via hill 472 to the sea.

[1] Yazy Tepe.   [2] The high ground due E. of Achi Baba.

APPENDIX 18

29TH DIVISION INSTRUCTIONS FOR THE HELLES COVERING FORCE

29TH DIVISION H.Q.,
20th April 1915.

1. A copy of the instructions issued by G.H.Q.[1] has been given **Map 2.** to O.C. Covering Force.
2. The personnel of a tent sub-division 87th Field Ambulance and a section of the 2nd London Field Company R.E. will be available to land with the 2nd South Wales Borderers (less one Coy.)
The tows provided for that battalion will only hold 720 men with their stores, and not more than 12 of the personnel of the Field Ambulance will be transferred to the trawlers unless it can be done without displacing fighting men.
One section of the 1st West Riding Field Co. R.E. is being transferred to B2, to land on beach W. The personnel of this section should be divided between H.M.S. *Euryalus* and H.M.S. *Implacable*, so as to equalize the number of men in each tow.
3. The O.C. 2nd Royal Fusiliers, with a staff of not more than 5, will proceed with the two companies and M.G. Section landing from H.M.S. *Implacable*.
4. The G.O.C. wishes the forces landed on beaches V, W, X to make good the line from the spur east of the E in Old Castle [2] to the spur which ends in square 175.Y.,[3] where a junction will be made with the force landed at Y.

O. W. DOD,
Colonel G.S., 29th Division.

[1] Appendix 4.
[2] ¼ m. N.E. of Sedd el Bahr village.
[3] East of Gully Ravine.

} The references are to the 1/40,000 Map.

APPENDIX 19

86TH BRIGADE OPERATION ORDER No. 1

BY

BR.-GENERAL S. W. HARE, COMMANDING (HELLES)
COVERING FORCE

23rd April, 1915.

Map 4. 1. *Information.*
   (*a*) Information points to any landing in Turkish territory being opposed.
   A sketch showing position of trenches and batteries located by aeroplane reconnaissance has been issued to all concerned.[1]
   (*b*) The detail of landing of detachments and covering force of the 29th Div. was issued in Preliminary Order No. 1.[2] Landings by the R.N.D., Australian Corps and French Expeditionary Force are taking place elsewhere.

2. *Intention.*
   The first objective of the covering force is the line points 141—138—114.

3. *Objectives.*
   1st R. Dublin Fus., Village of Sedd el Bahr and Hill 141.
   1st R. Munster Fus., Village exclusive to Fort 2[3] inclusive.
   1st Lancashire Fus., Trenches and redoubt on Hill 138.
      One Coy to assist 2nd Royal Fus. in taking Hill 114.
   2nd Royal Fus., Hill 114, and to secure flank towards N.E.

4. *Reserve.*
   The 2nd Hants. Regt. will form up clear of V Beach under cover, and will remain in temporary reserve.

---
[1] Not reproduced.   [2] Appendix 17.
[3] Gun emplacement N. of Fort No. 1. The reference is to the 1/40,000 Map.

APPENDIX 19

5. The W. Riding Field Co., R.E. will form up clear of V Beach under cover at place to be indicated by O.C. 2nd Hants. Regt. The O.C. will be prepared to give technical assistance to 1st R. Dublin Fus. or 1st R. Munster Fus. if required.
6. The 3 bearer subdivisions 89th Field Ambulance, will form up clear of beach under cover, at place to be indicated by O.C. 2nd Hants. Regt.
7. Reports to Brigade Headquarters at Lighthouse. O's.C. infantry battalions will send 2 orderlies to Brigade Headquarters soon after landing, giving the situation of their unit and any information. One of these orderlies will be returned to the Unit.

Central Military Base Signal Station on W Beach. Flank signal stations will be established subsequently on or near Hills 141 and 114.

T. H. C. FRANKLAND, Major.
Brigade Major, 86th Infantry Bde.

APPENDIX 20

INSTRUCTIONS TO G.O.C.
CORPS EXPÉDITIONNAIRE FRANÇAIS D'ORIENT

GENERAL HEADQUARTERS,
21st April[1] 1915.

Map 2. 1. With reference to para. 5 of my Secret Instructions, dated 18th April 1915,[2] issued as a supplement to Force Order No. 1, para. (4), orders as to the date and time of the eventual landing of the Corps Expéditionnaire near Cape Helles on the Gallipoli Peninsula will be issued later. Its disembarkation will take place in the order detailed in the annexed Table D,[3] the transports being brought up in divisions of six ships at a time.

2. The arrangements for the landing will be undertaken by the Royal Navy, by which the necessary boats and other appliances will be provided. The berths allotted to each division of transports will be notified later, and on arrival at their anchorage a Naval Transport Officer R.N. will be placed on board each transport in order to superintend the disembarkation of the troops. Since the naval personnel available will be few in number, I would ask you to arrange that the crews of your transports may be placed at the disposal of the Naval Transport Officer during his superintendence of the disembarkation; and that officers commanding troops on board may give him every assistance in their power in the matter of providing the necessary working parties for the holds and discharging gangways.

3. The task of the Corps Expéditionnaire will be to come up in line with the 29th Division preparatory to a general advance against the Kilid Bahr plateau. The date and time of the

[1] Despatched 22nd April.
[2] Appendix 6.
[3] Not reproduced. This table showed the distribution of the French transports to Beaches X, W and V and to the Kum Kale landing.

APPENDIX 20

disembarkation must depend upon the course of the action. In order to get the greatest number of fighting troops on shore on the first day, the 29th Division will land as small a number of animals and vehicles as possible. Should reinforcements be urgently required, you may be requested to land the fighting troops of the Corps Expéditionnaire before the remainder of the transport of the 29th Division is disembarked. In this case the vehicles of the 29th Division and of the Corps Expéditionnaire will be landed as opportunity offers. If the 29th Division makes good progress, all the ships of this division will be cleared before the disembarkation of the troops under your command is begun, and the landing of the Corps Expéditionnaire will then be able to continue without interruption.

4. I would ask you to keep me informed of the position of your Headquarters during the operations which you are undertaking at Kum Kale; and similarly where you propose to establish them during the disembarkation of the Corps Expéditionnaire on the Gallipoli Peninsula. Perhaps you would find it convenient to establish yourself in the first instance on board the French flagship, and the presence of English signallers on that vessel would facilitate our inter-communication.

W. P. BRAITHWAITE, Major-General,
for General Commanding Mediterranean
Expeditionary Forces.

APPENDIX 21

AN INSTANCE OF THE DIFFICULTY OF GETTING SHIPS' GUNS ON TO A SHORE TARGET

[Extracts from Signal Log of H.M.S. *Euryalus* (Flagship of Rear-Admiral Wemyss). The map references are to the 1/40,000 Operations Map in use at the time.]

27th April.
- 8.55 A.M. *Shore Station to Euryalus.*
  Open fire on 168.K.2.
- 9.16 A.M. *Euryalus to Swiftsure.*
  Can you open fire on 168.K.2. or shall Euryalus?
- 9.40 A.M. *Euryalus to Swiftsure.*
  Aeroplane has been sent for to spot on 168.K.2.
- 9.55 A.M. *Rear-Admiral Wemyss, Euryalus, to Rear-Admiral Nicholson, Swiftsure.*
  If you require an aeroplane for observing your fire on 168.K.2. will you communicate with aerodrome at Tenedos.
- 10 A.M. *Rear-Admiral Nicholson, Swiftsure, to Rear-Admiral Wemyss, Euryalus.*
  Request that Euryalus fire at 168.K.2. as we are firing at another important target.
- 10.5 A.M. *Implacable to Euryalus.*
  Borders report enemy advancing in large numbers in 168.K.2.
- 10.5 A.M. *Rear-Admiral Nicholson, Swiftsure, to Rear-Admiral Wemyss, Euryalus.*
  Your 09.55 I have already got an aeroplane spotting on 169. Our range is not quite clear for 168.K.2.

APPENDIX 21

10.20 A.M. *Vice-Admiral C.-in-C. to all ships.*
   Open fire on 168.K.2.

10.28 A.M. *87th Bde., X Beach, to Euryalus.*
   Enemy reported advancing down valley in 168.K.2.

NOTE: The report of Turks advancing subsequently proved to be false.

APPENDIX 22

29TH DIVISION ORDER
FIRST BATTLE OF KRITHIA

OPERATION ORDER No. 3[1]

29TH DIVISION HEADQUARTERS, 27th April 1915.
LIGHT HOUSE,
CAPE HELLES.

Sketch 14.
1. The Division will advance to-morrow to the line point 236 —knoll about 700 yards N.E. of Krithia—point 472—coast line in square 184 R.8.
2. The 175th Regiment French Expeditionary Force will take up the line from point 236 to square 176.T.9. (both exclusive). The 88th Brigade will take up from square 176 T.9 (exclusive) to centre of square 176 F (inclusive).
The 87th Brigade will take up from centre of square 176 F (exclusive) through hill 472 to the coast line in square 184 R.8.
3. The 86th Brigade will be in reserve and the officer commanding will report at Divisional Headquarters at 6.0 A.M. for instructions.
4. The advance will commence at 8.0 A.M.
5. The iron ration now in hand will probably have to last two days.
6. Infantry brigade commanders will report to headquarters the situation of any water supply which may be discovered.
7. Divisional Headquarters will move at 8.15 A.M. and will be re-established later at Knoll 176 Q.7.[2]

O. W. DOD,
Colonel G.S. 29th Div.

[1] The map references are to the 1/40,000 Operations Map in use at the time.
[2] 1¼ miles S.W. of Krithia.

Appendix 23

87th Brigade Order
First Battle of Krithia

O.C. 1st Rl. Innis. Fus.
O.C. 1st Border Regt.

B.M.1.   28th April.

Operation Order No. 1.[1]

    The divn. will advance to-day to the line point 236—knoll Sketch 14. about 700 yards N.E. of Krithia—472—coast line in square 184 R.8. The objective of the 87th Bde. is from centre of square 176 F exclusive, through hill 472—to coast line in square 184 R.8. The 88th Bde. are advancing on right of 87th Bde. the French on right of 88th Bde. The 86th Bde. will be in reserve. The advance will commence at 8 A.M. The R. Innis. Fus. will advance on the right of the Bord. Regt. each battn. will leave one company as brigade reserve the O.C. companies to report to Bde. Hd. Qrs. at 7 A.M. The objective of the Rl. Innis. Fus. will be from centre of square 176 F (exclusive) to hill 472 (inclusive) the Border Regt. from the Rl. Innis. Fus. to the sea. On reaching this line battns. will dig themselves in. The iron ration will probably have to last 2 days. Units will report to Bde. Hd. Qrs. the position of any water found. O.C. Bns. will report at Bde. Hd. Qrs. at 6 A.M. to-morrow for instructions. Acknowledge receipt.

87th Bde.
X Beach.
1.15 A.M.

[The filed copy is endorsed by the brigade-major: "Issued before S.W.B. arrived".]

---

[1] The map references are to the 1/40,000 Operations Map in use at the time.

APPENDIX 24

G.H.Q. ORDER
SECOND BATTLE OF KRITHIA

Force Order No. 5[1]

GENERAL HEADQUARTERS,
5th May 1915.

Sketch 18.

1. The enemy against whom we have been continuously fighting during the past ten days is known to have suffered very severe losses, more especially in the course of the recent night attacks. His troops now occupy a defensive position on and in front of the Achi Baba ridge, running roughly south-east to north-west, and hold the line of the Kereves Dere and Krithia village.

2. The advance against the Achi Baba position will be resumed on May 6th at 11 A.M. The main attack will be developed from the west and south-west by the left wing of the force.

3. The Corps Expéditionnaire will operate on the right with its right flank on the coast, and its left flank in touch with the right of the 29th Division.

The 29th Division, reconstituted for this operation as shown in the attached Order of Battle,[2] will operate on the left, its right in touch with the Corps Expéditionnaire and its left on the coast.

G.O.C. 29th Division will be responsible for the direction of the advance. The right flank of his right battalion will be directed along the stream running through square 169.H.7., H.2., C.5., C.3., 176.Y.7., Y.2., T.3., and thence on the eastern point of Achi Baba Peak square 177.N.1.

G.O.C. Corps Expéditionnaire will be responsible for the

---

[1] The map references are to the 1/40,000 Operations Map in use at the time.
[2] See page 323 of text.

APPENDIX 24

maintenance of connection between his own left and the right of the 29th Division.

4. The Composite Division constituted as in the attached Order of Battle [1] (less the Composite Naval Brigade) will form the General Reserve, and will be in concealed positions about 1000 yards north-west of the stone bridge on the Sedd el Bahr—Krithia road, 168.Z.4.,[2] by 5 A.M.

5. The 29th Division will move forward with one battalion with its right on the stream running through square 169.H. and C and 176 Y and T, as previously described in paragraph 3. The right of the remainder of the division will be directed in the first instance on the south-east edge of Krithia village.

In order to fill the gap thus formed between the right battalion of the division and the remainder of the division, the Composite Naval Brigade will man the trenches at present occupied by the 88th Brigade. The Motor Machine-gun Squadron Royal Naval Division will take up a position near the Sedd el Bahr—Krithia road immediately on the right flank of this brigade.

G.O.C. 29th Division will arrange to have sufficient troops echeloned in rear of the right of his main advance moving up the valley of the stream running through square 176.V.8., W.4., W.3., S.5.,[3] to deal with any attempt which may be made by the enemy to counter-attack down the valley on the left bank of that stream. He will also dispose the Motor Machine-gun Squadron with especial view to its employment in repelling any such counter-attack as may be attempted.

6. The Corps Expéditionnaire, reinforced by the 2nd Naval Brigade, will have as its first objective the line square 169.D.1., D.6., D.9., and thence crossing the Kereves Dere to the coast north-east of the mouth of that stream. During this movement the 2nd Naval Brigade will be echeloned in rear of the French left.

As soon as the line given as the first objective has been reached immediate steps are to be taken to strengthen it, special attention being paid to the spur in square 169.D.,[4] west of the Kereves Dere, which will form a point d'appui. This line must be secured throughout the operations, at all costs, as it will be the pivot on which the whole movement depends.

The Corps Expéditionnaire will not advance beyond this line until the 29th Division has taken Krithia village.

---

[1] See page 323 of text.
[3] Kirte Dere.
[2] Where road crosses Kirte Dere.
[4] A in Sketch 18.

G.O.C. 29th Division will be responsible for informing the G.O.C. Corps Expéditionnaire as soon as Krithia village is in his hands.

The Corps Expéditionnaire, until the time arrives for its further advance, will be so disposed as to bring the heaviest possible fire to bear against the enemy on the southern slopes of the Achi Baba ridge.

7. As soon as Krithia village is in the hands of the 29th Division, the further advance against Achi Baba peak will be undertaken. The right flank of the main body of the 29th Division will be directed on the eastern point of the peak, thus gradually closing the gap between it and the right battalion of the division.

The Corps Expéditionnaire will advance simultaneously against the ridge running south-east from Achi Baba peak to the sea, still maintaining connection with the right battalion of the 29th Division, and still holding the position across the spur in square 169.D.[1] west of the Kereves Dere.

8. The synchronizing of the movements ordered is of the highest importance. The advance as ordered in paragraphs 5 and 6 will commence on both flanks precisely at 11 A.M. A staff officer from Quartier Général, Corps Expéditionnaire, and from each division, will attend at W Beach barrel pier at 7 A.M. on the 6th, where they will correct their watches with General Headquarters time, which will be given them by a General Staff officer of G.H.Q.

9. Communications between General Headquarters and the Corps Expéditionnaire, the 29th Division and the Composite Division, will be established by the General Headquarters Signal Company.

Visual communication between Headquarters 29th Division and Quartier Général Corps Expéditionnaire will be established by G.O.C. 29th Division.

10. G.O's.C. Corps Expéditionnaire and 29th Division will concert arrangements for the mutual support of their respective movements by flanking artillery fire when opportunities occur, and for this purpose artillery liaison officers will be appointed by the G.O's.C. concerned.

The fire of supporting ships will be directed in accordance with the arrangements already made with the Rear-Admiral Commanding 3rd Squadron.

11. An officer of the Q.M.G.'s staff, General Headquarters, will be on the Sedd el Bahr—Krithia road, near the stone bridge at

---

[1] A in Sketch 18.

APPENDIX 24

square 168.Z.4.,[1] by 11 A.M. He will undertake the organization of all traffic on the road, both French and English, during the course of the operations, especially in respect of the passage of ammunition and supplies.

12. General Headquarters will be in H.M.T. *Arcadian*.

W. P. BRAITHWAITE,
Major-General,
Chief of General Staff, Med. Ex. Force.

---

[1] Where road crosses Kirte Dere.

APPENDIX 25

29TH DIVISION ORDER
SECOND BATTLE OF KRITHIA

OPERATION ORDER No. 4[1]

HILL 138,
5.5.1915.

Sketch 18.
1. The Force is advancing to-morrow to the attack of the Achi Baba position.

2. The French Division, to which is attached the 2nd Brigade, Royal Naval Division, will advance at 11 A.M. to a line extending from the neighbourhood of the mouth of the Kereves Dere to a position across the ridge west of the last e in Kereves Dere (169.D.6 to 169.D.1) and will entrench strongly on this line.

3. The 29th Division, consisting of 87th and 88th Brigades, Lancashire Fusilier Brigade, and the Indian Brigade, will advance from its present position and, when the French line is securely held, will move forward to the attack of Krithia, and subsequently to that of Achi Baba in accordance with the detailed orders for phases I, II and III of the attack.

4. The Composite Division will be in general reserve about 1000 yards N.W. of the stone bridge on the Krithia Road.[2]

Phase I.

5. The Composite Naval Brigade, to which is attached the 1st Lancashire Fusiliers, will occupy the trenches now held by the 88th Brigade. The Lancashire Fusiliers will move

---

[1] The map references are to the 1/40,000 Operations Map in use at the time.

[2] Where road crosses Kirte Dere.

forward at 11 A.M. in close touch with the French left, which is formed by the 2nd Brigade R.N.D. When the French have established their left on the line 169.D.6—169.D.1, this brigade will move up and entrench on the line from 169.D.1 to the nullah in 176.R.9 where contact will be established with 88th Brigade. The 1st Lancashire Fusiliers still keeping close touch with the French left. A proportion of the machine guns of the Drake and Plymouth Battalions will accompany the 1st Lancashire Fusiliers in their advance.

6. The 88th Brigade (less 1st Lancashire Fusiliers) will advance at 11 A.M. from the right of the present trenches held by the 87th Brigade, and will establish itself and entrench on a line across the ridge one mile S.W. of Krithia from the nullah in 176.R.9 (inclusive) to the nullah in 176.L.6 (exclusive) where they will be in touch with the Lancashire Fusilier Brigade. 2 Sections Lowland Field Company will be attached to the brigade.

7. The Lancashire Fusilier Brigade will advance at 11 A.M. from the left of the present 87th Brigade trenches and will establish itself and entrench on a line from the nullah in 176.L.6 (inclusive) where it will be in touch with 88th Brigade, to the coast in square 176.G.8. The Lowland Field Company (less 2 sections) will be attached to this Brigade.

8. The 87th Brigade, to which is attached the West Riding Field Company R.E., will remain about its present position under cover until the above line has been established.

9. During phases I and II, General Marshall, in addition to commanding the 87th Brigade, will assume general control of the operations of the 88th and Lancashire Fusilier Brigades.

10. The Indian Brigade will remain in reserve in a covered position about square 168.O. and the cyclist company at Divisional Headquarters.

11. The G.O.C., R.A. will arrange to open fire with howitzers at 10.30 A.M. on objectives in front of 88th Brigade and Lancashire Fusilier Brigade, and will support the advance of these brigades with shrapnel and cover them while they are entrenching on the new line. Artillery groups are allotted for the support of the advance as follows:—

Composite Naval Brigade —XV R.H.A. Brigade
                       Lieut.-Colonel Stockdale.
88th Brigade   —XVII R.F.A. Brigade,
                       Major Campbell.
Lancashire Fusilier Brigade—Artillery Group 3,
                Commander, Lieut.-Col. Wynter.

Artillery Brigade and Group Commanders will place themselves in communication with the Commanders of the Infantry Brigades which they are supporting.

The following artillery has been allotted under arrangements made by the G.O.C., R.A. to support the advance of the French:—

Two R.H.A. Batteries, two R.F.A. Batteries, one Section Heavy Battery.

12. Two cruisers will be operating on the left flank of the advance and the G.O.C. Lancashire Fusilier Brigade will arrange to keep communication with these through the observation officer on that flank and will also arrange to mark clearly with a flag the flank of his line as it advances along the coast. During this phase, the supporting ships will open fire on such of the enemy's batteries as may be ordered by the G.O.C., R.A., but will not fire without orders from the shore, except in the case of ships on the right flank which will support the French attack as opportunity offers.

13. Two depots of S.A.A. will be established, one at the ruined farm near 87th Brigade Headquarters in square 168.J.[1] and the other just west of Krithia road in square 168.U.[2]

14. One iron ration, in addition to the unexpended portion of the day's ration, will be carried by all ranks.

15. A dressing station is established by 87th Field Ambulance in the gully[3] leading down to Y Beach, square 168.C. Casualties of Lancashire Fusilier Brigade and 87th Brigade will be evacuated to this station by bearers 87th Field Ambulance.

    A dressing station will be established by the Krithia Road at square 168.Y.6.[4] by the Tent sub-division of 89th Field Ambulance. Casualties of the Composite Brigade and 88th Brigade will be evacuated to this station by bearers of 89th and 88th Field Ambulances respectively.

16. Reports to Divisional Headquarters on Hill 138.

[1] Pink Farm.   [2] About 2000 yds. from Sedd el Bahr.
[3] Gully Ravine.   [4] W. of road bridge over Kirte Dere.

APPENDIX 25

Phase II.

17. After the line detailed in phase I has been reached and made secure, the further advance will be made from that line in accordance with the following orders at a time which will be notified to all concerned.

18. The Composite Naval Brigade will hold the line of trenches in which they have established themselves. They will maintain connection between the French on their right and the 88th Brigade on their left.

19. The 88th Brigade will advance from the line on which they have established themselves and will attack Krithia and the trenches covering it from the S.W. and W. When this has been gained, they will move forward and establish themselves on a line from 176.T.9. to the knoll in 176.F.6. (inclusive) keeping touch with the Lancashire Fusilier Brigade on their left.

20. The Lancashire Fusilier Brigade will advance from the line on which they have established themselves and will seize the high ground about point 472, 1½ miles north of Krithia. They will establish themselves strongly there and hold the line from the left of 88th Brigade on knoll square 176.F.6. (exclusive) by point 472 to the coast in square 184.R.8. They will hold this position throughout the remainder of operations.

21. The 87th Brigade will move up and occupy the line from which the Lancashire Fusilier Brigade and 88th Brigade have advanced, and be prepared to support the leading brigades as may be necessary.

22. The Indian Brigade will move up and occupy the trenches originally held by the 88th Brigade, and will remain in general reserve.

23. In addition to the artillery support arranged for phase I, G.O.C., R.A., will detail one battery for the close support of each of the 88th and Lancashire Fusilier Brigade respectively.

24. When the order for the advance of this phase is given, the fire of the ships will be directed on Krithia and such objectives North and N.E. of it as may be hindering the advance. This fire will not be opened until the signal for it is given from the shore.

O. C. WOLLEY-DOD,
Colonel, G.S.,
29th Division.

Issued at 4 A.M. 6/5/15.

Phase III.[1]

25. After the line detailed in phase II to be reached by the 88th Brigade and the Lancashire Fusilier Brigade has been firmly established, the further advance will be made in accordance with the following orders, at a time which will be notified to all concerned.
26. The 87th Brigade will advance by the north of Krithia village eastwards against Achi Baba, with its right directed on the highest point.
27. The Indian Brigade will advance by the south of Krithia village and attack Achi Baba from the south-west, with its left directed on the highest point.
28. In support of the attack on Achi Baba, the CXLVII Brigade, the Mountain Artillery Brigade, and one section of each of the Australian and New Zealand Batteries will move up to the spur running S.W. from point 472, and the XV Horse Artillery Brigade to positions one mile S.W. of Krithia.
29. During this phase the ships will bring a heavy fire to bear on the works round Achi Baba peak from the S.W., West, and N.W. This fire will not commence until the order for it is given from the shore.

[1] Not to be issued till all was seen to be going well with phases I & II. Actually this part was never issued.

APPENDIX 26

29TH DIVISION ORDER
SECOND BATTLE OF KRITHIA (2ND DAY)

OPERATION ORDER No. 5[1]

1. A French infantry brigade and the Manchester Infantry Brigade arrived to-day. [Sketches 18, 19.]
2. The French have occupied approximately the position indicated in para. 2 of Divisional Operation Order No. 4 of 5th inst., but their left has only reached to a point in the North of squares 169.I. & J.
3. Brigadiers will consolidate their lines and ensure that the whole position is strongly entrenched and secure against counter-attack. They will report as soon as possible the position of all troops of their brigade.
4. The Composite Brigade is in touch with the French left and with the right of the 88th Brigade. The Lancashire Fusilier Brigade is on the left of the 88th Brigade.
5. The Indian Brigade is in reserve. The 87th Brigade is in Reserve near Y Beach. The Divisional Cyclist Coy. is West of hill 138.
6. Phase 2 indicated in Operation Order No. 4 of 5th May, will commence at 10 A.M. to-morrow, at which hour the advance of the infantry as laid down in paras 18 to 22 of that order will commence.
7. Brigadiers will report as soon as possible the position of any entrenchments, etc., of the enemy which have checked their advance to-day.
   These positions must be indicated as clearly as possible in order that artillery fire may be brought to bear on them to-morrow before the advance commences.
8. Divisional H.Q. remain in the same position as to-day.

O. C. WOLLEY-DOD, Colonel G.S.,
29th Division.

Issued at 10 P.M. 6/5/15.

[1] The map references are to the 1/40,000 Operations Map in use at the time.

APPENDIX 27

G.H.Q. ORDER
SECOND BATTLE OF KRITHIA (3RD DAY)

Force Order No. 6[1]

GENERAL HEADQUARTERS,
7th May 1915.

Sketches 1. The attack will be resumed to-morrow at 10.30 A.M. pre-
18, 19. cisely and will be pressed with the utmost possible vigour.
  2. The Lancashire Fusiliers Brigade will take the place of the New Zealand Brigade in the Composite Division, and the New Zealand Brigade will join the 29th Division.
  3. G.O.C. Composite Division will be prepared to move up one brigade to a convenient position on the left of the line held by the Composite Naval Brigade, in square 169.A., and will also be prepared, in case of the advance of the Composite Naval Brigade being ordered, to have its trenches taken over by another brigade of his division.
  4. The G.O.C. Corps Expéditionnaire will continue to consolidate his position in 169.D., and will endeavour to extend his right across the Kereves Dere as ordered in Force Order No. 5, para. 6. His further advance will be governed by the progress of the attack on Krithia as already described in Force Order No. 5, para. 7.
  5. General Headquarters will be established at Hill 114 at 10 A.M. to-morrow 8th inst.

W. G. BRAITHWAITE,
Major-General,
C.G.S., Med. Ex. Force.

10.25 P.M.

[1] The map references are to the 1/40,000 Operations Map in use at the time.

Appendix 28

29th Division Order
Final Phase of Second Battle of Krithia

Operation Order No. 6

8th May, 1915.

At 5.30 P.M. the 29th Division will advance in a North-Easterly direction General Paris' Division attacking parallel to them on their right. 87th Brigade will have as its objective the trenches West of Krithia its right on the ravine leading up to hill 472 inclusive. New Zealand Brigade objective village of Krithia and the trenches West of it will attack in a North-Easterly direction with its left flank resting on the ravine leading to 472 exclusive and its right flank on the stream flowing South-West from Krithia inclusive. The Australian Brigade will be passing through the Composite Brigade and will attack in a North-Easterly direction to the right of the New Zealand Brigade. 88th Brigade will support the attack of the New Zealand Brigade guarding its flanks and reinforcing it if necessary and keeping at least a battalion echeloned in rear of the right flank to meet any counter-attack from that direction. The Indian Brigade will remain in general reserve.

Sketches 18, 19.

O. C. WOLLEY-DOD, Col., G.S.,
29th Division.

Appendix 29

NOTES ON SIGNAL ARRANGEMENTS BEFORE AND AFTER THE LANDING

Visual signalling from ship to shore was to be established by landing Royal Navy ratings at each of the main beaches, V, W and X at Helles, and at Anzac. The personnel for these were to land in the first tows.

Two W/T stations (military) were allotted to Helles and Anzac respectively, and were to go ashore after the covering force. These wireless stations were to be flank signal stations for communicating with ships supporting the landing with their fire.

One Royal Naval Base Station (W/T and visual) was provided for each main landing.

One Central Signal Office (military) was provided for W Beach and Anzac.

One cable section was available for W Beach and Anzac to connect up the covering force with ships.

From the Diary of the D.A.S. it appears there was much delay and difficulty in getting messages through, owing to:—
    (1) Wave lengths.
    (2) Coding.
    (3) Retransmission.

The following notes with regard to co-operation between the Navy and Army for signal work emphasize some of the difficulties experienced.

Co-operation between Navy and Army

To remedy the deficiency of wireless sections, four pack W/T detachments were extemporized for G.H.Q. by withdrawing four Marconi pack W/T sets, and personnel to work them, from the Australian and New Zealand Light Horse Signal Troops, in Egypt. These detachments were sent early

APPENDIX 29

in April to Mudros to practise with the Royal Navy. Part of their old pattern apparatus was exchanged later on for two new pack W/T sets found among the stores brought out by the Royal Naval Division.

The amphibious nature of the projected operations necessitated the closest co-operation between the signal officers of the Navy and the Army. This was realized in good time, and even before the arrival of G.H.Q. in Alexandria a joint scheme for controlling intercommunication was in preparation, and a committee of naval and military officers drafted a pamphlet entitled "Signal Organization for Combined Operations". This pamphlet was issued to all troops and ships taking part in the landing, and it was also issued in French.

The provision of means of communication between transports at sea and in the harbour was a function of the Royal Navy, but the Royal Naval authorities were unable to provide the number of signal ratings necessary for the vast fleet of transports. The naval contention that the regimental signallers embarked in their respective ships would be able to pass the essential messages proved to be erroneous. The regimental signallers were able to cope with the work only at the short ranges at which Morse and semaphore flags could be used. They were quite unable to use or read the flag hoists necessary at long distances, or to attract the attention of individual ships.

The allotment of troops to transports and the order of landing of the various Army Signal detachments was arranged by the General Staff and Naval Adviser.

It was necessary to extemporize a signal unit to serve G.H.Q. in H.M.T. *Arcadian*, and to man the Central Signal Station at the principal (W) Beach. This was done principally at the expense of the Australian and New Zealand Corps Signal Company, and a detachment for this unit took over the visual and W/T signal work afloat on 7th April. The signallers were established on the upper bridge and a counter opened on the main deck. The P.N.T.O. arranged for steamboat communication at irregular intervals to convey despatch riders between transports in harbour.

Several conferences were held in H.M.S. *Queen Elizabeth*, at Mudros, to arrange signal working between ships, shore and aircraft. It was agreed that the general direction of wireless stations should rest with the Royal Navy, and that it should be used principally for fire control, or messages of extreme urgency. The Royal Navy undertook to provide base stations at each of the two principal beaches (W and Z) furnished with both visual and wireless gear and personnel. All other communication on shore and inland devolved on the Army Signal Service.

All work in connection with the maintenance and laying of submarine cables was undertaken by the Royal Navy. The working of these cables at the shore ends was a matter for the Army. The Eastern Telegraph Company's cable ship, *Levant*, was at the disposal of the Vice-Admiral, Eastern Mediterranean. The *Levant* carried at first about 30 miles of single core submarine cable; reserves of cable were held at Syra, Suez, and Malta.

The Royal Navy at first undertook the conveyance of despatch riders or packets between ships and shore in picket boats or other small craft. Also the transfer of cablegrams from and to the cable end at Tenedos. The number of steamships available proved to be insufficient, and much delay occurred in the delivery of written messages and other correspondence to troops in the transports, and also to and from the troops on shore. It became necessary for the Army to have independent means of carrying their correspondence. One motor launch, the *Sheltie*, purchased at Alexandria for G.H.Q. use, proved to be of inestimable value.

Other motor boats were obtained, after considerable delay, from A.S.C. sources, and were extremely useful in harbour.

Local Submarine Cables

On 29th April the cable ship *Levant* landed the end of a cable from Tenedos at W Beach. It was carried away on 1st May by the balloon ship *Manica*, and took all day to repair. The cable office was staffed by the Eastern Telegraph Company, and the personnel worked in a bell tent under the cliff on the east side of the beach. This cable carried all naval and military work to and from Great Britain, Egypt, and the East. By 7 P.M. on 2nd May a submarine cable had been laid from Anzac Cove to Cape Helles; and at 11 A.M. G.H.Q., in H.M.T. *Arcadian*, had been connected by cable to the Central Signal Office at W Beach. But the latter cable was carried away within four hours by a trawler. Next day two more cables were laid from the *Arcadian* to the beach by 7 P.M.

After the night attack on the 1st/2nd May, there was much congestion of messages—naval and military—at W Beach, especially at the naval base station. Important messages were delayed four hours.

APPENDIX 29

On the 6th May more trouble was experienced with submarine cables. The Anzac cable was dragged off shore by some ship, and could not be restored till 8th May. Merchant vessels totally disregarded the presence of the cables and the warning notices marking their places of landing.

www.ingramcontent.com/pod-product-compliance
Lightning Source LLC
Chambersburg PA
CBHW040319300426
44111CB00023B/2950